THE CANADIAN EXPERIENCE

If I had to sum up the lesson of the *Canadian experience* . . . I should put it like this: the life of a nation, like that of an individual, is not something to be lived in the innocent and happy illusion that other people can be made to like us, or to resemble us, but something to be endured on a basis of reality. The big problems are not the ones which can really ever be settled and "fixed" by some magic formula, some act of revolution, some political system. They are the problems we must teach ourselves to live with, just as all peoples, for the first time in human history, are now simply forced to learn to live with one another, if we are to survive at all.

Vincent Massey

Governor General of Canada, 1952-1959

THE CANADIAN EXPERIENCE

JOHN S. MOIR
Professor of History, Scarborough College,
University of Toronto

D. M. L. FARR
Professor of History, Carleton University

McGRAW-HILL RYERSON LIMITED
Toronto Montreal New York London Sydney
Johannesburg Mexico Panama Düsseldorf
Singapore Rio de Janeiro Kuala Lumpur New Delhi

SBN Cloth 7700 3159 5

SBN Paper 7700 3164 1

Maps by E. H. Ellwand
Charts and graphs by D. Hayward

ACKNOWLEDGMENTS

The authors and publisher wish to express their gratitude to those who have given permission for the use of copyrighted material. Specific acknowledgment of passages used in the Readings is given in the text. A detailed list of sources for the illustrations appear on page 590. Every effort has been made to trace and give credit to all copyright holders. The publisher would appreciate information leading to the correction of any errors or omissions.

Printed in Canada by the Bryant Press Limited

2 3 4 5 6 7 8 9 10 10 9 8 7 6 5 4 3 2

PREFACE

In writing *The Canadian Experience* we have tried to keep in mind several important points. We believe that history is much more than a dreary collection of dates or a review of "past politics". It should, rather, depict the whole of man's life—politics, society, economics, culture. We have attempted to represent all of these elements in our book. We have also tried to bring out, through incident and dramatic detail, our belief that history is made by men and women, that it is not the soulless product of impersonal forces. Finally, we believe that the writing of history should not be soulless and mechanical either. We have, therefore, not hesitated to express our own opinion forcefully. We hope that in so doing we will encourage our readers to read critically and with deeper understanding.

We would like to draw attention to the illustrations, maps, and charts in *The Canadian Experience*. They are more than a decorative addition to the book; they make their own integral contribution, and will reward study and analysis.

The belief that history is made by men and women appears to us a principal justification for studying it. Through history one is encouraged to formulate critical attitudes, to become, in Thomas Jefferson's words, "a judge of the actions and designs of men." Three hundred years ago Francis Bacon wrote that "histories make men wise". The desire to understand should be a principal consequence of the study of history, for such a desire is perhaps the most important contribution that any one of us can make to our own and to other societies.

J. S. M.

D. M. L. F.

CONTENTS

MAPS

CHARTS AND GRAPHS

N
A
B
G
H

1

THE COLONY OF NEW FRANCE

CHAPTER 1

BEGINNINGS IN NORTH AMERICA

THE GEOGRAPHICAL BACKGROUND

The geographical ancestor of North America was the ancient continent of Laurentia, whose history goes back to the earth's beginnings. This land mass possessed the rough outlines of the present continent, although it was much larger. Hudson Bay, for instance, was dry land; there was a land connection with Greenland and with Siberia; and on the Atlantic and Pacific coasts the present-day continental shelves lay above the waters. The nucleus of Laurentia was the Laurentian (Canadian) Shield, once two and a half million square miles of molten white rock which slowly cooled to a rigid, uneven crust. The Shield covered the entire north-eastern part of the continent, as it does today. Other rock formations of similar age are to be found in the Appalachian mountains running down the Atlantic coast and in the Selkirk range, lying west of the present-day Rockies in British Columbia. All of these rocks are called Precambrian to show that they date from the long span of geological time amounting to three-quarters of the three and a half billion year history of the earth before the beginnings of life appeared in the waters. Although each of the continents has shields of Precambrian rock, North America, and within it, Canada, can claim the largest expanse of the earth's original surface to be found anywhere. The oldest known rocks in the world are probably some located in the Shield region of northern Manitoba. Young in terms of recorded history, Canada is incredibly old from the point of view of geological time.

Present-day North America gradually took its shape from Laurentia. Through centuries of erosion the original mountains were worn down to low hills; sediment washed from them was deposited on their east and west flanks; and vast stretches of the continent subsided into the sea, so that water filled the wide troughs between the ancient mountains. Then gigantic pressures in the earth's crust caused Laurentia to be uplifted, beginning in the east and moving across to the west. The land surface was buckled and folded into new configurations and young jagged mountains, such as the Rockies, were formed. Finally the ice sheets, four times advancing relentlessly over the northern limits of the continent, scoured the surface into new patterns. The continent's drainage system was changed so that many streams that had once flowed south now flowed east. Surface soil was scraped away and pushed ahead of the ice sheets, and the land was strewn with debris. The "ancestors" of the Great Lakes came into being along

A coniferous forest in the Canadian Shield.

the southern rim of the Labrador ice cap. Through these cataclysmic alterations, most of which occurred before human life appeared in North America, the structure of the present continent was laid down.

Today Canada can be divided into five main physical regions, each of which has influenced the occupation and history of the country. To the east, covering the Atlantic provinces, part of the Eastern Townships and the Gaspé peninsula of Quebec, is the Appalachian region, the northern end of the chain of ancient mountains that runs parallel to the eastern seaboard of the United States. In Canada the Appalachians are so worn down by erosion that they do not rise above 4,200 feet. They form a surface of low rolling hills combined with valleys and uplands, the higher parts forested with conifers. Favoured by the moist climate of the Atlantic seaboard, this region supports an economy of mixed farming, fishing and lumbering.

To the west the St. Lawrence-Great Lakes Lowlands region runs up the St. Lawrence River and comprises the land lying immediately around Lakes Ontario and Erie. Small in area, this region offers fertile soil, a mild climate and a site beside a magnificent system of inland water communication. Its natural advantages of resources and position have made it the most

The Arctic wasteland, Grise Fiord.

densely populated and the most highly industrialized region of Canada. The entire area in both Canada and the United States is rapidly becoming one of the most highly developed and heavily populated regions of the world.

To the north of the Lowlands and extending in a great U around Hudson Bay, is the Canadian Shield, comprising over half of the territory of modern Canada. The rugged surface of the Shield is marked by rocky outcroppings, low hills, swamps, tortuous river systems and countless lakes. Highest in the east, in the Ungava peninsula (with elevations up to 5,500 feet), the Shield slopes under Hudson Bay and into northern Manitoba and the Northwest Territories. Its sheer size and inhospitable surface have made it a formidable barrier in Canada's history, although its minerals, water power and forests constitute some of the richest resources of modern Canada.

The prairies and the Mackenzie River Lowlands form a fourth principal physical region of Canada. They are a part of the Great Central Plain of North America, the vast trough that extends down the centre of the continent to the Gulf of Mexico. A slight height of land divides the Canadian prairies from the American plains to the south, separating the Saskatchewan River system from that of the Missouri-Mississippi. North of this height of land, the Canadian prairies rise in three discernible steps, each with a difference in elevation of about 1,000 feet, from the Manitoba plain to the rolling uplands of Alberta. One of the great wheat producing areas of the world, the prairies are also favoured with deposits of minerals, such as potash, and vast reserves of oil, gas and coal.

The Cordillera forms a high mountain wall along the Pacific coast of Canada. There are a series of ranges and plateaus: the Rockies, some of whose peaks reach 12,000 feet; the Selkirks; the Interior Plateau of British Columbia; the Coast Range, containing Mount Logan, the highest mountain in Canada, with an elevation of 19,850 feet. Beyond the deeply-indented, mountainous shoreline of mainland British Columbia lies a series of islands of which the largest are Vancouver Island and the Queen Charlotte Islands. The Cordillera receives heavy rain on the western slopes, causing the growth of dense forests and producing

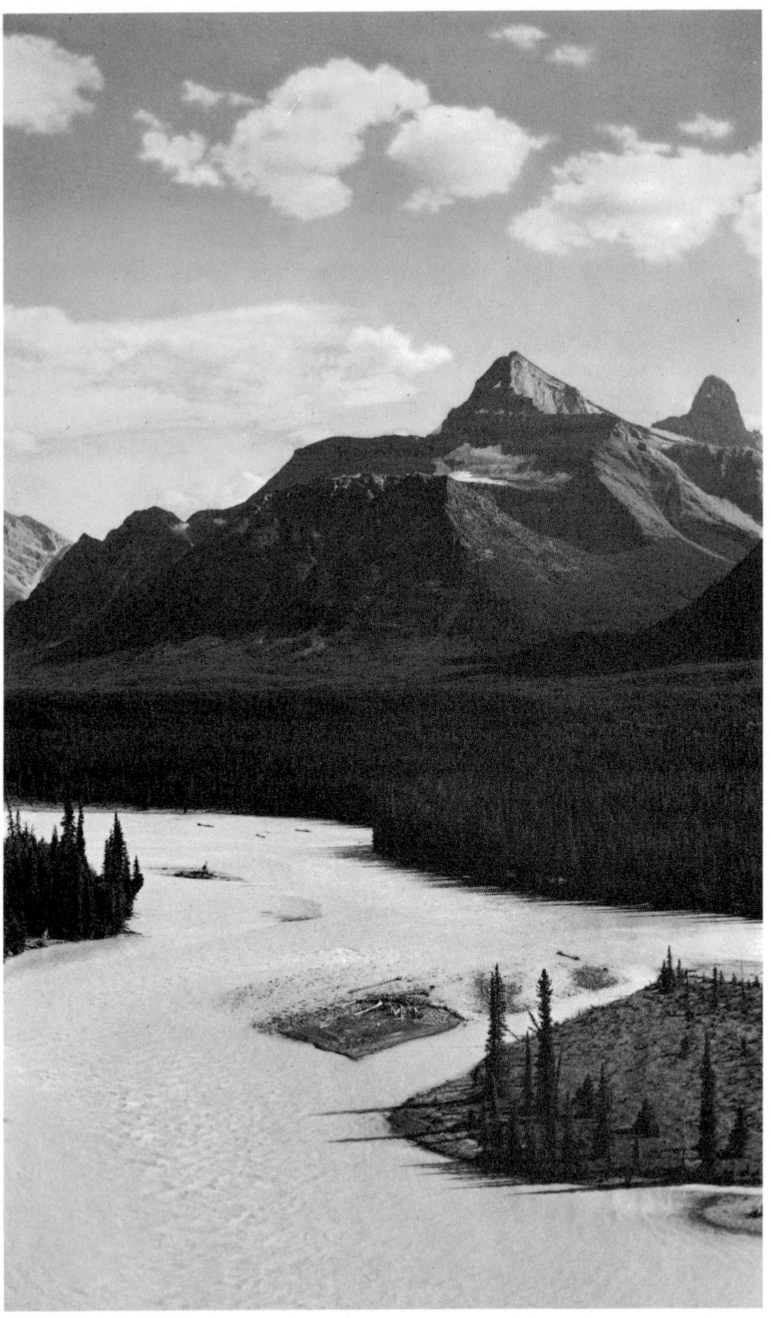

innumerable electric power sites. It also contains rich mineral deposits. The agricultural possibilities of the region are limited to fertile valleys along the coast and in the interior.

"History is geography set in motion." Of no country is this observation truer than of Canada. The size, the shape, the nature of the land have affected the human activity that has taken place on it over the centuries. First and most obvious is the sheer immensity of Canada, over 3,800,000 square miles, a state second only to Russia in size and larger than the continent or Europe. How much of the difficulty in governing, of the costs and effort of communications, and of the expenses of economic development, are due to the inescapable reality of the size of Canada? Then there is the variegated surface of the land. Areas suitable for agriculture comprise only 10 per cent of the total land mass and, except for the prairies, are found in dispersed pieces. Resources, too, are scattered and only rarely occur in economically desirable combinations (there is nothing in Canada similar to the grouping of coal, iron and oil that underlay the economic growth of Pennsylvania in the nineteenth century). There are also barriers of mountain, stream and forest between the five regions and even within individual regions. Finally, the climate is varied and much of it so extreme that it adds appreciably to the costs of settlement.

The determining consequences of geography have been far-reaching in Canadian history. The fact that North America lay open to easy access from the Atlantic and that no mountain barrier immediately obstructed inland penetration made for a rapid occupation by Europeans. Thus the French and the British successively dominated the eastern area of Canada. The sea provided a convenient and regular connection between Europe and North America, allowing Europeans to trade with Canada, to supply immigrants and to provide military and naval protection. Indeed some regions of Canada, such as Newfound-

The Bow River in the Canadian Rockies.

An aerial view of Riceton, Saskatchewan.

land and the Maritimes, have traditionally felt themselves part of an Atlantic world rather than a North American one. The sea reached into the interior of the continent, enabling the fur trade from Hudson Bay to be supplied by sea routes, and it allowed for immigration into the Pacific area by boat rather than by arduous overland travel. Thus geography helped to plant and maintain French, and later British institutions in Canada. Once settled in Canada, however, the nationalities developed in separate communities because of the geographical features of the country. The physical barriers between the Maritime area and the St. Lawrence Lowlands, between the Great Lakes region and the prairies, prevented the phenomenon of a continuously advancing frontier with a uniform settler outlook, such as was experienced in the occupation of the trans-Appalachian region of the United States. Geography in Canada helped to preserve the diversity of the country's peoples, maintained French and English-speaking Canadians in uneasy association rather than in union and assimilation, and dictated the loose federal structure of Canada's government. Canadian biculturism is, therefore, a consequence of geography as well as of "racial" experience.

THE SHIELD AND THE WATERWAYS

As the most massive physical feature of Canada, the Laurentian Shield dominates the country's history. Its rocky surface offered no immediate prospect for agriculture to early settlers, while its limits pressed close upon the arable land available along the St. Lawrence and the Great Lakes. That over half of Canada is composed of the hard igneous rocks of the Canadian Shield helps to explain why Canada's population is only one-tenth that of the United States. In the latter years of our history

Lobster traps and fishing craft in the Nova Scotian village of Mainadien, Cape Breton Island.

the Shield has contributed to the high costs of building and maintaining road and rail networks across Canada.

Yet the Shield has had a beneficial influence on Canada's development as well. From the beginning of the European occupation of northern North America it has supplied valuable staple products that have formed the exports of Canada: furs, timber, minerals, pulp and paper, and, more recently, hydro-electric energy. The lakes and rivers that fringe and traverse the Shield offered a means of easy access to the heart of the continent, an advantage which the French used to construct a far-flung trading empire. In the same way, the British trading companies operating from Hudson Bay and later Montreal pursued the wealth of the fur trade. It was no accident that the first overland crossing of the body of North America was completed by a Canadian fur trader, Alexander Mackenzie, in 1793, fully fourteen years before a comparable journey was made in the United States.

Along the southern edge of the Shield runs the most important waterway in Canada's history—the Great Lakes-St. Lawrence system. By this route were transported the staple commodities of early Canada: the wheat exports of the prairies, and the minerals and wood products needed for the industrial economy of the twentieth century. The original Canadian railway system paralleled this water route, reaching out to link the western prairies with the commercial and financial centres of Montreal and Toronto. The early development of the Canadian economy along east-west lines and the political structure which this orientation produced is the result of the existence of the Great Lakes-St. Lawrence waterway. Thus, even though geography has helped make the achievement of Canadian national unity more difficult, it has also helped to maintain the separate existence of Canada in North America.

THE NORTH AMERICAN INDIAN

The original inhabitants of North America were not native to the continent. No remains of human types as old as those found in other parts of the world have been discovered in North America, nor have any species of the higher apes been found on the continent. It is, therefore, believed that the continent's first inhabitants came to North America as immigrants from Asia, passing over the land bridge that almost joins Asia to North America at the Bering Strait. The migration of peoples of Mongoloid stock may have begun about 20,000 B.C., although recent archaeological evidence suggests that there may have been humans in North America before the last Ice Age. In any event the immigrants from Asia, after first occupying parts of Alaska and the Yukon, moved down the Pacific coast and over into the Great Central Plain of North America. For many centuries the early inhabitants of the continent, following a nomadic existence, dispersed throughout North America and penetrated into South America. The result was an extraordinary diversity of physical types, languages and social organization among the aborigines of the Americas. Over one thousand distinct languages have been identified, none of them bearing any relationship to languages of Europe and Asia. Differences in climate and in the nature of the land produced a wide variety of physical types, economic activities and social organizations among the native peoples of North America. In his physical characteristics the Eskimo differs markedly from the Indian of the plains, while the settled life of the Aztecs in the fertile valley of Mexico City bears no resemblance to the primitive existence forced upon the nomadic hunting Indians of the harsh Canadian Shield.

At the beginning of the sixteenth century, when Europeans first came to the shores of Canada, the Indian population of northern North America was scanty. Probably less than a quarter-million natives were scattered over the entire territory that now comprises Canada. A few places, such as the foothills of the Rockies, were completely uninhabited. And yet, in terms of the kind of life these peoples led (nomadic or semi-nomadic, and dependent largely on hunting, fishing, and in a few cases primitive agriculture) it is estimated that the population was about as large as the resources of the land could support. (In contrast, Mexico City, at the height of the much more sophisticated Aztec empire, is believed to have had 300,000 inhabitants.)

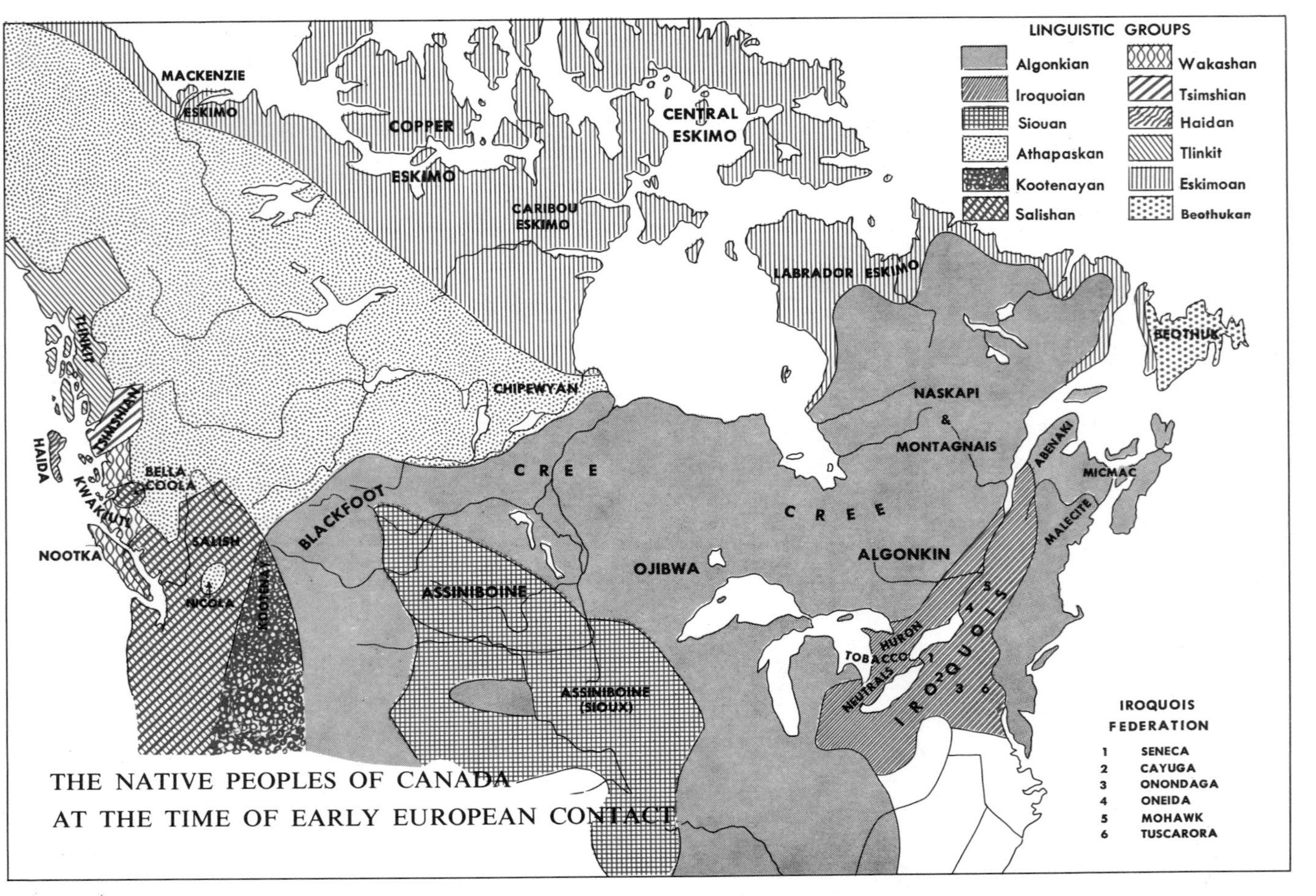

THE NATIVE PEOPLES OF CANADA
AT THE TIME OF EARLY EUROPEAN CONTACT

The Indians of Canada can be arranged into several main groups which correspond roughly with the various physical regions of the country they inhabited at the time of first contact with Europeans. With no political boundaries on the continent, the northern Indians moved freely back and forth between what is now Canadian and American territory.

The Indians of the Appalachians and the Shield regions in the eastern part of Canada were migratory, obtaining their food by hunting, and living in tents made of birch bark or caribou hides that could easily be moved. They used the snowshoe, the toboggan and the birch bark canoe, the last being their most valuable original invention. The family, usually joined with several others to form a band, represented the basic unit of social organization. There were really no "tribes" among these wandering Indians, for there was no common language among the groups and no common possession of territory. Thus the Indians of the eastern woodlands did not have a political structure strong enough to enable them to resist the European when he came to North America. The principal groups of nomadic Indians in eastern Canada were the Beothuks (now extinct) who lived in Newfoundland; the Micmacs, who occupied most of the Maritime area; the Montagnais, who lived on the Shield north of Quebec city; the Algonkins, who inhabited the Shield between the St. Maurice River and the Ottawa River, and the Ojibwas (Chippewas) and the Crees, who lived north of the Great Lakes.

More formidable to the white man than the nomadic Indian peoples were the agricultural Indians, the Iroquois and Huron peoples. They were more numerous, possibly numbering as many as 50,000 at the time of Champlain, the first white man to travel in their country, early in the seventeenth century. They possessed an assured food supply, gained from growing corn and squash, lived in large wooden houses grouped in semi-permanent, defensible villages, and engaged in an extensive trade in furs, ornaments and "wampum" (clam shell beads) over a wide territory from Hudson Bay to the coast of New England. But their principal achievement was a highly developed political and social organization, based on tribes that were linked (through federal councils) into confederacies for the conduct of war and

A Huron in aboriginal dress as shown in the 1613 edition of Champlain's Les Voyages.

the management of external affairs. The famous Iroquois confederacy was composed of five nations (tribes) that lived in the region south of the St. Lawrence and Lake Ontario. They were related in language and customs to the Hurons (who formed another confederacy), the Tobacco nation (so called because they cultivated and traded tobacco) and the Neutrals (a third confederacy), who lived between Georgian Bay and Lake Erie. It is believed that the Iroquois once occupied the St. Lawrence valley and were expelled from it by the nomadic tribes moving from the Shield. In any event, the Iroquois were bitterly hostile towards the Algonkins and other hunting Indians of the North, and frequently raided their territory for slaves and for the birch bark canoe, which they were unable to make themselves.

At the beginning of the seventeenth century the country of the Hurons was probably the most densely populated area in what is now Canada. Here lived about 17,000 people grouped in eighteen fortified villages.* The principal one, Cahiagué, is believed to have had a population of several thousand.

*It is impossible to be precise as to either the total Huron population or the number of villages. Champlain, for example, placed the population at 30,000. Later writers give a lower figure. It is difficult to determine if the difference is to be accounted for by a real reduction in population (possibly from diseases introduced by the Europeans), or by an error in Champlain's original estimate.

The Huron Feast of the Dead, shown here, was one of the most distinctive customs of the Hurons, and one which they shared only with the Neutrals and a few Algonkin (the latter probably modeling their ceremony after the Hurons', with whom they traded). The details of the ceremony are uncertain, as the available evidence from the writings of the Jesuit missionaries and the findings of archeologists tends to be contradictory on some points. However, we do know that it was held at intervals of between eight and twelve years. The Feast was the climax of elaborate and carefully observed ceremonies with which the Hurons surrounded death. The bodies of those who had died since the last Feast were taken from the cemeteries and any flesh that remained was cleaned away and burned. The bones of each corpse were then wrapped in new beaver skins, decorated with beads and necklaces, and placed in a bag, which was also decorated. Each family then carried its dead back to the village, where the corpses were stored in the house of the host. Near the village a large pit was dug and lined with skins and robes on which were laid a variety of gifts. A scaffolding was erected around this pit and all the bags of bones were carried to it. When all was ready, the bags of bones were emptied into the grave from the top of the scaffold, the grave was filled in with more new skins, tree bark, earth and wood. Wooden poles were placed in the ground around the grave and a covering was put over it. Finally, a feast was held and then all returned to their homes.

Although the Hurons followed the same way of life as the Iroquois, the political cohesion of their confederacy was weaker. But after the Hurons began trading with the French the Iroquois became jealous of their commercial success and fearful of the growing influence of the French. The result was intense rivalry that ended only with the virtual annihilation of the Hurons. For a long period the existence of the French settlement itself was imperilled by Iroquois attack.

Farther west, on the prairies, the Indians were nomadic, basing their livelihood on the presence of the vast buffalo herds that roamed the central plains. They gained the horse from tribes that were in contact with the Spaniards in Mexico. Although they succeeded in evolving a more advanced political organization than the eastern migratory bands, their groupings existed chiefly for war purposes and were not as permanent as the association of the Iroquois. Among these Indians, with whom the white men traded as they moved west from Hudson Bay, were the Assiniboines in the southern prairies, the Plains' Crees in northern Manitoba and Saskatchewan, and the Blackfoot in Alberta. To the north in the Mackenzie valley and over the Rockies in the interior of British Columbia lived other groups who depended on hunting and fishing for their livelihood. Finally, on the Pacific seaboard, a more settled Indian society appeared, drawing its food from the plentiful salmon runs of the coastal rivers. In particular, the Kwakiutl, the Salish and the Haida possessed a complex and stratified class society which was governed by an heriditary nobility and distinguished by the elaborate ceremony of the potlatch, a feast usually accompanied by masked dances and in which gifts were distributed to the guests.

The Eskimos (a Cree word meaning "eaters of raw meat") were derived from the same Mongoloid stock as the Indians, although their residence on the harsh Arctic coast and in Labrador gave them distinct characteristics and customs. They lived on the sea mammals and fish of the Arctic Ocean, journeying into the interior every summer to hunt the caribou and the musk-oxen. Anthropologists are divided as to whether the Eskimos were among the first or last groups to enter North

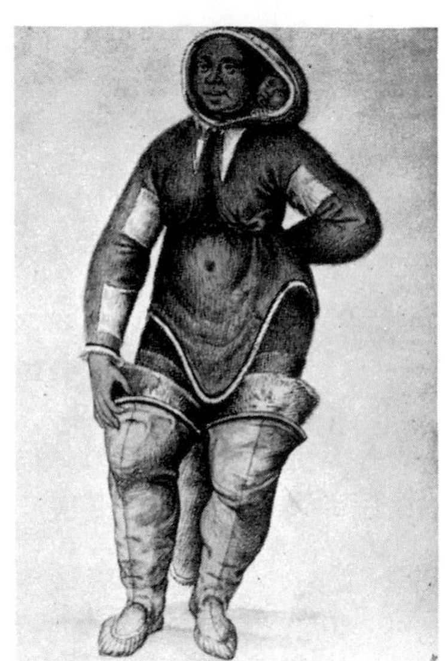

An Eskimo woman dressed in seal skins with a child in her hood, from a watercolour by John White, 1577.

America from Asia. Yet they are agreed that over many centuries the Eskimos adapted to the rigorous conditions of their Arctic existence with striking success. Indeed, it has been estimated that in pre-European times the Eskimo population of what is now Canada numbered 22,000, a figure that was to decline drastically after they encountered the white man.

The Indian was indispensable to the European settler. The fur trade depended upon the Indian's hunting or trapping the animal and exchanging the pelt for European trade goods. The birch bark canoe of the Shield Indian provided the white man with a means of rapid travel into the interior, while other Indian forms of transportation, such as the sled, the snowshoe, and the toboggan, were also adopted by the European. The white settler often grew the crops familiar to the Indian farmer—maize, pumpkins, squash—and was frequently helped through the difficult early years by the availability of these forms of food. Some tribes became the trading allies of the white man and moved ahead of him into new territory, seeking fresh supplies of furs and extending the European influence. Of course, the Indian paid a heavy price for his association with the European. In most cases his social organization was broken down, he was afflicted with the white man's diseases, especially smallpox, and in the end he found himself dispossessed of his land and uprooted from traditional habits. It is only in recent years that Canadians have begun to accept the responsibility for the unfortunate fate of this country's original inhabitants,

EUROPEANS COME TO NORTH AMERICA

The Vikings, the inhabitants of Scandinavia in the early Middle Ages, were the first European discoverers of North America. Driven from their homeland by economic pressure and impelled by a restless, aggressive spirit, they were possibly the finest sailors the world has ever known. Searching for trade and plunder, they raided the entire northern and western coast line of Europe, and moved out into the Atlantic. They came to North America in steps, first to Iceland about 850 A.D., then to Greenland, where they established several flourishing colonies after the tenth century, and finally across to the coasts of Labrador and Newfoundland. This was early in the eleventh century, when the Norsemen planted small settlements in a territory they called Vinland.

A Norse village, comprising the remains of eight houses, has been discovered at the tip of the northern peninsula of Newfoundland, at a place called L'Anse aux Meadows. Other sites around the Gulf of St. Lawrence, which may be of Viking origin, are being investigated. The Norse sagas, indeed, speak of several settlements in Vinland. Yet the mystery of Vinland, its location and its fate, remains unsolved. The sagas also speak of other settlements but these have never been found. The Norse settlers were probably driven away by hostile Indians or were assimilated into the native peoples; the legend of the "blond Eskimos" of the western Arctic islands survives. There does not, on the other hand, appear to be any support for the theory that the Vikings entered Hudson Bay and penetrated into the Great Lakes area. It is fitting that the honour of establishing the first European settlement in North America should belong to an adventurous maritime people such as the Norse, even though there was no sequel to their heroic achievement.

With the decline of the Viking age in Europe, the precarious links with North America disappeared into the Atlantic fog. Only a few scraps of information deriving from the Viking discoveries found their way onto maps of the world drawn by Europeans in later centuries.

Four centuries after the Viking contact, Europe again reached out to touch North America. This time the movement was part of a general awakening in western Europe that extended the influence of European civilization over much of the globe. This expansion of European influence was one of the most dynamic movements in history, a product of the restlessness that derived from profound changes in the political, economic and intellectual life in western Europe. The nation-state was emerging, to focus man's energies on a larger political community than the medieval village or town. In time this unit sought to enhance its power through the acquisition of territory at home or overseas. Colonies came to be valued for their economic worth: for the gold and silver, the fish and furs they supplied to an expanding commerce and industry in Europe. Trade with the Orient had once led Europeans to venture from their homelands; in the

"Indian Mask Dance" by Paul Kane (1810-1871). Born in Ireland, Kane came to Upper Canada in 1819 and grew up in York. He made frequent adventurous canoe trips in the Great Lakes area. He also made a two and a half year trip to the North-West to study, sketch and paint Indian life. His work stands with the writings of such earlier figures as Champlain, Sagard and the Jesuits as an important record of primitive society and customs in the northern regions of North America.

sixteenth century it encouraged men to seek a short route to the Orient by way of a northwest passage around America. Other men went forth carrying the Cross to bring competing forms of Christianity—Roman Catholic and Protestant—to the savages of foreign lands. Many journeyed out from Europe to escape intolerable political, economic or religious conditions at home. Most of the travellers did not discover the object of their search, but the act of searching often led to the realization of new purposes in expansion. Thus a variety of objectives, infused with man's natural curiosity and enterprise, led to the renewal of Europe's links with North America.

The first Europeans to seek the new route to the East knew almost nothing of the great American land mass. Therefore, they sailed across the Atlantic in a relatively straight line, only to find that the land they reached was not their original goal. The man credited with having first touched the Americas was, of course, Christopher Columbus. He was soon followed by others who were seeking to know more about this new land, as well as to discover the passage to the East.

Five years after Columbus, an Italian sailor employed by the merchants of Bristol, John Cabot, touched on the rocky shores of northeastern North America. He brought back exciting news of the teeming fishing grounds that lay off Newfoundland. In many fishing ports along Europe's Atlantic coast, this news may already have been known; in any event Cabot's voyage led to an increasing traffic across the Atlantic to exploit these new sources of food. The nameless and illiterate fishermen of the sixteenth century—Spaniards, Portuguese, French and English—were the real discoverers of Canada. Through their efforts a wide-ranging international fishery developed in the shallow waters of North America's continental shelf. Cod and other whitefish were salted at sea and sent home in the "green" state; during a later period they were dried on shore on rude platforms or "flakes." The latter activity led to the tentative beginnings of Canadian settlement, first on the island of Newfoundland and then at scattered points throughout the Maritime region.

The wandering Indians of North America introduced the Europeans to another natural resource of the area—furs. The

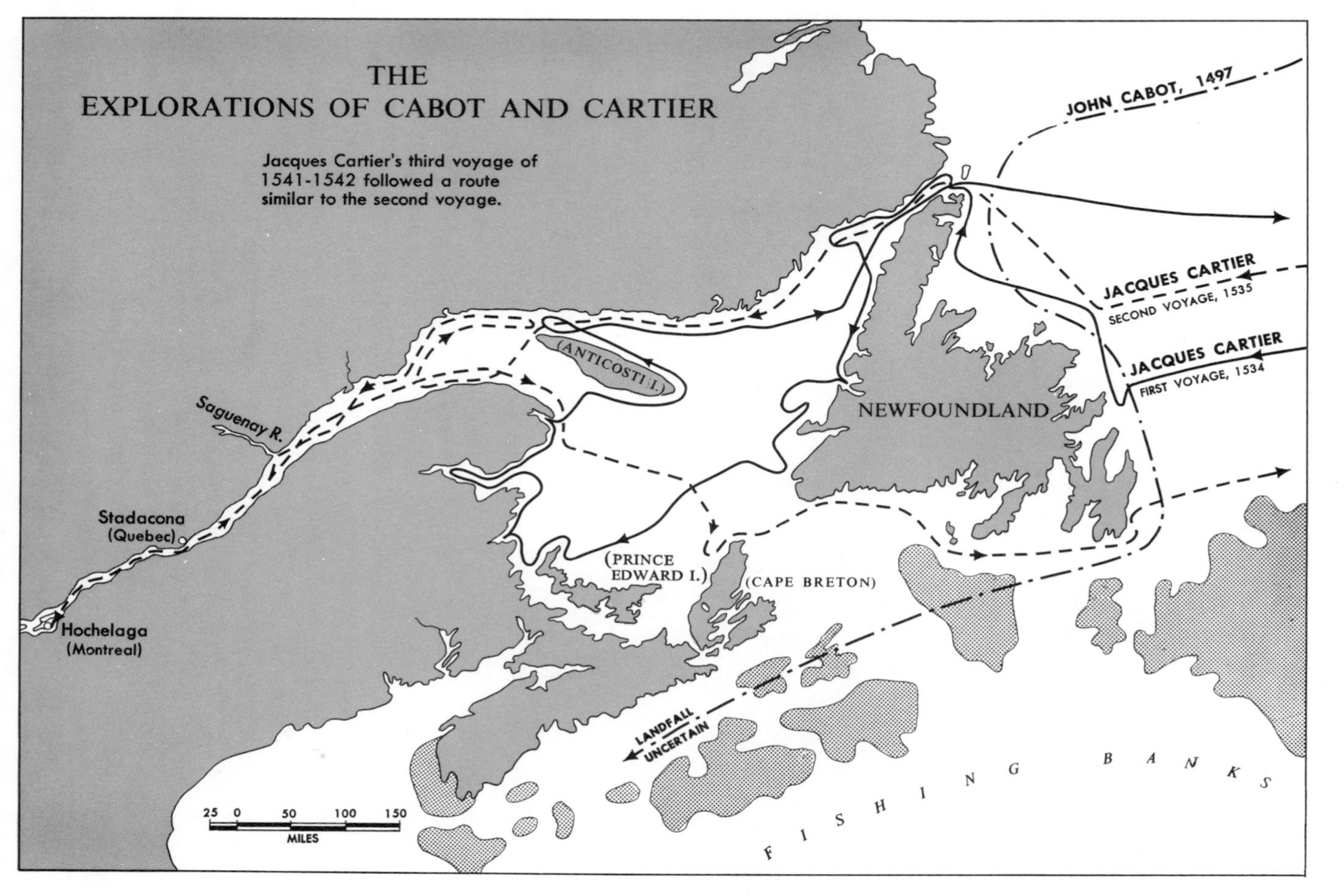
THE
EXPLORATIONS OF CABOT AND CARTIER
Jacques Cartier's third voyage of
1541-1542 followed a route
similar to the second voyage.
JOHN CABOT, 1497
JACQUES CARTIER
SECOND VOYAGE, 1535
JACQUES CARTIER
FIRST VOYAGE, 1534
NEWFOUNDLAND
(ANTICOSTI I.)
Saguenay R.
Stadacona
(Quebec)
Hochelaga
(Montreal)
(PRINCE
EDWARD I.)
(CAPE BRETON)
LANDFALL
UNCERTAIN
FISHING BANKS
25 0 50 100 150
MILES

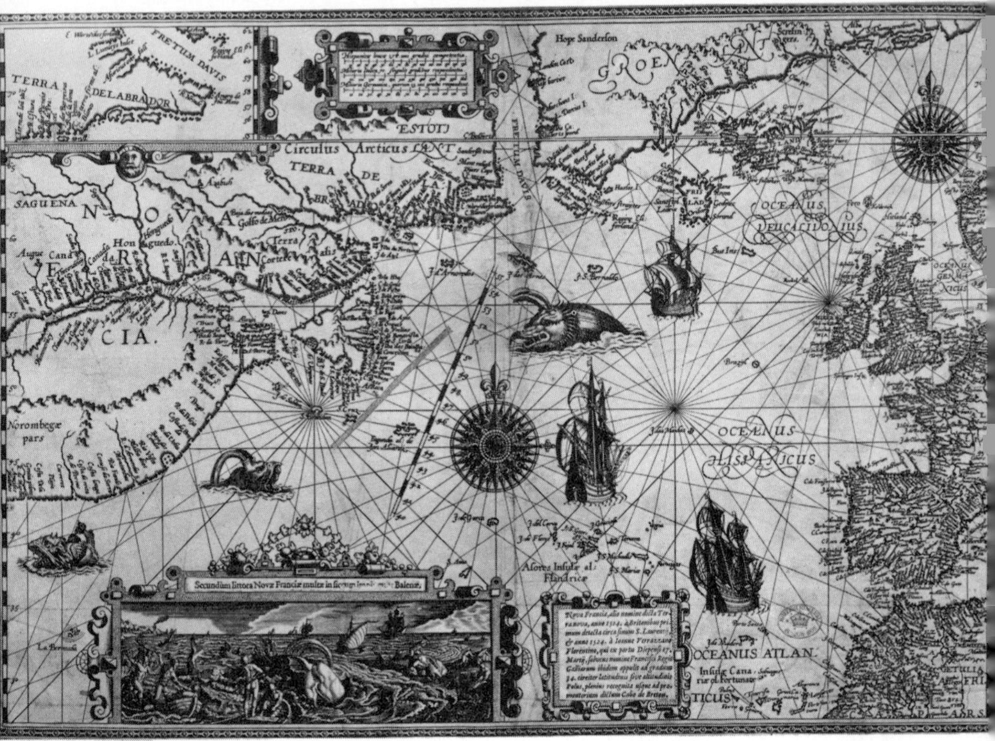

A map of "Nova Francia" by Petrus Plancius, 1592. Note that while the outline of the European coast is fairly accurate even in today's terms, the features of the North American coast are much less accurate and much less detailed. Even so, some familiar names are already shown (e.g. Terra De La Brador, Fretum Davis, Saguena).

Indians traded furs for European implements and the fishermen soon found that this could be a profitable side line. The Atlantic region was rich in beaver, an animal whose fur possessed qualities that allowed it to be felted and shaped into men's hats. The beaver hat was the fashionable male headgear of sixteenth-century Europe. Before the end of the century Europeans were voyaging to the New World, not for fish, but for the trade in beaver skins. This enterprise drew them inland, into the Gulf of St. Lawrence and up the mighty river of Canada.

A French sea captain from Brittany, Jacques Cartier, made the most extensive travels to that date in the Gulf of St. Lawrence on three voyages occurring between 1534 and 1543. On his second voyage he ascended the St. Lawrence River as far as the island of

Montreal, where he learned of the existence of the Great Lakes. He then spent a harrowing winter near the site of Quebec City. His third voyage was part of an ambitious colonizing venture sponsored by a French nobleman, de Roberval. Cartier passed the winter of 1541-42 at the narrows of the St. Lawrence near Quebec and de Roberval spent the succeeding winter in the same location. The severity of the climate discouraged them and their successors from planting a permanent colony in the St. Lawrence area for the rest of the century. The region was left to summer fishermen and fur traders. Tadoussac at the mouth of the Saguenay River, which flows into the St. Lawrence from the north, became the chief meeting place for this casual trade. Although the French did not manage to colonize the St. Lawrence region in the sixteenth century, they acquainted themselves with the main point of entry into the interior of North America. It was left to Samuel de Champlain, in the first decade of the seventeenth century, to plant a permanent French colony at Quebec and to begin the exploitation of the interior fur trade.

THE ENGLISH COLONIES IN NORTH AMERICA

France's empire in North America was eventually to be centred on Champlain's colony at Quebec. Hemmed in by the Canadian Shield to the north and by the Appalachian mountains to the south, Quebec's arable land was distinctly limited. Thus it could never become a flourishing colony of settlement.

The same limitation did not apply to the English who, at the same time as Champlain was founding a fur post at Quebec, began to settle on the seaboard south of the Gulf of St. Lawrence. Commencing with the establishment of Virginia, the first colony in the south, in 1607, and Massachusetts, the first in the north, in 1620, a string of British colonies was planted along a thousand miles of Atlantic coast. These colonies grew slowly over the years, but they grew, each finding the resources and developing the skills to sustain a healthy economic life. In the north were the four New England colonies, poorly endowed for agriculture

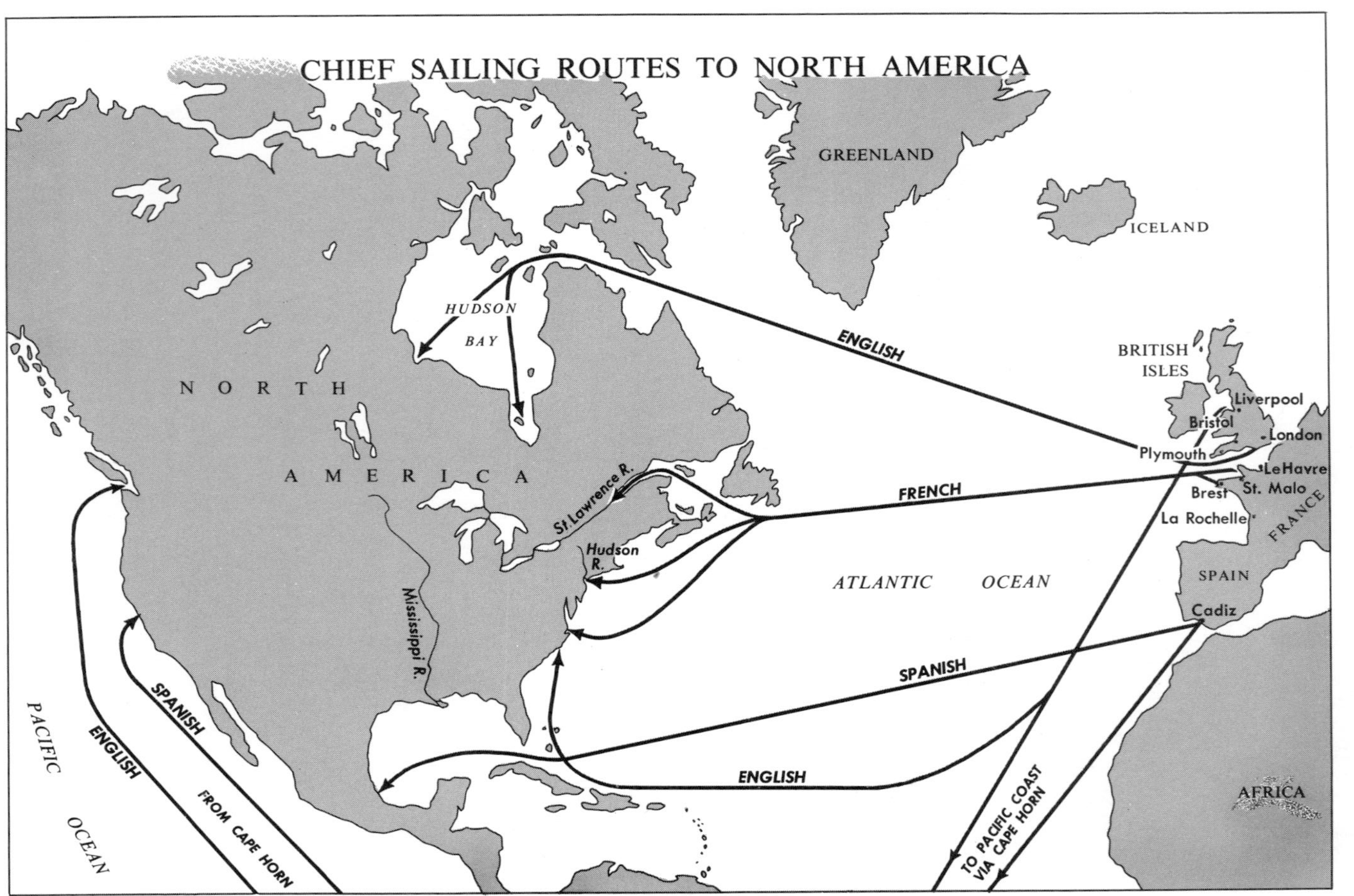

CHIEF SAILING ROUTES TO NORTH AMERICA
GREENLAND
ICELAND
HUDSON BAY
NORTH AMERICA
BRITISH ISLES
Liverpool
Bristol
London
Plymouth
LeHavre
St. Malo
Brest
La Rochelle
FRANCE
SPAIN
Cadiz
AFRICA
ENGLISH
FRENCH
SPANISH
ENGLISH
St.Lawrence R.
Hudson R.
Mississippi R.
ATLANTIC OCEAN
TO PACIFIC COAST VIA CAPE HORN
PACIFIC OCEAN
SPANISH
ENGLISH
FROM CAPE HORN

but actively engaged in fishing, lumbering, ship building and trading. The middle group of colonies, extending from New York to Pennsylvania and Delaware, were blessed with rich arable land lying in a broad coastal plain. They became prosperous "plantation colonies," producing grain and livestock that were traded up and down the coast and to Britain's possessions in the West Indies. Fur trading and lumbering were also carried out in the interior, and in the eighteenth century local manufacturing developed in these areas. South of Pennsylvania lay five more colonies, of which the oldest, Virginia, set an economic pattern for the others. Tobacco emerged as the staple commodity of the southern colonies, supplemented by food crops and by the cutting of timber, spars and masts.

The human ingredients in England's North American colonies were as varied as their means of livelihood. New England was a land of small proprietors—resourceful, hard working and independent. Peopled mostly from England, the northern colonies early possessed a rudimentary system of public education and political institutions distinguished by a high degree of individual participation. The middle colonies were more cosmopolitan in their racial composition, including Dutch folk, Rhineland Germans, Scots and Irish, English Quakers and other groups. Their landholding systems ranged from the large estates of wealthy Dutch farmers along the Hudson River to the frontiersman's clearing in the forests of the upper Susquehanna valley. Their towns, such as Philadelphia and New York, were beginning, by the middle of the eighteenth century, to acquire the adornments of older European communities: substantial brick houses, graded streets, printing presses, churches and colleges. The economy of the southern colonies was based on slave labour, a fact which resulted in the evolution of a stratified social system. Yet the white settler in these colonies was able to participate in a representative assembly such as the Virginia House of Burgesses, established in 1619—and the oldest legislature in the New World.

The English colonies lying to the north of the thirteen American colonies, in what is now Canada, were much less developed during the early period of European occupation. Newfoundland

The three panels on this and the facing page are from a copperplate engraving found in the Bodleian Library at Oxford University in 1929. It proved to be a major aid in the restoration during the present century of the eighteenth century town of Williamsburg, Virginia. Made sometime between 1732 and 1747, the plate shows several important buildings. At the top, left to right, are the Brafferton building, the Wren building and the President's House, the three original buildings of the College of William and Mary. In the top panel opposite, left to right, are the Capitol building of the Virginia Colony, a rear view of the Wren building, and the Governor's Palace. The lower panel depicts Indians and sketches of local flora and fauna.

began as a resident fishing station, with both the English and the French maintaining establishments on different stretches of the coast. The chief English settlement was at St. John's, on the eastern Avalon peninsula, later the capital of the island. For generations the growth of the colony was hindered by bitter conflict between the summer fishermen and the small body of permanent settlers, who were considered a threat to the traditional seasonal method of conducting the fishery. The island was governed by a British naval officer. A prize in the territorial struggle between England and France in North America, Newfoundland finally passed into British hands in 1713.

Nova Scotia was not really part of the British Empire in the seventeenth century, although its coastal waters were much visited by New England fishermen and one brief attempt at settlement had been made by a Scottish peer. Its inhabitants, most of whom lived around the Bay of Fundy, were Acadian French, a domestic, self-sufficient people who were content to till their farms and fish the coastal waters. It was not until 1710 that Port Royal, the main Acadian community, was captured by a force of British and New Englanders. After this event Acadia,

now called Nova Scotia by the British, began to attract settlers from New England and grew to resemble the New England colonies.

* * *

While the English were colonizing the eastern seaboard of North America and conducting a prosperous fishery from Newfoundland, the French moved inland to pursue the valuable prize of the fur trade. Established on the St. Lawrence by the early seventeenth century, they utilized the matchless waterways of the Canadian Shield to travel over most of the eastern area of North America. Thus they frequented and came to control a large part of present-day Canada. Early Canada was, therefore, an empire of the fur traders and the recipient of a culture, a faith and a government that derived from seventeenth century France. The French phase of Canadian history, lasting a hundred and fifty years, represents a major formative period in the experience of the country.

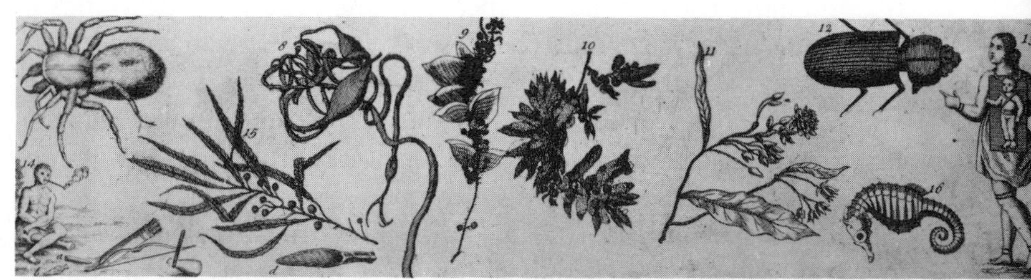

CHAPTER 2

THE ORIGIN OF NEW FRANCE

For half a century after the failure of the Cartier-Roberval attempt at colonization on the banks of the St. Lawrence, French interest in the New World was distracted by civil and foreign wars. Not until the accession of Henry IV to the French throne in 1589 was France to enjoy the domestic peace that would permit renewed attention to the prospects of building an empire in Canada. During the preceding decades, however, French fishermen continued to visit the waters of Newfoundland and the Gulf of St. Lawrence annually. Around 1580 it was reported that France had 150 ships engaged in the fishing trade. Some time around 1550 fishermen started a new and more valuable trade: they began to barter European manufactured goods, especially iron tools, for the furs worn by the natives encountered on the Canadian shore. More important than the furs used to trim expensive clothes were the beaver pelts that provided the fine hairs used to make expensive hats. The real beginnings of the fur trade occurred around 1600, when a beaver skin could be bought for a couple of knives or two ship's biscuits. Thus opened a new era in Canadian history; unlike the coastal fisheries that could be worked by Europeans without native aid, the fur trade depended on the Indians who trapped the valuable animals in the interior. Moreover, the fur trade drew the Europeans up the St. Lawrence River and set the stage for a new and significant development—permanent European settlement to maintain contact and friendship with the primary suppliers of the furs. Not forgotten, either, were the longer-range European interests in forming overseas colonies—the exploitation of the other resources in the new land, and the discovery of a short route to the fabled wealth of the Orient.

RENEWED PROJECTS FOR SETTLEMENT

The shift of European economic interest from fish to furs required new forms of organization on the part of the Europeans. The fur trade required larger capital investments, particularly if it was to be made permanent by the creation of trading settlements. Without small year-round settlements the fur trade would remain open to all comers, and the inevitable competition could easily destroy that trade by undermining relations with the Indians. But permanent settlements, however small, were expensive to maintain. Thus, interested merchants joined together to establish companies and sought to obtain from the king royal charters assuring them a monopoly of the trade. Chartered companies had long been established in Europe, but their extension to North America created persistent problems. No national boundaries existed in the New World, and kings were not reluctant to sell or rent monopolies to rival groups for the exploitation of areas over which their governments held only nominal control, or even over areas that other nations held by prior claim. Furthermore, European states were anxious to consolidate their claims to land by establishing colonies; one apparently inexpensive way was to impose on the chartered companies a requirement to transport and maintain colonists. The issue of conflicting claims was usually settled by superior naval strength; the provision for settlement by the companies was usually ignored by the monopolists, who were primarily interested in trading and correctly viewed colonization as an expensive competitor for the limited funds available.

The second French venture in settlement on the St. Lawrence was in 1600 at Tadoussac, the centre of the growing fur trade.

Pierre Chauvin, a Huguenot fishing merchant who had received a ten-year trading monopoly in New France, aided by Pierre du Gua de Monts, tried to form a settlement which lasted only one year. When other ambitious merchants protested against Chauvin's monopoly, Henry IV admitted them to the trade and appointed the governor of Dieppe, Aymar de Chaste, and others to investigate the fur trade and draw up rules for its conduct. When Chauvin died early in 1603, de Chaste was given the monopoly; he sent François Gravé Du Pont (sometimes called Pontgravé) in the same year to make an on-the-spot survey for a good settlement site. Gravé had already visited Trois Rivières with Chauvin. On this second trip he took with him Samuel de Champlain, a cartographer and acquaintance of de Chaste, to map the "river of Canada."

This was the first of Champlain's many trips to Canada (although it is believed he had previously visited the Spanish colonies in the West Indies). For the first, but not the last, time Champlain encountered the Algonkin Indians whom the French government had decided to support in their tribal war with the Iroquois Five Nations Confederacy. (This alliance, made to protect French interests in the fur trade, was fated to involve Champlain and later the French government in intermittent war that threatened at times the very presence of the French in the St. Lawrence valley.) On his first voyage Champlain ascended the St. Lawrence as far as the present site of Montreal. He was so impressed with the resources of the country and by Indian reports of a great sea to the west that he devoted the rest of his life to establishing French power in the region.

Before Champlain became irrevocably committed to his consuming passion for a "new" France on the St. Lawrence, he was involved in a separate French colonizing venture. When de Chaste died in 1603, de Monts acquired the monopoly of trade in New France (including Canada and Acadia) on condition that he form a settlement and Christianize the natives. De Monts' interest, however, was diverted from the St. Lawrence to the Bay of Fundy by rumours of a rich copper mine there, and in 1604 he established a small colony on the St. Croix River. Champlain, who was acting as de Monts' cartographer, then

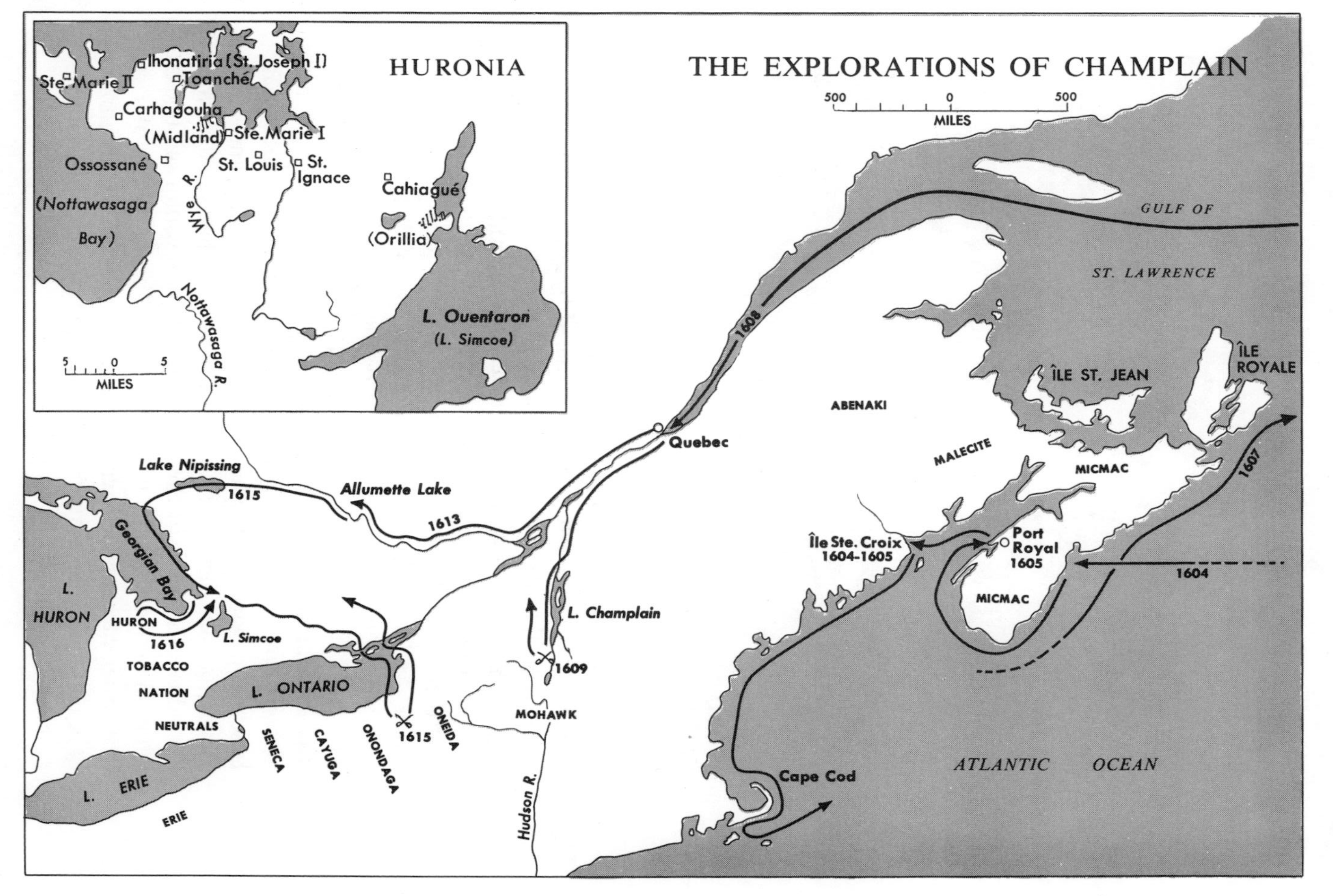
THE EXPLORATIONS OF CHAMPLAIN
500
0
500
MILES
GULF OF
ST. LAWRENCE
1608
Quebec
ÎLE ST. JEAN
ÎLE ROYALE
ABENAKI
MALECITE
MICMAC
1607
Port Royal 1605
Île Ste. Croix 1604-1605
1604
MICMAC
L. Champlain
1609
MOHAWK
Hudson R.
Cape Cod
ATLANTIC
OCEAN
Lake Nipissing
1615
Allumette Lake
1613
Georgian Bay
L. HURON
HURON
1616
L. Simcoe
TOBACCO
NATION
NEUTRALS
L. ONTARIO
SENECA
CAYUGA
ONONDAGA
1615
ONEIDA
L. ERIE
ERIE
HURONIA
Ihonatiria (St. Joseph I)
Ste. Marie II
Toanché
Carhagouha
(Midland)
Ste. Marie I
Ossossané
St. Louis
St. Ignace
Cahiagué
(Orillia)
(Nottawasaga Bay)
Wye R.
Nottawasaga R.
L. Ouentaron
(L. Simcoe)
5
0
5
MILES

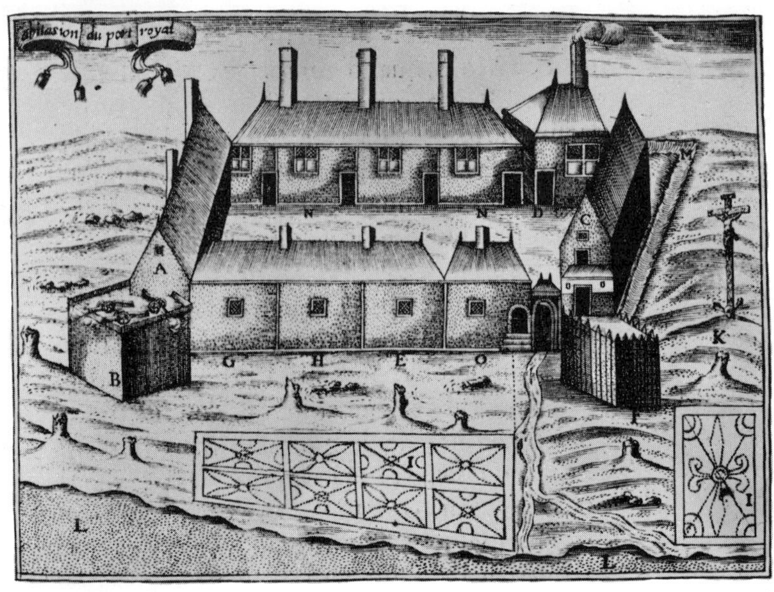

"The Habitation at Port Royal," as shown in Champlain's Les Voyages *(Paris, 1613).*

proceeded south along the coast of Maine in search of copper. The St. Croix colonists were so reduced by scurvy during their first winter that de Monts determined to resettle the group. The area eventually chosen was the sheltered Annapolis Basin. There, in a natural harbour they called Port Royal, the colonists were resettled.

The settlement survived its first winter. With the spring of 1606 more settlers came under Jean de Biencourt de Poutrincourt, who had been granted the land at Port Royal and whose family was to continue in the area for many years. Among the new arrivals were the lawyer and amateur playwright-poet Marc Lescarbot, who wrote the first history of Acadia, and Louis Hébert, an apothecary who later became Quebec's first farmer. To enliven the spirit of the settlers during the winter of 1606-07 Champlain founded the Order of Good Cheer, "a sort of carefree order of chivalry" whose members took turns organizing banquets and entertainments. At the same time he and Lescarbot became concerned about Christianizing the local Micmac Indians.

The Port Royal colony was abandoned in 1607 when the king cancelled de Monts' monopoly. Three years later, though, de Poutrincourt established at the same spot a new settlement that became the nucleus of the future Acadia, a colony that continued to grow through the next century and a half despite English attacks and internal strife.

THE FOUNDING OF QUEBEC

De Monts managed to have his monopoly renewed but he did not try to return to Acadia. After the costly experiment at Port Royal he was attracted by the quicker and larger profits promised by the fur trade of the St. Lawrence valley. In 1608 he took Champlain as his lieutenant on a new undertaking—a permanent trading post at Quebec, closer to the source of furs than the older post of Tadoussac. On July 3 the first lasting colony in New France was begun under the shadow of Cape Diamond.

Champlain built his wooden "habitation" at the water's edge and settled in with twenty-seven companions for the first winter. By the time the ships returned in 1609, over half of the small garrison was dead of scurvy. Nevertheless, the post at Quebec was reinforced as Champlain and de Monts considered what action should be taken against the two major problems confronting the colony: unlicensed traders who entered the St. Lawrence and drew off some of the trade de Monts felt was his exclusively, and the Iroquois Five Nations Confederacy, whose war with the Algonkins threatened to involve the French to the very point of ruining their colonizing venture. At this point the Hurons appeared, also asking French aid against the Five Nations. The Hurons, themselves an Iroquoian people, were involved in a struggle to retain their lucrative position as middlemen between the French and the western tribes. The Hurons' homeland on the shores of Georgian Bay was strategically located athwart the lines of the fur trade. The Iroquois

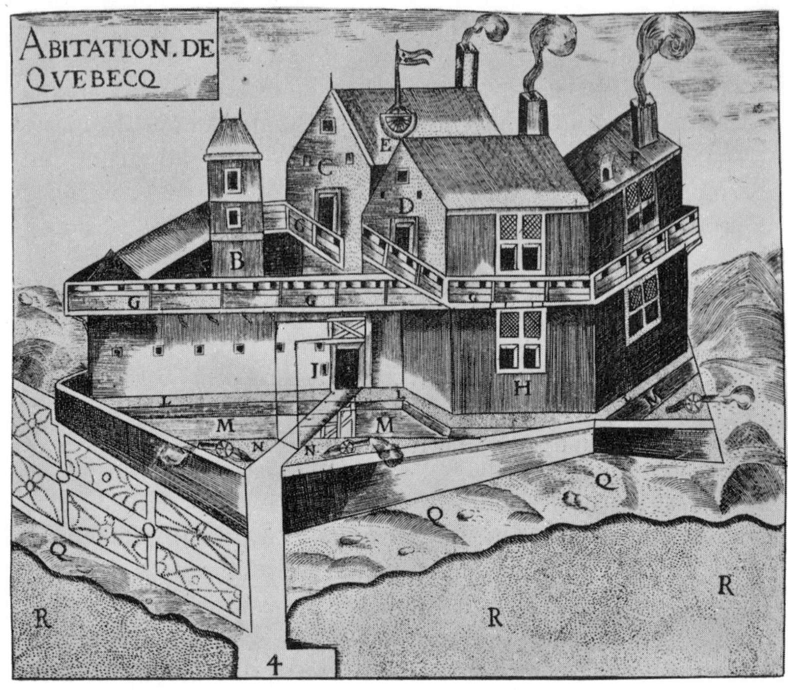

"The Habitation at Quebec," from Champlain's Les Voyages *(Paris, 1613).*

would have to destroy Huronia if they hoped to capture the trade for themselves.

Unlike de Monts, Champlain was primarily anxious to explore, to see New France settled by immigrants, and to see its natives converted to Roman Catholicism. For him the fur trade was the means to pay for settlement and the excuse to justify his own passion for exploration. But Champlain knew that if his dreams for a New France were ever to be realized, de Monts' investment in the fur trade must be assured. Therefore, with only two French companions Champlain accompanied a Huron war party to attack the Iroquois. Ascending the Richelieu River, he discovered Lake Champlain and was told by the Indians of nearby Lake George. At Ticonderoga he put the enemy to flight with shots from his arquebus. This incident, in which the Iroquois were shocked by their first encounter with European firearms, committed the French irrevocably to the Huron cause in a traditional war intensified by the competition for furs. Elated by their easy victory, the Hurons invited Champlain to visit their country. Reluctantly he refused, for the time being, but sent with them Etienne Brulé, one of the "young men" he hoped to train as interpreters and agents in the fur trade.

After wintering in France Champlain returned to Quebec for the summer season of 1611. He found that the unlicensed traders, working out of several French coastal towns, were now seriously reducing de Monts' profits; when he returned to France for the winter he attempted to arrange a solution for this persistent problem. Realizing the free traders could not be excluded simply on practical grounds, Champlain proposed a loose association of traders sharing fully in both the gains and the costs of the fur trade while excluding any newcomers. The idea was accepted and Champlain, acting as agent for the absentee Governor, was given full charge of the fur trade. He returned to New France in 1612.

Champlain's urge to explore had been curbed by the problem of the free traders but it was reawakened when Vignau, another of his "young men," claimed that he had reached the northern sea via the Ottawa River. Inspired by this report, Champlain followed the Ottawa in 1613 for some two hundred miles before Vignau admitted his story was a hoax. Bitterly disappointed, Champlain returned to Quebec and then to France. He spent the next two years publishing the records of his voyages and recruiting Récollet friars as missionaries to the Indians.

While in France after the 1613 season, Champlain made additional plans to settle the problem of the free traders. He arranged for the establishment of a Company of Merchants that would receive the fur monopoly for eleven years. The members of the Company were to share in both the profits and costs of the enterprise, to begin colonization and to provide Champlain with assistance in undertaking further exploration.

When he returned to New France in 1615, Champlain learned that the Iroquois continued to bar the Hurons from going to Quebec with furs to trade. The advantage gained at Ticonderoga had not endured, and the Hurons were talking of another attack into Iroquois territory. Champlain realized that the commerce with the Indians must be secured, and so he acceded to the Hurons' request that he join them in the attack. He also recognized that by aiding the Hurons he would be furthering his two main ambitions—exploration and the Christianizing of the natives. With one missionary and a small party of Hurons, he set out for Huronia, where he was to rendezvous with the war party.

Leaving Huronia, Champlain and the Huron war party travelled south through the Trent Valley and across the eastern end of Lake Ontario to the Finger Lakes district, where they attacked an Iroquois village. This time the encounter with the Iroquois ended inconclusively. After a short siege Champlain and the war party returned to Huronia. As the season was now too late for Champlain to reach Quebec, he spent the winter of

"Defeat of the Iroquois at Lake Champlain," from Champlain's Les Voyages *(Paris, 1613). Champlain himself is depicted as standing between the two bands of Indians. We have no authenticated portrait of Champlain. The figure here is too vague to reveal any significant facial features; it is not even known if the artist was trying to produce a likeness of his subject.*

1616 visiting the neighbouring Neutral and Tobacco peoples in Central Ontario, and establishing friendly relations with them.

In the next three years the tiny colony at Quebec made little progress. The dissident merchants in France, many of them Protestants, refused to spend money on colonization efforts, especially since these were linked to the propagation of Catholicism; they lobbied the government in Paris for their own benefit. When Champlain, who had visited the colony briefly in 1617 and 1618, set sail for Quebec in 1620, the prospects for New France seemed bleak indeed. The colony's population totalled only about ninety persons, very few of whom could be considered true settlers.

The ups and downs of New France were characteristic of most colonizing ventures of that period. The rivalry of commercial groups, the lack of any substantial support from the European mother countries, the complexities and uncertainties of relations with native peoples, and the conflict between settlement and trade were not unique to New France. But New France seemed to have more than its share of such troubles, and drastic changes in the fortunes of the colony seemed to come with bewildering rapidity.

The tiny colony's prospects brightened during the early 1620's. The monopoly was transferred in 1621 to a new group, which promised to be more aggressive in promoting settlement. In 1622 a peace was made between the Montagnais and the Iroquois. In 1625 the wealthy and influential Society of Jesus accepted the Récollets' invitation to join in their faltering missions to Christianize the natives, and in that same year the pious young Duc de Ventadour purchased the vice-royalty of New France and personally paid the expenses of six Jesuit missionaries. Finally, in 1627, the powerful Cardinal-Duc de Richelieu, Louis XIII's first minister, took a personal interest in the colony and organized the Company of New France, or Company of One Hundred Associates as it was called because of the number of wealthy subscribers.

Almost immediately New France's fortunes were dashed once more by the revival of Indian troubles and the appearance of a new European rival in North America.

NEW BEGINNINGS

In the summer of 1628, a hostile fleet of ships seized Tadoussac and demanded the surrender of Quebec. The excuse for this development was a war in Europe, begun by young King Charles I of England ostensibly to obtain his wife's dowry from his brother-in-law, the King of France. Seizing this opportunity, a number of London merchants led by Jarvis Kirke, a long-time resident of Dieppe, had obtained King Charles' warrant to capture "Canada" and its fur trade. The expedition, headed by David, the oldest of Kirke's five adventurous sons, failed to gain Quebec because Champlain refused to surrender. But the fate of Quebec was virtually sealed when the Kirkes captured the French supply fleet off the Gaspé peninsula. By the next summer, when the Kirkes returned, Champlain and the few settlers at Quebec had been reduced to eating wild roots. Having neither enough food nor ammunition to make resistance feasible, Champlain surrendered. Ironically, neither Champlain nor the Kirkes knew that the war had ended three months earlier, making the first English conquest of New France illegal.

Champlain, the Jesuit missionary Jean de Brébeuf, and all except five families were evacuated by the Kirkes, who seized the year's collection of furs and captured another French relief force on the St. Lawrence River. Although the English occupation of Quebec was illegal, the Kirkes refused to leave until they were assured that King Charles would compensate them for their large expenses. For four seasons the English merchants exploited the fur trade in the colonies, with the aid of renegade Frenchmen, and allowed Champlain's buildings to fall into ruins. Not until 1632, when a formal peace was signed between the two countries, did the French return to Canada under the energetic direction of the Company of One Hundred Associates. A new beginning was now to be made.

In 1633 Champlain returned to the shattered settlement with new colonists, and the Jesuits prepared to return to Huronia where they had opened missions in 1626. Each in their own way faced a huge task of reconstruction; but new settlers and new buildings rapidly appeared at Quebec. In 1634 Champlain

This nearly contemporary drawing of the first English conquest of Quebec shows that the Dutch artist had more imagination than information at his command. Champlain's modest fortification has grown into a formidable European-style fortress, while the French and English forces are locked in a battle that in fact never took place.

revived his passion for exploration as he sent Jean Nicolet west as far as Wisconsin in search of more furs and, hopefully, a route to the Orient. More Jesuits than ever now journeyed to the shores of Georgian Bay where, in 1639, they founded the permanent mission compound of Sainte Marie, near present-day Midland.

In the midst of the rebuilding of New France, Champlain died at Quebec on Christmas, 1635. His unremitting work and dedication to the exploring of a new world, to the founding of New France in North America, to the Christianizing of the native population and to the financial interests of his employers earned the gratitude of his contemporaries and the title, "Father of New France," from later generations. If Champlain had a fault it was his humanity in the midst of barbarity, or his reasonableness in an atmosphere of selfishness and deceit. Perhaps there was for him a satisfaction in his closing days to know that the settlement to which he had devoted almost a lifetime was recovering and showing a new vitality previously unknown, and that in old France powerful individuals were at last sharing his hopes for New France.

THREE DECADES OF UNCERTAINTY

New France had, in fact, entered a new era in 1627 when Cardinal Richelieu, the guiding hand behind the French throne, formed the Company of New France. The new company received a charter that granted "full title in perpetuity to property, justice and seigniory of the whole country of the New France. . . ." However, it also required them to transport four thousand settlers to New France within fifteen years and support three missionaries for every settlement established. Only "natural-born French Catholics" were allowed to immigrate, but a number of inducements were offered to eligible settlers. The Company had barely begun its operations, however, when the Kirkes seized New France, so that the full effects of Cardinal Richelieu's efforts for Canada were not felt until after 1633.

In the first decade of real Company operations, New France made considerable progress. Quebec was fortified, and under religious auspices schools for boys and girls were established and a hospital was built. While Quebec was taking on the physical appearance of a small European city, a new settlement was started at Trois Rivières. Ville Marie, the present Montreal, was begun in 1642 by a group of pious men and women under the direction of the experienced soldier, Maisonneuve. Montreal was the product of a great religious revival in France and inspired by the widely read reports of the Jesuit missionaries, their *Relations*. It was intended to be an advance post for Indian conversion. Ironically, the fur trade, which adopted Montreal as its natural headquarters, soon gave the small community a reputation as the site of lawlessness and wild scenes whenever the fur brigade arrived from the west. Nevertheless, New France experienced its first genuine progress during the early years under the Company of One Hundred Associates. A small but steady stream of immigrants arrived—smaller, however, than that required by the charter. New farmlands along the St. Lawrence were opened and settled. And everywhere in the colony the Jesuits tried to enforce a strict moral code of behaviour that left its mark for centuries in the form of a puritanical way of life.

The ominous threat of an Indian war still hung over the small colony. This danger increased after 1639 when the Dutch, from their trading post at Albany on the Hudson River, began to sell arms to the Iroquois. Champlain's peace treaty of 1624 with the Iroquois was still in effect, but he had always managed to prevent the sale of guns to Indians. These conditions could not last after another European state opened an arms race among the rival tribes, although the French still refused to sell arms to their allies. More trouble for New France came in 1641 when the Iroquois demanded French arms as their price for not attacking Trois Rivières. When this threat was successfully met by a show of French force, the Iroquois diverted their attention to raids against the fur trade routes and against the Jesuit missionaries who were binding the Hurons ever more closely to French interests. It became apparent that the Iroquois-Huron rivalry for the position of middleman in the fur trade could only be ended by the total submission or destruction of one group or the other; European competitors could do little to determine the outcome beyond supplying arms.

The undeclared Iroquois war against the French-Huron alliance increased in intensity each year. At first the Iroquois tried to intimidate the French and their Indian allies by hit-and-run raids against French posts—such as Fort Richelieu at

Sorel in 1642—or against isolated settlers, especially around Montreal in 1643. Terrifying as these raids were, they did little damage compared to the disaster inflicted on the fur trade, and hence on the economy of New France, by Iroquois ambushes of Huron canoes along the trade routes. Appeals for help to old France from New France brought one hundred regular soldiers, enough to halt Iroquois attacks temporarily. But the fate of New France was affected by other developments.

The Company of New France was already near bankruptcy and losing favour at the French court when Cardinal Richelieu, the protector of New France and friend of the Jesuits, died in 1642. In desperation the Company rented its fur monopoly in 1645 to a group of prominent residents in New France—the Community of Habitants of New France. Under this local management, and benefitting from a partial peace concluded with the Iroquois in the same year, the fur trade revived for a couple of years. But the final struggle for its control began in 1647 when the Iroquois killed two French agents trying to negotiate a lasting peace, and also attacked the Hurons.

Unable to win the Hurons away from the French by intimidation, it appears the Iroquois decided that nothing but the complete destruction of Huronia would do. In 1646 the Iroquois resumed sporadic attacks on the Huron fur canoes, and in 1648 they struck at the very heartland of Huronia. During the next three years they killed or captured 700 of the 12,000 Hurons. In 1648 the Jesuit missionary Daniel was killed; the next year Fathers Brébeuf, Lalemant, Garnier and Chabanel were martyred. Never as good at warfare as the Iroquois, the Hurons were seized by panic and fled from their land, some taking refuge with tribes to the south and west, and others going to Quebec with the surviving Jesuits. As a people the Hurons were reduced to a remnant, and their once populous homeland was left deserted.

The Iroquois victory bore heavily on the tiny colony's three major reasons for existence: the mission to the Indians was in ruins; the income from the fur trade was reduced by 50 per cent in one year; and the Iroquois now began to turn directly on the weak French settlements on the St. Lawrence. In desperation Governor d'Ailleboust sought a defensive alliance with New

England, but the request was rejected because the English feared Iroquois revenge. The Ursuline nuns, whose convent had been accidentally destroyed by fire, debated leaving New France and their school at Quebec. In 1653, 500 Iroquois laid siege to Trois Rivières. In the same year not a single pelt reached the fur market at Montreal. Suddenly, though, the Iroquois threat seemed to melt away, as tribal jealousy led each of the Five Nations to offer peace terms separately.

New France had fortuitously gained a breathing space. The arrival of one hundred male settlers, not to mention a dozen young ladies of marriageable age, and a sudden revival of the fur trade brought new hope to the colony. But the Community of Habitants was bankrupt; once again the One Hundred Associates were faced with the expensive problem of maintaining New France. Though only indirectly related to the Company's problems, in 1657 the appointment of a bishop to the colony proved to be a major step in the growth of New France. Competition between the Jesuits and the Sulpician priests, who had inaugurated the Montreal mission, had heretofore prevented any

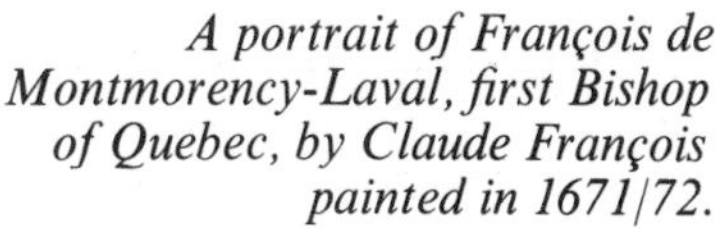

A portrait of François de Montmorency-Laval, first Bishop of Quebec, by Claude François painted in 1671/72.

appointment. At last François de Laval, a close friend to the Jesuits, was chosen by the young King, Louis XIV, over the Sulpician nominee, Gabriel Lévy de Queylus. The aristocratic Laval arrived in Quebec in 1659 as missionary bishop, despite the efforts of the Archbishop of Rouen to assert his own authority over New France.

Almost immediately Laval clashed with Queylus, and the latter was expelled from the colony. Behind this conflict between two strong-willed churchmen lay the larger question of the fate of religion in New France. The Sulpicians believed that the organized parish system of old France should be established, while Laval agreed with the Jesuits that the colony should be treated as one huge mission; his own policy was to concentrate control of all aspects of church life in his own hands.

Bishop Laval, like other aristocrats of his age, was extremely sensitive about the status of his class. Soon after his arrival he quarrelled with the Governor, d'Argenson, about their relative precedence at public functions. In the *ancien régime* of France church-state relations were close, the French monarchy traditionally viewing church officials as willing allies, if not outright servants of the state. However, this situation was not always accepted without question. Indeed, the quarrels between Laval and the civil authority in New France (represented chiefly by the Governor) were a partial reflection of the conflict in old France between Gallicanism (royal control of the church) and ultramontanism (papal supremacy over local secular authority). Laval's quarrel with d'Argenson was but the first of many in which the bishop seemed to be asserting the position of the church in New France to the detriment of royal authority.

As the unhappy decade of the 1650's closed, the fortunes of New France fell once more. Having defeated various other Indian tribes, the Iroquois prepared to renew their all-out war with the French. The spring of 1660 saw 900 warriors set out to surprise Montreal. At the same time, unaware that the Iroquois were massing for an attack, Dollard Des Ormeaux, with sixteen other Montrealers and about forty Indians, was preparing an ambush at the Long Sault rapids on the Ottawa River, where he hoped to intercept Iroquois fur traders and capture the precious pelts. Mistaking an enemy party of Onandaga scouts for returning fur traders, Dollard and his companions fell upon them. Although two of the scouts managed to escape, the Canadiens and their Indian allies, still unaware of the true intent of the Iroquois, held their position. On the following day a large and heavily armed force of Iroquois arrived. Thus began the battle of the Long Sault, which has passed into legend as a tale of heroism and courage. The Canadiens were overwhelmingly outnumbered from the beginning, and especially so after most of their Indian companions treacherously crossed to the enemy's side, and other Iroquois reinforcements arrived to more than double the enemy's strength. Nevertheless, it took the Iroquois eight days to achieve victory. When the battle was over the entire band of Canadiens lay dead; but the element of surprise had been wrested from the Iroquois war party, and they departed to their own territory. Montreal was left unharmed, and the French fur canoes arrived without being molested that year. In 1661 and 1662, however, the Iroquois were back in force, killing and burning at will throughout the length of the St. Lawrence valley. Only the outbreak of a smallpox epidemic among the Five Nations saved the French settlement from more attacks in 1663 and brought half the tribes to offer peace.

The position of New France seemed desperate indeed. The settlers knew that this peace, like the previous ones, would be broken whenever it suited the unpredictable Iroquois. The scattered farms along the edge of the St. Lawrence River were easy prey for raiding parties, and the fur trade that alone provided the wealth to keep New France alive could easily be cut off at any point in its long course up the Ottawa River and across to Lake Huron. New France needed more protection. Only troops could provide it—or hopefully eliminate the Iroquois threat by destroying Iroquoia. Moreover, New France needed many more settlers—after half a century of life it had only 2,500 inhabitants, and of these one-third lived in Quebec. Above all, New France needed a more diversified economy to give it a solid foundation and to end its dependence on the fur trade. France had the troops, the population, the finances and the political power to enforce new policies. Without French help the future of Canada seemed hopeless, as Pierre Boucher, spokesman for the Habitants, explained to the young King, Louis XIV, who had assumed personal control of his government in 1660. Spurred by the pleas of Boucher and the Governor, Louis decided on a new policy and a new status for the long-neglected colony. In 1663 he announced that New France would become a royal province of His Majesty and would receive the same support, government, institutions and care Louis and his ministers gave to old France.

* * *

In the sixty years between Chauvin's abortive settlement at Tadoussac and the establishment of the royal province of New France, the French empire had become firmly rooted in North America. The Acadian venture had admittedly languished from inattention, but along the banks of the St. Lawrence the foundations of a French colony had been laid despite innumerable difficulties. During the first thirty years Champlain had explored the hinterland, promoted the fur trade, striven for peaceful relations with the natives, and had dreamed of a strong French settlement in the New World. His dream of colonization had been hampered by the priority placed on fur trading, by the rivalries of commercial and religious interests, and by apparent apathy on the part of the royal government at home. Hopes of Christianizing and civilizing the Indians had suffered a serious setback in the destruction of Huronia, but the missionary enterprise went on in new fields. The brief English occupation of New France had proved to be but the prelude to intensified French interest in the colony, and the frictions between Sulpicians and Jesuits had been resolved by the appointment of a dynamic churchman in the person of Bishop Laval. Montreal, the pious and daring foundation of Maisonneuve, had survived repeated Iroquois threats to become the economic heart of the colony, while Quebec remained the administrative and cultural capital. By 1663 the small colony had survived in its struggle for existence and was prepared by its harsh experiences to fulfill its destiny in the golden age of New France.

CHAPTER 3

ROYAL NEW FRANCE

The assumption of personal political power by Louis XIV ushered in one of the most remarkable eras in French history. The half-century of French achievements in the arts and sciences and her military victories are conveyed by the phrase, "The Age of Louis Quatorze." Of all the countries in Western Europe, France had suffered least from the destructive Thirty Years' War, and now, led by this energetic and capable young king, she achieved unprecedented heights of wealth and power. This golden age of old France was also the golden age of New France. Between 1663 and the end of the century, Acadia was regained for France, Hudson Bay became virtually a French lake, and from the Great Lakes to the Gulf of Mexico French explorers claimed—and French soldiers ensured—the sovereignty of France over the heart of North America.

THE PEOPLE, THEIR LAND AND THEIR GOVERNMENT

In 1663, Canada, the settled portion of New France, consisted of only a few small communities, mere pock-marks in the forest's edge along the lower St. Lawrence from Montreal to Tadoussac. Some twenty miles below Quebec the pattern of life in New France had begun to emerge in the shape of long narrow farms

Louis XIV in a portrait by Rigaud. From 1613 on, Louis XIV adopted "a series of measures that were tantamount to the founding of a new French colony in America" (Trudel). Unfortunately, the King was preoccupied with the colony on the St. Lawrence and, therefore, Acadia continued to develop slowly and without any clearly defined policy goals.

fronting on the river, separated at intervals by the larger stone houses of the seigneurs. Quebec itself was dominated by the fort, the governor's house, the parish church, the Ursuline convent and the Jesuit college, all clustered on the top of the high cliff. At the foot of the cliff, houses and warehouses stood side by side in the lower town along the water's edge. One-third of Canada's 2,500 colonists lived in Quebec, five hundred more were sheltered under the low walls of Montreal, and a mere handful lived in the tiny settlement of Trois Rivières. All faced the constant threat of being driven from the land by the hostile Iroquois. Such was New France, the royal colony, that greeted the new governor, de Mésy in 1663, and started its golden century of development.

Acadia, France's other North American colony, was restored to the French crown by the Treaty of Breda, which ended the short war between Britain and France in 1667. For five years Acadia had been occupied by the English colonists from Boston, but now, like Canada, it hoped to claim a share of King Louis' attention. Instead, Acadia was largely ignored by the French government during the next forty-five years. A mere handful of troops was sent to defend its population of some four hundred souls. No steps for Acadia's growth were taken at a time when Canada was receiving capital, immigrants and protection from old France. Neglected by its mother country and (happily) ignored for the time by the neighbouring English colonies, Acadia grew quietly into a farming community of several thousand before its loss to Britain in 1713.

The decision of King Louis to end the long rule of the Company of One Hundred Associates meant that for the first time, money, soldiers, settlers and capable administrators were available to aid Canada's growth. The immediate needs were security from the Iroquois and a constitution. The Iroquois menace had become so serious that settlers dared not go out hunting or fishing. French soldiers soon made the hostile tribes more respectful of French military might. The second requirement, a constitution, was supplied by converting the colony into a province of old France.

At the heart of the new government was the Sovereign Council, composed of the governor and bishop, five councillors chosen by them, and an attorney general. In 1665 the membership of the Council was completed by the addition of the intendant, who served in the role of chairman. The Council's duties were to proclaim royal edicts, act as a court of law, and under careful royal supervision pass regulations for local matters. These limited powers were delegated by the Crown, which officially governed New France from Paris. In 1703 the Sovereign Council was renamed the Superior Council and its membership was expanded from eight members to twelve.

As direct representative of the King, the governor was primarily responsible for defence and diplomatic relations. The position of the bishop was more complicated. Because he was both a civil and an ecclesiastical official, the bishop might find himself opposed as a churchman to policies advocated by the King's other councillors. The third important government officer, the intendant, had many duties. He supervised justice, administration and finance. In co-operation with the minister of finance at Paris, he planned and carried out programmes to encourage trade and industry. While the governor was commander of the troops, the intendant was responsible for housing, feeding, arming, paying and transporting them, and for the construction and maintenance of fortifications.

As early as 1647 the King had authorized the election of two officials called syndics from each of the three major towns, to speak for the settlers, but not to vote in council. The system of syndics was ended in 1674, but a new office that would fulfil some of the same functions, that of captain of militia, had been created in 1669. Appointed from among the habitants, and unpaid for his work both as a military leader and a civil administrator, the captain of militia supervised the enforcement of royal and Council regulations, and performed a host of local duties. He was the eyes, ears and mouthpiece for the central administration. As a man of the people and of ability, as the go-between for both Council and populace, the captain of militia enjoyed an influential and respected position in the eyes of both his neighbours and of the government. Only occasionally, and on matters affecting all or most of the habitants, did the Council find it desirable to permit popular assemblies to meet and express opinions. In all matters of government the captain of militia remained the lynch-pin of administration in the colony.

The government of New France, like that of the motherland, was authoritarian and paternalistic. It was government for the people, by the King—the same as practised in most European countries of that period. Royal policies were shaped with a deep sense of the Crown's responsibility for its "children," and the "children" in turn accepted this leadership as being in their best interests. To claim, as some historians have, that this centralization of authority hampered the growth of individual initiative and made a sheep-like population is to ignore three facts: the system produced good government; no one in that

The Villeneuve House, Charlesbourg, Quebec. Built before 1700, this Norman-style house exhibits many of the characteristics of rural dwellings in New France of the period — the gable windows, steeply pitched roof and rough stucco-type siding.

age desired self-government as it was later understood; and the habitants showed remarkable independence when it suited them, as in the case of ignoring government attempts to control the fur trade. Under the fatherly care of Louis, the "Sun King," and of Jean-Baptiste Colbert, his minister of finance, New France grew and prospered.

SECURITY AND GROWTH

In Canada's last century under French rule the fur trade continued to be a major economic and social force in the colony's life, but of more lasting influence was the pattern of an agricultural society which evolved from a solid institutional basis. Before 1663 over fifty blocks of land had already been granted under the seigneurial (or manorial) system of old France, and this system expanded rapidly (60 seigneuries were granted in

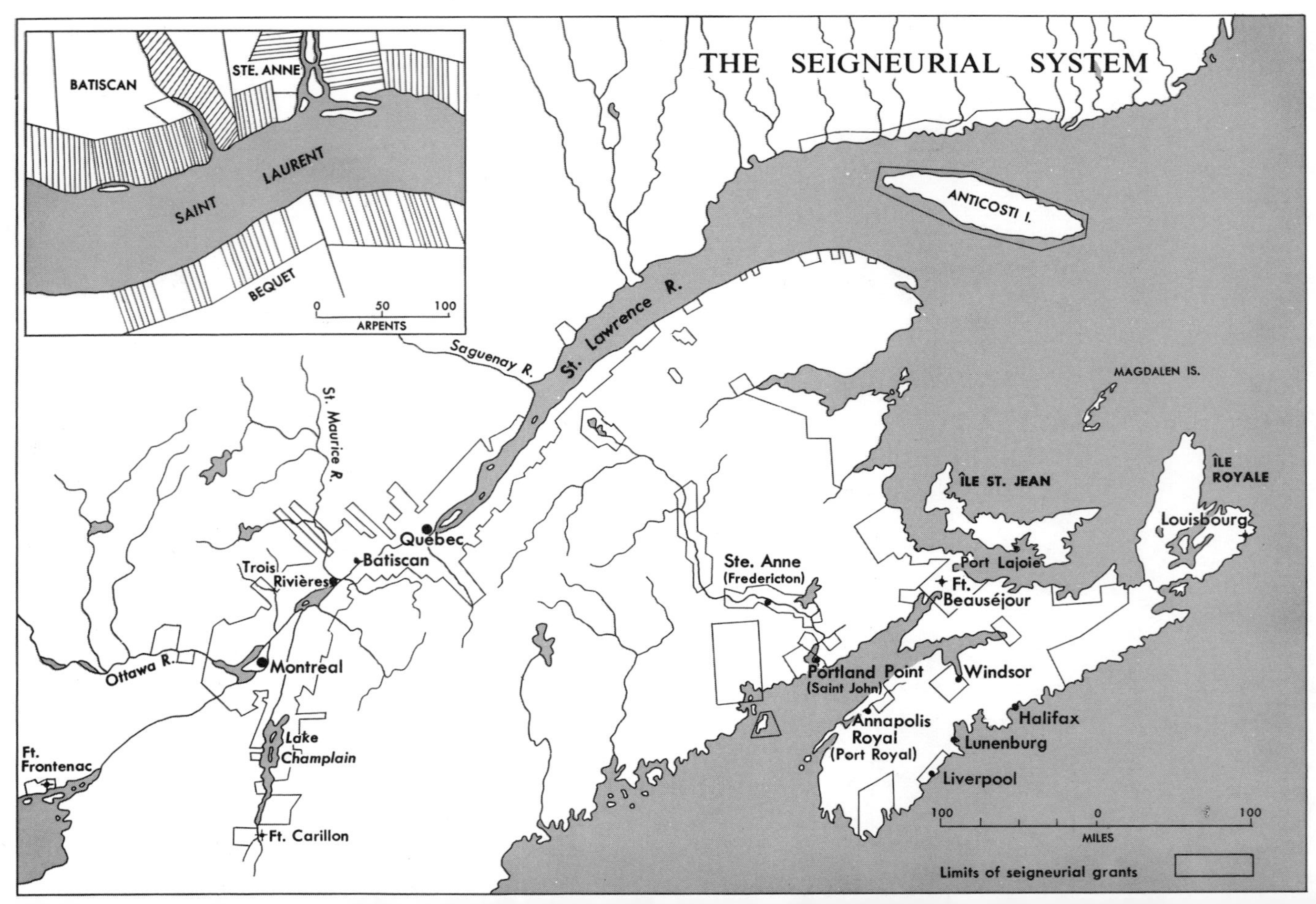
THE SEIGNEURIAL SYSTEM
BATISCAN
STE. ANNE
SAINT
LAURENT
BEQUET
0
50
100
ARPENTS
ANTICOSTI I.
St. Lawrence R.
Saguenay R.
St. Maurice R.
MAGDALEN IS.
ÎLE ST. JEAN
ÎLE ROYALE
Louisbourg
Port Lajoie
Ft. Beauséjour
Québec
Batiscan
Trois Rivières
Ste. Anne
(Fredericton)
Ottawa R.
Montreal
Portland Point
(Saint John)
Windsor
Halifax
Annapolis Royal
(Port Royal)
Lunenburg
Liverpool
Ft. Frontenac
Lake Champlain
Ft. Carillon
100
0
100
MILES
Limits of seigneurial grants

1672 alone) to become a basic part of the experience of the royal colony. Each seigneur, or grantee, whether an individual or a corporation such as the Church, received land on condition that he pay homage to the King, that he colonize it with tenants or *censitaires,* and that he provide the *censitaires* with a flour mill. In return the seigneur was accorded a prominent place in the parish church and given certain marks of social prestige. The obligations of the *censitaires* were to pay to the seigneur *cens et rentes* (small nominal ground rents), *lods et ventes* (a transfer tax when a *censitaire* sold his rights), *banalité* (a small portion of the flour ground at the seigneur's mill), and *corvées* (a few days of free labour on the seigneur's farm each year). Both seigneur and *censitaire* were subject to a *corvée* on the King's roads and bridges.

The seigneurial system involved mutual obligations on the part of both seigneur and *censitaire*, but the seigneur's burdens were the heavier. He paid a larger share of the cost of church building; he had to provide protection and occasional entertainment for his *censitaires*; and he alone paid the expense of building the mill. Yet his income from the various seigneurial fees was quite modest. One result of this was a general social and economic levelling in New France that was unknown in old France. Many prudent *censitaires* were able, in time, to buy their own seigneuries. Seigneurs were barely distinguishable in dress, habits and wealth from their tenants, and it was common to see the seigneur and his family doing manual labour on their farm. Thus a rough social equality arose in New France, largely because of a shortage of labour; but with that equality came a generally uniform higher standard of living compared to life in pre-revolutionary France.

Two opposing traditions of church-state relations underlay problems arising from the bishop's presence in the council. Laval was a believer in ultramontanism—the theory of papal supremacy over local secular authority—whereas French kings had long exerted royal control over the administration of the Roman Catholic Church in France, a practice known as Gallicanism. Conflict between these two views arose in the very early days of the royal government of New France. Although the first royal governor, de Mésy, was virtually Laval's appointee, the two men soon quarrelled over their respective authority. The Council supported Laval, as did the clergy for whom Laval had just founded his seminary. De Mésy died in 1665, but his successors encountered the same formidable opposition.

In 1665 important new arrivals came to Canada—the Carignan-Salières regiment, one thousand strong; General de Tracy, supreme commander of French forces in North America; Intendant Jean Talon, the royal instrument of King Louis and Colbert; and Daniel de Rémy de Courcelle, the new Governor. The arrival of Tracy, Talon and Courcelle marked the beginning of secular control over New France and the end of the clergy's influence on public affairs. Although Laval struggled valiantly to retain his former position of authority, each passing year brought more evidence of Louis XIV's intention to control the Church more closely. The practice of Gallicanism replaced the older tradition of ultramontanism, and became so firmly rooted in French-Canadian life as to remain an important political factor even after the British conquest.

A portrait of Jean Talon, Intendant of New France, by Claude François (1672). Talon was only 30 when he took up the extensive duties of Intendant in 1665. When he left New France in 1668, after his first term, Marie de l'Incarnation, foundress of the Ursuline order of nuns in New France, voiced the widespread regret: "Since he has been here as Intendant, the country has developed and business has progressed more than they had done since the French have been here."

The main causes of friction between church and state in royal New France during the next generation were the brandy trade and Laval's preference for centralized missionary institutions rather than parochial organization on the Old World pattern. As early as 1660 Laval had threatened to excommunicate any person selling brandy to the Indians. Merchants were convinced, however, that brandy was a necessity in the fur trade, especially after the British seized New Amsterdam (renamed New York in 1664) and offered their cheaper West Indian rum to the Indians. The brandy trade question dragged on for years, with the French government uncertain of its policy and merchants vying with theologians to justify their particular view of the trade.

The Iroquois threat was one of the first problems to be attacked by the new royal administration. Immediately upon his arrival in 1665, Tracy sent troops to fortify the Lake Champlain-Richelieu war route and in January, 1666, Courcelles left with 500 soldiers to make a surprise attack on the very heart of Iroquoia. This bold venture achieved no military success and was protested by the English at Albany as an invasion of British territory. Nevertheless, the march so impressed the Iroquois that they opened peace negotiations. When the Iroquois delayed their negotiations, Tracy and Governor Courcelles led a force that surprised and destroyed Iroquois villages in the Mohawk Valley late in 1666 at almost no cost to the French. The Iroquois Confederacy had not, of course, been destroyed, but henceforth it showed more respect for French power in North America.

With the Iroquois menace reduced, Talon set to work to build New France into a militarily and economically self-sufficient colony—one that would be a benefit, not a burden, to the mother country. The crying need of New France was for a more diversified economy to relieve its over-dependence on the uncertain beaver trade; to achieve this aim the colony required skilled workers, managers and capital. Unfortunately for New France, the success of Colbert, the King's finance minister, in expanding France's domestic economy offered equal if not better opportunities to men and investment capital. Nevertheless, subsidized immigration brought several hundred workers and a smaller number of single women across the Atlantic each year. Over 400 soldiers of the Carignan-Salières regiment settled along the Richelieu River when their tour of duty finished in 1668. Early marriages and large families were encouraged by cash bonuses—single men and girls were penalized. In the decade after 1665 the colony's population more than doubled (3,215 in 1665 to 7,832 in 1675).

Agriculture was stimulated by the importation of livestock and by the population explosion. The acreage under cultivation was nearly tripled between 1667 and 1687, and doubled again by 1713. As most river-front lots were quickly developed, a "European" pattern of compact inland settlement was attempted. It was not successful, though, for the habitants preferred the decentralized pattern of river-front seigneuries.

Other branches of the economy grew even more quickly than agriculture, thanks to the imaginative and energetic Talon, and to royal assistance, rather than to private enterprise. Talon provided large subsidies for the development of ship-building and lumbering, brewing and the raising of flax and hemp. Unfortunately, these enterprises did not have any enduring success: Baltic timber and French-built ships were still cheaper to produce; English and Dutch merchants could better supply the slaves and consumer goods for the French West Indies, and New France soon lost its small share of trade in that market. As a result of foreign competition and lack of business acumen and energy on the part of the habitants, New France soon reverted to dependence on furs and farming as the economic staples of the country. What seems surprising is the fact that industry was even planned for the colony in an age which supposedly accepted the mercantilist doctrine that colonies must only produce raw materials for the mother country and buy manufactured goods from her in return. The imagination and initiative shown by Jean Talon until he left New France in 1672 were not repeated by his successors.

Life in New France developed an independent spirit among the colonists who, always ready to accept and even demand aid, were equally quick to oppose any new responsibilities that the

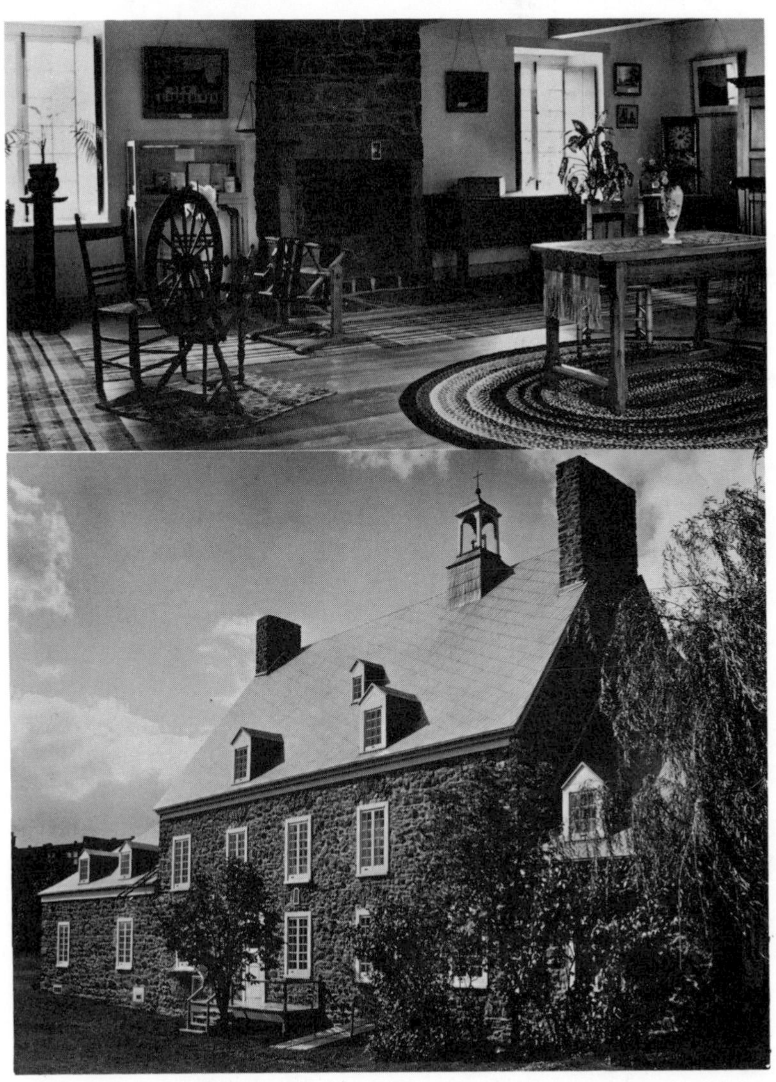

The "Ferme St. Gabriel," Point St. Charles, Quebec, built in 1698. The first house on this site was built in 1668 by Marguerite Bourgeoys, foundress of the Congregation of Notre Dame and one of the earliest inhabitants of Montreal. The present building, in spite of additions and reconstructions, is almost certainly the oldest continuously occupied house in Quebec. Marguerite Bourgeoys opened a school here, and at one time used it to house many of the "filles du Roi" while she attended to their matrimonial arrangements.

state, or even the Church, might try to impose. In this habit they differed little from the English colonists of that day, and even of later ages. But in New France, as in old, no sizeable or influential class of bourgeoisie developed because of a traditional disdain for commercial enterprises and the dominance of trade by visiting merchants from old France. Below the government administrators, most of whom came from France and left after a few years of service, society consisted of farm families. In the pre-machine age many hands made lighter work, and large families were an asset to the colony. But the lure of the forest and its furs was always present, and it was an accepted fact that every Canadian family had some relative involved in the trade.

FRONTENAC, THE FIGHTING GOVERNOR

The basic issues of New France's development—the brandy trade, Indian relations, Gallicanism and westward expansion—were beginning to come to a head in 1672 when the imperious Louis de Buade, Comte de Frontenac, became governor. Colbert's long-range plan was to make New France a compact, self-sufficient colony, but the only commodity that New France could produce competitively was furs, and the trade required continuous geographic expansion to maintain a supply of furs. The temporary removal of the Iroquois menace permitted just such an expansion towards the west. Despite official French policy laid down by Colbert to concentrate energy on developing the St. Lawrence valley, the fur trade was extended into the hinterland, weakening the settled area in direct ratio to the trade's success. Talon realized that the colony's existence depended on furs, and he began to send explorers into uncharted regions. Father Albanel, for example, went overland to Hudson Bay in 1671, only to discover that English traders were already there. (Pierre Radisson and his brother-in-law, Des Groseilliers, who had objected to paying the 25 percent tax on furs in New France, had received backing in England for a trading venture to Hudson Bay. They made such a profitable trip in 1668-69 that

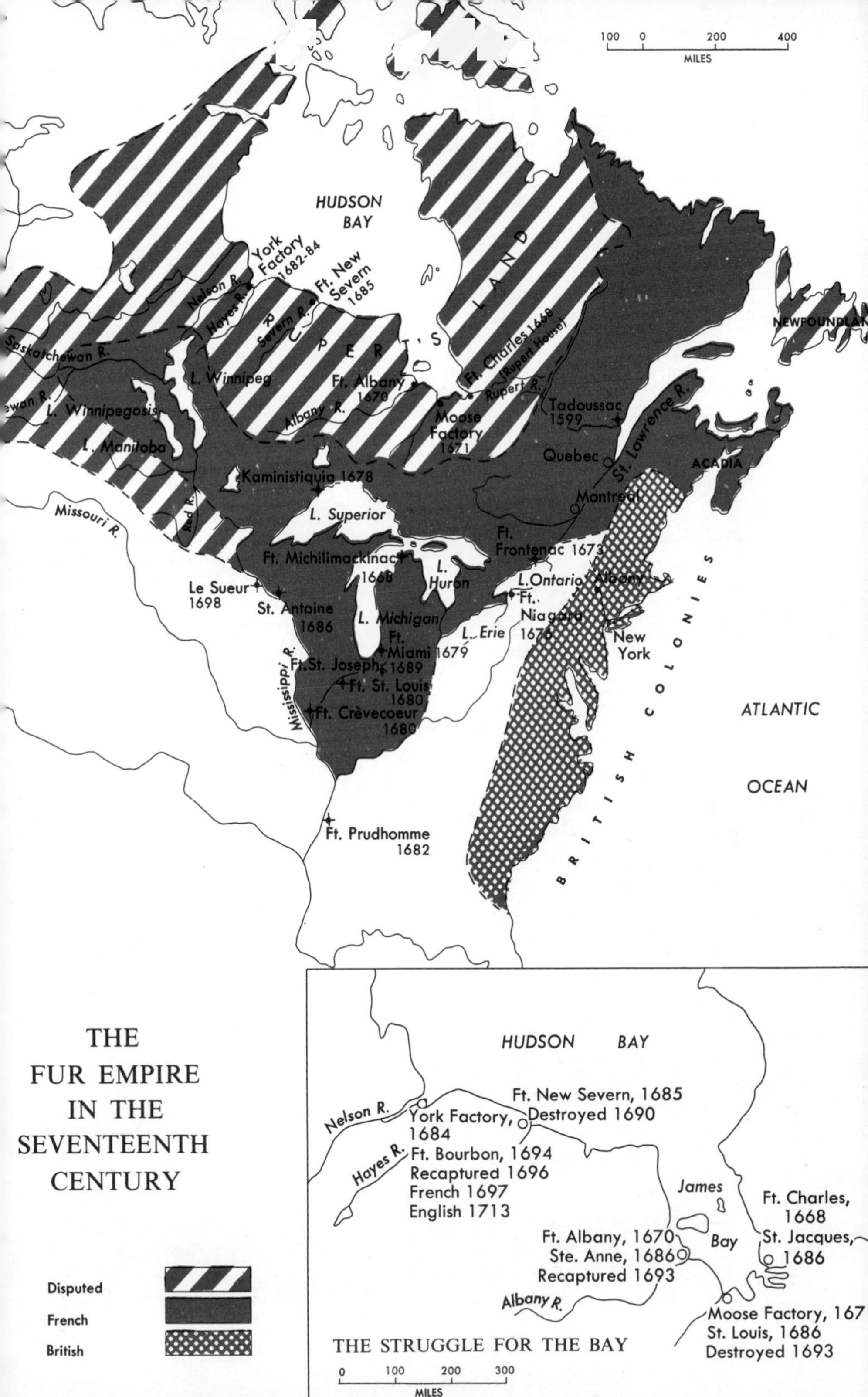
100 0 200 400
MILES
HUDSON BAY
York Factory 1682-84
Ft. New Severn 1685
Nelson R.
Hayes R.
Severn R.
RUPERT'S LAND
Saskatchewan R.
L. Winnipeg
Ft. Albany 1670
Albany R.
Ft. Charles 1668 (Rupert House)
Rupert R.
Moose Factory 1671
Tadoussac 1599
St. Lawrence R.
NEWFOUNDLAND
L. Winnipegosis
L. Manitoba
Quebec
ACADIA
Kaministiquia 1678
Montreal
Missouri R.
Red R.
L. Superior
Ft. Frontenac 1673
Ft. Michilimackinac 1668
L. Huron
L. Ontario
Albany
Le Sueur 1698
St. Antoine 1686
Ft. Niagara 1676
L. Michigan
L. Erie
New York
Ft. Miami 1679
Ft. St. Joseph 1689
Ft. St. Louis 1680
Mississippi R.
Ft. Crèvecoeur 1680
BRITISH COLONIES
ATLANTIC OCEAN
Ft. Prudhomme 1682
Disputed
French
British
HUDSON BAY
Nelson R.
York Factory, 1684
Ft. New Severn, 1685 Destroyed 1690
Hayes R.
Ft. Bourbon, 1694
Recaptured 1696
French 1697
English 1713
James Bay
Ft. Charles, 1668
St. Jacques, 1686
Ft. Albany, 1670
Ste. Anne, 1686
Recaptured 1693
Albany R.
Moose Factory, 1671
St. Louis, 1686
Destroyed 1693
THE STRUGGLE FOR THE BAY
0 100 200 300
MILES

THE FUR EMPIRE IN THE SEVENTEENTH CENTURY

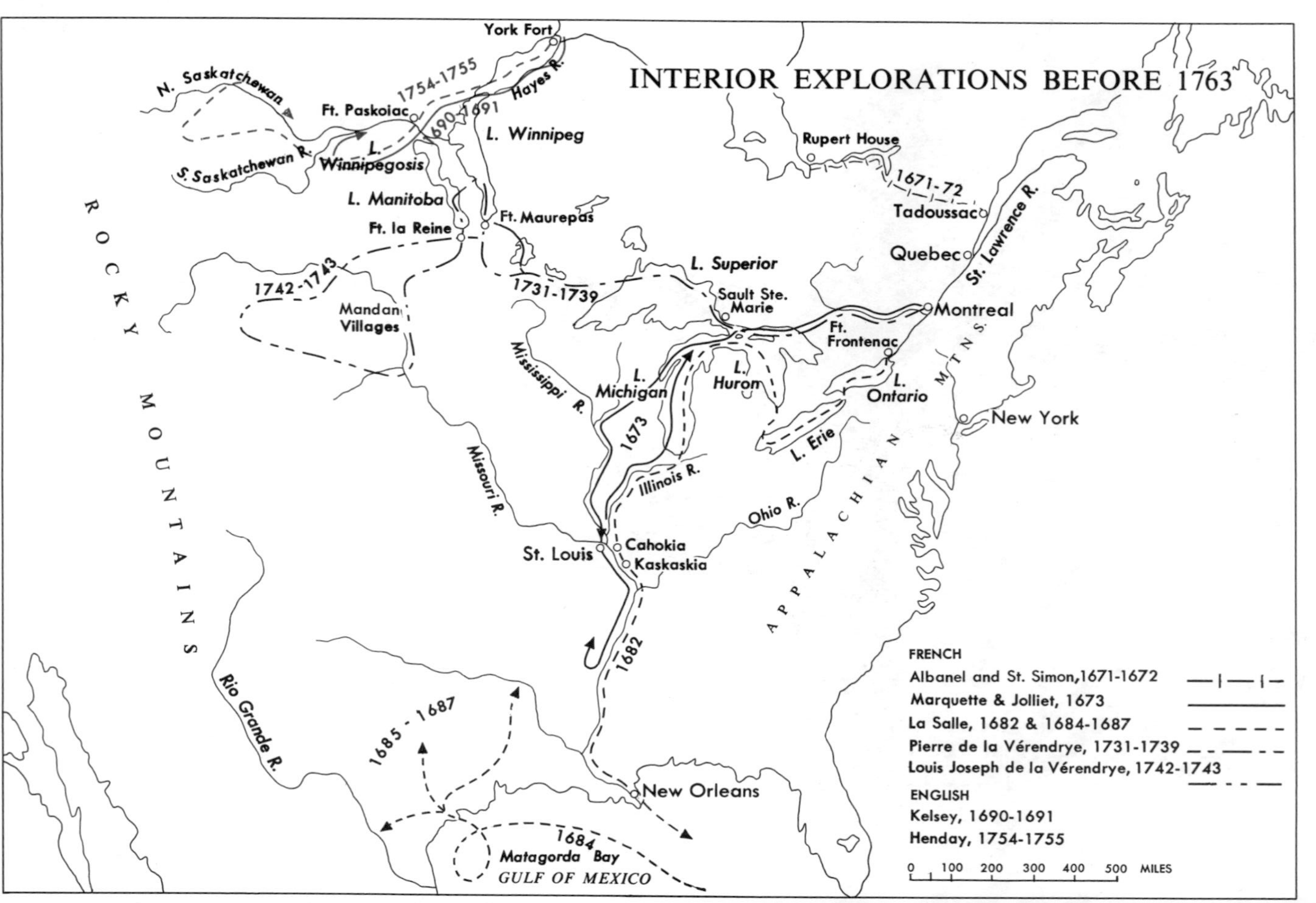
INTERIOR EXPLORATIONS BEFORE 1763
York Fort
N. Saskatchewan
1754-1755
Hayes R.
Ft. Paskoiac
1690-1691
L. Winnipeg
S. Saskatchewan R.
L. Winnipegosis
Rupert House
1671-72
Tadoussac
L. Manitoba
Ft. Maurepas
Ft. la Reine
ROCKY MOUNTAINS
Quebec
St. Lawrence R.
L. Superior
1742-1743
1731-1739
Sault Ste. Marie
Montreal
Mandan Villages
Ft. Frontenac
Mississippi R.
L. Michigan
L. Huron
L. Ontario
New York
1673
L. Erie
Missouri R.
Illinois R.
Ohio R.
APPALACHIAN MTNS.
Cahokia
St. Louis
Kaskaskia
1682
Rio Grande R.
1685-1687
New Orleans
1684
Matagorda Bay
GULF OF MEXICO
FRENCH
Albanel and St. Simon, 1671-1672
Marquette & Jolliet, 1673
La Salle, 1682 & 1684-1687
Pierre de la Vérendrye, 1731-1739
Louis Joseph de la Vérendrye, 1742-1743
ENGLISH
Kelsey, 1690-1691
Henday, 1754-1755
0 100 200 300 400 500 MILES

the Hudson's Bay Company was chartered in 1670.) Finally, on the eve of Talon's departure from New France, the new governor, Frontenac, accepted the "Great Intendant's" suggestion to send Louis Jolliet on an expedition that located the rumoured Mississippi River in 1673.

Traders followed the routes of explorers, and within a decade of Jolliet's great trip posts had been established at Sault Ste. Marie, Michilimackinac and in the Lake of the Woods and upper Mississippi regions. The greatly increased fur trade brought more wealth to New France, but it robbed the colony of some of its most energetic men, who abandoned farming to become *coureurs de bois* (independent trappers and woodsmen, estimated at as many as one quarter of the adult male population under 50). Jesuit missionaries soon followed the trade westward. When they found the natives debauched by the *coureurs de bois*, and the latter brutalized by contact with the Indians, they became, ironically, strong supporters of the policies of the anti-clerical Colbert.

One of the greatest achievements of Frontenac's governorship was the exploration and exploitation of the west, although undeniably it was in part responsible for destroying Colbert's plans for diversified colonial development. Defying the intentions of both Colbert and the King, Frontenac built a trading post at Cataraqui—the present site of Kingston—in 1673, and named it Fort Frontenac. The Governor encouraged and enabled his friend Robert Cavelier, Sieur de la Salle, to enlarge Fort Frontenac (of which he was seigneur), and to construct another fort at Niagara in 1678. La Salle also built the sailing vessel, *Griffon*, which was lost on its first voyage on the upper lakes. In 1678 La Salle got royal permission to explore the length of the Mississippi and to build forts thereon, which he did. Together, Frontenac and La Salle created a monopolistic fur empire in the west by issuing *congés* (trading licenses) only to their friends, with the result that the fur trade was divided into warring factions.

In 1682 Frontenac was abruptly removed from office and recalled to France by the King. The events leading to his recall had begun almost with his arrival in New France, when he had begun to antagonize Talon and Colbert. He asserted his social superiority to Talon and Talon's successor on every occasion, and usurped the council's powers after Talon left. When the governor of Montreal opposed Frontenac's arbitrary actions, Frontenac imprisoned him and punished one of his defenders, a Montreal priest. Despite royal censure, Frontenac's bullying of everyone around him continued. He accused the Jesuits of opposing the brandy trade so that they could monopolize the fur trade themselves. When Bishop Laval refused absolution to the sellers of brandy, Frontenac claimed the Church was interfering with royal authority. In 1679 the King himself ordered an end to the brandy trade, but this edict could be (and was) easily evaded by the Governor and his friends. By 1680 Frontenac had quarrelled with the clergy over the brandy trade and his own precedence at Church functions, had antagonized the council by his dictatorial methods, had favoured his friend La Salle in the western fur trade at the expense of the Montreal traders, and had provoked the royal government. When he arbitrarily ordered the arrest of his opponents in 1681, the King had no choice but to recall Frontenac for the good of the colony.

Frontenac's successor, La Barre, faced a triple challenge when he took office: the combined and well-armed forces of the Five Nations Confederacy, which in 1680 had renewed the French-Iroquois war with an attack on the Illinois valley; increased English activity on Hudson Bay; and New England's control of the Acadian fisheries. The French government which Frontenac had deliberately misinformed about conditions in New France in order to enhance his own reputation, seemed indifferent to La Barre's problems. His bungled and feeble show of force against the Iroquois near Oswego in 1684 ended in a diplomatic defeat when influenza struck down the French soldiers. The peace treaty concluded with the Iroquois on that occasion was the excuse for replacing La Barre in 1685 with the Marquis de Denonville. Denonville introduced much-needed administrative and military reforms, reduced drunkenness, controlled the fur trade and founded a navigation school. In order to reduce the English competition in the fur trade, he sent a military force overland to Hudson Bay. The expedition captured three of the Hudson's Bay Company's five posts, despite the fact that England and France were not at war. Denonville's march with 2,000 French and Indian allies into the Iroquois lands in 1687, however, achieved little more than the destruction of deserted villages. Thanks to his ineptness and poor judgment, the invasion destroyed hope of peace with the Iroquois: the Indians retaliated by attacking Forts Frontenac and Niagara. In 1688 the post at Niagara had to be abandoned.

When "King William's War" began between England and France in 1689, the first effect was renewed attacks by the Iroquois. They surprised and destroyed Lachine and then began random raiding among the settlements of New France. One result was that strategic Fort Frontenac had to be abandoned as indefensible. Not all the events of 1689, however, were tragic. Thanks to influential friends at Court, the Comte de Frontenac's earlier misdemeanours were forgiven by the King, and in the fall he returned to Quebec for a second term as Governor. Almost at the same time a record fur crop reached Montreal.

Frontenac, aiming to forestall a combined English-Indian attack on the colony, quickly took the offensive against the English, who were blamed—not altogether correctly—for the Iroquois raids. In February, 1690, a force of Canadiens and Indians massacred half the residents of Schenectady, New York. Two months later a second expedition fell on Salmon Falls, New Hampshire, and similar attacks were made on other Atlantic

Some eighteenth century impressions of the Canadian Indians from Lahontan's New Voyages *(1703). The artist demonstrates a delightful confusion—notice the fair, curly hair of the figure at the top of the page and the almost Grecian appearance of the costume worn by the figure.*

settlements. The response of the English colonies was Sir William Phips' capture and sack of the weak and divided post at Port Royal.

These savage attacks on isolated settlements did no serious harm to the English or their Iroquois allies, but they united New England and New York in the conviction that New France must be destroyed. A force sent to take Montreal in the autumn was too small for the task, but at the same time thirty-four ships from Boston under Phips' command and carrying 2,300 men approached Quebec and demanded its surrender. Frontenac, who had just returned from Montreal, haughtily stated that, "the mouths of my cannons and muskets" would give his reply. Faced by strong fortifications, superior numbers and Frontenac's spirit, the *Bostonnais* departed after a feeble land attack. Neither side attempted such a large-scale invasion again during the war, but contented themselves with harassing each other's outlying settlements.

The Canadiens were determined, however, to crush the Iroquois, who were a greater threat than the English. A raid against Mohawk villages in 1692 did no serious damage, but

A map of the English siege of Quebec of 1690 ascribed to Frontenac.

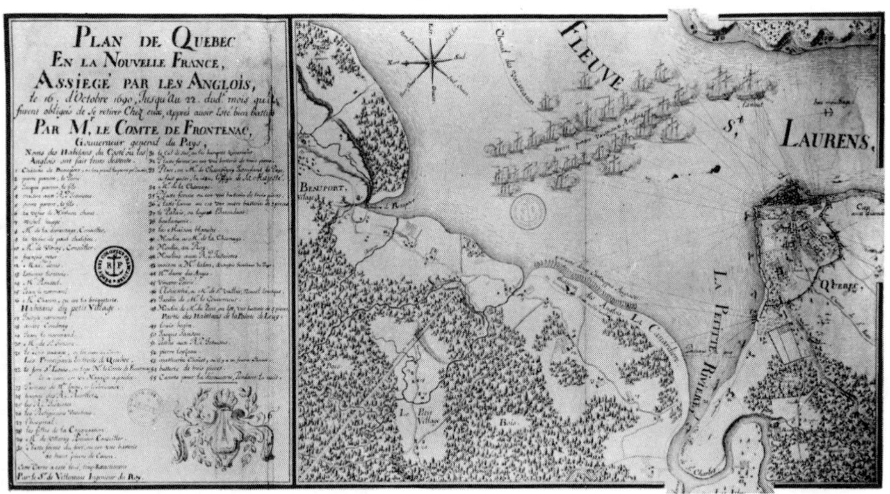

the Iroquois, who felt the English were shirking their role in the war, offered to make peace. By 1695, however, the Indian allies of the French, the Hurons and Ottawas, seemed likely to join the western Fox and Mascoutin tribes, who had deserted to the Iroquois. Frontenac decided to restore France's prestige with her Indian allies by striking at the Iroquois Confederacy. His large-scale invasion of Onondaga and Oneida territory in 1696 did little damage, but frightened the Iroquois into negotiating a peace, and saved the French fur trade by forcing the western Indians to continue their trade with Montreal.

As far as Acadia was concerned, the war after 1690 consisted of raids by the Abenakis against New England. The Acadians were too few to protect themselves or to prosecute hostilities, but the French sea power managed to contain the English colonists and control the disputed region of northern Maine. The French had their most notable victory far to the north, on the cold waters of Hudson Bay. Pierre le Moyne d'Iberville, whose ships had saved Acadia and had seized every British settlement in Newfoundland except Bonavista and Carbonear, in 1697 defeated the much larger force of Hudson's Bay Company ships and captured strategic Fort Nelson. Less than three weeks later the Treaty of Ryswick ended King William's War.

Although the treaty called for the restoration of York Fort to the English and returned Albany (on Hudson Bay) to the French, both sides simply kept what they had won. Elsewhere in Canada and Acadia, only minor changes were made. But the Treaty of Ryswick was more properly a truce than a peace—the Anglo-French struggle for empire in North America had, in reality, barely begun.

THE EXPANSION AND CONTRACTION OF NEW FRANCE

King William's War had just ended when Frontenac died in Quebec in December, 1698. His passing marked the end of an era in more ways than one. Despite all his high-handed actions, his two periods as governor had seen New France overcome major threats from its two greatest enemies, the Iroquois and the English. Never again would the colony have such a colourful leader. His successors were at best poor copies of the "Fighting Governor." Yet Frontenac's very drive and ambition had created a legacy for New France that hastened, if it did not cause, the end of French rule. French interests in North America, thanks largely to Frontenac's evasion of Colbert's policy for a compact colony, were committed to a westward expansion that the fur trade demanded but which over-extended all the colony's resources.

In July, 1701, as a result of Frontenac's Indian policy, more than 1,000 Indians of thirty-odd tribes met at Montreal, not for war but for peace. The treaty signed at that time pledged the Iroquois to stay neutral in any future wars between France and England and to live in peace with the western tribes. This agreement was of the highest importance, for in the entirely possible event of a new English-French war the treaty gave New France, for the first time, a decided military advantage over her English neighbours.

Meanwhile, Louis XIV, obsessed with his search for French glory, accepted the Spanish throne for his grandson. To protect the Spanish American colonies now under his control, he ordered the founding of New Orleans at the mouth of the Mississippi in 1701—"to halt the advance which the English of the colony of New York have begun to make in the lands which lie between them and this river." The lower Mississippi valley produced inferior furs, and New France had no colonists to spare for settlement, yet Frontenac's expansionist policy was now escalated to the level of French imperialism as a result of Louis XIV's European ambitions. Thus was established the French policy of containing the English on the Atlantic seaboard by encirclement; by the same token a half-century of conflict for total control of North America was made inevitable. Three wars would follow before New France disappeared, and the wonder is not that the wars occurred but that, considering the odds in favour of Britain, it took so long to conquer this outpost of the French empire.

Louis' action regarding the Spanish throne immediately

raised fears in Europe about the possible results of a strong union between France and Spain, and provoked the grand alliance of England, the Netherlands and Austria to open the War of the Spanish Succession. In North America there were, however, no Marlboroughs to fight "Queen Anne's War" (as the struggle in the New World has been called). While English regimental banners in Europe were inscribed with the battle honours of Blenheim, Ramillies and Malplaquet, the war in North America began with a series of French-Indian raids against English settlements. The first strike was made against New England in 1703, and was followed the next year

The art of wood carving, especially for the decoration of churches, thrived in New France. These pieces, now in a Quebec City museum, were done in 1748 by Noël and François Levasseur for the Church of Ste. Famille, on the Ile d'Orléans. They attest to the skill and sensitivity of the artist and are particularly fine examples of the art.

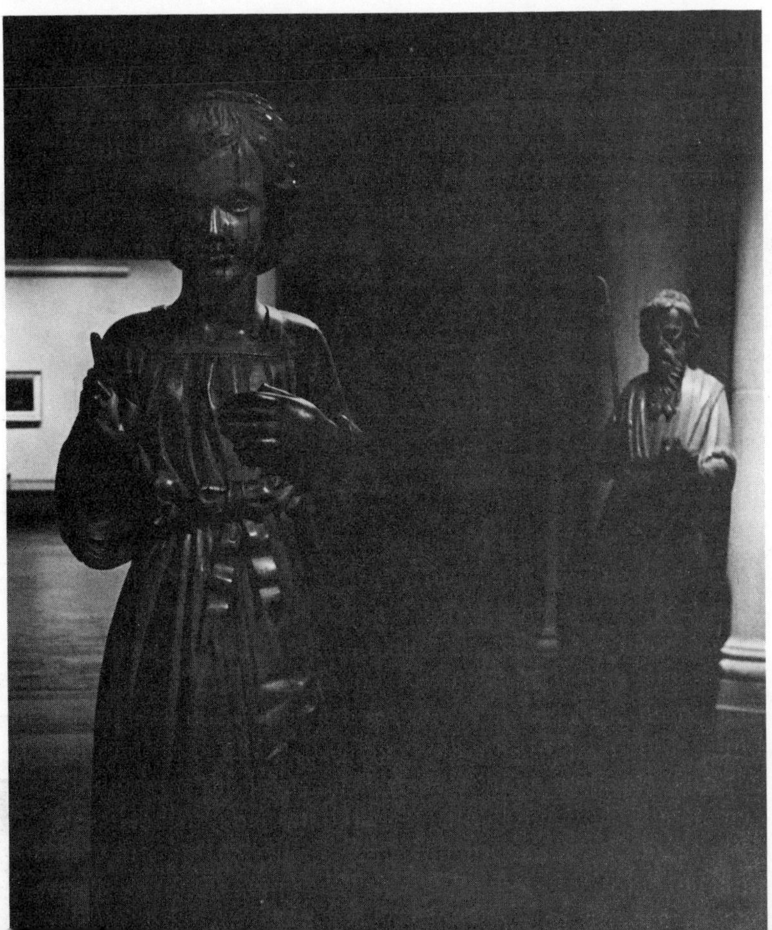

by an attack on Deerfield, Massachusetts. The New England colonists retaliated with raids on the Abenakis Indians and the Acadians. In 1705 the New Englanders sent envoys to New France with a proposal that the colonists remain neutral in the war being waged by their mother countries. But in spite of an encouraging response from Quebec, the New Englanders abandoned the scheme a year later. Once more the Abenakis struck southward, although they were now warned that Governor Vaudreuil would only pay bounties for English prisoners, not for English scalps. While hostilities continued between New England, the Abenakis and Acadia, the Canadiens carefully avoided attacks on New York and managed to maintain an uneasy balance between the Iroquois and the western tribes, lest the Iroquois be incited to break their treaty. For their part the Iroquois resisted British pressure and remained neutral until the later stages of the war. For these reasons both the New Yorkers and the people of New France were spared from a repetition of past savagery.

When the attacks on New England continued, the British decided to launch an attack on New France. Accordingly, in 1710, ships of the Royal Navy bearing New England troops seized Port Royal, which was then renamed Annapolis Royal. Encouraged by this easy victory, eighty-four ships carrying 7,400 men, set out in 1711 under Sir Hovenden Walker for Quebec. Two thousand soldiers with 600 Iroquois advanced towards Montreal. However, the expedition was abandoned and Quebec was delivered from almost certain defeat when 700 men of the British force were lost during a storm on the St. Lawrence. Neither side undertook further serious hostilities before the Treaty of Utrecht ended the war in 1713.

The Treaty of Utrecht confirmed Britain's claim to the Hudson Bay basin and Newfoundland, and to sovereignty over the Iroquois. It also transferred most of Acadia to Britain. Only Cape Breton and Isle St. Jean (Prince Edward Island) were left in French hands, as concessions of doubtful value in view of England's possession of both Nova Scotia and Newfoundland. The treaty also provided that the Acadian settlers, numbering some 2,500, were to be given one year to choose between emigrat-

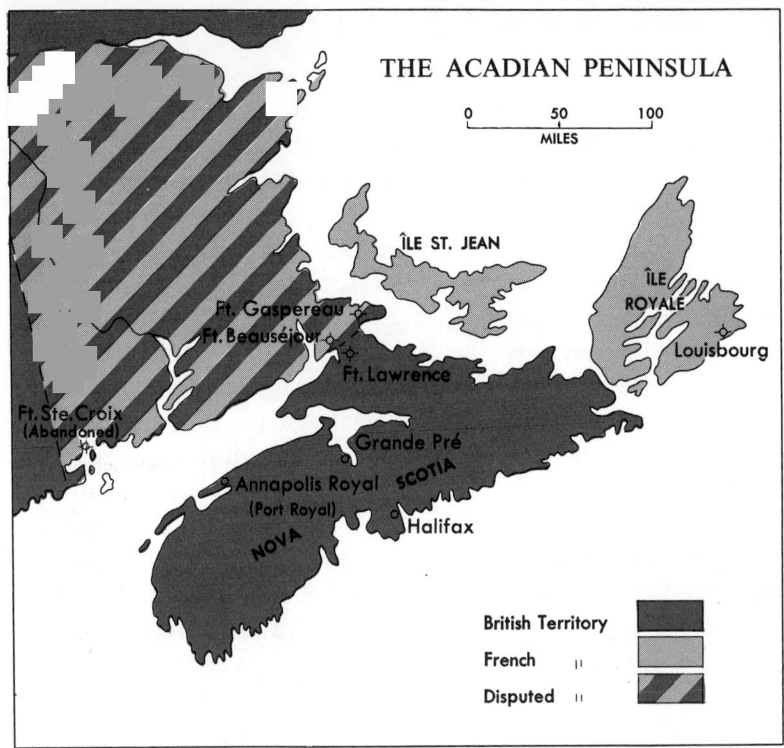

ing or remaining as British subjects. If they stayed they were to be guaranteed "the exercise of the Roman Catholic religion, insofar (sic) as this is permitted by the laws of Great Britain." This last phrase was highly ambiguous since the contemporary British penal code left Roman Catholic subjects of the King without many basic political rights. These laws were not, however, enforced in the colonies, and after 1713 the Acadians were permitted to receive missionary priests from Quebec as long as the priests avoided political interference.

When the Acadians were threatened with the imposition of a loyalty oath, they replied by planning a wholesale exodus of Isle St. Jean. Faced with the possibility of losing such useful citizens, no British governor seriously pressed the issue until the eve of the Seven Years' War. Under these circumstances the Acadians preferred to abandon their French citizenship rather than their farms. Life returned to its normal routine, with the British governor and his few troops at Annapolis Royal and Canso as the only marks of the change of sovereignty.

After the Treaty of Utrecht, both Newfoundland and Hudson Bay were fully, firmly and legally under British control. During the recent war the French had captured the British base of St. John's while the British had contented themselves in destroying French fishing stations. With the peace, however, the whole of Newfoundland, including the French settlement of Placentia, became British territory, France retaining only fishing rights in two designated areas.

France's territorial losses in North America had been extensive by European standards, but in terms of the North American situation they were only peripheral. Except for Acadia, the ceded lands were virtually uninhabited—their real importance to France had been economic and strategic. Even so, France retained a large stake in the Atlantic fisheries, while hoping that the furs of Hudson Bay might yet be replaced by greater exploitation of the western trade. The essential conflict remained, however, for France's possession of the great arc formed by the St. Lawrence and Mississippi basins seemed to restrict the British colonies to the Atlantic seaboard. As yet the population of those colonies was too small to challenge the French west of the Appalachians.

THE THIRTY YEARS' PEACE

The cessation of Anglo-French hostilities in North America ushered in three decades of dynamic, if quiet, development for both the French and British colonies. In that time British population along the seaboard grew from less than half a million to almost one and a half million. The population of New France also nearly tripled its 1713 total of eighteen thousand, largely by natural increase. Industry in the British colonies expanded and diversified to near self-sufficiency. But Canada underwent no basic economic change, except to find a larger market in the French West Indies.

The key to Canada's triangular trade with France and the West Indies was the great fortress at Louisbourg, on Isle Royale (Cape

Breton Island). Begun in 1719 to offset the loss of Port Royal, Louisbourg was a standing threat to English colonial commerce should war recur. Nevertheless, New France was never able to capitalize fully on the potential of this triangular trade, and the colony was forced to fall back on its traditional over-dependence on a single-staple economy. The fur trade, principally in beaver skins, remained the mainstay of New France's economy, despite a healthy revival of agriculture after the quarter-century of war.

Indian relations remained a problem for New France as the Iroquois sought to draw the western tribes into their orbit. English trade goods, of better quality and from two to four times cheaper than the French product, were a persuasive Iroquois argument that the French found hard to answer, although the intimidation of the Fox tribe by a French show of force in 1716 was a good beginning. But French expansion into the interior now actually worked against the traditional economic interests of Montreal as more and more furs from the Ohio and Upper Mississippi regions found their way to New Orleans instead of Montreal, and more Canadians moved west to settle in the Mississippi valley. The attractions of the fur trade—profits and untrammeled living—still drew young men from all classes. To control this unbridled trade, and to stop the widespread contraband with the British, the government attempted once more to enforce its system of licenses or *congés*. Private traders could still buy furs, but they could sell them only to the holders of the monopoly. The sale of foreign goods in the colony was prohibited and all buildings, even nunneries, could be searched for such merchandise. A campaign of fines, controls and confiscations (which remained in force until the British conquest), plus rising fur prices quickly produced the desired effect. By 1726 the volume of pelts reaching Quebec was double the previous annual average.

To intercept the southward flow of furs from the western tribes to the British colonies, Governor Vaudreuil built posts at Niagara and Toronto in the early 1720's. New York objected, claiming that these posts were in Iroquois territory and hence violated the Treaty of Utrecht. When Vaudreuil proceeded to fortify the Niagara base, the colony of New York countered by

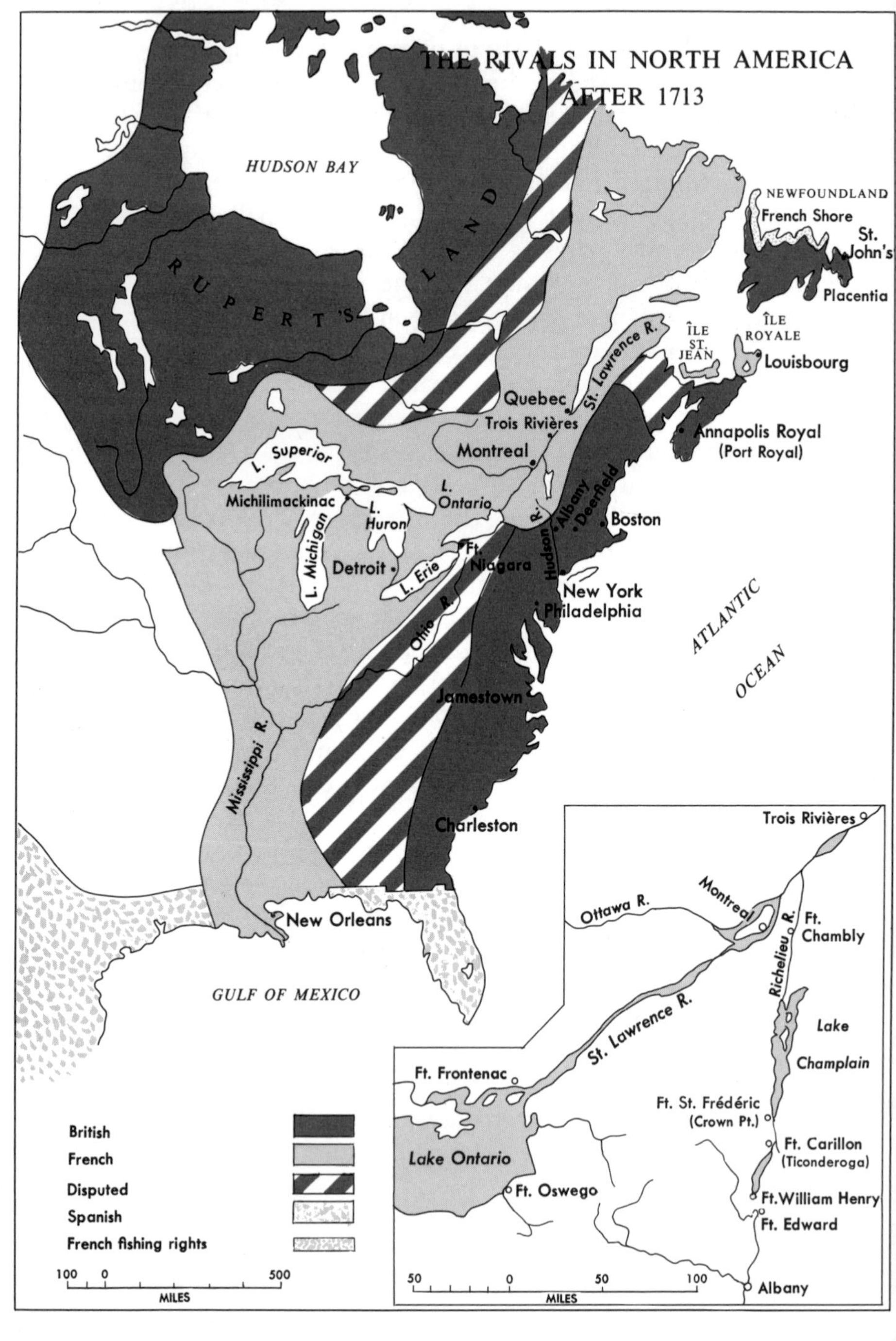
THE RIVALS IN NORTH AMERICA
AFTER 1713
HUDSON BAY
RUPERT'S LAND
NEWFOUNDLAND
French Shore
St. John's
Placentia
ÎLE ROYALE
ÎLE ST. JEAN
Louisbourg
St. Lawrence R.
Quebec
Trois Rivières
Montreal
Annapolis Royal
(Port Royal)
L. Superior
Michilimackinac
L. Huron
L. Ontario
L. Michigan
Albany
Deerfield
Boston
Hudson R.
Ft. Niagara
Detroit
L. Erie
New York
Philadelphia
Ohio R.
ATLANTIC
OCEAN
Jamestown
Mississippi R.
Charleston
New Orleans
GULF OF MEXICO
British
French
Disputed
Spanish
French fishing rights
100 0 500
MILES
Trois Rivières
Montreal
Ottawa R.
Ft. Chambly
Richelieu R.
Lake Champlain
St. Lawrence R.
Ft. Frontenac
Ft. St. Frédéric
(Crown Pt.)
Ft. Carillon
(Ticonderoga)
Lake Ontario
Ft. Oswego
Ft. William Henry
Ft. Edward
Albany
50 0 50 100
MILES

building a military post at Oswego on the south shore of Lake Ontario. This uneasy balance of power in the Great Lakes region continued until the Seven Years' War.

Far to the northwest a new chapter in Canadian explorations was being written during this period of relative peace. Still obsessed by the dream of a short route to the Orient, the French government sent the Jesuit, Charlevoix, westward in 1721, but he was stopped by wars with the Fox tribe. The exploratory project was revived in the 1730's as part of the fur trading operations of Pierre Gaultier de la Vérendrye and a company of Montreal merchants. They accepted the Indians' story that the "western ocean" was only ten days' travel from Lake Winnipeg. Expansion in this more northerly direction would bypass the Foxes. Despite financial difficulties with his partners and the government of New France, La Vérendrye had established a chain of forts on Rainy Lake, Lake of the Woods and the Red River by 1734. In 1738 he reached the site of Winnipeg and visited the upper reaches of the Missouri River. The following year one of his sons explored to the forks of the Saskatchewan River. Undeterred by a debt of 40,000 *livres* arising from his explorations, La Vérendrye sent two of his sons west in 1742-43, and they reached the Black Hills of Dakota. Until 1749 the French government refused to recognize these great achievements: La Vérendrye's death that same year virtually ended French exploration in the Canadian west. The only immediate sequel to these exploits was the building of Fort La Jonquière near the site of Edmonton, but La Vérendrye's work had opened the west to future fur trade, and had challenged the trade of the Hudson's Bay Company in the area.

While La Vérendrye was establishing France's claim to the prairie lands, the colony on the St. Lawrence was acquiring new signs of economic and social sophistication. By 1737 a one-track carriage road had been built from Montreal to Quebec, reducing the travelling time for the 170 miles to a mere four days. Montreal had now surpassed Quebec in size, but the capital had acquired the settled appearance of a European city, with imposing church and secular buildings rising behind the reconstructed walls of the Upper Town.

Bishop Laval had resigned in 1688 but lived on in Quebec untill his death in 1708. His successor, the stubborn Saint-Vallier, quarrelled with Laval and many of the clergy, and criticized the behaviour of laymen, including the governor, in the minutest

Typical of the marks of increased sophistication evident in Quebec City during the eighteenth century were houses like this, La Maison Chevalier.

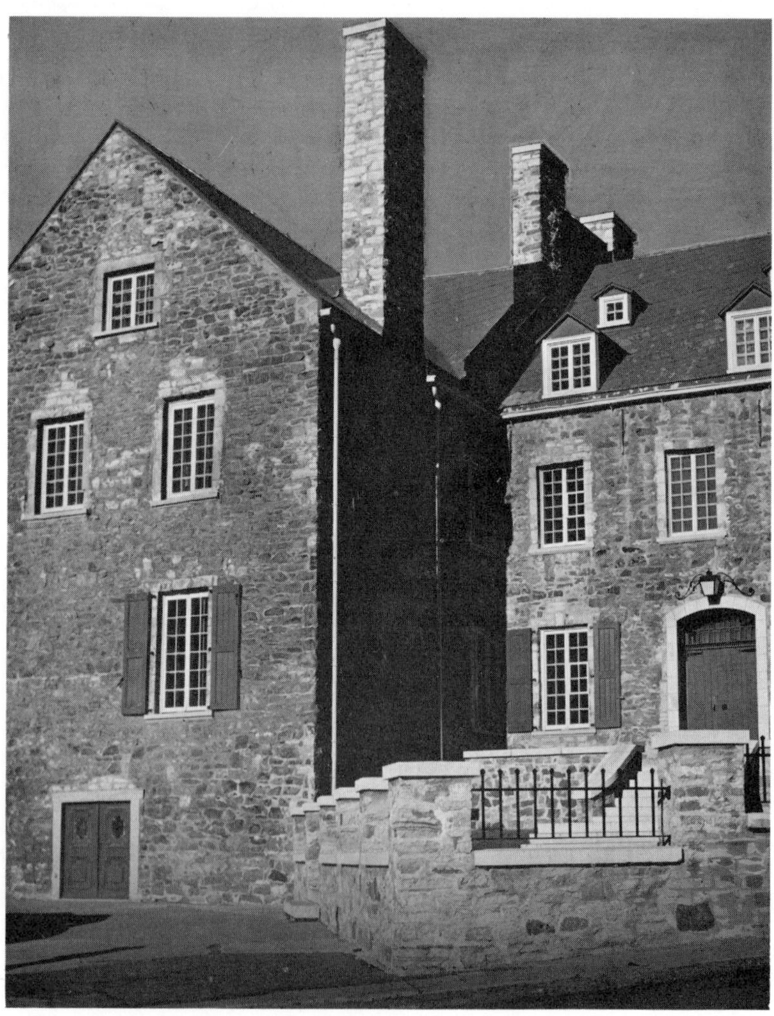

detail. Saint-Vallier died in 1728; of his three immediate successors the first never came to Canada, the second remained only two years and the third died less than a month after arriving. Not until 1741 did New France get an effective bishop, de Pontbriand, the last appointed by the King of France.

Since Frontenac's time the role of the Church in New France's political life had been minimized by the Gallican policies of the government, but its moral and religious influence at the parish level and in education was proportionately stronger. By 1722 the boundaries of eighty-four parishes had been defined, but only sixty priests were settled in parish work. Another ninety priests were attached to the seminary, in addition to the Jesuit and Récollet missionaries and the semi-independent Sulpicians of Montreal. Equally important for the survival of the French-Canadian identity, the parish priests were predominantly Canadian-born men whose sympathies and understanding lay with their people, whereas the upper ranks and senior offices of the church were filled by better-educated French clergy who tended to stay in the colony only for their period in office. This situation in the Church was but one aspect of the growth of an indigenous and homogeneous Canadian society which, like society in the English colonies, was developing in the eighteenth century as an entity distinct from its distant mother country in many ways of thinking and acting.

THE LAST DAYS OF NEW FRANCE

Thirty years of peace and progress in North America ended in 1744 when France declared war on Great Britain over the contested succession to the throne of Austria. Louisbourg, "the Gibraltar of America," was already marked as the prime target of the British colonies, and in 1745 a colonial force with Royal Navy aid captured the great fortress after a six-week siege, to the joy and relief of the Atlantic colonies. When the loss of Louisbourg left Quebec exposed, Governor Beauharnois seized the initiative by mounting raids against villages in New York and Massachusetts. He hoped that this would keep the

A view of Louisbourg in 1731.

British sufficiently off balance that they would not attack the capital. For two years both sides employed Indian allies against the enemy, but neither side could support any decisive campaign, nor were they really interested in doing so since they felt more was to be gained by putting the greatest effort into the war in Europe. The Treaty of Aix-la-Chapelle in 1748 ended hostilities for the time being, but the peace terms virtually insured a future renewal of war in North America. To the disgust of the British colonies, Louisbourg was restored to France. Equally provocative, the treaty did not define the disputed boundaries in the Ohio region or Acadia.

The issue of Acadian neutrality had now become critical. Though alternately threatened and cajoled by local representatives of both the French and British, most of the 13,000 Acadians had refused to bear arms for either side, although a few had responded to the invitations of one Abbé Le Loutre to rise against British rule. Faced with the presence of this potential "fifth column", the British government decided to colonize Nova Scotia with dependable settlers and to create a naval base to match Louisbourg. In 1749 Halifax was founded for this purpose,

and 2,700 "foreign Protestants," mostly German-speaking, were also settled there and at Lunenburg.

With this new strength Governor Cornwallis demanded an oath of allegiance from the Acadians in 1750. Some 1,500 preferred to emigrate to French territory—particularly to Isle St. Jean—but the majority procrastinated. The peaceful state of the Acadians and the increase of British settlers to 4,200 encouraged the British government to postpone a showdown on the matter. But French machinations continued among the Acadians, and France's Indian allies, encouraged by the missionary-agent provocateur, Le Loutre, began collecting British scalps. The new Lieutenant-Governor, Lawrence, then determined that the Acadians must be forced to take the oath or leave the colony. As a preparatory step he and Governor Shirley of Massachusetts captured Fort Beauséjour and Fort St. John, the only French protection fòr the Acadians, in June, 1755.

The way was now clear to force the Acadians either to accept an oath binding them to fight for Britain, or be deported. The oath was rejected, and during the remainder of that year Acadians were seized and deported to the more southerly colonies. Many avoided the explusion by fleeing to the forests, to Quebec or to Isle St. Jean. Further deportations followed the capture of Isle St. Jean and Isle Royale (Cape Breton) until, by 1762, about 70 per cent of the 15,500 Acadians had been removed. The plight of these refugees aroused the charity of the American colonists wherever they were landed, but Britain and France remained indifferent. Such wholesale deportations were common in European history; and in any case, France recognized the Acadians as British subjects to be disposed of entirely as it pleased the British government. For his part in the explusion of the Acadians, Lawrence was promoted to Governor of Nova Scotia. At his invitation thousands of New Englanders arrived to take up the vacant Acadian farms. In 1758 a legislative assembly was created, thus completing the establishment of Nova Scotia as a typical British royal colony in North America.

Even while Lawrence was planning the expulsion of the Acadians, the first shots in the Seven Years' War were fired, not in Europe, but in the Ohio valley. The population of the American colonies was now pressing forward beyond the Appalachians and challenging France's claim to the Ohio-Mississippi basin. The coming struggle would be no mere echo of European rivalries—this war in North America had North American causes.

In 1753 the Marquis Duquesne de Menneville, the new Governor of New France, began constructing a series of forts from Lake Erie to the Ohio, to block British expansion. The government of Virginia protested this French "invasion" of territory claimed by Britain, and then attempted to build its own forts in the valley. In May, 1754, George Washington, a Virginia militia officer, surprised a small French force and killed several men. The first blood had been spilled in an undeclared war that was destined to spread over three continents.

The undeclared war in North America began in earnest in 1755, although it was still unofficial. Two ships from a French relief fleet were captured near Newfoundland by a British naval force in an action that demonstrated how much New France was at the mercy of Britain's superior sea power. On land, however, Britain did not show as much strength. The march of General Braddock against strategic Fort Duquesne (Pittsburgh) ended in a disas-

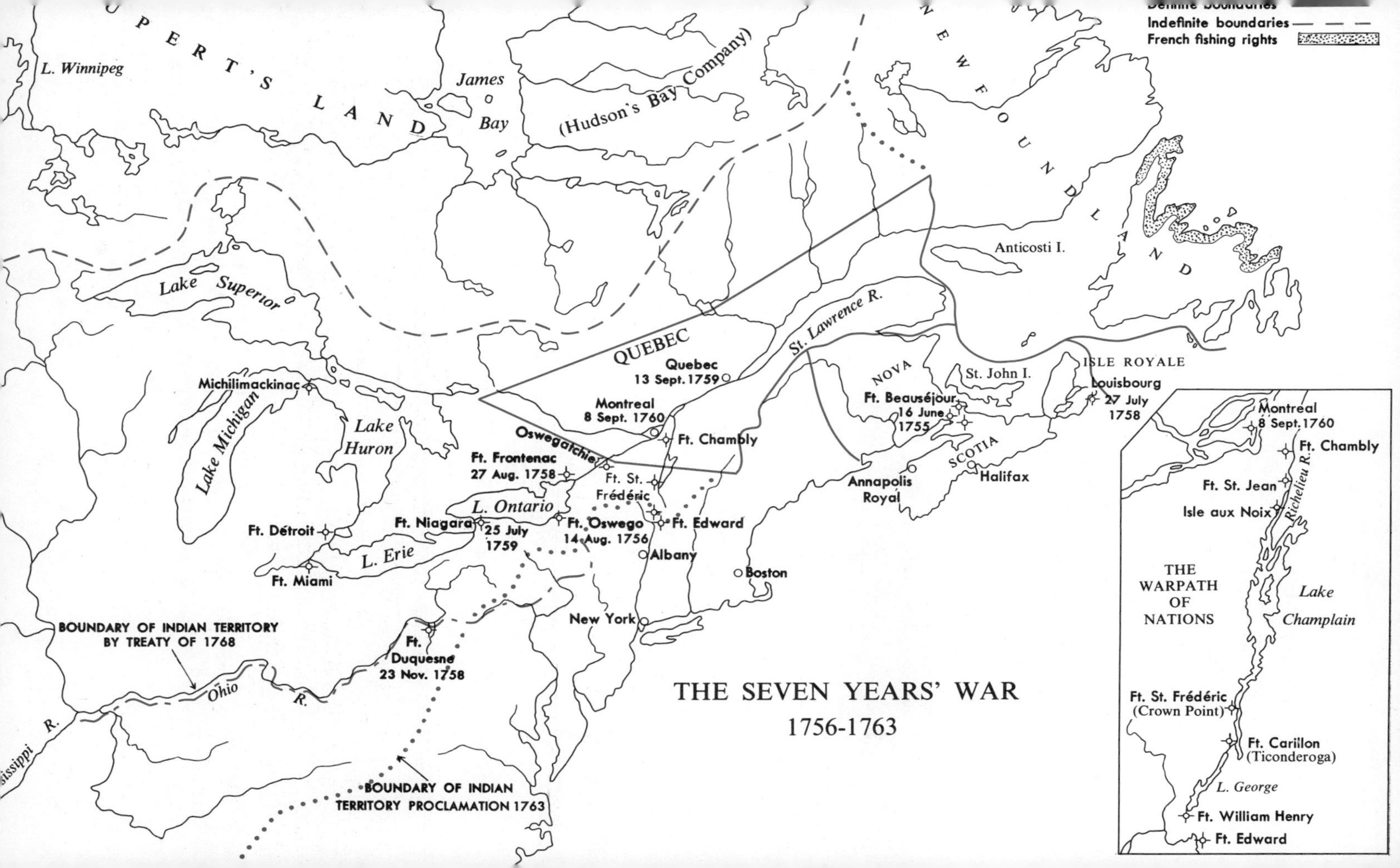

Indefinite boundaries
French fishing rights
RUPERT'S LAND
L. Winnipeg
James Bay
(Hudson's Bay Company)
NEWFOUNDLAND
Anticosti I.
Lake Superior
QUEBEC
Quebec 13 Sept. 1759
St. Lawrence R.
Michilimackinac
Montreal 8 Sept. 1760
Lake Michigan
Lake Huron
Oswegatchie
Ft. Chambly
Ft. Frontenac 27 Aug. 1758
Ft. St. Frédéric
L. Ontario
Ft. Niagara 25 July 1759
Ft. Oswego 14 Aug. 1756
Ft. Edward
Ft. Détroit
L. Erie
Ft. Miami
Albany
Boston
New York
NOVA SCOTIA
St. John I.
ISLE ROYALE
Louisbourg 27 July 1758
Ft. Beauséjour 16 June 1755
Annapolis Royal
Halifax
BOUNDARY OF INDIAN TERRITORY BY TREATY OF 1768
Ft. Duquesne 23 Nov. 1758
Ohio R.
Mississippi R.
BOUNDARY OF INDIAN TERRITORY PROCLAMATION 1763
THE SEVEN YEARS' WAR
1756-1763
Montreal 8 Sept. 1760
Ft. Chambly
Ft. St. Jean
Isle aux Noix
Richelieu R.
THE WARPATH OF NATIONS
Lake Champlain
Ft. St. Frédéric (Crown Point)
Ft. Carillon (Ticonderoga)
L. George
Ft. William Henry
Ft. Edward

Louis Joseph Marquis de Montcalm, a copy of a painting in the possession of the present Marquis de Montcalm of Paris. The eminent historian Gustave Lanctot describes Montcalm as, "a small man, but his expressive face and his wise and witty conversation made him an attractive figure. His native intelligence had been cultivated in the course of a rich classical education and in his profession as an officer in the army."

trous ambush. Along the Richelieu-Champlain war route military actions were inconclusive, but bloody Indian raids as far south as Georgia kept the British on the defensive during the following winter.

At last the war became official in the spring of 1756. In Europe and in America the opening battles went in favour of France and her allies. The Marquis de Montcalm, appointed Field Marshal for New France, captured Oswego in 1756, thereby gaining control of the lakes for New France. In 1757 he moved into the Lake Champlain frontier, taking Fort William Henry on Lake George, but he lacked the strength to follow up with an attack deeper into British territory. By the end of 1757 France's military prospects seemed bright, but economically the colony's plight was desperate. Economic inflation was a pressing problem, and poor harvests and food shortages, exacerbated by the hoarding of supplies by the corrupt Intendant Bigot and his dishonest associates, reduced civilians and soldiers to a daily diet of horse meat and two ounces of bread.

During 1758 the tide of war turned slowly in Britain's favour, thanks to her superior naval power. William Pitt, Britain's great "War Minister," was determined to end the French menace

Townshend's famous portrait of James Wolfe. A note at the top reads: "Although slight this is the most convincing *portrait of Wolfe I have ever seen . . . . R. Wright, 1864." Wright was the first biographer of Wolfe. Lanctot says of Wolfe: "[He] had the qualities of a tactitian rather than a strategist . . . ." And later: "He died . . . knowing that his audacious tactics had been crowned with victory."*

to the fourteen colonies in North America, and planned a three-pronged attack on New France. In the Gulf of St. Lawrence the objective was Louisbourg, which guarded the St. Lawrence approaches; on the Richelieu-Champlain route to Montreal the goal was Fort St. Frédéric; and in the west, Fort Duquesne, pivot of the Ohio valley defence system. When Louisbourg fell in July, 1758, after a two-month siege, and Fort Duquesne was destroyed by the retreating French, the centre of New France was left exposed and isolated, both from Louisiana and from old France. Total success eluded the British when they failed to take Carillon (Ticonderoga). The main war route to Montreal remained closed, but the western approach was laid bare when the British recaptured Oswego and swiftly destroyed Fort Frontenac at the head of the St. Lawrence River. It was obvious that only massive supplies of men and materials could save New France, yet with the spring of 1759 came word that France could not send sufficient help and that Britain's control of the sea lanes was almost impossible to evade. Montcalm was told that he must somehow retain a foothold in New France so that the lost territories could be regained at the peace table. The British plans to reduce the colony by simultaneous invasions from the St. Lawrence, Lake

Champlain and Lake Ontario were known to Montcalm as he prepared to defend Quebec.

By the end of May, 1759, forty-nine British warships had convoyed 11,000 troops under General James Wolfe to the gates of Quebec. British batteries across the river at Pointe Lévis began a bombardment that lasted for months and reduced much of the capital to rubble. Wolfe, however, was eager for a pitched battle, which Montcalm wisely avoided. A British attempt at the end of July to land at Montmorency cost them 500 casualties. The siege continued, with Wolfe destroying settlements downriver from the city to intimidate the habitants. As August ended, the British seemed no closer to capturing Quebec, and the approach of winter would soon necessitate withdrawal. Then on 10 September Wolfe discovered the steep and poorly guarded trail from the Anse Au Foulon to the plains above. In the early hours of 13 September Wolfe and some 4,000 men successfully scaled the high cliffs and took up positions to the west of the city walls, to the complete surprise of the French. Underestimating the size of the British force, Montcalm rashly abandoned his fixed defences and led 3,500 regulars and militia through the gates to meet his attackers.

The main French body advanced in formation until at forty paces from the British they were met by a withering musket volley followed by a bayonet charge that swept them back to the city in confusion. Wolfe had won a typical European battle, though he died on the field. He had not conquered Quebec's defences, but the city's defenders were disorganized and Montcalm lay dying. Five days later Quebec capitulated.

Although Quebec had fallen, the British had not conquered Canada. Montreal was still intact and from this foothold Lévis, Montcalm's second-in-command, launched an attack in April, 1760, to regain Quebec. The British General, Murray, made Montcalm's mistake of leaving the fortifications to fight on open ground at Ste. Foy. This time the French won and the British fled to the city. Eleven days later, however, as Lévis prepared to besiege Quebec, the vanguard of a British fleet dropped anchor in the harbour. Further French resistance was useless and on 8 September, with the British fleet advancing up the St. Lawrence,

3,400 men moving down the Richelieu to Montreal, and another 9,700 approaching from Oswego, Governor Vaudreil surrendered Montreal, the last vestige of French rule in New France. Sea power had been the deciding factor in the half-century of imperial conflict for control of North America.

* * *

The British conquest of Canada brought to an end France's only serious attempt at colonization in North America. French rule had lasted for one hundred and fifty years, yet only in the last century had settlement achieved any degree of success. Compared to the British colonies in North America, Canada at the conquest was retarded demographically, economically and technologically. Its fate had been sealed by several factors: by the fur trade which supported the colony and yet overextended its slim resources; by the lack of skilled labour and capital investment; and by France's preoccupation with territorial ambitions and resultant wars in Europe. But if the French lily flag disappeared from the shores of the St. Lawrence, the French nation did not. Generations of Canadiens had struck deep roots into the North American soil. Their language, their religion, their customs and their social organization were so firmly established by 1760 that they could and would survive any change of political allegiance. It now remained to be seen how this enclave of French and Roman Catholic culture could be accommodated within an English-speaking and predominantly Protestant empire.

READINGS

A French-Canadian Sense of Identity?

The physical separation of all American colonies from their European mother countries, and the differences in the New World environment—for example, climate, resources, vegetation and topography—produced new patterns of living in the colonies. This development of a culture similar to, yet distinct from, that of the homeland was intensified in New France by the long winters that froze the St. Lawrence River. All contacts with old France were severed for one-third of each year.

How soon did the Canadiens develop distinctive habits, customs and attitudes? When did they become aware of their separate identity as Frenchmen *in* Canada? Before the conquest New France did not have any printing presses, and education was largely restricted to the small professional class; therefore, a literary tradition, one of the common mirrors of culture, did not appear. As a result, historians must look to other sources for clues to the cultural environment of New France. For example, evidence of particular Canadien customs is recorded incidentally in government documents, in court records and religious decrees, and from these sources some knowledge of Canadien attitudes can be inferred. The best evidence of a Canadien sense of identity before the conquest must be sought in the reports of visitors to the colony. Even this source of material, however, is slim and scattered, consisting mostly of casual references embodied in a few general descriptions of New France by travellers who were more interested in the life of the native Indians and in the plants and animals of the New World than in the changes appearing in the Canadien way-of-life.

The Baron de Lahontan (1666-1715?), soldier and writer, first came to Canada in 1683 at the age of seventeen to fight the Iroquois. Later he did some exploring in the west. He gained fame and fortune when his book, *Nouveaux Voyages de M. le Baron de Lahontan dans l'Amerique Septentrionale* (1703), became a best seller. Despite the Baron's exaggeration of his own exploits, the book provides one of the earliest commentaries on the Canadien character.

The Canadians are well built, sturdy, tall, strong, vigorous, enterprising, brave, and indefatigable. They lack only the knowledge of literature. They are presumptuous and full of themselves, putting themselves ahead of all the nations of the earth; and unfortunately they do not have the respect that they might for their relatives (the French). The blood of Canada is very good; the women are generally pretty; brunettes are rare, the wise are common, and the lazy are found in great enough number; they love luxury dearly, and it falls to the one who best traps a husband.

R. G. Thwaites (ed.), *New Voyages to North America by the Baron de Lahontan* (Chicago: A. McClurg, 1905), vol. I, p. 391.

Gilles Hocquart (1694-1783), who served as Intendant of New France longer than any other man (1731-1748), had a well-deserved reputation for honesty and ability. In 1737 he sent home a long report on the state of the colony. The following excerpt, from an unsigned appendix to that report, was certainly written for Hocquart, although probably not by him.

Canadians are by nature tall, well-built and of a vigorous temperament. As the trades here are not controlled by guilds, and because from the beginning of the establishment of the colony craftsmen were scarce, necessity has made the Canadians self-reliant from one generation to the next. The country folk handle an axe most adroitly. They make for themselves most of the tools and utensils for farming; they build their own houses and barns. Several are weavers who make coarse linen and a coarse woollen cloth called drugget, which they use to clothe themselves and their families.

They love distinctions and flatteries, priding themselves on their bravery, are extremely touchy about criticisms and the smallest punishments; they are selfish, vindictive, subject to drunkenness, make much use of brandy and are considered not to be truthful.

This characterization applies to most and particularly to the country folk. Those in the cities have fewer faults. All are very devout. You see few scoundrels. They are flighty, have too good an opinion of themselves, which keeps them from succeeding as they could in the arts, agriculture and commerce. Add to this the laziness that the length and rigor of the winter causes. They love hunting, sailing and travelling and have none of the crude or rustic air of our peasants of France. They are commonly pliant enough when their honour is flattered and when they are governed with justice, but they are by nature unmanageable. It is necessary to strengthen more and more that precise subordination which should exist in all classes, particularly among the country folk. This aspect of policy has been at all times the most important and the most difficult to accomplish. One means of achieving it is to choose as local officials those inhabitants who are wisest and most capable of leading, and on the government's part to give all convenient attention to supporting them in their authority. One might venture to say that the lack of firmness in past administrations had very much injured subordination. For several years past, however, crimes have been punished and disorders curbed by suitable corrections. According to reports the policing of public roads and cabarets has been more carefully enforced and in general the people have been happier than ever before.

W. B. Munro (ed.), *Documents Relating to the Seigneurial Tenure in Canada, 1598-1854* (Toronto: Champlain Society, 1908), pp. 186/87 (trans. J. S. Moir).

Father Pierre François Xavier de Charlevoix (1682-1761) was a Jesuit professor at the college of Quebec who travelled the length of the Mississippi River in 1721/22. His *Histoire et Description Générale de la Nouvelle-France*, published in 1744, is the first general history of Canada. In this passage from the *Journal of a Voyage to North America* (which formed part of the *Histoire*) Charlevoix describes the Canadiens and then compares them to the English settlers in the Thirteen Colonies.

I have already said, that they reckon no more than 7,000 souls at Quebec; yet you find in it a small number of the best company, where nothing is wanting that can possibly contribute to form an agreeable society. Enough, in my opinion, to enable all sorts of persons whatever to pass their time very agreeably.

They accordingly do so, every one contributing all in his power to make life agreeable and cheerful. They play at cards, or go abroad on parties of pleasure in the summer-time in calashes or canoes, in winter, in sledges upon the snow, or on skates upon the ice. Hunting is a great exercise amongst them, and there are a number of gentlemen who have no other way of providing handsomely for their subsistence. The current news consist of a very few articles, and those of Europe arrive all at once, though they supply matter of discourse for great part of the year. They reason like politicians on what is past, and form conjectures on what is likely to happen; the sciences and fine arts have also their part, so that the conversation never flags for want of matter. The Canadians, that is to say, the Creoles of Canada, draw in with their native breath an air of freedom, which renders them very agreeable in the commerce of life, and no where in the world is our language spoken in greater purity. There is not the smallest foreign accent remarked in their pronunciation.

You meet with no rich men in this country, and it is really a great pity, every one endeavouring to put as good a face on it as possible, and nobody scarce thinking of laying up wealth. They make good cheer, provided they are also able to be at the expense of fine clothes; if not, they retrench in the article of the table to be able to appear well dressed. And indeed, we must allow, that dress becomes our Creolians extremely well. They are all here of very advantageous stature, and both sexes have the finest complexion in the world; a gay and sprightly behaviour, with great sweetness and politeness of manners are common to all of them; and the least rusticity, either in language or behaviour, is utterly unknown even in the remotest and most distant parts.

The case is very different as I am informed with respect to our English neighbours, and to judge of the two colonies by the way of life, behaviour, and speech of the inhabitants, nobody would hesitate to say that ours were the most flourishing. In New England and the other provinces of the continent of America, subject to the British empire, there prevails an opulence which they are utterly at a loss how to use; and in New France, a poverty hid by an air of being in easy circumstances, which seems not at all studied. Trade, and the cultivation of their plantations strengthen the first, whereas the second is supported by the industry of its inhabitants, and the taste of the nation diffuses over it something infinitely pleasing. The English planter amasses wealth, and never makes any superfluous expence; the French inhabitant again enjoys what he has acquired, and often makes a parade of what he is not possessed of.

P. F. X. Charlevoix, *Journal of a Voyage to North America*, trans. L. P. Kellogg (Chicago: Caxton Club, 1923), vol. I, pp. 116/17.

BIBLIOGRAPHY

*INDICATES VOLUMES AVAILABLE IN PAPERBACK.

*Bishop, Morris. *Champlain: the Life of Fortitude*. Carleton Library (McClelland and Stewart), 1963—the most reliable and readable of the several biographies of Champlain.

*Brebner, J. B. *The Explorers of North America, 1492-1806*. Doubleday Anchor Books, 1955—a short but authoritative account of explorations from Columbus to Lewis and Clark.

Clark, T. H. and Stearn, C. W. *The Geological Evolution of North America: A Regional Approach to Historical Geology*. Ronald, 1960—not an elementary text, but one of the few available books describing the geological evolution of Canada.

Cranston, J. H. *Etienne Brulé, Immortal Scoundrel*. Ryerson, 1949—a popular biography of this early Canadian hero.

Currie, A. W. *Canadian Economic Development*. (4th ed.) Nelson, 1963—Chapter 1 discusses the relationship between Canada's geography and its economic development.

Eccles, W. J. *Canada under Louis XIV, 1663-1701*. ("The Canadian Centenary Series," Vol. 3.) McClelland and Stewart, 1964—an excellent survey of the period.

*———. *Frontenac: the Courtier Governor*. Carleton Library (McClelland and Stewart), 1959—a biography that has aroused controversy by its criticism of Frontenac.

*Frégault, Guy. *Canadian Society in the French Regime*. Canadian Historical Association Booklets, 1954—a brief but provocative description of the social structure of New France.

*Glazebrook, G. P. de T. *A History of Transportation in Canada*. 2 vols. Carleton Library (McClelland and Stewart), 1964—the first chapter of Vol. I describes transportation in New France.

Innis, H. A. *The Cod Fisheries*. Yale and Ryerson, 1940—opening chapters examine the role of the cod fisheries in early Canadian history.

*———. *The Fur Trade in Canada.* University of Toronto Press, 1964—a revised edition of the 1930 classic, which devotes one chapter to the fur trade before 1763.

Jenness, Diamond. *The Indians of Canada.* (4th ed.) Queen's Printer, 1938—the standard introduction to the subject.

Lanctot, Gustave. *A History of Canada.* 3 vols. Clarke, Irwin, 1963-1965—a thorough study of New France by a noted Canadian historian, the volumes cover, respectively, from Canada's origins to 1663, from 1663 to 1713, and from 1713 to 1763.

Lower, A. R. M. "Geographical Determinants in Canadian History", in Flenley, R. (ed.), *Essays in Canadian History.* Macmillan, 1939—a useful short essay.

*Mackintosh, W. A. "Economic Factors in Canadian History". In Easterbrook, W. T. and Watkins, M. H. (eds.). *Approaches to Canadian Economic History.* Carleton Library (McClelland and Stewart), 1967—a brilliant essay on the way geography has affected the economic history of Canada.

*Mealing, S. R. (ed.). *The Jesuit Relations and Allied Documents.* Carleton Library (McClelland and Stewart), 1963—a selection from one of the most important sources for the history of New France.

Nettels, C. P. *The Roots of American Civilization.* Appleton-Century-Crofts, 1938—a comprehensive treatment of the English colonies in North America.

*Nish, Cameron (ed.). *The French Regime.* ("Canadian Historical Documents Series," Vol. I.) Prentice-Hall, 1965—documents relating to the history of New France.

Oleson, T. J. *Early Voyages and Northern Approaches, 1000-1632.* ("The Canadian Centenary Series," Vol. I.) McClelland and Stewart, 1963—the most recent scholarly account of early exploration in Canada, including the Norse voyages.

*———. *The Norsemen in America.* Canadian Historical Association Booklets, 1963—a summary account of the Norse voyages.

Parry, J. H. *Europe and a Wider World, 1415-1715.* Hutchinson's University Library, 1949—an excellent brief discussion of European expansion.

Paterson, J.H. *North America, A Regional Geography.* (2nd ed.) Oxford University Press, 1961—a physical and economic geography, with attention to the regions of Canada.

Pleva, E. G. (Advisory Editor). *Canadian Oxford School Atlas.* Oxford University Press, 1957—gives a good introduction to the physical features of the country. (See also the atlases mentioned in the General Bibliography.)

*Ragueneau, Paul. *Shadows Over Huronia.* Midland: The Martyrs' Shrine, 1965—eyewitness descriptions of the destruction of the Huron Mission drawn from the letters of Ragueneau, the Jesuit Superior of the Mission.

*Rothney, G. O. *Newfoundland, From International Fishery to Canadian Province.* Canadian Historical Association Booklets, 1959—a convenient short history of Newfoundland.

Sage, W. N. "Geographical and Cultural Aspects of the Five Canadas", *Report of the Canadian Historical Association, 1937*—a short introduction to the relationship between geography and history in the five main physical regions of Canada.

Scott, H. A. *Bishop Laval.* Oxford University Press, 1926—although obviously partisan in its interpretation, this is the latest biography of Laval available in English.

Stanley, G.F.G. *Canada's Soldiers.* (2nd. ed.) Macmillan. 1960—includes military history of New France.

———. *New France, The Last Phase, 1744-1760.* ("Canadian Centenary Series," Vol. 5.) McClelland and Stewart, 1968—solid history brilliantly written.

*Steele, Ian K. *Guerillas and Grenadiers: The Struggle for Canada, 1689-1760.* ("The Frontenac Library," No. 3.) Ryerson, 1969—a study in depth of the patterns of conflict using representative source material.

*Talbot, F.X. *Saint Among the Hurons.* Doubleday Image Books, 1956—a highly readable biography of the Jesuit martyr, Jean de Brébeuf.

*Trudel, Marcel. *The Seigneurial Regime.* Canadian Historical Association Booklets, 1956—a succinct account of the land-holding system on which New France was built.

Walsh, H.H. *The Church in the French Era. (A History of the Christian Church in Canada,* ed. J.W. Grant, Vol. 1.), Ryerson, 1966—a modern and definitive work on the religious life of New France.

*Wright, L.B. *The Atlantic Frontier: Colonial American Civilization, 1607-1763.* Cornell, 1947—an interesting history of the American colonies, bringing out social factors.

2

BRITISH NORTH AMERICA

CHAPTER 4

REMNANTS OF EMPIRE

There was never any doubt that Great Britain would keep New France when the Seven Years' War ended. A primary British war objective had been to remove forever the threat of French encirclement that had hung over the fourteen British colonies and confined them to the Atlantic seaboard. Ironically, the removal of the French threat unleashed forces within the colonies that led to civil war, and independence from Britain for thirteen of them.

But what was to be the future of a French-speaking, Roman Catholic colony within an English-speaking and officially Protestant empire? The Peace of Paris closed a global war, so it was not surprising that few of the treaty's clauses referred specifically to the fate of New France. By a stroke of the pen Canadiens became British subjects. Their religious freedom was guaranteed, but what precisely did this mean when Roman Catholics in Britain had no political rights? How would His Majesty's "new subjects" cope with such British institutions as English common law and the parliamentary system? And what would be the economic role of the new colony in the dynamic, aggressive and far-flung British empire? What, for instance, would be the place of the fur trade and the Canadien fur traders, so important in the history of New France, now that Canada had become part of the diversified, British mercantilist system? Would Canada still be neglected under British rule as it had been under French, or would she receive the kind of development so long desired and so long postponed? In short, would the conquest prove to be the destruction of, or a new beginning for, the French Canadians and their distinctive way-of-life?

NEW SUBJECTS AND OLD

The only reference to British policy in the Articles of Quebec's Capitulation was provision for "the free exercise of the Roman religion." Montreal's terms of surrender one year later were much more explicit regarding the future of her civilian population. Religious freedom and Church property were again guaranteed, although the request that future bishops should be named by the King of France was refused. Any of the 65,000 civilians could leave the colony and take their goods with them. Few left, and in fact half of the French troops preferred to settle in Canada rather than return home. So the population remained and, with necessary adjustments to the British presence, life generally went on in the pre-conquest pattern.

Physically, war damage had been confined to the city of Quebec and the adjacent farms that Wolfe had burned. The efficient and charitable military government of the occupation period soon reconciled the population to its new status as British subjects and helped to heal the wounds of battle. During the winter of 1759-60 British General James Murray at Quebec ensured the good will of the colonists by enforcing a rigid discipline on his troops: soldiers were released from duty to aid in harvesting; each soldier donated one day's rations per month to the needy; the feelings and customs of the conquered were scrupulously respected by the conquerors. As new British subjects the Canadiens responded warmly to these benevolent policies. By European standards the conquest of New France was amazingly lenient, and the reconciliation that followed was a happy omen for future relations between French and British in Canada.

An engraving after Richard Short's drawing, "The Bishop's House With the Ruins Going Down the Hill, Quebec, 1759." Short was purser on H.M.S. Prince of Orange *and served at the siege of Quebec. His drawings are the most accurate record we have of Quebec and the devastating effect upon it of the English naval bombardment.*

In contrast to the peaceful takeover in Quebec, British-Indian relations in the interior caused a crisis. Fearful that a British victory would bring a flood of settlers and the loss of hunting grounds, the tribes south of the upper Great Lakes rose suddenly in 1763. Under the Ottawa chief, Pontiac, they captured every post west of Niagara except Detroit and massacred their British garrisons. Pontiac's rebellion was soon suppressed by fresh troops, but it showed the British government the urgency of settling this conflict between settlement and the fur trading interests.

The details of Britain's policy to meet the problems in her new possession were laid out in a Royal Proclamation of 1763. The colony of Quebec was to be modelled after other royal colonies in North America, with English laws and an elected assembly to encourage immigration from the colonies to the south. Territorially, Quebec was confined to a relatively small rectangular area on both sides of the St. Lawrence from the Gulf to a line running east and north of Lake Ontario. Prior to Pontiac's rebellion it had been anticipated that there would be trouble with the Indians and a policy had been devised to meet the possibility. It was now put into force by the Proclamation: the east portion of the Mississippi drainage basin and the Great Lakes watershed were turned into one vast Indian reserve from which settlement and unlicensed traders were excluded.

The aims of the Proclamation of 1763 were never fully realized. The Canadiens were, of course, Roman Catholics and therefore by British law ineligible to sit or vote in the assembly. Few Canadiens could speak English and none had any knowledge of common law, and therefore could hardly take active part in judicial or legal affairs. The territorial settlement was equally unsuccessful because it did not provide for proper administration of the vast area. Few American settlers entered the colony, rendering the political settlement even more useless. But more important was the storm of protest raised in the American colonies over the prohibition of westward migration. Had the Americans not fought in the recent war expressly to open the west to settlement, as well as to remove the French threat? With official policy being so inadequate, it was the policies of Quebec's first governors that set the early pattern for future development.

General Murray, the colony's first British governor, had a soldier's respect for the disciplined and docile society which he professed to find in Quebec. He protested the government's plan, which he said would disrupt a peaceful society merely to meet the political demands of the small group of English-speaking merchants who were settling in the colony. "Little, very little, will content the New Subjects but nothing will satisfy the Licentious Fanaticks Trading here," he reported to the Board of Trade. "Unless the Canadiens are admitted on Jurys, and are allowed Judges and Lawyers who understand their Language, His Majesty will lose the greatest part of this Valuable people."

The Roman Catholic Church was the sole institution to survive the change of sovereignty intact, yet in the immediate post-conquest period it faced two major interrelated problems. Its influence had been reduced by the death of Bishop Pontbriand at Montreal just before the surrender of that city. Without a bishop

Sir Guy Carleton's attitude of magnanimity toward the Quebecois did not go unnoticed. One Ursuline nun wrote: "His mild and paternal administration, his personal merits and kindness have rendered him dear to all ranks. . . ."

the sacramental life of the Church would disappear. Murray foresaw that without the Church British sovereignty would lose the support of the greatest stabilizing influence in the colony. Yet the King of England could neither constitutionally nor politically allow either the King of France or the Pope to appoint a bishop. By quiet diplomacy Murray arranged instead for the appointment in 1765 of Bishop Briand as "Superintendent of the Romish Church in Quebec." The continuing work of the Church was thus assured, the imperial government was not compromised openly and the Canadiens rejoiced at "the King's Paternal Goodness to them." The religious phase of the programme to anglicize the Canadiens by protestantizing them had now been dropped. But on the very day that Bishop Briand arrived in Quebec in 1766, his friend and patron, Governor Murray, departed for London to defend himself against charges levelled by a clique of English merchants, specifically, "most flagrant Partialities," "discountenancing the Protestant Religion," and "the Deprivation of the open Trade."

Murray's successor, another career soldier, Guy Carleton, was even more emphatic in his praise of the superior institutions and spirit of New France and in his condemnation of the purpose of the Proclamation of 1763. Carleton wanted to appease the Canadiens, on whose goodwill depended the defence of the colony in any future war. British immigrants were not coming to Quebec as expected, and the Canadiens still comprised some 95 percent of the colony's population. Common sense, political realism and simple justice to the French Canadians demanded a new constitution to ensure them membership on juries, protection for seigneurial rights, and use of their customary laws. The home government was by this time well aware of the difficulties of assimilating a population foreign in language, religion and law into the established pattern of empire, and it was engaged in hearing representations on all aspects of the Quebec question. To make his points in person, Carleton went home in 1770, although seigneurial tenure and French juries had by then been approved.

A solution to the Quebec question was evolved by 1774, but the decisions made may have been influenced by the serious unrest occurring in the thirteen oldest American colonies. The Quebec Act of that year restored a semblance of the former constitution of New France. The governor was to rule through a council only—the assembly promised in 1763 was dropped as inapplicable. Roman Catholics were to be eligible for public office (which they were not elsewhere in the Empire). After a decade of uncertainty the Roman Catholic Church was now given legal power to compel payment of the tithe, and the seigneurs resumed their pre-conquest status. Civil cases were to be judged by "the Laws of Canada," but English criminal law was instituted because it was considered more humane. Finally, the Quebec boundaries were extended to take in the whole Great Lakes-St. Lawrence basin and all the land between the Ohio and Mississippi rivers, in order to bring civil government to the area and to provide central administration of the fur trade.

The Quebec Act pleased Governor Carleton, the Roman Catholic Church and the seigneurs. The reaction of the average habitant was less certain. But the Quebec Act raised a storm of

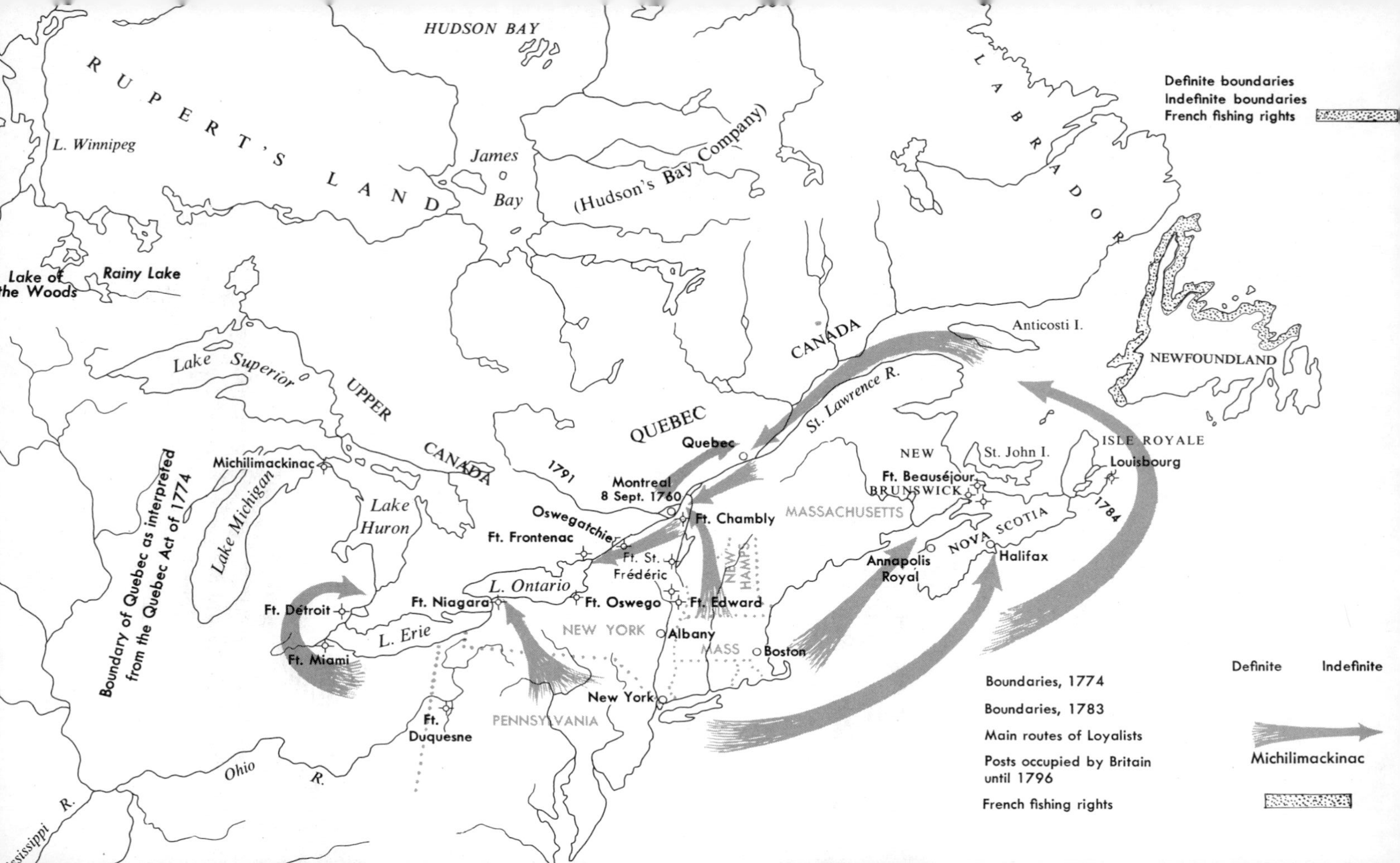

HUDSON BAY
RUPERT'S LAND
L. Winnipeg
James Bay
(Hudson's Bay Company)
LABRADOR
Definite boundaries
Indefinite boundaries
French fishing rights
Lake of the Woods
Rainy Lake
Lake Superior
UPPER CANADA
Anticosti I.
NEWFOUNDLAND
CANADA
St. Lawrence R.
QUEBEC
Quebec
ISLE ROYALE
Louisbourg
NEW BRUNSWICK
St. John I.
Ft. Beauséjour
Michilimackinac
1791
Montreal 8 Sept. 1760
Boundary of Quebec as interpreted from the Quebec Act of 1774
Lake Michigan
Lake Huron
Oswegatchie
Ft. Chambly
MASSACHUSETTS
NOVA SCOTIA
1784
Ft. Frontenac
Ft. St. Frédéric
NEW HAMPS
Annapolis Royal
Halifax
L. Ontario
Ft. Niagara
Ft. Oswego
Ft. Edward
Ft. Détroit
L. Erie
NEW YORK
Albany
MASS
Boston
Ft. Miami
New York
Ft. Duquesne
PENNSYLVANIA
Ohio R.
Mississippi R.
Definite
Indefinite
Boundaries, 1774
Boundaries, 1783
Main routes of Loyalists
Posts occupied by Britain until 1796
Michilimackinac
French fishing rights

protest in the American colonies, coming as it did in the same parliamentary session as the four "Intolerable Acts" against the rebellious citizens of Massachusetts. The alliance of priest, seigneur and governor, the absence of an Englishman's right to representative government, and the transfer of the Ohio valley to Quebec made the new British colony look so much like the old enemy, New France, that the Declaration of Independence by the thirteen colonies accused King George of "establishing therein an arbitrary government . . . so as to render it at once an example and fit instrument for introducing the same absolute rule into these colonies."

THE END OF THE FIRST BRITISH EMPIRE

The outbreak of the American Revolution put the Quebec Act to the test. Carleton returned to Quebec in 1774, confident that he could raise 6,000 Canadiens in the event of that "catastrophe shocking to think of" which had preyed on his mind for several years. American propaganda inviting the Canadiens to rise against Britain in the cause of "Englishmen's rights" flooded the colony in 1775, but disaffection was limited to a few British merchants in Montreal and a handful of habitants. Canadiens refused to fight America's battles, but Carleton was dismayed to discover that they were equally unprepared to fight for Britain, despite encouragement from the Church and the seigneurs. Carleton was forced to flee Montreal in the face of a successful American invasion along the Champlain-Richelieu route in November, 1775. A second American army under Benedict Arnold joined in a siege of Quebec, but after a futile assault on New Year's Eve, during which the American general, Montgomery, was killed, the enemy forces spent a miserable winter in the neighbourhood before withdrawing on the arrival of British reinforcements.

At Montreal, which lived as a captured city during that winter, Benjamin Franklin (the Philadelphia publisher, statesman and scientist, and soon to be the first United States ambassador to France) established the Montreal *Gazette* as the mouthpiece of the "liberators." But the American Jesuit, John Carroll, failed to win over the Canadian clergy, and the army of occupation with its worthless "Continental Congress" paper money became extremely unpopular. The American retreat from Quebec left Montreal vulnerable to Carleton's advancing forces, but for reasons unexplained Carleton allowed the Americans to escape in June, 1776. Once rid of these invaders, the colony was untouched by hostilities during the remainder of the long war for American independence. Yet, the Quebec Act had not won the Canadiens' loyalty to Britian—if indeed that was its purpose. Although Carleton managed to recruit roughly 2,000 habitants, at least as many joined the rebels. Bishop Briand brought against the latter the full force of his Church in punishment for their disloyalty to the king whom Providence had placed over them. Even France's entry into the war on the side of the rebellious colonies did not cause any change in the general attitude of indifference among the Canadiens to the war.

For the Maritime colonies of Nova Scotia and Prince Edward Island (the latter had obtained representative government in 1769) and for the Newfoundland settlements, the American Revolution was never a real threat, nor for long an attraction. Nevertheless, Newfoundland fishermen suffered economically when the island's supply of American flour was cut off, and some Maritime towns, like Charlottetown, the tiny capital of Prince Edward Island, were raided by American freebooters until British control of the seas was re-established. The most crucial area in the Maritimes was the Bay of Fundy. In the generation since the expulsion of the Acadians, several thousand "planters" from New England had taken up farms along the coast from Annapolis, around the Chignecto peninsula and as far west as the St. John River. Often they came in groups and retained connection with their home colonies, where they still visited and traded.

Given such potentially rebellious settlers in Nova Scotia it is not surprising that in 1776 Maine rebels and some local settlers surrounded Fort Cumberland (formerly Beauséjour) until reinforcements from Halifax drove them off. The "Cumberland Rebellion" was the only incident of its kind—for the

Joseph Brant, the Mohawk Chief. For his services to the British during the American War of Independence, Brant and his people were given land in the Grand River valley, east of Lake Ontario. This portrait is believed to have been painted in 1797 near Brant's own home, which he called Wellington Square, near Burlington Bay on Lake Ontario.

remainder of the war the worst damage the American forces could inflict on Nova Scotia was to prey on merchant ships while the Royal Navy was away from base or to try, vainly, to incite local Indians against the British. Most Nova Scotians profited from the wartime demands for foods and materials, but their aim was the same neutrality that the Acadians had sought. If the "neutral Yankees of Nova Scotia" did not engage directly on Britain's side in the hostilities, at least their continuing presence in the British Empire was assured by their tacit loyalty to the mother country.

The Treaty of Versailles in 1783 established the independence of the United States, but its also ensured the continuance of a British North America. Nevertheless, the territorial settlement, at least in retrospect, was less than favourable to British North America. Although there were no military reasons for the British being conciliatory in the negotiations, they were motivated by a strong desire to establish reasonably friendly relations with their former colonies, especially in view of the economic desirability of recapturing the North Atlantic trade. American demands for the cession of all Canada were rejected completely, but the British delegates were willing to bargain on the question of boundaries. The final decision was to run the boundary up the St. Croix River to the highlands between the St. Lawrence and the Atlantic, thence west along the 45th parallel to the St. Lawrence and from there along the centre line of the river and the Great Lakes. From the lakehead the boundary was to follow the route of the fur traders to a point on the Lake of the Woods and then due west. Thus, for no strong historical, geographic or military reason, British North America lost large areas that might otherwise have remained hers—specifically the south bank of the St. Lawrence, and the area between the lakes and the Ohio and Mississippi rivers.

The Empire had been shattered, but it was not destroyed. Significantly, with the end of hostilities came assurance that the remaining colonies would be populated with settlers whose loyalty had been tested in the crucible of war. This became plain in the closing days of 1782, when the first 30,000 refugees, many of them members of Loyalist regiments, were transported from New York to Nova Scotia. When this great exodus was completed in the next year, Nova Scotia's population had tripled. St. John's Island (Prince Edward Island) received a very modest 600 Loyalists; Newfoundland acquired hardly any. The two largest Loyalist centres in Nova Scotia were Shelburne and Saint John, but the harbours of the Atlantic shore were dotted with new villages, and whole regiments settled along the St. John River. These Loyalists were a cross-section of American society, although the harsh postwar conditions caused many of the professional class to leave for the more sophisticated society of old England. Similarly, inhospitable conditions caused some internal shifts in population; in particular, the rocky soil of Nova Scotia's south shore soon gained the nickname "Nova Scarcity" and in a few short years Shelburne was virtually a ghost town.

From the interior parts of the former northern colonies, particularly New York and Pennsylvania, a second and markedly different stream of Loyalists was working its tedious way overland through the forests to reach asylum in the province of Quebec. Over 5,000 of these settlers, predominantly backwoods farmers, entered at Quebec, Sorel and Niagara. Because the government wanted to keep the area south of Montreal vacant, as a *cordon sanitaire* against possible American influences or incursions, these Loyalists were offered free land in the interior. Loyalist regiments were placed along the upper St. Lawrence, around Kingston, and close to Niagara. The record of Loyalist hardships has been often told, but difficult as their lot undoubtedly was, most of these Loyalists were better equipped by experience to make a new start at pioneering than their fellow sufferers in Nova Scotia.

In both Nova Scotia and Quebec the migrations soon caused political difficulties. Nova Scotia Loyalists demanded more recognition of their sacrifices and complained of their inferior lands, of Governor Parr's supposed indifference, and of political domination by the older settlers whose loyalty to Britain was questioned. To pacify these unhappy people, the imperial government created the separate colonies of New Brunswick and Cape Breton, reducing the old province of Nova Scotia to the peninsula. (The governors of both Cape Breton and St. John's Island were, however, made subordinate to the governor of Nova Scotia.)

Along the upper St. Lawrence the Loyalist immigrants were also complaining, but for different reasons. The lack of an

An encampment of Loyalists at Johnstown, on the banks of the St. Lawrence, June 6, 1784.

assembly and of English common law, and the absence of freehold tenure under the Quebec Act seemed a punishment rather than a reward for their allegiance to Britain. The Revolution had in fact destroyed the basic assumption underlying the Quebec Act—that Quebec would forever be completely French in character. A new pattern for this remnant of empire was needed. The path of policy had been plainly marked in Nova Scotia when the British government had acceded to the wishes of the Loyalists for a separate political identity. But of greater magnitude and difficulty was the problem of fitting the colonies into the mercantilist scheme of trade, now that one of the key areas of the old triangular Atlantic trade (between Britain, the mainland colonies and the West Indies) had become the independent and hostile United States.

THE BAY VERSUS THE RIVER

One of the immediate consequences of the Conquest was a heavy influx of American and British merchants into the Montreal fur trade. The fur brigades continued their annual westward journeys, but the capital was now provided by the new commercial elite who employed the muscles and knowledge of the voyageurs. The more strategic location of Montreal, as compared to Albany, attracted Americans into the trade, and the superior and cheaper trade goods from Britain added a further stimulus.

Competition among the independent fur traders forced them deeper into the interior. Men like Alexander Henry (the elder) and Peter Pond, both colonial veterans of the Seven Years' War, combined trading with random exploration. In 1772 the Hudson's Bay Company realized that the "pedlars from Quebec" (as they were disparagingly called by the "Bay men") had intercepted most of the furs destined for York Fort. The Company had always insisted on the Indians bringing their pelts to the post on the Bay, but in 1774 the Company sent Samuel Hearne to build their first inland factory, Cumberland House, close to the Saskatchewan River. This was but the beginning of a westward race between the rival fur empires of "the Bay" and "the River" that carried the voyageurs over the Rockies and north to the Arctic in the space of two generations. Rival posts began springing up side by side at every advantageous site from the Red River to Great Slave Lake and the foothills of the Rockies. The Montrealers were obviously uninhibited by the Bay Company's chartered rights in Rupert's Land, for eight of their posts stood on Hudson's Bay property.

Because this race for furs created ever-lengthening lines of communication and hence higher costs to the "pedlars," a number of leading merchants in 1779 formed an association called the North West Company. Each year the shareholders, or *bourgeois*, individually provided a certain number of "outfits" of trade goods, and a year later, when their "wintering partners" in the interior had delivered the pelts at the Fort William rendezvous, the profits were divided in proportion to the investments. This cash-cropping system left the "Nor'Westers" without a capital reserve for bad seasons or for development of the trade, and without continuity in personnel, policy or administration. By contrast, the Hudson's Bay Company was heavily capitalized and its control centralized in London. It also had a shorter and cheaper ocean route to the European markets. Under such conditions it seems surprising that the North West Company managed to survive until 1821. In that year the Bay finally beat the River and established a monopoly in the fur trade by buying out the Nor'Westers.

The north-westward extension of the Montreal fur empire had been necessitated in part by the Peace of Paris, which had made the western lands south of the Great Lakes—the Old Northwest—American territory. In that area a rival American fur empire was being built by men like John Jacob Astor, who later created the American Fur Company in 1808. The full effects of the loss of the Old Northwest were not felt immediately because Britain retained the western posts (partly as security for debts claimed by the Loyalists) until the signing of Jay's Treaty in 1794. Even the Montreal merchants kept a minor interest in the trade of the region until excluded by American authorities in 1817. Nevertheless, the relentless search for new fur areas resulted in major

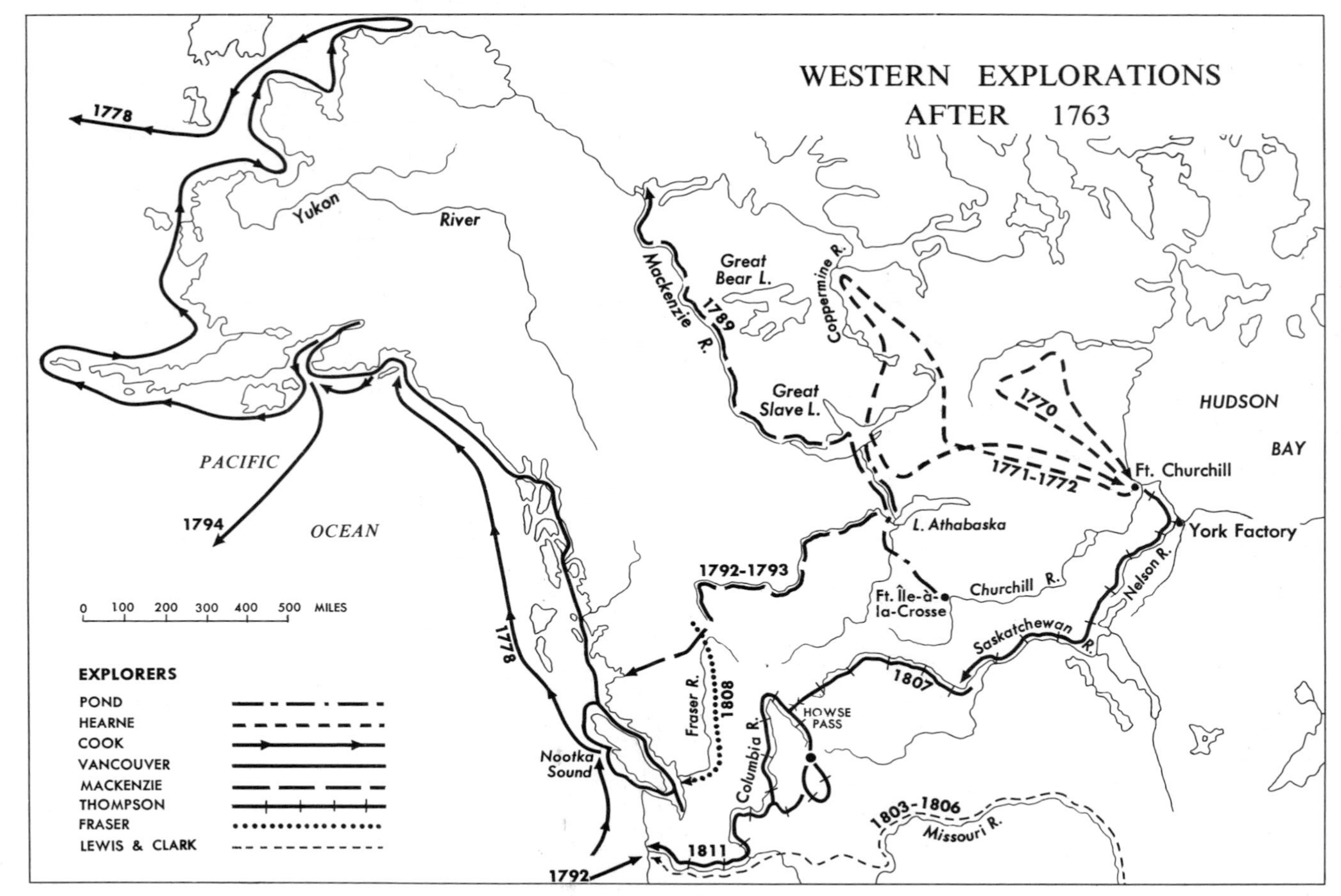
WESTERN EXPLORATIONS
AFTER 1763
1778
Yukon
River
Mackenzie R.
1789
Great Bear L.
Coppermine R.
Great Slave L.
HUDSON
BAY
1770
1771-1772
Ft. Churchill
York Factory
L. Athabaska
PACIFIC
OCEAN
1794
1792-1793
Ft. Île-à-la-Crosse
Churchill R.
Nelson R.
Saskatchewan R.
1807
HOWSE PASS
Fraser R.
1808
Columbia R.
Nootka Sound
1778
1803-1806
Missouri R.
1811
1792
0 100 200 300 400 500 MILES
EXPLORERS
POND
HEARNE
COOK
VANCOUVER
MACKENZIE
THOMPSON
FRASER
LEWIS & CLARK

exploration ventures in the Canadian west. In 1789 Alexander Mackenzie of the North West Company discovered the river now named for him and descended it to the Arctic Ocean. Four years later he travelled up the Peace River and over the Rockies to become the first white man to cross the northern part of North America to the Pacific coast. Another Nor'Wester, Simon Fraser, began building posts west of the continental divide in 1805, and in 1808 followed the dangerous Fraser River to its mouth, believing it was the Columbia. Most of the Columbia was explored in 1811 by David Thompson, a cartographer and former Hudson's Bay employee. Thompson was disappointed to find Astor's employees already installed at the mouth of the Columbia, but aggressive trading by the Nor'Westers led Astor to sell them his post when the War of 1812 threatened its existence. For a few brief years thereafter the fur trade empire of the St. Lawrence was a truly transcontinental enterprise, Canada's first.

While the two eastern gateways to the interior—Hudson Bay and the St. Lawrence—were being exploited and expanded by the rival fur companies, a new approach to the continent had been made, from the Pacific Ocean. Captain James Cook of the Royal Navy touched Vancouver Island in 1778 while mapping the coastline from California to Alaska during his third journey of discovery in the Pacific. When Cook's detailed records were published, British and American fur traders began sailing to the North Pacific in search of the valuable sea otter. The Spanish government seized several British ships in 1789 as interlopers, but the threat of a retaliatory war with Britain caused Spain to abandon all claims to the Pacific coast north of 42 degrees.

To confirm this surrender and to complete Cook's mapping of the coast, the British government dispatched Captain George Vancouver, who had sailed with Cook's last expedition. At Nootka Sound, scene of Cook's landing in 1778, Vancouver met the Spanish emissary Bodega y Quadra and signed the Nootka Sound Convention giving the North Pacific coast to Britain. Vancouver spent three years mapping the coast, and although he circumnavigated Vancouver Island he mistook the mouth of the Fraser for a coastal inlet. His discovery of a large river farther

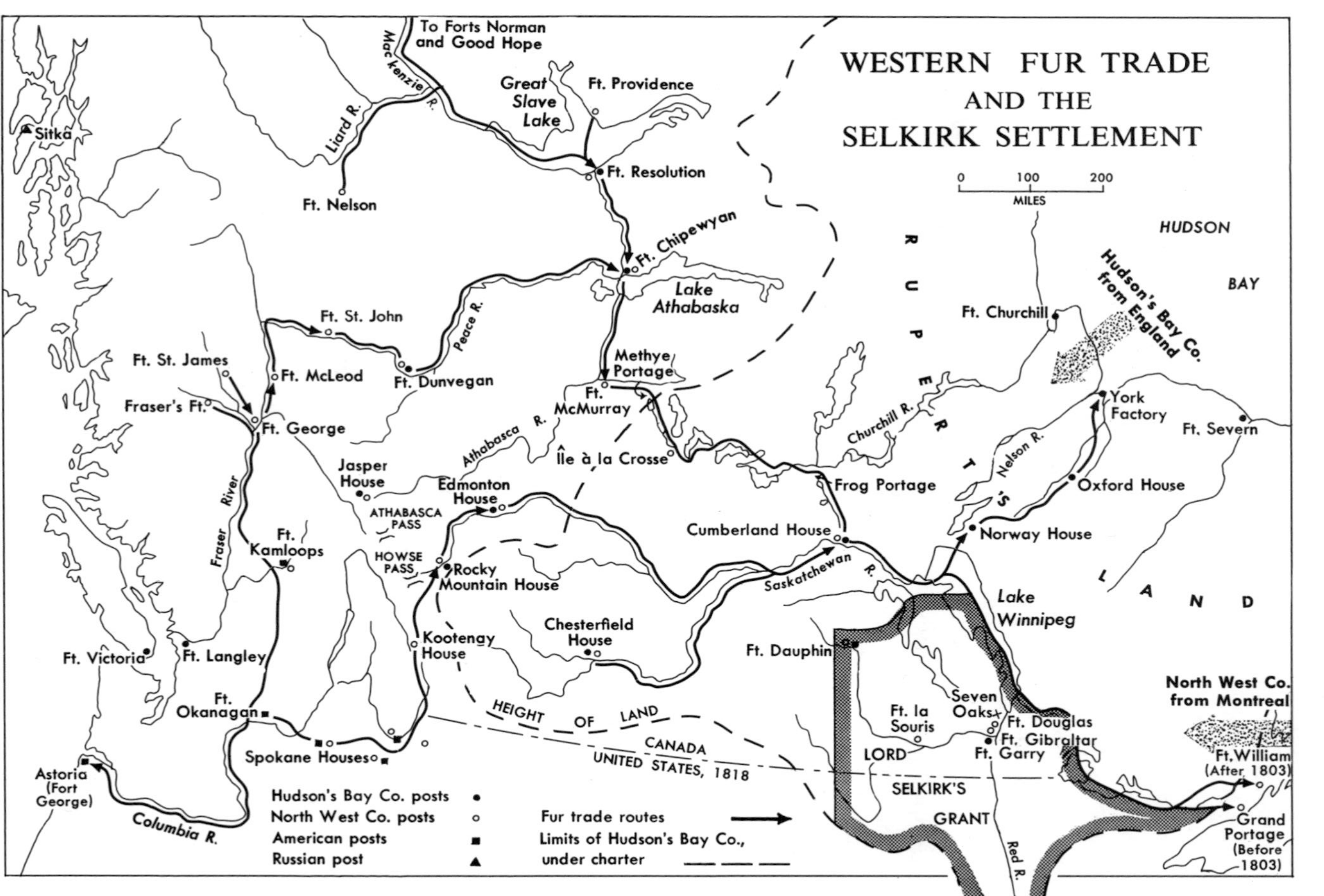
WESTERN FUR TRADE
AND THE
SELKIRK SETTLEMENT
0
100
200
MILES
To Forts Norman and Good Hope
Mackenzie R.
Liard R.
Sitka
Ft. Nelson
Great Slave Lake
Ft. Providence
Ft. Resolution
Ft. Chipewyan
Lake Athabaska
Ft. St. John
Peace R.
Ft. Dunvegan
Ft. St. James
Ft. McLeod
Fraser's Ft.
Ft. George
Methye Portage
Ft. McMurray
Athabasca R.
Île à la Crosse
Jasper House
Edmonton House
ATHABASCA PASS
HOWSE PASS
Rocky Mountain House
Fraser River
Ft. Kamloops
Kootenay House
Chesterfield House
Ft. Victoria
Ft. Langley
Ft. Okanagan
Spokane Houses
Astoria (Fort George)
Columbia R.
HEIGHT OF LAND
CANADA
UNITED STATES, 1818
R U P E R T 'S L A N D
HUDSON BAY
Hudson's Bay Co. from England
Ft. Churchill
Churchill R.
York Factory
Ft. Severn
Nelson R.
Oxford House
Norway House
Frog Portage
Cumberland House
Saskatchewan R.
Lake Winnipeg
Ft. Dauphin
Seven Oaks
Ft. la Souris
Ft. Douglas
Ft. Gibraltar
Ft. Garry
LORD SELKIRK'S GRANT
Red R.
North West Co. from Montreal
Ft. William (After 1803)
Grand Portage (Before 1803)
Hudson's Bay Co. posts
North West Co. posts
American posts
Russian post
Fur trade routes
Limits of Hudson's Bay Co., under charter

south came five months after an American captain had claimed the river for the United States and named it after his ship, the *Columbia*. Thus the existence of the Columbia River was already known in Canada when Fraser and Thompson sought its headwaters on behalf of the Nor'Westers. The rival claims of Great Britain and the United States to the Oregon region of the Pacific coast were destined to remain unsettled until 1846.

In the east the Nor'Westers overcame two more challenges before their absorption in 1821. A rival Montreal group, the New North West Company, popularly known as the "XY Company" from the markings on its goods, was formed in 1798, by a merger of independent traders. A bitter struggle between the two groups ended in 1804 when the old North West Company absorbed the New.

The second challenge to the Nor'Westers came indirectly from the Hudson's Bay Company. Thomas Douglas, fifth Earl of Selkirk, a wealthy and philanthropic Scot, had tried after 1803 to relieve the suffering of Highland crofters (tenant farmers) and Irish subtenants who had been evicted from their small farms. Selkirk had founded settlements for them on Prince Edward Island and at Baldoon on Lake St. Clair. In 1809 he revived a project for another settlement on the Red River. Taking advantage of a war-time recession in the Hudson's Bay Company's trade, he bought control of the Company and obtained 110,000 square miles in the Red River-Lake Winnipeg basin.

Selkirk's first settlers arrived in Assiniboia, as the area was called, via York Fort in 1812. It was, perhaps, inevitable that their arrival should produce tension, for the new settlement sat astride the routes from Montreal to the west and in the midst of one of the pemmican-producing areas. Pemmican, a mixture of dried meat, fat and berries, was an important part of the diet of the traders, the local half-breed Métis and the Indians. Because of the relative ease with which it could be stored and transported, it was considered a valuable product and it had become an important item of trade. In addition, the local half-breed Métis saw in this colonizing venture a portent of the end of the buffalo hunt, on which they depended for their livelihood.

Lord Selkirk.

In 1814 open conflict broke out, and under pressure from the pedlars the settlement broke up. But the following year it was re-established by an influx of new settlers. The Nor'Westers refused to give in and enlisted the support of the local Métis, whose attacks against the Red River settlers culminated in 1816 with the "Massacre of Seven Oaks," in which Governor Semple and twenty colonists were killed. When news of Seven Oaks reached Selkirk, he was en route from Canada to the Red River with a small force of Swiss mercenaries who had been disbanded in Canada at the end of the War of 1812. Changing his original plans, Selkirk attacked and captured the Nor'Westers' base at Fort William before completing his journey. This act exceeded Selkirk's powers, for Fort William was in Canadian territory. As a result, he became enmeshed in a protracted series of lawsuits with the North West Company. Despondent at the sad results of his philanthropic efforts and with his health and finances impaired, Lord Selkirk died in 1820. But his tiny colony on the Red River became the nucleus of Manitoba.

The problems surrounding Lord Selkirk and his settlement on the Red River typified two significant conflicts: the competition between the Montreal pedlars and the Hudson's Bay Company; and the interests of the fur traders and buffalo hunters on the western plains in opposition to the settled life of the farmer. The former conflict was resolved in 1821 with the absorption of the Nor'Westers by the Bay Company; but the latter problem was to lie dormant for a half century when open hostilities would shatter the peace of Assiniboia once again.

THE TWO CANADAS

The problems created by the influx of English-speaking, Protestant Loyalists into the French-speaking and Roman Catholic colony of Quebec during and after the American Revolution demanded a new British policy for the St. Lawrence valley. Since the Loyalists were unhappy with the terms of the Quebec Act, the imperial parliament in 1791 passed an amendment popularly known as the Constitutional Act. By its terms the region, which constituted a single economic unit, was to be divided politically into two colonies, Upper and Lower Canada, in which English and French could maintain their separate identities. Both colonies were granted elected assemblies, thus reversing the decision of 1774. But the Constitutional Act also tried to encourage loyalty by establishing Anglicanism as the state religion, with an Anglican bishop of Quebec. One-eighth of the existing Crown land was to be reserved as an endowment for the support of "the Protestant clergy" (a term then applied to the Church of England but later claimed to include others).

The granting of an assembly to Lower Canada was a major step in the development of the colony's political character. Once given the vote and admitted to the assembly (privileges denied to Roman Catholics in Britain until 1829), the French Canadians dispelled any notions of their political indifference or ineptness by quickly learning to use the parliamentary system for their own ends. From the beginning the French (their numbers soared from 65,000 in 1759 to 335,000 in 1814) controlled the rural constituencies, and their representatives, almost equally divided among lawyers and farmers, constituted a majority in the assembly. In a minority position were the English-speaking representatives of the commercial class of Montreal. The real balance of power, however, was more even than it appeared in the assembly, for the English "party"—a social and economic élite—benefited greatly from its close alliance with the "English" governor and his predominantly English-speaking executive and legislative councils, and civil servants.

Political divisions in Lower Canada, though coinciding closely with linguistic divisions, were primarily formed by economic interests. English-speaking merchants and their representatives were vitally interested in the economic development of the colony, especially in such public works as canals that could help open Upper Canada as a hinterland for Montreal's trade. The merchants naturally favoured land taxes to pay for such expenditures, but the French majority voiced the farmers'

"The Woolsey Family" by Wilhelm von Moll Berczy. This is the first example of a type of painting known as a "Conversation Picture," that is, an animated group of figures. Woolsey was a prominent merchant in Quebec. A note on the back, written by Woolsey (standing), reads: "The family group represented in this picture was painted in 1809, by Mr. Berczy, an amateur, assisted by his own son William. The eight portraits cost ten pounds each, the dog Brador was added without cost."

preference for higher customs duties which would primarily affect the merchants. In 1805 the assembly majority, called the "Popular party," defeated a proposed land tax designed to replace higher duties on trade and jailed the editor of the English party's organ, the Quebec *Mercury*, for criticizing their behaviour. To speak for the "Popular party" and to educate French Canadians in the use of political power, they founded the *Canadien* in 1806. The leading intellectual of the Popular party, and a founder and contributor to the *Canadien* was Pierre Bédard. A great admirer of the British constitution, he came close to expounding the ideal of responsible government when he suggested in 1809 that the operation of the colonial constitution depended on "ministerial responsibility implicit in the King's grant of self-government" in 1791.

Sir Robert Milne, the Lieutenant-Governor and acting administrator, had remained fairly neutral in this political conflict, but in 1807 Lower Canada received its first and only anti-French Governor General, Sir James Craig. He was a veteran of the American Revolution, during which he had acquired a skepticism about French-Canadian loyalty to the Crown. Craig's civil secretary, H. W. Ryland, had a bigot's fear of the French Canadians and their religion. If more provocation were needed—in addition to these personal prejudices and the province's political divisions—to create a constitutional crisis in Lower Canada, it was provided by the serious international situation. Britain, already on the defensive against Napoleon, now faced the threat of war with the United States. Fearing French-Canadian disloyalty, Craig showed his partiality by supporting the "English" party and dismissing the owners of the *Canadien* from all government positions for their attacks on the practice of permitting judges to hold seats in the legislature. The extremism of the French-Canadian Popular party made compromise impossible on the issues of financial control and the political position of judges. The printer and major supporters of the *Canadien* were jailed in 1810 for treasonable writings against Craig. When Craig called a general election in 1810, the voting went against him but the uprising he feared did not occur. Craig's "Reign of Terror" had convinced the

Popular party of the necessity of compromise and the arrival of a new and friendly governor general, Sir George Prevost, in 1811 reduced the political tension in Lower Canada.

In contrast to Lower Canada's troubled growth, the colony of Upper Canada developed quietly during its early years. Like Craig, the first Lieutenant-Governor of Upper Canada, John Graves Simcoe, had fought in the American Revolution, and had a considerable knowledge of North American conditions. Although nominally under the Governor General at Quebec, he communicated directly with the Colonial Office regarding policy. He dreamed of building a little England, complete with old world social classes, in the wilderness. To populate his province Simcoe advertised in the United States that there were free grants of land for immigrants. He relied on the established Church of England and on what he believed to be the obvious superiority of British institutions to convert Americans into loyal British subjects. Upper Canada's government, he told the first legislature, was the very "image and transcript" of the English constitution. He also believed his plans for Anglican schools to educate "the superior classes" would ensure the next generation of Upper Canadians against infection by democratic notions from the neighbouring United States.

Simcoe's plans for an aristocratic Upper Canada were doomed to failure in such a sparsely-populated, frontier and egalitarian society. His administrative work in establishing the machinery for justice, local government and in promoting road building and land settlement was, however, most creditable. American settlers came in droves as Simcoe desired, but he was distressed that an almost total lack of Anglican clergymen left the religious life of the colonists largely in the hands of Methodist preachers from the United States. The Loyalists had been followed by "late Loyalists"—people whose loyalty was sometimes suspect. In later years the loyalty issue became even more pressing as the ratio of American settlers to Loyalists increased. The Loyalists, including Chief Joseph Brant's Mohawks, viewed with alarm the continuing American pressure that forced the tribes of the Ohio region to surrender their lands in 1795 at the same time that Britain gave up the western posts. Gone was the buffer that might have forestalled invasion by a land-hungry American nation.

After population, the most pressing need in the province was development capital. Unoccupied fertile lands were the province's greatest asset but it would take years to realize a return thereon. In the meantime, the colony relied heavily on British government grants and on its share of the duties collected by Lower Canada on goods proceeding to the upper province.

After Simcoe's departure in 1796 his successors were honest but unimaginative, and Upper Canada grew by fits and starts. Political life in the frontier colony never rose above the pettiest of issues promoted by unimportant men. Outside of the tiny capital of York (later Toronto) with its few hundred residents, social life was simple in the extreme. The economy of the young colony came to be based on an increasing grain trade with Britain, although in the process of land-clearing squared timber and potash were produced for export. Upper Canada's population became increasingly heterogeneous: settlements of Roman Catholic Highlanders were formed in Glengarry County; French royalist refugees tried farming along Yonge Street north of York; and large groups of German-speaking Mennonites, Dunkards, Quakers and other "plain folk," and Lutherans arrived from Pennsylvania and New York to form block agricultural settlements around York and in the upper Grand Valley. By 1812 Upper Canada had almost 100,000 residents, but only 20,000 of them could boast the designation "U.E.L." (United Empire Loyalist). The province might be British in government, but socially and economically it seemed more like a part of the American frontier. The War of 1812 was destined to prove whether the American settlers had been truly assimilated into a British colony, or whether they still retained the prejudices and loyalties created by the American Revolution.

THE WAR OF 1812

After the British surrendered their posts in the Old Northwest in 1796, in accordance with the terms of Jay's Treaty, imperial policy concentrated on building up the new colonies of New Brunswick and Upper Canada. But tension in the Northwest

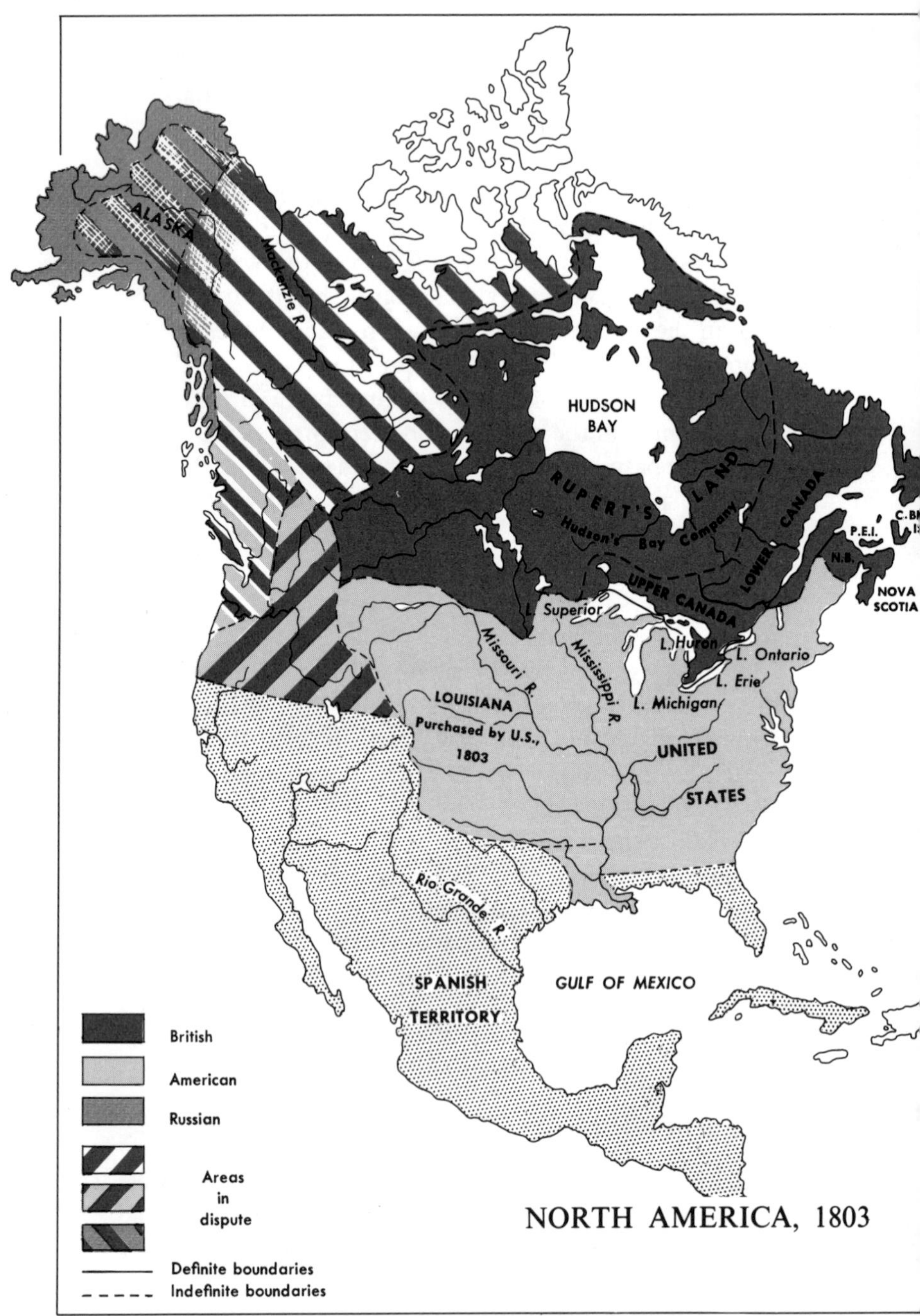

ALASKA
Mackenzie R.
HUDSON BAY
RUPERT'S LAND
Hudson's Bay Company
LOWER CANADA
UPPER CANADA
P.E.I.
N.B.
NOVA SCOTIA
L. Superior
L. Huron
L. Ontario
L. Erie
L. Michigan
Missouri R.
Mississippi R.
LOUISIANA
Purchased by U.S., 1803
UNITED STATES
Rio Grande R.
SPANISH TERRITORY
GULF OF MEXICO
British
American
Russian
Areas in dispute
Definite boundaries
Indefinite boundaries

NORTH AMERICA, 1803

continued as American fur traders, followed by settlers, invaded this last refuge of the eastern Indian tribes. Behind every conflict with these Indians the Americans believed they saw evidence of British interference. The fact was that until 1807 British policy was aimed at strict neutrality, but after that date the Indian Department in Canada looked to the Indians for support in case of an unwanted war with the United States. American relations with the Indians continued to deteriorate until 1811, when the battle of Tippecanoe ended in defeat for the Indians and the removal forever of Indian resistance to settlement in the Old Northwest.

Another cause of Anglo-American friction arose from the Napoleonic wars. Both Britain's Orders-in-Council and Napoleon's Berlin Decree offended America's national pride by forbidding her from trading with the belligerents. In 1809, under the impetus of pressure from the "war hawks" (politicians from the American south and midwest who sought advantage from traditional American animosity toward Britain), the United States retaliated by imposing her own embargo on American trade with both belligerents. Ironically this step alienated New England by damaging the commercial basis of her economy. A related grievance arose from the British practice of searching neutral ships on the high seas for deserters from the Royal Navy. When sailors claiming American citizenship (sometimes honestly, sometimes not) were pressed into British service, the United States protested vehemently that her rights on the high seas were being infringed. War between Britain and the United States seemed imminent by 1808, and although the crisis was delayed, both sides assumed that it was inevitable.

A further cause of the Anglo-American war of 1812 lay in American expansionism. The land hunger of a growing population in the United States was the excuse for the continuing Indian-settler wars and for the anti-British propaganda of the "war hawks." The rich but underdeveloped lands of British North America seemed to invite American occupation. With Britain fighting France for her very existence, it appeared that the conquest of British North America would be easy and profitable.

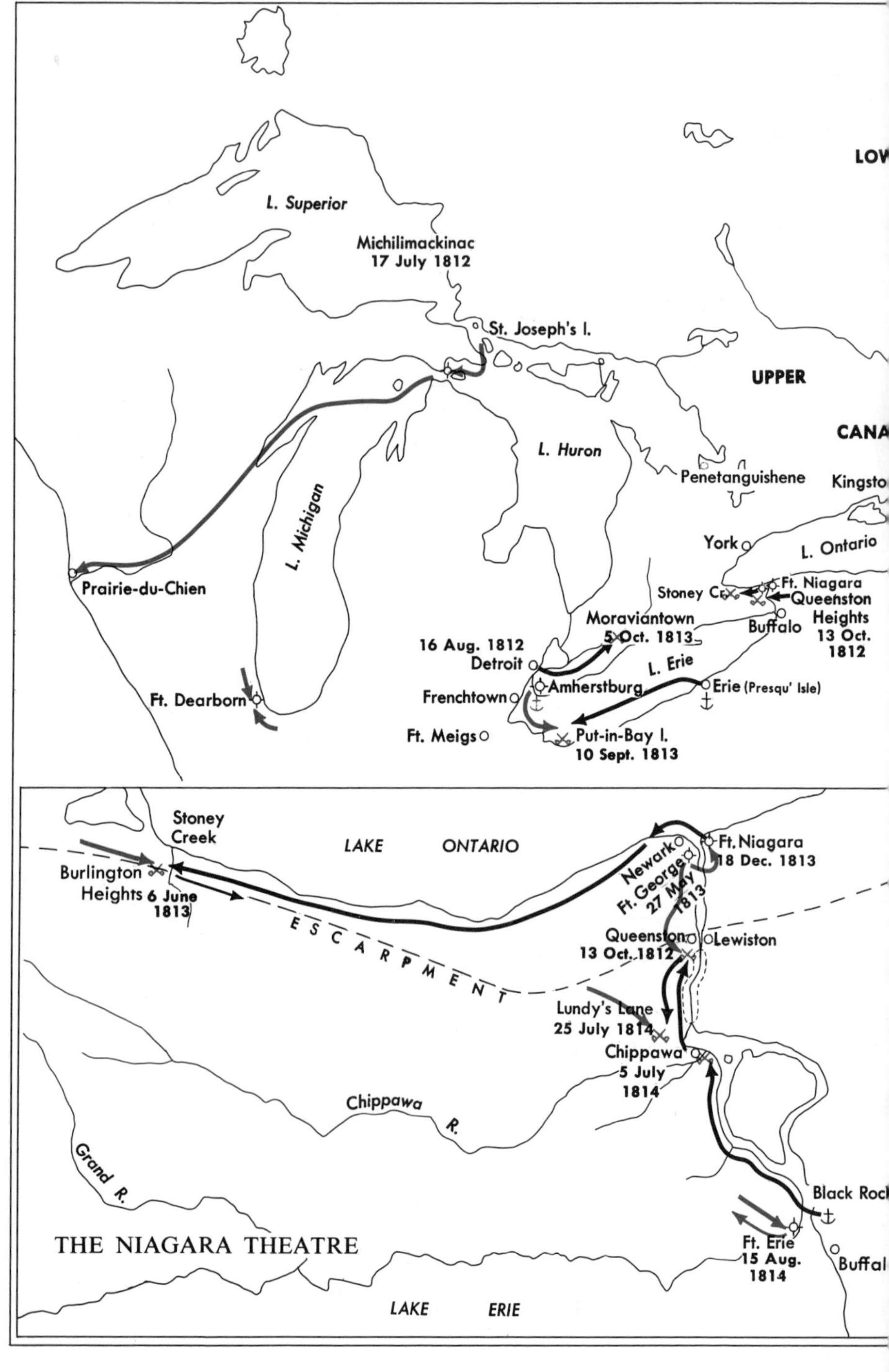
L. Superior
Michilimackinac
17 July 1812
St. Joseph's I.
UPPER
CANA
LOW
L. Huron
L. Michigan
Penetanguishene
Kingsto
York
L. Ontario
Prairie-du-Chien
Stoney Cr.
Ft. Niagara
Queenston
Heights
13 Oct.
1812
Buffalo
Moraviantown
5 Oct. 1813
16 Aug. 1812
Detroit
L. Erie
Amherstburg
Erie (Presqu' Isle)
Frenchtown
Ft. Dearborn
Ft. Meigs
Put-in-Bay I.
10 Sept. 1813
Stoney
Creek
LAKE
ONTARIO
Burlington
Heights 6 June
1813
Newark
Ft. George
27 May
1813
Ft. Niagara
18 Dec. 1813
ESCARPMENT
Queenston
13 Oct. 1812
Lewiston
Lundy's Lane
25 July 1814
Chippawa
5 July
1814
Chippawa R.
Grand R.
Black Rock
THE NIAGARA THEATRE
Ft. Erie
15 Aug.
1814
Buffal
LAKE
ERIE

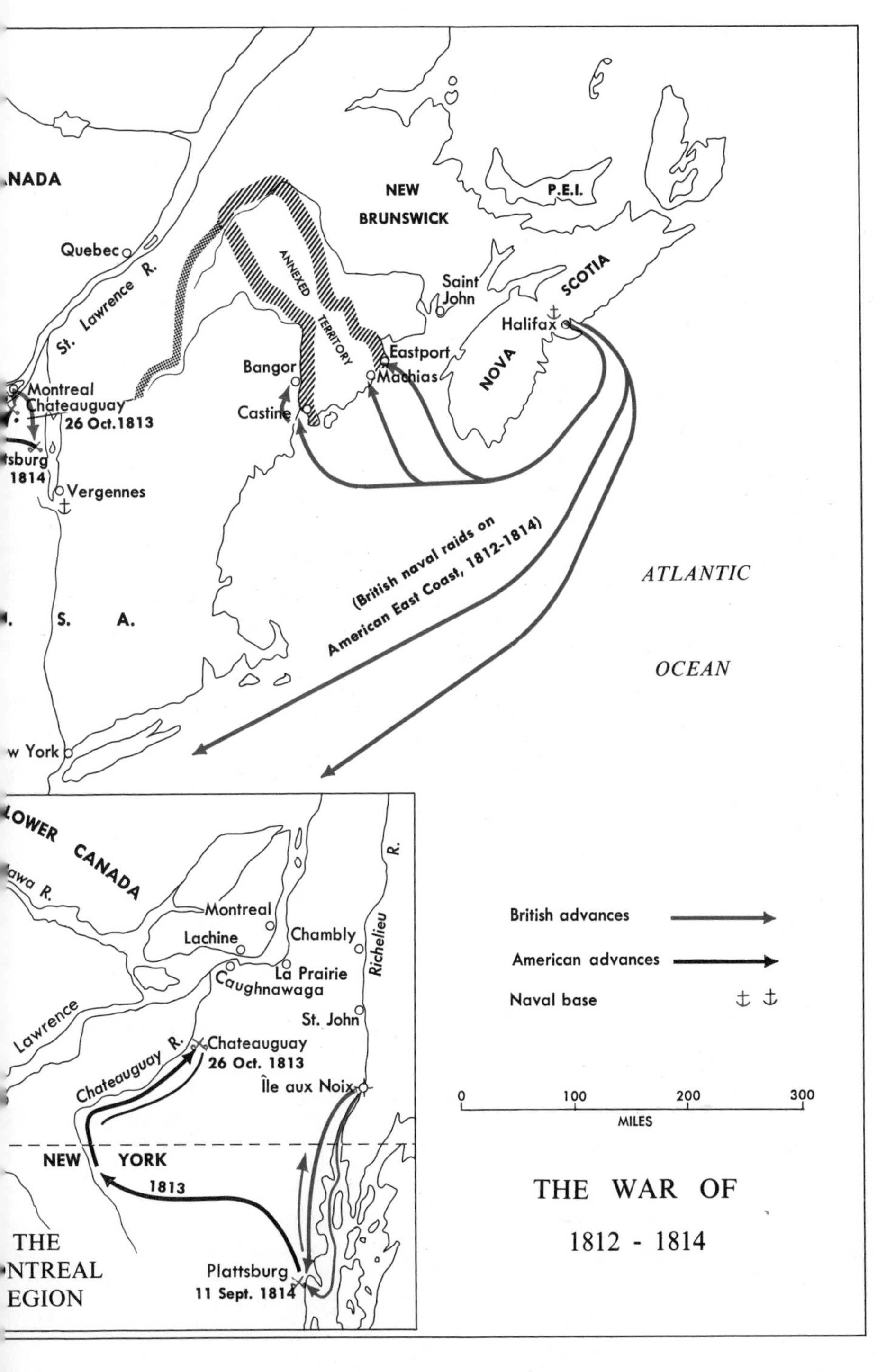
NADA
NEW
BRUNSWICK
P.E.I.
Quebec
St. Lawrence R.
ANNEXED
TERRITORY
Saint
John
SCOTIA
NOVA
Halifax
Eastport
Machias
Bangor
Castine
Montreal
Chateauguay
26 Oct.1813
tsburg
1814
Vergennes
(British naval raids on
American East Coast, 1812-1814)
ATLANTIC
OCEAN
S.
A.
w York
LOWER
CANADA
awa R.
Montreal
Lachine
Chambly
La Prairie
Caughnawaga
Richelieu
R.
St. John
Lawrence
Chateauguay R.
Chateauguay
26 Oct. 1813
Île aux Noix
NEW
YORK
1813
Plattsburg
11 Sept. 1814
THE
NTREAL
EGION
British advances
American advances
Naval base
0
100
200
300
MILES
THE WAR OF
1812 - 1814

Under such strong, yet diverse, pressures President Madison reluctantly declared war on Britain in the summer of 1812. Ironically, the offending Orders-in-Council had just been cancelled, and the Indian problem had already been reduced. Almost from the moment of declaring war the American government began to make peace overtures to Britain. But national passions generated by "war hawk" propaganda ran high, and once begun, the war could not easily be stopped.

British naval strength limited American activities on the Atlantic Ocean and around the Maritime colonies to isolated encounters of individual ships, but the inland frontiers of the Canadas were not as easy to defend. The brunt of war fell with devastating effect upon Upper Canada in particular. Upper Canada's line of communication, the St. Lawrence River, lay open to easy attack. Even so, the American military commanders aimed nearly all their futile, ill-directed and poorly planned war campaigns against the western region from Niagara to Windsor. Almost as great a threat as the enemy armies was the apathy of some Upper Canadians who felt their province was doomed, and the open disloyalty of a few—though surprisingly few—of the thousands of recent American settlers in the province.

The first year of war went in Britain's favour. Learning of the outbreak of hostilities before the local American authorities on the frontier, General Sir Isaac Brock, the British commander in Upper Canada, carried out a series of lightning campaigns that inspired the province and disheartened the enemy. His forces seized Michilimackinac without a shot; then, supported by the Shawnee warriors of Tecumseh, the tragic hero of Tippecanoe, Brock frightened the aging General Hull into surrendering Detroit. Together these two victories gave the British control of the upper Great Lakes and the Old Northwest. Weeks later Brock's men halted an American invasion across the Niagara River at the battle of Queenston Heights, during which the General himself was killed. Brock's success in routing the Americans during this early period had depended on his own imagination and daring, and on British control of the Great Lakes.

"The Battle of Queenston," an engraving after a drawing by one Major Dennis, published in 1836. As is frequent in drawings of military engagements from that period, the artist has compressed time and depicts a whole series of events as if they were happening at the same time. Note the small group of figures surrounding the fallen Brock, on the hill above the town.

The Americans saw control of the Great Lakes as vital to their campaign against Upper Canada. Therefore, in 1813 both sides became engaged in a navy-building race—Sackett's Harbour and Kingston at the eastern end of Lake Ontario being the rival bases. At the same time, the uninspired American commanders persisted in their misdirected attacks on the western region instead of cutting Upper Canada's lifeline, the St. Lawrence. During 1813, although the British suffered serious reverses, their vital supply line from Montreal remained unthreatened. On Lake Erie, the British commander, Barclay, unaccountably allowed the American fleet commanded by Oliver Perry to escape a trap. Barclay was then defeated by the larger American force in the battle of Put-in-Bay. This engagement restored Michigan to American control.

In April of that year, an American force seized York, destroyed supplies, and burned the parliament buildings before withdrawing. On the Niagara frontier the invaders took Fort George at the mouth of the Niagara River and advanced almost to

Hamilton before being driven back by a daring night bayonet charge at Stoney Creek. Forewarned of another American attack in the Niagara region by Laura Secord, a local woman who has become a legendary heroine, a band of Indians and a handful of British regulars under James FitzGibbon won another victory at Beaver Dams. A British raid against Sackett's Harbour failed miserably, and naval skirmishes on Lake Ontario were indecisive. In the western region, the British general, Proctor, abandoned Amherstburg on the Detroit River and retreated up the Thames valley. When his pursuers overtook him at Moraviantown the result was a complete victory for the Americans. Thus, by the end of 1813 the western peninsula region of Upper Canada was at the mercy of the Americans. But as insurance against its loss the British continued to hold the Old Northwest and to control the upper lakes.

In the autumn and winter of 1813-14, the Americans belatedly turned their power against the St. Lawrence route. At the end of October an American invasion was routed at Chateau Guai south of Montreal by the Canadien, de Salaberry, and on 11 November a mixed force of regulars and militia inflicted a second major defeat on the Americans at Crysler's Farm. After these reverses the Americans again turned to the Niagara region in 1814. Their early successes there came to an end with the bloody battle of Lundy's Lane. Before winter arrived they had abandoned Fort Erie and had retired to the American shore of the Niagara River.

Elsewhere in North America the British took the offensive in 1814 with mixed results. Maine was invaded, Washington captured and partly burned in retaliation for the destruction of York, and several Niagara frontier towns were razed. But a British invasion of the United States along the Richelieu-Lake Champlain route was abandoned by General Prevost when his supporting fleet was destroyed at Plattsburg. The final battle of the war, fought at New Orleans after a peace treaty had been signed in Europe, was a costly British defeat at the hands of a future American president, Andrew Jackson.

The Treaty of Ghent, signed on Christmas Eve, 1814, was an acknowledgment that the war between Britain and the United

In 1813 this medal was struck to raise the spirits of Upper Canadians. A British lion and a Canadian beaver quietly guard one side of the Niagara River against an American eagle that appears to be excitedly menacing them from the other side.

States had been fought to a draw. If Britain, now freed of the menace of Napoleon, held a military advantage, she failed in her attempt to use it at the bargaining table to reverse the unsatisfactory settlement of 1783. The boundaries remained unchanged after 1814—the strategic lands of the Old Northwest were still in American hands. The issue of "freedom of the seas" was not mentioned in the treaty. The Peace of Ghent was simply a return to the *status quo* before 1812. Obviously Canada was vulnerable to a determined and well-executed American invasion, but equally the Atlantic seaboard could be dominated by the Royal Navy. It was in the interests of both nations to seek peaceful solutions to any future difficulties.

To the Maritimes the war had brought prosperity. Halifax bustled with naval and merchant sailors. Increased trade and the capture of American ships put money in the pockets of enterprising individuals. The demand for food benefited farmers and fisherman. In New Brunswick the war stimulated the lumber industry, which continued as the basis for the colony's peacetime economy. This new wealth in turn encouraged the cultural life of the colonies.

In Lower Canada the war had been a golden opportunity for French Canadians to prove their loyalty and to confirm their own identity. Cut off from France since 1763, French Canadians now firmly identified themselves with the Canada which they had defended at Chateauguay.

Although Upper Canada had suffered physical damage, that province, like Lower Canada, gained immeasurably from the psychological reactions to the war. Gone was the small pro-American minority. From this time forward the loyalty of Upper Canadians—even American-born ones—was unquestioned and unquestionable. Upper Canadians gloried in such memories as Lundy's Lane and the militiamen who had shared the heat of battle with the small but decisive forces of British regulars. Like French Canadians in Lower Canada, the English-speaking Canadians in Upper Canada had experienced the birth pangs of nationalism.

* * *

Thanks to Britain's policy of "leniency," French Canada culturally survived the Conquest of 1763. In turn, the British empire in North America survived the catastrophe of the American Revolution, although half of the economic empire of the St. Lawrence-Great Lakes basin was lost by the boundary settlement. The migration of the Loyalists into the Maritimes had altered the character of that region and had led to the establishment of two new colonies, New Brunswick and Cape Breton Island; yet in the post-Revolutionary decades the Maritime colonies grew but slowly because they were unable to displace the United States in the Atlantic trading triangle.

In the colony of Quebec the arrival of the Loyalists had necessitated a basic revision of the Quebec Act to provide for the establishment of British institutions in a distinctly British colony, Upper Canada. While Upper Canada's early years were filled with the physical problems of growth and settlement, her sister province of Lower Canada felt the first strains of the political and linguistic animosities that were to plague her later development. By the beginning of the War of 1812 both of the Canadas were emerging as agricultural societies for whom the grain trade to Britain was a new staple, replacing the traditional dependence of the St. Lawrence economic region on furs. The fur trade itself had been stretched westward to the shores of the Pacific Ocean. British North America, having survived the second American challenge to its existence in the War of 1812, was ready to enter an age of solid political, social and economic growth.

CHAPTER 5

REFORM REACHES THE COLONIES

The year 1815 saw the end of both the Anglo-American war and Europe's long struggle against Napoleon. "Pax Britannica"—a century of general peace—was beginning. For the six colonies of British North America the next fifty years would be a golden era of demographic, economic, political and cultural growth. They would also be years of self-assessment, of domestic strain even to the point of rebellion, and ultimately of a new relationship to the mother country and to the rest of the empire.

The recent war had brought prosperity to the Maritimes and self-awareness to the Canadas. In Lower Canada the course of political activity, suspended during the war, would now be resumed with French-Canadian politicians increasing their opposition to the colonial government. For Upper Canada the war had given form to the idea of "loyalty" to British institutions, an idea held with increasing conviction as those in authority sought to curb what they considered to be destructive and insidious influences of democratic Americanism.

BRITAIN AND HER EMPIRE

One immediate result of the War of 1812 was the settlement (at least provisionally) of most North American issues between Britain and the United States. In 1817 the Rush-Bagot Agreement ended naval rivalry on the Great Lakes by restricting the number of armed vessels in these waters to one for each nation on Lake Ontario, and two on the upper lakes. By another convention, signed in 1818, the forty-ninth parallel was fixed as the international boundary from the Lake of the Woods to the Rockies. The mountain and Pacific coast regions were to be jointly occupied, no final boundary settlement being made there until 1846. The Convention of 1818 excluded American fishermen from the territorial waters of British North America (except for the inshore fisheries of Labrador and Newfoundland), but this created no hardship for Americans because the main fishing ground lay in international waters beyond the three-mile limit. Only the disputed Maine-New Brunswick border remained a source of irritation, until settled by the Webster-Ashburton Treaty of 1842.

The most significant changes for British North America after the war were those occurring in Britain. Britain was now feeling the full impact of the Industrial Revolution and was soon to become the most powerful manufacturing and trading nation in the world. The technological changes were producing a revolution in British society. A steadily increasing population was matched by a higher standard of living. Britain needed new and larger markets, which her overseas colonies could not provide, and she needed new sources of such raw materials as cotton, which again the older colonies could not provide. British attention, therefore, naturally shifted to Africa and Asia, and opinion in Britain began to accept the idea of an enlarged empire composed of people of many races and creeds—an empire in which the older, British-settled colonies would have a less significant role. One justification for this changing empire was offered by writers like Jeremy Bentham (1748-1832), father of the Philosophic Radical or Benthamite group, and his eloquent disciple, James Mill. They felt that colonies in the old style were a burden on the British taxpayers from which no return could be expected. Colonies could also be a cause of war, as in the case of British North America. Both arguments—the economic and the military—were soon accepted by the manufacturing and commercial classes whose sole interest was profit.

"Bush Farm near Chatham, Upper Canada, about 1838." As can be seen in this contemporary watercolour, early settlers in Upper Canada led a life of isolation.

Equally important, British politics in the post-Napoleonic era underwent a process of liberalization of aims and modernization of structure exemplified by the Great Reform Act of 1832. Colonial politics, with their petty issues and oligarchic administration, seemed sadly out of step in this new age. From a more liberal Britain the colonies received a double legacy: the attitude of the mother country toward them became more permissive, or apathetic; and a wave of politically active immigrants arrived. The newcomers unsettled the conservative outlook of colonists who had just survived war's challenge to their way of life.

Another obvious gain for the colonies from the post-Napoleonic conditions was increased population. Demobilized soldiers settled in British North America individually, or in such groups as the two battalions given land at Perth, Upper Canada. Post-war unemployment and distress in Britain brought thousands more to North America in search of new opportunities. Of the colonies, Upper Canada received the greatest number—her population jumped from 95,000 in 1814 to 150,000 by 1824, and to 236,000 by 1831—but all of the British North American colonies benefited in terms of population and economic growth.

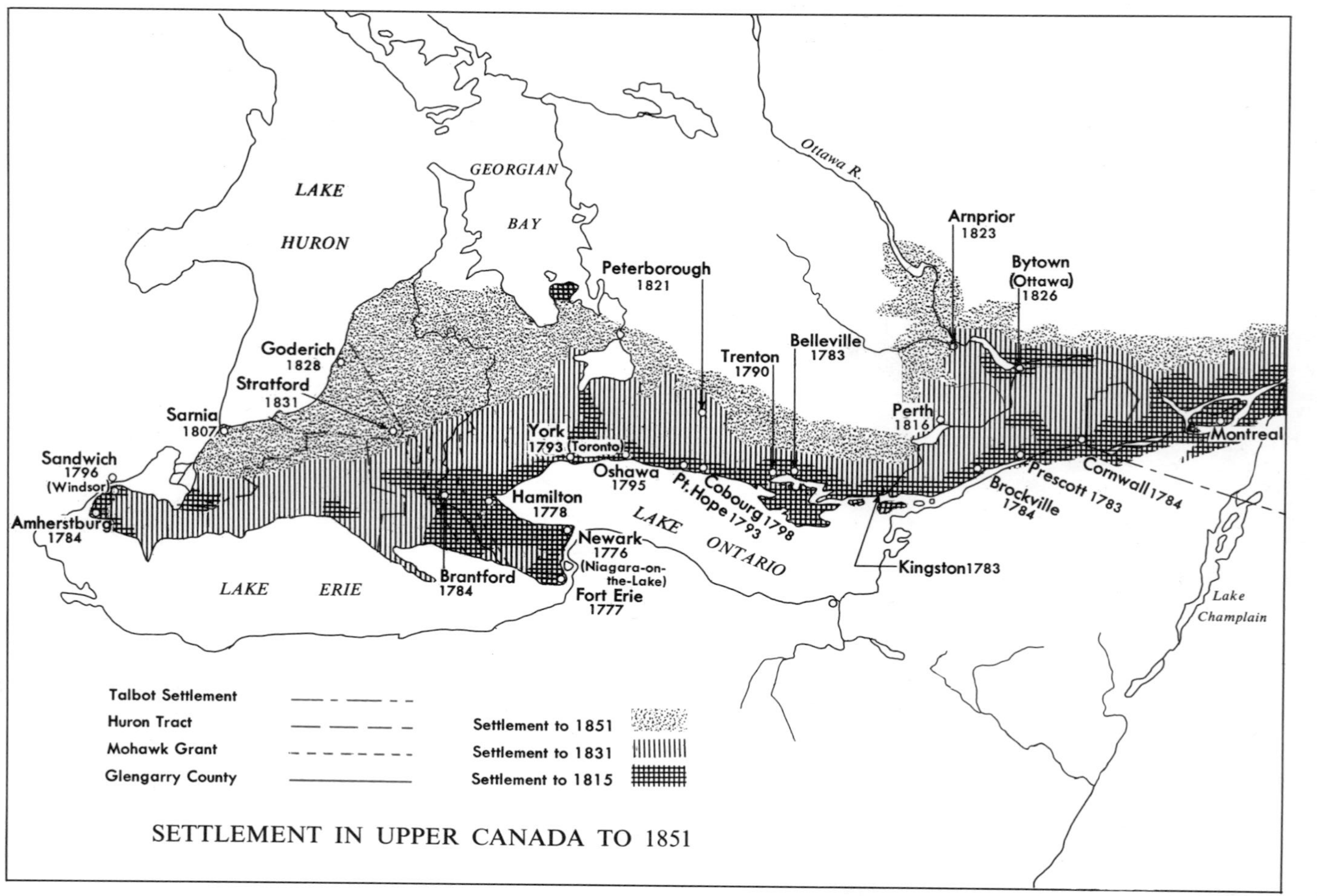
LAKE HURON
GEORGIAN BAY
Ottawa R.
Arnprior 1823
Bytown (Ottawa) 1826
Peterborough 1821
Goderich 1828
Stratford 1831
Sarnia 1807
Belleville 1783
Trenton 1790
Perth 1816
York 1793 (Toronto)
Montreal
Sandwich 1796 (Windsor)
Oshawa 1795
Cobourg 1798
Pt. Hope 1793
Cornwall 1784
Prescott 1783
Brockville 1784
Hamilton 1778
Amherstburg 1784
LAKE ONTARIO
Newark 1776 (Niagara-on-the-Lake)
Kingston 1783
Brantford 1784
Fort Erie 1777
LAKE ERIE
Lake Champlain
Talbot Settlement
Huron Tract
Mohawk Grant
Glengarry County
Settlement to 1851
Settlement to 1831
Settlement to 1815

SETTLEMENT IN UPPER CANADA TO 1851

CHANGING ECONOMIC PATTERNS

In the three decades following the end of the Napoleonic wars and the War of 1812, the British North American colonies, and particularly Upper Canada, assumed the form of settled societies. Nova Scotia (to which Cape Breton was reunited in 1820) continued to grow, though more slowly, as a colony based on a mixed economy of farming, fishing and lumbering. The life of New Brunswick centred predominantly on lumbering. Prince Edward Island still suffered from the problem of absentee landlords, and as a consequence its social and economic development were retarded for at least another two generations.

British North American timber had a decisive advantage in the British and West Indian markets, thanks to Britain's 275 percent tariff on foreign timber that remained even after a reduction in 1821. With this encouragement, enterprising lumbermen in New Brunswick, the Ottawa valley and on the shores of the Great Lakes annually sent huge rafts of squared timber to the depots at Saint John and Quebec. As a by-product the cutting of timber also made cleared land available for new settlers, who arrived by the rough but cheap means of steerage passage in the returning timber ships. By the 1840's a large trade in sawn lumber, that also extended to the United States, was rapidly replacing the squared timber business, dotting the more remote areas with sawmills.

Economic development was not achieved without dramatic change. The war with the United States had barely ended when the fur trading empire of the St. Lawrence collapsed. Given the ever-lengthening line of trade, the rising cost of goods and transportation, and the fall of fur prices on the international market, the North West Company succumbed to the inevitable when it sold out to the Hudson's Bay Company in 1821. The "wintering partners" in the western interior found employment with the new monopolists and all furs now moved from the ports on Hudson Bay to the warehouses of London. The Montreal merchants, forced to seek new commercial empires of their own, now entered the carrying trade of the Great Lakes.

The export from the Canadas of grain, flour and timber,

which had just commenced before the War of 1812, was stimulated by post-war shortages of food and building materials in Britain and Europe, at the same time that the new settlers needed European-made manufactured goods. For at least another generation the supply of inexpensive manufactured goods from Britain forestalled any sizeable industrial growth in British North America. A new economy was emerging based on the rich agricultural resources of the colonies. The "Bay" had beaten the "River" in the struggle for the fur trade, but the "River" was building a more solid, if less romantic, economic empire on the rich resources of field and forest.

The old dream that Montreal might capture the trade of the hinterland, including the American midwest, seemed close to realization, but a second blow fell with the opening in 1825 of the Erie Canal, linking the Great Lakes to the port of New York. The produce of the American midwest could now flow to an American port, and Upper Canada appeared doomed to become

An 1843 sketch of a stage coach equipped with runners for winter travel. Pioneer travel was slow and at times could be almost unbearably uncomfortable. A common type of road, especially in swampy places, was the corduroy road in which logs were laid side by side. The result was to create a bone-jarring ride quite unimaginable to the motorist using modern super highways.

The Royal William, *built in Quebec in 1831, to link Quebec and Halifax. In 1833 it became the first vessel to cross the Atlantic using steam as the main source of power. The introduction of steam vessels reduced the time for an Atlantic crossing from several weeks to fourteen days. One of the most prominent of Atlantic steamship operators of the day was Samuel Cunard of Halifax, who founded the firm that still bears his name.*

a part of this American commercial empire unless measures were taken to offset its disadvantage in transportation. Since only water transport was economically feasible for such bulky commodities as timber and grain, the St. Lawrence route would have to be improved by the building of expensive canals. (The Rideau Canal, conceived during the recent war, and completed from Kingston to Ottawa in 1832, was not intended to fill an economic role.) The first canals would have to bypass the series of rapids on the St. Lawrence from Lachine to the Long Sault; the second would have to skirt Niagara Falls. The staggering cost of such projects seemed too great for colonial resources, particularly when the St. Lawrence economic unit was divided politically into two provinces.

The five-foot deep Lachine Canal was opened in 1825 by the Lower Canadian government, but the farmers who composed the majority of the assembly in that province refused to share in canal ventures outside of Lower Canada because they seemed to offer no direct return. The four other canals on the Upper

Canadian section of the St. Lawrence were then constructed piece-meal, whenever funds could be obtained, between 1845 and 1847. The first Welland Canal across the neck of the Niagara peninsula was financed by private enterprise (largely American) and by imperial subsidies. It was opened for business in 1829 and was expanded four years later, only to become a political issue because of its financial difficulties.

The long delay in finishing the necessary canal system meant that trade from the American midwest continued through the Erie Canal and that Upper Canadian trade usually crossed Lake Erie or Lake Ontario to take advantage of that canal route. When the St. Lawrence canal system was complete at last in the late 1840s, it was on the point of being rendered obsolete by railways. In any case, the whole economic structure of the empire was about to be shaken by Britain's decision to replace the mercantile system of "imperial preferences" by free trade with the world.

THE REFORM MOVEMENTS

The political reform movements that appeared in the Canadas and in Nova Scotia after 1815, culminating in the achievement of responsible government, were the result of a variety of forces at work inside and outside of British North America. In none of the colonies were the internal forces identical, and even the impact of contemporary British and American influences produced differences in the degree of response. In Nova Scotia the reform movement was British in expression—conservative and constitutional—and led by native sons. In Lower Canada basic political issues were confounded by the elements of "race," language and religion, and influenced by the romantic nationalism so prevalent in contemporary Europe. In Upper Canada reform leadership was provided by such disparate personalities as the two Scottish radicals, Robert Gourlay and William Lyon Mackenzie; Egerton Ryerson of Loyalist stock; and Robert Baldwin, a native Upper Canadian. Although Upper Canada was untroubled by language issue, the reform movement there was more complex than those in the other colonies. The colony was so much more a battleground for ideas imported from Britain and the United States that several distinct reform groups existed.

The basic problem of all the colonies was the same one that had beset the Americans before the Revolution—the impossibility of imposing the popular will on an appointed executive. Other complaints common to all colonies were favouritism in granting lands and political jobs, and delay in developing roads and schools. Still other issues were peculiar to specific colonies: the fear of French Canadians that they would be swamped by British immigration; the lack of opportunities for the French-Canadian professional class; the Upper Canadian grievances over the preferred position of the Church of England in education, marriage and burial rites, its monopoly of the clergy reserves and, after 1835, the legal endowment of forty-four Anglican rectories without similar compensation for the other denominations.

Constitutionally the colonies has representative government, but not responsible government (wherein the cabinet is formed from the party comprising a majority in the assembly). Lacking the practice of cabinet government, in which the executive council or cabinet finds seats in the assembly in order to explain and gain support for government policy, a hiatus existed between these two elements of the constitution: the royally appointed executive and the popularly elected assembly. Within the British constitution a solution had been evolving for over a century in the form of cabinet responsibility, but it is important to remember that the full implications of cabinet government were still being worked out in the mother country at the time when the reform movements appeared in the colonies.

The British North American colonies were ruled by local oligarchies. The so-called "Family Compact" in Upper Canada, for instance, was not a party but a loose alliance of prominent conservatives at the capitals with similarly-minded local leaders throughout the colony. In Lower Canada the equivalent was the Château Clique, although the picture there was complicated by the disproportionate dominance of the "English". The

The Reverend Egerton Ryerson. Ryerson began his career as a Methodist circuit rider in an area west of York, Upper Canada's capital. His influence in his own day is well-known, but it is often forgotten that the principles on which he established the educational system of Upper Canada continued, with few changes, to govern educational policy in Ontario and other parts of Canada until recent decades.

The Reverend John Strachan, when he was Archdeacon of York. ". . . the great Bond of attachment between the Colonies and Great Britain depends entirely upon the progress and influence of Church principles." Strachan to the Colonial Office.
It need hardly be said that when Strachan speaks of the "Church" he is thinking of the Church of England.

colonial toryism represented by such groups was more a shared political point of view than a political organization. The members of the oligarchies almost without exception were men of ability and dedication in a society where education and trained leadership were rare. These men were usually rigid defenders of British institutions, including a privileged position for the Church of England.

John Strachan, the Scottish school teacher, Anglican priest,

Despite the comic-opera nature of the rebellion he led in Upper Canada, William Lyon Mackenzie (1795-1861) was far from being a clown or figure of fun. As a politician he frequently overcame the stigma of official disapproval to win considerable popular support, both as a candidate for the provincial legislature and for the mayoralty of Toronto. As a journalist he exerted influence upon both farmers and businessmen.

and later first Bishop of Toronto, moulded a generation of young conservatives and stamped his mark indelibly on the educational, political and religious life of his adopted province. A strong believer in the virtues of Anglicanism, the British constitution and an aristocratic society, Strachan had been projected into prominence and given a sense of self-assurance and destiny when he took charge of affairs in York during its brief American occupation in 1813. Successively he had been made a legislative councillor, an executive councillor and in 1826 president of his projected King's College. Neither flamboyant nor popular, Strachan was content to manage men and direct political developments from behind the scenes. Strachan was devoted to what he considered the best interests of Canada, and in many fields he showed quite early a remarkable grasp of Canada's needs. But he was prepared to defend both the privileges of his own church and the "correct" political principles of the Compact against all comers, particularly against what he believed to be American and democratic influences.

Contrary to the tradition popularized by an older generation of Canadian historians who accepted the radical propaganda of the period uncritically, the colonies, in fact, got good government from the oligarchies. Colonial governors came and went with considerable frequency, but the local oligarchies who ruled in fact held their positions virtually for life. The charges against these oligarchies was not bad government—their members were able and dedicated men and abuses of power were few—but that good government was no substitute for government in which the popularly-elected representatives could put into practice the desires of the majority.

Radical demands for changes in government policies or personnel were generally unsuccessful because they were misdirected and overly concerned with trivia. The Halifax-based group that composed both the executive and legislative councils of Nova Scotia had early found a way of circumventing political opposition in their province by using government jobs and social recognition as a means of silencing grumblers. In Prince Edward Island the assembly succeeded in obtaining the removal of the unpopular Lieutenant-Governor C. D. Smith. But the basic problem of colonial politics remained—the concentration of too much power in the hands of too few people. In their earlier years the provincial reform movements lacked both cohesion and policy. Isolated clashes occurred between the government and outspoken critics, but as long as people retained the eighteenth century attitude that organized opposition was somehow disloyal, no true parties in the modern sense emerged, and without the restriction of parties local oligarchies were able to silence their critics by various means.

Individual critics of the oligarchies appeared at various times, but none was able to organize enough popular support to effect any changes in the political system. In Upper Canada Robert Gourlay, an erratic Scot who threatened to cause trouble by calling local protest meetings, was easily banished from the province in 1819 on a legal technicality. Similarly, the erratic newspaper publisher Robert Collins of York was temporarily silenced by imprisonment. Egerton Ryerson, a young Methodist preacher, attacked the privileged position of the Church of

An election—pioneer style. Until the secret ballot was introduced in 1872, Canadian elections were entirely open affairs and too often were accompanied by violence. Each poll followed a popular and prescribed ritual. The local sheriff would proclaim the election to the assembled crowd and then call for nominations. Each mover and seconder followed with a long speech praising the virtues of his candidate. Often, as part of the game, several people were nominated who promptly withdrew after making speeches in favour of one or other of the favourites. Several hours later, when nominations and acceptance speeches had finally ended, the returning officer called for a show of hands, and by tradition announced that he could not decide who had won, no matter how loud the voices for either candidate. Then close to a hotel where strong drink was available to "refresh" officials and voters, a register for votes was opened in a booth or on a platform.

The property qualification for voters was so small that almost all men could be electors. The voter cast his vote by stating publicly the candidate he supported. If the friends of the other candidate were numerous, drunk or just in a fighting mood, the voter might be attacked with stones or clubs when he left the voting table. Each poll was kept open for several days, and candidates tried to hold back some of their votes for a last-minute rush.

Provincial general elections might go on for several weeks because polls were held at different times in different places, in contrast to today's one-day elections. At each poll opposing groups tried to keep a small gang and lots of grog to "persuade" any reluctant voter. The unhappy results of these prolonged and open elections were frequent riots, numerous cracked heads, and occasional murders. Such interference made "controverted elections"—appeals to parliament to unseat the winner—very common, but because the final decision was made by the majority in the Commons every appeal meant that the majority added to its strength by voting in their own candidate.

This unusual sketch portrays a nomination day at Perth, Upper Canada, in July, 1828.

England regarding marriages and its monopoly of the clergy reserves funds. But it was William Lyon Mackenzie, a fiery Scottish immigrant, who led in demands for reforms. Mackenzie produced an endless stream of grievances—both real and imaginary—charging favouritism in land grants, discrimination against non-Anglicans, injustices in the law courts, delay in educational and economic developments, and a host of others, which he published in his newspaper, *The Colonial Advocate*. His main support came, significantly, from small farmers in the more recently settled areas, often recent immigrants who brought to Canada reform ideas then popular in Britain. What made Mackenzie and the radicals suspect in the eyes of most Upper Canadians was their constant reference to the more advanced conditions in the United States.

Mackenzie was rescued from bankruptcy (and historical oblivion) when he won a large damage suit against some scions of the "Family Compact," who had wrecked his printing shop. Two years later, amidst widespread discontent with Compact policies, the reformers won a majority in the assembly at a general election, and promptly chose American-born, moderate reformer Marshall Spring Bidwell for the influential post of Speaker of the House.

As prominent in the reform cause as the radical Mackenzie or the moderate Bidwell was young Robert Baldwin, related to several Compact members, incisive of mind, but lacking both oratorical ability and the qualities of political leadership. Yet it was Baldwin who, as early as 1828, formulated the basic principle of all the reform movements—the principle that members of the executive council must be drawn from that party which controlled a majority of seats in the assembly. This was no more than cabinet government, yet for twenty years Baldwin's "great principle" was rejected by the Colonial Office for the sound reason that it would give sovereign power to a colony.

The election of 1830 proved to be the turning point in the political growth of Upper Canada. When Robert Baldwin was defeated in that election the ever-vocal Mackenzie appeared to assume the leadership of the reform movement.

For a few years Mackenzie believed he had an ally in Egerton

Ryerson, who was editing the weekly Methodist *Christian Guardian,* the most influential of the many newspapers existing in the 1830's. Ryerson spoke for the Methodists, Baptists, some Presbyterians and even some Anglicans when he denounced the inequity of church establishment. But on a trip to England he discovered that Mackenzie's friends in the British parliament, particularly the radical Joseph Hume, were unprincipled and irreligious. Ryerson's publication of this information in 1833 turned all moderates against Mackenzie, and particularly separated the Methodists who were interested only in religious equality.

Since colonial governors were usually conservatives and veterans of the battle of Waterloo, and since they were dependent on the local oligarchy in forming policies, the Colonial Office in London received dispatches that put the reformers in the worst possible light. In addition, colonial reformers who tried to by-pass the governor and his council by visiting the Colonial Office personally, got a cool reception, if they were received at all. As a result the reformers realized that the key to colonial reform must be control of the public purse. In 1831 the Upper Canadian assembly was given control over customs revenues—but not over the valuable fees and rents that made up the Casual and Terri-

The Alpheus Jones house, Prescott, Ontario, built about 1820. Domestic architecture such as this provided a significant sign of increasing sophistication in the growing towns of Upper Canada. The style is Georgian, a popular one at the time among Loyalist families.

torial Revenues. In exchange the assembly granted a permanent civil list (schedule of salaries for civil servants), insuring public officers of their salaries and of executive independence from the assembly's control. Mackenzie denounced this measure in unbridled language. He was expelled four times from the assembly, and re-elected as often! At last Mackenzie's opportunity came in 1834 when the reformers won a general election. During the next parliamentary session he chaired a so-called Seventh Committee on Grievances, at which every imaginable complaint was trotted out, and for which Mackenzie offered a single solution—replacement of the appointed legislative council by an elected one.

THE DRIFT TO REBELLION

At this point a new Lieutenant-Governor, Sir Francis Bond Head, an unknown Poor Law Commissioner, was sent out to Upper Canada with instructions to give Mackenzie a fair hearing. Head, who claimed he was no more partisan than his carriage horses, soon discovered to his own satisfaction that the reformers were really republicans bent on destroying the imperial connection. After appointing Baldwin and two other moderates to his executive, he quarrelled with them about political patronage and called another election in the summer of 1836. In Head's opinion this election would make or break Upper Canada as a British colony, and he made personal appeals to voters to support the right cause, the royal cause. The result was a striking victory for the Governor—in practice governor-prime minister—and such an ignominous defeat for the radicals that Mackenzie at once began to plan drastic action that would end "irresponsible government" and his own frustration.

In Lower Canada the agitation for reform was complicated by the language factor, but otherwise its development showed numerous parallels with the movement in Upper Canada. An abortive attempt of the Montreal business groups to arrange a political reunion of the two Canadas in 1822 accidentally started the movement in the lower province. Reunion would have

"Louis Joseph Papineau (1786-1871) . . . was a democrat, but he was also the spokesman of French-Canadian nationalism. Because of this double dimension, his personality is more difficult to analyse than that of his Upper Canadian counterpart, William Lyon Mackenzie."

saddled Lower Canada with Upper Canada's debts, and popular opposition to such a burden brought together John Neilson, editor of the influential Quebec *Gazette*, and Louis-Joseph Papineau, an aristocratic, eloquent, but essentially conservative, French-Canadian nationalist. Neilson, like Baldwin and his friends in Upper Canada, thought of reform in terms of British political experience. Papineau, like Mackenzie, became progressively more radical and more obstinate in his opinions. Papineau led the assembly (of which he became a member as early as 1809) in attacks on executive policies and personnel. Besides the common problem of all colonial governments—the frustrating inability of the elected assembly to control the local executive—the Lower Canadian political scene was complicated by French domination in the assembly and English control of the council and administration. In 1834 only 47 of 244 government officials spoke French, although the population of the province was about 85 percent French-speaking. Papineau set the tone of reform obstructionism when he rejected the imperial government's offer of limited financial control in exchange for a permanent civil list. Year after year the reform majority adamantly refused any co-operation, but this obvious obstructionism and Papineau's increasingly republican and anti-clerical speeches estranged both French-speaking moderates and sympathetic English Canadians. The breaking point came with Papineau's Ninety-two Resolutions, an omnibus collection of grievances both serious and trivial, passed by the assembly in 1834. Typical of the moderates' reaction was Neilson's comment that sixteen of these resolutions were false, fourteen merely abusive, and twelve ridiculous. Most English-speaking reformers and virtually all of the clergy withdrew from a movement that seemed determined to cause a critical confrontation with the imperial government. Yet, in justice to Papineau, it must be remembered that his aim was to conserve the French-Canadian way of life by using the political power put into French-Canadian hands by the Constitutional Act.

The colonial agitation for reform was both helped and hindered by the liberal developments in Britain. Colonial reformers drew inspiration from the movement in the mother country; but that movement also diverted British attention from colonial problems. Moreover, the Whig leaders such as Lord Melbourne, who was Prime Minister in 1834 and again from 1835 to 1841, were essentially conservatives. They felt that reform in Britain had now gone far enough, and conscientiously believed that the colonial reformers' demand for a right not yet clearly established in the mother country could, if conceded, only lead to a break-up of the Empire. Typical of these men was Lord John Russell, Colonial Secretary, who earned the nickname "Finality Jack" for his statement that no further reforms would be needed for a lifetime after the Great Reform Act of 1832. British officials were not, however, simply reactionary; they sincerely wanted the colonists to be content. But the deluge of petitions, counter-petitions, advice and complaints that reached them from the colonies left them uncertain of what policy to pursue.

In 1835 Lord Gosford was sent to Canada as Governor General with instructions to seek a reconciliation with Papineau's party. This good will was nullified by Sir Francis Bond Head who injudiciously published Lord Gosford's instructions and showed that the Colonial Office had attached many restrictive strings to the offer of a settlement. Angered by this evidence of duplicity, the Lower Canadian assembly refused to vote supply (the funds for government operations). The reply of the imperial government to this obstructionism was Lord John Russell's famous Ten Resolutions of 1837, which rejected the radicals' demand for elective councils and authorized the Governor to spend money without the approval of the assembly.

The Ten Resolutions proved to be the spark that ignited rebellion in the two colonies. Tension was already high in Montreal where revolutionary groups calling themselves *Patriotes* and *Fils de la Liberté* were opposed by a "Constitutional Society," whose followers saw in French-Canadian political domination an end to the economic progress of the province. A sharp recession that struck the colonies in 1836 was compounded by serious crop failures in the Montreal-Richelieu area. Economic interests joined political and "racial" factors to create a dangerous climate.

A bivouac at St. Hilaire de Rouville, November 23 and 24, 1837, in Lithographic Views of Military Operations in Canada . . . During the Late Insurrection. *London, 1840. The British troops and colonial militiamen were billeted in the out-buildings of what the artist described as "a Canadian gentleman."*

The gathering storm broke on 7 November, 1837, when rival groups of youths clashed in the streets of Montreal. Shocked that his inflammatory speeches should have resulted in open hostilities, Papineau fled to the United States, leaving to others the management of the rebellion he had fostered. Troops sent to arrest the ringleaders were at first repulsed by the habitants of St. Charles, but in a matter of days these rebels and others at St. Denis and St. Eustache had been defeated and sharply punished by regular soldiers and militia volunteers from Upper Canada.

The radicals in Upper Canada followed events in the lower province closely. During the summer of 1837 Mackenzie had barn-stormed around the Toronto (its name having been changed in 1834 from York) area trying to organize a protest march on the provincial capital. When news of the outbreak in Lower Canada reached him, he determined to strike a similar blow in Upper Canada, taking advantage of the absence of the troops sent to Montreal. But the Upper Canadian rebellion was so badly planned and so poorly supported that Lieutenant-Governor Head and the militia easily scattered the rebel gathering at Montgomery's Tavern just north of Toronto on 7 December.

The rebellions in the two Canadas did not really pose a serious threat to authority, and the events in Upper Canada especially had had an almost comic opera appearance. Significantly, the population in both provinces did not support this resort to violence and the abortive rebellions were limited to the immediate vicinities of Montreal and Toronto.

All danger did not, however, end with the crushing of the rebellions. Lower Canadian rebels who fled to the United States were received as the victims of British tyranny. Mackenzie escaped after the fiasco at Toronto and entrenched himself on Navy Island in the Niagara River, where he was joined by American sympathizers bent on liberating Upper Canada in the name of democracy and freedom. In the neighbouring United States, along the border, secret societies called "Hunters' Lodges" were formed to promote armed aggression against British Canada. For a full year the border regions were kept in a state of agitation by filibustering raids, but the only result was to

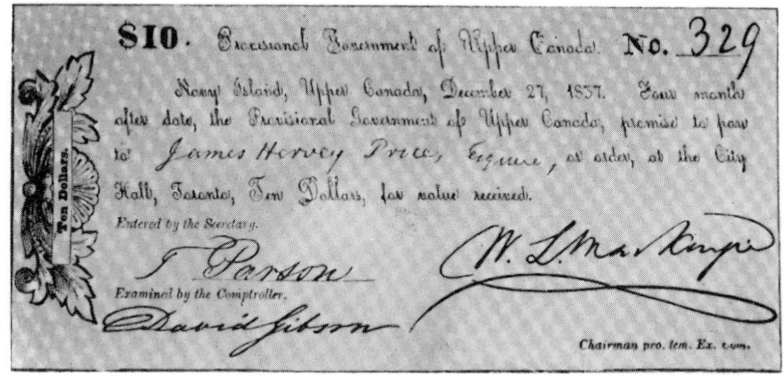

$10. Provisional Government of Upper Canada. No. 329

Navy Island, Upper Canada, December 27, 1837. Four months after date, the Provisional Government of Upper Canada, promise to pay to James Harvey Price, Esquire, or order, at the City Hall, Toronto, Ten Dollars, for value received.

Ten Dollars.

Entered by the Secretary.

T. Parson

Examined by the Comptroller.

David Gibson

W. L. Mackenzie

Chairman pro. tem. Ex. com.

Shown above is a ten dollar note issued by Mackenzie's "Provisional Government of Upper Canada" on Navy Island. Mackenzie obviously believed he would be able to succeed in his attempted coup d'état, *but one wonders if James Harvey Price ever received his ten dollars.*

deepen Canadian mistrust of the Americans. The largest raid, at Prescott, Upper Canada, ended with the capture of over one hundred American "Patriots" and the execution of their leader, a misguided Polish soldier, Nils von Schoultz. Of the captured Canadian rebels a few were hanged (only two in Upper Canada) and most were transported to the prison colony of Van Dieman's Island. The so-called "Patriot War" dwindled away as the American government belatedly began to enforce strict neutrality on its citizens. Thus the double threats of domestic revolt and foreign intervention were virtually removed in the space of one year, but the problem of coping with colonial unrest and the conditions that had led to rebellion remained to be dealt with by the mother country.

LORD DURHAM'S SOLUTION

It was ironic that Sir Francis Bond Head, the major irritant in Upper Canada, was being recalled to Britain when Mackenzie took up arms. It was also both ironic and auspicious that Prime Minister Lord Melbourne had already decided on an investigation of the whole colonial problem before the street rioting began in Montreal. Privately, Melbourne was not opposed to ultimate independence for the colonies, but he was concerned about the political repercussions in Britain of such a development. The commissioner chosen to report on the "Canada question" was John George Lambton, "Radical Jack," first Earl of Durham, a handsome and wealthy, but emotional, statesman and diplomat. Durham was already recognized as leader of the "radical imperialists," a Whig faction that favoured colonial self-government within a new structure of empire.

Durham was given the unprecedented title of Governor General of British North America. Although he spent less than five months of 1838 in Lower Canada, only eleven days in the upper province, and no time in the Maritimes, his report on colonial affairs is the most important document in the history of the British Commonwealth. Aided by a corps of brilliant minds, Durham sounded public opinion of every hue in the two provinces, and received factual reports on the Atlantic provinces, which had been spared the horrors of rebellion. At first Durham contemplated recommending a federation of all British North America, but he soon realized that inadequate communications would make the plan impossible for many years. Instead, he recommended a legislative union of the two Canadas, relying on the combined English-speaking majority in the two provinces to ensure English domination of the union. Since there would be a few English-speaking representatives from the lower province in the new assembly, this plan would have given political control to the English. Next he suggested the importance of a system of local government to avoid clogging the provincial parliament with heavy administrative problems. He also recommended judicial reforms and a new land holding system for Prince Edward Island. But most important he recommended a new relationship between colony and mother country by which the colonies would be entrusted with the management of internal colonial affairs. His only reservations were that the imperial government must continue to control the colonial constitution, trade and diplomatic relations, the latter two being of concern to the Empire as a whole. He also recommended the plan of Gibbon Wakefield, one of his secretaries, to keep all public lands

John George Lambton, first Earl of Durham. By forecasting the complete assimilation of French Canadians within a united province of Canada, Durham's Report *had the unforeseen effect of creating such a vehement reaction among French Canadians that, if anything, they redoubled their efforts to preserve their racial and cultural identity.*

under imperial control so that a system of self-supporting colonization could be introduced.

Durham's recommendations were both sweeping and imaginative, but some were not practical. His proposed division of powers between mother country and colonies was ultimately unworkable because colonial interest in the reserved jurisdiction of constitution, trade, and diplomacy was bound to grow with the colonies. His imperial lands scheme could not be implemented because virtually all good land in the colonies had already been granted away. His most serious miscalculation, however, was his assumption that the French could be anglicized, that eighty years of British encouragement to French-Canadian nationalism could be reversed by a mere political decision.

Lord Durham's most lasting achievement was his new concept of empire—of colonies allied to, rather than subject to, the mother country. While historical evidence indicates that Durham did not accept the interpretation of responsible government

Baldwin submitted, nevertheless, his Report and his recommendation that colonists be trusted to govern themselves became a bible for colonial reformers. In a few years this group managed to implement that broader concept of responsible government in the colonies which made possible the evolution of the British Commonwealth of Nations.

In Britain during 1839 the fate of Durham's recommendations hung in the balance because of the circumstances surrounding his return home. Armed though he was with extensive power as Governor General and High Commissioner, Durham had exceeded the limits of his authority in one detail during the summer of 1838 when he banished a number of convicted rebels to Bermuda. He had no jurisdiction in that colony and his personal enemies and enemies of Melbourne's government were quick to attack Durham's action in the imperial parliament. Lord Melbourne had always distrusted the quixotic Durham, and his defense of Durham's action in the face of this criticism was so weak as to constitute a virtual condemnation of the Governor General. Stung by this lack of loyalty from his chief, Lord Durham petulantly announced that he would leave Canada, and he sailed for home on 1 November. Barely had he left the shores of Canada when a second brief, but equally futile, revolt broke out in a few counties of Lower Canada.

The return of Durham to Britain posed a serious threat to Melbourne's government. If Lord Durham wanted revenge for his betrayal over the Bermuda affair, he had only to side with the opposition and Melbourne's tottery government would be defeated. But being a man of nobler principles, the High Commissioner to the Canadas kept silent and plunged into the work of preparing his monumental Report. By February, 1839, the task was complete. Colonial newspapers avidly serialized the document in their columns and Lord Durham's findings electrified the colonial political atmosphere. But the final decision on what action, if any would be taken on his recommendations still rested with "Lord M." and his government. Would they have the necessary political fortitude to endorse policies that seemed positively revolutionary to conservatives at home and in the colonies?

MODERATION AND HARMONY IN THE MARITIMES

The Maritime colonies of British North America were fortunately spared from rebellion. This fact stemmed more from their closer traditional ties to Britain and from the spirit of moderation that marked their local politics, than from any lack of complaints against the workings of the colonial system. New Brunswick, Prince Edward Island and also Newfoundland had not experienced the development of a reforming government; their political condition was closer to that of the "upper colonies" around 1820, when reform sentiment was still unorganized. The situation in Nova Scotia, however, was somewhat different. There, reform found a spokesman in the person of Joseph Howe, son of a Loyalist who was Nova Scotia's King's Printer. In 1828 the twenty-three year old Howe began his own newspaper and printing business when he purchased the *Novascotian.* Howe was basically a conservative—his principle was "the Constitution, the *whole* Constitution, and *nothing but* the Constitution," which he would defend against "the misguided zeal of the People, and the dangerous encroachment of Rulers." Soon, however, he became convinced that "the People" were more to be trusted than the Halifax clique that ruled Nova Scotia.

After 1830 the provincial councils (which were identical in membership) and the assembly engaged in a series of petty quarrels that impeded provincial development. Howe, critical of councils and assembly, concluded that electoral reforms were needed, particularly the secret ballot. But fame came to Joseph Howe more by accident than as a result of his writings. In the issue of 1 January, 1835, his *Novascotian* carried an anonymous letter accusing the Halifax magistrates of dishonesty. For printing this Howe was tried for libel. He argued his own case and won an acquittal, even though the letter had undoubtedly been libellous. The day after this famous trial the Halifax magistrates resigned *en masse*—and Howe became a popular hero. He could not, however, be considered a party leader, for political parties had not really appeared in the province, and Howe himself, like many Nova Scotians, looked upon organized parties as disloyalty

During his early career Joseph Howe gained a remarkable popularity in his province. Popularly known as "The Tribune of Nova Scotia," he was an indefatigable worker in the interests of his fellow Nova Scotians. Government, education, agriculture, railways, mail service, fisheries—all these and many other matters came under his penetrating scrutiny and were influenced by his forceful opinions and activity.

to the constitution. When the next elections were held in December, 1836, Howe won a seat in the assembly and launched into his campaign for reform:

All we ask is for what exists at home—a system of responsibility to the people, extending through all the Departments supported

Early in the session of 1837, Howe and other reformers drew up Twelve Resolutions outlining the ills of Nova Scotia and requesting the Crown to grant an elective legislative council, or "such other re-construction of the local Government as will ensure responsibility to the Commons, and confer upon the People of this Province, what they value above all other possessions, the blessings of the British Constitution." The ills of Nova Scotia were basically the same as those in the other British North American provinces, and the blessing of the British constitution was the very promise to Upper Canada made by its founding governor, John Graves Simcoe. Howe had grasped the essential colonial problem—the lack of governmental responsibility to the elected representatives—but as yet he had not seen the solution so obvious to Baldwin, namely cabinet government.

Although Howe withdrew the Resolutions (because he knew they would not pass), they were answered by Lord Glenelg, the liberal-minded Colonial Secretary. He agreed that the assembly should control all revenues and that the executive and legislative councils should be separated. But Howe now realized that such reforms fell short of curing the basic maladies. By April, 1839, his reading of Durham's Report provided an answer that did not conflct with, but actually reinforced, his loyalty to Britain:

> Let the *majority* and not the *minority* govern, and compell every Governor to select his advisors from those who *enjoy the confidence of the people* and *command a majority in the popular Branch*.

The principle of responsible government for the colonies had now found its most able advocate in Joseph Howe.

* * *

The quarter century that followed the decisive War of 1812 proved to be years of unprecendented development in the Canadian experience. Thanks to the large immigration to British North America and to the demand of industrialized Britain for foodstuffs and lumber, the two Canadas had built a firm foundation for the grain trade and for timber; New Brunswick's forest industries had boomed; and Nova Scotia and Prince Edward Island had prospered on the sale of fish and agricultural products. But paradoxically, those same years of solid economic development had witnessed growing political unrest, an unrest compounded in Upper Canada by religious strife and in Lower Canada by "racial" tensions. In the two Canadas unrest had culminated in the outbreak of armed rebellions in 1837. What had caused this appeal to violence? Did the colonies have legitimate grievances against the political system? What policies could be found that would prevent a repetition of the imperial disaster of 1776, would satisfy the desire for greater colonial self-government, and would promote the peaceful development of the British North American colonies within the structure of the Empire? Were Lord Durham's recommendations (for reunion of the Canadas and application of "the principles of the British Constitution" in all the colonies) the solution to the "colonial question"? Would they work, not only in the troubled Canadas, but also in the more moderate political climate of the Maritime provinces?

CHAPTER 6

THE DECLINE OF THE OLD COLONIAL SYSTEM

The American Revolution had destroyed the great promise of a British continental empire in North America, but the remnant of empire lived on for over half a century in the old political and economic colonial system. The rebellions of 1837 had challenged this imperial unity once more. In the 1840's the old colonial, political and economic systems finally dissolved. As a result, by the late 1840's the colonies were faced with a question—did the "imperial connexion" still have any value, or would the colonies be better off asserting their complete independence?

LORD SYDENHAM—PRO-CONSUL

What action, if any, would Lord Melbourne's Whig government take on Lord Durham's recommendations for reforms? In June, 1839, Colonial Secretary Lord John Russell clarified the British government's intentions by introducing a bill to reunite the two Canadas, strengthening Durham's anglicization aims by giving each of the old provinces equal representation in the new legislature despite the larger population of Lower Canada. At the same time Russell declared that responsible government as advocated in the colonies was inadmissible. Since every colonial governor, he said, was responsible to the Crown through the Colonial

Secretary he could not be answerable to a colonial cabinet too. Sovereignty could not be divided—a colony could not be both a colony and a sovereign state at the same time. The Crown could not have two sets of advisors in the form of two cabinets and still maintain the unity of empire. No British statesman, excepting perhaps Lord Durham, could see any practical alternative to dependence or independence for the colonies. The British government still faced the problem of pacifying colonial complaints while maintaining imperial principles. Who would finally "bell the cat" of colonial politics?

Despite various proposals to leading statesmen, the British government found no one willing to undertake the task of governing British North America until late in the summer of 1839, when Charles Poulett Thomson, protégé of Jeremy Bentham and the first member for the new industrial seat of Manchester, volunteered his services. Just thirty-nine years of age, Thomson was the third son of a rising mercantile family active in trade with Russia and allied to London banking interests. Well-schooled by an apprenticeship in the family business at St. Petersburg, Russia, Thomson was an undisputed master of the House of Commons in commercial matters, making up for lack of debating ability by his unrivaled knowledge of business methods. Typical of the new nineteenth-century class whose bible was the company ledger, Thomson was also ambitious, conceited and capable—a combination that made him respected but not loved by his more aristocratic colleagues. As a strong contender for the post of Chancellor of the Exchequer, Thomson confidently agreed to settle the "Canadian question" in return for a peerage.

Before leaving for Canada Thomson had several conversations with Lord Durham and presumably understood the problems and Lord Durham's proposed solutions. He arrived at Quebec in October armed with a secret promise of a £1,500,000 imperial loan to prime the colonial economic pump, and with a despatch authorizing him to replace colonial executive councillors whenever "the interests of the public service . . . require such a change." This despatch of 16 October, 1839, was originally written to the Governor of South Australia, but Thomson had asked for an identical one to give him more control over the councils in the

Charles Poulett Thomson, Lord Sydenham. "I have told the people plainly that, as I cannot get rid of my responsibility to the home government, I will place no responsibility on the council; that they are a council *for the governor to consult, but no more." Thomson to a friend, 12 December, 1839.*

Canadas. Ironically, it proved to be the sword that slashed the Gordian knot of irresponsible colonial government by permitting the creation of party government. For the moment, however, Thomson was ordered by Russell to "consider yourself precluded from entertaining any proposition" or even offering "any explanation" regarding responsible government. As Governor General, Thomson was directed to defend "the honour of the Crown" by "maintaining the harmony" between appointed executives and elected representatives. Since Russell had no positive suggestions as to how this miracle could be accomplished, he told Thomson to implement "the practical views of colonial government recommended by Lord Durham, as I understand them"!

Governing Lower Canada presented no problem for Thomson: the constitution had been suspended following the rebellion and the colony was still ruled without hindrance by the special council established by Lord Durham. Upper Canada, however, posed a more difficult situation: the assembly was acting in a very independent manner. Union could be imposed on Lower Canada, but Upper Canada must be won over by political means. After arranging Lower Canadian matters to his satisfaction, Thomson hastened to Toronto in December to meet the Upper Canadian parliament in person. By personal flattery, by appeals to loyalty, by private banquets with much wine, by vague references to responsible government, by veiled hints about the £1,500,000 loan, by backroom politicking in the best (or worst) North American tradition, Thomson got his resolution in favour of reunion of the Canadas (with equal representation for the smaller population of Upper Canada and the transfer of Upper Canada's crushing public debt to the new province of Canada). He also obtained an Upper Canada statute creating district councils for local government and another to settle the vexed clergy reserves question by dividing the income among all denominations. The small and futile opposition to both measures had been led by "your confounded Bishop," Strachan, who had just been elevated to the new diocese of Toronto. Pleased with these successes, Thomson asked for his peerage and in the summer of 1840 received word that he had been made Baron, Lord Sydenham.

The union naturally aroused hostility amongst most Lower Canadians. Its anglicizing purposes were clear and, in addition, the larger province would be saddled with reduced representation and Upper Canada's debts. But the two unsuccessful rebellions in Lower Canada, her suspended constitution and the crushing of radical opinion meant that the most influential voice in the province was that of the Montreal merchant group who had tried to promote a union in the early 1820's.

Before the union was proclaimed in February, 1841, however, new difficulties arose for Lord Sydenham. His Upper Canadian Clergy Reserves Act was disallowed on legal grounds and its imperial replacement left all religious groups dissatisfied—the Anglicans because they had to share the reserves, the Presbyterians because their share was so small, and voluntarists (proponents of the separation of church and state) because the settlement multiplied rather than abolished the number of state-supported churches. Conflict between the Lieutenant-Governor and the assembly in Nova Scotia forced the Governor General to travel to the Maritimes to seek a compromise solution. In 1841, on the eve of the meeting of the First Parliament for the united Province of Canada, Robert Baldwin, who had earlier been appointed to Sydenham's executive council, resigned in an unsuccessful effort to force the conservatives out of the administration. Baldwin's ill-timed demand for responsible government made him seem merely stubborn and unco-operative, and this played into the hands of Lord Sydenham.

Sydenham, like Head before him, had acted as his own prime minister and party chief during the recent election in order to win the support of a solid bloc of moderates in the assembly. Against this "Governor's party" stood a disunited opposition, comprising unconnected factions of Family Compact men from Upper Canada, Tories from Lower Canada, French-Canadian reformers and a handful of Baldwinites. Lord Sydenham had little difficulty during the summer of 1841 in getting his own measures for local government, public works and elementary education passed into law. He was convinced that Canadians needed such practical projects to divert them from their theorizing, and he was equally convinced that once his personal influence had rallied all reasonable men to the cause of union and progress, the new constitution would "run in grooves." He was already planning his triumphal return to Britain when a fall from his horse led to medical complications and his tragic death in September, 1841.

Most Canadians mourned Sydenham's passing. In less than two years he had brought about significant changes in the political life of British North America. After years of bickering and frustration the colonists now seemed to have grasped a vision of a brighter future. Now they spoke proudly of the prosperity that would soon be theirs. Good laws, sound institutions and enlightened leadership had silenced their speculations about responsible government. Such, at least, was Lord Sydenham's deathbed appraisal of his own achievements, but events soon proved he had overestimated his own influence and underestimated the political aspirations of British North Americans.

FORCES IN BALANCE

Short weeks before Lord Sydenham's death the shaky Melbourne government in Britain was defeated at a general election. The new Conservative ministry of Sir Robert Peel, with Lord Stanley as Colonial Secretary, sent to Canada Sir Charles Bagot, career diplomat and negotiator of the Rush-Bagot Treaty of 1817. Sir Charles soon realized that Sydenham's successes had been largely due to the late Governor General's personal interference in politics and to the temporary confusion of opposition groups in the Canadian assembly. He believed that the Sydenham system of managing men through patronage was self-defeating, and that the union of the Canadas had merely papered over the deep fissures while leaving the Lower Canadians "powerless" but "sulky." The "deformity" that he saw in Sydenham's regime was already being challenged by a new political force.

Unlike Baldwin, who had vainly tried to promote a resolution on responsible government in the last days of the 1841 parliamentary session, Irish-born Francis Hincks, reform journalist and financier, had joined Sydenham's government in the belief that by working from inside, reformers could use the union to gain responsible government. During 1839 and 1840 Hincks had laid the foundations for a genuine Reform party and its future success by bringing Baldwin and Louis Hippolyte Lafontaine, Baldwin's opposite number among Lower Canadian reformers, into alliance. Hincks had convinced Lafontaine that responsible government could ensure the French-Canadian way of life; he had convinced Baldwin that Lower Canadian reformers shared Baldwin's faith in responsible government. When Lafontaine was defeated in the election of 1841, Baldwin found him a seat as a member for York County, Upper Canada (popularly called Canada West after 1841). The basis of future co-operation between French-speaking and English-speaking Reformers had thus been laid and Bagot faced a united party such as Sydenham had not seen or foreseen.

As Bagot surveyed the Canadian political scene in 1842, he became acutely aware of the fact that Sydenham's coalition government, led by William Henry Draper, had no support

Louis Hippolyte Lafontaine (left) and Robert Baldwin. In his youth Lafontaine was an ardent supporter of Papineau; however, he stubbornly opposed the call to arms by the Patriotes *in 1837. One Canadian historian has remarked that Lafontaine and Baldwin "buried the biggest hatchet in Canadian history." Their alliance was sealed in the elections of 1841, when Baldwin suggested Lafontaine's candidature in Protestant, Anglo-Saxon York.*

among French Canadians and could not withstand the combined forces of Baldwin and Lafontaine. There seemed no alternative but to broaden the coalition to include the French Canadians, whom Sydenham had deliberately ignored because he shared Durham's reservations on them. In reply, Lord Stanley, the Colonial Secretary, urged Bagot to try "all other means" before admitting the French party and its suspected rebel leaders into office. This advice came too late, for Bagot, unable to continue the government without French-Canadian support, had been forced to accept Lafontaine's terms for entering the ministry, namely, the inclusion of Baldwin as well. Bagot's "Great

Measure" (as he called it)—the conciliation of the French Canadians "as a Race"—was received with regret by Peel's government, although Stanley privately admitted that the measure was probably inevitable. The regret concerned Lafontaine who, less than five years earlier, had been accused of treason for his part in the rebellion. Bagot insisted that the issue at stake was not responsible government, since he had frequently stated that his changes meant only a broadening of Sydenham's coalition. This was not a recognition of any political party, let alone the practice of government by party. Sir Charles Bagot did not live to see the next phase of his "great experiment." Worn out by the heavy duties of office, just as Sydenham had been, Bagot died in the spring of 1843.

Sir Charles Metcalfe arrived in March when it was evident that Bagot could not continue his work. The new Governor had already won a reputation as a civilian administrator in India and Jamaica, but he had never dealt with the likes of Canada's House of Assembly. Like Bagot, Metcalfe was genuinely concerned to see justice done to French Canadians within the framework of union. He declared that Bagot's Great Measure had produced "many beneficial effects," and he condemned Durham's policy of enforced anglicization. As part of Durham's policy, Kingston in Upper Canada had been chosen for the seat of government, but in line with his sympathy for the French Canadians Metcalfe now welcomed the executive council's plan to move the capital to Montreal. For the same reason he adopted and brought to completion Bagot's proposed amnesty for all rebels of '37. He also successfully urged the repeal of that clause in the Union Act which made English the only official language for what was in actual fact a bilingual province.

On the question of responsible government Sir Charles Metcalfe agreed with Lord Stanley that no further advances should be made beyond Bagot's concessions. He was convinced that the Baldwin-Lafontaine alliance was based on the friendship of the two leaders, rather than on acceptance of the principles of responsible government, and he believed that if French aspirations were satisfied the alliance would dissolve. Therefore, his support for the use of the French language and for Montreal

Sir Charles Bagot (left) and Sir Charles T. Metcalfe.
"... the keystone of my policy ... was to admit the French as a part of, or an addition to my old Council, and not to reconstruct my Council with Mr. Baldwin and the French as the steeple of it."
Bagot to Lord Stanley, 26 September, 1842.

as the seat of government was really intended to split the Reform alliance along linguistic lines.

Between Metcalfe and the Reformers in his executive council there remained two possible areas of conflict over the implications of responsible government. The first area was the permanent civil list established by the Union Act, reminiscent to Reformers of the "everlasting salary" bills that had put control over the executive and civil service beyond their grasp in pre-rebellion days. To avoid trouble Metcalfe intended to have this clause repealed as soon as the assembly settled on a new salary schedule, but the change was not completed until 1847.

Metcalfe's second possible area of conflict with the Reformers was the question of political patronage. It was on this issue that he chose to fight what he called the "responsible government cry." Were the "spoils of office" to be used by party leaders as rewards for their followers, or should the governor dispose of public jobs in the interests of the whole country? In brief, must the governor accept the advice of his advisors, as Baldwin had demanded unsuccessfully of Sir Francis Bond Head in 1836? Soon after his arrival in Kingston, Metcalfe decided that Baldwin was uncompromising, intolerant, arrogant, and fanatical on the subject of responsible government, and that he had usurped power in the government during Bagot's illness. Metcalfe, to Baldwin's dismay, proceeded to conduct the business of government himself. The stage was set for a confrontation between a Governor who believed in the responsibility of his position and in the moderate policies of his superiors in London, and a colonial politician of great ability and influence who believed himself to be the only pure patriot in the country.

The clash was months in the making. Metcalfe strongly opposed what he considered to be Baldwin's encroachments on the governor's authority and his partisan discrimination against loyal subjects. Late in November, 1843, Metcalfe rejected a demand by Baldwin and Lafontaine that he make no appointments without consulting them. All but one of the executive councillors resigned and Canada was plunged into a major political crisis over patronage, or responsible government as Baldwin described it. The issue was confused by the fact that several proposed government measures—one to outlaw the Orangemen's parades, another to exclude religious influences from the provincial university—had aroused popular opposition, giving the resignations the appearance of being an easy way for the ministers to escape their responsibilities.

Metcalfe arranged for the moderate W. H. Draper, and D. B. Viger, a popular French Canadian and rebel of '37, to join his other councillor, Dominick Daly, and managed to run the government with surprising success for several months without having to face a hostile assembly. After the initial shock, public opinion began to rally to the side of the Governor. More sympathy for Metcalfe was aroused by the cruel nickname he was given by the Reformers—"the old squaw," a reference to discoloration caused by a cancer which was eating away his face, slowly blinding his vision, and which would in time bring him a lingering, painful death. In the autumn of 1844, unable to continue the government any longer without support in the assembly, the Governor called a general election. He hoped that French-Canadian votes would be drawn away from Lafontaine. The results were disappointing: the French Canadians did not desert their leader and the Reformers continued to comprise a large minority. Metcalfe still faced the problem that had beset Bagot—how to govern without sizeable French-Canadian support. He had erred in believing that Lafontaine could be separated from Baldwin. He had not realized that French Canadians now believed responsible government was necessary for their *survivance* (cultural survival).

Metcalfe's new government, led by the moderate Draper, struggled on, beset by internal strife and external obstruction, and deserted on crucial issues by some of its own members. The only answer to the government's dwindling strength was the inclusion of some representatives from the French-Canadian bloc, but an approach to Lafontaine in 1845 failed. Lafontaine would not accept office without Baldwin, but Metcalfe, like Bagot, would not acknowledge Baldwin. A true political party had emerged from the Reform ranks of Upper and Lower Canada, although the sole cement of this alliance was the principle of responsible government, which the two wings of the party supported for quite different reasons. The political forces of Canada were still poised in uneasy balance when Metcalfe, the Governor who refused to be a "cipher," sailed late in 1845 for England and an early death. Until a successor could be appointed, Lord Cathcart, the senior military officer and interim administrator, was content to leave that balance undisturbed.

THE END OF MERCANTILISM

The Act of Union had reunited the commercial empire of the St. Lawrence, which had been politically divided since 1791. At the same time, by giving equal representation to the smaller population of Upper Canada, the Act sought to ensure the new province's economic development as a unit. No longer would Lower Canadian farmers be able to block the building of the transportation system that Upper Canada still desperately needed to reach overseas markets and to compete with American commerce and its southward pull on the St. Lawrence economy.

Canadian grain and flour (and large quantities of American grain milled in Canada) had found a market in Great Britain since 1825, when the import duty for Canadian wheat had been fixed at the low preferential rate of twenty-five shillings per quarter (a measure equalling eight bushels). In 1843 this trade received further stimulus from the imperial Canada Corn Act, which reduced the duty on Canadian-grown wheat and Canadian-milled flour to one shilling per quarter, the lowest possible rate under the British tariff. This step allowed Canadian commerce to tap the trade of the American midwest by importing American grain and exporting it as "naturalized" wheat after milling. The results were startling; Canadian exports of wheat doubled in one year to 260,000 quarters, and Canadian imports of American grain doubled to 67,000 quarters. In an attempt to counter the attraction of the St. Lawrence trade route, the American Congress passed its Drawback Act of 1845, which allowed overseas goods destined for Canada to pass through the United States duty free. This was intended to boost traffic on the Erie Canal route. Nevertheless, in anticipation of a boom in Canada's trade, some Canadian mill owners increased the capacity of their mills at considerable expense—the number of pairs of millstones in Canada increased from 584 in 1842 to 1200 in 1848.

The possible long-range effects of the advantageous Canada Corn Act can, however, never be known, for the whole British policy of colonial tariff preferences was overturned in 1846 with disastrous consequences for Canada. The cause of this change lay far beyond the confines of the St. Lawrence basin. Since the Napoleonic wars a growing body of opinion in Britain had been voicing its belief that mercantilism was more profitable to the colonies than to the mother country. Colonies were an economic burden on the British taxpayer, and a potential cause of war between Britain and other nations. The £800,000 imperial debt for building the Rideau Canal was proof of the former, and the

Canadian rebellions of 1837 and the subsequent Patriots' War certainly supported the latter point. To the anti-colonial sentiment was added in 1839 the influence of the Anti-Corn Law League formed by Richard Cobden, a Manchester textile manufacturer. The League contended that the Corn Laws, designed to protect British farmers by restricting grain imports, actually increased the cost of British manufactures and reduced exports by raising the price of food at the expense of all consumers. Since British manufacturing succeeded by its own efficiency, not by government protection, why should not British agriculture be forced to become self-supporting? The same argument of efficiency could be, and was, used against the trade of the colonies which prospered behind the complex tariff shield of the old colonial system. To the "Manchester school" the solution was simple—apply Bentham's yardstick of "utility" to the workings of the economy by adopting unilateral free trade.

Undoubtedly the persuasive arguments of the Anti-Corn Law League won converts in the early 1840's, but in the last analysis it was potato blight, not propaganda, that ended Britain's mercantilist empire. Beginning in 1845 the potato crop, which formed the staple diet of millions of poverty-stricken Irish tenant-farmers, was ruined for three successive years by black rot. Famine and starvation stalked Ireland as an estimated 700,000 died. Sir Robert Peel met this catastrophe by abolishing the restrictive Corn Laws in 1846, so that flour could be imported as cheaply as possible. The preference on colonial grain was actually phased out over three years so that the full impact of the laws' abolition was only felt in 1848. Having begun the work of demolishing the mercantilist economic structure, Peel went on to reduce the preference on colonial timber (which had already been halved in 1841), and by successive measures the whole mercantilist system was dismantled in the space of a few short years. The repeal of the Corn Laws meant that Canadian grain and flour would have to compete on equal terms with American grain and flour, which had a much cheaper and shorter route across the Atlantic to Great Britain. Adding to these colonial difficulties, a world-wide recession began in 1847, and the Americans enacted a new Drawback Law permitting the shipment of Canadian

Emigrants on the quay at Cork, Ireland, wait to embark on ships that will take them from famine in their homeland to such places as Boston, New York and Quebec.

produce in bond for export from American harbours. The commercial empire of the St. Lawrence was reeling under the impact of these fatal blows to the old colonial system.

The Irish potato famine had more than economic effects on the British North American colonies. Irish landlords eased their consciences by shipping more than 100,000 Irish to the colonies in the empty holds of returning timber ships. The crowded, unsanitary conditions on those ships took a high toll of the wretched immigrants. Many more carried a typhus epidemic to the quarantine station below Quebec City, where more than 5,000 died; self-sacrificing persons who went to their aid also fell victims to the disease. Other immigrants, penniless but apparently in good health, proceeded to Montreal, Kingston or Toronto, only to come down in their turn with typhus, which then spread among the panic-sticken local inhabitants. Altogether some 20,000 immigrants died in Canada and another 17,000 perished during the Atlantic crossings.

Uprooted from their home soil and unable to finance a beginning in the New World, the Irish peasants flocked to the rising cities where they were forced to accept the most menial of unskilled labour and to live in the cheapest and most depressed urban areas. Destitute widows and orphans wandered the streets of Canadian cities, dependent on the charity of the inhabitants, since the Canadian government had neither the funds nor the organization to cope with the tide of misery and disease. Canadians protested loudly against the inhumanity of such immigration, in vain asking the imperial government to forbid the practice of dumping Ireland's unwanted surplus population on their soil; but these appeals were largely unheeded. Canada, on the other hand, was only a colony and as such had no power to stop the inflow of destitute immigrants.

The repeal of the Corn Laws and the Irish famine threw into bold relief the disadvantages under which the colonies laboured. Destruction of part of the old colonial system now made necessary the complete removal of all remaining political and economic restrictions on colonial development.

COLONIALISM AT THE CROSSROADS

If free trade shook the economic foundations of the British Empire, it also ended Sir Robert Peel's political career and forever damaged the Tory party that had drawn its strength from the landed gentry. In June, 1846, the protectionists revolted against Peel's leadership and defeated his government.

Almost the last achievement of Peel's regime was the signing of the Oregon Treaty with the United States. For over a year President Polk had supported the American expansionists whose rallying cry "fifty-four forty or fight," loudly proclaimed America's right to possession of the Pacific seaboard as far north as the Russian territory of Alaska. Since 1818 Britain and the United States had jointly occupied the disputed Oregon territory, but during those years American settlers had entered the area, giving their nation a strong claim to ownership. Nevertheless, Britain's proposal that the forty-ninth parallel should form the

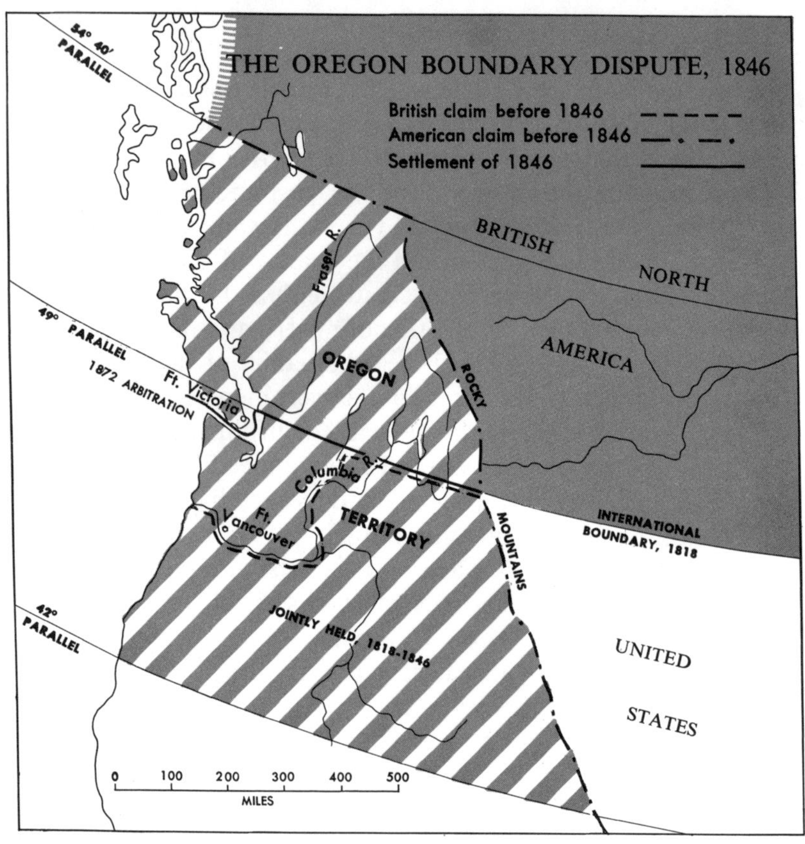

boundary from the Rockies to the Pacific was accepted by the American Congress because war with Mexico over ownership of Texas had just begun.

The settlement of the Oregon dispute removed a potential source of Anglo-American conflict and eased the task facing Canada's new Governor General, Lord Elgin. Elgin, thirty-five years old, a former Governor of Jamaica and a moderate conservative in politics, had been appointed by the Peel government and confirmed by the new Liberal ministry led by Lord John Russell. His wife was a daughter of the late Lord Durham and a niece of Earl Grey, Colonial Secretary in Russell's cabinet. Elgin reached Canada in the early days of 1847 and immediately set to work "to raise Canadian politics from the dirt." Replying to an address of welcome in Montreal, he announced that he would adopt "frankly and unequivocally Lord Durham's view of government," but he did not attempt to define his interpretation of those views. He saw clearly that no government could succeed without support from the French party.

From the outset Elgin tried to show the French Canadians that he trusted them. He intended to draw them into a coalition through the agency of A. N. Morin. The French bloc, he believed, was an unnatural formation, disguising the essential material for two political parties parallel to the "English" parties. The subsequent failure of Elgin's attempt at coalition convinced him that the French party did not understand the meaning of responsible government:

> The French seemed incapable of comprehending that the principle of constitutional government must be applied against them as well as for them. . . . Whenever there appears to be a chance of things taking this turn they revive the ancient cry of nationality and insist on their right to have a share in the administration not because the party, with which they have chosen to connect themselves, is in the ascendant, but because they represent a people of distinct origin.

In his efforts to prove that the Governor was neutral toward all Canadian parties, Elgin had Lord Grey's fullest approval. Soon after the provincial parliament met in June, however, the government was in difficulty. Draper resigned to become a judge, leaving a floundering administration under the uninspired leadership of two long-time Tories, Henry Sherwood and Dominick Daly. Exemplifying the government's confusion was the fate of a bill to divide the endowment of the provincial university among various denominations. Introduced by a young Kingston Lawyer, John Alexander Macdonald (whom Draper had chosen as Attorney General for Canada West), the bill was dropped before second reading because of lack of support within the executive and opposition both inside and outside the assembly. Public attention was distracted by the Irish potato famine refugees, whose arrival and plight were made into a political issue against the government and against colonial status. The disorganized parliamentary session ended after only eight weeks amidst rumours of an election.

Lord Elgin.
". . . you must accept such a Council as the newly elected Parl^{t} will support, & that however unwise as relates to the real interests of Canada their measures may be, they must be acquiesced in, until it shall clearly appear that public opinion will support a resistance to them. . . ."
Lord Grey to Lord Elgin, 22 February, 1848.

The election was not, in fact, held until December. The campaign of the Upper Canadian Reformers emphasized the university endowment issue more than that of responsible government. In Lower Canada the campaign was confused by a manifesto in favour of republicanism, issued by the "notorious" rebel, L. J. Papineau. When the votes were counted, however, the country had rejected both republicanism and Lord Metcalfe's English-dominated conservative government. Baldwin, Lafontaine and the Reformers had been victorious in both parts of the province, Canada East and Canada West. But was this also a victory for the ideal of responsible government?

In his assessment of the new political situation Elgin recognized the trials that lay ahead. He concluded that Papineau still had great influence among the French Canadians and that Lafontaine's constitutional understanding was suspect. Above all, Elgin feared the victors would try "to deal harshly, Yankee fashion," with political opponents. The bugbear of political patronage might yet arise, as it had in 1836 and 1843, to test Elgin's claim that he was above party considerations. The government, Elgin insisted, must either resign at once or meet the challenge in a parliamentary session immediately. The ministry chose to test its strength in parliament and was overwhelmingly defeated on the first vote. As a result, on 11 March, 1848, Lafontaine, Baldwin and their colleagues were asked to form a cabinet and were sworn in as the province's first recognizable party government.

Lord Elgin's acceptance of the new government had been made easier by the publication of a despatch from Lord Grey to Sir John Harvey, Lieutenant-Governor of Nova Scotia, in which the Colonial Secretary said:

> The direction of the internal policy of the Colony should be entrusted to those who enjoy the confidence of the Provincial Parliament.

To Lord Elgin the Colonial Secretary wrote:

> You must accept such a Council as the newly elected [Parliament] will support & that however unwise . . . their measures may be, they must be acquiesced in until it shall pretty clearly appear that public opinion will support a resistance to them.

The principle of responsible government was thus conceded—the governor must accept the advice of his ministers as long as those ministers retained the support of a parliamentary majority. How responsible government would work in practice, if such issues as political patronage or the imperial connection arose between governor and government, remained to be seen as the "Great Ministry" of L. H. Lafontaine and Robert Baldwin took office in 1848.

MODERATION AND PROGRESS IN THE ATLANTIC COLONIES

Although Joseph Howe had doubted that colonial executive councils could be converted into cabinets after the British model, the recommendations of Lord Durham's report won him completely to the cause of colonial responsible government in its fullest sense. From this position he never departed, although he did falter on the way to its achievement.

Lord John Russell's statement that a colonial governor must accept the directions of the Colonial Office over the advice of his colonial executive council brought from Howe a series of open letters addressed to Russell through the columns of the *Novascotian* in the autumn of 1839. These letters have been described as the colonial counterpart to Durham's Report. Howe argued that irresponsible government threatened imperial unity, that only the fullest granting of British institutions could retain the tie of loyalty between colony and mother country. He saw, as no one else did, that Russell's despatch to Sydenham (p. 154) on the tenure of offices was the simple instrument that made the peaceful evolution of responsible government possible. Howe and the Nova Scotia reformers took the first step along the path to responsible government by challenging Russell's interpretation of responsibility. They produced a resolution demanding the recall of Lieutenant-Governor Sir Colin Campbell (a man whom they actually held in high personal esteem) when he refused to change his advisors without Russell's approval.

Faced by this minor crisis Lord Sydenham hastened to the Maritimes in the summer of 1840. His grand tour of these colonies was a success from the moment he announced in Halifax that henceforth the colonies must be governed in accordance with the "well understood wishes of the people." Sydenham listened so attentively to Howe's personal explanation of the theory of responsible government that Howe was convinced the day was won. Accepting Sydenham's appeal to his loyalty, Howe joined a coalition government with the conservative James W. Johnston. On Sydenham's recommendation Campbell was replaced by Lord Falkland. Sydenham left Nova Scotia believing the province's government, like Canada's, would "run in grooves," provided the Lieutenant-Governor avoided dependence on a single party when forming his ministry.

In New Brunswick Sydenham faced problems unconnected with responsible government. Here political harmony reigned and parties were unknown, but in 1839 the invasion of provincial

In 1838 the first steam locomotive in Canada, the Samson *(above), went into service on the Albion Railway, a private six-mile line transporting coal to Pictou harbour in Nova Scotia. Although the line itself was only of local and temporary importance, the* Samson *is of great historical interest since it introduced the age of steam to Canada.*

timber lands by Maine lumbermen had produced the bloodless "Aroostook War." When Lieutenant-Governor Sir John Harvey, hero of the 1813 battle of Stoney Creek, failed to take a firm stand against the American intruders, Sydenham arranged his removal to Newfoundland. A settlement of the disputed Maine-New Brunswick boundary was reached in 1842 by Daniel Webster and Lord Ashburton. This Webster-Ashburton Treaty secured for New Brunswick the Acadian areas north of the St. John River and the vital Temiscouata portage route linking the province to Canada. Harvey's replacement, Sir William Colebrooke, introduced a system of municipal government and concentrated provincial financial controls in the hands of his executive. These internal reforms ensured the continuance of political harmony and the absence of party politics from the provincial scene.

Like New Brunswick, the island colonies of Prince Edward Island and Newfoundland also lacked political parties and issues sufficiently urgent to produce parties. Prince Edward Island had its own version of a Family Compact—the absentee landlords—and against this group the tenant farmers were slowly becoming more vocal in their request that the original land grants be abolished in favour of freehold tenure. Newfoundland was put under a new constitution in 1842 by an imperial statute that created a mixed legislature of elected and appointed members. Socially and politically Newfoundland was divided into two groups: the wealthy and powerful merchants of St. John's, and the more numerous but less effective small shopkeepers and fishermen. The lack of a solid middle class undoubtedly contributed to the belated development of parties based on ideologies rather than on economic class interests.

In Nova Scotia alone, among the Atlantic colonies, did responsible government become a political issue. Falkland and Johnston contrived to exclude Howe from any effective voice in the executive. Not until Johnston had won an election late in 1843, though, did Howe realize that the Sydenham-inspired coalition had prevented, not promoted, responsible government. His resignation from the executive in 1844 left him free to pursue

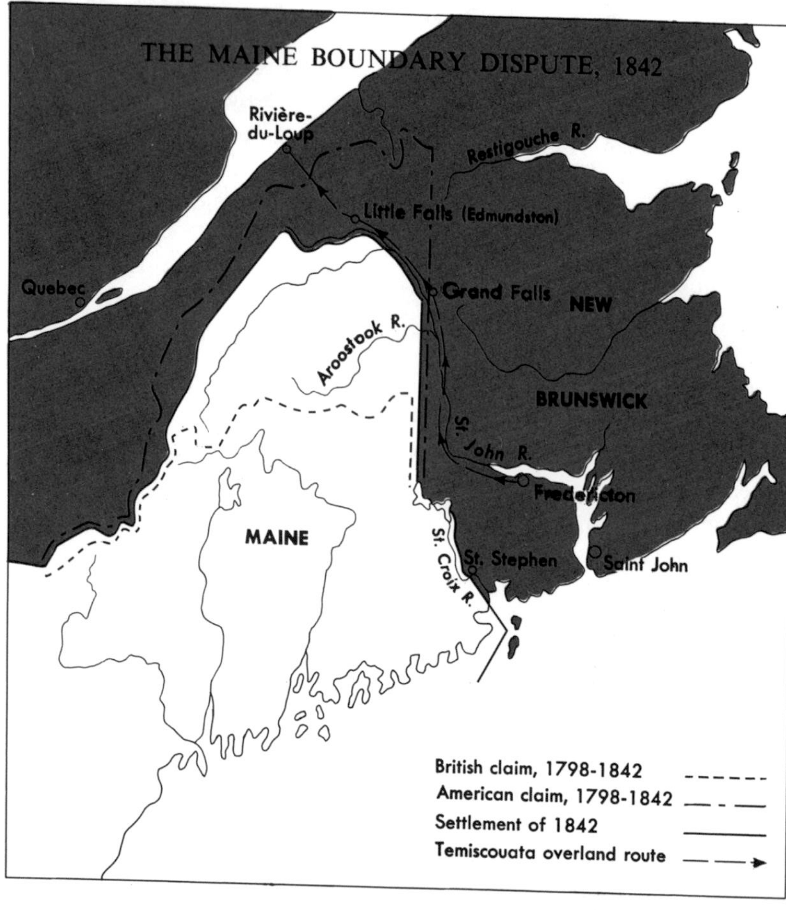

the ideal of a single-party government, although he was not acknowledged as a leader of the Nova Scotia reformers in the way that Baldwin was undisputed chief of the Canadian party. Howe had already estranged many groups, in particular the numerous Baptist communion, of which Johnston was a member, by opposing in 1843 government grants to the small denominational colleges and by his demand for a single provincial university like Baldwin's projected University of Toronto. Howe now began to rebuild his political power at the grass roots by conducting speaking tours in the farming areas.

As in Canada, the Nova Scotia struggle over responsible government was really a struggle over political patronage. In the election of 1847, as in the Canadian election of that year, the principle of responsible government was only one issue. Other more tangible questions, such as retrenchment of government spending, college endowments and religious arguments, attracted more public attention. Despite a clear Reform victory at the polls, Johnston did not resign until defeated by a vote in the assembly on 27 January, 1848. The Reform or Liberal government that now took office was the first colonial administration in the history of the British colonies to be formed on the principle of responsible government, and to be accepted as such by the British government. James Boyle Uniacke became the first Prime Minister, rather than Joseph Howe, who had been the journalistic spokesman but hardly the party chief of the Reformers.

This concession of responsible government in Nova Scotia opened the way for its concession in other colonies and for the eventual growth of autonomous dominions within the British Commonwealth. The Lafontaine-Baldwin government came to power several weeks later in Canada. In the other British North American colonies the change came without the political controversy that marked its achievement in Nova Scotia and Canada. Indeed, in New Brunswick the principle of responsible government was officially acknowledged by the new Lieutenant-Governor, Sir Edmund Head, less than two months after the change of executive in neighbouring Nova Scotia, even though political parties (in the sense of disciplinary groups) still did not exist in the province.

A room in Uniacke House, near Halifax, Nova Scotia. The house was built by R. J. Uniacke, the father of J. B. Uniacke in 1815. Now maintained in the style of the period for public viewing, it is one of the most interesting examples of colonial architecture in Canada.

The economic revolution within the empire begun by the adoption of free trade did not immediately affect the Atlantic provinces as seriously as it did Canada. Nova Scotia, Prince Edward Island and Newfoundland were largely unaffected. New Brunswick's experience, however, was less happy. That province's dependence on timber exports had already been affected by earlier reductions in its preferred position in the British market, and the double blows of free trade and the end of the Navigation Acts fell on the colony when it was unprepared for American competition. Total exports began to fall sharply in 1847 and did not recover until 1853. In 1847 New Brunswick imports were almost twice the value of exports, but this apparently serious imbalance in trade was not new and in the past had been offset by the sale of wooden ships and the earnings of New Brunswick's shipping industry.

By the end of the 1840's the Maritimes found themselves increasingly excluded from their former markets by a combination of high tariffs in the United States and American initiative in the trade with Britain. Small in size, heavily dependent on exports, but separated from each other by strong provincial loyalties, the Maritimes were awakening to their need for a newer or stronger economic foundation, perhaps through reciprocity of trade with the United States, perhaps through a regional union, or even (a more remote possibility) in union with the large and inviting market of Canada.

* * *

The introduction of the full practice of responsible government in Nova Scotia and Canada, in the face of the coldly logical constitutionalism of Lord John Russell and Lord Stanley, preserved the political unity of the British Empire and made possible the evolution of the modern Commonwealth as an association of autonomous states sharing common ideals and a common heritage. At the end of the 1840's, however, autonomy was still far removed from either the experience of the desires of the colonies. Lord Durham's reservations of ultimate political and economic controls in the hands of the imperial authorities were as yet unchallenged by provincial politicians.

The problem of the immediate future was to find a new imperial relationship for the mother country and her colonies after British adoption of free trade had destroyed the old economic basis of their unity. How would the separate British North American colonies survive the strong competition, especially from the United States, in British markets? One answer to this question might be a shift in economic emphasis to draw the colonies closer to the United States in a continental economy. Whatever the long-range destiny of British North America—as part of a North American trading bloc or within a North Atlantic economic community—the beginning of the second half of the nineteenth century marked a significant turning point in the experience of the colonies. In less than a generation the Industrial Revolution and all its technological ramifications would reach British North America and transform every aspect of life—economic, social and political. In varying degrees, but with irresistible force, the colonial components of the future Dominion of Canada were about to pass from an age of agriculture to an age of industry.

CHAPTER 7

THE WATERSHED

The decade of the 1850's witnessed a many-sided revolution in the development of British North America. The last vestiges of the old colonial system (or mercantilism) disappeared and the colonies entered the new economic world of free trade, a world in which the colonies' trade pattern began to shift away from Britain and towards the United States. Politically, these years witnessed the full acceptance of responsible government and the emergence in Canada of new alignments in the form of modern political parties. At the same time, the appearance of strong sectional rivalries so threatened the union of the Canadas that its dissolution seemed a desirable inevitability. But the most striking aspect of the revolution was symbolized by the technological and social changes produced by the steam engine. Industrialism, admittedly still in its infancy, came to British North America and particularly to Canada. The factory system and the growth of cities clearly marked the watershed which the older agricultural society had passed. Railways, telegraphs, manufactured goods—all were symbols of revolutionary change and of a new and more affluent standard of living. In the span of a handful of years British North America was transformed, both physically and psychologically, from a community of farmers, fishermen and lumbermen into the embryo of modern Canada.

THE GREAT MINISTRY

In its first parliamentary session (1848) the Lafontaine-Baldwin government was so busy laying plans for a sweeping program of reforms that only eighteen statutes were enacted. The year passed peacefully with no forewarnings of the storm to come. As parliament reconvened in January, 1849, hopes for a revolution by legislation ran high among Reformers, and they were not disappointed.

Among the 200 acts introduced by the government were several items of Reform policy that had been pending when Lafontaine and Baldwin resigned in 1843. A Municipal Corporations Act for Canada West established the system of local government that functioned, without any basic changes, for the next century. Complementing this legislation, a new Assessment Act, passed in 1850, modernized the system of local taxation. Baldwin's ideal of a nondenominational provincial university was put into effect by a controversial statute of 1849 that secularized King's College and left its Presbyterian and Methodist rivals, Queen's and Victoria, without government aid. This university act failed, however, to end denominational colleges, for Queen's and Victoria managed to survive, and the aging but energetic Bishop Strachan promptly began to organize a new Anglican institution, which the government reluctantly incorporated in 1852 as Trinity College.

The most controversial legislation, however, was an act to recompense Lower Canadians for losses suffered in the rebellion of 1837. Compensation for losses in Upper Canada had already been paid by 1845. The act of 1849 was more controversial because it was so worded that even convicted rebels could claim compensation from the government. Lord Elgin was concerned by the proposed increase in the provincial debt, but he could see no other political way for his ministers to redress "the alleged injustice to Lower Canada." He was more concerned that the leaders of the Tory opposition were using the issue "to work on the feelings of old Loyalists as opposed to rebels, of British as opposed to French, and of Upper Canadians as opposed to Lower. . . ." The Governor General had the constitutional power to disallow this "payment of rebels." When it became clear that Lord Elgin would conform to the principle of responsible government by accepting the advice of his ministers, the violence of the opposition was turned against him personally. In the assembly the small but vocal Tory minority began a bitter and prolonged debate that reopened old political and racial wounds dating from the rebellion. Outside the assembly the "loyalist" press and "loyalist" protest meetings stirred English-speaking Montrealers to action. On 9 March the Rebellion Losses Bill was passed by 47 votes to 18; all Canada now waited to see if Lord Elgin would give royal assent to the law. Elgin knew he faced a difficult decision. Disallowance of the bill would negate the principle of responsible government; approval of this "payment of rebels" was certain to antagonize the large body of "loyal" opinion. Confident of Lord Grey's full support, he refused to shirk the unpleasant responsibility. On 25 April he drove to parliament and gave assent to this and several other bills. His words of assent were greeted by shouts of outrage from the gallery and his carriage was stoned as he left for Monklands, his official residence. The same evening a mob attacked the legislative building, drove out the members and caused a fire which destroyed the building, its libraries and its archives.

For the next few days Montreal was at the mercy of a mob, which roamed the streets threatening life and property, and which actually sacked Lafontaine's house. Elgin and his ministers refused to use troops to stop the rioting for fear of causing bloodshed. Slowly the violence subsided, but when Lord Elgin returned to the temporary parliament buildings on 29 April to receive an address of loyalty, a mob pursued his carriage through the streets and smashed every panel of it with rocks. Throughout the whole episode of the Rebellion Losses Bill riots, Elgin never once lost his composure or self-control.

Approval of the law by the imperial parliament sobered its opponents in Canada. "The Canadian Tory Rebellion of 1849" was punished by the removal of the capital from Montreal to Toronto; it alternated between Toronto and Quebec every two years thereafter until Confederation. The Tories' thirst for revenge on Lord Elgin had been expressed by personal insults

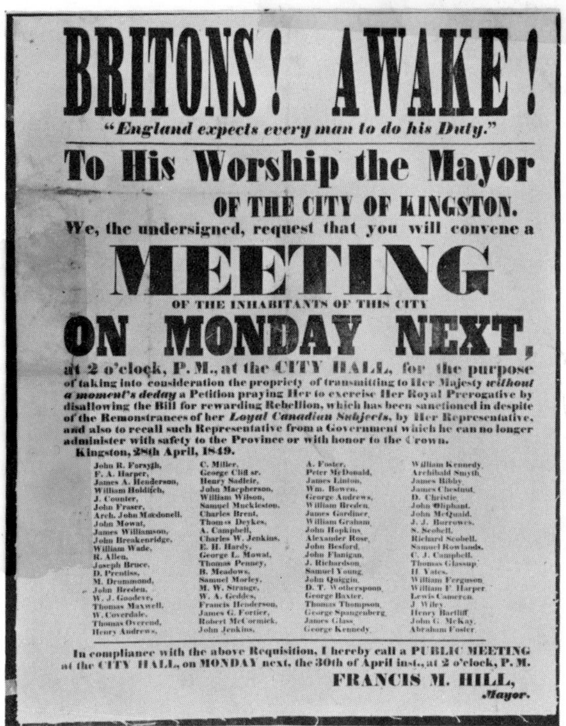

BRITONS! AWAKE!

"England expects every man to do his Duty."

To His Worship the Mayor

OF THE CITY OF KINGSTON.

We, the undersigned, request that you will convene a

MEETING

OF THE INHABITANTS OF THIS CITY

ON MONDAY NEXT,

at 2 o'clock, P. M., at the CITY HALL, for the purpose of taking into consideration the propriety of transmitting to Her Majesty *without a moment's delay* a Petition praying Her to exercise Her Royal Prerogative by disallowing the Bill for rewarding Rebellion, which has been sanctioned in despite of the Remonstrances of her *Loyal Canadian Subjects*, by Her Representative, and also to recall such Representative from a Government which he can no longer administer with safety to the Province or with honor to the Crown.

Kingston, 28th April, 1849.

John R. Forsyth,
F. A. Harper,
James A. Henderson,
William Holditch,
J. Counter,
John Fraser,
Arch. John Macdonell,
John Mowat,
James Williamson,
John Breakenridge,
William Wade,
R. Allen,
Joseph Bruce,
D. Prentiss,
M. Drummond,
John Breden,
W. J. Goodeve,
Thomas Maxwell,
W. Coverdale,
Thomas Overend,
Henry Andrews,
C. Miller,
George Cliff sr.
Henry Sadleir,
John Macpherson,
William Wilson,
Samuel Muckleston,
Charles Brent,
Thomas Deykes,
A. Campbell,
Charles W. Jenkins,
E. H. Hardy,
George L. Mowat,
Thomas Penney,
B. Meadows,
Samuel Morley,
M. W. Strange,
W. A. Geddes,
Francis Henderson,
James G. Fortier,
Robert McCormick,
John Jenkins,
A. Foster,
Peter McDonald,
James Linton,
Wm. Bowen,
George Andrews,
William Breden,
James Gardiner,
William Graham,
John Hopkins,
Alexander Rose,
John Besford,
John Flanigan,
J. Richardson,
Samuel Young,
John Quiggin,
D. T. Wotherspoon,
George Baxter,
Thomas Thompson,
George Spangenberg,
James Glass,
George Kennedy,
William Kennedy,
Archibald Smyth,
James Bibby,
James Chestnut,
D. Christie,
John Oliphant,
John McQuaid,
J. J. Burrowes,
S. Scobell,
Richard Scobell,
Samuel Rowlands,
C. J. Campbell,
Thomas Glassup,
H. Yates,
William Ferguson,
William F. Harper,
Lewis Cameron,
J. Wiley,
Henry Bartliff,
John G. McKay,
Abraham Foster.

In compliance with the above Requisition, I hereby call a PUBLIC MEETING at the CITY HALL, on MONDAY next, the 30th of April inst., at 2 o'clock, P. M.

FRANCIS M. HILL,
Mayor.

but his was the victory. Reason, not bayonets, had won the day. "And what is the result?" Elgin asked rhetorically. "Seven hundred thousand French reconciled to England . . . because they believe the British government is just."

The Tory rebellion had, however, deeper causes than the Rebellion Losses Bill, and potentially more serious consequences than rioting. Britain's restrictive Navigation Laws, repeal of the Corn Laws, and reduction of the colonial timber preference hurt the provincial economy and particularly the Montreal merchants. Elgin warned his superiors in London that British North Americans, feeling there was no longer any advantage in the imperial connection, might seek annexation to the United States as a solution for their economic problems. In the autumn of 1849 annexation associations did begin to appear in Montreal and Toronto. A manifesto in favour of "a friendly and peaceful separation from British connection and a union upon equitable terms" with the United States was issued over the signatures of more than 300 leading businessmen. Elgin promptly dismissed any public servants who had signed this treasonable document. The return of prosperity in 1850 virtually ended all support for annexation.

Lord Elgin was well aware that the annexation movement, like the recent riots, was primarily an expression of frustration and bewilderment at the rapid political and economic changes taking place, but he was also aware of the need for a more permanent solution to British North America's trade problems. As early as 1847 he had become convinced that reciprocity in trade with the United States would be the antidote rather than the antecedent to annexation, and in 1849 he was instrumental in reopening trade negotiations with Washington. After prolonged delays in the early 1850's Elgin went to Washington in person in 1854, and taking advantage of America's deep sectional cleavage over the slavery issue, convinced the southerners that reciprocity could prevent the annexation of Canada and the consequent strengthening of the North. Generous hospitality aided the negotiation of an advantageous treaty for free trade in natural products; Elgin's secretary reported that the treaty had been "floated through on champagne."

The government of Lafontaine and Baldwin survived the outbursts of hostility against its reform program only to fall victim to the "extravagant expectations" of its own radical wing. Old reformers of '37, such as Peter Perry and John Rolph, joined young liberal idealists in 1849 to form the Clear Grit group, which advocated retrenchment, judicial reform, complete separation of church and state, and application of the republican elective principle to all public offices.

At first George Brown, owner of the influential ministerial newspaper, The Toronto *Globe*, defended the conservatism of the government. But Brown's support became a doubtful asset when he unwittingly became embroiled in a religious controversy that pitted Protestants against Roman Catholics and embittered Canadian life for a decade. Commenting in 1850 on the so-called "papal aggression"—the recreation of a Roman Catholic

THE GOVERNMENT THIMBLERIG.
Here I am, Sporting Bob from York!—Rowl in here, gentlemen, and stake your money. Now, Mr. Sherwood! I see you looking at one of the thimbles;—walk up, sir, like a man, and go your length upon it in goold or silver,—Debentures taken at a small discount. Here you are, Mr. What-d'ye-call him, the coroner from Kingston! Sport your jinglers here upon the lucky thimble; —a quick eye and a ready observation takes the tin. O, there's the French gentlemen from Montreal feeling for their purses!—step this way, gentlemen, and the day's your own. Rowl in.— (Here Punch clandestinely tilts ub a thimble, and discovers the pea.)
Punch in Canada, September, 1849.

A cartoon by J. W. Bengough on the movement of the seat of government in the Province of Canada between Toronto, Montreal and Kingston. In a period of twenty-five years the provincial legislature changed its location six times.

hierarchy in Britain—Brown extolled separation of church and state and criticized the interference of the Roman Catholic Church in Upper Canadian political life. The following year when he was defeated in a by-election by the returned rebel, William Lyon Mackenzie, Brown blamed both the Roman Catholic Church and the government, which had failed to support him.

Disgusted at the pettiness of provincial politics, Baldwin resigned later in 1851; Lafontaine followed him into retirement soon after. Their Great Ministry was at an end. It had achieved responsible government and many other reforms; but the scene was now set for a period of political flux and cultural unrest out of which would emerge new and more permanent political alignments, both in Canada and in British North America.

THE AGE OF STEAM

As the Province of Canada descended into a maelstrom of factious politics, sectional rivalry and religious antagonism in the early 1850's, a revolution in technology was changing the face of the countryside and the life of its inhabitants. This revolution was precipitating British North America into the modern industrial age by producing interacting changes in communications, transportation, manufacturing, agriculture, and even social relations. At the very moment when Britain was displaying her industrial might to the world at the Great Exhibition of 1851, her North American colonies were copying

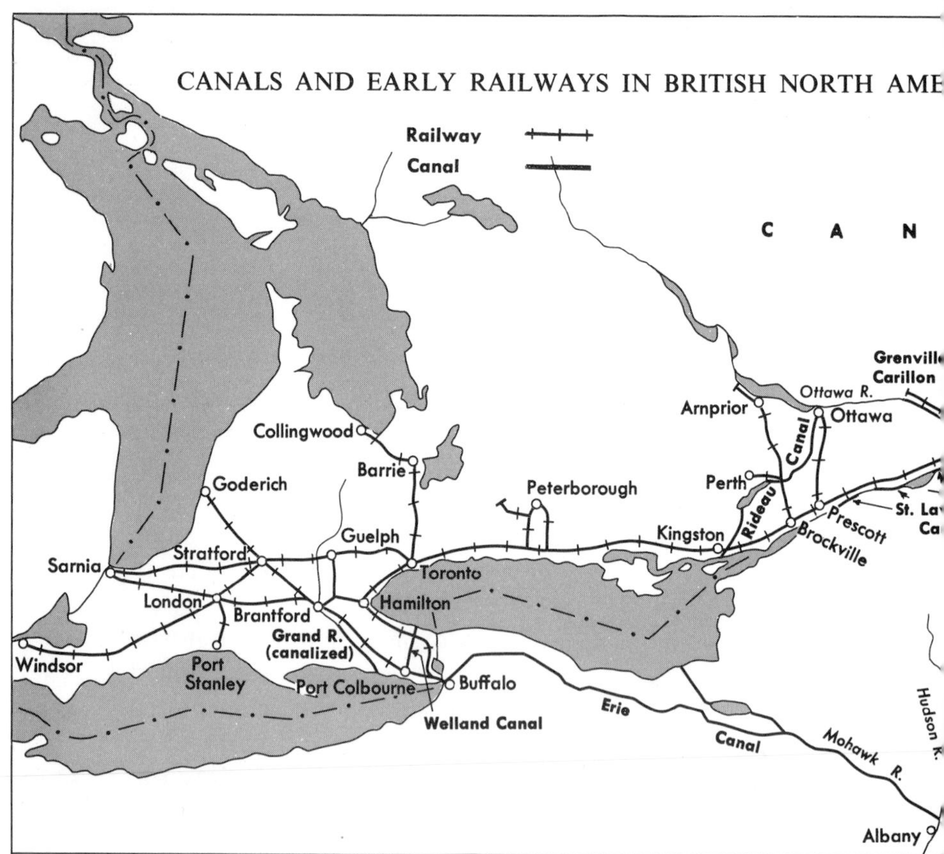

the techniques that had produced Britain's pre-eminence and would soon produce its rival in the United States.

Harbingers of the new age were the telegraph lines that first carried instant news from Toronto to Hamilton in 1847 and which, by 1861, had stretched nearly 3,500 miles, linking the commercial empire of the St. Lawrence to Detroit, New York and New Brunswick. In 1849 Canada got her first daily newspaper, the Kingston *Whig*. But the most obvious symbols of the new age were the railways, which mushroomed in the 1850's. Wood-burning engines hauled farm produce to market and brought machine-made products to the farm. Not only factory-made necessities but sheer luxuries such as pianos appeared in

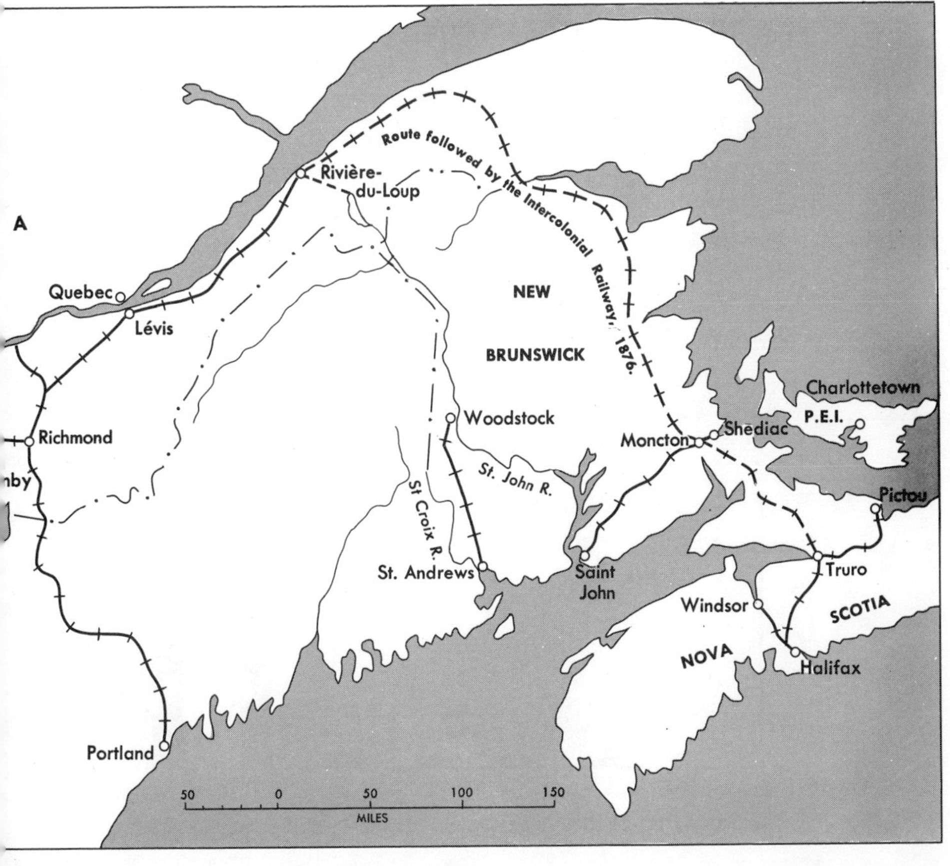

well-to-do rural homes, providing an air of genteel sophistication to the formerly pioneer society. Thanks to the new rapid transportation, politicians could visit their constituencies, clergymen could attend conferences, travelling salesmen could transport their sample cases of fancy clothes or fine china to customers, and families could enjoy reunions with distant relatives, all in comparative ease and comfort. The railway worked a revolution on every aspect of day-to-day life in the country.

British America's first railway, the Champlain-St. Lawrence Railway, a short portage line sixteen miles long, was built in 1838. Though many lines were chartered in subsequent years, no other railways were constructed until the railway age was opened by the Northern, which joined Toronto to Georgian Bay in 1853. In rapid succession short lines linked the interior areas with neighbouring Great Lakes ports. But the most imaginative railway scheme was the Grand Trunk, which was planned to traverse Canada West from Sarnia to Montreal. This was not a portage system to supplement the Great Lakes and the St. Lawrence canals, but a genuine, year-round rival for water communications.

The railway-building mania soon produced financial problems; some short lines failed within a few years. But the Grand Trunk seemed so essential to the revival of the commercial empire of the St. Lawrence that the government inevitably became involved in its controversial career. "Railways are my politics," remarked Sir Allan MacNab, speaking for all Canadian legislators. In 1853 the Grand Trunk Company had predicted

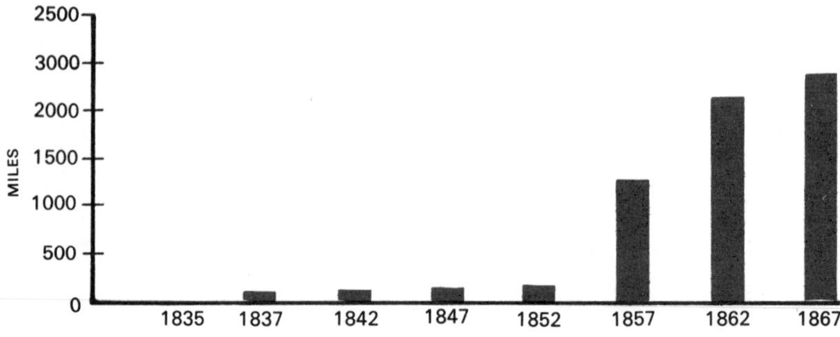

Railway Mileage in Operation in British North America, 1835-1867

$11\frac{1}{2}$ per cent profits by 1853, but by that date unrealistic construction cost estimates had brought bankruptcy. A £900,000 loan from the government was exhausted within a year. The government of Francis Hincks (successor to Baldwin and Lafontaine), which had been so generous with the taxpayers' money, fell, in part because of its Grand Trunk associations. Even so, more capital and concessions disappeared into the Grand Trunk morass until 1860, when the deficit was $13 million and the government foreclosed on the railway. "I am in the position," remarked A. T. Galt, the government solicitor, "of the man who had the good luck to win an elephant."

Despite the over-optimism of the railway builders, much was accomplished in the railway decade. By 1860 Canada had 1,900 miles of track—more than Scotland or Ireland—although two-thirds of the Canadian mileage was in Canada West. This disparity was but one indicator of the growing gap in the economic development of the two parts of the province that underlay the rising sectional conflict. At the 1851 census Canada East had 900,000 population; Canada West surpassed this by 50,000. A decade later Lower Canada's population had increased by 220,000, but Canada West's had grown by 450,000. Actual immigration (predominantly British) was larger than census figures indicated. For every ten immigrants who reached Canada, four went on to the United States. Of the remaining six, five settled in Upper Canada. Thus, most of Lower Canada's population growth came from natural increase.

The new arrivals in Canada West were making significant contributions to the human, capital and political resources of the region. Unlike the unskilled workers of the great Irish migration, the new British immigrants were highly trained workers with modest bankrolls for investment. Equally important, they brought mid-nineteenth century British ideas about progress and nationalism, and soon became active in the political life of their chosen home. However, the strait-jacket of equal parliamentary representation for the two Canadas frustrated that very spirit of expansion.

Not all the new arrivals settled in the rapidly growing industrial cities, but little good land remained in the Province of Canada

"The Habitant Farm," by Cornelius Krieghoff, Quebec, 1856. No other artist was as successful as the German-born Krieghoff in reproducing the spirit of nineteenth-century rural Quebec. Sleigh races and sleighing scenes were among his popular subjects. The Quebec farmhouse with people and some of the farm animals was also a popular and often repeated Krieghoff study. With a frequently meticulous attention to detail, Krieghoff captured the time, the place and the people and has left a most important and appealing record of early French Canada.

for those who took up farming. This accounts for English-speaking Canadians' interest in the west during the late 1850's. The prairies offered a potential farm estimated at 65,000 square miles. The Clear Grits were quick to see in that vast region an agricultural hinterland for an industrializing east.

Meanwhile, Canadian agriculture was undergoing its own revolution. Crop rotation and drainage were becoming common. New and more efficient implements were being made in Canada West, such as better plows and the revolutionary reaper-binder. Despite several bad harvests, wheat production in Canada West actually doubled between 1851 and 1861, and prices were steady and good throughout the decade. The increase in production was partly due to the introduction of disease and rust resistant Red Fife wheat. Of greater significance for agriculture was the trend to more diversified farming through the planting of root crops and the emphasis on dairying to meet the food needs of an urban society. Canada West's farm animal population reflected this change; the number of pigs and cows rose by 50 percent in the decade. This new pattern of agriculture was officially recognized by the formation of a Department of Agriculture in 1857. At that time there were nearly 130 agricultural societies and farm fairs, not to mention such groups as the Fruit Growers' Association, and botanical and horticultural societies.

The disparity in growth between the two sections of the Province of Canada was also indicated by their relative agricultural efficiency. Canada West's farmers got sixteen bushels of wheat per acre, whereas Canada East's farmers got only ten.

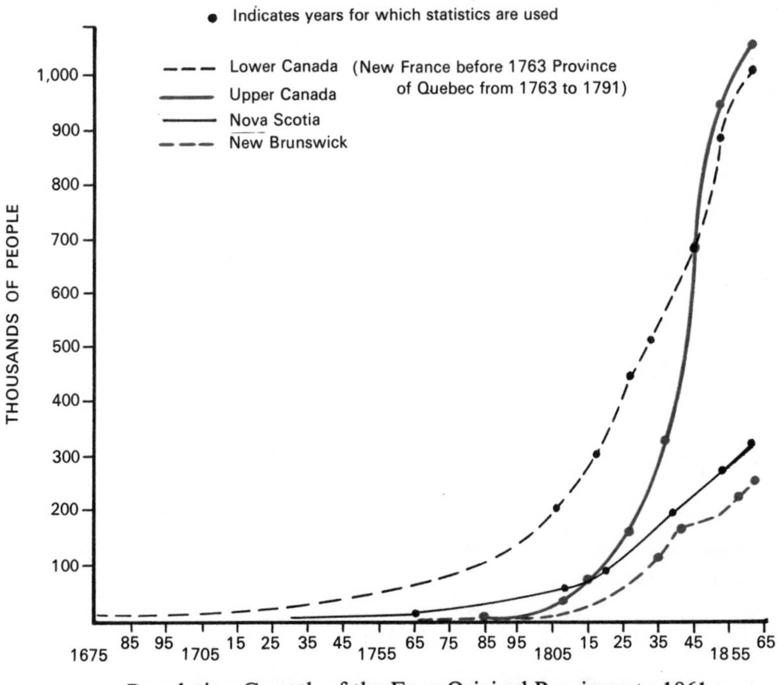

Population Growth of the Four Original Provinces to 1861

Canada West produced twenty-six bushels of oats per acre to Canada East's twenty bushels. Butter production in Canada West was fifty-four pounds per cow; in Canada East it was only thirty-three. Canada West produced four times as much cheese as Canada East. Obviously the impact of the agricultural revolution was felt and seen much more in dynamic Canada West than in conservative Canada East. But the difference was even more marked in urban society. Montreal's population more than doubled in the score of years after 1851. Toronto's population merely doubled in the same period; but Montreal was virtually the only industrial centre in Canada East, whereas Toronto had many rivals, including Hamilton, Brantford, London, Guelph, Kingston and Ottawa, where clothing, boots, agricultural implements, hardware and household utensils were being manufactured. Canada's economy, and hence her way of life, was still dominated by agriculture, but the decisive decade of the fifties marked the beginning of change from pioneer to modern society, from agriculture to industry, from rural to urban living.

In that same decade the old imperial economic system disintegrated. With the repeal of the Navigation Laws in 1850 and the reciprocity treaty with the United States, Canada's economy shifted to a north-south axis. After the economic revival of 1850, Canadian trade with Britain continued to expand; imports from Britain rose by 50 percent and exports to the mother country doubled between 1852 and 1856. But a new trade pattern was emerging, as Canadian imports from the United States rose 150 percent and in total value surpassed imports from Britain between 1852 and 1855. During that time Canadian exports to the United States quadrupled and in total value rose to equal exports to Britain. Despite her favourable trade balance with Britain, Canada incurred a constant trade deficit because of her increased dependence on the United States. During the 1850's total Canadian trade doubled, but in nine of those ten years imports exceeded exports. In the natural products covered by the reciprocity treaty, Canada had an annual credit balance of over $8 million. This was proof that her natural resources could win foreign markets. Conversely, Canadian manufacturing could not hope to compete against more industrialized countries without tariff protection and large transfusions of capital from abroad. Britain, the workshop of the world, was also the world's banker, and provided most of Canada's needs for development capital.

In retrospect the 1850's—the decade of railways, telegraphs and agricultural improvements, of the beginnings of light and heavy industry, of the modernization of government administration, and of government participation in developmental policies —constituted a watershed in the Canadian experience. To understand the Canada of Macdonald and Laurier, one must seek its roots in the 1850's. It was the paradox of that decade that deep technological and social advances should be taking place while the union was being destroyed by sectional conflicts, political disintegration and religious strife. The strange combination of expansionism and frustration was carrying Canada and her sister colonies inevitably towards a new vision of transcontinental nationhood, wherein they could find the challenge and fulfilment denied to them as small and separate entities.

SECTIONAL RIVALRIES AND POLITICAL REALIGNMENT

The retirements of Baldwin and Lafontaine from the Great Ministry led to the reorganization of the government under Francis Hincks (whose political integrity was doubted by many) and A. N. Morin (whose unquestioned honesty was weakened by indecisiveness). Arrayed in opposition within parliament were the handful of Tories from both parts of Canada, the revolutionary Clear Grit group of radical Reformers, John Sandfield Macdonald (the Roman Catholic Baldwinite from Glengarry) and his few followers who had been estranged by Hincks, and the small Lower Canadian contingent of anti-clerical reformers known as the *Rouges*. Outside parliament George Brown and his influential *Globe* took an independent position openly critical of the slow pace of reform and especially of Hincks' inactivity regarding the clergy reserves question.

Sir Allan Napier MacNab, in a portrait taken by the Montreal photographer William Notman in 1863. MacNab's colourful career included service in the War of 1812, in which he gained the name "Boy Hero." Later he was a vigorous promoter of early Canadian railways. In 1834 he began construction of a large and lavishly appointed mansion overlooking Hamilton Bay, giving it the grandiose name, Dundurn Castle. When Sir Allan died his personal finances were so strained by his ambitious and extravagant plans that Dundurn itself was threatened by bailiffs. Today Dundurn is a public museum.

By reconstructing the Reform government Hincks was able to gain the support of most of the Clear Grits, and when a general election was called late in 1851 the government was returned with almost the same strength as before. One significant change, however, was the appearance in parliament for the first time of Hincks' avowed enemy, George Brown. The government's policy remained basically that of Lafontaine and Baldwin, but there was now more emphasis on reform, to meet the complaints of its uneasy supporters. The government was also actively involved in various railway projects. It was in connection with a proposed inter-colonial railway, to link the British North American colonies, that Hincks and a New Brunswick cabinet member went to Britain in 1852 to seek financial aid from the imperial government. In Britain a recent change of government had produced a Conservative ministry under Lord Derby which was unwilling to help build an intercolonial railway along the route desired by the colonies. More threatening to Hincks' political position was the Derby government's rejection of the Canadian parliament's request for legislation to permit the abolition of the clergy reserves.

Despite bitter criticism of the government by a frustrated George Brown, a republican Papineau and an ambitious John A. Macdonald, the parliamentary session of 1852-53 passed several significant measures, including acts incorporating the Grand Trunk Railway and a transatlantic steamship line. Another series of resolutions against the clergy reserves, passed to show Canadian dissatisfaction with the Derby government's decision, proved to be unnecessary. In December, 1852, a Liberal ministry came to office in Britain and promised to let the Canadians settle the vexing issue themselves. This news temporarily stole some of George Brown's thunder against the Hincks-Morin government, but before the year 1853 ended a number of unconnected incidents and political decisions reversed the fortunes of the coalition and doomed it to eventual defeat.

To begin with, popular opinion demanded that the Legislative Council be made an elective and hence, supposedly, a more democratic body. Next, a redistribution of parliamentary seats increased the number of constituencies from 84 to 130 but ignored the demands of Canada West for representation by population ("rep by pop"). Equality of seats for each half of the province was retained despite Canada West's larger population as recorded in the 1851 census. Then the government announced that secularization of the clergy reserves and abolition of seigneurial tenure in Canada East would be postponed until after parliamentary redistribution. The good faith of the ministry was vehemently questioned by its opponents and even doubted by some of its supporters. These attacks on the government, originating mostly in Canada West, increased when the government's generous contract terms to the Grand Trunk Railway were announced. The dissent was redoubled when the government gave public money to various denominational colleges.

The final blow to Hincks' prestige in Canada West came in June, a few days before parliament adjourned, arising from an incident in the continuing "papal aggression" controversy.

The Gavazzi riot in Montreal, as it was shown to the readers of The Illustrated London News *in the issue of July 9, 1853.*

Alessandro Gavazzi, an ex-monk and Italian patriot, had arrived in Canada on a speaking tour in favour of Italian independence and against papal interference in politics. At Quebec City a mob attacked him during his speech. In Montreal Gavazzi finished his lecture without any serious interruption, but as the audience began to disperse, troops who had been called out to maintain order fired into the crowd, killing five persons and wounding a dozen others. The government's tardiness in ordering an investigation into the tragedy brought charges of collusion with the Roman Catholic Church to prevent free speech in a British colony.

During the following summer the cabinet was weakened by the resignation of several prominent members. Hincks' personal involvement in certain highly profitable deals in railway stocks and lands did nothing to enhance his political image. As for the coalition, it had become trapped, largely because of its own actions, in a rising tide of sectional conflict between the two parts of the Province of Canada. The conflict was reflected in political, religious, economic and social tensions between predominantly French-speaking, Roman Catholic and conservative Canada East, and aggressively reform-minded, English-speaking and Protestant Canada West. Virtually every public matter, from education to economic development, became an issue in this confrontation as the two regions viewed with alarm, envy, disapproval or outright fear the aspirations, decisions or events in the other section. The whole problem of two diverse approaches to life was compounded by the legislative union that gave each equal representation but failed to foster any genuine unity.

When parliament met in June, 1854, the two major issues on the public's mind were secularization of the clergy reserves and abolition of seigneurial tenure. The government, however, intended to postpone action until a general election could test popular opinion again. One week after the session began the Government was defeated on precisely these two issues, and two days later a snap election was called before the customary constitutional formalities of the session were completed. Public anger with these unusual proceedings was shown by the cooperation of George Brown, the Clear Grits, William Lyon Mackenzie, and even the Upper Canadian Conservatives, during the election campaign. When the votes were counted Hincks had lost control of Canada West to the Conservatives and radicals. Morin, however, still had the solid backing of Canada East.

As soon as the new parliament met in September the government candidate for Speaker was rejected, and five days later, after a second defeat, the Hincks-Morin ministry resigned. The successor would obviously have to contain Morin and his supporters. Since a coalition of Morin with the Clear Grits and *Rouges* was impossible, the natural and inevitable result was the fusion of the Lower Canadian Reformers with the Upper Canadian Conservatives of Sir Allan MacNab. The driving force behind this newest coalition was John A. Macdonald, one of MacNab's supporters.

Macdonald saw in the events of 1854 an opportunity to reconstruct the Conservative party along more liberal lines, to attract the support of moderates from both sections of the province. He believed that Canadian Conservatism was ready to abandon such outmoded ideas as its uncompromising defence of church establishment. Thus, the MacNab-Morin coalition of six Reformers and four Conservatives, which now took office under the name Liberal-Conservative, fulfilled its pledge to enact several Reform measures, including secularization of the clergy reserves, abolition of seigneurial tenure and the creation of an elective Legislative Council.

The new political alignment left the Grits, *Rouges* and a few old-line Tories in a hopeless position as small minority parties. Outwardly at least, the Liberal-Conservative coalition seemed to ensure a strong government that could reconcile sectional interests; certainly, for the next few years sectionalism was lessened as a divisive force in the Canadian union. But in fact, the differences and antagonisms between the two Canadas had been only temporarily suppressed, more from exhaustion of energy than from their solution by the Liberal-Conservative coalition. In 1855 two new causes of sectional and religious conflict appeared—Lower Canadian votes for the creation of a system of separate Roman Catholic schools in Upper Canada; and the brutal and unpunished murder near Quebec of a Protestant, Robert Corrigan, at the hands of a Roman Catholic mob.

The birth of the Liberal-Conservative government was followed by the disappearance from Canadian politics of several familiar figures. Lord Elgin was replaced as Governor General late in 1854 by Sir Edmund Walker Head, a distant relative of Sir Francis Head but completely dissimilar in his breadth of political wisdom. Francis Hincks was appointed Governor of Barbados and the Windward Islands. He reappeared but briefly in Canadian politics after Confederation as Minister of Finance. A. N. Morin resigned as leader of the Lower Canadian Reformers in January, 1855, to become a judge. His place as co-premier with MacNab was taken by E. P. Taché. The aging and ailing MacNab resigned one year later. Sir Allan's leadership of the coalition had not satisfied many of his colleagues, especially former supporters of Hincks. When his government was defeated for its weak handling of the Corrigan case all the other cabinet members deserted Sir Allan, and the ambitious John A. Macdonald was promoted to the post held by his former chief. This forced change in leadership was but the visible conclusion of a process of political and ideological change, and party realignment in Canada that had begun when the Great Ministry achieved its objective of responsible government. The stage was now set for new developments led by new men.

PROGRESS IN THE ATLANTIC COLONIES

Between 1849 and 1857 the Atlantic colonies faced many of the same challenges as Canada, but their transition from the colonial to the modern era was both slower and easier than that of their sister colony on the St. Lawrence. Economic, more than political, factors shaped developments on the seaboard. The most urgent problem was the need for new policies to counter the effects of British free trade. Like the businessmen of Canada, the residents of the Atlantic provinces seized on the possibility of increased trade with Canada and reciprocity with the United States as solutions to their economic ills.

The first step towards a new alignment of trade was taken in 1849 when official delegates of New Brunswick, Nova Scotia and Prince Edward Island exchanged views at Halifax. The rapid industrialization of the New England states had created a huge market for the natural products of the Maritimes—fish, lumber and farm products. The real question was, how could the British North American colonies gain an entry to this market through the high American tariff walls? The best and only offer that the colonies could make to the United States would be access to their inshore fisheries, from which Americans had been excluded by the Convention of 1818. Maritimers themselves had not exploited the fisheries in any systematic way, partly because the American tariffs and bounties designed to protect American fishermen discouraged foreign competition. If opening the inshore fisheries to the Americans could obtain a reciprocal opening of American markets to Maritime products, the legislature of Prince Edward Island was prepared to ask Britain to relax the Convention of 1818.

Nova Scotia, with its more diversified economy, did not share this sense of urgency; but in New Brunswick, where trade had dwindled to a third of its previous volume, the Council expressed fears that annexation might result if reciprocity were refused.

Compared to the rapid economic progress of both the United States and Canada, the economy of the Maritimes seemed becalmed in the doldrums of free trade. Immigration and trade were passing their region by. Reciprocity offered one hope of economic survival.

By 1852, however, the urgent interest of the Maritimes in reciprocity was declining as prosperity returned. At the insistence of Nova Scotia the British navy began enforcing the fishery clauses of the 1818 Convention with unprecedented stringency. Reciprocity was still their aim, but as far as the Maritime provinces were concerned, the Americans could not have it at a low price. When Lord Elgin succeeded in winning a reciprocity treaty from the United States in 1854, the Maritimes realized most of their wishes—free trade in natural products in exchange for inshore fishing rights for the Americans. Nova Scotia even obtained free entry for its coal into the American market. New Brunswick's hopes of sharing the rich American coastal trade on equal terms were, however, disappointed. Each of the Atlantic provinces ratified the treaty in accordance with its new status as a self-governing colony. The reviving trade of the region thus got a further stimulus thanks to Lord Elgin's diplomacy and champagne. The golden age of the Maritimes had arrived, but Fate decreed that steam and steel would soon replace wind and wood, to the lasting detriment of those provinces.

Railways, and particularly an intercolonial railway linking the Maritimes to the Canadian market of 2,000,000 people, had been discussed for several years, but, as in Canada, a lack of capital had prevented their development. New hope for an intercolonial railway was raised in 1848 when a British survey reported the feasibility of a line following the east coast of New Brunswick. This route would give Canada a year-round port at Halifax and give the Maritimes access to the Canadian market. The route could also expect to receive official British support, since it met the imperial defence requirements of an intercolonial communications link at a safe distance from the American border. British construction of such a line would be accepted by Maritimers as compensation for their loss of protected British markets.

Maritime hopes for a free intercolonial railway were crushed by Earl Grey's announcement in 1850 that Britain would not pay for such a railway. Maritime eyes now turned away from Canada and towards the much larger market of the United States. American railroad interests proposed to join Portland, Maine, to Saint John and Halifax, because of the greater proximity of these seaboard cities to Europe than any American ports. Together, New Brunswick and Nova Scotia began the piecemeal construction of lines to Portland in 1853. By 1857, under the energetic supervision of Joseph Howe, President of the Nova Scotia Board of Railway Commissioners, the railway from Halifax to Truro was completed. But the American capitalists had made no move to advance from Portland, and the international recession compounded the financial troubles of the Maritime railways. Eventually the governments of Nova Scotia and New Brunswick were forced to take over the incomplete lines. As late as 1867 railways in the two provinces totalled less than 350 miles.

On the political scene the precedent of responsible government in Nova Scotia was soon applied in her sister provinces. Prince Edward Island got her first responsible administration in 1851, but factional politics came close to wrecking the experiment in 1854. In Newfoundland, as in Prince Edward Island, true parties had barely emerged and the granting of responsible government to Britain's oldest colony was made with reluctance in 1855. The island's population was almost equally divided among Roman Catholics, Anglicans and Methodists; denominational conflicts, particularly over education, influenced the colony's politics even to the extent of dictating unofficial denominational representation in the cabinet. A further step beyond responsible government towards autonomy was taken in 1857 when the British government admitted Newfoundland's right to be consulted regarding any alterations of French fishing rights along the province's shores.

The working of responsible government in Nova Scotia and New Brunswick also encountered difficulties. In both colonies the opposition refused to accept government by the other party as proof of the existence of responsible government and deplored

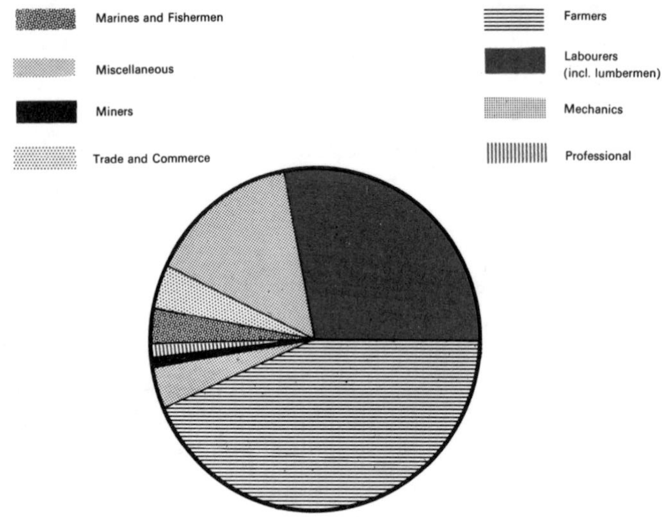

Labour Force of the Four Original Provinces, 1861.

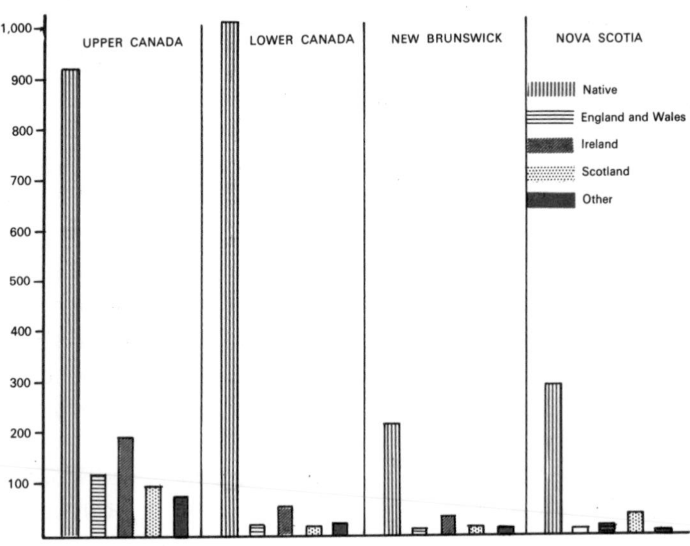

Population of the Four Original Provinces by Origin, 1861

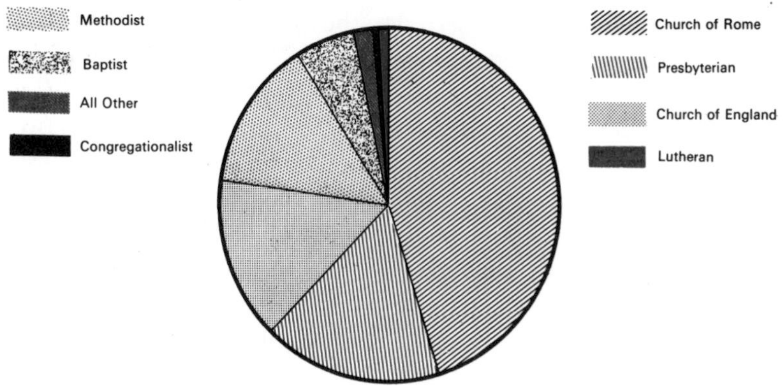

Population of the Four Original Provinces by Religion, 1861.

the new dispensation which increased the power of the executive councils at the expense of the lieutenant-governors. Local political habits and traditions changed but slowly and in neither province did party organization achieve the sophistication shown in the Province of Canada. Patronage was just beginning to be used for party purposes. Other basic weaknesses of their political systems were the absence of strong municipal governments and the belated adoption of financial control by the assemblies (1857 in New Brunswick and 1860 in Nova Scotia), which alone could make responsible government effective through the power of the purse.

During the 1850's denominational controversies over education in the Maritimes began to resemble the Canadian disputes over separate schools and church colleges. The spirit of secularism brought about the secularization of King's College, Fredericton, which became the provincial university in 1854. But Joseph Howe never succeeded in his campaign against denominationalism in the Nova Scotia colleges. When the Roman Catholic Church, strengthened by recent Irish immigration, demanded separate schools in Nova Scotia, Protestants responded not with demands for separation of church and state in education, but with demands for equal denominational privileges. The government of William Young and Joseph Howe in Nova Scotia was ended in 1857 when its Roman Catholic supporters in the assembly deserted to the opposition. This estrangement continued through the election of 1859 and even after Howe became premier in 1860, despite attempts at reconciliation. Howe's attacks on Roman Catholic doctrines during the election campaign reproduced, although on a smaller scale, the "papal aggression" controversy that had rocked Canada short years before. Despite all these issues, political life in the Maritime provinces remained relatively peaceful in comparison with the violence of the experience of the united Province of Canada.

The decade that followed the introduction of responsible government in Nova Scotia and Canada had been one of the most revolutionary in the experience of the British North American colonies, and perhaps in the whole of the Canadian experience. The dramatic changes wrought in the everyday life of the colonists marked those years as a watershed in their development from an agricultural society towards a modern industrialized nation. But the very changes that occurred created both new problems and new opportunities.

The new economic trends posed basic questions about the colonies' trade relations to Great Britain, to the United States and among themselves. Industry was also establishing modern cities, with all the social problems of poverty, housing, law and order that urbanization brings in its wake. In a broader perspective, however, the individual colonies were made more aware, through transportation and communications, of their place in the Atlantic community of nations and, paradoxically, of their isolation from each other. A sense of identification with the land was slowly growing into a dream of nationality, a dream of unity in North America under the British flag. In the next decade forces at work both within and without the colonies would convert that dream into the reality of a British North American confederation stretching tenuously, but hopefully, from sea to sea.

CHAPTER 8

THE ROAD TO NATIONHOOD

With her best lands already occupied and her economy experiencing the multiple impacts of the age of steam, the Province of Canada, especially Canada West, felt a pressing need to expand in two directions. Eastward lay a year-round port at Halifax, the Atlantic Ocean and European markets; westward lay the vacant prairie lands and the Pacific seaboard, ensuring access to the Orient. The interest of the Canadian government in acquiring the west had begun before 1858 when the Hudson's Bay Company's license from the British government came up for renewal. In 1856 Chief Justice William Henry Draper went to London to press Canada's case for acquiring the western lands. The discovery that year of gold on the Fraser River added a note of urgency to his discussion. As thousands of American miners flocked north from the declining gold fields of California, the possibility of American acquisition of the Pacific coast became a real threat to Canadian ambitions; the fate of Oregon only a decade earlier was still a fresh memory. No less important than the west, yet of more immediate concern, were Canada's future connections with the four Atlantic provinces.

ATLANTIC UNION OR BRITISH NORTH AMERICAN CONFEDERATION?

The Atlantic colonies were not only isolated from Canada—they were also separated one from the other by a strong sense of provincial identity and pride. Newfoundland was obviously the most isolated; by the mid-1850's her population of roughly 120,000 was still entirely dependent on the fisheries, which in turn were largely under the indirect control of the St. John's merchants. In 1855 responsible government was introduced to Newfoundland, but political parties were slow to evolve because of religious antagonisms between the equally-balanced groups of Roman Catholics, Anglicans and Methodists, and because of the economic jealousies between the wealthy merchant group in the capital and the depressed residents of the outports. In the late 1850's Nova Scotia, so long marked by its "moderation and harmony," was experiencing some of the religio-political strains between Roman Catholics and Protestants with which Canada was too well acquainted. At the same time Nova Scotia was enjoying prosperity; her wooden sailing ships carried fish, lumber and farm products to the markets of the United States and the British West Indies. It was a golden age doomed to disappear within a generation, as steam and steel became the rulers of the waves. Nova Scotia, more than either Prince Edward Island or New Brunswick, was vitally interested in the proposed intercolonial railway that could give access to the Canadian market, but the failure of plans to finance the railway in Britain was blamed by Joseph Howe on Canadian duplicity. This unhappy relationship prejudiced the later movement towards Confederation.

The lumber industry, the basis of New Brunswick's economy, was also that province's greatest disadvantage, for other forms of industry such as agriculture had been so overshadowed by lumbering that they were grossly underdeveloped. This produced a too-heavy dependence on a single staple, and left the province with insufficient diversity in economic development when the lumber trade declined in later years. In the political sphere, the most prominent individual in New Brunswick was the urbane and

The Montreal photographer William Notman was an enthusiastic traveller, and as a result he has left an important photographic record of Canada in the mid-nineteenth century. These photographs give two views of New Brunswick. Above is the harbour of Saint John in 1870. Note the number of large wooden buildings. Below, lumbermen prepare for operations in the bush near the Washawaak River in 1871.

capable Leonard Tilley, whose destiny it was to carry his province into Confederation. The most potent force in New Brunswick politics was, however, a group known as "the Smashers" (because their liberal, democratic ideas were destroying the traditional habits of political moderation in that colony during the decade before Confederation). Less obvious at the time, but of long-range importance, was the awakening sense of identity among New Brunswick's sizeable Acadian population. This Acadian cultural revival in language and education was led by a handful of Roman Catholic clergy, the most notable being the French-born Abbé J-M. Sigogne.

The physical isolation of Prince Edward Island created an even deeper provincial loyalty and sense of self-satisfaction than in the other Maritime colonies, but Prince Edward Island's most immediate problem was still that of the absentee landlords. In 1861 "the Island" had only 80,000 people, compared to 250,000 in New Brunswick and 330,000 in Nova Scotia. These population figures indicated that the great wave of immigration in the recent decade had passed the Maritimes by, in favour of Canada or the United States. Such population growth as the Maritime provinces showed stemmed very largely from natural increase.

These economic and demographic conditions caused little immediate concern in the Maritimes. Public interest was directed more towards the idea of a union of all the colonies, which could open the Canadian hinterland market to the products of the Atlantic regions. As early as 1840 Howe's imagination had been stirred by Lord Durham's dream of a British North American federation, but even then Howe was painfully aware of the physical and psychological obstacles in the way of such a union. The federation idea was reawakened in the 1850's by the possibility of building an intercolonial railway linking the Maritimes with the St. Lawrence at Quebec, the terminus of the Grand Trunk. Despite the subsequent failure of negotiations, the railway was the strongest attraction that a British North American federation held for the Maritimes, particularly for New Brunswick and Nova Scotia, who would benefit most from its construction. The vague concept of a larger British-American nationality held little appeal for the provincially-minded Maritimers. Only concrete advantages were likely to win their hard-headed allegiance to any federation scheme.

"FATHER DEADLOCK"

After the exciting events and developments in the Canadas during the early 1850's, a period of adjustment began about 1857. The political and "racial" tensions remained, but the most important development was the beginning of a major recession that acted as a catalyst on the political and economic attitudes of the colonies. On the economic scene public attention was directed to the changing pattern of life: to the increasing trade with the United States and the decreasing trade with Britain; and to the more rapid growth of Canada West in comparison to Canada East. One result was a deepening sense of frustration and confinement on the part of Canada West, which began to view Canada East as a millstone retarding the province's development in various fields. Canada East's conservatism was evident in her slower agricultural production, her retarded industrial growth, and her lack of interest in territorial expansion (particularly westward expansion which appealed to land-hungry Canada West). Canada East's equal voice in the united parliament not only enabled it to stall progressive measures that Canada West deemed necessary, but even to impose its solution on Canada West's problems, as in the case of separate school legislation. Within the Union the two Canadas were equal partners politically, but Canada West, now larger in population and more dynamic, complained of French domination and of minority rule—thanks to the alliance of Macdonald's Liberal-Conservatives with, and dependence on, the solid voting support of its wing in Canada East.

The first answer to this growing stalemate between Canada East and Canada West came from George Brown and the Clear Grits in their policy of "rep by pop" (representation by population), the very principle denied Lower Canada in the Union of 1841 and demanded by the *Rouges* in 1849. The Union had

George E. Cartier in 1871

John A. Macdonald in 1863

John Sandfield Macdonald in 1863

George Brown (about 1865)

Thomas D'Arcy McGee in 1866/67

imposed equal representation on the more populous lower province as one means of swamping the French. Now, however, the shoe was on the Upper Canadian foot and it pinched Upper Canadian ambitions. It was understandable that John A. Macdonald should reject this Grit policy of "rep by pop" because the French Canadians, on whom his political power depended, refused to surrender their newly-acquired political advantage.

A second answer to the stalemate, proposed by John Sandfield Macdonald and the rump of the old Baldwin-Lafontaine Reform group, was adherence to the "double majority" principle, whereby no legislation should be passed for one section of the province without the approval of a majority from that section. As both Grits and Liberal-Conservatives pointed out, the double majority would perpetuate sectionalism and violate the spirit of responsible government. Two other solutions—a federation of the two Canadas or simple separation—were soon to be suggested for Canada's dilemma.

The Canadian parliament met in 1858 after a general election had given the Clear Grits a majority of the Canada West seats. Members learned that in response to their request Queen Victoria had chosen Ottawa as a permanent capital for the province. Before the seat of government question was debated, however, Alexander Tilloch Galt, the young Liberal-Conservative member from Sherbrooke, introduced resolutions for a division of the two Canadas, federation of British North America, and territorial government for the North-West. His proposals were rejected because the Macdonald-Cartier government withheld its support. Three weeks later sectional rivalry defeated the government: a motion rejecting the Queen's choice of Ottawa was carried by a majority of fourteen. The ensuing events showed clearly the impasse that had been reached in the political life of the Union as a result of sectionalism.

The Macdonald-Cartier government resigned on 29 July, and when Governor General Sir Edmund Head called on George Brown to form a new ministry, Brown accepted despite the fact that his Clear Grits numbered only thirty-three in a House of 130 members. Brown won the co-operation of nine *Rouges* led by

A. A. Dorion, and the new government was sworn in on 2 August. That same day it was easily defeated on a no-confidence vote. Head then refused the cabinet's request for a general election, as he had already warned Brown that he would. The new ministry, embittered by this action which they viewed as partisan, resigned on 4 August. At the Governor General's request George Cartier then formed a government that included Macdonald and Galt.

The new Cartier cabinet immediately found itself in a highly dangerous position. The law required that a member of the House who accepted a paying office of the Crown, including a cabinet post, must resign his seat to seek personal re-election. The government could ill afford to risk the absence from the House of any of its supporters, let alone the whole cabinet. But there was one way out of the predicament. A law existed, originally intended simply to allow incumbent ministers to exchange portfolios more easily, stating that a minister taking up a new office within one month of leaving an old one did not have to seek re-election. The Cartier cabinet, composed mostly of members of the former Macdonald-Cartier ministry, seized upon this loophole. On 6 August they assumed portfolios other than those they had resigned one week earlier, but on the following day they reverted to their old offices. The letter of the law had been observed and the ministers were safely in their accustomed posts. This famous, or infamous, incident became known as the "double shuffle"—a perfectly legal action but an undeniably devious one that dramatized the difficulty of forming any stable government in the fragmented political scene of Canada.

Both parties profited from their experiences in the summer of 1858. By co-operating with the *Rouges,* Brown and the Clear Grits had laid the foundations of a "desectionalized" (united) Liberal party. At the same time, Galt joined the Liberal-Conservative government on the express promise that federation would be made government policy. Cartier, Galt and another minister left in October for talks with the Colonial Office about the North-West, an intercolonial railway and Galt's scheme for union. At the same moment New Brunswick and Nova Scotia

A view of Ottawa at about the time it was chosen by Queen Victoria as the capital of Canada in 1858. The vantage point is adjacent to the present location of the Parliament Buildings.

delegations broached the subject of an intercolonial railway in London.

Although the Conservative government of Lord Derby in Britain was more favourable to an Atlantic regional union, Governor General Head had written to the Colonial Office supporting the larger federation. Thus, the colonial delegations received a kindly, although ultimately unsatisfactory, welcome. The refusal of an imperial guarantee for financing the intercolonial railway—the third such refusal—disappointed all three delegations. The Canadian federation proposal was also rejected because it was still a matter of partisan debate in Canada and one as yet unsupported by the other colonies. Equally unsatisfactory was the decision to leave the disposition of the North-West to negotiation. Ten years of uncertainty were to follow as Canada, the Hudson's Bay Company and the imperial government discussed a transfer of the North-West. Thus, in 1858, the three-fold plan for political and economic expansion of British North

America failed to win imperial approval, and the colonies remained in difficult circumstances.

In 1859 Galt, as Finance Minister, offered Canada one solution to the problem of declining revenues and the critical indebtedness of the Grand Trunk Railway—a protective tariff, which he argued would actually reduce costs to Canadian consumers. Although British manufacturers protested loudly about discrimination by a colony, the imperial government allowed the tariff to stand. This action was a significant break with the policy established by Durham, whereby certain powers had been reserved exclusively for the imperial government. It was, therefore, a large step towards colonial independence in colonial economic matters.

By late 1859 a new Liberal-Whig government in Britain was anxious that Canada's credit be restored and so offered to consider any joint colonial proposal for federation. But the necessary forces to unite colonial sentiments were just emerging. In December the Reform party held a convention in Toronto at which Brown, with some difficulty, convinced the delegates to pass a resolution in favour of a federation of the two Canadas, in place of one calling for simple dissolution of the Union.

Both parties in Canada were now pledged to the federal ideal when a unifying crisis for all British North America arose with the outbreak of the American Civil War in 1861. British North American interests and sympathies lay with the abolitionist North, but the North was antagonized by British imperial policies that favoured the rebellious Southern states.

Against the background of the American Civil War, the Canadian Union staggered from one crisis to another. In a general election in 1861 the Cartier-Macdonald government won a reduced majority at the polls. In the same election Brown resigned the Reform leadership after suffering personal defeat. Late that year the American seizure of two Confederate agents from the British ship *Trent* brought Britain and the United States to the brink of war. The Cartier-Macdonald government tried in 1862 to improve Canada's defences by enlarging her militia, but suffered defeat in parliament on the issue. The patchwork cabinet now put together by Sandfield Macdonald and

Louis Sicotte remained in office less than two years. As the war in the United States intensified, the intercolonial railway project was revived as a defence measure, this time on the initiative of the imperial government. Nova Scotia and New Brunswick agreed to share the cost with alacrity, only to find to their disgust that the Canadian government refused at the last moment to participate because of certain financial details.

The Macdonald-Sicotte minority government was already losing public confidence when George Brown returned to parliament in 1863 and attacked its passing of another Upper Canadian separate school act with Lower Canadian votes. John A. Macdonald completed the disruption of the government by attacking its railway and militia policies. Defeated in parliament, Sandfield Macdonald announced another general election and reconstructed his cabinet with A. A. Dorion as co-premier.

The election of 1863 had no real issues, and when it was over there was still no real change in the confused welter of Canadian politics. The government of the province was still cursed by sectionalism that prevented a stable majority on crucial issues, a fact that was reflected in double-name ministries. The intercolonial railway project was stalled, for which Canada was blamed. British North America was no better prepared to defend itself, but the American North was talking of taking revenge on Britain and British North America for their sympathy towards the South. Cancellation of the Reciprocity Treaty, and even conquest had been suggested, but British North America's defences remained inadequate. When the Province of Canada's eighth and last parliament resumed in the winter of 1864, George Brown had assumed the leadership of the militant confederationists, but it was E. P. Taché and John A. Macdonald who formed yet another coalition government in March. Three months later that cabinet also fell—by two votes. Unable to muster a majority from the splintered groupings in the House, it was the fourth victim of sectionalism in two years.

The deadlock in Canadian politics was complete; only a miracle could make effective government possible. That miracle occurred on 23 June when George Brown broke the crisis by offering to join his old enemies, the Liberal-Conservatives, in a coalition dedicated to seeking a solution to the problems of sectionalism, defence, the North-West and the intercolonial railway, through a union of British North America. Deadlock was indeed a "father" of Confederation, at least for the Province of Canada.

THE MOVEMENT FOR CONFEDERATION

The Confederation movement seemed to grow suddenly out of political deadlock during the early 1860's in the Province of Canada, and to mushroom almost overnight to absorb the separate movement for union among the four Atlantic colonies. In fact, however, the seeds of Confederation had been sown as far back as the American Revolution, when Nova Scotia and the newly-conquered province of Quebec remained loyal to Great Britain. The legislative union of Upper and Lower Canada had very quickly become an embryonic federation, with separate educational systems and duplicate public officers to serve the two distinct regions. From this federal experience of the supposedly unified province of Canada came many of the practices adopted in the Dominion of Canada after 1867.

By the early 1860's no political party or coalition of parties could produce a working majority in the Canadian assembly; four governments and two general elections in the space of two years were proof of the deadlock that had seized the province. A last chance to escape this frustration came when George Brown offered in June, 1864, to support his political enemy, John A. Macdonald, if Macdonald would agree to work for a federation of all British North America. The offer was accepted and the course of the future was set.

On the first day of September, 1864, delegates from New Brunswick, Nova Scotia and Prince Edward Island were gathered in Charlottetown to discuss Maritime union when two-thirds of the Canadian cabinet arrived without formal invitations. After five days of hard arguing and generous entertainment, Macdonald, George Cartier, A. T. Galt (the financial expert) and George Brown (the Clear Grit newspaper editor) so dazzled their Maritime counterparts with the vision of a greater, stronger, transcontinental nationality that the project of Maritime union was put aside. At this point the federation movement expanded from the Province of Canada to sweep up all British North America in its headlong rush.

The idea of Confederation held little attraction for most Maritimers. Aside from the possible advantage of the railway line to Canada and a new market of two and a half million people, Confederation offered few concrete gains and many drawbacks. Maritimers had deep and abiding loyalties to their own provinces, that seemed stronger than any dream of empire, and they were understandably suspicious of becoming enmeshed in the jungle-like politics of Canada. Nevertheless, the colonial leaders agreed to meet again at Quebec in October, 1864. At this second conference, to which Newfoundland sent a delegation, they hammered out the framework of a federal constitution for British North America. The resulting document has become known as The Seventy-Two Resolutions.

Compromises were made at Quebec. No colony got all it wanted in the Resolutions. Most Canadians shared the sense of satisfaction of their provincial leaders in the prospects of a British North American federation. But the hard-headed Maritimers were still suspicious of the motives behind the whirlwind courtship that had begun so unexpectedly at Charlottetown. In New Brunswick the voters defeated Leonard Tilley's pro-Confederation government at a general election in March.

The "Fathers of Confederation" in Charlottetown, September 1, 1864.

Samuel Leonard Tilley (left) of New Brunswick and Charles Tupper of Nova Scotia.

In Nova Scotia Premier Charles Tupper avoided the same fate by not bringing the Confederation issue before the provincial legislature. Prince Edward Island and Newfoundland, following the trend set in New Brunswick, decided against joining the proposed federation.

The prospects for Confederation looked black indeed by the spring of 1865, but new pressures outside of British North America were about to provide the required impetus to bring the movement to fruition. In New Brunswick the new premier, A. J. Smith, failed to revive the Maritime union project, or to ensure reciprocity in trade with the United States, or a railway to the United States. These failures should have been sufficient evidence to prove there was no practicable alternative to Confederation. But public opinion was still not ready to accept the scheme. On orders from the British Colonial Office, Lieutenant-

Governor Gordon, in a move that negated the principle of responsible government, dissolved the New Brunswick legislature. With financial aid from the Canadian confederationists and the support of the Lieutenant-Governor, Tilley was able to win the ensuing election. One explanation for these developments was to be found in the United States, where the North had recently emerged victorious from the Civil War. Popular annoyance in the United States with Britain's support of the rebellious South had been expressed by threats to annex the British colonies in revenge, and through the decision taken in January, 1865, to cancel the Reciprocity Treaty of 1854 that had proved so profitable to British North America. At the same time American Fenians, an Irish organization dedicated to freeing their homeland from British rule, were preparing to invade the colonies to teach Britain a lesson. Faced with increased responsibilities and costs in defending the North American colonies, the British government became the enthusiastic supporter of a federation that would reduce some of these burdens.

The British government's change of heart explains the irregular actions of Lieutenant-Governor Gordon in New Brunswick, and the known presence of Fenian bands on the borders of New Brunswick and Canada provided the pressure that enabled Tilley and Tupper to continue actively pursuing their Confederation programme. By the summer of 1866 the road to Confederation had been cleared of all obstacles in these three colonies, thanks to American and Fenian threats, and it only remained to convert the Seventy-Two Resolutions into a statute of the imperial parliament. To this end, delegates from the three colonies met the British officials at the Westminster Palace Hotel Conference in December of 1866.

A NEW CONSTITUTION

The Seventy-Two Resolutions had been approved in 1865 by the Canadian legislature, but they had never been debated or approved in the legislatures of New Brunswick and Nova Scotia.

New Brunswick had never gone beyond passing a resolution supporting the general principle of Confederation during a Fenian scare in 1866. Nevertheless, with only minor changes in wording, the Resolutions were accepted as the basis of Confederation by the Westminster Conference and were embodied in the British North America Act of 1867. The Act itself forms only the written part of the constitution established for Canada. True to British traditions, the colonists accepted as their own many of the unwritten constitutional customs and practices of the Mother of Parliaments. The preamble of the British North America Act describes the Canadian constitution as "similar in principle to that of the United Kingdon." Nevertheless, the Act was a departure from previous imperial practice in two important respects: it was a written constitution, and (obviously influenced by the United States) it created a federation.

The British North America Act was a statute of the imperial parliament. Only that parliament had the power to change the Act, and until 1949 the court charged with its interpretation was the Judicial Committee of the British Privy Council. Legally the new dominion was still a creature of the imperial parliament, unable to change the written basis of its constitution, unable to pass legislation contrary to British law and, in theory, unable to have any direct dealings with foreign states. Indeed, except for the implementation of responsible government and the acknowledged right to establish its own tariffs, the constitutional powers of Canada were much the same as those of the colonies in Lord Durham's day. In 1867 Canada was no more than a supercolony. But it was generally understood that changing circumstances in the future might give it more, if not all, the powers of a sovereign and independent country.

The new federal constitution provided for a Canadian parliament. The House of Commons, with 181 members in 1867, was elected to represent population. The upper house, called a senate, was composed of members appointed by the Crown for life to represent the Maritimes, Quebec and Ontario *as regions*, not as provinces. Finally, a Privy Council was created as the formal vehicle for an executive or cabinet, functioning in the name of the Queen and responsible to the House of Commons.

In the formation of the Commons and the cabinet, British traditions were followed. But the Senate was modelled more on its American namesake than on the British House of Lords, although the inclusion of property ownership as a qualification for membership was an attempt to make the Senate representative of property and conservatism, in the manner of the House of Lords.

American political experience was reflected in the British North America Act for the simple reason that both Canada and the United States faced the same problem of governing vast and diversified regions. In Canada's case there was also the fact that her people were of two quite distinct cultural and racial origins. But in the final analysis Canada's new constitution was in the British tradition of a largely unwritten constitution. The British North America Act is only one part—the written part—of the Canadian constitution. The greater part is unwritten parliamentary custom, evolved over centuries of British experience and always changing to meet new conditions. The weakness of any written constitution is that it can quickly become dated and is usually difficult to change. This inflexibility has been a problem in the British North America Act. For example, even the Fathers of Confederation, astute though they may have been, could not possibly have foreseen the contemporary issues of conflicting federal and provincial jurisdiction in such areas as modern transportation, the mass communications media and education.

The British North America Act preserved many existing colonial and British institutions in the new provinces. The provinces were to have legislatures not unlike their old colonial assemblies. The new provincial legislatures were also copies of the new federal House of Commons. The 150-year-old British practice of making money bills the sole responsibility of the government of the day was now introduced into the legislatures of the Maritime provinces. Each province also had an executive, or cabinet, functioning according to the principles of responsible government. In other respects the Act was very British in its practices: there was no Bill of Rights, no separation of the legislature and executive, and no election of judges.

In one important respect the British North America Act was strongly influenced by the example of the United States—in the adoption of the federal principle. But even here there was obvious suspicion of the American precedent. With the American Civil War fresh in their memories, the Fathers of Confederation deliberately planned for a central government that would be stronger than the provinces. The new provincial governments might look and act much like their colonial namesakes, but there was an essential difference. The provinces were subordinate to the federal power; they were the creations of the British North America Act and had only such powers as the Act gave them. Although some politicians in 1867 and later years might talk of Confederation as a "compact" between the colonies to establish a new level of government between themselves and Britain, the legal facts were otherwise.

The powers of the provinces were precisely stated in Section 92 of the Act. Section 91, after listing the powers of the central government, included the "peace, order and good government" clause that gave all unspecified powers to the central government. Section 91 also contained the "post enumeration" clause giving priority to federal over provincial rights in the event of conflict. Specifically, Section 91 gave to the federal government all the powers that any national government would need to promote national policies—control of money and banking, trade and commerce, shipping, defence, criminal law and prisons, fisheries, and most important of all, "the raising of money by any mode or system of taxation." In other ways the national government was made strong at the expense of the provinces. The federal government was given the power to appoint lieutenant-governors, to disallow provincial legislation, to appoint and pay all senior judges, and to create federal courts. Only in education did the Fathers of Confederation admit as a provincial responsibility a field that in most countries has been deemed a national interest.

The intentions of the Fathers were clear in 1867, but time and circumstance were fated to frustrate some of their wishes during the coming century.

THE PEOPLE AND THE LAND

Of the three British colonies (Canada, New Brunswick and Nova Scotia) that were joined in 1867 to form the new Dominion of Canada, the old colony of Canada—now the provinces of Ontario and Quebec—was by far the largest and richest. Its population of 2,500,000 massed in the fertile St. Lawrence valley and lower Great Lakes region was largely employed in agriculture, though lumbering was also an important primary industry. In addition, a wide variety of manufacturing was already carried on in numerous towns and cities, particularly Montreal and Toronto. But the colony of Canada suffered two major drawbacks—the granite Canadian Shield blocked northward and westward expansion (all good farmland was occupied by the 1840's); and the St. Lawrence, the colony's commercial highway, was ice-bound for one-third of the year.

New Brunswick's population of some 275,000 was still heavily dependent on lumbering and related industries, as its farms did not produce enough to feed its residents. By contrast, Nova Scotia had a diversified economy for its 375,000 people, with farming, fishing, lumbering, coal mining, ship building and

"Bellevue," a mid-nineteenth century house in Kingston occupied for a short period by John A. Macdonald. Aside from its connection with Canada's first Prime Minister, Bellevue, with its almost whimsical appearance and Italian flavour, demonstrates the taste for the unusual and exotic that is frequently evident in homes of the period.

ocean transportation. Prince Edward Island, which joined Confederation in 1873, was already established as an international supplier of potatoes and coarse cereals.

In Quebec and Ontario more people were moving into the towns and cities each year, but in New Brunswick and Nova Scotia the rural areas were growing faster than either the cities of Saint John or Halifax. This fact was indicative of certain weaknesses in the Maritime economy. The Maritimes were short of much-needed capital to promote their growth. The slow progress of railway building was one obvious indication of this shortage. Only 250 miles of track had been constructed in the Maritimes, compared to nearly 2,200 miles in the colony of Canada. But the real weakness of the Maritime economy was the dependence on wooden sailing ships. Confederation coincided with the change in transportation from wood and wind to iron and steam. The golden age of the Maritime colonies was closing imperceptibly just as a new political day was dawning.

The British colonies had lost their protected market in Britain when the mother country adopted free trade in the 1840's. The end of the old mercantilist system had caused some dislocations in the colonies, but these had been largely offset by the negotiation of the reciprocity or free trade treaty with the United States in 1854. Reciprocity with the United States had brought prosperity to the colonies. But that prosperity had been in large

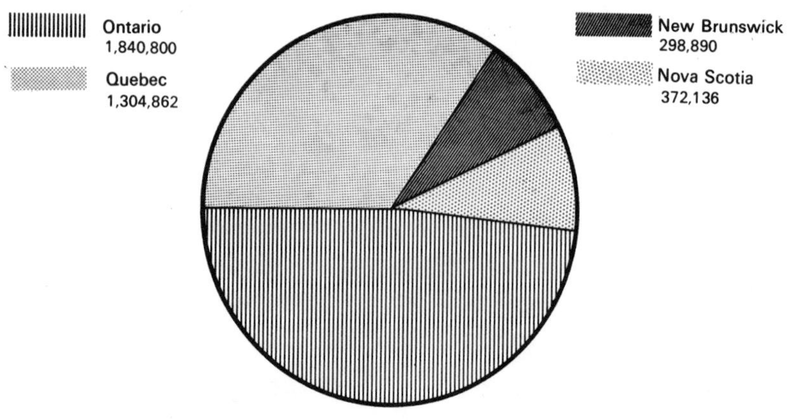

Population of Canada, July 1, 1867 (estimate)

measure promoted by accentuated American needs for food and lumber during the Civil War. After Confederation, however, some of the economic difficulties returned, for the Americans had cancelled the reciprocity treaty in 1866. Without any preferred position in Britain's market and without reciprocity, the new Dominion of Canada was forced to rely on its limited home markets and on its weak position in the international market where European nations were beginning to adopt high protective tariffs against all trading nations.

Confederation could not offer any quick or easy solution to the economic problems of the colonies. The provinces were just as isolated from one another as ever, both geographically and economically. No railways linked them together; the building of an intercolonial railway from Quebec to Halifax and Saint John was still part of the Confederation dream. Neither products nor people moved in any quantity from one colony to another before Confederation, nor for several years after. Each region had its own traditions, its own way-of-life and its own economic interests. More often they were rivals than partners or fellow provinces, as certain incidents of that first Dominion Day demonstrated.

"Died! Last night at twelve o'clock, the free and enlightened Province of Nova Scotia," read the black-edged announcement in the Halifax *Morning Chronicle* of 1 July, 1867. A more optimistic Nova Scotian citizen recorded in his diary at Lunenburg that same day,

> Monday, 1st Dominion Day!! this first day of July, in the year of our Lord 1867, is the Birth Day of the Dominion of Canada. Nova Scotia has entered to-day into a new state of things, having now entered into a partnership, forever, with New Brunswick and the Canadas.

At midnight in Ottawa a 101-gun salute, the pealing of bells and the lighting of a public bonfire had started the festivities. Now, as the sun rose auspiciously across the new nation, guns at Halifax, Saint John and Kingston boomed out their own welcome to the historic day. That morning, from Sydney to

ELLIOT'S
DENTIFRICE
FOR PRESERVING AND CLEANSING THE TEETH.

This Powder, after twenty-six years' experience is regarded by many as
THE BEST IN USE!

Dignitaries of the Church, the Bench, Officers of the Army and Navy, M's. L. C., M. P's., M. D's., D's. D. S., all unite in testifying in its favour.

Du Révérendissime l'Evêque de Cydonia, Coadjuteur de Montréal.

MONTRÉAL, 3 Novembre, 1855.

Cette excellente poudre m'est connue par mon expérience personnelle, depuis plusieurs années. Je la trouve éminemment propre à produire l'effet désiré, sans faire craindre, pour les dents ou pour les gencives, les inconvénients causés par ces poudres où il entre des ingrédients corrosifs.

Dans l'occasion je me ferai un plaisir de la recommander. Avec considération, Messieurs, votre reconnaissant serviteur.

† JOSEPH, EVEQUE DE CYDONIA.

From the Reverend Dr. Bethune, Dean of Montreal.

MONTREAL, 7th October, 1854.

I have used Elliot's Dentifrice for the last four months, and have found it very efficacious in cleansing the teeth and strengthening the gums, as well as agreeable to the taste. Your obedient servant.

JOHN BETHUNE,
Dean of Montreal.

Many imitations are sold. Ask for Elliot's Dentifrice and take no other.

TRADE MARK SECURED.

Sold by all the Druggists. 3

These two advertisements from issues of The Canadian Illustrated News *of the 1860's provide some interesting opportunities for comparisons with modern advertising.*

CARBOLIC SALVE.—The discovery of the remarkable healing qualities of Carbolic Acid is the most remarkable result of modern research. The purifying power of Carbolic Acid has long been known. It is now presented in scientific combination as a salve, and it has proved the most rapid and effectual remedy yet discovered for all sores of no matter how long standing. Every abrasion of skin or flesh rapidly healed. Sold by all Druggists. Price, 25 cents.

JOHN F. HENRY, Sole Proprietor,
8, College Place, New York.

HENRY, SIMPSON & CO., MONTREAL, Wholesale Agents for Canada.

Sarnia, local bands and militia units paraded through flag-bedecked streets as Queen Victoria's proclamation of the new dominion was read to excited crowds. At Ottawa, in front of the still unfinished Parliament buildings, Lord Monck reviewed the troops in his first public act as Governor General. Rejoicing prevailed in all parts of the dominion—very few people did not share in the popular enthusiasm. In the Maritimes some anti-Confederationists did decorate their doorways with mourning crepe. But the voices of gloom were barely noticed amid the public celebrations and private picnics that were the order of the day on 1 July, 1867.

Still, the happy throngs that celebrated Canada's birth were celebrating only a legal fact. The Dominion of Canada existed as a political entity, not as a social or economic unit. In addition, most of British North America still lay outside the boundaries of the new dominion. Obviously, the task that lay ahead was awesome—to turn this new dominion into a real nation, to bind together the scattered parts with transportation and communications, to instill in the inhabitants a sense of national unity that would rise above local or provincial loyalties, and to expand the boundaries from sea to sea. This challenge to build a new nation was both inspiring and formidable, but the very fact that a federation had been established was proof of a will to achieve greatness in spite of all obstacles.

* * *

The challenges and the opportunities facing this new dominion were numerous and great. Canada needed more markets for its products and more jobs for its people. Close by was the United States, a potential market of 30,000,000, a land of apparently limitless prospects for economic growth, especially in its rapidly developing midwestern states. Could the new dominion find a way to re-enter the American market on competitive terms, and could it at the same time find or make the necessary opportunities in Canada to keep Canadians at home? Much would depend on the future of Rupert's Land, the prairie region to the west of Ontario. Could Canada acquire those vast areas before the westward tide of American population spilled into them? And could Canada conquer the forbidding Shield country with a railway to carry Canadians to the west, to make the west a home market for the products of the eastern provinces? On the morning of Confederation the new dominion faced great problems on two different fronts. In the settled east Canada must overcome its traditions of separateness to make Canadian nationhood and Canadian unity more than mere legal phrases. At the same time, the new dominion must acquire, keep and develop the west as part of its inheritance for future generations.

READINGS

Economic Disparity—The Real Source of Sectionalism?

The obvious cultural differences between Upper and Lower Canada, such as language and religion, have been regularly and correctly identified as sources of sectional loyalties and conflicts during the decade and a half before Confederation, and as problems that propelled the political leaders of the Province of Canada to find a more hospitable constitutional framework. A more subtle factor, economic disparity, has received much less attention from historians. In terms of sectional conflict, the Clear Grits and many other Upper Canadians were, essentially, protesting that equal representation in the Union was retarding the economic development of Canada West. Canada West was growing more rapidly in population, agriculture, industry, transportation and communications than Canada East. Canada West was producing more goods, services and taxes. But Canada East, it was felt, by demanding equal treatment in terms of government expenditure and by blocking reforms that Canada West deemed necessary, was actually draining the strength from the more ambitious and industrious half of the province even while it retarded Canada West's further growth.

Addressing the Reform Convention at Toronto in 1859, George Brown repeated his familiar charges against "French domination" in the Union and undoubtedly summarized the feelings of many Upper Canadians.

> What is it that has most galled the people of Upper Canada in the working of the existing Union? Has it not been the injustice done to Upper Canada in local and sectional matters? Has it not been the expenditure of Provincial funds for local purposes of Lower Canada which here are defrayed from local taxation? Has it not been the control exercised by Lower Canada over matters purely pertaining to Upper Canada—the framing of our School laws, the selection of our ministers, the appointment of our local officials? Has it not been that the minority of Upper Canada rule here through Lower Canada votes—that extravagant expenditures are voted by men who have not to provide the means—that fresh taxes are continually imposed by those who have not to pay them? . . .

The Globe, Toronto, 16 November, 1859

How valid were these economic, sectional complaints against the union? Statistics cannot, admittedly, portray accurately the full extent of economic disparity between the two Canadas; they are, however, undeniable indicators of an increasing gap in progress and productivity. By 1862, twelve of the sixteen railways and 880 of the 1030 miles of track in the province were concentrated in Canada West. Canada West had spent nearly $6.4 millions on roads since the Union, to Canada East's $1.9 millions. Similarly, the bulk of the province's telegraph lines and eleven of the sixteen branch lines were in Canada West. The following comments and tables suggest the same sectional disparity in the areas of population, agriculture and industry.

With the increase of population, and the love for the paternal roof, which distinguishes the *habitans* of Lower Canada, their farms have been again subdivided longitudinally, sometimes into three parts, or one arpent in breadth by thirty in depth, or in the proportion of 66⅔ yards broad to 2,000 long; and in the older seigneuries the ratio of breadth to length is not unfrequently as one is to sixty or 33⅓ yards broad to 2,000 yards long. These are some of the heirlooms of that old feudal system which sat like a huge incubus on Lower Canada, and whose depressing influence will long leave its mark on the energies and character of its people. . . .

The following table will show the progress made in Lower Canada [in agricultural production] between 1827 and 1852, a period of twenty-five years, and it will strikingly illustrate the fact that, ten years since, real improvement was scarcely visible in aggregate results, while in some instances a retrograde movement seems plainly discernible.—

Year	POPULATION	WHEAT Bushels.	OATS Bushels.	BARLEY Bushels.
1827,	471,876	2,931,240	2,341,529	363,117
1852,	890,261	3,073,943	8,977,380	494,766

	PEAS Bushels.	RYE Bushels.	INDIAN CORN Bushels.	POTATOES Bushels.
1827,	832,318	217,543	333,150	6,796,310
1852,	1,415,806	325,422	401,284	442,016

Year	HAY Tons	FLAX Pounds	HORSES	OXEN
1827,	1,228,067	731,696	140,432	145,012
1852,	755,579	1,189,018	184,620	112,128

	COWS	SHEEP	SWINE	AREA CULTIVATED —acres
1827,	260,015	829,122	241,735	2,946,565
1852,	295,552*	647,465	257,794	3,605,167

*183,972 calves or heifers not included under the head 'cows.'

The diminution of oxen and sheep is remarkable; the small increase in the production of wheat is probably owing to the "fly" [see below]. In two articles only do we recognize any advance commensurate with the increase of population in twenty-five years, viz., in oats and flax. The area under crop in 1827 was 1,002,198 acres, in 1852, 2,072,341 acres, or more than double, yet while the area under crop had doubled, the yield appears to have uniformly diminished, a fact strongly shown in the subjoined comparative table of average produce per acre in Upper and Lower Canada in 1852, according to the census of 1851—2:

	Upper Canada Bushels per acre	**Lower Canada** Bushels per acre
WHEAT	$16\frac{14}{60}$	$9\frac{50}{60}$
INDIAN CORN	$24\frac{4}{60}$	$18\frac{14}{60}$
RYE	$12\frac{17}{60}$	10
PEAS	$14\frac{16}{60}$	$9\frac{56}{60}$
OATS	$26\frac{19}{34}$	$20\frac{26}{34}$

In 1851—2, each person in Lower Canada cultivated 4 acres, 0 roods, 8 poles; in Upper Canada, 3 acres, 3 roods, 20 poles; and while each family in either section of the province had on an average 2 cows, in Upper Canada 53 pounds of butter per cow was produced, and in Lower Canada the quantity was only 33 pounds. With respect to cheese, the proportion was as $7\frac{1}{2}$ is to $1\frac{3}{4}$, or about 4 to 1 in favor of Upper Canada. . . .

In 1828, when the whole population of Upper Canada amounted to 185,500 inhabitants, the number of acres under agricultural improvement was 570,000, or about $3\frac{3}{16}$ for each individual; in 1851 the average for each inhabitant was very nearly four acres. The comparative progress of Upper and Lower Canada, in bringing the forest-clad wilderness into cultivation, may be inferred from the following table:

Year.	Lower Canada No. acres cultivated	Upper Canada No. acres cultivated
1831,	2,065,913	818,432
1844,	2,802,317	2,166,101
1851,	3,605,076	3,695,763

Hence, in a period of twenty years, Lower Canada increased her cultivated acres by 1.9 and Upper Canada by 4.5. . . .

AGRICULTURAL PRODUCTIONS.

WHEAT

Among farm products, wheat takes the first rank in the husbandry of Upper Canada. Formerly it occupied an equally prominent position in Lower Canada, but for many years this cereal has not been successfully cultivated in the eastern part of the province, in consequence of the Hessian fly, wheat midge, and an exhausting system of culture; it is now, however, slowly regaining its position in Lower Canada.

The following table shows the amount of wheat produced in Lower and Upper Canada in different years:

Lower Canada		Upper Canada	
Year.	Bushels of Wheat	Year.	Bushels of Wheat
1827,	2,931,240	1842,	3,221,991
1831,	3,404,756	1848,	7,558,773
1844,	942,835	1851,	12,674,503
1851,	3,045,600	1861,	24,620,425
1861,	———		

OATS

The total average of oats in Upper Canada was 34½ bushels per acre in 1859; in 1858 the average was only 32 bushels. In Lower Canada the returns show an average of 22½ bushels per acre.

BARLEY

The average return of this grain in Upper Canada is 27½ bushels to the acre; in Lower Canada it is 23 bushels.

H. W. Hind *et al*, *Eighty Years' Progress of British North America*. . . . (Toronto: L. Stebins, 1863), pp. 34, 35/6, 41, 52, 59.

SUMMARY

	Upper Canada	
	1851	1861
Land occupied	9,828,655	13,354,896
Land improved	3,705,523	6,051,609
Horses	201,670	377,681
Cattle	744,264	1,015,278
Sheep	967,168	1,170,225
Swine	571,496	776,001
Wheat, bushels	12,682,550	24,620,425
Oats, bushels	11,395,467	21,220,874
Farmers	86,224	132,064

	Lower Canada	
	1851	1861
Land occupied	8,113,408	10,375,418
Land improved	3,605,167	4,804,235
Horses	184,620	248,505
Cattle	591,652	816,972
Sheep	647,465	682,829
Swine	257,794	286,400
Wheat, bushels	3,073,943	2,654,354
Oats, bushels	8,977,380	17,551,296
Farmers	78,264	105,784

Canada Census, 1870-71, vol. IV (Ottawa, 1876), pp. 194/5, 220/1, 272/3, 320/1.

The following additional statistical tables are based on the Canadian census returns of 1851 and 1861. Note the marked difference in the number of steam mills and the number of employees in each part of the united province.

Saw Mills—1851-52

	TOTAL	EMPLOYEES
Upper Canada	1567	3670
Lower Canada	1065	n.a.

1860-61

	STEAM	WATER	EMPLOYEES
Upper Canada	305	689	7073
Lower Canada	26	634	4991

Grist Mills—1851-52

	TOTAL	EMPLOYEES
Upper Canada	692	1150
Lower Canada	541	n.a.

1860-61	STEAM	WATER	EMPLOYEES
Upper Canada	61	386	1630
Lower Canada	13	353	756

Woollen Mills—1851-52

	TOTAL	EMPLOYEES
Upper Canada	74	632
Lower Canada	18	n.a.
1860-61		
Upper Canada	85	615
Lower Canada	47	119

Foundries—1851-52

	TOTAL	EMPLOYEES
Upper Canada	97	925
Lower Canada	38	n.a.
1860-61		
Upper Canada	124	1601
Lower Canada	60	665

Canada Census, 1870-71, vol. IV (Ottawa, 1876), pp. 198/9, 218, 270/1, 313 315, 317.

The following table of occupations compiled from the Canadian census of 1860-61 provides further interesting comparisons in the relative economic development of the two sections of the Province of Canada. Of the thirty-four selected categories, Canada West ranks higher than Canada East in twenty-five. Significantly, Canada West leads in occupations connected with or stimulated by the new industrialism—blacksmiths, carpenters, coopers (men who make or repair barrels, casks, etc.) labourers, machinists, mechanics, railroad employees, saddlers and harness makers, and wagon and cart makers. Canada West also leads strikingly in "clergymen, priests, and ministers". The much higher proportion of men in the teaching profession in Canada West no doubt reflects secular influences in that section of the province. Similarly, Canada East's large number of "notaries" is a product of the nature of that section's legal system. Some interesting anomalies, such as the disparity in "boat and bateau men" and the much greater proportion in Canada East of "tailoresses" to "tailors", are difficult to explain. In comparing and contrasting these statistics it should be kept in mind that the populations of the sections as given in the 1860-61 census were as follows: Canada East, 1,111,566, Canada West, 1,396,091.

Occupations, 1861

	CANADA EAST	CANADA WEST
Advocates, Barristers, etc.	489	632
Blacksmiths	3,460	5,431
Boat and bateau men	2,816	68
Boot and shoe makers	4,916	6,270
Carpenters	7,291	9,866
Carters	2,999	604
Clergymen, Priests and Ministers	948	1,716
Clerks	4,717	4,262
Coopers	611	1,798
Dentists	32	114
Farmers	105,784	132,064
Fishermen	4,149	258
Grocers	725	1,010
Inn-keepers	225	1,568
Labourers	44,984	96,543
Lumbermen	3,815	4,114
Machinists	172	614
Manufacturers	82	253
Masons	1,099	1,650
Mechanics	377	700
Merchants	1,165	586
Millers	764	1,816
Notaries	571	32
Physicians and Surgeons	603	886
Railroad employees	307	855
Shopkeepers	2,407	3,661
Tailoresses	1,526	237
Tailors	833	2,739
Teachers, female	1,995	1,119
Teachers, male	957	2,956
Traders	1,312	168
Saddlers and harness-makers	467	1,152
Waggon and cart makers	364	1,509
Weavers	92	1,110

Census of the Canadas, 1860-61, vol. I (Quebec, 1863), pp. 534-575 *passim.*

The economics of sectionalism have not as yet been carefully examined by Canadian historians, but the main outlines of the problem were sketched by D. G. Creighton in a study prepared in 1939 for the Rowell-Sirois Commission, which was itself created to examine the economic disparity of Canadian federalism during the Great Depression.

. . . Canada, after the union of 1841, was in form a unitary state; in fact, it was an unacknowledged federal system; and the division of portfolios, moneys and parliamentary places between the people of Canada East and Canada West was the inevitable consequence of inward and fundamental social differences. Ministerial places were apportioned with fair equality between the members from the two sections of the Province. Certain government departments, such as that for education, were split into two distinct divisions, equipped with separate staffs and granted approximately equal appropriations. Legislation affecting one section of the Province only was passed at every session of the provincial parliament: and even when, as in setting up the Municipal Loan Funds, no essential differences of treatment were contemplated, separate statutes were often passed for Canada East and Canada West. Expenditures in one section of the Province could not go uncompensated by comparable expenditures in the other. On the extinction of the seigniorial tenure, by which the Province was committed to the payment of substantial sums, efforts had to be made to recompense the Eastern Township of Lower Canada and the Upper Canadian municipalities; and these indemnities increased the financial burdens of the Province and complicated its accounts, without really satisfying the demands of the western section.

These administrative difficulties, serious as they were, were only one aspect of a fundamental political problem. The political system of the time was suspended in uneasy balance; but the economic and social forces of the period threatened disequilibrium. The straining energies and ambitions of the western section of the Province could find no scope within the *de facto* federalism of the existing union; and the cultural interests of the eastern section were thought to be endangered by anything but a *de jure* unity. The demand of the Grit Party for representation by population, and the urgings of Canada West for expansion into the territories of the Hudson's Bay Company, were alike inadmissible for they would alike destroy that rough political equality by which alone the Union of 1841 had been made acceptable to the French. The social composition of the country seemed to necessitate a static political dualism; the economic ambitions of the St. Lawrence appeared to encourage an expanding political unity. It was certain that these two different though equally legitimate interests could not both find peaceful satisfaction within the existing political system. Burdened with debts, inhibited from expansion, and distracted by its sectional differences, the Province reached the end of its difficult and erratic course in the ministerial crisis of 1864.

D. G. Creighton, *British North America at Confederation: A Study Prepared for the Royal Commission on Dominion-Provincial Relations* (Ottawa: King's Printer, 1939), Appendix 2, p. 21.

BIBLIOGRAPHY

*INDICATES VOLUMES AVAILABLE IN PAPERBACK.

*Beck, J. M. (ed.). *Joseph Howe: Voice of Nova Scotia.* Carleton Library (McClelland and Stewart), 1964—a collection of Howe's writings and speeches.

*Burt, A. L. *Guy Carleton, Lord Dorchester, 1724-1808.* Canadian Historical Association Booklets, 1955—a brief study of Carleton's relationship to the Quebec Act.

———. *The Old Province of Quebec.* 2 vols. Carleton Library (McClelland and Stewart), 1968—a masterly analysis of Quebec between the Conquest and 1790.

*———. *The United States, Great Britain and British North America.* Ryerson, 1966—a classic study of international relations and colonial development from the American Revolution to the War of 1812 (reprint).

Campbell, Grace. *The North West Company.* Macmillan, 1957—a highly readable account of this romantic organization.

*Careless, J. M. S. *Brown of the Globe.* 2 vols. Macmillan, 1959, 1964—an outstanding biography of the journalist-politician.

———. *The Union of the Canadas, 1841-1857.* ("The Canadian Centenary Series," Vol. 10.) McClelland and Stewart, 1967—the most recent and most scholarly study of development in the Province of Canada.

Cornell, P. G. *The Alignment of Political Groups in Canada, 1841-1867.* University of Toronto Press, 1962—a scholarly analysis of voting patterns in parliament.

*———. *The Great Coalition.* Canadian Historical Association Booklets, 1966—analyzes the background of the Macdonald-Brown government formed in 1864.

Coupland, Sir Reginald. *The Quebec Act.* Oxford University Press, 1925—describes the Quebec Act as evidence of British statesmanship.

Cowan, H. I. *British Emigration to British North America, 1783-1837.* University of Toronto Press, 1961 (rev.)—an excellent study of population growth and policy.

*Craig, G. M. (ed.). *The Durham Report.* Carleton Library (McClelland and Stewart), 1963—an abridgement of the most famous document in Canadian history.

———. *Upper Canada: The Formative Years, 1784-1841.* ("The Canadian Centenary Series," Vol. 7.), McClelland and Stewart, 1963—an excellent survey of the period.

Creighton, D. G. *Empire of the St. Lawrence, 1760-1850.* Macmillan, 1956—a study of the commerical interests of the region as they influenced politics.

*————. *John A. Macdonald: The Young Politician.* 2 vols. Macmillan, 1952—superb biography of the founder of the Conservative party.
————. *The Road to Confederation.* Macmillan, 1964—a scholarly study of the Confederation movement in Canadian history.
*Dunham, Aileen. *Political Unrest in Upper Canada.* Carleton Library (McClelland and Stewart), 1963—a classic on its subject.
The Elgin-Grey Papers, 1846-1852. 4 vols. King's Printer, 1937—the most important documentary source on responsible government.
Fairley, Margaret (ed.). *The Selected Writings of William Lyon Mackenzie, 1824-1837.* Oxford University Press, 1960—a topical arrangement of Mackenzie's opinions drawn mostly from his newspaper editorials.
Gates, Lillian F. *Land Policies of Upper Canada.* University of Toronto Press, 1968—the most recent and authoritative study of the subject.
Gray, J. M. *Lord Selkirk of Red River.* Macmillan, 1963—concentrates on Selkirk's Canadian career.
Guillet, E. C. *Life and Times of the Patriots, 1837-1842.* Nelson, 1938—traces the aftermath of the rebellion in Upper Canada through the lives of participants.
*Hitsman, J. M. *The Incredible War of 1812.* University of Toronto Press, 1965—a narrative account of the war in North America.
*Innis, H. A. *The Fur Trade in Canada.* University of Toronto Press, 1964—later chapters deal with the fur trade after the British Conquest.
Kennedy, W. P. M. *Lord Elgin.* Oxford University Press, 1926—the best of several biographies of the Governor General who implemented responsible government.
Kerr, D. G. G., and Gibson, J. A. *Sir Edmund Head: A Scholarly Governor.* University of Toronto Press, 1954—treats particularly of Head's relation to Confederation.
*Kilbourn, William. *The Firebrand.* Clarke, Irwin, 1964—a penetrating interpretation of William Lyon Mackenzie.
*Landon, Fred. *Western Ontario and the American Frontier.* Carleton Library (McClelland and Stewart), 1967—a survey of social conditions in Upper Canada.
Longley, R. S. *Sir Francis Hincks.* University of Toronto Press, 1943—the best biography available on the subject.
MacKay, Douglas. *The Honourable Company: A History of the Hudson's Bay Company.* ("Canadian Best-Seller Library," No. 22.) McClelland and Stewart, 1966—the standard history of the Company.
MacNutt, W. S. *The Atlantic Provinces, 1712-1857.* ("The Canadian Centenary Series," Vol. 9.) McClelland and Stewart, 1965—a survey of regional development.
Manning, H. T. *The Revolt of French Canada, 1800-1835.* Macmillan, 1962—a scholarly analysis of Reformism and French-Canadian nationalism.
Martin, Chester. *Empire and Commonwealth.* Oxford University Press, 1928—Chapter 3 considers the Quebec Act as a threat to British liberties.
*Masters, D. C. *The Reciprocity Treaty of 1854.* Carleton Library (McClelland and Stewart), 1963—a scholarly study of an important event in Canadian economic history.
Moir, J. S. *Church and State in Canada West.* University of Toronto Press, 1959—religious issues in the Province of Canada.
Morton, W. L. *The Critical Years: The Union of British North America, 1857-1873.*

("The Canadian Centenary Series," Vol. 12.) McClelland and Stewart, 1964—survey of the Confederation era to the inclusion of Prince Edward Island.

*———. *The West and Confederation, 1857-1871.* Canadian Historical Association Booklets, 1958—outlines the role of the Canadian west in relation to the Confederation movement.

Neatby, Hilda. *Quebec, The Revolutionary Age, 1760-1791.* ("The Canadian Centenary Series," Vol. 6.) McClelland and Stewart, 1966—the most recent and comprehensive study of the period.

*New, Chester. *Lord Durham's Mission to Canada.* Carleton Library (McClelland and Stewart), 1963—extracted from New's distinguished biography of Lord Durham.

*Ouellet, Fernand. *L. J. Papineau.* Canadian Historical Association Booklets, 1960—a brief interpretive essay on Papineau's ideas.

Shortt, Adam. *Lord Sydenham.* ("Makers of Canada Series") Oxford University Press, 1926—the only modern biography of this important Governor General.

———, and Doughty, A. H. (eds.). *Documents Relating to the Constitutional History of Canada, 1759-1791.* 2 vols. King's Printer, 1918—the most complete collection available on this topic.

Sissons, C. B. *Egerton Ryerson, His Life and Letters.* 2 vols. Clarke, Irwin, 1937, 1947—the standard biography of this prominent leader in education and religion.

*Skelton, O. D. *Life and Times of Sir Alexander Tilloch Galt.* Carleton Library (McClelland and Stewart,) 1966—an abridgement of the standard biography written in 1920.

*Tucker, G. N. *The Canadian Commercial Revolution, 1846-1851.* Carleton Library (McClelland and Stewart), 1964—describes the impact of the end of the old colonial system.

*Wade, Mason. *The French Canadians,* 1760-1967. 2 vols. Macmillan, 1968—originally published in 1955, this is the only survey in English devoted specifically to this topic.

*Waite, P. B. *The Charlottetown Conference.* Canadian Historical Association Booklets, 1963—reconstruction of the events at this famous meeting.

*———. (ed.). *The Confederation Debates.* Carleton Library (McClelland and Stewart), 1963—abridgement of the debates on the 72 Resolutions in the Canadian Parliament.

*———. *The Life and Times of Confederation.* University of Toronto Press, 1963—an account of the three years before Confederation drawn from contemporary newspapers.

*——— (ed.). *Pre-Confederation.* ("Canadian Historical Documents Series," Vol. II.) Prentice-Hall, 1965—documents covering the period from the British Conquest to Confederation.

Wallace, W. S. *The Family Compact.* ("The Chronicles of Canada Series," Vol. 24.) Glasgow, Brook, 1915—a short and sympathetic account of this group's role in Canada's development.

———. *The United Empire Loyalists: A Chronicle of the Great Migration.* ("The Chronicles of Canada Series," Vol. 13.) Glasgow, Brook, 1914—brief, balanced, and highly readable.

*Whitelaw, W. M. *The Maritimes and Canada before Confederation*. Oxford University Press, 1966—describes the background of British North American Confederation.

*———. *The Quebec Conference*. Canadian Historical Association Booklets, 1966—background and work of the meeting which formulated the 72 Resolutions.

Wilson, Alan. *The Clergy Reserves of Upper Canada*. University of Toronto Press, 1968—deals primarily with the administrative history of the Reserves.

Wilson, G. E. *The Life of Robert Baldwin*. Ryerson, 1933—the only separate study of Baldwin.

Winks, Robin. *Canada and the United States: The Civil War Years*. Johns Hopkins Press, 1960—examines the role of the United States as a factor in Confederation.

Zaslow, Morris (ed.). *The Defended Border*. Macmillan, 1964—a collection of reprinted essays dealing with the War of 1812 in Upper Canada.

3

CREATING A NEW NATION

CHAPTER 9

A NEW DOMINION

Happy throngs celebrated Canada's birth on 1 July, 1867, but they were celebrating only a legal fact. The Dominion of Canada existed as a political entity, not as a social or economic unit. In addition, most of British North America still lay outside the boundaries of the new dominion.

For Macdonald, Confederation had created problems as great or greater than those it was expected to solve. The first and most pressing requirement was to put the machinery of the new government into operation—to breathe political life into the constitutional framework, to reconcile divergent views within the new nation, to drive the disparate elements in "double harness." Macdonald's next task was to realize his vision of a British nation in a state stretching from the Atlantic to the Pacific, incorporating the still unfederated colonies in the east and the vast, empty lands west of the Great Lakes. When these aims were achieved—and not before—Canada would be able to face the challenge of nationhood.

THE FORMATION OF PARTIES

From 1865 until Confederation, Narcisse Belleau had been titular prime minister of the Province of Canada, but John A. Macdonald had wielded the real power and had been the moving force in Confederation. Even before Confederation was officially proclaimed, it was obvious that Macdonald had won for himself the right to form the first government of the dominion. In the words of one of his friends, Macdonald would only be putting "the topstone on the dominion of which you have been the artificer-in-chief." So it was that on 24 May, the Queen's Birthday, Governor General Viscount Monck asked Macdonald to form a government. His cabinet, Macdonald decided, would be federalized like the Senate:

I do not want it to be felt by any section of the country that they have no representatives in the Cabinet, and no influence in the Government.

Then, as now, the choice of cabinet ministers posed a four-dimensional problem—political, racial, religious and regional.

This view of Ottawa by Notman in 1872 demonstrates clearly the two dominant preoccupations of the city. Lumber barges are loaded in the foreground, while the still incomplete Parliament Buildings can be seen in the background.

But the "cabinet maker" set to work again, this time with even more difficult pieces of lumber to put together.

The government put together by Macdonald in 1867 included seven Conservatives and six Reformers. Ten of these men were Fathers of Confederation. Five of them came from Ontario, four from Quebec and two each from Nova Scotia and New Brunswick, thereby giving regional representation roughly in proportion to population. Five of the thirteen ministers were senators, two being from Ontario and one from each of the other provinces. Having adroitly met the demands of regionalism, Macdonald had also managed to give due attention to political opinion. In fact, he had succeeded in creating a government representing the major political factions—a government of no party. It was true that at the moment there were no issues and therefore no reasons for parties, but issues would soon arise and when they did party organization would follow.

On 22 May, seventy-two senators were appointed by proclamation, half of them being Reformers and half of them Conservatives. On that day also Monck announced his own appointment as governor general of the new dominion. Then, just before noon on 1 July, in the Privy Council Chamber of the Parliament Buildings (which were still under construction) the Governor General, judges and members of the administration were sworn into office. The Governor General surprised the august gathering by announcing honours bestowed by the Queen upon her Canadian ministers. John A. Macdonald became a Knight Commander of the Bath, while Cartier, Galt, McDougall, Howland, Tilley and Tupper were each made a Companion of the Bath for their share in bringing about Confederation. Cartier and Galt refused the proffered honours. Cartier, in particular, felt entitled to equal distinction with Macdonald; after all, his Lower Canada majorities had made Confederation possible and had kept Macdonald in office. The rift between the two was only partially closed a year later when Cartier was given a baronetcy, an honour greater than that of Macdonald.

Four days before the dominion of Canada came into existence, the Reform party held a convention in Toronto where Howland and McDougall repeated Macdonald's dictum that a new era was dawning and that old party lines were no longer relevant. For such intrepid realism, George Brown, whose influence was still strong, managed to have the two men read out of the party. This action, however, only evaded the basic question raised by Howland and McDougall—what alternative policies could the Reformers offer to the people of Canada that would justify their existence as a separate political party? Their problem was that Macdonald's coalition platform embraced all policies that would benefit the new dominion. Therefore, if Reform was to become a national party, the only possible strategy was to seek the votes of the anti-Confederationists. But this left the Reformers facing a dilemma, for they had been among the strongest proponents of Confederation.

The first general election proved the strength of Macdonald's coalition and the bankruptcy in policy of Reform. In Ontario (formerly a Reform stronghold) Confederation was endorsed and George Brown was personally defeated. The Reform party, already without a programme, now found itself leaderless. In the new parliament, where Macdonald's coalition held 100 of the 181 seats and controlled all the patronage, the Reformers were disorganized and internally divided. Their ranks included such old Reformers as the cultured A. A. Dorion, the inflexible Alexander Mackenzie (a stonemason turned journalist and politician), P. J. O. Chauveau, John Sandfield Macdonald and the volatile Joseph Howe, who led the Nova Scotia "antis." A newcomer to Reform ranks was the stocky Edward Blake, only thirty-four years old but already the leading equity lawyer of Ontario and destined to be a premier of that province. Blake and Mackenzie were strong contenders to succeed Brown as leader, and, of the two, Blake certainly had greater intellectual powers. But Blake was very like that other great Reformer, Robert Baldwin—oversensitive, high-principled, cautious and honest, but at times tactless and cold, incapable of inspiring the personal loyalty that political leadership demands.

Macdonald had asked the Canadian people to give his government a "fair trial," and George Brown advised Mackenzie to follow a "quiescent" policy. "Give (the government) the full length of their tether and they will soon quarrel." Mackenzie, however, found it hard to be a member of an opposition that did not oppose. The main political objectives of the Reformers were a new reciprocity treaty with the United States and George Brown's old dream of westward expansion. But the only real bond of agreement among the opponents of the government was mistrust of the administration. Maritimers felt they had been sold out at Confederation; the *Rouges* feared the loss of French-Canadian identity in the larger English-speaking nation, and the Grits of Ontario had good reason to consider Macdonald a slippery and dishonest customer.

Although Confederation was now an accomplished fact, opinion was by no means universally behind the new federation or its first government. For some time before 1867 it had been obvious that considerable antagonism to Confederation still existed. In Quebec the *Rouges* had opposed Confederation, preferring annexation to the United States. Even in Ontario, where approval was almost unanimous, George Brown's *Globe* had denounced W. T. Howland and William McDougall as political traitors for joining Macdonald's coalition. The seat of strongest anti-Confederation feeling, though, was in the Maritimes, particularly in Nova Scotia. Denouncing the means by which Confederation had been imposed and demanding repeal of the union, Joseph Howe had assumed the leadership of the "antis." Their success in the general election was almost complete, for Dr. Tupper was the only coalitionist elected from Nova Scotia; the other eighteen provincial seats were taken by Howe's followers.

Sir John viewed developments in Nova Scotia with concern lest Howe's demand for the repeal of Confederation meet with British approval and thereby threaten the very existence of his young dominion. Macdonald's overriding objectives remained the consolidation of national unity and the expansion of the new nation from sea to sea by the absorption of the North-West and all other British North American colonies. The federal government therefore proclaimed its intention of pushing on with its program of nation-building—especially the promised inter-colonial railway, which was probably the one, universally acceptable aspect of Confederation in the Maritime provinces.

The funeral procession in Montreal of D'Arcy McGee as shown in The Illustrated London News. *Early in his life McGee was a passionate Irish nationalist, but he later became an eloquent supporter of the concepts of Canadian nationhood and the British connection. He was assassinated on 7 April, 1868 by a Fenian on the steps of his Ottawa boarding house, after returning from the House of Commons.*

But Joseph Howe continued his attempts to take Nova Scotia out of Confederation. The compensation for loss of certain provincial tax sources had been, he said, only "eighty cents per head, the price of a Nova Scotian as well as a sheep." Howe now set off with a delegation to London, where he hoped to gain the support of imperial authorities for repeal.

By the time parliament met in 1868, the route of the intercolonial railway was still undecided, and although Dr. Tupper had gone to London to oppose Howe's demands for repeal, no positive policy to settle the grievances of Nova Scotia was in evidence. By July, 1868, Joseph Howe was back from London, where his appeals had failed to gain approval. The British government had refused to consider any move that might endanger Confederation. Howe now began to demand "better terms" for Nova Scotia.

It was Macdonald who opened the way for negotiations by personally going to Halifax. Howe warned the "antis" against useless demonstrations. "If we have lost our constitution, let us preserve our manners." After a private chat, neither Howe nor Macdonald would make any public statement. Rumours were rife that "Old Man Eloquent" had been bought by Macdonald and was "going to Ottawa." Indeed, Macdonald did intend to have Howe in his government, but it took many months and many letters to persuade the disillusioned "Bluenose." Howe's reluctant surrender and "better terms" for Nova Scotia came early in 1869 through the adroit management of Macdonald. Howe was made President of the Council in Macdonald's government and, soon after, Secretary of State for the Provinces. When the new Governor General, Sir John Young (later Lord Lisgar) opened parliament, he announced the "better terms" for Nova Scotia: the federal government assumed an additional $2,000,000 of the province's debt and would grant an annual subsidy of $82,698 to the province for ten years retroactive to 1 July, 1867.

CANADA'S WESTERN HERITAGE

For almost half a century after the Hudson's Bay Company absorbed the Montreal-based North West Company (1821), there was little contact between the Red River settlement and the British colonies in the east. In 1836 Lord Selkirk's son sold his interest in the settlement to the "Bay," and for the next thirty years Rupert's Land and the North-West Territories continued under the quiet, efficient management of the Company. But the great western plains, though separated from the busy St. Lawrence basin by the rugged Canadian Shield, were not forgotten in the east. As the good farming land south of the Shield filled up with settlers, Canadians looked westward for new land. Since the American frontier of settlement had now reached the political boundaries of the United States, little good land remained unoccupied in that country. By the late 1850's most Upper Canadians were agreed that the acquisition of the

North-West was an economic necessity, and one that could not be long delayed.

The North-West was composed of the northern reaches of the continent, including the Hudson Bay basin, the prairies and thousands of miles of muskeg and tundra stretching still farther north and west up to and beyond the Arctic circle. Its few thousand inhabitants were Indians or Métis, the half-breed descendents of Indian women and French or Scottish fur traders, who combined the endurance and initiative of the Indian with the physical strength and perseverance of the European. The Métis were devout Roman Catholics and intensely aware of their racial identity. The buffalo hunt was their main occupation, followed by trading and farming. Métis settlement, small as it was, centred around the Red and Assiniboine rivers and the Hudson's Bay post at Fort Garry. There the influential Roman Catholic bishop, Alexandre Taché, had his cathedral, and from there a governor and council appointed by the Company to represent the various racial, religious and economic interests of Assiniboia (as the Red River colony was known) ruled the North-West.

Since 1858 the annexation of western lands had been a plank of the Clear Grit platform. But covetous American eyes were also watching the northern portion of the great plains. In 1866 Congress had considered a bill for the admission of all British North American territories into the United States, and in 1867 Secretary of State Seward had arranged the purchase of Alaska as a "flank movement" to forestall westward expansion by Canada. In the words of the New York *Tribune*, British North America would soon be "a hostile Cockney with a watchful Yankee on each side of him."

In view of the strained Anglo-American relations during the Civil War, Macdonald had looked upon the North-West primarily as a strategic area:

> If Canada is to remain a country separate from the United States, it is of great importance to her that they should not get behind us by right or force, and intercept the route to the Pacific. . . .

"The Situation," a political cartoon on the entry of Manitoba into Confederation.

Two years later, in 1869, Macdonald saw the economic value of the North-West, which the Grits had stressed:

The rapid march of events and the increase of population on this continent, will compel England and Canada to come to some arrangement respecting this immense country.

"Some arrangement" had been a long time in the making. For years the Hudson's Bay Company had striven to exclude the colonists who would inevitably drive out fur-bearing animals. In 1857 the Province of Canada had challenged the validity of the Hudson's Bay Company territorial rights in the North-West under the charter granted in 1670. The British government of the time was sympathetic, but legal procedures and three-sided negotiations between the Company, the Colonial Office and the Province of Canada delayed any solution until after 1865. But Canada's whole attention was by then concentrated on the Confederation scheme, and it was December, 1867, before the

Bishop A. A. Taché (left), and William McDougall.

new dominion took up the matter of negotiating for the North-West once more.

In July, 1868, the imperial parliament passed the Rupert's Land Act, which authorized the Crown to act as middleman in the transfer of the North-West to the dominion. Three months later Sir George Cartier and William McDougall, the former Grit, arrived in London as Canada's delegates. After months of haggling, the terms were finally settled. Canada would pay £300,000 for the Company's rights and privileges, but the Company would retain its posts, the right to trade and one-twentieth of all fertile land. 1 December, 1869, was fixed as the date of transfer of the North-West.

In recognition of his interest and efforts, William McDougall was appointed first lieutenant-governor of the North-West. He left for the west in September, 1869, in order to be in Assiniboia before the transfer took place. About the end of October McDougall reached Pembina, on the northern Minnesota border. To his utter astonishment he was met by a messenger from the "National Committee of the Métis of the Red River" with the order "de ne pas entrer sur le Territoire du Nord-Ouest sans une permission spéciale de ce Comité." This ultimatum, barring the Lieutenant-Governor from his jurisdiction, was signed by the president of the "National Committee," John Bruce, and by its secretary, Louis Riel.

What had inspired the Métis to set up an *ad hoc* government utterly disregarding the treaty between Canada and the Hudson's Bay Company? The causes were many and varied. For twenty years the Métis had been gaining a larger voice in the Council of Assiniboia, and this power had reinforced their convictions that they were *La Nation Métisse*, a racially distinct people with a God-given right to determine their own destiny free of outside interference from the Company, the United States or Canada. The Métis were sure that Canadian authority in Assiniboia would inevitably be followed by Canadian settlers with democratic, anti-French and anti-clerical ideas, and that the whole

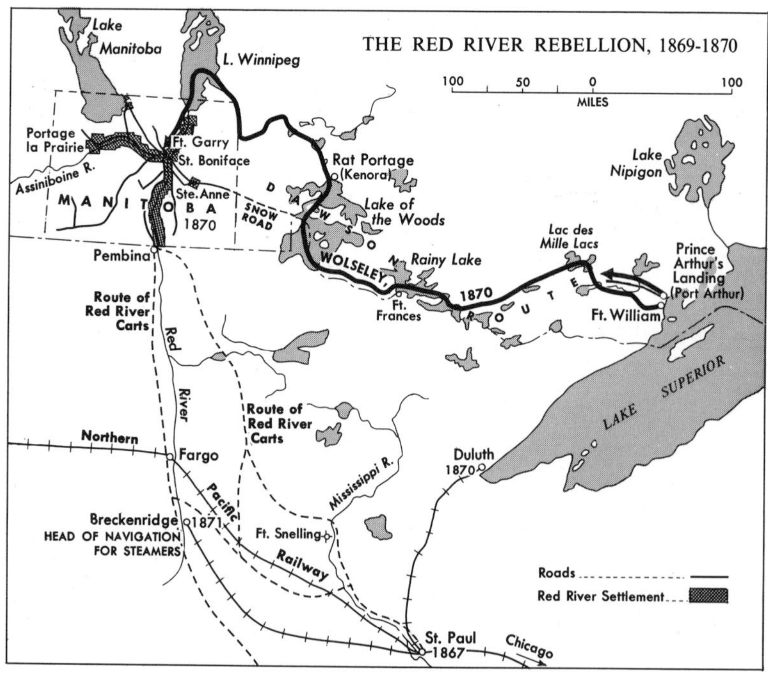

Métis way of life—economic and cultural—would be destroyed. Nor did this threat appear suddenly in the Red River valley. Since 1860 a small "Canadian party," led by an ambitious, young Kingston doctor, John Christian Schultz, had been loudly advocating transfer of authority from the weakening grasp of the Hudson's Bay Company to the Province of Canada. So far, however, recurrent droughts during the sixties had slowed the economic tempo of the settlement and had discouraged any large-scale migration from the Canadas. As long as the area was isolated from the aggressive easterners, Canadian or American, the Métis had felt secure. But the decline of the buffalo herds, the booming development of nearby Minnesota, the breakdown of Company rule, Canadian plans for a railway and telegraph to British Columbia, and Dr. Schultz's speeches had aroused deep fears among the Métis. To add to their troubles, a plague of locusts devastated the crops in 1867 and threatened the inhabitants of Assiniboia with starvation. "Within the whole colony not one bushel will be harvested," wrote Bishop Taché. Close on the heels of the locusts came a Canadian construction outfit to build a road from the Lake of the Woods to the Red River. These Canadians, especially Charles Mair, a poet and writer, proceeded by bad manners to make themselves extremely unpopular.

What finally broke Métis patience was the question of land ownership. About 90 percent of the settled population had no legal proof of ownership of their land. When a Canadian surveyor, Colonel J. S. Dennis, began laying out prospective farms, the Métis were not given an explanation of his activities. This, coupled with the news of McDougall's imminent arrival, alarmed the Métis, who then established a "National Committee" and declared a "Bill of Rights." With Bishop Taché in Rome and Governor William MacTavish ill, the Métis encountered no opposition when they occupied Fort Garry, the strategic and geographic centre of the settlement.

Who was to blame? The Company had apparently deliberately kept the Métis ignorant of the transfer of ownership. The Macdonald government had turned a deaf (and uncivil) ear to the warnings of the Right Reverend Robert Machray, Anglican

Bishop of Rupert's Land, and to those of Governor MacTavish. In addition, the choice of the haughty McDougall as lieutenant-governor proved unfortunate. Still at Pembina, McDougall issued a peremptory proclamation asserting his authority in the North-West and calling on all loyal elements for support. This, of course, did nothing to soothe Métis fears. Macdonald unfairly blamed all the Red River trouble on Colonel Dennis and Lieutenant-Governor McDougall:

The two together have done their utmost to destroy our chance of an amicable settlement with these wild people.

But personalities were only the occasion, not the cause, of conflict. Nor were "these wild people" merely factious French-Canadian nationalists. They had legitimate grievances, and their

A Notman photograph of a Red River cart and a Métis camp.

opinions and wishes as to a territorial transfer had been ignored from start to finish.

The quixotic Riel, now President of the National Committee, had the support of all but the Canadian party in the settlement. A convention drew up a new "List of Rights" to be sent to Ottawa and established a "Provincial Government" with Riel as president. The new "government" hailed its creation on 9 February, 1870, by setting off fireworks originally purchased by the Canadian party to welcome McDougall.

Louis Riel was at this time twenty-five years old, tall, bearded and imposing, the son of a Métis. Sent to Montreal by Bishop Taché to be trained as a priest, his egotism and lack of humility had soon disqualified him for any such training. While in Montreal, however, Riel had drunk deeply of political ideas in ferment in the early 1860's. Indeed, he was much more attracted by politics than by religion. Handsome, educated, eloquent in both French and English, devoted to the cause of the Métis, Riel was a natural leader of insurrection. His position in the Red River was unquestioned, but he soon undid his success by resorting to violence. Fearing an attack by the Canadian party, Riel seized his leading opponents and proceeded to try one of them, Thomas Scott, an Ontario Orangeman, on charges of disorderly conduct, insubordination and open opposition. Scott was executed by a Métis firing squad. This "barbarous murder" by a "sham court," as Macdonald rightly described it, came close to lynching, an opinion strongly supported by Riel's admission that he had intended to make an example of Scott— "We must make Canada respect us."

Five days after Scott's execution Bishop Taché returned to the settlement from Rome, where he had been attending the first Vatican Council, intent on restoring peace. But irremediable damage had been done to the Métis cause. Although the execution had caused little excitement along the Red River, Protestant, Orange Ontario was howling for revenge, and Macdonald was on the horns of the old racial-religious dilemma that had rocked the Province of Canada in the fifties. To punish Riel would unite all French Canada against a "Protestant-dominated Government"; to ignore the "murder" would convince Orange Ontario voters that the government was protecting French Roman Catholic killers. Under such circumstances Macdonald played for time.

Meanwhile, the Métis delegates had carried their "List of Rights" to Ottawa and had seen most of their demands incorporated in the Manitoba Act of 1870. Assiniboia became the Province of Manitoba, with responsible government; French and English were declared official languages; local customs were to be preserved; treaties were to be made with the Indians; and financial aid was to be granted the new province. A general amnesty for the "rebels" was promised (verbally). On 15 July, 1870, Manitoba became the fifth province of Canada, the first Lieutenant-Governor being A. G. Archibald, a Nova Scotian and a Father of Confederation.

The creation of Manitoba did nothing to erase Ontario's anger over Scott's "martyrdom." (The Manitoba delegates to Ottawa had been arrested by Ontario authorities for complicity in his death and then released for lack of evidence.) Two militia battalions and a detachment of British regulars under Sir Garnet Wolseley were despatched by Macdonald in May to give Archibald's administration armed support and, incidentally, to muffle Ontario's demands for vengeance. Three months later, after an exhausting trip through the wilderness of forest and water between Ottawa and the Red River, Wolseley's force entered Fort Garry on 24 August, only to find it abandoned. Louis Riel had fled.

Was Louis Riel a patriot or a rebel, a hero or a murderer? He had gained provincial status for his people, but he had done nothing to stop the westward march of settlement. He had preserved the west as Canadian territory by rejecting American overtures for annexation, but he had severely strained the unity that Canada so badly needed. He had virtually destroyed the coalition of nation-builders in Ottawa. Anti-Orange, anti-Protestant feeling in Quebec now answered the anti-French, anti-Catholic agitation in Ontario. Riel had given the Liberals (as the Reformers were now being called sometimes) a cause round which to rally and a bludgeon with which to beat Macdonald and smash his bi-racial, bipartisan political machine.

FROM SEA TO SEA

One thousand miles west of the Red River, beyond the almost impassible ranges of the Cordillera, the Crown Colony of British Columbia had not shared in the many activities that culminated in Confederation. British Columbia's life in the first half of the nineteenth century had been entirely wrapped up in the fur trade of the Hudson's Bay Company, and no settlement had occurred. Vancouver Island had indisputably became British Territory by the Oregon Treaty of 1846, and in 1849 it had been made a Crown Colony. But the Hudson's Bay Company had so discouraged colonization that as late as 1851 there were scarcely thirty settlers in the island colony, and none on the mainland. When Vancouver Island was given a legislative assembly in 1856, the colony still had less than 800 settlers. However, the discovery of gold along the Fraser River in 1858 changed this situation almost overnight. When twenty-five thousand people, mostly Americans, rushed in to join the search for gold, the mainland area was made into the separate colony of British Columbia. James Douglas, Governor of Vancouver Island, became Governor of British Columbia as well.

Douglas took immediate steps to preserve British sovereignty from American encroachment and to develop the colony. Law and order were imposed on the wild elements who scrabbled and fought for gold on the mainland; New Westminster, a by-product of the gold rush, became the capital. The Cariboo Road was built between 1862 and 1865 through 480 miles of difficult terrain, connecting Fort Yale on the lower Fraser and Barkerville in the Cariboo. Farming, fishing and lumbering activities began to develop, although both Vancouver Island and British Columbia still depended heavily on gold mining for government revenue. In 1866, two years after Governor Douglas retired, Vancouver Island was reunited with the mainland in a move to reduce administrative costs. After 1868 the capital of British Columbia was permanently established at Victoria.

As early as March, 1867, an eccentric democrat, William Alexander Smith, was proposing federation with Canada. Nova Scotian by birth, a gold miner, peripatetic journalist and politician by profession, he blandly assumed the name Amor de Cosmos (very freely translated as Lover of the World). He moved a resolution in the British Columbia assembly for the inclusion of the colony in the terms of the British North America Act. The Colonial Office felt, however, that consideration of the subject must await conclusion of the negotiations for transfer of the North-West to Canada. There the matter rested officially.

By now the young colony had plenty of settlers, many of whom were American-born and naturally favoured union with the United States—a cause being actively promoted by interested parties in the Pacific Coast states. The United States had purchased Alaska from Russia in 1867, and the acquisition of British Columbia would shut the young dominion off from the Pacific. If British Columbia were to continue British, it had to develop closer political and economic ties within the empire. The desirable political solution was federation with Canada. But what was politically desirable was physically unobtainable because of the barriers of uninhabited mountains, prairies and rocky Shield. In the cold light of reason, federation seemed an almost laughable ambition.

Governor Anthony Musgrave, an intelligent man with experience in other colonies (including Newfoundland), arrived in Victoria in 1869 with instructions to promote British

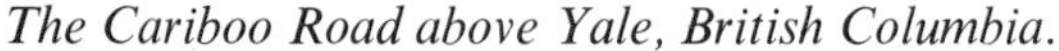

The Cariboo Road above Yale, British Columbia.

Columbia's union with Canada. Upon arrival Musgrave found three rival groups: the American minority that favoured annexation to the United States; British Columbians who saw in Confederation greater opportunity and a chance to throw off British control; and officials of the government and the Hudson's Bay Company—the "Crown Colony clique"—who deplored any change in the colony's status. Indeed, the absence of responsible government in the colony was producing the same type of friction that had been generated by the entrenched compacts in the east two generations before.

When the British Columbia legislature met in 1870, a resolution for union with Canada was debated at great length. The politicians were practical, not sentimental; they wanted to see concrete advantages from such an important move. Musgrave realized that a railway to the east was a *sine qua non* if federation with Canada was to be more than a legal instrument. In addition, British Columbia's debt would have to be wiped out and Canada's financial resources would have to be made available for public works in the province. These terms were unanimously approved by the legislature and were carried by a delegation to Ottawa, where an anxious Macdonald viewed with pleasure the prospects for his vision of a truly transcontinental union.

The main street of Barkerville, British Columbia, in the 1860's. The town was the terminus of the Cariboo Road and a typical gold rush community.

The final terms agreed upon for British Columbia's entry into Confederation included the liquidation of the million-dollar debt of the colony, establishment of a responsible government, and the construction of a transcontinental railway, the line to be begun in two years and completed within ten. These generous terms for union were promised by Macdonald's ambitious government, though opposed by the federal Reformers (and some Conservatives) as being too heavy a burden for the young dominion to undertake. For that matter, some British Columbians complained that their colony had become a "conquered country" to satisfy the greed of certain Canadian and British Columbian politicians. Nevertheless, on 20 July, 1871, British Columbia became the sixth province in the dominion amid general rejoicing.

The provincial constitution, which was modelled on that of Ontario, seemed too elaborate in view of the small population—"an elephant to drag a dog cart," as one politician described it. But full provincial status was a small price for Canada to pay for a foothold on the Pacific coast. British Columbia's problems now became Canada's problems; provincial deficits continued to pile up, and the transcontinental railway seemed agonizingly slow in starting. By 1874 British Columbians were asking aloud if Canada ever intended to fulfill its railway promises and if Confederation had not really been a great sell-out. The complaint was but one more in the loud chorus beginning to be heard across the land, proclaiming the sins of centralization at Ottawa and the virtues of provincial rights.

THE NEW DOMINION AND ITS PEOPLE

By 1871 tremendous changes had occurred in British North America in terms of population, economy, communication and its way of life, especially since 1860. The census of 1871 showed a total population in the six provinces of a little over 3.5 million people, of whom three-quarters lived in the central provinces of Quebec and Ontario. The population was still largely confined to French-speaking and English-speaking persons, though the

English now outnumbered the French by two to one. As her resources were exploited, Ontario was rapidly outstripping Quebec in development. The Maritime provinces had, in many respects, reached a high mark in their growth and were soon to be beset by major economic dislocations. West of the St. Lawrence basin, Manitoba was just freeing itself from the restraints imposed by the fur trade. The prairies were virtually untouched, and British Columbia was only in a pioneer boom stage induced by the recent gold rush.

The most significant factors changing the face of Canada had been an increased population and the use of steam power. Aside from the massive immigration from Britain during the 1840's and early 1850's the spectacular population growth of 1.2 million between 1851 and 1871 was due to a high birth rate—in Ontario four times as high as the death rate, and in Quebec three times as high. The second factor, the application of steam power, also brought decisive changes in nearly every aspect of life by 1871. Steam engines drove the wheels for sawmills and flour mills, and powered a variety of manufacturing industries. Steam-powered ships had reduced the transatlantic trip from several weeks to a mere ten days and had made Montreal the main seaport in the country. Woodburning railway engines rattled over more than 2,000 miles of track in central Canada and some 400 miles in the Maritime provinces. The railways transported the produce of field, forest and factory to distribution and export centres, brought a variety of manufactures to the farmer and drew urban and rural dwellers closer together into a more recognizable modern society.

The face of the country was changing, too, in other ways. Industry was concentrating in areas where raw materials, labour and transportation were available, and Canada was becoming urbanized. By 1871 Toronto boasted 56,000 persons and Montreal almost twice as many; villages that had once been mere distribution centres were growing into towns that produced export goods.

Available capital was the key to economic growth, and after Confederation this growth became more and more concentrated in the St. Lawrence basin. The industrial and commercial

Montreal in 1863. It was only after 1853 that Montreal became a trans-Atlantic shipping centre. Previously, the undeveloped channel above Quebec City had been too dangerous for ships of large draught to navigate.

revolution occurring in Ontario and Quebec between 1850 and 1870 involved family industries, as opposed to joint-stock companies, but at the time of Confederation these two provinces had nineteen banks when Nova Scotia had only six, New Brunswick four, British Columbia one and Manitoba none. In the decade after Confederation twenty-one Canadian banks were chartered, fifteen of them in Ontario and Quebec. The terms of the Federal Bank Act of 1871, introduced by Sir Francis Hincks, encouraged the concentration of capital in a few financial institutions.

In the fifties and sixties trade unions had been organized among skilled labourers. The unions were small and localized and as much concerned with benevolence to members as with raising wages, reducing working hours or improving working conditions. By 1870 they embraced some twenty trades with

5,000 members in Ontario and in Quebec. Being essentially craft guilds to regulate their own occupations, these unions were not interested in other unions, nor in unorganized or unskilled labour. In 1870 they had a six-day work week and their only immediate objective was a nine-hour day. Although American in their style of organization, the Canadian unions were more strongly influenced in their attitudes by British trade union practices. They preferred arbitration to the strike. In the words of the first president of the Canadian Labour Union, their aim was to present an image of themselves as "honest, earnest, prudent workers." This essential conservatism of early Canadian trade unionism militated against its becoming an effective force on the industrial scene.

The countryside of every province was now dotted with elementary schools to which children, books and lunchpails in hand, trudged miles every day to be drilled in the three R's and some geography. Virtually all children spent five or six years in elementary school, but attendance was irregular, for chores at home had first call on children's time. Secondary school systems had been slow to develop because secondary education was specifically intended to prepare the student for university. Each province had several universities, usually under church control. The most frequent criticism of the universities was that they were too numerous for such a small population, few of whom even progressed beyond elementary school. The universities prepared men for the ministry, for medicine and for law; modern science was just appearing in the curricula, and such professional studies as engineering, business management or journalism had yet to be inaugurated. At a humbler level, the Mechanics' Institute movement through evening classes and lectures brought from Britain the ideal of self-help for working men. The Mechanics' Institute, with its meeting-hall and lending library, was a local centre for enlightenment and culture in every town of any importance in the dominion.

Canadians in 1871 were, if anything, more church-going than in the pioneer period. But the churches themselves had changed. As members grew wealthier, the log or board church was replaced by a massive structure of stone or brick, and church services became more formal. Confederation had inspired the union of most of the Methodist denominations in 1874 and of all the Presbyterian churches in 1875. In the Canada of 1871 Roman Catholic adherents now comprised only 40 percent of the population, the Methodists and Presbyterians each 17 percent and the Church of England 14 percent.

The indigenous cultural life of the new dominion was still in its infancy. Canadians looked to Britain, and to a lesser extent to the United States, for both inspiration and material in all the arts. Confederation stimulated the production of literature, and successful magazines were now appearing in every province. Among English-speaking Canadians, novels, dramas and poems inspired by Canadian nationalism were slower to appear, the earliest important writer being Sir Charles G. D. Roberts. Not until the 1890's was he joined by other authors who could claim even national recognition. The Nova Scotian humourist, T. C. Haliburton, had no worthy successor until Stephen Leacock in the twentieth century. The field of drama was also empty until the twentieth century. In French Canada, however, a succession of historians, novelists and poets fostered a distinct literary tradition, although their works were too exclusively concerned with the ethnic and cultural survival of French Canada to gain more than regional attention.

In the field of painting there were a number of artists besides the well-known Cornelius Krieghoff, but only Paul Kane, still valued for his studies of the Indians, achieved international recognition. Except for Madame Emma Albani, who made her singing debut in London in 1872, no Canadian musician, performer or composer attracted attention at home or abroad until the end of the Victorian era. Canadians were generally content to be entertained by barnstorming "road shows" that brought prominent British and American stars to the larger Canadian communities.

Canada in 1871 may have been a cultural backwater, but in every other respect it was a beehive of activity. Every day of the week except Sunday her many small towns resounded to the hoofbeats of horses drawing produce from farm to railway, and manufactured goods from warehouse to store. The board side-

In addition to the more commonly acknowledged arts of the day, photography was beginning to make a place for itself in the latter half of the nineteenth century. One of the most outstanding Canadian practitioners of this new art was William Notman, who settled in Montreal in 1856. He established a studio catering to a clientele that included many of Canada's most prominent political and social figures. Notman also travelled widely in Canada, recording on fragile glass negatives many invaluable details of life in the new nation. Notman's photographs frequently combine great historic value with artistic merit, as can be seen in these views of lumbering in Canada, one of his favourite subjects. Above is an 1872 photograph of a timber cove near Quebec City. Below, an 1871 view (left) shows trees being hauled in the Ottawa valley. Another photograph from 1872 shows timber being loaded at Quebec City for export.

walks echoed the tread of lawyers, doctors and tradesmen of an energetic community. Black smoke belched from the chimney of the blacksmith's shop, the local sawmill or gristmill, foundry or carriage factory. Ladies examined the latest imported fashions and materials at the merchants' long counters, while their husbands chatted and waited in the crowded post office to receive their letters and newspapers. The rattling trains rapidly transported Canadians (with as much comfort as the era could provide) to visit distant relatives or to meet business associates. Well-to-do citizens in stiff collars or bustled dresses embarked at Montreal on the luxuriously appointed steamships to fulfill that educational and social necessity, the "Grand Tour." Farm, forest and fishery mirrored the intense activity of a people who fervently believed Confederation had made them a new nation with unlimited opportunities for material progress.

* * *

The years immediately following Confederation witnessed the completion of the first stage of Canada's national development. Prospects for the nation's economy looked bright as new areas were added to the dominion, giving the necessary variety on which a sound east-west economy could be built. Macdonald had now formed a middle-of-the-road party—the Liberal-Conservatives—dedicated to policies of national expansion.

Yet, storm-warnings should have been noted and pondered. Riel's uprising had plainly indicated the forces of religious-racial conflict that lay barely hidden beneath an apparently calm surface. Similarly, Howe's "better terms" campaign had indicated how delicate was the balance of regionalism and centralism on which Confederation rested. Symbolic of the magnitude of the nation's problems was the proposed transcontinental railway that held the promise of a new political, economic and social unity and that, at the same time, promised to severely challenge the nation's resources.

CHAPTER 10

YEARS OF DECISION

With Nova Scotia apparently reconciled to Confederation, with the Métis problem apparently settled in the west and with British Columbia safely incorporated within the fold of the dominion, the time had come for Macdonald to tackle long-term projects for Canada's growth. A railway to the Pacific was needed; reciprocity, or failing that a national tariff policy, was needed. But, before these projects could be attended to, Macdonald was compromised by his involvement in British-American relations and suffered political disgrace through the indiscretions of his colleagues. Yet, in the end, these reversals proved not only temporary but profitable to Macdonald. It was his Liberal opponent, Alexander Mackenzie, who, as prime minister through five disappointing years, had to face the stultifying effects in Canada of a world-wide depression.

"JOHN A."

Canada's first quarter-century has been fittingly called "The Age of Macdonald." Sir John had been the foremost personality in creating Confederation, and after Confederation his figure dominated the national scene. Except for a period of five years, he was to be prime minister of Canada from 1867 until his death in 1891.

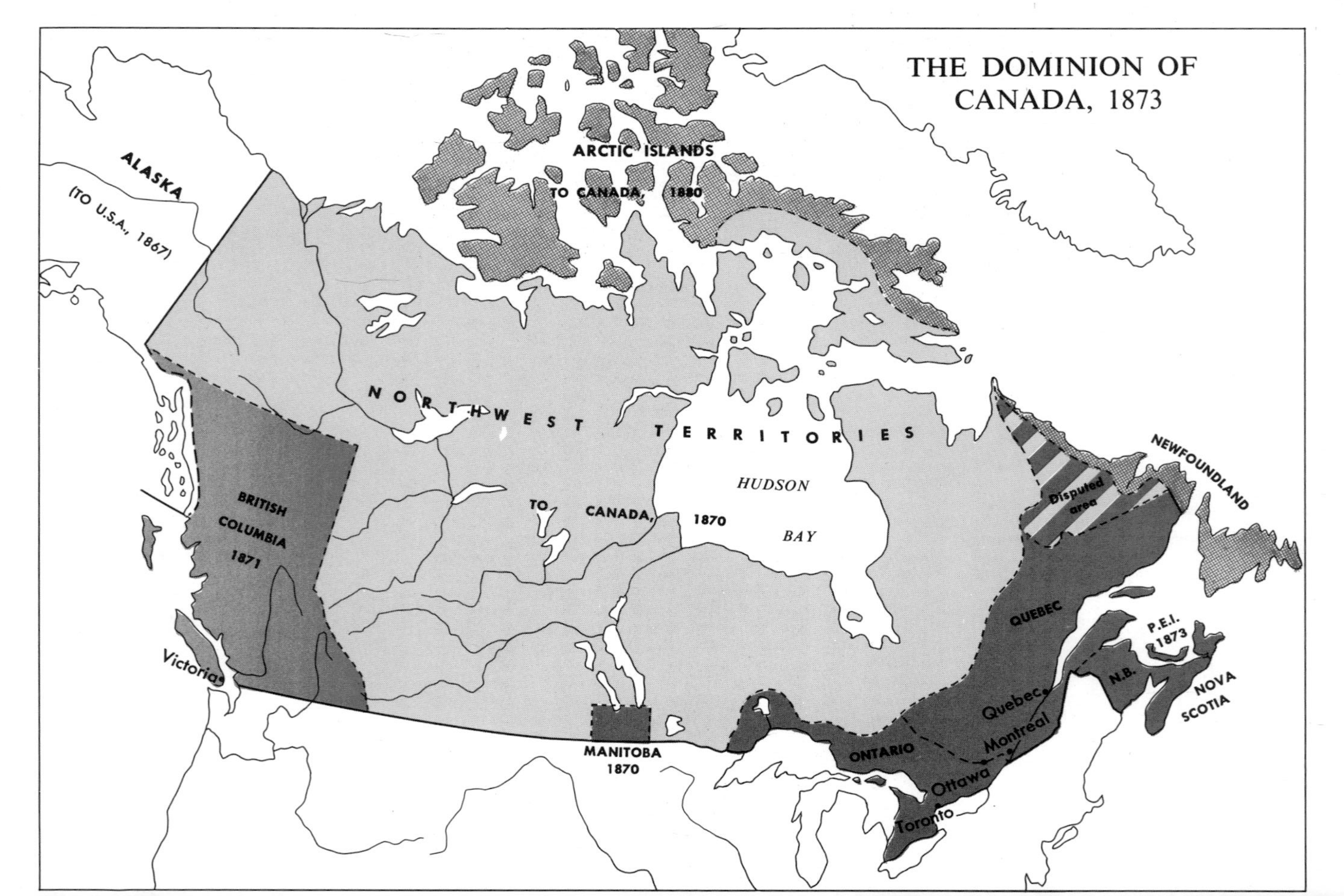
THE DOMINION OF
CANADA, 1873
ALASKA
(TO U.S.A., 1867)
ARCTIC ISLANDS
TO CANADA, 1880
NORTHWEST TERRITORIES
TO CANADA, 1870
HUDSON
BAY
BRITISH
COLUMBIA
1871
Victoria
MANITOBA
1870
ONTARIO
Toronto
Ottawa
Montreal
Quebec
QUEBEC
Disputed
area
NEWFOUNDLAND
P.E.I.
1873
N.B.
NOVA
SCOTIA

Six years after Confederation the new nation had acquired the immense North-West, British Columbia (1871) and Prince Edward Island (1873). The addition of the Arctic islands in 1880 almost completed Canada's modern boundaries. With the major geographic limits of Canada thus established, there remained the important task of charting the dominion's political and cultural course. True to his own British heritage, Macdonald's vision of Canada was based on one overriding principle—Canada must be British. Although it was *in* North America and peopled by various races, Canada had to remain *of* the British tradition. To this end the central government had been made the stronger element in the federal constitution, and the British parliamentary system and its usages had been adopted. Canada was not to become a mere miniature copy of its powerful republican neighbour to the south, a possibility consistently rejected by British North Americans since 1775. Although Macdonald felt that Canada had to remain of the British tradition, he sought for Canada a junior partnership within the British Empire rather than colonial dependence. He would prove the error of the "Little England" claim that Canadian self-government was the prelude to separation. Canada would remain British, if necessary in spite of Britain.

In Sir John's eyes the most serious threat to the dominion's growth was the possibility of American economic domination. Canada's principal weaknesses were her own great size and diversity. Nature, it seemed, intended a North American economy to flow north and south, but Macdonald was determined that the east-west axis of the St. Lawrence, which had linked the colonies to Britain, must now be extended westward across rolling prairies and forbidding mountains even to the shores of the Pacific. When the political unity of Confederation was translated into economic unity, Canada would become the bridge between Britain and her Asian dominions. A transcontinental railway would open Canada's back door to the rich trade of the Orient, bind together the separate regions of the nation, carry settlers westward to fill and to exploit the empty hinterland and preserve the country forever as part of the British inheritance.

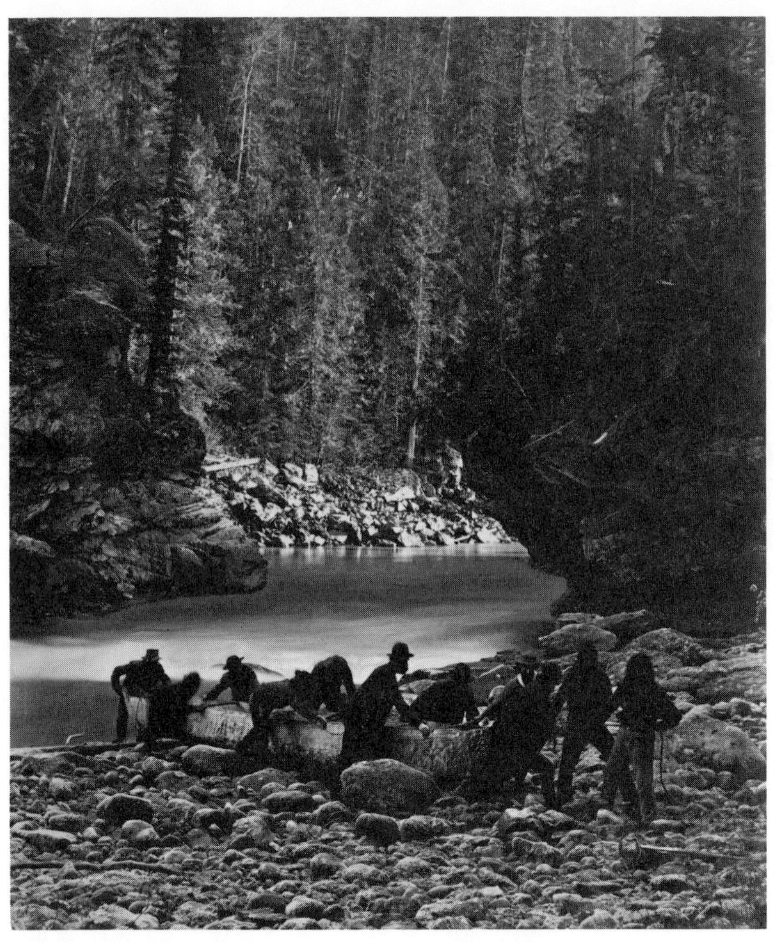

The task of building a railway to the Pacific involved almost insurmountable obstacles, not the least of which were geographic. This Notman photograph shows a joint government-C.P.R. survey crew portaging a dugout canoe around the Murchison Rapids on the North Thompson River in British Columbia in the fall of 1871.

Macdonald also believed that the interests of Canada were identical with those of his party. It was not a desire for power itself, but a sense of obligation to his adopted country that drove him, time and again, to ensure the continuance of a Conservative government. Fully aware that changing times bring changing conditions, he was always prepared to seek compromise and conciliation, to handle each crisis as gently and as slowly as possible without, however, losing sight of the ultimate end to be achieved. Macdonald seemed to understand intuitively, as no one else in Canadian political life, the many hopes, fears and conflicts of the Canadian people. He stood in this regard head and shoulders above his contemporaries.

Above all, Macdonald enjoyed the game of politics and played it like a master. He knew his fellow Canadians and knew them personally. On crowded railway platforms, at thronged political picnics, on the flag-bedecked platforms, in the stuffy, overheated community halls of innumerable towns and villages, he had met Canadians, had shaken their hands, had listened attentively to their complaints, had chatted about prospects for the year's crops and had then greeted them by name on his next visit. "He threaded his way through the intricacies of Canadian politics like a man crossing a room which is crowded with his friends," writes one of his biographers.

Yet Macdonald often longed for release from the burdens of office. His personal life had seen more than its share of sorrow and tragedy, and his health was weakened by recurrent illnesses. His sense of mission, however, drove him on. As he remarked in 1871:

> I greatly desire to complete the work of Confederation before I make my final bow to the Canadian audience before whom I have been acting my part for so long.

THE TREATY OF WASHINGTON, 1871

The abrogation of the reciprocity treaty by the United States in 1866 brought to an end the American right to enter the rich fishing grounds of Canada's Atlantic coastal waters (although American fishermen continued to exploit the inshore fisheries under licenses until the licensing system was cancelled in 1870). That year, Macdonald's government sent out eight ships to patrol the Gulf of St. Lawrence fisheries and to arrest American poachers. Canada was not unwilling to share her fisheries, but she wanted compensation—a new reciprocity treaty and payment for the damages done by the Fenians—and the fisheries were the only lever that might pry open American customs barriers.

The United States showed no interest in renewing reciprocity, which, it believed, had worked unduly to Canada's advantage. Besides, the victorious North had not forgotten the *Alabama* depredations during the Civil War. British shipyards had built a number of vessels, including the *Alabama*, that were subsequently used by the South to raid and destroy Northern ships. American authorities now saw—and used—Canada as a whipping-boy to even old scores with Great Britain. As it happened, the Gladstone government in Britain was at this time deeply preoccupied by the continued strain in Anglo-American relations, especially after the German victory over France in 1870 had seriously upset the fragile balance of power in Europe. Britain was anxious to appease the United States, and the fisheries dispute seemed—to everyone except Canadians—a heaven-sent opportunity to arrange a rapprochement. For his part, Macdonald clearly saw that the fisheries might be given away for the sake of peace and that Canada, as yet lacking treaty-making powers, could be left uncompensated.

In December, 1870, President Grant acidly sounded a warning:

> The colonial authority known as the Dominion of Canada . . . this semi-independent but irresponsible agent has exercised its delegated power (over the inshore fisheries) in an unfriendly way. . . . It is hoped that the government of Great Britain will see the justice of abandoning the narrow and inconsistent claim to which her Canadian Provinces have urged her adherence.

Whatever the justice of the matter, the British government also believed that the Canadian government's approach was too rigid and that Canada's policy of exclusion was perpetuating Anglo-American difficulties. To consider all these related problems, Britain agreed to an Anglo-American commission. Macdonald was appointed as one of the five British members. The inclusion of a colonial statesman in an imperial commission was certainly a diplomatic innovation, but Macdonald was reminded that he represented the British, not the Canadian, government. Thus the honour accorded the Canadian prime minister was somewhat tarnished by the ambiguous position in which it placed him; he was made, for all practical purposes, answerable to both the British government and the Canadian parliament.

The commission deliberated in Washington from March to May, 1871. Macdonald's first problem was posed by an understanding between the British and American representatives that the fisheries problem could easily be settled if Canada would sell in perpetuity her fishing rights to the United States. Such a settlement would nullify the Fenian damage claims and Canada's dreams of renewed reciprocity. Macdonald was adamant; the fisheries were Canada's and could only be sold with her consent—though they might be exchanged for an advantageous trade agreement. To the annoyance of his British colleagues on the commission, Macdonald also spurned an offer of reciprocity in coal, salt, salt fish and firewood. Gladstone's government now authorized any agreed settlement, providing that the articles affecting Canada were ratified by the Canadian parliament. Macdonald was trapped. To withdraw from the commission would be to play completely into American hands; to remain would be to make himself responsible for the final treaty, thus rendering it very difficult to refuse ratification. Macdonald stayed, fully aware that his bargaining power was virtually gone.

Despite an American offer to add lumber to the previous paltry list of duty-free commodities, Macdonald would not budge, and in proportion to his determination the anger of his colleagues increased. But Macdonald had support. His cabinet in Ottawa stood solidly behind him. In London, Gladstone's government was sympathetic to Canadian demands and unwilling to force Macdonald to accept the insulting American offer, despite a warning from the British chairman, Lord Ripon, of the possible "unpleasant consequences" of Canadian obstinacy. By mid-April, however, Macdonald was confronted with a new and final offer from the United States—an offer that eventually was fully accepted by the British government. The United States

Sir John A. Macdonald (third from left) with the other British High Commissioners at the Treaty of Washington. In commenting on the Treaty, Edward Blake, a leading Liberal said: "It produced a feeling [in Canada] that at no distant period the people of Canada would desire that they should have some greater share of control than they now have in the management of foreign affairs; that our Government should not present the anomaly which it now presents—a Government the freest, perhaps the most democratic in the world with reference to local and domestic matters . . . while in your foreign affairs . . . you may have no more voice than the people of Japan."

would buy entry into the fisheries for ten years and would permit the free entry of Canadian fish into its markets. No compensation for the Fenian raids would be included. To win the reluctant consent of Canada to the American offer, the British government was ready (Macdonald believed) to indemnify the victims of Fenian aggression, and the value of the fisheries was to be decided by arbitration. Macdonald surrendered with poor grace and dire fears of strong political reaction in Canada. The Treaty of Washington was signed on 8 May, 1871.

The major clauses of the treaty affecting Canada covered free navigation for both countries of the St. Lawrence River and Lake Michigan (but not the Canadian canals), bonding privileges to and from New York City, Boston and Portland, the free entry of both countries to each other's inshore Atlantic fisheries (north of the 39th parallel in the case of the United States), and consideration by a commission of the superior value of Canadian concessions of the fisheries. A boundary dispute over the San Juan Islands on the Northwest Pacific coast, in the strait between Vancouver Island and the mainland, was referred to the German Emperor, who awarded the islands to the United States.

Back in Ottawa Macdonald maintained an official silence, waiting for the storm of protest over the treaty terms to break and to blow itself out. To Lord Ripon he wrote:

> The feeling in Canada against the Treaty has increased and is increasing and I cannot foresee the results. An utter feeling of distrust in the imperial government has arisen in the public mind and every clause in the Treaty is therefore discussed in a jealous and prejudiced spirit.

The last session of the dominion's first parliament did not open until April, 1872. Throughout the fall and winter months Macdonald had used ratification of the treaty as a lever to pry from the imperial government a firm promise of compensation for the Fenian damages, in the form of a guaranteed loan for railway and canal construction. In the debate in the Canadian Commons Macdonald stressed that the treaty ensured peace for the British Empire and markets for Maritime fishermen. Mackenzie, appealing in reply to Canadian nationalism, denounced the treaty as detrimental to Canada's interests and called on parliament to preserve its "dignity and independence" by rejecting it. But the criticism of the opposition had been at least partially gagged by Macdonald's plea for loyalty, and ratification of the Treaty of Washington became an accomplished fact just one year after it had been signed. The climax of the affair came when a High Commission of three members (one British, one American and one Belgian) determined in 1877 that the United States should pay $5,500,000 for the use of the Canadian fisheries for ten years. The American representative dissented from this decision, and American public opinion considered it unfair to the United States. Technical and economic changes, plus the fact Canada was using the award money to subsidize Canadian fishermen, led the United States to cancel the unpopular fisheries article in 1885.

MAKING HASTE SLOWLY

In view of the forthcoming general election, Macdonald deliberately delayed the 1872 session of parliament until the latest legally permissible date. By the time the session closed, he was able to face the voters with three substantial pieces of legislation —the ratification of the Treaty of Washington, a Trade Unions Act giving the unions the right to strike and a Dominion Lands (homestead) Act that followed the American practice of giving free land to settlers. (This Lands Act of 1872 offered a settler a quarter section—160 acres—of western farming land plus an option to an adjoining quarter section, at a nominal price, after he had completed three years of occupation.) Sir John could also take pride in the preparations for Prince Edward Island's anticipated entry into Confederation. Bankrupted by railway-building, the Island was to be given $800,000 to buy out its absentee landlords and a generous credit of fifty dollars per person toward payment of the provincial debt.

One major phase of Macdonald's plan to develop Canada still remained on the drawing board—the transcontinental railway that was the price of British Columbia's entry into Confederation. In 1872 two rival companies were bidding for the honour of binding the dominion with ribbons of steel. Sir Hugh Allan, the Montreal shipping magnate, had formed the Canadian Pacific Railway Company; however, much of his financial backing came from Americans associated with the Northern Pacific Railroad, which skirted the 49th parallel in an obvious attempt to draw Canada's western economy into the American orbit.

The second, all-Canadian syndicate, the Interoceanic Railway Company, had been formed by David L. Macpherson, a loyal Conservative and a personal friend of Macdonald, and other Toronto financiers connected with the Grand Trunk Railway. Unfortunately, Macpherson lacked the experience and international prestige of the older Allan. The Pacific railway charter could not go to an American-controlled company—nor to the Interoceanic standing alone. But all attempts by Macdonald to bring about a merger of the Toronto and Montreal interests failed, since Allan refused to desert his American associates.

Macdonald had already secured the dominion's territory. In the election of 1872 he sought the time and the means with which to weld Canada into an economic unity. "Confederation is only yet in the gristle, and it will require five more years before it hardens into bone," he remarked. A strongly industrial east, a transcontinental railway and a settled, agricultural west would make the gristle hard. In the election of 1872, however, Allan was sowing seeds of political catastrophe for Macdonald. By indirectly opposing Cartier's re-election in Montreal, Allan cunningly forced the ailing Sir George to seek election funds from him, and Sir George compounded his mistake by virtually promising Allan the Pacific railway charter. (Cartier received $85,000, but he was not the only Conservative politician indebted to Allan. Allan gave a total of $200,000 to the Conservative cause.) When the new parliament met, Macdonald's railway troubles were just beginning. Allan promised to jettison his American colleagues and merge with Macpherson, but only on his own terms, which virtually amounted to absolute control of the new railway company. It was only gradually that Macdonald realized that the Americans refused to be dismissed so easily and that Allan had blindly mismanaged the whole affair. Eventually, in the early months of 1873 an agreement between the rival capitalists was reached, a charter was awarded, and Allan left for England in search of further funds. The prime minister was well aware of Allan's manoeuvering, but he did not know of Cartier's promises—nor of the theft of potentially incriminating documents from the Montreal offices of Allan's lawyers.

THE IRREPRESSIBLE SHOWMAN.
BARNUM WANTS TO BUY THE "PACIFIC SCANDAL."

J. W. Bengough on the Pacific Scandal.

On 2 April, 1873, L. F. Huntington, the Liberal member for Shefford, rose in the House of Commons to charge that Sir Hugh Allan's railway company was American-controlled and that Sir Hugh had provided the Macdonald government with huge election funds in return for the promise of the coveted railway charter. Ignorant of all the evidence that the Liberals now possessed, Macdonald, after considerable delay, appointed a commission to investigate the charges. The commission did not open its hearings until September, but in the interval Cartier died, Allan's attempts to raise money in England were completely blocked by reports of scandal, and the opposition released most of the purloined documents that detailed Macdonald's receipts of election funds from Allan. However, the commission failed to reveal any "deal" involving Macdonald and the grant of the railway charter.

When parliament met again in the autumn of 1873, Macdonald's government seemed to have weathered the "Pacific Scandal." But its slim majority in the House soon melted away, and Macdonald, finding no escape in alcohol, decided to resign. The Pacific railway, and all it stood for, was shelved. Apparently British Columbia was going to remain isolated from the rest of

Canada. No settlers would reach the west by an all-Canadian route. The Conservative party had been disgraced by the foolishness of the ailing Cartier and the overconfidence and the machinations of Allan and his American financial friends. On 7 November, 1873, Alexander Mackenzie was sworn into office as Canada's first Liberal prime minister. Mackenzie's first act was to call an election for January, 1874. Its results showed clearly how Canada had reacted to the Pacific Scandal. The Liberals gained a clear majority of sixty over the party of Sir John A. Macdonald.

The Liberal party, however, proved to be unprepared for the responsibilities of office. Its first problem was Mackenzie himself. In Lord Dufferin's words, "He is honest, industrious, and sensible, but he has very little talent." The bearded Scot was neither sufficiently ruthless nor persuasive to be a strong party leader. His party, primarily a regional one based in Ontario, was loosely organized and dependent for strength on provincial party "machines," which dictated conflicting policies of regional interests to the federal party. Mackenzie's cabinet, nicknamed the "Incapables," contained one minister from Prince Edward Island and none from British Columbia (which had not returned any Liberals anyway); it had no Irish Roman Catholic and no Englishman. The party at large contained too many conflicting elements; as Mackenzie admitted, its leadership was "no sinecure." The equivocal position of the able Edward Blake epitomized these difficulties, for Blake left the cabinet after only three months and then returned as virtual co-leader a year later in the wake of conspiracies against Mackenzie. As prime minister, Alexander Mackenzie failed to meet the challenges of office, although in fairness to him some of those challenges were perhaps greater than any that Macdonald had had to face.

A problem that greatly vexed the Liberal government was ultramontanism—the movement in the Roman Catholic Church that defended the absolute authority of the papacy—which was particularly strong in Quebec. Added to the vital tradition of religious conservatism inherited by the province from New France, had been the impetus of the papal *Syllabus of Errors* in 1864—a condemnation of the liberal, anti-clerical movement then active in Europe. The *Parti Rouge,* the Liberals' Quebec wing, which had drawn much of its original inspiration from European liberalism, came under clerical attack when its educational organization, the *Institut Canadien*, was formally condemned by the papacy in 1869. The *Institut* rapidly declined under a barrage of clerical fire Ultramontanism had already infiltrated Canadian politics by 1875 with its "catholic programme" for protecting the purity and power of the Church. In that year a pastoral letter of the Quebec bishops defended priestly interference in politics and condemned voting for an unacceptable candidate as a sin. Despite the protestations of Mackenzie's party, political liberalism was popularly identified in Quebec with the condemned liberalism in the Church, and during by-elections held in 1876 the ultramontanists gave decisive support to the Conservative cause. Macdonald cynically advised his party organizers to "use the priests for the next election, but be ready to fight them in the Dominion parliament." Not all Roman Catholics, nor all the bishops, agreed with the extreme ultramontanists, but the Liberal party had to await the passing of another generation and the appearance of a French Liberal whose Catholicism was beyond question before the Conservative-ultramontanist hegemony in Quebec could be broken.

Far more serious, however, than the political threat posed by ultramontanism was the onset of the great depression of the late nineteenth century. Macdonald might well congratulate himself and his party that they were out of office when the full effects of the world-wide trade stagnation struck Canada after 1873. Companies went bankrupt, prices fell steadily, unemployment became chronic and widespread, and the total volume of Canadian trade declined, while the government's annual deficit rose. The Liberal government had before it three possible economic policies: reduce expenditures; increase Canada's export trade; raise tariffs for revenue. Each policy was tried in turn by Mackenzie and each failed to lift Canada out of the economic doldrums.

Retrenchment of government expenditure was a Liberal aim hallowed in Canada since Clear Grit days, but the attempt to cut down on the most obvious burden, the Pacific railway commitment, soon involved Mackenzie in political difficulties. Was the

J. W. Bengough on Ultramontanism

Liberal government bound to fulfill the overgenerous promises of its political enemies? Most Liberals, unimpressed by the popular demand for unifying measures, such as the railway, said no; British Columbia, understandably, said yes. Mackenzie proposed spending one and a half million dollars annually to build a coach road westward and a railway from Esquimalt to Nanaimo on Vancouver Island (as the first part of the trans-continental railway) in compensation for waiving the original completion time of ten years. His offer was rejected in British Columbia, and the Esquimalt-Nanaimo Railway Bill was defeated in the Senate. Macdonald's promises and British Columbia's intransigence went a long way towards wrecking the Liberal party. The railway question remained unsettled and gave Mackenzie "many a painful hour and sleepless night." With a general election approaching, it appeared that Macdonald might have to find a solution to his own promises and the depression.

The second hope of the Liberal government—to expand Canada's trade—had led Mackenzie to send George Brown (now a Senator) to Washington in an attempt to renew reciprocity with the United States. The American government agreed to renew the 1854 treaty for twenty-one years and to expand the list of free products, but Canada was required to forego compensation for the fisheries and to deepen its canals to accommodate American vessels. The tariff concessions alone were going to cost Canada $3,000,000 in revenue each year, but the offer of reciprocity was too attractive for any free-trade Liberal to resist. The treaty was signed by the American administration, only to be rejected by the United States' Senate. The failure to gain reciprocity was a political disaster for the Liberals and probably an economic disaster for Canada. More significantly, however, the fears of Canada's nascent manufacturing industries had been aroused at the prospect of American competition, and Macdonald was quick to see the election potential of a protectionist programme.

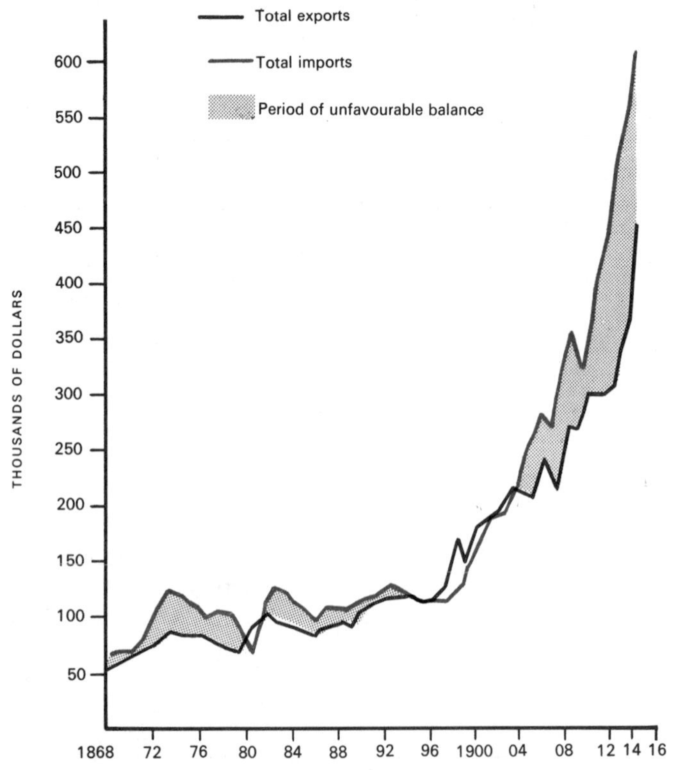

The Balance of Trade, 1868-1914

Alexander Mackenzie in 1876. The Governor General, Lord Dufferin, in assessing the Prime Minister, wrote to the Colonial Secretary: "He is honest, industrious and sensible, but he has very little talent. He possesses neither 'initiative' nor 'ascendancy'."

Having failed to obtain reciprocity, there remained the final, and in Liberal eyes, least desirable choice—an increase in tariffs. A measure of this kind was bound to split a party that contained such opposed elements as adamant free traders and mild protectionists. And, publicly at least, the Liberals had always espoused free trade. When the budget of 1874 increased the old Conservative tariffs from fifteen to seventeen and a half percent on manufactured goods and from 5 to 10 percent on certain semi-finished goods, the opposition was filled with glee. Tupper, opposition financial critic, proceeded to blame the depression on the Liberal government. Liberal times were hard times, the Conservatives claimed, and the government soon found itself defending higher tariffs against its own avowed principles. By 1876 the depth of the depression had been reached. Canada faced a major economic crisis, and the Liberals faced a dilemma; the Maritime provinces opposed any further tariff increases, but Liberals from the manufacturing provinces of Ontario and Quebec favoured outright protection. The Liberal government's rigid adherence to the ideal of the lowest possible tariff inspired

Macdonald to adopt protection as a Conservative plank. Macdonald, though, was not a protectionist—he was a politician. A young Liberal newcomer. Wilfrid Laurier, remarked:

The question of free trade and protection in any country is not to be applied to political motive: but to be treated as a matter of pure economy.

He would soon learn from Macdonald that in Canada protection was politics.

NATIONAL POLICY

As the life of Canada's Third Parliament drew to a close, Mackenzie's government could look back on a record of considerable achievement. The Royal Military College had been founded at Kingston, the Supreme Court of Canada had been established, the secret ballot was now employed in elections, and the recording of parliamentary debates had begun (in the volumes popularly known as "Hansard"). True, only a few miles of the transcontinental railway had been built west and east of Fort Garry, but the whole line to the Pacific had been surveyed. Yet over the whole political scene hung the huge, lowering, black cloud of the depression, a cloud that showed no sign of dispersing.

In September, 1878, the Liberals went to the country on their record. "Honesty, integrity and economy" was their slogan. The "demon of protection" was their warning cry. The Conservatives attacked the government's record from all sides. Canadians needed prosperity and leadership—and had been given austerity and Liberal indecision. Canada's economy needed tariff protection—and the Liberals had chased that "will o'the wisp," reciprocity. Canada needed a transcontinental railway—and the fainthearted Liberals had built virtually nothing. What Canada needed most, shouted the Conservatives, was Sir John A. and his "National Policy." Canadians listened, reflected and agreed.

The phrase "national policy" had been used by the Conservatives as early as 1870 to describe moderate tariff protection.

National Policy meant, in fact, economic nationalism, but in a broader sense it implied national development through a combination of tariffs, industry, immigration and railways. "Now you are, I know, a free-trader; so am I," Sir John had written to David Macpherson in 1872, "but . . . our game is to coquet with the protectionists. The word 'protection' itself must be taboo, but we can ring the changes on National Policy, paying [the] U.S. in their own coin. . . ." Canada had not been ready for the National Policy in 1872, but six years of depression and the American rejection of reciprocity had ripened public opinion. By the time the general election was held, protection had become the foremost question in Canadian politics.

"If we do well, we shall have a majority of sixty; if badly, thirty," Macdonald told his wife. In fact, the election gave the Conservatives a majority of sixty-eight. Canada had overwhelmingly endorsed the National Policy. Not only the manufacturers and industrial workers, but also the traditionally free trade farmers had voted for protection.

The election of 1878 gave Macdonald the opportunity to implement his National Policy. In the budget of 1879 the general tariff was raised from 17.5 to 20 percent. Duties on semi-finished goods ranged from 10 to 20 percent, but on fully manufactured equipment and machinery they averaged 25 percent, and on such finished goods as glass, china, boots, shoes and furniture they went as high as 30 percent. (A tariff on agricultural products did not really help farmers but made them feel they had not been forgotten.) Finally, a duty of fifty cents per ton on coal gave Nova Scotian mines a strong grip on the markets of central Canada.

In vain did Richard Cartwright, Mackenzie's Minister of Finance and now the opposition financial critic, denounce the National Policy as an unjust scheme to tax one part of the nation for the benefit of another. The government was giving privileges in exchange for contributions to the party funds, he charged. Combines and trusts would soon dominate the Canadian economy, he prophesied, leaving the labourer and consumer without protection against price increases. To some extent at least Cartwright was right—the era of Big Business (on a small scale) began when Canada deserted a revenue tariff for a protective tariff.

How successful in fact was the National Policy in reviving the lagging economy of Canada and in encouraging infant industries? Certainly Canadian industry was well protected from American and British competition, perhaps in some cases over protected. Certainly the National Policy encouraged manufacturing in Canada, but at the cost of higher consumer prices. It also created jobs and strengthened Macdonald's planned east-west economy. Since Canadian industry could not possibly meet the total national demand for manufactured goods, tariff revenues increased and so provided the government with the capital needed for such projects as the transcontinental railway.

Some early settlers on the prairies built their first homes of sod because of the very short supply of suitable timber. The photograph above shows a sod hut at Souris, Manitoba. Three men spent the winter of 1882 here caring for the cattle of settlers who had returned to the east for the winter.

Begun as a Conservative programme and adopted by later Liberal governments, the National Policy was a resounding political success. Economically speaking, if the National Policy did not quickly create an industrial giant, at least it laid the foundations for later industrial growth and produced a stable and ever-growing source of revenue for later governments.

"THE STEEL OF EMPIRE"

Macdonald now turned his attention to the next (and long-overdue) step in his grand design for Canada—the construction of the Pacific railway and the settlement of the west. The railway would tie together the far-flung regions of Canada. But the railway had two broader purposes. It would provide a link between Britain and the Orient, and it would open prairie land for settlement, providing new homes to relieve unemployment and over population in Britain. Indeed, the railway was as much a part of Macdonald's imperial vision as it was of his Canadian vision.

The project of a transcontinental railway was so gigantic that it dismayed all but the most daring minds. It called for the construction of a rail route two-thirds longer than any then in existence, at a cost that defied imagination. To make the railway pay, its builders would have to create—and maintain—a constant stream of human traffic by attracting settlers through immense, prolonged overseas advertising campaigns. Private capital alone would be quite incapable of tackling the stupendous job. The solution lay in the co-operation between government and private enterprise. Negotiations with a Montreal syndicate of financiers began in the spring of 1880. The Grand Trunk Railway was interested, but only if the Pacific railway followed a southerly route from Sault Ste. Marie through Chicago and around the south shore of Lake Superior. The Montreal men were headed by James J. Hill, a Canadian who had earned wealth and fame in American railroading, and George Stephen, who had risen from shepherd boy in Scotland to bank president in

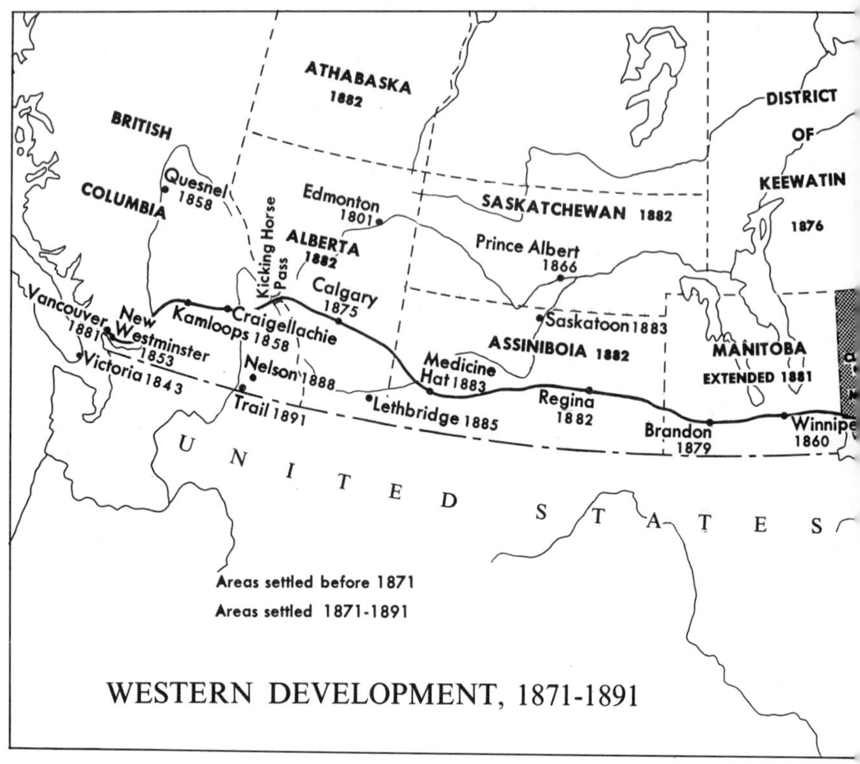

WESTERN DEVELOPMENT, 1871-1891

Canada. They accepted Macdonald's insistence on an all-Canadian route. Money for the project was promised by American, French and German, as well as Canadian sources. But only one small British company was willing to invest, and the British government itself was uninterested in the scheme.

Terms for the railway charter were arranged late in 1880. The government would give the Canadian Pacific Railway Company a subsidy of \$25,000,000 and 25,000,000 acres of prairie land "fairly fit for settlement" in alternate mile-square sections in a belt twenty-four miles deep on each side of the railway. The Company was also to receive some 700 miles of railway already under construction from Port Moody to Kamloops in the west and from Fort William to Winnipeg in the east. All materials and construction equipment would be tax-free and tariff-free, and subsidy lands would be tax-free for

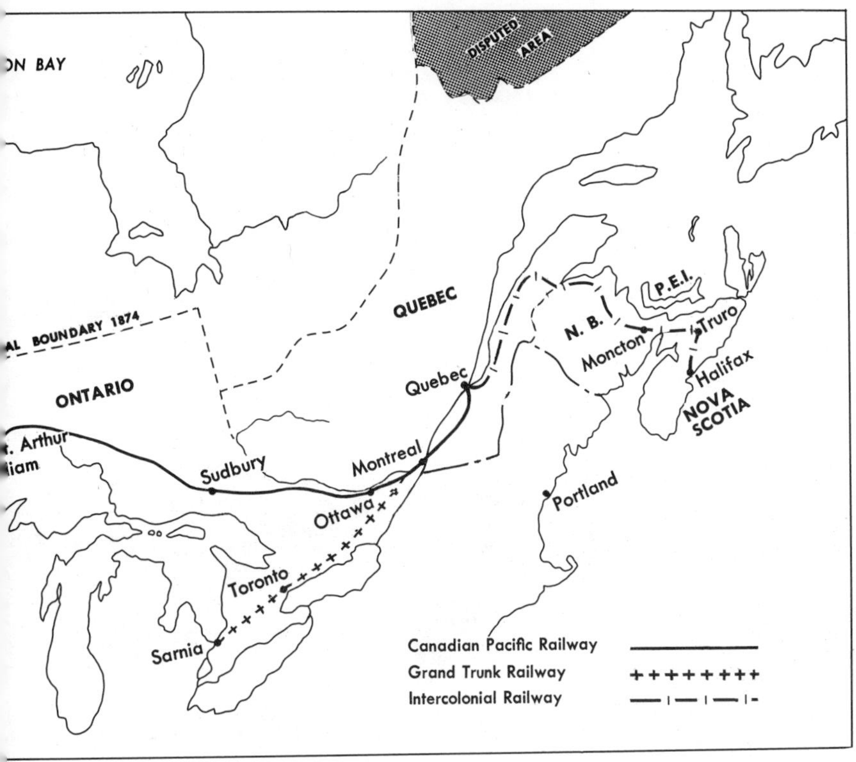

twenty years. Most controversial of all was the "monopoly" clause, which prohibited for twenty years the construction of any rival railway between the C.P.R. line and the United States' border. In return for these fantastically generous handouts the Company promised to complete a railway to the Pacific by 1891.

The reaction of the opposition and the rival Grand Trunk Railway was immediate and vociferous. The whole scheme was a colossal giveaway; the terms were unnecessarily generous; the subsidies in cash and land were too large; the tax and tariff concessions were discriminatory and the monopoly clause was patently unjust. The C.P.R. charter was obviously an extension of the protectionist National Policy into the world of railways. The government replied (with justice) that the undertaking was so immense that every possible aid and encouragement to the Company was necessary.

An early C.P.R. poster.

After the C.P.R. Act was passed in February, 1881, the Company purchased railways that would link its western construction with the proposed intercolonial and thus ensure access to Atlantic ports and unified control of the full route. Shorter lines were also purchased to tap the wealth of western Ontario in competition with the Grand Trunk, while construction in British Columbia and in northwestern Ontario was pushed forward. Early in 1882 the C.P.R. acquired as general manager, William Cornelius Van Horne, a blunt, hard-driving American railroad man. They also hired as purchasing agent, Thomas G. Shaughnessy, who was to perform miracles of organization and supply. Van Horne, dazzled by the vision of a route to the Orient, announced that he would lay an unheard of five hundred miles of track across the prairies in 1882. As soon as spring arrived, an army of 5,000 men and 1,700 teams of horses moved west from Winnipeg. Men and horses toiled and sweated from dawn to dusk through the long summer days, averaging three miles per day. But still the ambitious Van Horne, "Czar of the C.P.R.," was not satisfied, and night shifts carried on by the light of kerosene lamps. When the winter of 1882-83 closed in, Van Horne had broken all construction records by laying 445 miles of main line and enough miles of sidings and branches to more than fulfill his promise. Beyond the Rockies the American engineer, Andrew Onderdonk, was pushing the C.P.R. eastward up the Fraser Valley alongside the Cariboo Trail. Three portable dynamite factories produced supplies of this new, powerful explosive to blast a way through the rocks, and coolies brought from China provided cheap labour.

Money, however, proved to be a greater problem for the Company than any of the engineering difficulties encountered. Buoyant optimism in the future of the Canadian west faded with the return of a trade depression in 1882. Immigration dwindled, and the western land boom suddenly collapsed. The 1883 crops in the west were a failure, and by October, with the railhead in the Kicking Horse Pass, the funds of the Company were exhausted.

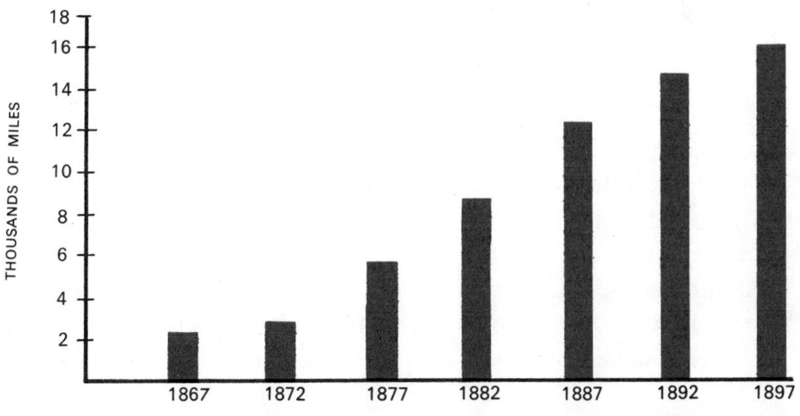

Railway Mileage in Operation in Canada, 1867-1897

The hall in the home of George Stephen, Montreal financier and President of the C.P.R. This could hardly be described as a typical home of the period, but it does demonstrate Victorian taste in home furnishings and the degree of sophistication present in the major Canadian cities of the time.

To complicate matters, the C.P.R. proved to be a particularly unattractive investment in what was already a "bear market"; C.P.R. stock was simply not selling the way the Company had anticipated. Construction on the North Shore section had begun, and although the route was moved closer to Lake Superior to utilize water communications, the cost of blasting and building through the ancient granite of the Shield was appallingly high. Late in 1883 George Stephen was frantically trying to borrow money in England. The bankruptcy of the Northern Pacific Railroad that year had had a depressing effect on all railway shares, and European capitalists were particularly shy of Canadian investments. London financial houses, influenced by the Grand Trunk's propaganda against "The Canadian Pacific Bubble", turned a deaf ear to Stephen's pleas, and the New York market remained uninterested. Stephen and his cousin and co-director, Donald Smith, had already used their personal fortunes to pay the most insistent creditors, but there were many others only slightly less impatient. The Company asked Macdonald's government for help. Sir John delayed —but not for long. The future of Canada was tied up with the C.P.R., and the Conservative party was equally tied to Canada's destiny. The Company could not be allowed to fail. Parliament authorized a $22,500,000 loan in return for a mortgage on the C.P.R. main line.

A real estate office in Vancouver, 1886. Port Moody had originally been designated as the Pacific terminus of the C.P.R., but the company secured permission to extend the line a further twelve miles to a new terminus that was named "Vancouver." As the actual end of steel on the C.P.R., Vancouver experienced a tremendous boom. Dubbed "the City of Imperial Destiny", it had 800 business establishments and a population of 2,000 within weeks of its incorporation in April, 1886.

Craigellachie, the spot where the last spike of the C.P.R. was driven, was named by George Stephen after the great rock that had been the rallying-place of the Clan Grant in Scotland, and had given the clan its battle cry—"Stand fast, Craigellachie!" It was the spot that symbolized Stephen's defiance of the forces that had stood in the way of his monumental undertaking. This famous photograph shows Donald Smith driving in the last spike. Behind him is Sir Sandford Fleming (who devised the system of standard time zones used today) and to his right is William Van Horne.

By the end of 1884 the Company was again unable to meet its bills and again Stephen appealed to Macdonald for help. This time Macdonald, facing a divided cabinet, hesitated longer. Then suddenly the Company's prospects brightened. Riel's second insurrection gave the C.P.R. a golden opportunity to show its worth. Troops were hurried westward over the line to Winnipeg and points farther west. Opponents of the North Shore line were impressed, and the value of the C.P.R. project was at last brought home even to British investors. A complicated but highly favourable arrangement was offered by the Canadian government and when $3,000,000 of bonds were offered to the public some months later, the whole issue was bought up at 90 percent of face value by the famous London investment firm, Barings. The C.P.R. was saved from its immediate difficulty and its ultimate success was assured. Public confidence in the vision of Macdonald, Stephen, Smith and Van Horne had finally been won. In 1886 Canada was at last joined from sea to sea by "the steel of empire," and that summer the entire railway was open for service—five years ahead of schedule.

* * *

Since 1874 a dozen busy years had passed, and for Canada and Macdonald they had latterly been years of achievement. The shame of the Pacific Scandal had been forgiven by electors weary of Liberal indecision and captivated by the appeal of the National Policy. With the magnificent project of the C.P.R. completed, the electors not only forgave but forgot many past shortcomings of "Old Tomorrow." Even Edward Blake, that incarnation of Liberalism, confessed when his C.P.R. train reached Vancouver that he was "converted" to Macdonald's vision of a great nation, unified by steel, and an integral part of the British Empire.

Macdonald was now in his seventy-first year, but the few years of life left to him were not to be years of peace or rest. Confederation, the central fact of his political life, was about to be threatened by a revolt of the provinces against the very principles of Confederation; Louis Riel was fated to die, and his ghost would revive old racial hatreds and fears; Macdonald's closest associates would betray his trust and blight his hopes; the danger of American domination would be raised—and defeated—once more. And through it all, Macdonald would play the game of politics to the end.

CHAPTER 11

A DECADE OF FRUSTRATION

Sir John A. Macdonald's design for the east-west economic integration of the dominion had two major bases—the development of manufacturing industries in eastern Canada and the exploitation of the agricultural resources of the west. To achieve development in the east, the National Policy had been instituted, providing Canada's infant industries with sizeable tariff protection against both American and British competitors. To achieve the exploitation of the west, the C.P.R. had been built to carry settlers and manufacturers to the prairies and to bring back grains to feed the east. These policies, however, were not very successful, largely because of a trade depression that continued for twenty-three years, broken only by a brief economic upsurge between 1879 and 1883. In addition, Macdonald's policies were so interwoven and so interdependent that the failure of any one affected and damaged his whole economic plan.

UNFULFILLED POLICIES

The first problem arising from the depression was the decline in the value and volume of Canadian exports between 1873 and 1879. There was a brief revival in the early 1880's, but it was more than a decade before trade again improved. The farmer was the person most seriously affected by falling prices. World wheat prices were halved as grain from the midwestern United States flooded world markets. At the same time, the National Policy required the farmer to pay higher prices for the manufactures of Canada's protected industries. To add to the farmer's burden came recurrent droughts and pest and disease infestation. Since the farmer, the "backbone of the national economy," had less to spend, manufacturers were forced to reduce production and to lay off employees.

Even Macdonald's railway-building programme did not bring prosperity. The Intercolonial Railway and the C.P.R. did not produce the interprovincial trade that had been expected, nor did they succeed in creating any noticeable flow of people from one region to another. The construction of the C.P.R. had been politically and economically a necessary gamble, but it had its own built-in problems. For years the Company would be burdened with heavy debts. Its economic future depended on the success of western settlement, and unless settlers came in large numbers, the Company would have neither purchasers for its lands nor customers exporting grain and importing manufactures. The Dominion Lands Act of 1872 was a blow to the C.P.R., for settlers naturally preferred free land to that being sold by the Company. The railway land grants system, which continued until 1894, brought charges, however unjustified, of "land-lock" against the government and the Company. Adding to the troubles of western farmers was the "monopoly" clause of the C.P.R. charter, which excluded competition in transportation and thereby kept railway rates high. The simple fact was that Canada could not afford a railway that served only the purpose of political unity—the success of the railway ultimately depended on its being able to pay its own way.

The area suffering most from this period of frustration was Manitoba. By the terms of the Manitoba Act the natural resources of the province had been retained by the federal government as "public domain." Thus, the provincial government received no revenues from land, forest or mine, but did acquire additional financial responsibilities with every settler that entered the province. If Manitoba was the hardest hit financially, it was certainly not alone in its difficulties. Other

At the top is a Blackfoot sun dance camp in the 1880's. The sun dance was an elaborate annual festival observed by the plains Indians. Among the Blackfoot, it included a ceremony in which several young warriors inflicted various forms of torture upon themselves in order to gain the favour of the Great Spirit. On the bottom (left) is a group, including Mounted Police, in front of a theatre in Banff in 1888. Being easily accessible by railway once the C.P.R. had been completed, Banff quickly developed as a resort area. On the right are Kootenay Indians at Donald, British Columbia, about 1885.

provinces had tried to promote expansion by railway-building and immigration, only to find themselves in a financial strait-jacket imposed by the rigid terms of Confederation. By 1887 every province was clamouring for "better terms" except Ontario. Ontario (and to a lesser extent Quebec) was not so adversely affected by the depression, due to its more diversified economy and also to its greater municipal development. The municipal governments established in the Province of Canada before Confederation were able to provide many services that elsewhere depended upon provincial administrations.

Canadians saw their economic problems amply reflected in the grim statistics of the 1891 census. In the previous decade the country's population had grown by only 500,000 to 4,833,000. Urban centres had expanded, but the farming population had not. The Canadian annual population increase of less than 12 percent contrasted sadly with the 25 percent increase in the United States. What were the reasons for this disappointingly slow growth? For one thing, fewer people were coming to the dominion and more were leaving. In addition, the United States now had about one and a half million Canadian-born persons, almost one-third of Canada's total population. In the nineties the population grew by only 538,000, barely surpassing the meagre increase of the 1880's. Between 1871 and 1901 the population rose by one and a half million—but over two million people left the country.

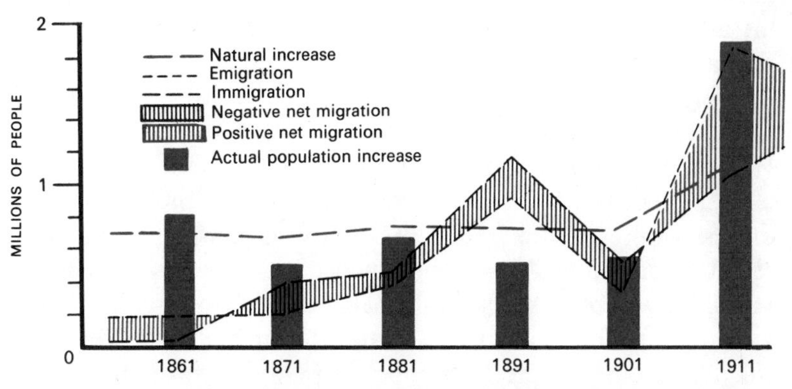

Demographic Trends, 1861-1911

Under the impact of depression Canada's economy had stagnated. Macdonald's policies had failed to create prosperity. Instead they had created hardships, especially in the Maritimes, by weighing the country down with debt. Confederation in its first quarter-century had apparently failed.

RACE, RELIGION AND RIEL

As Wolseley's force approached Fort Garry in August, 1870, Louis Riel fled into the countryside and awaited the general amnesty expected from the Canadian government. But the anger of English Ontario at Thomas Scott's murder made it politically impossible to include Riel in any amnesty. To add to the federal government's embarrassment, Riel reappeared in Red River in the autumn of 1871, offering the services of Métis horsemen to meet a threatened Fenian raid into Manitoba. The Lieutenant-Governor further complicated matters by publicly thanking Riel for his offer. Ultimately, Riel did retire to the United States (in 1872) at the urging of Bishop Taché and with money supplied by Macdonald's government.

Riel might have drifted into obscurity had he not felt a compulsion to obtain the promised amnesty. By 1873 he was back in Manitoba, contesting the constituency of Provencher, which he won not only in the by-election of that year, but also in the election of 1874. Despite an Ontario government warrant for his arrest, Riel audaciously slipped into Ottawa and into the Parliament Buildings, where he took the oath as a member of the Commons. However, he did not try to take his seat and was formally expelled from the Commons by a resolution of the House. In 1875 he was exiled from Canada for ten years.

Riel's exile was soon interrupted. Brooding on past events and on the future of the Métis, his sanity gave way and he was secretly committed to various Quebec asylums for almost two years. He was obsessed with the belief that he possessed a divine "mission" to found a new theocratic state in the Canadian west, ruled by a North American pope. In 1878 he returned to Montana, where he worked as an interpreter and trader. But he never

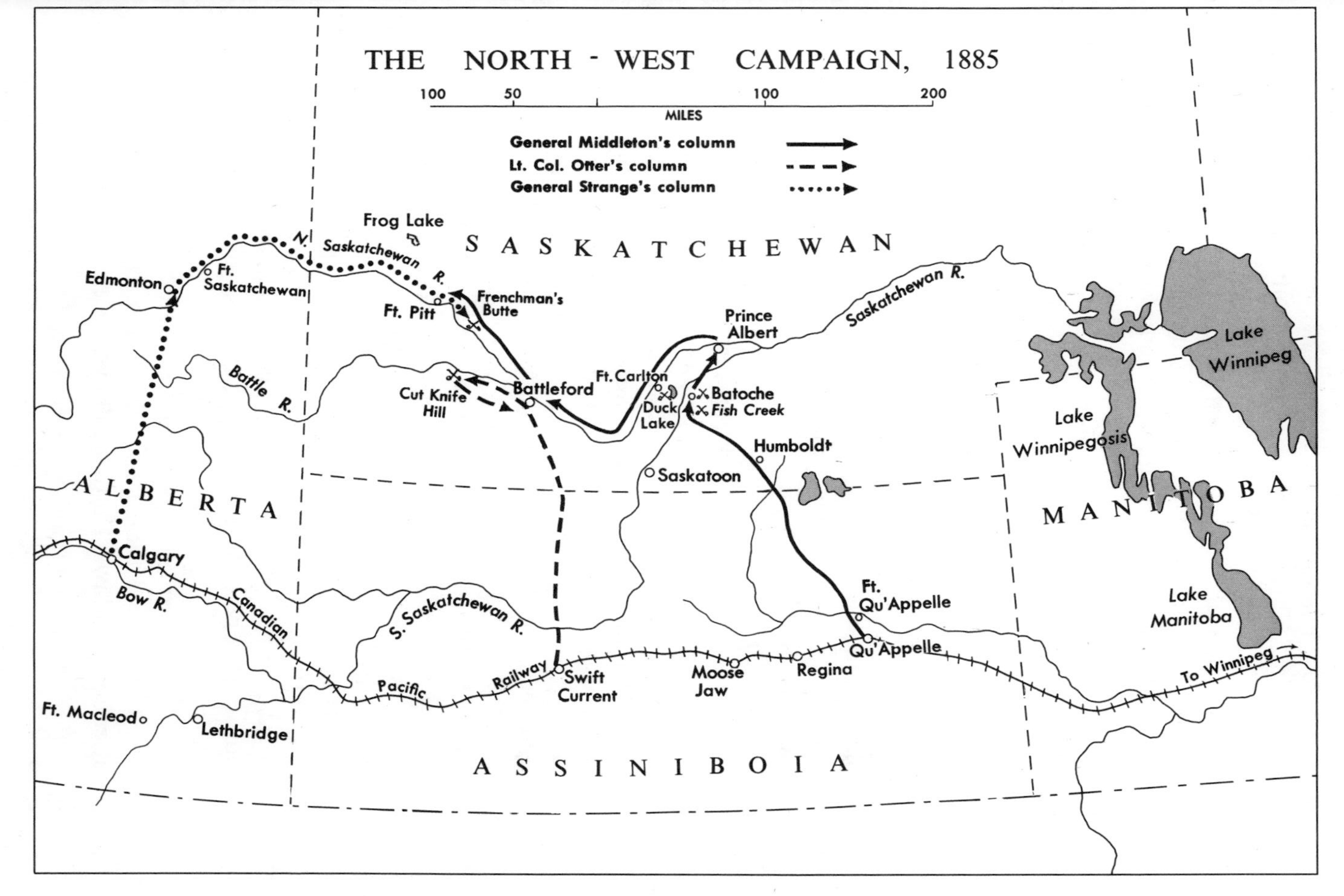

THE NORTH - WEST CAMPAIGN, 1885
100
50
100
200
MILES
General Middleton's column
Lt. Col. Otter's column
General Strange's column
Frog Lake
SASKATCHEWAN
N. Saskatchewan R.
Edmonton
Ft. Saskatchewan
Ft. Pitt
Frenchman's Butte
Saskatchewan R.
Prince Albert
Battle R.
Cut Knife Hill
Battleford
Ft. Carlton
Duck Lake
Batoche
Fish Creek
Humboldt
Saskatoon
Lake Winnipeg
Lake Winnipegosis
MANITOBA
Lake Manitoba
ALBERTA
Calgary
Bow R.
Canadian
S. Saskatchewan R.
Ft. Qu'Appelle
Qu'Appelle
Regina
Moose Jaw
Swift Current
Railway
Pacific
To Winnipeg
Ft. Macleod
Lethbridge
ASSINIBOIA

forgot his "mission" and when, in 1883, he visited Métis friends in Manitoba, his old ambitions came flooding back.

The Métis had been unable to accommodate themselves to the Anglo-Saxon agrarian society that began to occupy the west. Settlers had arrived, and the buffalo, the basis of the economy of the old North-West, had almost become extinct. The Métis had sold their land and scrip to speculators and had followed the few remaining buffalo westward. For ten years petitions of complaint to Ottawa had produced nothing. Under similar pressure, the Indians had given up their hunting grounds under treaties they barely understood, and they had been herded like cattle into reservations. Louis Riel was French and Indian, and Métis and Indian alike appealed to him for guidance and leadership. In June, 1884, messengers came to Riel with an urgent plea that he leave Montana and return to the North-West to lead another protest against the indifference and procrastination of the Macdonald government. Louis Riel did not hesitate—his "mission" called him to save the west.

Once established in the region that is now northern Saskatchewan, Riel sent an omnibus petition to Ottawa embodying the complaints of the west and reflectingthe diversity of his support. For the Indians, it requested more liberal treatment; for the Métis, legal proof of their ownership of the land; for the white settlers, a provincial legislature with responsible government, representation at Ottawa, amendments to the homestead and tariff laws, and the construction of a railway to Hudson Bay. Many westerners, however, opposed the agitation because of its leadership. The memory of Scott's death was fresh in English minds, and the Roman Catholic clergy, aware of Riel's mental instability, were fearful that the movement would end in violence. For its part, Macdonald's government was disinclined to do business with a man who had privately let it be known that he could be bought for $100,000. Ottawa merely promised an investigation, despite persistent warnings that the Saskatchewan situation was explosive.

While Macdonald procrastinated through the winter of 1884-85, Riel decided that only a show of force would secure the attention of Ottawa. His plan followed the precedent of 1869—he would arm his Métis and Indian followers, form a provisional government and then, from a position of strength, negotiate a revision of Confederation as it affected the North-West. But this was 1885, not 1869; the clergy no longer supported Riel, and the Mounted Police, few but disciplined, now enforced law and order and could be quickly reinforced, thanks to the C.P.R. Ignoring these facts, Riel announced on 19 March that the North-West Mounted Police were about to attack Batoche. Using this pretext, a provisional government was established, and from headquarters in the Batoche parish church Riel began organizing military operations.

One week later Riel's "adjutant general," Gabriel Dumont, ambushed a Mounted Police force at Duck Lake, while Riel looked on, crucifix in hand. At the same time Cree Indians pillaged stores in Battleford. Isolated settlers were murdered, but the rebels were too few and too disorganized to attack the larger villages. Atrocities were perpetrated by small bands of roving Indians who did not acknowledge Riel's leadership. Most of the tribes, however, had harkened to the appeal of the influential missionary, Father Lacombe, that they stay on their reservations. The English-speaking half-breeds and many French Métis refused to join a rebellion that looked increasingly like an Indian uprising.

When word of the fighting reached Ottawa, a militia force was hastily entrained for the west under the command of stolid, unimaginative Frederick Middleton. "Localize the insurrection," was Macdonald's order. Leap-frogging the seventy miles in the North Shore railway line during foul, late winter weather, the force reached Winnipeg in eight days. There they gathered 2,000 local reinforcements and then divided to attack Batoche, relieve Battleford (besieged by Chief Poundmaker and his Indians), and capture Chief Big Bear's band of Crees. Batoche was taken, and fugitive Riel soon surrendered. Despite initial success, Poundmaker surrendered when he learned of Riel's defeat. Chief Big Bear temporarily avoided the same fate, but his Indian band scattered and forced him to surrender, thereby bringing the rebellion to a close.

Heavy vengeance was meted out to the defeated Métis. Their

On the left is Poundmaker, and on the right is Big Bear.

homes and property were destroyed and their leaders imprisoned. Indeed, within a generation the Métis ceased to exist in any real sense as a social and cultural group. As for the Indians, they were disarmed, a few leaders were hanged, Big Bear and Poundmaker were imprisoned, and the rebels' annuities were used to compensate victims of the rebellion; on the whole, the Indians paid less dearly than the Métis. Yet the cause of rebellion was not a total loss. The Canadian government had been awakened at last to the grievances of the Métis, and those Métis who had not joined the rebellion were given title to their lands.

Riel's trial for treason began at Regina on 20 July, 1885. The self-styled "Prophet of the New World" repudiated the plea of insanity that his lawyers made for him. "I cannot abandon my dignity," he said. His trial was conducted amid all the revived fury of racial and religious hatred. Orange Ontario demanded Riel's life for Scott's; Roman Catholic Quebec demanded clemency for this "gallant," "religious" Frenchman. An English-speaking jury found Riel guilty, but recommended further consideration before sentencing.

Riel's eventual death sentence only intensified the racial and religious feeling that threatened the unity of Canada and its government. Ignoring Riel's heresy, French Canada insisted that he live. (His heresy was, in their eyes, proof of his insanity.) Ignoring Riel's record of insanity, English Canada insisted that he die. Macdonald could commute the death sentence and lose Ontario, or let justice be done and lose Quebec; either course would harm the Conservative party. When a medical commission declared Riel sane but irresponsible, Macdonald rallied the

This important photograph shows Louis Riel addressing the court from the prisoner's dock during his trial in Regina in 1885. During the course of his long speech he said: "I am glad that the Crown have proved that I am the leader of the Half-breeds in the North-West. I will perhaps be one day acknowledged as more than a leader of the Half-breeds, and if I am I will have an opportunity of being acknowledged as a leader of good in this great country. . . ."

"Justice Not Satisfied" by Bengough. Sir John—"Well madam, Riel is gone; I hope you are satisfied." Justice—"No, I am not. You have hanged the effect *of the Rebellion. I must now punish you as the* cause."

"Had there been no neglect, there would have been no rebellion; if no rebellion, no arrest; if no arrest, no trial; if no trial, no condemnation; if no condemnation, no execution. They, therefore, who are responsible for the first are responsible for every link in that fatal chain."—Edward Blake.

support of his French colleagues and the Roman Catholic hierarchy against the storm that would break when he let Riel hang. In the chill, grey dawn of 16 November, the fatal trap dropped from under the tragic and pathetic figure of Louis Riel. As one commentator remarked: "The madman became a martyr."

"Riel, our brother, is dead," announced Honoré Mercier, "victim of his devotion to the cause of the Métis . . . , victim of fanaticism and treason. . . ." One English Canadian described Riel as "a cur of a self-interested conspirator." Was he a murderous traitor or the misguided victim of religious bigotry? Of his treason there can be no legal doubt, but of his sanity there is considerable medical doubt. Certainly his fate was influenced by political considerations. In 1886 French-Canadian *"nationalistes"* led by Honoré Mercier avenged Riel by ousting the Conservative government of Quebec, and in the general election of 1887 Macdonald retained a majority of only one seat in the province. As long as Macdonald's influence was alive in Hector Langevin, the Conservatives retained a foothold in Quebec; but for sixty years after Macdonald's death Quebec voted overwhelmingly against the party that had hanged Riel.

UNREPENTANT PROVINCES

In the first quarter-century of the dominion's existence, Canada discovered that a federation is the most difficult form of constitution to operate. Every federation is an artificial creation, its existence a recognition of the distinctiveness of its component parts. Canada was (and is) no exception, and in the years immediately following 1867 the local loyalties of the pre-Confederation era remained strong.

The Fathers of Confederation deliberately strengthened the federal government at the expense of the provinces to overcome the sectionalism that had cursed the Province of Canada and to avoid the "states' rights" issue that had caused the American Civil War. Section 92 of the British North America Act had enumerated sixteen exclusively provincial "classes of subjects," but Section 91 left residual powers of legislation in federal hands. Legal demarcation lines between two authorities are never absolute, but the intention of the BNA Act was clear. Yet after Confederation the Ontario Liberal party, feeding on many of the prejudices of Upper Canada tradition, spearheaded a movement for "provincial rights" which, within twenty-five years, upset and partially reversed the balance of power established in 1867.

The provincial rights agitation had two important aspects—a demand for revision of the financial settlement of the BNA Act, and a demand for greater "provincial autonomy." Adopting the arguments used by the southern states prior to the American Civil War, advocates of provincial rights argued a "compact theory" of Confederation and announced that the provinces were partners, not subordinates, of the dominion government. The Toronto *Globe* put the basic assumption of this theory succinctly: "The Dominion is the creation of these Provinces."

The financial aspect of provincial rights first arose in 1869 when Joseph Howe won "better terms" for Nova Scotia. Edward Blake, Premier of Ontario, protested that the federal government could not revise the 1867 settlement without the agreement of all the provinces and implied that Ontario, too, had to get equal treatment. Yet the per capita grants rule could not be applied

Left, John Norquay, Premier of Manitoba, 1878-1886. Right, Oliver Mowat, Premier of Ontario.

rigidly, or the smaller provinces would suffer. The disparity in grants became even greater when Manitoba and British Columbia entered Confederation. When Prince Edward Island joined the dominion in 1873, it received such exceptional financial treatment that the old formula was destroyed, leaving no semblance of equality in the grants. Federal-provincial relations were further complicated by the depression, which fell so heavily on the smaller provinces, and by the clash of political personalities. Unlike Ontario, which had budget deficits in only three of its first twenty-one years, the other provinces were almost continually in financial difficulty and were forced to look to Ottawa for help.

When Blake resigned the Ontario premiership in 1872 to devote all his time to federal politics, Oliver Mowat succeeded to a term of office that lasted until 1896. Blake's policy of opposing "the infringement of provincial interests" was vigorously pursued by Mowat. This squint-eyed former student of Macdonald's law office had become Sir John's most dogged, bitter and able political enemy even before Confederation. Their rivalry affected both Canadian and Ontario politics.

The first real clash over provincial rights, however, was delayed until 1879, because Liberals were ruling on both Toronto and Ottawa. The Liberal truce was ended by Macdonald's success at the polls, and the battle of provincial rights began, the pretext being an issue that did not concern the federal government—the disputed boundary between Manitoba and Ontario. At the time, Manitoba was surrounded on three sides by the North-West Territories, whose boundary with Ontario was the height of land between Hudson Bay and the St. Lawrence basin. During the Mackenzie regime the delineation of Ontario's western boundary was referred to three arbitrators, whose decision in 1878 gave Ontario 144,000 square miles of land between Port Arthur and the Lake of the Woods. Once back in office, Macdonald referred to the award as "a scrap of waste paper" and in 1881 passed an act establishing the western boundary of Ontario as Manitoba's eastern boundary—but failed (deliberately) to define the boundary.

Macdonald's action had political and economic motives. The Liberals were his enemies, especially Mowat and the Ontario Liberals. Federal support for Manitoba's claim would demonstrate to Ontario the advantage of electing a Conservative provincial government (as Manitoba had just done). Then, too, the eastward extension of Manitoba's boundary would be partial compensation for federal ownership of its natural resources and would make Manitoba a province in central Canada. Predictably, Ontario rejected Macdonald's plan. As far as Ontario was concerned, the award of 1878 had been "final and conclusive." Tension in the disputed area rose as the federal and Ontario governments both granted timber licenses; Manitoba and Ontario both held elections there, and Manitoba sent an artillery battery to enforce its sovereignty. In this crisis, it was agreed to put the issue before the Judicial Committee of the British Privy Council, which, in 1884, upheld the 1878 award to Ontario. Manitoba had perhaps, as some authorities have suggested, the better historical claim to the territory, but Macdonald's scheming against Mowat had worked to the disadvantage of Manitoba.

Other Macdonald techniques were backfiring, too. His use of

"Let the Big Chief Beware," a Bengough cartoon on Manitoba and the railway monopoly issue.

the federal government's power to disallow provincial acts considered undesirable in the national interest had led to a series of court cases, many of which were decided only by a final appeal to the Judicial Committee of the Privy Council. In *Russell v. the Queen* (1882) the Judicial Committee decided that federal legislation for "peace, order and good government" might affect property and civil rights in the provinces, but that every act must be judged "in the particular instance under discussion." One year later, in *Hodge v. the Queen*, it was determined that the exclusive provincial jurisdictions under Section 92 might not ordinarily be infringed by the federal government. This latter decision began a long trend in the courts that altered the intended balance of the Canadian constitution. By the mid 1890's the true residual power had come to rest with the provinces by virtue of their power, given in Section 92, to legislate for property and civil rights. Ironically, Macdonald's centralist interpretation of the BNA Act and his stress on the federal residual powers of Section 91 had been the real reasons for his frequent use of disallowance, which had precipitated the Judicial Committee's curiously illogical decisions in favour of the provinces.

Thus far, Mowat's Ontario had been the driving force in the struggle for provincial rights. Alone of all the provinces Ontario was solvent and prosperous and could not be bribed into silence by financial concessions from Macdonald. But the incident that brought all the forces of provincialism together was, paradoxically, the execution of Riel. In Quebec a Liberal-Conservative coalition had formed *Le Parti National*, a French-Canadian party based on race and dedicated to avenging Riel. In 1886, headed by the stirring orator Honoré Mercier, chosen as leader in 1883, the *Nationalistes* defeated the Conservative government of Quebec and raised the cry of provincial autonomy. The following year Mercier called an interprovincial conference to discuss "the autonomy of the Provinces and their financial arrangements with the Dominion." Ontario, Nova Scotia and New Brunswick, all Liberal provinces, accepted Mercier's invitation, as did John Norquay, the Conservative premier of Manitoba, who had been constantly frustrated by financial problems and Macdonald's defence of the C.P.R. monopoly. Macdonald and the Conservative premiers of Prince Edward Island and British Columbia were unrepresented.

With Mowat as chairman, the conference proceeded to challenge Macdonald's basic assumption that governmental powers should be predominantly centralized. It passed a series of resolutions, most of which reflected Ontario's particular interest in the provincial rights struggle and all of which were clearly aimed at decreasing federal powers. Perhaps doubting their ultimate success, the conference members also passed a resolution calling for larger federal subsidies. Ultimately nothing concrete resulted from the interprovincial conference because Macdonald would not co-operate and the provinces could do nothing alone. Later, however, successive court decisions sustained Mowat's views on the power of the provincial executive and legislature.

The apparent harmony of the Liberal provinces at Quebec in 1887, in opposition to the federal government, was soon replaced by a violent return of those very cultural problems that had weakened the Union of 1841. In the wake of the row between Quebec and Ontario over the fate of Riel, Mercier, who owed his power to Riel's death, re-opened the question of "one Canada, or two" with his Jesuit Estates Act. Following the demise of the Jesuit Order after its suppression by the Papacy in 1773, the income from the Order's Quebec property (some 900,000 acres) had been directed to educational purposes. But when the Order was re-established and had returned to Canada in the 1840's, the legal ownership of the estates was placed in doubt. Mercier's Act sought a final settlement of the various claims. The sum of $400,000 was to be divided by the Papacy to settle the claims of the Jesuits and the Quebec bishops, and $60,000 was to be paid to the Protestant schools of Quebec. Immediately, Ontario voices denounced this intervention of a "foreign potentate" in Canadian affairs. Dalton McCarthy, a leading Conservative, founded the Equal Rights Association which, with Orange support, crusaded against "Romish aggression." Here were all the elements of the fiery fifties repeated—Protestant ascendancy, religious endowment, and French Catholic separatism. In the House of Commons eight Conservatives and five Liberals, the self-styled "Noble 13" (or "the devil's dozen") voted in vain for disallowance of the Quebec Jesuit Estates Act. Macdonald, the centralist and nationalist, refused to interfere with provincial rights in this instance. At a mass protest rally in Toronto McCarthy announced the issue as he saw it—"whether this country is to be English or French." Unlike Macdonald, McCarthy equated unity with uniformity.

Frustrated in the east, McCarthy and the Ontario Equal Rights Association turned westward to that "little Ontario," the Province of Manitoba. Since 1871 its population had changed radically. The French and Métis were now a minority in an Anglo-Saxon society, with no prospect of ever regaining numerical superiority. The Manitoba Act had guaranteed an educational system for this minority at the time of federation, but no legal system then existed in fact. Subsequently, a dual system of Roman Catholic and Protestant schools, patterned after that of Quebec, had been created. But in 1890, inspired by McCarthy and the Manitoba Orange lodges, Thomas Greenway, Liberal successor to Premier Norquay, abolished the official use of the French language in the province and established a duplicate of Ontario's educational system, *without* its separate school provision.

Macdonald hesitated to disallow the Manitoba school and language acts; there had been too much disallowance in Manitoba already. The Manitoba courts upheld both acts in 1891. Since the School Act was within the letter, though admittedly not the spirit, of 1871, what could the federal government do to restore French educational rights in Manitoba and thereby pacify Quebec and the Roman Catholic bishops? The answer was remedial legislation to create separate schools as in Ontario; and the Conservative party was pledged to introduce it. The Liberals at Ottawa defended the right of Manitoba to reject separate schools, and the Liberal government of Manitoba rejected the proposal of separate schools. Ironically, it was Wilfrid Laurier, a French-speaking, Roman Catholic and a Liberal, who called for the conciliation, not the coercion, of Manitoba when Macdonald's Conservative heirs failed to pass the remedial bill. It was Laurier who inherited the Manitoba schools question with all its cultural, religious and political implications when the generation of Conservative supremacy at Ottawa was ended in 1896.

SIR JOHN'S LAST TRIUMPH

The closing years of Macdonald's life were disturbed by many conflicts. The cultural conflict raised by the Jesuit Estates Act was projected westward into the Manitoba schools question which, in turn, overflowed into the North-West Territories, starting a row there over the place of the French language. There were disputes with Stephen and the C.P.R. regarding relations between the Company and the government. The United States had rejected a fisheries treaty with Canada and was disputing

Canadian sealing rights in the Bering Sea. Over all these difficulties hung the daunting cloud of depression that had frustrated Macdonald's fondest dreams.

A general election was called early in 1891. Macdonald's campaign strategy was to attack the Liberal policy of unrestricted reciprocity as *the* threat to Canada's existence. A national transcontinental railway and a National Policy of protection had been the basis of his design for Canada. Unrestricted reciprocity would be the antecedent to annexation. "A British subject I was born and a British subject I will die!" was Sir John's rallying cry. He charged the provincial rights Liberals with virtual treason for conniving with United States annexationists. Following his lead, the Conservatives linked the Union Jack with the National Policy, shouting long and loud their election slogan: "The old flag, the old man, the old policy!"

Macdonald set himself a killing electioneering pace in the changeable winter weather. Before the end of February he was physically exhausted, unable to finish his tour. When the ballots were counted on 5 March, the Conservatives had been returned, but seats had been lost in Quebec and Ontario. The depression and the McKinley tariff had combined to convert many farmers to the Liberal ideal of unrestricted reciprocity. Macdonald's "loyalty" cry, however, had been more effective in the end.

Macdonald was recuperating slowly from the campaign. When the new Parliament met on 29 April he was his old, good-humoured self again. But on 12 May he suffered a mild stroke. He recovered rapidly and refused to excuse himself from work. Two weeks later he was again stricken, and again two days later, on 29 May. This third stroke racked his frail body and left him completely helpless and speechless. Still he clung to life for another week until, in the stillness of an early June evening, he died.

For forty-seven years John A. Macdonald had served in the Canadian political arena; for nineteen of those years he had been prime minister of the dominion that he had done so much to create. In the House of Commons Hector Langevin, Macdonald's faithful follower for over thirty years, was obliged to leave his eulogy of Sir John unfinished. "My heart is full of tears. I cannot

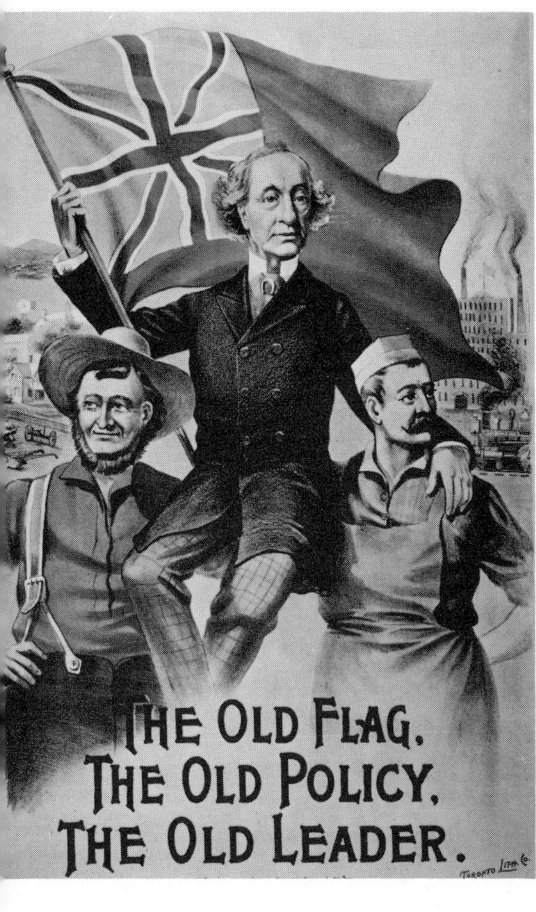

A Conservative election poster of 1891.

proceed further." Before being taken to Kingston for burial, the Old Chieftain's body lay in state in the red-carpeted Senate Chamber, and on his breast was a wreath of roses inscribed: "From Her Majesty Queen Victoria, in memory of Her faithful and devoted servant."

Whatever his personal shortcomings may have been, Macdonald had indeed served his Queen and his adopted land with faith and devotion. At much personal cost he had held fast to his vision of a great national destiny until that vision had become Canada's vision. Macdonald's friends and enemies alike were deeply moved by the death of this great Canadian.

THE CONSERVATIVES WITHOUT MACDONALD

The death of Macdonald was a serious blow to Canada and a crushing one to the Conservative party. The depression, strained relations with the United States, internecine religio-racial controversies, and the struggle over provincial rights still plagued the country. As for the party, the Old Chieftain had had no heir apparent. Sir John had been the Conservative party. Without him it was a headless body. Dalton McCarthy, once marked as Sir John's successor, had committed political suicide by fostering political Protestantism. Hector Langevin lacked the magnetism and drive of a leader. Sir Charles Tupper had no interest in returning to political life. George E. Foster, the slim, bespectacled Minister of Finance, directed the best-run government department and was a possibility for prime minister. John S. Thompson, Minister of Justice, could best have filled Sir John's empty shoes, but the fact that he was a convert to Roman Catholicism had singled him out for political and religious persecution. The final choice—at Thompson's insistence—was the aged but able Senator J. J. C. Abbott.

In 1892 Conservative prospects seemed to improve. The party won more than a dozen by-elections, and in the Province of Quebec the corrupt Mercier regime, which had led the province deeply into debt, was condemned by a royal commission, dismissed by the Lieutenant-Governor and finally overwhelmed in a general election. In Ottawa, Abbott resigned after eighteen months in office and Thompson, who had been virtual head of the government because of his ability and his position in the Commons, became prime minister. Thompson's appointment was generally received with approval, although some denounced him as the tool of ultramontism because of his defence of the Jesuit Estates Act. Thompson's wise insistence on keeping his religion separate from his role as public servant did much to allay opposition to any future Canadian prime minister on grounds of faith.

Thompson's policies were essentially those of Macdonald.

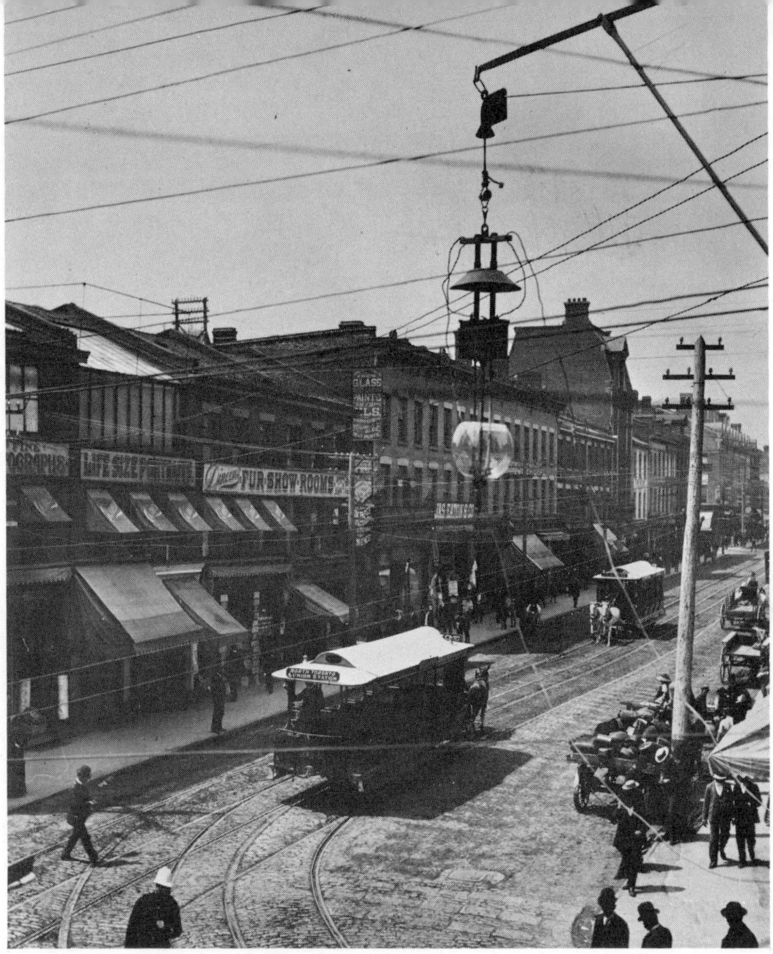

Yonge Street, Toronto, in the 1890's. The scene is typical of many large communities in Canada at the time. Within a few years, however, many changes were to take place; the street cars would be electrified; automobiles and trucks would displace horse-drawn vehicles; and the streets would be lighted by electricity.

He tried in vain to keep the Manitoba schools question out of politics by leaving it to the courts. He strongly upheld Macdonald's rejection of reciprocity with the United States, fearing that it would lead to annexation. A major achievement of Thompson's period in office was the settlement of the long-standing dispute between the United States, Canada, Britain and Russia over seal fisheries in the Bering Sea. Britain successfully rejected the American claim to sovereignty, but all the countries

Sir Charles Tupper in 1893.

agreed on regulating the fur-sealing industry to conserve the declining herd of these valuable animals.

The sudden death of Thompson in December, 1894, raised again the vexatious problem of party leadership. George Foster was now party leader in the Commons, but Governor General Lord Aberdeen chose Senator Mackenzie Bowell, the senior cabinet member, as prime minister. Foster, like several of his cabinet colleagues, had little confidence in Bowell, and what little he did have disappeared during 1895. Early that year the Judicial Committee of the Privy Council decided that the federal parliament could constitutionally pass remedial legislation to deal with the Manitoba schools question. Bowell, however, delayed for a year, precipitating resignations from the cabinet and widespread dissatisfaction within the party. Finally, in January, 1896, a compromise was reached; Bowell remained prime minister, but Sir Charles Tupper entered the cabinet with the clear understanding that he would replace Bowell very shortly.

Tupper soon obtained a Commons seat, assumed the party leadership in the House and introduced the long-awaited remedial bill. The moment of truth in the Manitoba schools question had arrived for both parties. After six weeks of obstruction by McCarthy, his Orange followers from Ontario, and the Liberals, Tupper withdrew the remedial bill. Soon after, parliament was dissolved and Tupper succeeded Bowell and went to the country on the issue of the remedial bill. In the course of his energetic campaign Tupper defended the bill in the face of noisy, hostile crowds in Ontario. It was not Ontario, however, that defeated the Conservative's remedial bill, but Roman Catholic Quebec—despite a warning from the Bishop of Trois Rivières that a vote for "Barabbas" Laurier was a sin. Laurier, the favourite son, took forty-nine seats in Quebec, Tupper and the bishops held sixteen, while Orange Ontario gave a majority to the Conservative supporters of Manitoba separate schools. On that strangely discordant note ended seventeen years of Conservative rule in Canada. The Age of Macdonald—and its dismal postlude—was over. The Age of Laurier was about to begin.

* * *

The Liberals achieved political victory at an opportune moment; the long depression was lifting at last. Perhaps Laurier, who was French, Roman Catholic and Liberal, could repair the damage done to the cause of national unity by Riel's execution and the prolonged struggle over provincial rights. In any case, the Liberals now had their chance to implement their favourite policies of freer trade, retrenchment and honest administration.

CHAPTER 12

THE POLICY FULFILLED

The election of 1896 is a watershed in Canadian history because it marks the dissolution of Macdonald's party and his political system, which together had dominated the Canadian scene since Confederation. The new prime minister, Wilfrid Laurier, was destined, however, to achieve a place in Canada's history second only to that of Macdonald.

Affable and jaunty, Macdonald had capitalized upon his homely appeal to Canadians. By contrast, the suave and sophisticated Laurier captivated his audiences with his silver-tongued oratory and his appeal to the highest principles of public policy. Laurier, his high-browed, balding head fringed with a shock of prematurely greying hair, was the new leader and the image of his nation in a new age. Still, much that was basic to the Age of Macdonald lived on in the Age of Laurier. The same problems of national development and external relations, the same internal stresses of race, language and religion remained, and they were met by policies effected by a Liberal who called himself a disciple of the "Old Chieftain."

LAURIER AND "SUNNY WAYS"

Laurier's first act as prime minister was to choose his cabinet members. The Liberals were fortunate in having a large number of able men, many of them still relatively young, in their ranks.

From them Laurier selected one of the strongest cabinets in Canada's history, "The Ministry of all Talents" as contemporaries described it. It included the redoubtable and experienced Sir Richard Cartwright at Trade and Commerce, Sir Oliver Mowat as Minister of Justice, W. S. Fielding, a former premier of Nova Scotia in Finance, and Clifford Sifton, Manitoba's Minister of Education, as Minister of the Interior.

Before this strong team could begin planning a Liberal program for Canada, it was called upon to close the Manitoba schools question once and for all. Laurier had promised that there would be no coercion—only the "sunny ways" of conciliation. He and the Liberal provincial ministers agreed to a solution of the religious question that avoided any coercive action from Ottawa, while establishing by law, among other things, the right of religious denominations to give religious instruction in the public schools at specified times. But this was a settlement in name only, for the Roman Catholic bishops of Quebec continued to denounce the terms and all supporters thereof. In Quebec, Roman Catholics were forbidden to read the Liberal newspaper, *L'Electeur*, on the threat of being excluded from the Church. Sir Charles Tupper, the seventy-five-year-old Conservative leader, took full advantage of the Church's opposition to Laurier and his government by echoing the bishops' contention that justice had been denied to the Roman Catholic minority in Manitoba. As a last resort to overcome the opposition of the bishops and the political opportunism of the Conservatives, several Roman Catholic Liberals appealed to the Pope, who sent a legate (representative) to investigate. The legate managed to impose a grudging silence on the bishops, and so the Manitoba schools question was closed. Henceforth, the bishops avoided open political involvement.

The second issue that had played a prominent role in the recent general election was the tariff. Traditionally the party of free—or at least freer—trade, the Liberals had unequivocally reaffirmed their stand against protection at their 1893 convention. Yet even before the election, Laurier had stated publicly that genuine free trade was impossible for Canada and that a Liberal government would have to maintain a tariff for revenue purposes. Immediately after the election, Laurier announced: "The tariff should not be reformed, in my estimation, except after ample discussion with the businessmen. . . ." And so a tariff commission was appointed, which visited commercial and industrial centres to hear opinions. Then, in April, 1897, Fielding introduced the first Liberal budget, a budget that set the tone for the future. A number of nuisance duties were abolished, *ad valorem* duties (duties in proportion to the estimated value of goods) replaced specific ones, and tariffs protecting Canadian monopolies and combines were reduced. Most significantly, the budget provided for high and low tariff schedules, the lower one being for countries that gave equally favourable rates to Canada. This last provision was intended to permit a preference to free-trading Britain, an aim espoused by the Liberals for several years past. In 1898 a special British preference, one-quarter less than the regular rate, was established.

At first sight this Liberal tariff did seem more liberal than

Barr colonists prepare their wagons to leave Saskatoon for Lloydminster, May 1, 1903. Isaac Barr, an Anglican priest born in Ontario, was a great admirer of Cecil Rhodes. Frustrated in his ambition to work with Rhodes in Africa. Barr decided to start his own colony of English settlers in western Canada. From the beginning the venture was plagued by trouble. Originally the plans called for three ships to transport the colonists but in the end the entire party of over 1,900 was crammed into one ship. Barr himself proved to be aloof, and an unhappy rivalry developed between him and his assistant G. E. Lloyd, another Anglican priest, who was very popular among the colonists. The settlers, most of whom were used to city life, were totally unprepared for the rigours of life on the Canadian prairie. Barr became personally discouraged by what he considered to be his failure and left for the United States. Traditionally it has been held that he absconded with the colony's funds, but more recent research has shown this accusation to be unjustified.

Macdonald's National Policy, yet by some clauses the protectionist aims of the National Policy were achieved by roundabout means. The reduction of the tariff on iron and steel was offset by government bounties for Canadian production. Most of the tariff reductions were so minimal that few manufacturers ever complained about loss of protection. Some industrial interests in succeeding years actually got as much as 5 percent more tariff protection than the original National Policy had given. For the consumer, British preference did bring some relief from the burden of a protective tariff, but it became less important with each passing year, since Canada continued to import more from the United States than from Britain.

IMMIGRANTS AND RAILWAYS

There was a bitter irony in the ending of the depression, for now with the return of prosperity Laurier, the embodiment of Liberalism, was able to fulfill one plan which Macdonald, the soul of Conservatism, had conceived. Macdonald had promoted the C.P.R. to populate and develop the west, but his hopes had largely met with failure. It was left to Laurier, and particularly to his imaginative, energetic Minister of the Interior, Clifford Sifton, to fill the fertile western plains with farmers who turned this region into the granary of the empire and the breadbasket of the world.

During 1896 only some 1,800 homesteads had been taken up in the west, and less than 600 settlers had come from the older Canada. Between Port Arthur and Victoria there were only 300,000 souls, and almost a third of these were Indian. But now, thirty years after Confederation, the tide of fate turned. The development of early-maturing, frost-resistant varieties of wheat, the introduction of the roller-milling method of making flour, the intensive use of such aids as the superior chilled-steel plough and binders, government aid in the construction of grain elevators, docks, grain-boats and new railways gave the grain producers of the west great technical advantages over European agriculture. All over the world the price of farm products rose as more

KINGS

people settled in industrial cities and as new supplies of gold from Australia, South Africa and Canada filled international coffers. The American west that had drained off so much of Canada's population was now almost all occupied, and the flow of settlers seeking land flooded northward into western Canada.

But it was not land alone that brought settlers, for the empty spaces of Australia beckoned and American railroads still had millions of acres for sale. The difference for Canada was the unparalleled promotional campaign conducted by Clifford Sifton, a man who knew the Canadian west, its opportunities and its needs. This dapper man, who epitomized the Ontario Grits that had settled in the west, was outwardly reserved and publicly reputed to be ruthlessly impersonal. In fact, he was friendly and outgoing, though inclined to be impulsive and hot-tempered. Now, stemming from Sifton's faith in the future of the west, a vast flood of booklets, posters and advertisements in many languages told the people of Europe and the United States of Canada's great promise, free land, and assisted passages to immigrants. Paid agents were appointed to obtain settlers. Newspapermen and a number of British M.P.s were entertained with trips to "the last, best West." Even the help of philanthropic societies was enlisted. This systematic, energetic campaign bore astounding fruit.

First came Europeans—Germans, Hungarians, Ukrainians, Ruthenians (from the Balkans), Scandinavians, Icelanders, Russian Doukhobors, all by the thousands. Then followed American immigrants, whose numbers jumped from a mere 700 entries in 1896 to nearly 13,000 in 1911. Finally, waves of British settlers arrived, even more numerous than the Americans. When total immigration during the fifteen years of Liberal government was reckoned up, over 2,000,000 people had arrived in Canada. The southern regions of the North-West Territories were largely filled and their population expanded five-fold. Sifton's magnifi-

Top, homesteaders, Mr. and Mrs. Tom Ogden from Boston, en route to their new home in Alberta, 1910.
Centre, branding calves on an Alberta ranch, 1904.
Bottom, a real estate office in Wainwright, Alberta, around 1910.

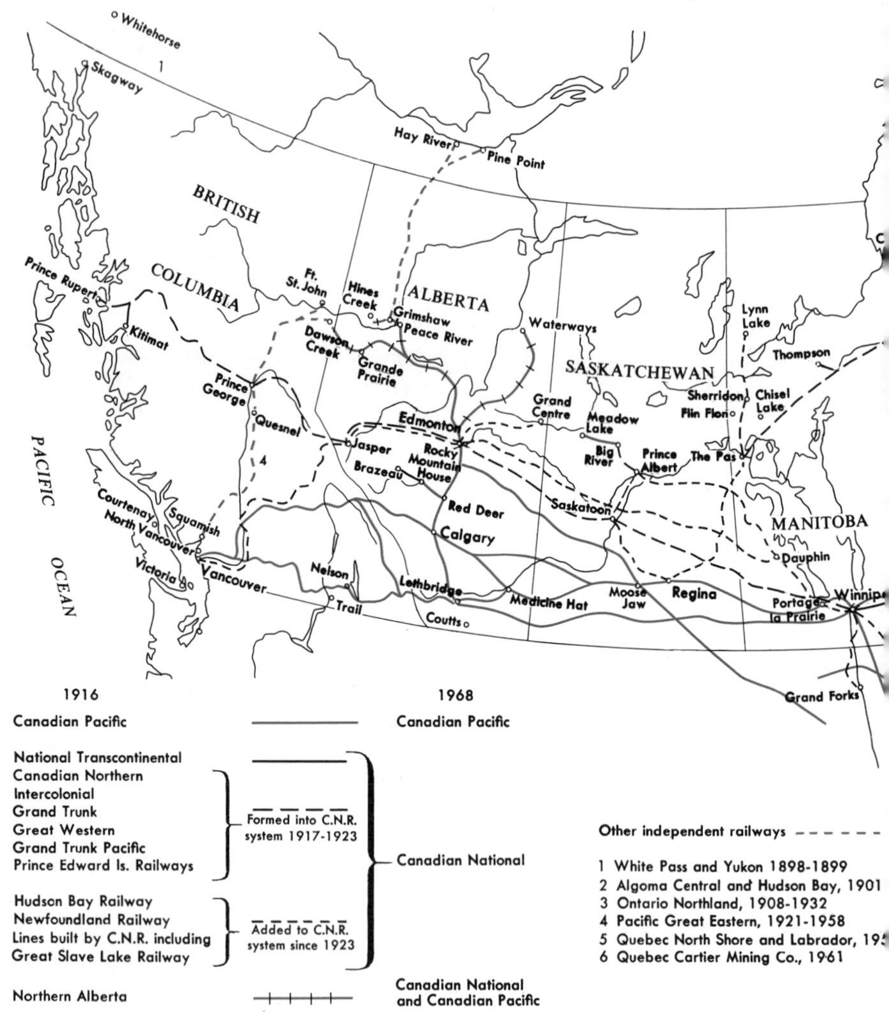

cent advertising attracted these new Canadians, and the free homestead system settled many of them. (In 1908 an area almost as large as Portugal was given away under the homestead system, and grants in 1909 equalled an area five times that of Prince Edward Island.)

Hand in hand with the exploitation and population of the prairie wheatlands went another aspect of economic nationalism,

CANADIAN RAILWAYS, 1916 AND 1968

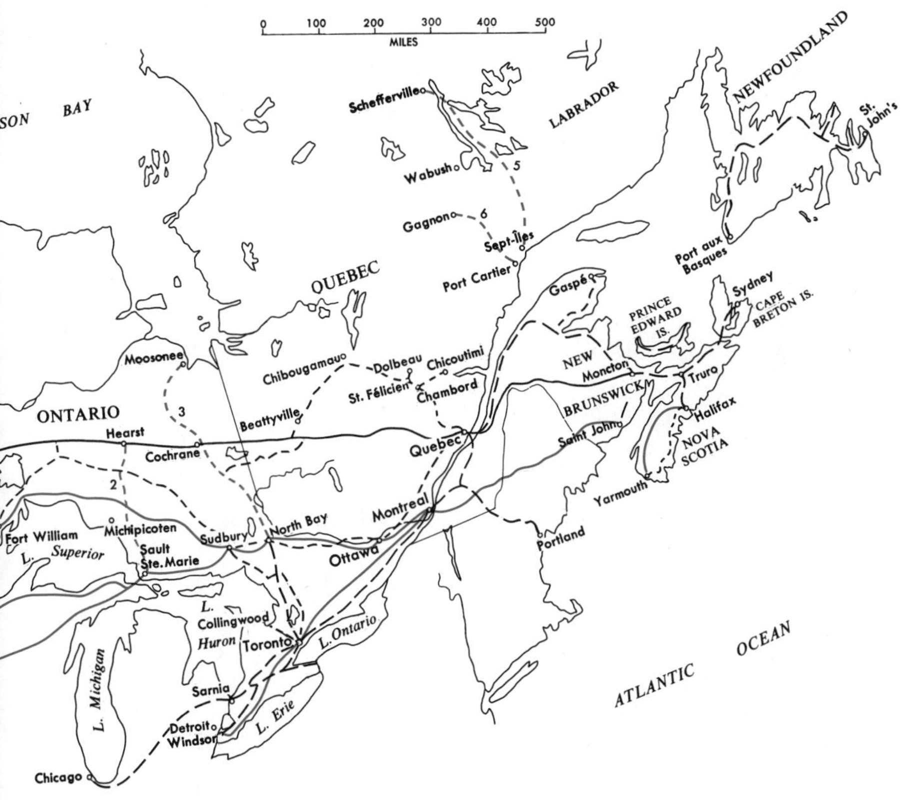

the development of communications. In the fifteen years following 1896 nearly 20,000 miles of railway track were laid, and much of that mileage was in the west. Railways served several purposes —immediately getting settlers into the west, hauling grain out and, looking to future years, gradually creating more settlement and thus creating more business. In 1901 and 1902, however, C.P.R. facilities were unable to handle the increasing volume of eastbound wheat. In the words of Van Horne, "the hopper was too big for the spout." An obvious need for more railways in the west existed. Late in 1902 the Grand Trunk, Canada's oldest railway system, offered to build a second transcontinental line from Winnipeg to the Pacific coast if given a subsidy of 5,000 acres and $6,000 a mile for construction costs. Soon the Canadian Northern Railway publicized its interest in constructing a transcontinental line. Sifton believed three lines would be wasteful and proposed a division of labour—the Canadian Northern would build and service a western line in conjunction with the Grand Trunk, which would build a line from the edge of the prairies to Canada's eastern ports. Unfortunately, such was the excessive confidence and optimism of the time that Laurier was pressured within and without parliament to support both a Grand Trunk Pacific Railway, in the form of a *government-built* line (the National Transcontinental) from Moncton to Winnipeg, and certain cash subsidies for the Grand Trunk Pacific's Winnipeg-Prince Rupert section. At the same time Laurier permitted the Canadian Northern to build a line from Winnipeg to the west coast, parallel to and very close to the Grand Trunk Pacific line. Admittedly, the C.P.R. was unable to serve the entire Canadian west, but *two* new transcontinental lines were at least *one* too many. The old, tragic railway story of eastern Canada—too many uneconomic and competing railways—was blithely repeated in western Canada half a century later.

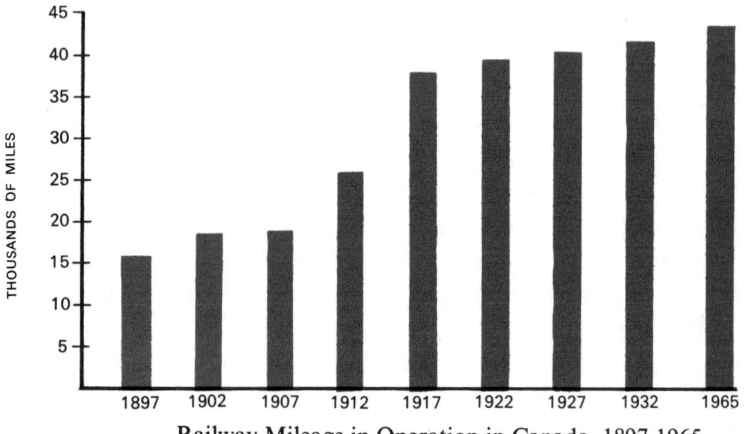

Railway Mileage in Operation in Canada, 1897-1965

Prominent among those who settled in Manitoba early in the new century were Ukrainians. At the top is a view of a Ukrainian church around 1910. The lower photograph is of a steam threshing outfit in Manitoba.

By 1907 the Grand Trunk Pacific was in extreme financial difficulty. Costs had exceeded estimates by as much as 200 per-cent, and Ottawa had to lend money to the company again and again. By the time the last spike had been driven in, early in 1914, the Grand Trunk Pacific was hopelessly in debt. The same story holds true of William Mackenzie and Donald A. Mann's

Canadian Northern. Together, these two remarkable promoters were able to transform various shoestring-financed companies into a vast transportation empire that ran westward from Winnipeg through the Yellowhead Pass to Vancouver, and eastward as far as Quebec City. Mackenzie showed a positive genius at wheedling money out of financiers, while Mann lobbied in Ottawa for financial support with amazing success. But even before the Canadian Northern system was finished (1915), Mackenzie and Mann had used up their government subsidies, had sold government-guaranteed bonds, had given up $40,000,000 in stock to the federal government and were again begging further loans from Ottawa.

By its encouragement of railway construction the Liberal government gave Canada infinitely more railway mileage than was necessary, and a financial headache into the bargain. (By the early twenties, the Canadian taxpayer had to bear the cost of the bankruptcies of the National Transcontinental, the Grand Trunk Pacific, the Canadian Northern *and* the Grand Trunk itself.) Yet, once committed to an expansionist railway policy, the government was either too deeply committed or too blind to the economic facts of Canadian life to draw back. Macdonald's unswerving support of the C.P.R. in its early days had been justified because that bond of steel was absolutely necessary to the young nation's existence. Laurier's blank cheques to both the Grand Trunk Pacific and the Canadian Northern can only be accounted examples of irresolution—if not of irresponsibility.

"CANADA'S CENTURY" BEGINS

During the years that the Canadian prairies resounded to the clang of spike-hammers and the whirr of binders, and the babel of foreign tongues filled the air of eastern ports, the Canadian nation and its Liberal government underwent a variety of strains and stresses. In 1900, 1904 and 1908, Laurier's party had won increasing strength at the polls, but these victories had their price. The support of the Canadian Manufacturers' Association had been won in exchange for an upward revision of the tariff.

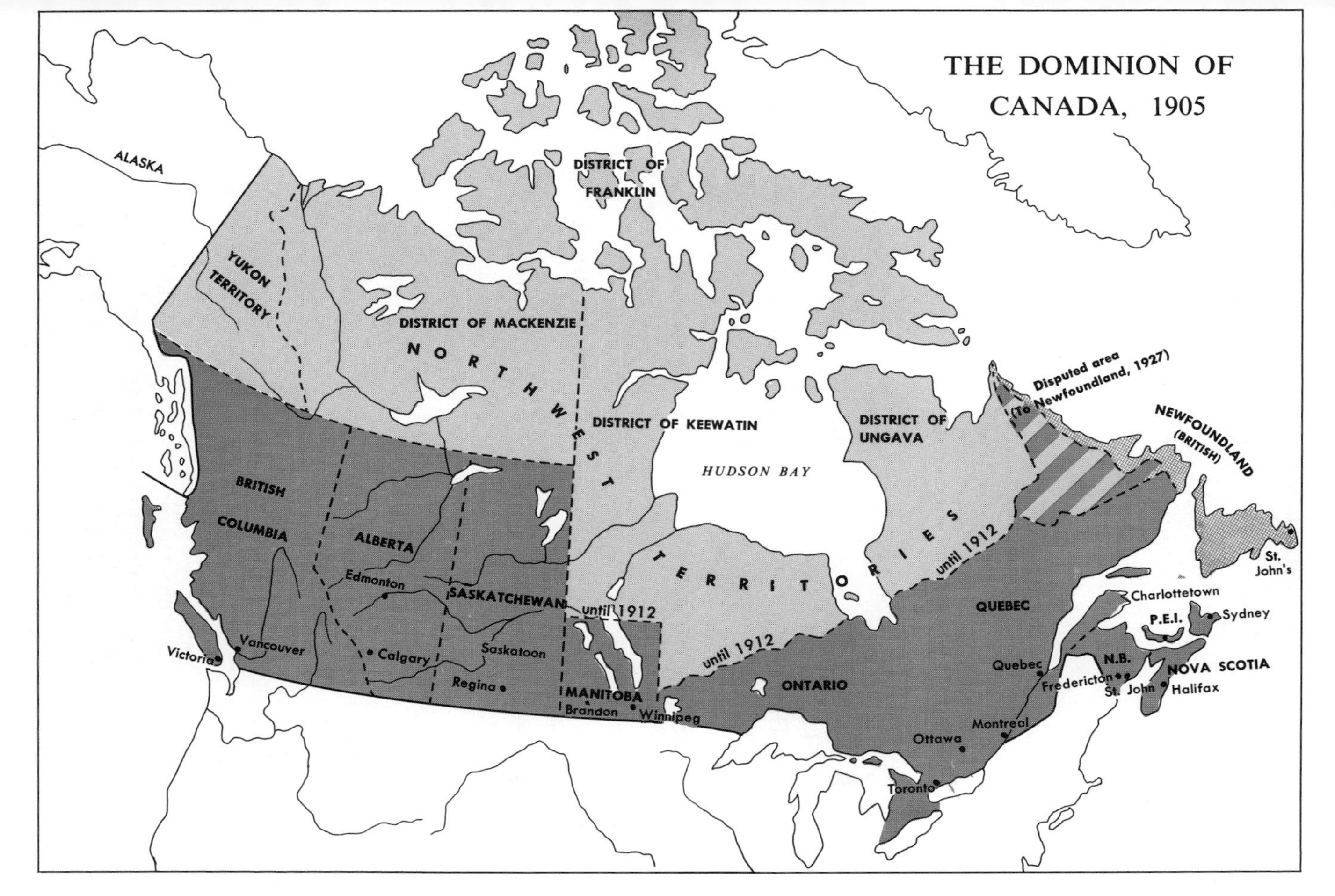
THE DOMINION OF
CANADA, 1905
ALASKA
YUKON
TERRITORY
DISTRICT OF
FRANKLIN
DISTRICT OF MACKENZIE
NORTHWEST TERRITORIES
DISTRICT OF KEEWATIN
HUDSON BAY
DISTRICT OF
UNGAVA
Disputed area
(To Newfoundland, 1927)
NEWFOUNDLAND
(BRITISH)
St. John's
until 1912
until 1912
until 1912
BRITISH
COLUMBIA
ALBERTA
SASKATCHEWAN
MANITOBA
ONTARIO
QUEBEC
N.B.
P.E.I.
NOVA SCOTIA
Victoria
Vancouver
Edmonton
Calgary
Saskatoon
Regina
Brandon
Winnipeg
Toronto
Ottawa
Montreal
Quebec
Fredericton
St. John
Halifax
Charlottetown
Sydney

In 1905 Clifford Sifton had resigned from the government when it tried to limit the educational autonomy of the new provinces of Saskatchewan and Alberta by saddling them with denominational schools. Although a compromise was reached with Sifton, he did not return to the cabinet, for in these two policies—the tariff and provincial autonomy—Laurier Liberalism had departed significantly from traditional Liberal policies and from the platform of 1896. More serious for Canada's future at this time were problems that involved external relations.

Towards the end of the nineteenth century the settlement of a number of minor issues between the United States and Canada became imperative, and a Joint High Commission of British, American and Canadian representatives met in 1898 to consider these difficulties. One issue in particular, the boundary between Alaska and Canadian territory on the Pacific coast, defied solution.

The Anglo-Russian Treaty of 1825, supposedly defining the Alaska boundary, had been worded very vaguely. Its statement that the boundary was to "follow the summit of the mountains situated parallel to the coast" was interpreted by Canada to mean the line of mountains nearest the sea and by the United States to mean a line of mountains that would ensure an unbroken strip of coastal land. The question had been discussed in 1888, but it became a live issue when gold was discovered along the Klondike River in 1896. The tens of thousands of gold-seekers who poured into the Yukon, especially in '98, entered the interior from the deep coastal inlets of the Stikine River or via the Lynn Canal. Were they crossing Canadian or American soil, and which country should police the gold route? The Alaska boundary now posed a very real problem—the gold rush had ended all academic discussion.

The dispute was referred to the Joint High Commission, but the commissioners could not arrive at an agreeable interpretation of the 1825 treaty. The imperialistic President Theodore Roosevelt denounced the Canadian claim to the coastal inlets as "dangerously close to blackmail." Finally, after American troops had been posted close to the Yukon in 1903—a move interpreted by Canadians as yet another Roosevelt "Big Stick" threat—

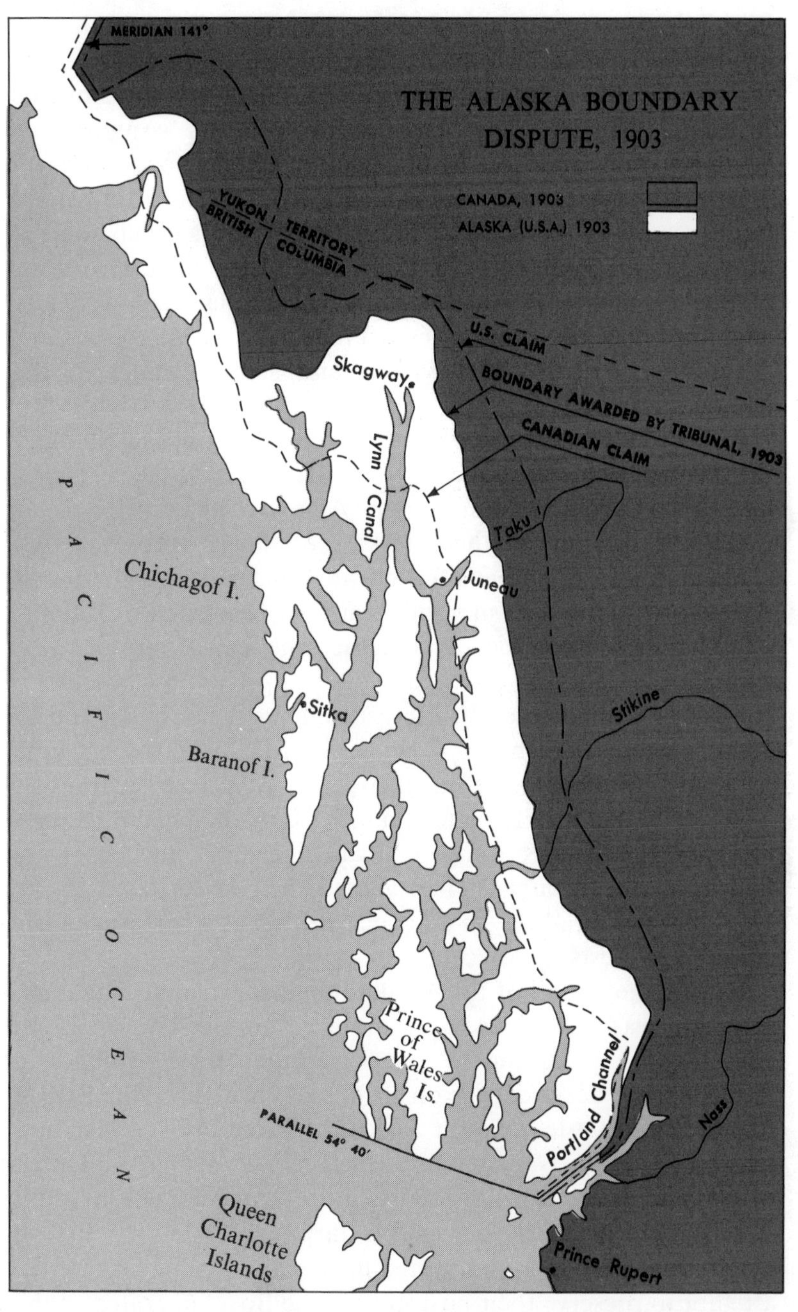
THE ALASKA BOUNDARY DISPUTE, 1903
CANADA, 1903
ALASKA (U.S.A.) 1903
MERIDIAN 141°
YUKON TERRITORY
BRITISH COLUMBIA
U.S. CLAIM
BOUNDARY AWARDED BY TRIBUNAL, 1903
CANADIAN CLAIM
Skagway
Lynn Canal
Taku
Juneau
Chichagof I.
Sitka
Baranof I.
Stikine
PACIFIC OCEAN
Prince of Wales Is.
Portland Channel
Nass
PARALLEL 54° 40′
Queen Charlotte Islands
Prince Rupert

Laurier's government accepted the American proposal that an arbitration tribunal be formed of six "impartial jurists of repute," three to be chosen by the American President and three by His Britannic Majesty. The American arbitrators—Anglophobe Secretary of War Elihu Root, Senator Cabot Lodge and ex-Senator George Turner—were all outspoken defenders of United States' rights in the Alaska "Panhandle," but it is debatable if the Canadian members—Sir Louis Jetté, Lieutenant-Governor of Quebec, and A. B. Aylesworth, a Toronto lawyer—were any less impartial. In these circumstances the opinion of Lord Alverstone, British Chief Justice and sixth member of the tribunal, was decisive.

Roosevelt considered the American claims unimpeachable and the tribunal as merely a means to let Britain "save face." Therefore, when Lord Alverstone and the American jurists rejected the Canadian version of the Alaska boundary, Roosevelt felt vindicated and Canadians felt cheated and robbed. (Jetté and Aylesworth refused to sign the award.) It was true Lord Alverstone had been more friendly with the American arbitrators than with his two Canadian colleagues, but trapped as he was between conflicting Canadian and American interests, he was bound to make enemies whichever way he voted. In retrospect, the tribunal's findings were justified; the American claim was historically and legally better than the Canadian claim. Nevertheless, Canadians were angered by the means as much as by the finding of the tribunal. They vented their spleen against the United States as a bully and against Britain as a betrayer of her colony's interests.

During the period of the Alaska boundary dispute Canadian attention was also focused on another, more distant crisis. In 1899 the Transvaal and Orange Free State, Boer republics in South Africa, declared war on Britain. Almost since the British had begun to settle in South Africa there had been conflict and tension. The Boers, a religious, self-reliant people of Dutch origin, and descendents of the first European colonists in South Africa, were primarily engaged in farming, while their British neighbours were more interested in trade and commerce. In an attempt to preserve their pastoral life the Boers migrated to the

During the winter of 1898/99 one of the main routes to the Klondike gold field led over the Chilkoot Pass (above). Day and night a steady stream of men, lurching under heavy packs, snaked across the steep pass. It is said that if a man lost his footing his place was immediately taken by those who followed and he might have to wait for hours before finding an opening in the line that would permit him to continue. The main town in the Klondike region was Dawson City (below). It sprung up quickly and flourished briefly as a supply centre. With the departure of the miners Dawson became a ghost town, its few inhabitants surrounded by decaying relics of those brief raucous months.

The front page of The Klondike News. The picture is of George Carmack, said to be the person who first discovered gold in the area.

north of the British settlements and established their own states, to which the British colonial authorities were eventually forced to grant independence. The tension, however, did not disappear and flared into open hostilities again in 1899.

Whatever the rights or wrongs of Boer and Briton in South Africa, the British Empire had been challenged, and the call to arms was heard in far-off Canada. Many English-speaking Canadians demanded that Canada defend the cause of empire; French Canadians (and a few English Canadians) denounced the war as an imperialistic "grab" of no concern to Canada and expressed their sympathy for two tiny republics attempting to defend their heritage.

Such a serious division of opinion, fed by the still-fresh memories of Riel, the Jesuit Estates and the Manitoba schools question, posed a major problem for Laurier. To eschew participation in the South African War would insult and incense pro-British sentiment in Canada, but to support the Empire in this struggle would anger and estrange Quebec nationalists and isolationists. In the face of mounting public pressure from Ontario Laurier gave way (as Macdonald had over Riel's death sentence) and authorized the raising, equipping and transporting of a Canadian contingent to serve in South Africa. Later, nearly 7,000 Canadians were recruited by the British government to serve in British units, while one private Canadian, Lord Strathcona (Donald Smith), organized a cavalry unit at his own expense.

For Canada, her limited participation in the South African War had results out of all proportion to her involvement. Canadian losses in action were few, and Canadian soldiers had distinguished themselves. Patriotic fervour was aroused, and a sense of participation in a great imperial destiny was imbued in many who had previously been indifferent to the idea of imperial unity. On the debit side, however, Laurier's early indecision and belated support of the mother country only perpetuated the political-cultural conflict within Canada. Such French Canadians as the arch-nationalists Israël Tarte, federal Minister of Public Works, and Henri Bourassa, who resigned his parliamentary seat in protest, roundly condemned this meddling in foreign affairs, while such Ontario imperialists as Sam Hughes branded Laurier's policy as inadequate and half-hearted. Neither group forgot or forgave Laurier's unsuccessful attempt to compromise on the question of Canada's relationship with Great Britain and the Empire.

THE QUESTION OF EMPIRE

In 1884 an Imperial Federation League was formed in Britain to promote closer political ties within the Empire. Three years later, on the occasion of Queen Victoria's fiftieth year as monarch, the Salisbury government (at the League's urging) invited representatives of the colonies to attend a colonial conference, the first of its kind. This invitation was a recognition of the new spirit of the Empire—an alliance of semi-dependent nations. As bonfires lit the night skies over Britain and as the venerated Queen attended a thanksgiving service in the company of princes and potentates from around the world, the colonial delegates discussed the prospect of political union, defence and commercial union.

Macdonald had not been present on that occasion, and Canada's delegates had deliberately taken no initiative in the discussion. Ordinary subjects might have been dazzled by the prospect of an Empire "mightier yet," but political leaders had been too well aware of the inherent difficulties in each of the three proposals under discussion to allow themselves to be hurried into any new imperial relationship. The only positive achievement of the conference was a small grant towards the cost of the imperial navy from the Australasian colonies.

Ten years passed and Victoria, now a small, enfeebled lady, celebrated her Diamond Jubilee. Another colonial conference was called, and Laurier was invited to attend in person. By this time many things besides the Canadian government had changed. Joseph Chamberlain, the most popular British statesman of the period, was now Colonial Secretary, a post he had coveted for more than a decade. Traditionally, the Colonial Office had been a very inferior cabinet position, but the dynamic and determined Chamberlain made it one of the most important ministries and was himself virtually "co-premier" with Lord Salisbury. Equally important, Chamberlain had broken completely with the previous *laissez-faire* attitude of indifference (and even of antagonism) towards the colonies voiced a generation earlier by such British politicians as Richard Cobden. Chamberlain intended to make the British Empire more than a name; he was prepared to advance British interests in every quarter of the globe. Naturally, he expected full support from the older, English-settled colonies.

As Colonial Secretary, Chamberlain presided at this third Colonial Conference (a less formal meeting of Empire statesmen at Ottawa in 1894 had been designated the second Conference).

Imperial organization along the three lines first suggested in 1887—political union, defence and commercial union—had been widely discussed during the decade, so that Chamberlain's call for an Imperial Council with certain executive powers "to develop into something still greater" came as no surprise. But, to the colonies, Chamberlain's vague approach towards imperial federation posed a thinly veiled threat to their highly prized autonomy, and all except New Zealand and Tasmania supported a resolution that "the present political relations between the United Kingdom and the self-governing Colonies are generally satisfactory under the existing condition of things." Imperial federation was now certainly dead, if not buried. On the matter of imperial defence the third Conference made virtually no progress since Canada, the senior colony, refused to consider any form of contribution to a truly imperial army or navy, on the grounds that this would mean commitment to action without consultation on policy. Similarly, the third issue, commercial union, had little prospect of success because the colonies, especially Canada, would not abandon tariff protection entirely and Britain would not give up free trade. As the twentieth century dawned, it was a self-satisfied but disparate Empire which faced the unknown future.

When the fourth Colonial Conference met in the summer of 1902 on the eve of Edward VII's coronation, Chamberlain was still Colonial Secretary and was still hopeful of achieving a great imperial unity. For a brief period the South African War had brought together the many parts of the Empire in a common cause, but pride in the achievement of their own soldiers had only served to foster nationalism in each colony. The centrifugal nationalism of peace was far stronger than the centripetal imperialism of war. Chamberlain again urged his plans for an Imperial Council; the colonies proved less interested than ever. Chamberlain again proposed colonial aid to meet the staggering costs of imperial defence (on which Britain was spending fourteen and a half times as much per capita as Canada); Canada spoke for all when she said she felt neither obligation nor danger. Chamberlain again advocated "free trade within the Empire"; the colonies would not give up their tariffs. The net

In honour of the coronation of Edward VII in 1902, Canada erected an arch in Whitehall, London. Loyalty to the crown and the promoting of immigration could obviously be combined to good effect.

achievement of the conference was a resolution in favour of imperial tariff preference and British abandonment of free trade.

As a sequel to the 1902 Conference, Joseph Chamberlain publicly announced his conversion to the ideal of imperial preference, which meant, in effect, condemning the cherished principle of free trade. His opinion was that if the colonies would not abandon their policies of protection, Britain would have to back down and abandon free trade. When, in 1903, Chamberlain found himself alone and without support in the cabinet, he resigned, a disappointed man.

When the fifth Colonial Conference (the first to call itself an Imperial Conference) met in 1907, a Liberal government was in office in Britain, and the Colonial Secretary, the eldest son of

Lord Elgin (of responsible government fame), offered no effective leadership at the meeting. The colonial prime ministers returned home after agreeing to substitute the term "dominion" for "colony," to establish a permanent secretariat for their conferences and to meet in future every fourth year. Thereafter, each succeeding conference seemed to be less useful than the one before, and prospects for imperial co-operation declined drastically from the popular enthusiasm of the early 1890's. Yet, within a year of the 1907 Colonial Conference, the revelation that Germany was building a fleet that would soon challenge Britannia's command of the seas produced a sudden, if temporary, reversal in the general attitude towards imperial defence. The British government began in 1909 a crash program of battleship-building to counter the threat of German naval supremacy, and invited the colonial governments to attend a special imperial defence conference in London.

At this particular conference, held in the summer of 1909, the British government urged "laying the foundation of future Dominion navies to be maintained in different parts of the Empire." This new policy represented a victory for the colonial point of view: previously, the Admiralty had adamantly defended the concept of a single Imperial Navy under Britain's command. But in the face of the German threat, Britain agreed that "room must be found for the expression of national sentiment" in the form of separate and distinct dominion navies. The Australian decision to acquire a navy at once was not copied by Canada. Canada had two seaboards to protect; in any case she felt that the Monroe Doctrine offered her a large measure of security. (This statement of American policy first enunciated by President Monroe in 1823 declared that the United States would not interfere in European affairs, but by the same token would resist any outside interference in the affairs of the Western Hemisphere.) Canada would accept British naval opinion on the possibility of a two-squadron navy and would consider the matter. Laurier's representatives would go no further.

When the Canadian parliament met in 1909, Britain's "sense of peril" had obviously crossed the Atlantic. George E. Foster, Minister of Finance in Macdonald's last government, and Robert

This interesting group was photographed at the first anniversary of Wellesley Hospital, Toronto, in 1913. In the centre are Sir Wilfrid and Lady Laurier. Third from the left is Sir Edmund Osler, financier, Conservative politician and brother of the renowned physician, Sir William Osler. At the extreme right is Sir William Mulock. Mulock had been Postmaster General in Laurier's "ministry of all talents" and had been the moving force behind the establishment of penny postage rates throughout the Empire. He later became Chief Justice of Ontario.

Borden, the Nova Scotia lawyer who had assumed the Conservative leadership in 1901, moved that "Canada should no longer delay in assuming her proper share of the responsibility and financial burden" of her own defence. Laurier promptly turned this into a government resolution which was passed unanimously. But what form of sharing was implied—Canadian contributions to the Royal Navy or a separate Canadian navy? The latter was preferred by both Liberals and Conservatives, but Laurier would not be rushed into any hasty decision. When parliament met again in January, 1910, Laurier introduced his Naval Service Bill by which, in easy stages, a small Canadian navy would be established. Laurier's proposal of a modest naval force that could be placed at the disposal of the British Admiralty came under heavy fire from the opposition. Many Conservatives were now filled with a sense of urgency and felt that "Laurier's tin-pot navy" would be too little and too late. They wanted an immediate and direct contribution to the building program of the Royal Navy. Laurier would not be swayed. His Naval Service Bill became law, and Canada now possessed its own, albeit useless, navy.

In the bitter debate over naval policy the positive achievements of Laurier's government in defence preparations were largely overlooked. Beginning in 1909, the size of the permanent militia (today the regular army) was increased, corps of supporting arms (signals, service, ordnance, etc.) were created, army administration was largerly reorganized, cadet and rifle corps were encouraged, the acquisition of up-to-date equipment was begun and the defence budget was so increased that by 1911 it was six times that of 1896. These measures did not, and could not, produce an effective war machine overnight, but when hostilities began in 1914, Canada's soldiers were much better prepared for conflict than they could ever have been in 1908.

* * *

In many ways the Age of Laurier was the fulfillment of the Age of Macdonald. Liberal tariff policy was no more than a continuation of Macdonald's protectionism despite the traditional Liberal leaning toward free trade. The west had finally been peopled by the migrations that the depression had delayed under Mackenzie and Macdonald. The National Policy was now in truth national, for it had been adopted by both parties.

Yet some elements of the Age of Laurier were distinctly Liberal. It was Laurier's "sunny ways" that had settled the Manitoba schools question, while at the same time defending the Liberal principle of provincial rights. In these years, too, Canada's external relations had assumed a new importance, thanks to the Alaska boundary dispute and the Boer War; the Liberals had responded with a new emphasis on Canadian nationhood. Similarly, colonial and imperial conferences had served to accentuate the disunity of the Empire arising from national interests and national aspirations. However, the nature of Canada's equivocal position on imperial trade and defence would soon be brought home by an American offer of reciprocity and by the drift to war in Europe.

CHAPTER 13

THE CONSERVATIVE RESTORATION

The achievements of Laurier had been considerable, but not considerable enough to keep the Liberals in power when he estranged, for different reasons, both French and English Canada. Having raised strong opposition to his naval policy in his native Quebec, Laurier unwittingly turned a decisive portion of the rest of Canada against himself by accepting an American offer of reciprocity. The result was the defeat of Laurier Liberalism and the restoration of Conservative rule. Under the leadership of Robert Borden Canadians forgot reciprocity and turned their attention once more to defence. Britain's need for imperial naval support was now urgent, but a Liberal-dominated Senate smashed Borden's plan for direct aid to the Royal Navy. By 1914 Canada had neither established a worthwhile navy of her own nor contributed to Britain's defence burden.

LAURIER'S DOUBLE DEFEAT

In 1896 Quebec had given forty-nine of its sixty-five seats to Laurier. It was obvious that Quebec had voted for Laurier and against the bishops. What was not obvious then was the fact that Quebec had voted for its favourite son, Laurier, but had not voted for the Liberals. The election of 1896 disguised for a while the inherent conservatism of French Canadians.

Laurier's victory at the polls had been largely due to the temporary alliance of two provincial factions: the *Bleus*, moderate Liberals in the Lafontaine tradition of Reformism, and the *Rouges*, disciples of the anti-clerical, doctrinaire liberalism of nineteenth-century European politics, who had once counted Laurier as one of their number. (After 1896 the Rouges no longer existed as a separate political entity. Their extreme policies were softened and their identity virtually submerged within the Bleus.) A third faction in Quebec, the conservative Castors, ultraclerical and ultramontane, had been brought low by a series of provincial scandals, beginning with the resignation of Sir Hector Langevin as a result of corruption in his federal department. As it happened, the process of Castor decline had joined together Laurier and the nominally Bleu Joseph Israël Tarte, who had been a Castor but who now became Laurier's lieutenant in Quebec. Yet Tarte, ambitious and domineering, never really became a Liberal, and his policies seemed to be aimed at leading Laurier's party along the path to Liberal-Conservatism. In 1896 Tarte (and also the Bleus) had preferred Laurier to the Castors and the bishops, but this alliance of Liberal and Bleu was doomed to destruction as soon as the threat of clerical domination was removed. Using his control of patronage as Minister of Public Works, Tarte proceeded during and after 1896 to extinguish the political power of his former associates, the Castors, and to replace even Laurier Liberals with friends of his own and of Joseph A. Chapleau, Lieutenant-Governor of Quebec, a long time Conservative but also a political opportunist. Yet Laurier was dependent upon these men, whom Tarte was alienating, and upon the decisive bloc of votes they controlled. Even after the defeat of the Quebec bishops over the Manitoba Schools Remedial Bill, Laurier remained fearful that the issues of race, religion, and education might re-appear (as in fact they were about to do in connection with the creation of Saskatchewan and Alberta). The resentments created in Quebec by the Manitoba crisis went underground, to revive when the zeal of the Castors and the bishops merged with the Quebec nationalism fostered by Henri Bourassa.

The slim, handsome, dark-eyed Bourassa was an accomplished

Henry Bourassa never strayed very far from journalism, first as owner and editor of L'Interprète, published in Clarence Creek, Ontario, and later as founder, co-owner and editor-in-chief of the Montreal Nationaliste daily, Le Devoir. Like his famous grandfather, Papineau, he was a brilliant orator but a poor politician, unable to work with men who held views different from his own. His parliamentary career was confined to the years 1896-1899 and 1900-1907.

orator with a flair for the dramatic. A grandson of Louis Joseph Papineau, he had entered parliament in 1896 at Laurier's suggestion but had resigned in protest against Laurier's decision to allow Canadians to fight in South Africa. With a handful of followers Bourassa founded in 1903 the *League Nationaliste*, dedicated to safeguarding and to increasing the rights of French Canada. Yet Bourassa was no separatist. An admirer of British parliamentary and legal traditions, he advocated an honest and frank acceptance of the co-existence of two races within Canada. To him, Canadianism was always more than language, and patriotism was always broader than race. In the last analysis, the *Nationalistes* believed that there were more advantages than disadvantages in maintaining a bicultural Canada.

In 1902 Tarte's ambition finally caused his downfall, for with Laurier rumoured to be seriously ill during a short visit to England, Tarte sought the Liberal leadership and publicly announced his support for much higher tariffs. On his return home Laurier immediately removed his scheming lieutenant from his cabinet, and Tarte spent the remaining five years of his life as a repentant Conservative, attacking Laurier and the Liberals in the editorial columns of his newspaper, *La Patrie*.

The educational provisions of the 1905 autonomy bill for Saskatchewan and Alberta resurrected again the racial and religious issues that repeatedly confronted Laurier. The problem was occasioned by Laurier's mistaken belief that all his cabinet colleagues would accept denominational schools. The opposition of Clifford Sifton (who aimed to mould western Canada into an English-speaking society) and other English-speaking Liberals was successfully checked by Laurier, but only at the cost of Sifton's resignation. As has been remarked of this episode, "the storm blew over but the wreckage remained." Not only had Laurier raised lasting suspicions in the English provinces by his apparent willingness to let Sifton go and by his mild support of denominational schools, but his later acceptance of a compromise that destroyed those schools made him appear in Quebec to be the betrayer of French Catholic interests, a charge that Bourassa voiced long and loud. From this point forward in time the strength of the *Nationaliste* movement grew rapidly as French Canada reacted against English "domination" and Laurier Liberalism. The showdown came in the general election of 1911 when two separate Laurier policies, his Naval Service Act of 1910 and his Reciprocity Bill of 1911, combined to cause his defeat in both French and English Canada.

It was the proposal of a reciprocity agreement with the United States, rather than Quebec's opposition to a navy, that really ended the fifteen-year Age of Laurier. Throughout Canada's history, the tariff question has been an explosive and emotion-charged issue because industrialization has made more evident the diverse and conflicting regional economic interests within the nation. A low tariff (or even free trade) increases foreign sales of Canada's natural products, especially wheat; it also brings a flood of inexpensive American manufactured goods—and with them the threat of American economic (and perhaps political) domination. High tariffs, in contrast, promote industry and employment to the benefit of the manufacturers, financiers and workers (primarily in eastern Canada); high tariffs also raise

A Montreal woman in a Packard attended by the family chauffeur in 1911. At this time the automobile was only just beginning to become a popular means of transportation. Cheaper models, such as Ford's "Model T", were mass produced, but luxury models, such as the Packard, still required considerable hand work. Notice the solid rubber tires, the carriage lamps and the impressive-looking horn mounted behind the front fender.

domestic prices at the expense of the primary producer. Since any tariff policy affects every Canadian pocket, every Canadian has some reason either to hail it or to hate it.

In 1904, on the eve of a general election, the government had bowed to demands by the Canadian Manufacturers' Association for increased protection against British products, especially woollens. "Canada for Canadians" and "Business before Politics" became the rallying cries of the politically minded Canadian Industrial League. "'Made in Canada' should be the watchword of the people of Canada," announced one Liberal member of parliament (who owned a woollen mill). Virtually every manufacturer demanded increased protection for his product, whether it was baby carriages or coffins, pickles or suspenders. Increased tariff protection for the woollen industry was followed in 1907 by further bounties and privileges to the Canadian steel and iron industry. With reason, free traders complained of the "Liberal National Policy." Despite the increasing prosperity of Canada, upward revisions of tariff schedules were proposed in 1904 as retaliation against the American Dingley tariff. The revisions suggested three schedules: the regular tariff for such protectionist countries as the United States and Germany; lower tariff for countries with revenue tariffs only; and an even lower preferential rate for Britain and the Empire. The Canadian Manufacturers' Association now gave its full support to Macdonald's tariff heirs—the Liberal party. The combined opposition of western farmers' associations blocked these revisions, demanding instead a revenue tariff and a reciprocity treaty with the United States. Nonetheless, upward revisions were made two years later, a triumph for manufacturers, for the "big business" of trusts and combines (but not for infant industries as originally described under the National Policy).

Laurier's tariff policy had turned out to be as "national" as Macdonald's, and many doctrinaire free traders talked openly of Laurier's betrayal of Liberal principles. Laurier might have found it easier to justify the continuation of the National Policy if the depression had continued, but the depression had ended almost at the moment the Liberals entered office. Canada, along with most of the western world, was enjoying a fifteen-year bonanza, an era of prosperity unequalled since the booming early 1850's; it was an era that was to last almost to the beginning of World War 1. In that golden age Laurier's prediction that the twentieth century would be Canada's century seemed an economic truism.

Late in 1910 a delegation of a thousand farmers, representing the Grain Growers' associations of the three prairie provinces, marched into the House of Commons to condemn price-fixing by industrialists and to urge reciprocal free trade with the United States in farm products. A little later that year the Liberal editor of the Toronto *Globe*, in the course of an interview with President Taft, was encouraged to believe that a Canadian proposal for the old Liberal continentalist dream of commercial reciprocity between the two neighbours would be received kindly. Laurier grasped this invitation gladly as an answer to western farm dissatisfaction with the Liberal National Policy and as a diversion of public opinion from recent scandals involving his government. W. S. Fielding, Minister of Finance, and William Paterson, Minister of Customs, proceeded to Washington where they negotiated an agreement for reciprocity in a number of Canadian natural products (e.g. grain, timber, fish, fruit), and the reduction of tariff rates on certain American manufactures to the level of Canada's intermediate tariff (designed to protect the imperial preference and many Canadian manufactures). The agreement was to be implemented by parallel legislation in each country.

A few weeks after the farmers had harangued Laurier and his cabinet, Fielding introduced the terms of the agreement in the House. Fielding stressed the Canadian desire, felt since Confederation, for a renewal of reciprocity and recalled Sir John A. Macdonald's standing offer of reciprocity that had accompanied the National Policy in 1879. The opposition, aware that the agreement would, in Borden's words, give the Liberals "another term in office," replied with a brief warning that some Canadian industries might be hurt by reciprocity, but the Conservatives were so confused and divided that the government might easily have carried their bill then if they had pressed for an immediate decision. Instead, the government delayed until the American Senate passed the legislation. While it delayed, the opposition, the bulk of the press of English Canada and "big business" whipped public opinion into an emotional frenzy against reciprocity.

The reaction against reciprocity appeared first—and most significantly—in the Toronto and Montreal Conservative newspapers, and vocal support was soon heard from Canadian manufacturers, bankers, boards of trade and the railways. Two points were emphasized by all opponents of reciprocity—the proposed agreement was an economic threat to Canada and a political threat to the imperial connection. Canada, they insisted, would lose the benefits purchased so dearly by the National

A Toronto News anti-Reciprocity cartoon entitled "Looking Our Way," August 23, 1911.

Policy, while commercial union would lead inevitably to a political union that would destroy Canada's separate identity. The second point was given particular emphasis by the flag-waving opponents of reciprocity.

The anti-reciprocity campaign was soon in high gear, and a flood of propaganda deluged the country. Every major newspaper came out against the proposed agreement, echoing the Conservative charge of Liberal disloyalty to Britain. "Which will it be?" demanded the Toronto *World*, "Borden and King George or Laurier and President Taft?" Laurier protested that reciprocity would benefit Canadian farmers without hurting Canadian manufacturers and that reciprocity was the antidote, not the antecedent, to annexation. The Maritime and prairie provinces generally favoured reciprocity, but Montreal and Toronto remained unconvinced. President Taft's impatience, however, played into the hands of Laurier's opponents when he was heard predicting American exploitation of Canadian resources. Another American politician publicly hailed the approach of "the day when the American flag will float over every square foot of British North American possessions clear to the North Pole." Picking up these marvellous cues, Conservatives and other opponents of reciprocity stressed the political consideration, not the economic. Laurier's reasoned answer that reciprocity would give Canada a "Ninety Million Market" simply could not offset the highly emotional charge that the agreement would rob Canada of its independence and would sever the tie with Britain. As Laurier wryly remarked:

> I am branded in Quebec as a traitor to the French, and in Ontario as a traitor to the English. In Quebec I am branded as a Jingo, and in Ontario as a Separatist. In Quebec I am attacked as an Imperialist, and in Ontario as an anti-Imperialist.

The Conservative premiers of Ontario and Manitoba had been instrumental in having the federal Conservatives take up anti-reciprocity as a party issue. But an infinitely more dangerous threat to reciprocity and to Laurier as Liberal leader was the action of eighteen Liberals prominent in Toronto financial circles, who published a manifesto repudiating the reciprocity plan. The "Revolt of the Eighteen" (including such eminent personages as Sir Edmund Walker, President of the Canadian Bank of Commerce, and John C. Eaton of the T. Eaton Co.) led to the establishment of the Canadian National League, which seriously damaged the Liberal party in Ontario and also spurred the founding of an anti-reciprocity league by Montreal businessmen. Sir Clifford Sifton, though not associated with the Eighteen, left the Liberals to join the opposition in parliament, while Sir William Van Horne emerged from retirement in Montreal to support the Conservatives in their fight against reciprocity, claiming that he was "out to do all I can to bust the damned thing." Eastern businessmen talked patriotism, but they thought profit.

The causes of war and the lines of battle were now clearly drawn. Every group with a vested interest in the historic east-west trade pattern as established by the National Policy was arrayed against a north-south trade axis (which the continentally-minded Liberals had sought phlegmatically to create since the day George Brown had travelled to Washington in 1874). What Canadians—including the Conservatives—had sought in vain was now being offered by the United States. Yet many Canadians suddenly became unwilling to let their natural resources leave the country. The arguments over reciprocity soon became a jumble of economic theories and conflicting political and emotional prejudices.

Because of their inadequate planning in parliament, the Liberals had been outmanoeuvered politically by the opposition. After twenty-five days of debate, during which the opposition used every means to delay a vote, the reciprocity issue was still undecided as parliament adjourned on 18 May to permit Laurier's attendance at the coronation of George V and also at the Imperial Conference of 1911. When parliament reassembled one month later, Conservative obstructionist tactics were resumed. After ten more days of this filibustering, the harassed Laurier made a fateful decision. A snap election was called for 21 September, two years before the sitting parliament was due to expire. Ostensibly, this election was to be a straight fight for or against reciprocity.

The Conservatives made the most of such indiscreet political statements as President Taft's remark that "Canada was at the parting of the ways." "Beware of Americans bearing tariff concessions," trumpeted American-born Van Horne. Reciprocity, he warned, would be "a bed to lie in and to die in." But elections are seldom decided on a single issue, and in the fiercely fought contest of 1911 the "tin-pot" navy was as damaging to Laurier in Quebec as reciprocity was in Ontario, while beneath both these issues smouldered the troublesome questions of race and religion. Without any solicitation from Borden, Henri Bourassa and all like-minded *Nationalistes* who saw behind the Naval Service Act the spectre of conscription allied themselves with the anti-reciprocity imperialists of Ontario who viewed the same Act as "too little, too late." Thus, for totally different (and even opposing) reasons, an "unholy alliance" was formed to overthrow Laurier, the moderate who could claim to be a Canadian nationalist and an Anglophile. Obviously, Canadianism had a different meaning to different Canadians.

When the ballots were counted, Laurier and reciprocity had been defeated by "nationalisme" in Quebec and by the old loyalty cry in Ontario. Quebec had reduced its Liberal seats from 53 to 37, while Anglo-Saxon, imperialistic Ontario gave no less than 72 of its 86 seats to Borden and the Conservatives. Every constituency in British Columbia had gone Conservative, and even in the Maritimes the government lost seats. Only in the prairie provinces had Laurier's party gained any new strength. Fielding and Paterson, the negotiators of the reciprocity agreement, had gone down to defeat along with five other cabinet ministers. The inflammatory attacks of the *Nationalistes* had undoubtedly hurt the Liberals in Quebec, but Laurier's verdict on the election, "It is the province of Ontario which has defeated us," pointed out the basic cause of this almost exact reversal of the 1908 election.

NEW MEN AND NEW MEASURES

The new prime minister, Robert Laird Borden, had shown he possessed the qualities of leadership: cool judgment, the ability to inspire confidence and win co-operation and political astuteness without narrow partisanship. His silvery hair parted in the middle, his beetling brows, his heavy moustache and his handsome face and solid stature all combined to give an impression of rugged vigour and strength of character that contrasted sharply with the urbane, polished, almost decorative appearance of Laurier.

In choosing his cabinet Borden was faced by a legacy of recent party divisions, divisions so serious that he had actually considered abandoning the Conservative leadership during the reciprocity debate. He had always insisted that the party achieve unity before it achieved power. In 1911 it was given power, but unity was harder to secure. Many elements had contributed to the electoral victory, and it was no simple task to meet their diverse claims. Borden suffered from a lack of prestige within his own cabinet. Some cabinet ministers believed that they, not Borden, had won the election, and it took Borden five years to force his team to pull in harness. Furthermore, this cabinet was heavily weighted with businessmen, four of whom were millionaires, and all ministers were tried and true Conservatives except the Minister of Finance, Thomas White, a Liberal deserter who was still suspect to some Conservatives. The *Nationalistes* were represented in the cabinet by F. D. Monk, a known opponent of Borden's naval policy and one who was to resign in 1912 in protest against Borden's Naval Aid Bill. But the only cabinet appointment that was to prove dangerous was the man chosen for the fatefully important post of Minister of Militia and Defence, Sam Hughes—bulky, imperialistic, tactless, boastful and naïve.

When the new parliament met in November, 1911, the Speech from the Throne announced the establishment of a tariff commission to institute a scientifically designed National Policy; no mention whatever was made of naval policy, which in English Canada had become the question of questions, thanks to the recent election. In the debate that followed, government speakers referred to Laurier's navy as economically "ruinous" and militarily "useless," yet offered no positive alternate policy. Laurier was quick to suggest that the "*Nationaliste* lamb" had "swallowed the Imperial lion," and that Borden was too afraid of Quebec to implement his "cash contribution" plan of 1909. Borden refused to be goaded into premature action, but the serious amendment of his Tariff Commission Bill at the hands of the Senate's Liberal majority must have given him an inkling of what would happen to any measure involving a Canadian navy.

During the summer of 1912 Borden met members of Britain's Liberal government. From Winston Churchill, First Lord of the Admiralty, he learned of the threatening growth of German naval power; the need for help in imperial naval defence was serious and immediate. Convinced that Canada had to adopt a positive policy of co-operation with the Royal Navy, Borden obtained from Churchill a full statement of Britain's need for capital ships and, when parliament met late that autumn, Borden introduced his Naval Aid Bill. The Bill provided for a grant of $35,000,000 towards three battleships, to be built in Britain as part of the Royal Navy. To placate the *Nationalistes,* the ships could be used to train Canadian sailors and might, at some future date, become a Canadian unit within the Royal Navy. The "hazardous and costly experiment of building up a naval organization" solely for Canada would be abandoned. Aside from the savings involved, the rationale of this new policy was simply the pressing urgency for stronger imperial forces to meet the warlike preparations of Germany. "Confronted with the problem of combining co-operation with autonomy," explained Borden ". . . it seems essential that there should be such co-operation in defence. . . ."

As soon as Borden had finished his speech, most of the House began to sing "Rule Britannia" and then switched to "God Save the King." Laurier's reaction was merely a motion calling for the stationing of Canadian naval units on the Atlantic and Pacific coasts. Debate on the Bill was resumed in earnest in January, 1913, after the Christmas recess. The Liberals, who refused to admit the existence of any defence emergency, now began employing the same obstructionist tactics against the Naval Aid Bill that the Conservatives had used so effectively against the reciprocity agreement. Indeed, the latter stages of debate became so heated that disorderly scenes occurred in the Commons, and members came close to exchanging blows. As a last resort, Borden introduced the closure rule (to cut off debate after a stated time), a procedure never before used in the Canadian parliament. Despite the threat of closure, the Liberals still argued against the Bill; but at last, on 15 May, 1913, more than five months after Borden had introduced it, the Naval Aid Bill was passed by the Commons.

The struggle was not yet over. The Bill had to be passed by a Liberal-dominated Senate, and the Liberal Senators refused to accept the Bill for the simple reason that Laurier had threatened to resign if they did. Borden's policy of a direct cash contribution to the Royal Navy had been checkmated as effectively as Borden had killed the Liberal plan for a Canadian navy. The result of this prolonged and bitter discussion of naval policy was that Canada failed entirely to provide support of any kind towards the pre-war defence of the Empire. The controversy had shown all too clearly how divided public opinion was and how uncertain were the relations of the self-governing, self-conscious dominion with Britain and with the Empire.

BORDEN: IMPERIAL NATIONALIST

Borden's rejection of the Liberal Naval Service Act of 1910 and his substitution of the ill-starred cash contribution plan of 1912 give a very misleading impression of his policies on Canadian-British relations. Borden was far from being an imperialist. In many ways he was as nationalistic as Laurier, or even Bourassa. "I stand first in all matters," Borden had announced long before, "for the rights of Canada which must be maintained." Laurier and Bourassa saw Canadian nationalism as autonomy, the power to make one's own policy for one's own destiny isolated from the "vortex of European militarism" and apart from any obligation incurred by membership in the British Empire. Borden's aim for Canada was neither colonial subservience nor national separatism, but a partnership within the Empire, a partnership to be shared with Britain and with the other self-governing dominions.

For over half a century the British-settled colonies had enjoyed full control of their domestic politics, thanks to the grant of responsible government. For almost as long a period of time they had controlled one aspect of their external relations, tariff policies. Of all the powers that Lord Durham had wished reserved to the mother country, only external political policies had not been fully transferred to the self-governing colonies. Even in this area Canada had been granted some voice in treaty-making where it concerned her and had, since 1879, maintained a High Commissioner in London to act as liaison officer between Canada and the imperial government. What Canada could not do was appoint ambassadors, sign treaties independently of Britain, or declare war. As dark, threatening clouds of battle loomed large on the horizon of European affairs after 1909, this last point became the crucial issue in Anglo-Canadian relations.

Legally, Canada would be at war when Britain was at war, even though Canada could expect no voice in policies that might lead to war. The sharing by the dominion in the making of foreign policy seemed to most British statesmen to be both legally and physically impossible. How could one colony be allowed to interfere in the foreign affairs of the whole Empire? How could equal status be given where equal responsibility was obviously impossible? And what kind of machinery would provide a means of consultation between mother country and colonies, considering the great distances that separated the various parts of the Empire and considering the need for instant decision when there was an international emergency or crisis? Undeterred by the logic of these arguments, Borden pressed Canada's claim for full partnership with Britain on every occasion. Introducing his Naval Aid Bill, Borden had stated his view bluntly:

> When Great Britain no longer assumes full responsibility for defence upon the high seas, she can no longer undertake to assume sole responsibility for and sole control of foreign policy, which is closely, vitally and constantly associated with that defence in which the Dominions participate.

This was Borden's imperialism and his nationalism.

During his 1912 visit to England Borden had put his view clearly before British statesmen:

> The people of Canada are not the type that will permit themselves to become merely silent partners in such a great Empire. If there is to be Imperial co-operation, the people of Canada propose to have a reasonable and fair voice in that co-operation.

British statesmen had applauded this statement, and Borden had come home convinced of their change of heart and prepared to earn for Canada a voice in policy-making through his Naval Aid Bill. In both matters he had been frustrated. Naval co-operation had been blocked by a Liberal-dominated Senate, and British statesmen had only been giving lip service to Borden's proposal

Prime Minister Robert Borden and Winston Churchill (then First Lord of the Admiralty). This photograph was taken during Borden's 1912 visit to England to discuss with Prime Minister Asquith and his cabinet the problem of unified Imperial defence.

of partnership. Those statesmen were still conducting imperial policy without consultation or reference to Canada when that policy brought Britain and the whole Empire into World War I.

When the war that Borden had expected did begin, Borden hastened to assure the British government of Canada's resolve to render "every possible aid, every effort and . . . every sacrifice to ensure the integrity and to maintain the honour of the Empire. A considerable force," he promised, "will be available for service abroad." Like that other great Canadian, Robert Baldwin, Borden saw no cause or occasion for conflict between Canadian nationalism and British imperialism. Robert Baldwin's "single idea" had been responsible government for the colonies—autonomy in domestic affairs; Robert Borden's "single idea" was dominion status—the blending of national autonomy within an imperial partnership.

*   *   *

Robert Borden, the imperial nationalist who saw no conflict in that description of himself, had kept Canada British by defeating Laurier and reciprocity, but a Liberal-dominated Senate had kept Canada North American by defeating Borden's Naval Aid Bill. As yet, however, Borden had not been faced with the old problem of racial animosity in Canada. This problem and the financial crisis that descended on the new transcontinental railways were to be forced upon him by the impact of World War I upon Canada.

CHAPTER 14

THE TEST OF WAR

On 28 June, 1914, in the small town of Sarajevo, capital of the Austrian province of Bosnia, the heir to the Austro-Hungarian Empire was assassinated. To Canadians the incident was just another unfortunate episode in European affairs, but within a few short weeks this event was to bring Canada into World War I. For Canada a major consequence of the war was that she assumed a new and important role in world affairs.

THE CANADIAN WAR EFFORT

The German invasion of Belgium on 4 August, 1914, and the request of King Leopold for aid brought Britain into World War I, and it followed that, since Britain was at war, the British Empire was also at war. For Britain and the Empire the war had come almost without warning, and no special preparations had been made to meet the crisis. British policy looked to Canada primarily for men and food to supply the imperial war effort. It was not anticipated that Canada's small industrial plant would make any significant contribution. Conflicts in the past century had been short affairs, and no one could foresee that this one would drag on for four, long years.

Canada's response to the cry "the Empire in danger" was immediate and overwhelming. By Christmas of 1914 the 1st

Canadian Division, some thirty thousand strong and largely composed of volunteers, had been dispatched overseas, and by 7 February it was in France. Just two months after the Division entered the trenches at Ypres, the Germans unleashed a new and frightful weapon of war, poison gas, against the Allied lines. The effect of the thick, sweeping, greenish-yellow clouds of chlorine gas was disastrous. A four-mile gap was torn open when three French battalions broke and ran, gasping, choking and dying, from the new and destructive weapon. It fell to the British and the Canadians to close this gap in the lines. Two days later, at 4 a.m., the Canadians received the full brunt of another gas attack. The Canadians again held their lines without flinching, but by the time fighting at Ypres died down, almost one-third of the Division had become casualties. Four weeks later the Canadians were engaged in the battle of Festubert where, in five separate days of fighting over enemy trenches, they gained 600 yards at the cost of almost 2,500 casualties.

During the remainder of 1915 the Division was not engaged in heavy fighting. In September, the 2nd Canadian Division arrived, and the Canadian Corps was born. In later months the 3rd and 4th Divisions arrived. When the Corps was transferred from Ypres to take part in the Battle of the Somme in 1916, it was to earn a reputation that marked Canadian troops as second to none in the Allied armies—but the cost was 24,000 casualties in eleven weeks of fighting.

Sir Douglas Haig, the commander of British and Imperial forces in France, had long planned a great offensive in Flanders to break through into Belgium and seize the German U-boat bases at Ostend and Zeebrugge. In the spring of 1917, as a prelude to this offensive, the Canadian Corps was ordered to capture Vimy Ridge. For Canadians on the western front, one of the greatest and most historic battles of the war was about to take place.

Vimy Ridge dominates the flat country of Flanders, and on this strategic position the Germans were heavily entrenched. The battle for Vimy Ridge—"the most perfectly organized and the most successful battle of the whole war"—began with almost a thousand guns and mortars softening up the enemy, and then, at

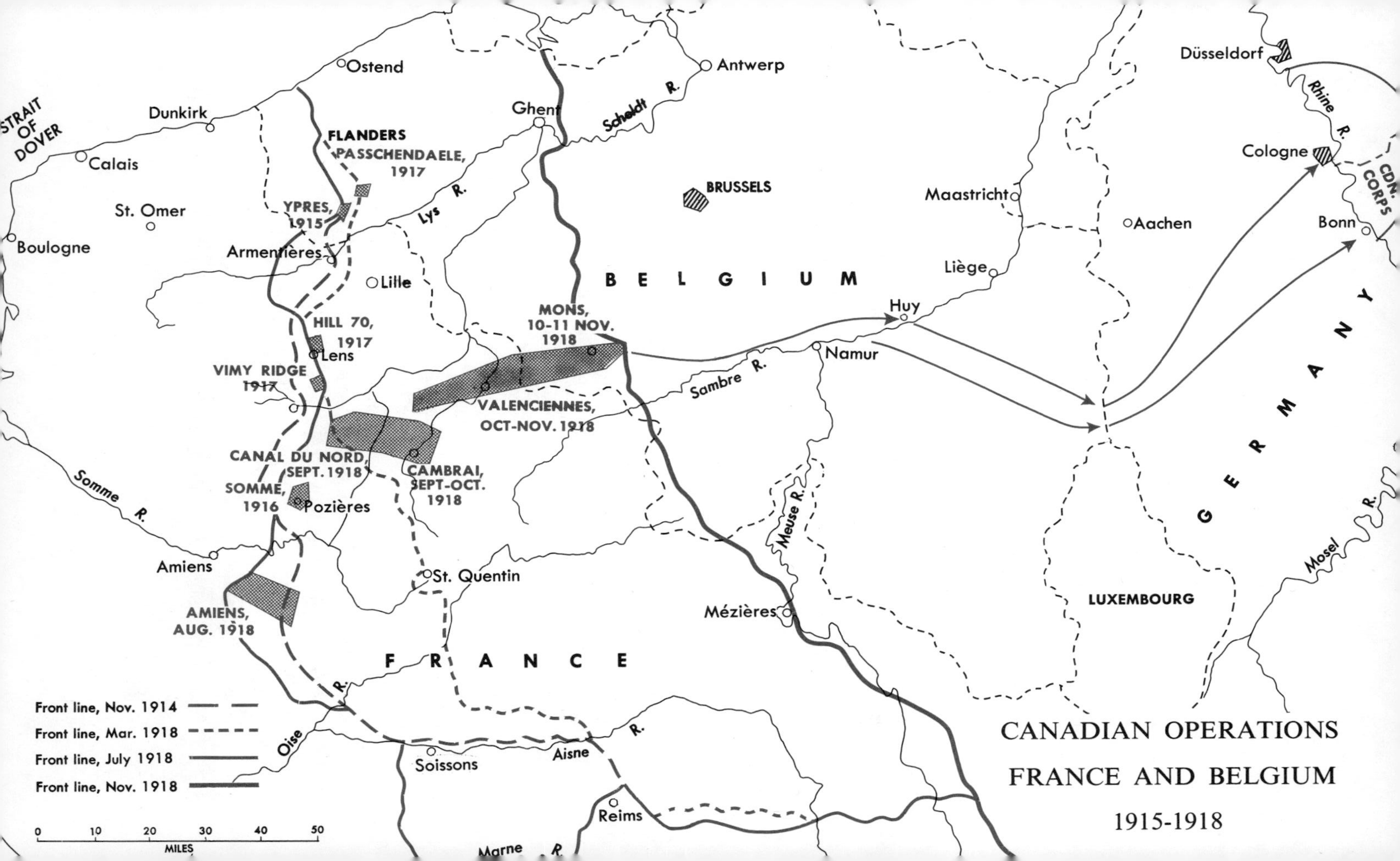
CANADIAN OPERATIONS
FRANCE AND BELGIUM
1915-1918
STRAIT OF DOVER
Dunkirk
Calais
Boulogne
St. Omer
Ostend
FLANDERS
PASSCHENDAELE, 1917
YPRES, 1915
Armentières
Lille
Lys R.
Ghent
Scheldt R.
Antwerp
BRUSSELS
BELGIUM
HILL 70, 1917
Lens
VIMY RIDGE 1917
MONS, 10-11 NOV. 1918
VALENCIENNES, OCT-NOV. 1918
CANAL DU NORD, SEPT. 1918
CAMBRAI, SEPT-OCT. 1918
SOMME, 1916
Pozières
Somme R.
Amiens
AMIENS, AUG. 1918
St. Quentin
FRANCE
Oise R.
Soissons
Aisne R.
Reims
Marne R.
Sambre R.
Namur
Huy
Liège
Maastricht
Aachen
Meuse R.
Mézières
LUXEMBOURG
GERMANY
Mosel R.
Düsseldorf
Rhine R.
Cologne
CDN. CORPS
Bonn
Front line, Nov. 1914
Front line, Mar. 1918
Front line, July 1918
Front line, Nov. 1918
0
10
20
30
40
50
MILES

dawn on Easter Monday, 9 April, the four Canadian divisions and a British brigade attacked across "no-man's-land" on a four-mile front. The Ridge was taken from the Germans within ten hours. The Corps went on to take part in other desperate battles of the long and bitter Flanders offensive—Arleux, the Scarpe, Hill 70, Passchendaele. The Passchendaele campaign, fought in October, 1917, was a particularly bloody, murderous one. Following one of the wettest summers on record in Flanders, the Canadians were confronted by enemies ensconced in concrete pillboxes that by now were embedded in a veritable sea of mud. Over what was described as "utterly impassable ground," Canadians won, in two nightmare weeks of fighting, two miles (an amazing advance by western front standards); but the cost to the Corps was one thousand men a day.

As 1917 merged into 1918, it became obvious that time was running out for the Central Powers. A war of attrition favoured the Allies in the long run. The United States was mobilizing men and resources. In an attempt to end the war before American reinforcements could reach the western front in quantity, the Germans mounted their great spring offensive of 1918. When the Allied counterattack commenced, the Canadian Corps played a vital role. On 8 August, Canadians gained some eight miles in a surprise attack that opened the battle of Amiens. There followed the "hundred days" of rapid advances by the Allies, advances that were only ended by an armistice on 11 November.

For Canada, World War I had been very much a soldiers' war, but this was not the sum of her war effort. Although the abortive naval service established in 1910 had never become effective, submarine warfare forced Canada to equip 134 vessels for coastal patrol, and the Royal Canadian Navy enlisted almost ten thousand men in the course of the war. Canada had no active air force, but many Canadians enlisted in the British flying services (the Royal Naval Air Service and the Royal Flying Corps, later the Royal Air Force). At first the main duties of pilots were artillery observation and reconnaissance, but new uses were continually being found for aircraft. Air drops of supplies were made occasionally, and as early as 1914 airplanes dropped smoke bombs in support of ground forces. In 1917 and

Passchendaele, 1917. The conditions under which this battle was fought are almost beyond description. One historian relates the following incident: "For weeks the dead lay buried amid the mud. In the spring, when the Newfoundlanders held the ridge, corpses rose out of the softening ooze and were cleared away. One morning stretcher parties blundered into a pair of bodies, perhaps symbolic of the whole campaign. One was Canadian, the other German, grappling still in death. They had fought desperately and, sucked into the swamp, had died in one another's arms. . . ." (John Swettenham. To Seize the Victory. *Ryerson, 1965). At the top a German soldier helps a wounded Canadian soldier through the mire at Passchendaele to an aid post.*

In order to entertain the troops a group known as the "Dumbells" was organized. They gave concert parties that included music-hall songs, dancing and skits. The group, which included female impersonators, was very popular among the troops and became well known throughout Canada after the war.

1918 airplanes were used to machine-gun enemy positions, and in one battle a hundred French planes actually broke up two German divisions. Bigger and faster planes—some flying 150 miles per hour and others carrying several tons of bombs—were developed, and in the last months of the war Allied bombs fell on German industrial cities 120 miles behind the western front. The most spectacular—if strategically unimportant—development was the aerial dog fight, in which Canadians won particular fame. Ten of the twenty-seven leading R.F.C. "aces" were Canadian, and three Canadian V.Cs. were won in the air. Maj. W. A. (Billy) Bishop ranked third among the aces of all belligerents with seventy-two "kills" to his credit, and Maj. Raymond Collishaw stood fifth with sixty victories.

On the home front, industry was fostered by the demands of war. In fact, for the first time industrial output in Canada surpassed that of agriculture. The production of base metals, wood pulp and newsprint expanded under the demands of war. Aircraft and great quantities of munitions poured from factories in central Canada. It is said that 60 percent of the shrapnel fired by the Allies on the western front came from Canada. Large numbers of merchant ships and small naval craft were launched in Canadian shipyards, while the products of Canadian agriculture flowed overseas to supply the population of Great Britain and the Allied armies in France with most of the food they ate. The country's expenditure quadrupled and its debt, mostly borrowed from Canadians themselves in "Victory Bond" drives, increased sevenfold by 1921 as a result of wartime expenditures. World War I showed that Canada could produce the armed forces and the economic support for a major war effort.

THE CONSCRIPTION ISSUE

World War I created problems of a magnitude and kind never before encountered by Canada. The provision and maintenance of the Canadian Corps imposed strains on an economy already burdened with the responsibility of producing food and war supplies for the Allied war effort. Added to these physical problems were the deep-seated differences inherent in the nation's cultural and political structure, differences which threatened to limit, if not disrupt, Canada's participation in the conflict.

For the first year and a half of war there was no serious problem in finding recruits for the armed forces—in fact more men were available than could be absorbed. Then, in January, 1916 (with two Canadian divisions already in the field), Sir Robert Borden, on his own initiative, pledged half a million men for the Allied armies. This figure was double the existing establishment of Canada's army and would require the addition of 300,000 men per year. Sam Hughes, Minister of Militia, believed Borden's pledge could be redeemed, but many responsible persons felt that half a million men in arms was quite beyond the country's capabilities.

After the initial surge of patriotism in 1914, voices could be heard, particularly in Quebec, criticizing participation in a war that did not concern Canada and that was not of her making. The most outspoken critic of the "imperialist war" was Henri Bourassa, Laurier's rival for the affections of Quebec, who now denounced Laurier's support of voluntary recruiting. In 1912 the Province of Ontario had restricted the use of the French language in provincial elementary schools by its controversial Regulation 17. Despite pleas from Quebec and French ecclesiastics in Ontario, Borden had refused to intervene in what he considered a provincial matter. Bourassa now used Regulation 17 as a club with which to belabour Laurier, the Borden government and all those who would send Canada's sons to war while denying justice to a large section of the nation at home. For his efforts to rouse anti-war sentiment, Bourassa was accused of virtual treason and dubbed "von Bourassa" by the press of English Canada.

Overseas, the administration of Canada's war effort was bedevilled by confusion, thanks to Sam Hughes' reliance on favourites as agents of his extensive powers. The administrative problem was only solved late in 1916 when Borden appointed Sir George Perley (Minister without Portfolio and acting High Commissioner in London) as Minister of Overseas Military Affairs, to the great annoyance of Hughes, who felt his powers were being reduced. At home a committee enquiring into charges of irregularities in the awarding of shell contracts disclosed in 1916 that Hughes had been guilty of gross naïveté in allowing contracts to go to personal friends. Borden charged that the Minister of Militia was trying to run his department "as if it were a distinct and separate Government in itself," and he asked for Hughes' resignation. Thereafter, the conduct of Canada's war effort proceeded with more despatch and efficiency and with less conflict of personalities in both government and army.

Borden's pledge of 500,000 men in January, 1916, seemed for a while to stimulate the already high rate of enlistment, but it soon became apparent that Canada's resources of manpower could not produce soldiers and at the same time produce workers to turn the wheels of war-expanded industry and agriculture. Industry had already lost to the army skilled workers who could not be readily replaced. Complicating this problem were the high casualty rate in France and a marked decline in voluntary recruiting, first apparent in June, 1916, and so serious by December that less than 20 percent of the monthly reinforcement requirements were being obtained. As early as mid-1916 there was evidence of a popular demand for selective, compulsory conscription to safeguard the needs of industry and agriculture while ensuring a steady supply of replacements to the Canadian Corps. Yet the very word "conscription" roused violent reactions among Canadians. To French Canadians it connoted coercion—being forced to fight, not for Canada, but in the interests of European imperialism. To most English Canadians conscription seemed the only fair way to defend Canada and, to their minds, the defence of France and Britain was the defence of Canada.

In April, 1917, less than 5,000 volunteers came forward, yet in six days of fighting at and beyond Vimy Ridge that month, Canada had suffered over 10,000 casualties. A fifth division had to be broken up to provide reinforcements for the Canadian Corps, and plans for a sixth division had to be scrapped. It was becoming quite obvious that compulsory military service would be necessary to fulfil Borden's promise of half a million men in arms. Yet, an inventory of manpower had failed to produce any

Sir Sam Hughes, Canada's Minister of Militia and Defence, steps ashore at Boulogne on his visit to France in August, 1916.

worthwhile results, and Sam Hughes' incredible stupidity while Minister of Militia—for example, in using an English, Protestant clergyman in Quebec as a recruiting officer and in ordering the use of English training manuals in French-speaking army units—had provided much ammunition for Bourassa's attacks on "Britain's war," Laurier's "imperialism" and Borden's "Anglo-Saxon, Protestant policies."

On 15 May, 1917, a greatly worried Borden returned from a visit to the Canadian Corps and from meetings of the Imperial War Cabinet where the critical, Allied manpower shortage had been anxiously discussed. The following day he announced in the Commons the government's intention to introduce legislation for "compulsory military enlistment on a selective basis" to provide the 100,000 reinforcements necessary "to maintain the Canadian Army in the field as one of the finest fighting units in the Empire." Borden added fuel to the English-Canadian outcry against Quebec "shirkers" by stating that the enlistment of English Canadians had been nine times as great as that of French

Canadians, an opinion that is not supported by statistics but which, in the supercharged atmosphere of 1917, provoked manifestations of violent anger from both groups.

Laurier proposed a referendum on conscription, but Quebec newspapers denied that any need for reinforcements existed. South Africa did not have conscription, and Australia and New Zealand had voted against it. Did Canada really *need* conscription? The Canadian Corps was indeed one of the finest fighting units in the Empire. But was it not true that one cause of the manpower crisis was the Canadian policy of maintaining military autonomy? This policy, unlike the policy of imperial integration accepted by other imperial forces, imposed upon Canada the need to maintain a steady supply of reinforcements for her own Corps. Was not Canada's pride in the Corps weakening the effectiveness of her contribution? In the midst of all this violent and bitter debate Borden congratulated Lieutenant General Arthur Currie on his appointment as the first Canadian to become Corps commander, and Currie answered (following Borden's enquiry) that the Corps had to be reinforced. When Laurier's referendum amendment came to a vote in the Commons, party allegiance was shattered: twenty-two English Liberals voted for conscription (among them Sir Clifford Sifton and W. S. Fielding), while several Quebec Conservatives revolted against Borden's "coercion." Several Liberal newspapers (including the influential Toronto *Globe*) deserted Laurier and backed conscription. This, however, was the beginning, not the end of the conscription crisis.

Borden's Military Service Act of August, 1917, was followed by his Wartime Election Act, designed to enfranchise female relatives of servicemen and disenfranchise Canadians born in enemy countries or naturalized since 1902. While Borden might defend this law on patriotic grounds, its obvious result would be to give more votes to the Conservatives, who now appeared as the party of patriotism in contrast to the Liberals, who seemed to be lukewarm—if not hostile—towards Canada's war effort and sacrifice of life. Laurier and the opposition vainly denounced the law as discrimination against loyal British subjects, but popular sympathy was undoubtedly with the government.

Propaganda, such as that shown above, was directed at Canadian soldiers in France prior to the election of 1917.

The passing of the Wartime Election Act was followed in December, 1917, by a general election—the "Khaki Election," so called because it focused on wartime issues. Before the election, however, Borden announced the formation of a Union government that included ten Liberals and brought the government the support of most English-speaking members of the Liberal party. When the returns were counted, Laurier had won as many as 62 of Quebec's 65 seats, but outside Quebec the Liberals held only 20 ridings. The Wartime Election Act had played its part. English Canada had shown overwhelming confidence in Borden, in conscription and in the Allied cause. Sectionalism, that "unloved bogey of Canadian national life," seemed to have triumphed. After twenty years of growing national unity, Quebec faced a united, English-speaking Canada. But worse was to come.

Despite repeated requests for delay, and warnings by responsible persons that conscription would precipitate a racial-religious war in Quebec, Borden was adamant that the Military Service Act be enforced. By March, 1918, the machinery of conscription was at work, and late that month the predicted trouble occurred in Quebec City. Resentment against the arrest of a supposed draft dodger by federal police officers flared into rioting; rioting grew into arson and pillage. Finally, when rioters fired on 700 English-speaking troops sent to restore order, the soldiers retaliated, and four persons were killed. No further public disturbances on this scale occurred, but the reinforcement situation was so serious that the government next decided to cancel exemptions granted to certain categories of draftees. Almost 94 percent of the conscripts had claimed exemption on various grounds, and 84 percent of these claims had been accepted. The decision to cancel the exemptions to farmers' sons and to skilled industrial workers brought bitter charges of bad faith from both organized labour and farmers' associations. Nevertheless, the government insisted on cancelling exemptions.

Of almost 402,000 men called up under the Military Service Act, more than half had been exempted, almost 28,000 either failed to report or deserted, and after deductions had been made for other reasons, about 120,000 were actually inducted. Yet reductions by medical and other discharges cut this number to just under 100,000—the goal originally set by Borden as the justification of conscription. In this respect the Act was a success—even though less than 25,000 conscripts actually saw action. The necessary reinforcements had been produced, but the cost to national unity was to prove high.

The conscription crisis and the election of 1917 shattered the Liberal party, but the long-term effects on the Conservatives were more drastic. The party was anathema in Quebec for decades as the party that forced Canadians to fight Britain's wars against their will, whereas the Liberals were able to regain much of their English-speaking support after the war. The explosive conscription issue had shown how thin a thread joined the elements that supposedly made up Canadian unity. It was a sharp reminder that the continuance of Canada's national life depends upon the application of the principle of compromise.

THE RAILWAY MESS

The conscription crisis may have been of Borden's making, but the wartime bankruptcies of two major railways, the Grand Trunk Pacific and the Canadian Northern, were certainly not. From their earliest days these railways had been burdened with debt, their lines overextended, their own competition (and that of others) too stiff for profitable operation. Indeed, the financial troubles of the Grand Trunk Pacific and the Canadian Northern had begun the day that Laurier authorized two more transcontinental lines. The company most seriously in trouble was the Grand Trunk Pacific, but many small feeder lines were also in difficulty. By 1916 the president of the C.P.R. was advocating the nationalization of all lines in the country.

The government was hesitant to underwrite further railway costs, especially since its own wartime expenses were high and no end to the conflict was in sight. On the other hand, railways could not be allowed to stand idle. In the end loans were approved by parliament, but a royal commission was appointed to investigate the country's railways. The commission reported in 1917, recommending nationalization of the Canadian Northern, the Grand Trunk, the Grand Trunk Pacific, the Intercolonial and the National Transcontinental. Borden's government was not prepared to do this, and instead introduced a bill in August, 1917, which called for a large loan to the Grand Trunk Pacific and the nationalization of the Canadian Northern. (Since the previous November the government had been *operating* the National Transcontinental.) The bill was passed, and a second bill placed the Canadian Northern under the control of a crown corporation.

Despite the Railway Commission's statement that Canadian Northern stock was worthless, the government paid $10.8 million for Mackenzie and Mann's interests in order to compensate in part the unfortunate creditors of these two spectacular speculators (who never went bankrupt themselves). Settlement with the Grand Trunk Pacific Company took longer to arrange; the parent Grand Trunk Railway held out until 1919, hoping against hope to make some profit from its valueless shares. The

Canadian National Railways Act of 1919 was not made effective until 1922, but as early as 1919 the Minister of Railways had to be appointed receiver in bankruptcy of the Grand Trunk Pacific, and in 1920 capital stock of the Grand Trunk itself was bought up by the government. In 1923 the Canadian Government Railways, the system begun by the wartime purchase of the Canadian Northern, became the Canadian National Railways.

WOMEN'S SUFFRAGE

One further development that arose from wartime conditions—women's suffrage—was important for its long-term influence rather than for the controversy aroused by its introduction during the war.

The movement demanding votes for women had appeared in Canada in the late 1800's soon after similar campaigns were begun in Europe and the United States. Unlike their counterparts elsewhere, Canadian suffragettes never engaged in such militant actions as disrupting public meetings, destroying public and private property and flouting the law. The Canadian movement was, in fact, part of a larger movement for equal rights for women, and the vote was merely the first objective. The vote would be a means of achieving full legal equality between men and women. Many groups supported the suffrage movement for their own reasons (the Women's Christian Temperance Union, for example, saw in the vote a means of establishing prohibition). Many supporters were men, and the movement had the approval of many farm and labour organizations.

By 1910 the suffrage movement had gained much respect throughout Canada, but it took a war to achieve the final political equality of the sexes. Opponents of women's suffrage claimed, with some truth, that many women did not want the vote. Nevertheless, war work by women, especially in factories, earned them the franchise. Their services to Canada were equal to those performed by many men. To the municipal franchise, won for women around 1900, was now added the federal vote in

The war hastened the emancipation of women, giving them hitherto unheard of responsibilities. These girls, under female supervision, are operating lathes in a war factory manufacturing brass shell cases. Caps were worn as a safety measure to contain long hair.

the provinces. The Federal Franchise Act of 1898 had given control of the franchise to the provinces, and in 1916 the three prairie provinces gave women the vote. British Columbia and Ontario followed suit in 1917. But Borden's government now insisted that only a federal statute could confer the federal franchise on women. Women in the five provinces where enabling legislation had been passed now felt cheated, yet a breach in the Conservative government's position came suddenly with the Wartime Election Act of 1917. The limited grant of the vote to the female next-of-kin of Canadian soldiers opened the way for full women's suffrage. It would henceforth be unjust and politically impossible to refuse the vote to all adult women at some near date, and so the Elections Act of 1918 granted women full federal voting rights.

Although women could henceforth vote for members of Parliament, they still had no legal right to sit in Parliament. This anomaly was corrected by a temporary law of 1919 (made permanent the following year). In 1921 Miss Agnes MacPhail, a school teacher running as a candidate of the United Farmers of Ontario party, became the first woman member of the Canadian House of Commons.

THE PEACE CONFERENCE AND CANADA'S NEW STATUS

From the moment that Britain declared war on Germany, Canada's constitutional relations with the mother country became a matter of deep concern to Borden. Canada and the other dominions shared with Britain the trial of war, and thus the Empire was drawn together in a manner impossible, even unimaginable, in peacetime. Yet the very events that encouraged imperial unity—the contributions of the dominions to the imperial war effort and the achievements of their soldiers in battle—also stimulated a strong sense of nationalism.

The Imperial Conference scheduled for 1915 was postponed by the war. When an Imperial War Conference was convened in 1917, David Lloyd George, who had become prime minister of Britain late in 1916, invited the dominion prime ministers to join the deliberations of the five-man British War Cabinet. Thus was formed the Imperial War Cabinet, a means of co-ordinating the war efforts of the mother country and the dominions, an innovation considered so successful by Lloyd George that he announced that it would meet at least once a year henceforth.

Many months before the Imperial War Cabinet first met, Borden had spoken bitterly, but privately, of the lack of information and consultation between the British government and his own:

> Is this war being waged by the United Kingdom alone, or is it a war waged by the whole Empire? It can hardly be expected that we shall put 400,000 or 500,000 men in the field and willingly accept the position of having no more voice and receiving no more consideration than if we were toy automata.

Borden found in the Imperial War Cabinet an opportunity to sound once more "the note of Canadian nationhood." He was determined that out of it would come "a new conception of the status of the Dominions in their relation to the governance of the Empire." With the aid of J. C. Smuts of South Africa, he moved a resolution that, although constitutional changes within the Empire should be postponed to a special postwar conference, "any such readjustment, while thoroughly preserving all existing power of self-government and complete control of domestic affairs, should be based upon a full recognition of the Dominions as autonomous nations of an Imperial Commonwealth." Borden insisted that the dominions had a "right to a voice in foreign policy through continuous consultation," and Smuts stated bluntly that imperial federation was an impossibility.

Despite the good intentions of the 1917 and 1918 meetings of the Imperial War Cabinet, forces of disunity, largely hidden by the war, were already at work within the Empire. Some were economic, since the dominions were competitive, not complementary, in their economies. The tariff policies of the dominions, especially those of Canada, were proof of this. Canada seemed, by its role in the war, to have been bound even closer to the mother country, but in fact the war had bred a spirit of national pride of self-consciousness and self-confidence in the dominion, and this centrifugal force soon became apparent after the Armistice. Again, each dominion was bound to express a different foreign policy because of its location. Canada, for example, was anxious to be the intermediary between the United States and Great Britain. In addition, Canada shared the general North American suspicion of what Laurier had called "the vortex of European militarism." Then again, the contribution of the dominions to victory had been important. Next to the major powers, they had supplied the greatest number of men and had suffered the greatest casualties. Canada, a country of 9,000,000 that mourned 60,000 dead in Flanders fields, had lost more men than the United States, a nation with ten times the population.

The Imperial War Cabinet meeting of 1918 set the stage for the post-war settlement as far as the dominions were concerned. The

The Peace Conference, Paris, 1919. Sir Robert Borden, Canada's Prime Minister, can be seen second from the right at the right hand arm of the table.

delegates to this meeting moved to Paris as the British Empire delegation, and dominion leaders spoke on behalf of the Empire. But the dominions also gained the right to speak on their own behalf at the Peace Conference. Led by Borden, the dominions demanded and received separate representation as sovereign nations, both at the Peace Conference and in the League of Nations—a far cry from their colonial status of 1914 when they had dutifully followed Britain into war.

At the Peace Conference (and later) Canada sought precise and limiting definitions of national responsibility in maintaining international peace, especially with regard to Article X of the Covenant of the League of Nations (by which member nations guaranteed the territorial integrity and political independence of each other). To the newly created states of post-war Europe, Article X appeared "the central pillar of the temple of peace," but many Canadians believed that it imposed an "unlimited liability," "an obligation direct and absolute" to assume responsibilities that might drag Canada into further European wars. "We do not," remarked one Liberal member of parliament, "want to be governed by and from Geneva," while another added, "we are placing the Canadian people at the beck and call of a Council not responsible to the nation for its actions." Clearly, Canadians were more interested in national sovereignty than in international security.

When the Treaty of Versailles (including the League Covenant) was completed, Great Britain signed for the Empire, but the four dominions signed individually, as autonomous nations within the Empire. When the first assembly of the League of Nations met in 1920, the seating of Canadian and other dominion delegates signified a new stage in the gradual metamorphosis of the British Empire into a Commonwealth of Nations.

* * *

No period in Canada's century-and-a-half in the British Empire was so pregnant with change as the years 1914 to 1919. If, as it has been said, the seed of Canadian nationalism was planted in the War of 1812, then World War I saw the tree of nationhood blossom. The magnitude of Canada's contribution to victory was recognized in Canada's new stature at Versailles and Geneva. Canada was now a nation among nations, and if she looked forward with hope and confidence to a new and greater age, she would always look back in sorrow to the blood-drenched fields of Flanders where her nationhood had been so dearly purchased.

READINGS

Policies for an Emerging Nation

The bases of Macdonald's policies for developing a strong Canada can be expressed in three words—railways, population, tariffs. How successful were these policies as employed by both Macdonald and Laurier? Was their success due to their intrinsic merits or to accidental circumstances outside of Canada? What disadvantages ensued from the implementation of these policies? Finally, what was, and is, Canada's economic destiny—to be a self-sufficient nation, or a hewer of wood for the British or American empires?

One of the most cogent defences of the National Policy—and a politically successful one—was made by the policy's author, Sir John A. Macdonald, in the course of his last election campaign in 1891.

... Our policy ... is to-day what it has been for the past thirteen years, and is directed by a firm determination to foster and develop the varied resources of the Dominion, by every means in our power, consistent with Canada's position as an integral portion of the British Empire ....

When, in 1878, we were called upon to administer the affairs of the Dominion, Canada occupied a position in the eyes of the world very different from that which she enjoys to-day. At that time a profound depression hung like a pall over the whole country, from the Atlantic Ocean to the western limits of the province of Ontario, beyond which to the Rocky Mountains stretched a vast and almost unknown wilderness. Trade was depressed, manufactures languished, and, exposed to ruinous competition, Canadians were fast sinking into the position of being mere hewers of wood and drawers of water for the great nation dwelling to the south of us. We determined to change this unhappy state of things. We felt that Canada, with its agricultural resources, rich in its fisheries, timber, and mineral wealth, was worthy of a nobler position than that of being a slaughter market for the United States .... So we inaugurated the National Policy. You all know what followed. Almost as if by magic, the whole face of the country underwent a change. Stagnation and apathy and gloom—ay, and want and misery too—gave place to activity and enterprise and prosperity. The miners of Nova Scotia took courage; the manufacturing industries in our great centres revived and multiplied; the farmer found a market for his produce, the artisan and labourer employment at good wages, and all Canada rejoiced under the quickening impulse of a new-found life. The age of deficits was past, and an over-flowing treasury gave to the Government the means of carrying forward those great works necessary to the realization of our purpose to make this country a homogeneous whole.

To that end we undertook that stupendous work, the Canadian Pacific Railway. Undeterred by the pessimistic views of our opponents —nay, in spite of their strenuous, and even malignant opposition, we pushed forward that great enterprise through the wilds north of Lake Superior, across the western prairies, over the Rocky Mountains to the shores of the Pacific, with such inflexible resolution, that, in seven years after the assumption of office by the present Administration, the dream of our public men was an accomplished fact, and I myself experienced the proud satisfaction of looking back from the steps of my car upon the Rocky Mountains fringing the eastern sky. The Canadian Pacific Railway now extends from ocean to ocean, opening up and developing the country at a marvellous rate, and forming an Imperial highway to the east, over which the trade of the Indies is destined to reach the markets of Europe. We have subsidized steamship lines on both oceans —to Europe, China, Japan, Australia, and the West Indies. We have spent millions on the extension and improvement of our canal system. We have, by liberal grants of subsidies, promoted the building of railways, now become an absolute necessity, until the whole country is covered as with a network; and we have done all this with such prudence and caution, that our credit in the money market of the world is higher to-day than it has ever been, and the rate of interest on our debt, which is a true measure of the public burdens, is less than it was when we took office in 1878 . . . .

. . . Disappointed by the failure of all their predictions, and convinced that nothing is to be gained by further opposition on the old lines, the Reform Party has [now] taken a new departure, and has announced its policy to be Unrestricted Reciprocity—that is (as defined by its author, Mr. Wiman, in the *North American Review* a few days ago), free-trade with the United States, and a common tariff with the United States against the rest of the world. The adoption of this policy would involve, among other grave evils, discrimination against the mother country . . . .

It would, in my opinion, inevitably result in the annexation of this Dominion to the United States. The advocates of Unrestricted Reciprocity on this side of the line deny that it would have such an effect, though its friends in the United States urge, as the chief reason for its adoption, that Unrestricted Reciprocity would be the first step in the direction of Political Union . . . .

. . . For a century and a half this country has grown and flourished under the protecting ægis of the British Crown . . . .

Under the broad folds of the Union Jack, we enjoy the most ample liberty to govern ourselves as we please, and at the same time we participate in the advantages which flow from association with the mightiest Empire the world has ever seen . . . .

The question which you will shortly be called upon to determine resolves itself into this; shall we endanger our possession of the great heritage bequeathed to us by our fathers, and submit ourselves to direct taxation for the privilege of having our tariff fixed at Washington, with a prospect of ultimately becoming a portion of the American Union?...

As for myself, my course is clear. A British subject I was born—a British subject I will die. With my utmost effort, with my latest breath, will I oppose the 'veiled treason' which attempts by sordid means and mercenary proffers to lure our people from their allegiance. During my long public service of nearly half a century, I have been true to my country and its best interests, and I appeal with equal confidence to the men who have trusted me in the past, and to the young hope of the country, with whom rests its destinies for the future, to give me their united and strenuous aid in this, my last effort, for the unity of the Empire and the preservation of our commercial and political freedom.

Joseph Pope, *Memoirs of the Right Honourable Sir John Alexander Macdonald, G.C.B., First Prime Minister of the Dominion of Canada* (Toronto: Oxford, 1930), pp. 272-277 *passim.*

Sir John A. Macdonald always linked the fate of the C.P.R. to the fate of his party and of Canada. Originally planned to prevent American encroachment on the Canadian west, the C.P.R. in 1890 was still to Macdonald's mind a bulwark to keep Canada British.

Earnscliffe, Ottawa, November 10/90.

My Dear [Sir George] Stephen.

Many thanks for your reminder of the birthday of the C.P.R. What a change that event has made in this Canada of ours! And to think that not until next year was it expected that the infant prodigy would arrive at maturity. . . .

I think you have great cause for thankfulness at the success of the line, instead of feeling disappointed. Its pecuniary returns within such a short period after construction, are almost as remarkable as the unprecedented speed of construction. You, personally, have had an enormous amount of strain, responsibility and worry, but the enterprize has been a success from the beginning.

The Government and Parliament will do what they can to sustain and help the line, but it must be remembered that in 1891 we are to go to the electors, and one cannot foresee the result. If left to ourselves, I have no doubt of a decision in our favour, but I have serious apprehensions which are shared by all our friends here, that a large amount of Yankee money will be expended to corrupt our people. I have no doubt that that rascal Wiman is already raising a fund for the purpose. Sir C. Tupper will tell you that every American statesman (and he saw them all in 88), covets Canada. The greed for its acquisition is still on the increase, and God knows where it will all end. If Gladstone succeeds, he will sacrifice Canada without scruple.

We must face the fight at our next election, and it is only the conviction that the battle will be better fought under my guidance than under another's, that makes me undertake the task, handicapped as I am, with the infirmities of old age. . . .

Sir Joseph Pope (ed.), *Correspondence of Sir John Macdonald* (Toronto: Oxford, c. 1921), pp. 477/78.

On the eve of the election of 1891 Goldwin Smith, self-appointed thinker and voice of the Liberals, reiterated that party's belief in Canada's continental destiny when he published *Canada and the Canadian Question.* To him the existence of the Commerical Union movement was proof that not all Canadians were convinced of the benefits of Macdonald's National Policy of tariffs.

The movement in Canada originated with a Farmers' Convention in Toronto, and was taken up by the Farmers' Institutes of the Province. On the farmer's mind had dawned the fact that he was the sheep, and the protected manufacturer was the shearer. The special organ of the movement has been the Commercial Union Club, an association independent of political party. The policy of Reciprocity, however, has been embraced by the Liberal Party now in Opposition; it forms the main plank in the platform of that party; and will, in all probability be the issue at the coming elections. . . .

That the market of her own continent is the natural market of Canada, both as a seller and a buyer, even so strong an Imperialist as Sir Charles Dilke admits, and no one but a protected manufacturer or a fanatical Tory would attempt to deny. The Conservative leader, Sir John Macdonald, has always professed to be doing his utmost to bring about reciprocity. His motto has been Reciprocity of Trade or Reciprocity of Tariffs, meaning that if he had recourse of reciprocity of tariffs it was only because he could not get reciprocity of trade, and in order to enforce it. His Protectionist Tariff Act contained a standing offer of reciprocity in natural products. This, as has been said before, was illusory, inasmuch as the Americans evidently could not, in common justice to their own interests, allow their manufactures to be excluded while they admitted the natural products of Canada; but it was at all events the homage paid by political strategy to commercial wisdom....

It is alleged by Protectionists that there cannot be a profitable trade between Canada and the United States, because the products of the two countries are the same. The products of the two countries, even their natural products, leaving out of sight special manufactures, are not the same. In the United States are included regions and productions almost tropical. Canada, on the other hand, has bituminous coal, for which there are markets in the United States, and plenty of nickel, of which the United States have but little. Canada has lumber to export, and the United States want all they can get. Both countries produce barley, but the Canadian barley is the best for making beer, and its exclusion by the M'Kinley Act brought out a heavy vote at Buffalo against the party of Mr. M'Kinley. This is the first answer. The second and the most decisive is that, in spite of the tariff, Canada has actually been trading with the United States more than with England or any other country in the world, and nearly as much as with all the other countries in the world put together....

To Manitoba and the North-West, which neither have manufactures, nor, as farm products are their staple, are likely to have them, the tariff is a curse, without even a shadow of compensation....

Canadians are told, to scare them from Commercial Union, that if the tariff wall were out of the way they would become "hewers of wood and drawers of water for the Yankees." Hewers of wood for the Yankees they are already to their own great profit. It is not obvious why the producer of raw materials should be deemed so much beneath the factory hand; perhaps looking to the effect of manufactures on national character in England we might think that a nation would be wise in contenting itself with so much of factory life as nature had allotted it. Whatever yields most wealth will raise highest the condition of the people, their standard of living and their general civilisation....

To make up for the dearth of economical arguments against Reciprocity its opponents appeal to Loyalty and the Old Flag. "Discriminate against the Mother Country! Never!" So with uplifted hands and eyes cry Protectionists who are running to Ottawa to get higher duties laid on British goods, and would not be sorry to shut the gate, if they could, against British importation altogether. Canada does already discriminate against Great Britain, if not on any specific article, on the aggregate trade. It has been shown that she collects about four per cent more in the aggregate on British than on American goods, and admits more American than British products free. When the privileges enjoyed by the colonies in the British market were withdrawn and the commercial unity of the Empire was broken up, notice was in effect given to each member of the Empire to do the best that it could for itself under its own circumstances. The circumstances of Canada are those of a country commercially bound up with another country much larger than itself and with a high tariff. It is surely too much to expect that all Canada shall remain in a state of commercial atrophy for the sake of a few exporting houses in Great Britain.

Goldwin Smith, *Canada and the Canadian Question* (Toronto: Hunter, Rose, 1891), pp. 282, 283, 287/88, 289, 294, 295.

A letter addressed by Edward Blake to his former constituents in West Durham during the 1891 election, but not released until after the voting, denounced Macdonald's policies for corrupting national political life.

It has left us with a small population, a scanty immigration, and a North-West empty still; with enormous additions to our public debt and yearly charge, an extravagant system of expenditure, and an unjust and oppressive tariff . . . and with unfriendly relations and frowning tariff walls ever more and more estranging us from the mighty English-speaking nation to the south, our neighbours and relations, with whom we ought to be, as it was promised that we should be, living in generous amity and liberal intercourse. Worse, far worse! It has left us with lowered standards of public virtue and a death-like apathy in public opinion; with racial, religious and provincial animosities rather inflamed than soothed; with a subservient parliament, an autocratic executive, debauched constituencies, and corrupted and corrupting classes; with lessened self-reliance and increased dependence on the public chest and on legislative aids, and possessed withal by a boastful jingo spirit far enough removed from true manliness, loudly proclaiming unreal conditions and exaggerated sentiments, while actual facts and genuine opinions are suppressed. It has left us with our hands tied, our future compromised, and in such a plight that, whether we stand or move, we must run some risks which else we might either have declined or encountered with greater promise of success.

The Globe, Toronto, 6 March, 1891, reprinted in O. D. Skelton, *Life and Letters of Sir Wilfrid Laurier* (Toronto: Oxford, 1921), vol. I, pp. 419/20.

As Prime Minister, Laurier accepted and perpetuated Macdonald's principles for nation-building, and explicitly announced his acceptance of protective tariffs in a speech to the Canadian Manufacturers' Association in 1905. A private letter of Liberal Senator James McMullen (who in 1892 had opposed the erection of a national monument to Sir John A. Macdonald) to the Canadian correspondent of *The Times* of

London in 1904 shows why even Liberals had come to accept Macdonald's policies as the most *practical* ones for Canada.

If Canada adopted the policy of England there would not be one of our institutions that would be in existence in twelve months from now, American competition would wipe them out in one year. If we adopted a revenue tariff on a revenue basis the American competition would wipe out every one of these institutions in about two years. Free trade is a good thing if you can get people to free-trade with you, but in the face of first the McKinley Bill and then the Dingley Bill that struck at Canada as clearly and distinctly as a tariff can be adjusted and in face of the fact that the United States is drawing over 70 million dollars in gold from our Treasury every year, after all *The Globe* refuses to sanction a measure that would tend to equalize our trade with that country. . . .

I am not a protectionist by choice, but where our manufacturers are denied the privilege of trade on equal terms I refuse that nation advantages in our market so much in excess of what she gives us as in the case of the United States.

A. H. U. Colquhoun (ed.), *Press, Politics and People: The Life and Letters of Sir John Willison, Journalist and Correspondent of* The Times (Toronto: Macmillan, 1935), p. 121.

When European migration was filling the west and western grain was jamming the C.P.R. facilities, Laurier stated his reasons for supporting another transcontinental railway in terms reminiscent of Macdonald's speeches on development policies.

. . . To those who urge upon us the policy of tomorrow, and tomorrow, and tomorrow; to those who tell us, Wait, wait, wait; to those who advise us to pause, to consider, to reflect, to calculate and to inquire, our answer is No, this is not a time for deliberation, this is a time for action. The flood tide is upon us that leads on to fortune; if we let it pass it may never recur again. If we let it pass, the voyage of our national life, bright as it is today, will be bound in shallows. We cannot wait, because time does not wait; we cannot wait because, in these days of wonderful development, time lost is doubly lost; we cannot wait, because at this moment there is a transformation going on in the conditions of our national life which it would be folly to ignore and a crime to overlook; we cannot wait, because the prairies of the North-west, which for countless ages have been roamed over by the wild herds of the bison, or by the scarcely less wild tribes of red men, are now invaded from all sides by the white race. They came—last year 100,000—and still they come in still greater numbers. Already they are at work opening the long dormant soil; already they are at work sowing, harvesting and reaping. We say that today it is the duty of the Canadian government, it is the duty of the Canadian parliament, it is the duty of all those who have a mandate from the people to attend to the needs and requirements of this fast growing country, to give heed to that condition of things. We consider that it is the duty of all those who sit within these walls by the will of the people, to provide immediate means whereby the products of those new settlers may find an exit to the ocean at the least possible cost, and whereby, likewise, a market may be found in this new region for those who toil in the forests, in the fields, in the mines, in the shops of the older provinces. Such is our duty; it is immediate and imperative. It is not of tomorrow, but of this day, of this hour and of this minute. Heaven grant that it be not already too late; heaven grant that whilst we tarry and dispute, the trade of Canada is not deviated to other channels, and that an ever vigilant competitor does not take to himself the trade that properly belongs to those who acknowledge Canada as their native or their adopted land.

House of Commons Debates, 30 July, 1903, p. 7659.

Instead of one more transcontinental railway, Laurier actually permitted the building of both the Grand Trunk Pacific and the Canadian Northern. When a world depression struck in 1913 both lines faced bankruptcy. A Royal Commissioner investigated the railway crisis and reported in 1917. The nub of his findings is contained in the following extract from the report:

The policy of government aid makes the need for regulation of railway building more necessary even than where private capital is depended upon, for in the latter case the proposal must at least have a promise of commercial success before capital can be induced to come in and give it support. To the absence of such regulation must be charged responsibility for no small part of the railway problem today. . . .

The records show that the Canadian Northern had a large mileage on the prairies before the projection of the Grand Trunk Pacific; so that when the extension plans of the Grand Trunk became a part of the national policy, as they did become, the Canadian Northern was added to the number of those who wanted to own a transcontinental system and one as fully complete and self-contained as was that of the Canadian Pacific. Hence, we find two new companies, both built largely upon public credit, striving for first place in a field which, as for transcontinental transportation, or even as for connecting Eastern and Western Canada, was already occupied. Besides having the Great Lakes waterway, there could have been barely enough business to support one additional line, and that only by the exercise of economy in operation and prudence in investment. . . .

This brings us fairly to a recognition of the fact that while the policy of public aid to railways had originally been founded on the urgent need for transportation to open up a new country, to develop its resources, and to unify Canada commercially and politically, it was carried far beyond the limits warranted by the original exigency. It appears to me that the responsibility is as much the Government's as the private companies'. Without enabling legislation and the extension of Government credit from which all received their essential support, the companies could not have expanded and overbuilt. . . .

Report of the Royal Commission to Inquire into Railways and Transportation in Canada (Ottawa: King's Printer, 1917), pp. xci-xcii.

BIBLIOGRAPHY

*INDICATES VOLUMES AVAILABLE IN PAPERBACK.

Armstrong, E. H. *The Crisis of Quebec, 1914-1918*. Columbia University Press, 1937—a balanced view of the conscription issue.

Borden, Henry (ed.). *Robert Laird Borden: His Memoirs*. 2 vols. Macmillan, 1938—an autobiography of Canada's war-time Prime Minister.

Brown, R. C. *Canada's National Policy, 1883-1900*. Princeton University Press, 1964—an analysis of Canadian economic nationalism as practised by the Conservatives and Liberals.

*Careless, J. M. S. *Brown of the Globe*. Vol. II. Macmillan, 1964—covers the period from 1859 to Brown's death.

Cook, Ramsay. *The Politics of John W. Dafoe and the Free Press*. University of Toronto Press, 1963—an analysis of the political ideas of a leading Liberal journalist.

*Creighton, D. G. *John A. Macdonald: The Old Chieftain*. Macmillan, 1955—the second volume of the definitive biography of Canada's first Prime Minister.

Dawson, R. M. *William Lyon Mackenzie King, A Political Biography*. Vol. I. *1894-1923*. University of Toronto Press, 1958—a sympathetic treatment by King's official biographer.

Ellis, L. E. *Reciprocity, 1911: A Study in Canadian-American Relations*. Yale and Ryerson, 1939—a detailed study of an important event in Canada's economic growth.

Farr, D. M. L. *Canada and the Colonial Office, 1867-1887*. University of Toronto Press, 1955—early developments towards dominion status.

Ferns, H. S., and Ostry, Bernard. *The Age of Mackenzie King: The Rise of the Leader*. Heinemann, 1955—a highly critical account of King's early career.

Gibbon, J. M. *Steel of Empire*. McClelland and Stewart, 1935—the most readable history of the C.P.R.

Glazebrook, G. P. de T. *Canada at the Paris Peace Conference*. Oxford University Press, 1942—Canadian aims and practices analyzed.
*————. *A History of Canadian External Relations*. 2 vols. Carleton Library (McClelland and Stewart), 1966—a general survey with emphasis on the post-Confederation period.
*————. *A History of Transportation in Canada*. 2 vols. Carleton Library (McClelland and Stewart), 1964—the second volume is devoted to post-Confederation developments.
Nicholson, G. W. L. *The Canadian Expeditionary Force, 1914-1919*. Queen's Printer, 1962—an official account of all military aspects of the war concerning Canada.
Penlington, Norman. *Canada and Imperialism, 1896-1899*. University of Toronto Press, 1965—the background of Canadian involvement in the Boer War.
Schull, Joseph. *Laurier: The First Canadian*. Macmillan, 1965—the most recent and comprehensive of several available biographies.
*Stanley, G. F. G. *The Birth of Western Canada: A History of the Rebellions*. University of Toronto Press, 1963—survey of the Canadian west in the first two decades of Confederation.
————. *Louis Riel*. Ryerson, 1963—the definitive biography of the Métis leader.
Swettenham, J. A. *McNaughton:* Vol. 1, *1887-1939*. Ryerson, 1968—the authorized biography of the great Canadian soldier-scientist.
————. *To Seize the Victory*. Ryerson, 1965—Canadian military operations in the First World War set against the background of Canadian politics.
Thomson, Dale. *Alexander Mackenzie, Clear Grit*. Macmillan, 1960—a biography of Brown's successor as Liberal leader.
Wallace, Elizabeth. *Goldwin Smith*. University of Toronto Press, 1957—a stimulating biography of the controversial political writer.

4

THE ERA OF MACKENZIE KING

CHAPTER 15

THE RISE OF MACKENZIE KING

World War I, with its strong demand for both raw materials and manufactured goods, had continued the boom conditions of the Laurier period. With the end of the war, there was a period of uncertainty while prices climbed down from their inflated wartime levels and production adjusted itself to the new conditions of peace. In Canada this uncertainty produced a short depression, but much of the country soon entered a period of prosperity. This prosperity, which was closely related to a flourishing United States economy, was to last through the decade of the twenties.

The issues raised by Canada's transition from war to peace were epitomized in the general election of 1921. This contest saw new leaders at the head of Canada's major parties—Arthur Meighen for the Conservatives and Mackenzie King for the Liberals. It also witnessed the appearance of a new party from the west, aggressively determined to end the dominance of the old parties in Canadian politics. The duel for power between Meighen and King, begun in the 1921 election, reached its climax in the dramatic constitutional crisis of 1926. King, standing on the brink of political oblivion in 1926, turned the tables on his opponent and went on to win Britain's recognition of Canada as an independent state.

THE PATTERN OF PROSPERITY

Canada's first industrial revolution had been based on iron, coal and the railway; the economic revolution of the twentieth century involved base metals, oil and hydro power. Central Canada's possession of these resources gave it an immense advantage in meeting the demands of this technological revolution. No longer did the lack of coal in central Canada hamper industrial efforts, for at hand was the enormous power potential of the Great Lakes and the rivers of the Shield. The scarcity of iron in the industrial heartland presented no problem in an age when automobile manufacturers were calling for non-ferrous metals and alloys.

Quebec and Ontario clearly reflected the economic growth of the decade. Hydro-electric power production in the two provinces, largely obtained from the Shield, jumped from 2 million to almost 5 million horsepower between 1920 and 1930. Hydro-electric power encouraged the location of a major aluminum industry in Quebec on the Saguenay River, which drops over 300 feet in its first thirty miles after leaving Lake St. John. The town of Arvida, containing the largest aluminum smelter in the world, was founded in 1926. Again, thanks to water power, the production of non-ferrous metals in the central provinces almost doubled in the decade, while the output of paper and newsprint increased threefold. Inevitably, manufacturing also expanded and its concentration in central Canada became even greater. Ontario emerged as the centre of the Canadian automobile industry, while both Ontario and Quebec broadened the range of consumer goods they produced. Westward, in Manitoba, expansion occurred along the same lines, again based on the Shield. Extensive zinc and copper deposits were mined at Flin Flon on the Manitoba-Saskatchewan border. Hydro-electric power and pulp and paper production were developed on a large scale.

In the prairie provinces a large proportion of total income was still derived from wheat farming. The 1920's saw a strong demand for wheat, primarily from Europe. Canada's success in meeting this need is revealed by the fact that in the mid-twenties she supplied almost 40 percent of the world's wheat (as compared with about 12 percent in 1909). However, it was now apparent that the geographic limits of wheat production had virtually been reached. A few large blocks of unoccupied land remained (for example, the Peace River valley), but the great days of agricultural settlement in the west were over. The prairie farmer would now have to depend on mechanization and more efficient methods of cultivation to increase his annual harvest and to reduce his cost per bushel.

In British Columbia the 1920's was also a period of lively economic activity. Here, in the interior and coastal mountains, were base metal deposits, pulpwood and lumber, forests and hydro-electric power in abundance. Transportation for British Columbia lumber was greatly assisted by the opening of the Panama Canal in 1914. Now it was possible, using the Canal, to compete in the large eastern United States market against timber from the southern states or the American northwest. Much of the province's lumber was also exported to Great Britain and to the Orient. The same was true of its fish, its minerals and its apple crop.

While central Canada and British Columbia prospered immensely, and while Manitoba, Saskatchewan and Alberta enjoyed steady annual wheat sales, the Maritime provinces found themselves producing less railway track and rolling stock for the west. True, they still could count on selling fish and lumber to some extent in world markets, but what future had the east coast iron and steel industry now that the settlement of the western plains was practically accomplished? No one seemed to know.

The economic activity of the 1920's produced a regional rather than a national prosperity. This circumstance resulted directly from the relative decline of agriculture in the Canadian economy and from the rise of the new export staples. Agriculture, although it enjoyed large overseas markets for its products, did not show anywhere near the same growth as mining, pulp and paper and manufacturing. Moreover, there was little hope of the expansion of wheat farming on the prairies, and farm workers (there and elsewhere in Canada) were being drawn off to better-paying industrial jobs in the cities. The markets for Canadian wheat, which looked stable in the 1920's, were, in reality, precarious. Europe's buying power depended to a great extent on the continuance of loans from the United States, and an ominous trend towards economic nationalism overseas was to appear before the end of the decade. The declining position of agriculture was underlined by the ever-growing importance of mining, manufacturing and the forest industries. Their share of the national income increased and they began to employ a greater proportion of the Canadian labour force. Their output—gold, copper, nickel, chemicals, lumber, pulp, newsprint—went south to the United States rather than east to Great Britain.

Economic development in the twenties cut across the east-west unity that had been created by Macdonald's National Policy. The prosperity of the 1920's spread itself unevenly across Canada, a condition which was destined to rouse tensions in the federal political system and to weaken the basis of Canadian unity.

NEW FACES AND NEW MOVEMENTS

In 1919 Canada's government, the Union government of 1917, was still in the hands of the Conservative party, led by Sir Robert Borden. Borden, however, was an exhausted man. Worn out by the stresses and strains of office during the war years, he resigned in the summer of 1920. He was succeeded by his right-hand man, Arthur Meighen, to whom he had entrusted the difficult task of executing the Union government's conscription programme.

Born and educated in Ontario, Meighen had gone to Manitoba as a young man to practise law. In time he had become widely known in the west as a successful trial lawyer. In 1908 he was elected to parliament, and thereafter his political advancement was rapid. He entered Borden's government as Solicitor General in 1913 and became a member of the cabinet two years later.

Meighen possessed many of the qualities that bring success in political life. Intellectually he was a giant, with a razor-sharp intelligence he used to shred an opponent's arguments. Forceful in debate, he was equally clear and effective in his writings. His courage and personal integrity were of the highest order. He was hard-working and determined to play a constructive role in the affairs of his country. Yet Meighen had less desirable qualities. A gaunt appearance and a reserved manner suggested the new prime minister's upright character, but they also concealed arrogance and an uncompromising sense of rectitude. He never went out of his way to seek friends and indeed he lacked the little personal graces that are the very essence of political leadership. An "upright figure of ice" he has been called; a man respected, but not loved, by those around him.

The new Liberal leader was William Lyon Mackenzie King. Born in 1874 (the same year as Meighen), King's career was always consciously influenced by the fact that his mother's father had been William Lyon Mackenzie, the fiery rebel of 1837. A contemporary of Meighen at the University of Toronto, "Rex" King worked during the summers as a reporter for a Toronto newspaper, thereby gaining much experience of people outside his own middle-class background. Already interested in labour and social questions, he decided to pursue graduate studies at the new University of Chicago. Instead of staying in a students' residence at the university, he lived at Hull House, a social service centre founded in the slums near the Chicago stockyards. There, King observed at first hand the social problems that accompanied industrialism.

From Chicago King went on to Harvard, where he ultimately submitted a brilliant thesis on "sweat shop" conditions in the garment trades of the United States and Britain, a subject that he had previously investigated as a young reporter in Toronto. His studies of industrial conditions brought him to the attention of Laurier. In 1900 he was asked to come to Ottawa as editor of the *Labour Gazette*, a publication of the new Department of Labour created by Laurier. A little later, King became Deputy Minister of Labour.

King had no intention of remaining a civil servant, no matter how influential. Since boyhood his secret desire had been to enter politics, "for which my whole nature and ambition longs," he had confided to his diary in 1902. With Laurier's blessing, he

Arthur Meighen (left) and Mackenzie King.

contested North Waterloo in the election of 1908, won his seat and entered parliament (at the same time as Meighen). Within a year Laurier had invited the young man into his cabinet as Minister of Labour. Here, he drafted acts for the regulation of labour disputes and the curbing of business combines. In the 1911 defeat of the Liberals King was among the casualties. For a time he served as a Liberal party organizer and then decided to return to the study of industrial problems. He carried out industrial research for the Rockefeller Foundation and became a labour relations adviser to John D. Rockefeller, Jr. In 1917 he returned to Canada to support Laurier against conscription in the "Khaki Election," but was defeated again. King returned to the United States.

Laurier's death early in 1919 necessitated a party convention, which King was careful to attend. In the course of the convention, the Liberals adopted a platform that in many respects differed radically from past aims. It broke with the notion of passive government that Liberals had traditionally favoured and suggested that government should act boldly in order to meet the problems that industrialism had brought to Canada. (King's hand had clearly been at work in these sections of the platform that called for legislation on behalf of the working man—a national system of insurance for unemployment, sickness, disability and old age.) There was a distinct effort to attract the western farmer back into the party with the promise of lower tariffs on farm implements, fertilizers and clothing. The urban dweller was promised a reduction in living costs by the removal of duties on foodstuffs. Reciprocity with the United States, an historic Liberal doctrine, was reaffirmed. In foreign policy the party promised to oppose any suggestion of centralized imperial control over Canada's external affairs. The platform, in general, reflected the contemporary spirit of reform and included something for almost everybody.

By a narrow margin Mackenzie King won the leadership nomination. He had shown an unswerving loyalty to Laurier throughout the dark days of the party's fortunes. He possessed a famous name. He was young and energetic. He was known to be a talented and successful mediator in labour disputes, and this ability would be very useful if transferred to party politics. Above all, the party was still weak and divided and required a leader who could unite the various factions and lead them to victory at the polls. Observers noted that King had gained the support of the large Quebec delegation at the convention. All in all, he seemed to be the leader the party needed.

As a person and as a politician Mackenzie King stood in complete contrast to Arthur Meighen. A short, stocky man with a round face and a mincing manner, he possessed none of Meighen's force and directness. King's speeches were long and prolix, so qualified and rambling that it was often difficult to determine just what he was saying. Yet, behind his bland, slightly pompous appearance resided a will as implacable as Meighen's and a political shrewdness that the Conservative leader sadly lacked. In addition, King had cultivated the art of managing men; he knew the importance of organization, whether in industry, in trade unions or in political parties, and he was soon to display his mastery of this particular art.

The election of 1921 witnessed the appearance of a new political party, the Progressive Party. For the first time in Canadian history a third party challenged the position of the two older political parties.

The Progressive movement drew support from two important groups in the country—trade unions, and farmers in Ontario and the west. Organized labour, which had doubled in size as a result of the war, began to stir restlessly during the early twenties. The high cost of living, evidences of war profiteering, the unemployment that resulted from the shift to peacetime production—all these factors contributed to labour discontent. In western mining towns a new organization, the "One Big Union," tried to line up all workers in common opposition to the leaders of business and industry. Its methods were violent and it won few converts in the east, but it represented a more militant force within the ranks of Canadian labour.

This militancy was displayed at Winnipeg in the early summer of 1919. A demonstration by construction and metal workers in favour of shorter hours, higher wages and union recognition spread to become a general strike of 30,000 working men in Winnipeg. In the "Red Scare" that gripped North America at the time, the strike was immediately interpreted as a revolutionary conspiracy. The strikers, it was claimed, were led by dangerous foreign elements and were about to establish a Bolshevist state on the banks of the Red River. The Royal North-West Mounted Police and the militia were called in and violence, leading to at least two deaths, occurred. The trial of the leaders of the Winnipeg strike resulted in a new bitterness on the part of labour and led to demands that trade unions play a more active role in politics.

Labour's restiveness was matched by dissatisfaction among Canadian farmers. (In the twenties, one out of every two Canadians lived and worked on the land.) Economic difficulties stemming from the transition from war to peace provoked discontent. Farm sales in the immediate postwar years slumped, bringing particularly serious hardship to the prairie farmer, who depended on one crop—wheat. Farmers in Canada, however, had been critical for years of the economic and political systems under which they lived. They opposed the protective tariff, which only increased their costs of operation. They wanted the railways taken over by the state and freight rates reduced. They demanded higher taxes on the profits of business and industry. Western farmers, in particular, felt that government was influenced far too much by the wealthy, eastern capitalists who occupied a commanding position in both the Conservative and Liberal parties. Big Business, in short, was felt to represent a combination of economic and political power that was detrimental to the welfare of the farmer, who considered himself the mainstay of the economy. A statement at this time by the founder of the western farmers' newspaper, the *Grain Growers Guide*, recalls the point of view of the Populists in the United States twenty years before:

> The history of Canada since Confederation has been a history of heartless robbery of both the people of the Maritimes and of the Prairie Sections of Canada by the Big "Vested" interests—so called from the size of their owners' vests—of the Central Provinces.

In 1918 the national farmers' organization, the Canadian Council of Agriculture, issued a statement called the "New National Policy" in which it set forth the economic and political aims that many farmers had been seeking for years. Shortly afterwards Ontario farmers decided to found a political party to contest the provincial elections of 1919. To the surprise of many people, the United Farmers of Ontario won a majority of seats in the legislature and proceeded to set up a government under E. C. Drury. This victory in Canada's largest province suggested that a powerful new political force had appeared in the dominion.

The exciting possibilities of political action appealed to farm groups all across Canada, and it was decided to establish a national political party. Out of a convention at Winnipeg in 1920 came the National Progressive Party. The New National Policy was adopted as its platform. Here was a bold challenge to the older parties to justify their claim to leadership in the rapidly changing conditions of post-war Canada. The first leader of the

On Saturday June 21, 1919, the Winnipeg general strike took a turn toward violence. Already convinced that the strike was part of a "revolutionary plot," the civic authorities became alarmed when returned servicemen organized a "silent march" on the Manitoba legislative buildings, to ask the government for information on plans to settle the strike. Mounted police and members of a "citizens' militia," swinging baseball bats, charged the marchers on Winnipeg's Main Street (above). Shots were also fired, although it was a matter of dispute as to who fired first—the police or one of the marchers. The Western Labor News *commented that it was unlikely the marchers had planned violence, for they had brought their wives with them.*

party was T. A. Crerar, a Manitoba farm boy who had been president of the United Grain Growers Company for many years. His patriotism had caused him to join Borden's Union government as Minister of Agriculture, but in 1919 he had resigned to protest against high tariffs. Now, at the age of forty-five, he prepared to lead the protest movement of farm and labour in the federal election of 1921.

The election campaign of December, 1921, while an exciting campaign, failed to present a list of clear-cut issues. Each party offered a program for the future. Crerar put forward the western farm view and appealed to urban workers to support the Progressives in their new approach to national politics. Meighen emphasized the importance of tariff protection as the economic basis of national existence. King cunningly pursued a middle course, skilfully underlining different aspects of the Liberal platform in different parts of the country. Evasive though his own platform was, King branded the Meighen government a war government, a high-tariff government, the patron of big business and an administration that had failed to deal with the social problems of Canada. The results of the election showed a country divided along regional and racial lines. The Liberals captured all 65 Quebec seats and 52 others, mainly in Ontario and the Maritimes. The Conservatives dropped to 50 seats, most of which were in Ontario, the English-speaking areas of New Brunswick, and British Columbia. The Progressives showed remarkable strength by winning 24 seats in Ontario and 41 in the west.

The election of 1921 was a disquieting indication of how fragile was the unity for which Macdonald and Laurier had laboured so hard and so long. The structure of Canadian unity seemed to lie in pieces. Who would undertake the task of rebuilding it?

THE LIBERAL RESTORATION

The man who became prime minister of Canada in 1921 was destined to be the most successful political leader of his age. For the next thirty years until his death in 1950 Mackenzie King was to dominate the public life of Canada. As Macdonald and Laurier had done before, he gave his name to an era of Canadian history.

On the surface King seemed to possess few of the qualities of greatness. His personality lacked colour, and he could not command the warm loyalty that Macdonald, and to a lesser extent Laurier, had evoked. As a young politician he was inwardly unsure of himself, and as an older one he continued to worry over the impression he made upon others. Yet for a generation he held off challenges to his leadership of the Liberal party and outwitted new political movements that were determined to topple him from power. What was the secret of King's astounding success?

King's genius lay in his realization that because Canada is not a united country its political life must rest on certain principles of action. Foremost among these was the principle that no major

"Still Waiting," is the title of this 1921 cartoon on Meighen's unsuccessful efforts to win support in Quebec. The reputation earned by Meighen and the Conservatives in the conscription crisis of 1917 was too much to overcome.

decision should be taken unless it had the support of all the important interests in the country. Thus, policies had to be framed with a view to meeting the needs of the various sections and groups in the country. King had an uncanny ability of gauging what his fellow Canadians wanted—or what they were prepared to accept. He took endless pains to analyze the outlook of different parts of Canada; he was prepared to wait for long periods before coming to a decision; he then proceeded by means of innumerable compromises and bargains. He refused to commit himself beforehand to any course of action, but insisted on full discussion—in the party caucus, in parliament and in the nation. The result of these practices was a cautious, uninspiring but effective direction of affairs that maintained unity. "Mr. King for twenty-five years was the leader who divided us least," wrote one observer at the time of his death.

King's minority government was sustained in power after 1921 by the support of the Progressive members of parliament. Although he had refused to coalesce with the Progressives in 1921, King lavished attention upon them. He looked upon the sixty-five Progressives as potential allies, to be attracted into the Liberal party if possible. Emphasizing the general similarity between the aims of the two parties, King brought about an informal alliance between Liberals and Progressives in parliament. But once committed to co-operation with the Liberals, the Progressives faced the loss of their identity. The renewal of prosperity after 1923 made it more difficult to maintain the crusading fervour of the immediate post-war years, and the Progressives became divided among themselves. Crerar resigned the leadership, while others formally joined the Liberal caucus. On the provincial scene as well the movement soon lost its momentum. The Drury government in Ontario collapsed through scandal and mismanagement in 1923; the Manitoba Progressives merged with the Liberals after 1928. King began to implement parts of the Liberal platform of 1919 during these years. (The tariff was lowered, particularly on items that the western farmer used and on foodstuffs consumed by the general public. In 1926 a national system of old age pensions was enacted.)

Political life in the early 1920's centred on the parliamentary struggle between King and Meighen, a contest between two intensely ambitious men. The rivalry of Meighen and King was intensified by their personal attitude towards each other, which can only be described as one of mutual loathing. While King concealed his true feelings under a mask of exaggerated politeness and urbanity, Meighen took no pains to hide his contempt.

His clear, logical mind was exasperated beyond measure by King's almost perpetual evasiveness. The burden of a complaint he had made in 1919 was constantly on his lips:

If I have one suggestion to offer to the [honourable member], it is that when we have a concrete subject before the House for debate, he would be good enough to offer some remarks which really bear upon the merits of the issue....

Meighen accused King of confusing issues, of failing to put forward clear goals, of attempting to satisfy all parts of Canada through contradictory policies. King, however, refused to be pinned down or to be ruffled by such scornful thrusts. He met his rival's jibes with infinite patience and continued to conduct himself in his usual bland manner.

As a contest, the election of 1925 was a dull one, reflecting the prosperity of the country and an apathy towards politics. King stood on the record of his government and asked that it be given a stronger mandate to carry on. Meighen proposed a return to the historic principle of tariff protection in order to safeguard the domestic market and thus increase the nation's prosperity. (It was typical of the man that he made the appeal, without qualification, in all sections of the country, including the traditionally low-tariff west.) Meighen increased the standing of the Conservatives in the House to 116. The Liberals were reduced to 101, one of their casualties being the Prime Minister himself; however, they did retain a solid Quebec bloc. The Progressives saw their strength fall away to 25 members. Once again no party had a majority. Although the Conservatives were now the largest party, they could not gain office, for King managed to win the support of the Progressives.

Disaster soon overtook the shaky administration headed by King (who had been returned to parliament in a by-election). Early in 1926 the Conservatives accused the Customs Department of grave scandals involving the smuggling of whisky into the prohibitionist United States. It was said that the Customs Department, and even the Minister himself, had been remiss in their duties. The Liberal party, it was reported, had profited through "kickbacks" from smugglers. A select committee, appointed to study the evidence, reported in June, upholding the accusations. King was in an unenviable position, because he knew that a motion of censure against the government would undoubtedly be introduced. It stood an excellent chance of passing, for the Progressive members had shown unmistakable signs of repugnance at the sordid disclosures made before the committee. His back to the wall, King asked the Governor General to grant him a dissolution of parliament so that he could appeal to the Canadian people in another election.

Normally a governor general accepts the advice of his prime minister on the matter of a dissolution. But in 1926 there were circumstances that made Governor General Lord Byng hesitate. King's government was facing a vote of censure in the House; should it be allowed to avoid this vote before it went to the country? Would another election, the second in eight months, serve any useful purpose? Should not Arthur Meighen, the leader of the largest group of members in the Commons, be given a chance to form an alternative government? Three times, in a dramatic weekend, Mackenzie King advised the dissolution of parliament, and three times Byng refused. King thereupon indignantly resigned, leaving Canada without a prime minister and without a government.

Byng called upon Meighen to form an administration. Three days later the new ministry was defeated in the Commons.

In engineering this defeat, Mackenzie King displayed consummate political skill. In those days it was necessary for a member of parliament who had been appointed to the cabinet to resign his seat and to stand for re-election. Meighen, therefore, when he was sworn in as prime minister, resigned his Commons seat. He appointed six Conservatives, all but one of whom were ex-cabinet ministers, as acting ministers of various departments. King immediately challenged the legality of the new ministry, charging that it was composed of men who had not taken the oath of office and were therefore not properly ministers of the Crown. King also pointed to the fact that the ministry was headed by a prime minister who did not have a seat in parliament. The Progressives were impressed by the charges of

Meighen and King—Une voiture, là, m'sieur? This cartoon from Montreal's La Presse *shows Meighen and King eager to please the Progressive leader, who holds the balance of power in the first parliament of 1926.*

illegality. On 1 July they voted with the Liberals on a motion of censure to defeat the government. Meighen immediately advised the Governor General to grant a dissolution of parliament.

In the ensuing election King took the initiative, charging that the Governor General had acted in an unconstitutional manner in originally denying him a dissolution. Recalling his grandfather's struggle in 1837, Mackenzie King heatedly proclaimed that the same problem—the actions of an irresponsible governor—was evident in 1926. He went on to claim that the Governor General's actions threatened Canada's autonomy and reduced her to the status of a crown colony. Knowing that self-government was one of the most sensitive subjects in the Canadian experience, King kept coming back to the theme of aggrieved nationhood (and, in the process, completely obscured the grave charges against his administration). Meighen indignantly sought to counter this attack, which he considered grossly oversimplified, by an appeal to reason. He repeatedly pointed out that there was no constitutional crisis at all. The Governor General had acted quite properly in the circumstances. Moreover, he charged, King had committed the unprecedented sin of dragging the Crown into political controversy. To say that the episode had threatened responsible government was absurd, Meighen declared, for the British government had not dictated Lord Byng's actions in any way.

The election of 1926 was a confused one, for other factors—a Liberal budget promising tax reductions, the proposal of an old age pension—were involved. When the shouting died away, the Liberals had won 116 seats to the Conservatives' 91 and the Progressives' 13.

In 1926 the Liberal party emerged from an election for the first time since 1917 as a genuine national party. It still relied on Quebec support, but it had increased its standing considerably in Ontario and in the Maritimes. It had absorbed so many Progressives that the farmers' party virtually disappeared as a political force after 1926. (The new Progressive leader, Robert Forke, entered King's cabinet after the election.) The Conservatives were now restricted to support in Ontario, the Maritimes and British Columbia. Meighen, crushed by what he felt to be an unfair verdict, retired in 1927. With the exception of a brief return to power (1930-1935), the Conservative party was destined to inhabit the wilderness of opposition for the next thirty years. The long reign of Mackenzie King had begun.

THE ACHIEVEMENT OF AUTONOMY

One plank in the Liberal party platform of 1919 read:

> Resolved, that we are strongly opposed to centralized Imperial control.

This sentence sums up King's attitude towards the conduct of foreign policy within the British Empire. He disagreed with

Borden's view that there should be a common foreign policy for the dominions and Great Britain. To King, a common foreign policy was unrealistic. In the first place, the individual interests of the various parts of the Empire differed widely. Secondly, it was beyond all reason that Britain would allow the dominions a hand in making *her* foreign policy. Thirdly, a common policy would obscure the new status that Canada and the dominions had gained through their efforts during the war. A common foreign policy would, in point of fact, be a British foreign policy that Canada could not endorse without losing her self-respect.

Borden's concept of an imperial foreign policy broke down in 1922. The occasion was the so-called "Chanak crisis," arising from Britain's decision, as a signatory of the 1920 peace treaty with Turkey, to garrison a neutralized zone along the Straits of the Dardanelles. Turkey, repudiating the treaty in 1922, sent troops to occupy the zone. For some weeks there seemed to be every possibility of war between Britain and Turkey. The British government, which had taken its stand without consulting the dominions, now cabled to ask them for aid should war break out. Unfortunately, the request for aid was made known to British newspapers before it was received in the dominions. Mackenzie King was attending a political picnic in Toronto when the request for aid reached Ottawa. First hearing of it from a reporter, he felt, as he wrote in his diary, "annoyed" at the message. "It is drafted designedly to play the imperial game, to test out centralization vs. autonomy as regards European wars." Britain's request for aid, he thought, revealed that her government had not appreciated the implications of the new status Canada had gained at the Paris Peace Conference. It raised the delicate question, lurking so close to the surface in Canadian politics, of the pull between loyalty to Britain and the assertion of Canada's autonomy.

King told the British government that Canada could not furnish aid without a full discussion of the subject in parliament. While he had not refused aid, King had let it be known that he was not prepared to be responsible for supporting British foreign policy. The Chanak crisis clearly revealed the serious difficulties that were inherent in the practice of a diplomacy common to all the dominions. Britain obviously assumed that she could take the support of her dominions for granted. Canada had little interest in certain parts of the world (such as the Middle East), whereas Britain had many concerns in many distant places. There was also the practical problem of arranging consultation with far-flung dominions in the light of swiftly moving events.

The concept of a common foreign policy was seriously weakened by Chanak. This was confirmed a year later when Britain signed a new treaty with Turkey. King indicated that since Canada had not taken a part in negotiating the Treaty of Lausanne, he did not feel bound to support it. King confided to his diary:

> Only in matters in which we have a direct and immediate interest will we expect to . . . participate . . . in all others . . . we will decide "on merits of the case" what it is wisest do do. . . .

If a common foreign policy was an impossibility, it was obvious that Canada would have to devise a foreign policy of her own. She had some of the means with which to effect foreign policy in the Department of External Affairs, that Laurier had created in 1909 as an adjunct of the prime minister's office. Its existence, however, did not change the fact that Canada needed to exercise two essential functions before she could claim to conduct her own foreign policy. In the first place, she would have to gain the power to make her own treaties with foreign nations; secondly, she would require the authority to send diplomatic representatives to other lands. In the course of his first administration Mackenzie King assumed the first of these powers.

For some years Canada had exercised the right to negotiate commercial treaties with foreign countries. However, she did so under certain limitations. For example, her negotiators received their authority from the Crown on the advice of the British government; a British representative was required to sign the completed treaty along with the Canadian negotiators; the treaty had to be ratified by the Crown on the advice of British ministers. Of course the British government willingly performed these tasks at the request of the Canadian government, but it was still humiliating to undertake diplomacy in this roundabout way. For treaties which involved political subjects, the British participation was much greater, usually involving Foreign Office approval.

King resolved to change these practices. He began with a treaty between Canada and the United States on a matter that had no interest for other parts of the Empire: the Halibut Fisheries Treaty, that concerned the regulation of this fishery on the Pacific coast of the United States and Canada. The treaty was negotiated by Canadian officials with "full powers" derived from the Crown at Canada's request. It was signed in March, 1923, by the American Secretary of State and Ernest Lapointe, the Canadian Minister of Marine and Fisheries. When the British government decided that the British ambassador in Washington should sign the treaty, King flatly refused any such signature. The treaty was later ratified by King George V, after the *Canadian* parliament had approved it and after the *Canadian* government had made a formal request for ratification. Canada had thus concluded a treaty with a foreign power in her own right.

The idea that each dominion should be free to conduct its own foreign policy where no Empire interests were involved was accepted at the Imperial Conference of 1923. This was King's first meeting with the other prime ministers of the Empire, most of whom were in favour of restoring the principle of a common foreign policy. King stoutly resisted this attempt, putting forward his concept of the autonomy of each partner in the Empire. In 1923 King's view prevailed, and the Empire began moving towards a looser form of association of sovereign nations—the modern Commonwealth.

The second power that Canada required if she were to pursue an independent diplomacy was the right to appoint representatives to foreign countries. Representatives abroad were needed to give her accurate knowledge of conditions in other countries, to look after her interests in these countries and to conduct negotiations with them. Obviously the United States, the foreign country with whom she had the most numerous dealings, should be the first to receive a Canadian diplomatic agent. (There had, of course, been a Canadian High Commissioner in London since

1879.) Such a plan had been put forward at the close of World War I, with a view to strengthening the workings of a common foreign policy. At that time it had been envisaged that a Canadian agent would be appointed to the United States with a rather shadowy status as second-in-command at the British Embassy in Washington. The British and American governments had accepted this proposal. However, for a variety of reasons (one of them being the unstable political situation in Canada in the early 1920's) the plan had not been put into practice.

In the meantime, the Irish Free State had opened a legation in Washington in 1924. When King returned to office after his temporary absence in 1926, he decided to take the same step. Mr. Vincent Massey was appointed first Canadian minister to the United States in 1927. Before the decade was over, other Canadian ministers had been appointed to countries such as France and Japan, which had large commercial dealings with Canada.

At the Imperial Conference held in London in the autumn of 1926, King returned to the question of defining Canada's new freedom of action. Still smarting over his treatment by the Governor General, he was determined to clarify the relationship between Canada and Great Britain in such a way that it would accurately reflect Canada's independent status. He was supported by General Hertzog, Prime Minister of South Africa, who was interested in a redefinition of the British Empire that would indicate South Africa's separate nationality. (Australia and New Zealand, with more homogeneous English-speaking populations, were less interested in this question of definition.) A compromise was reached between the dominions on the matter of a new constitution for the British Empire.

The essence of the new relationship was contained in the report of a conference committee headed by Lord Balfour, a former British prime minister. The Balfour report recognized that nothing like the British Empire of 1926 had ever existed before. It proceeded to define the self-governing dominions as:

autonomous communities within the British Empire, equal in status, in no way subordinate one to another in any aspect of their domestic or external affairs, though united by a common allegiance to the Crown and freely associated as members of the British Commonwealth of Nations.

Throughout the last fifty years, the report went on, the dominions had steadily followed the road to autonomy. Now the end of the road had been reached and "every self-governing member of the Empire was now the master of its destiny. Free institutions are its [the Commonwealth's] life-blood. Free co-operation is its instrument. Peace, security, and progress are among its objects." The British Commonwealth of Nations, based securely on positive ideals, had emerged.

While equal in status, the dominions were hardly equal in function, the conference agreed. Britain's power and experience meant that she would have to bear special responsibilities in the attainment of Commonwealth objectives. But there was no longer to be any pretence of diplomatic unity within the British Empire; each dominion was to conduct its own foreign policy, even though it might diverge from that of the others. With the principles of the new Commonwealth defined, the 1926 conference turned to some of the practical features of the relationship. One such aspect was, clearly, the position of governor general. In the past he had acted both as an agent of the British government and as the Crown's representative in the dominion. Now he was judged simply to be the Crown's representative, holding the same relationship to his ministers as the monarch in Great Britain. He was not to reserve dominion legislation for the approval of Great Britain; nor was he to serve any longer as the official channel of communication between the dominion and the British government. He was to become, in fact, a viceroy, a constitutional head of state in the dominion. These important steps were complemented a few years later when Britain began the practice of appointing representatives in the dominions to act on her behalf. Canada received a High Commissioner from the United Kingdom in 1928, the counterpart of the Canadian High Commissioner in London.

The remaining stages in the progress of the dominions toward their new role as sovereign states were quickly taken. The most important requirement was that the changed status of the dominions be translated into law. These changes were embodied in the Statute of Westminster, which was passed by the Westminster parliament in 1931. The Statute provided that no law of a dominion could be considered invalid on the grounds that it conflicted with English law. The Colonial Laws Validity Act (1865), which had asserted this doctrine prohibiting conflict, was now repealed. No act of the British parliament was to extend to a dominion unless a dominion specifically requested it. In addition, the dominions were also empowered to legislate extra-territorially, that is, to supervise the movements of their citizens beyond three-mile national limits. Thus each dominion would now be able to exercise jurisdiction over its merchant shipping on the high seas. Henceforth the parliament of Canada would possess co-ordinate powers with the parliament of Great Britain.

The Statute of Westminster translated into law the principle of equality among Commonwealth countries. Only two points of subordination remained in Canada's relations with the United Kingdom: appeals could still be carried from the Supreme Court of Canada to the Judicial Committee of the Privy Council in England; and it was still necessary to ask Westminster to amend Canada's constitution. These were legal survivals from earlier days of dependence. Time and circumstance, it was thought, would ultimately remove them.

For Canada, the significance of the Statute of Westminster is that it completed the eighty-year process, dating from the achievement of responsible government, by which Canada acquired freedom of action. This Statute of 1931 secured complete legislative independence. The principles of political freedom and popular government, matured in Britain and carried to the New World three hundred years before, had produced a new nation.

* * *

Most Canadians, while recognizing the importance of the constitutional advances their country had made in the decade since the end of World War I, were more interested in the benefits of material prosperity. The 1920's had been a decade of economic progress for Canada, just as it had been for the United States. By 1929 it was estimated that the average per capita income of Canadians stood one-third higher than in 1920. Buoyed up by the insatiable demands of the American market, the Canadian economy had achieved new records in the 1920's. The possibilities of expansion seemed unlimited; the confidence of the people unshakeable. In April, 1929, Prime Minister King remarked:

> Our prosperity has been very general and has been shared in some measure by all classes throughout the country. . . . The prosperity of the present year succeeds the prosperity of the year previous . . . and we intend to maintain it and, if possible, to increase it.

In that age of optimism it seemed as if an earthly paradise had been established in North America. Few noted how precarious were the supports of that paradise and how easily they could be disturbed.

CHAPTER 16

THE POLITICS OF DEPRESSION

The confident optimism of Canada in the 1920's was replaced in the 1930's by despair and disillusionment resulting from the devastating impact of world-wide depression upon a country whose prosperity depended upon international trade. Economic distress led, as it had in the 1880's, to strains on the Canadian federal system. The remedies adopted to meet the crisis failed to provide a uniform measure of recovery. Protest parties appeared —some criticizing the workings of the National Policy, some proclaiming the old slogan of provincial rights, whilst others challenged the methods of capitalism itself and advanced socialist aims. Beset by such harsh criticism, Canadian unity, as Macdonald and Laurier had fashioned it, was severely shaken.

THE GREAT DEPRESSION

The decade of the 1930's in Canada was dominated by the worst depression the world has ever known. The economy of the United States, weakened by over-production and speculation, collapsed in 1929, to be followed by financial and commercial chaos in every country in the Western world. The response of most nations to the crisis was simple: they lowered the prices of their exports in order to sell more abroad, at the same time raising tariff walls in

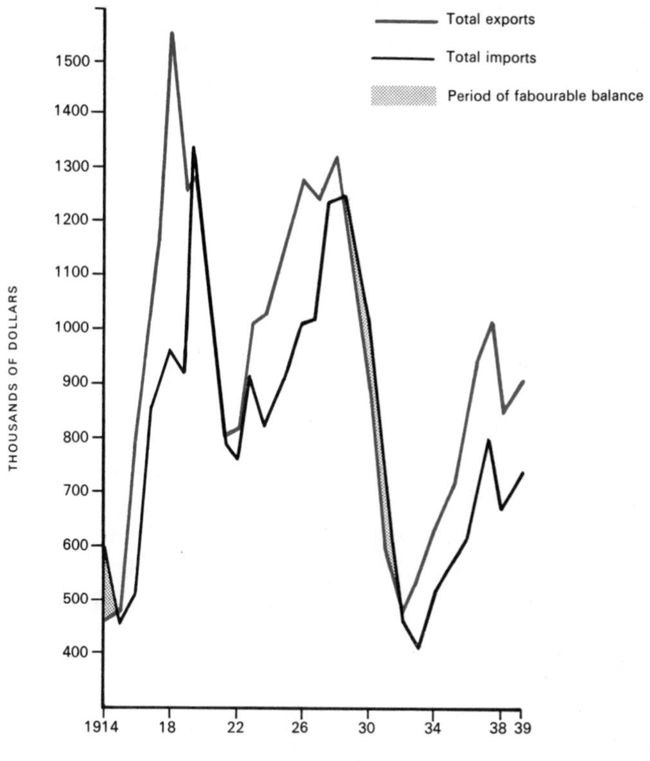

The Balance of Trade, 1914-1939

an attempt to shut out others' exports. Everywhere countries poured forth goods, but there were few takers. The dimensions of world trade shrank alarmingly as nations adopted import quotas or engaged in simple barter. Economic nationalism appeared throughout the Western world.

Canada, which had laboured for years to create an economy that produced for world markets, was almost mortally stricken by these developments. She derived one-third of her national income from foreign sales, and two-thirds of those sales involved raw materials. The international prices of raw materials fell to the lowest levels in recorded history. Wheat, which had sold for $1.60 a bushel in the boom year of 1929, fetched only 38 cents a bushel in 1932. Newsprint prices fell so drastically that half the Canadian mills were forced out of business. Fish dropped to a mere fraction of its former price, as did the prices of potatoes, lumber, dairy products and apples. Across the dominion primary producers watched their markets vanish.

One of the most disquieting features of the depression in Canada was the uneven manner in which it affected the various sections of the country. The Maritimes, although a region of primary production, did not experience the economic shock that struck other parts of the dominion. This was partly because the Maritimer frequently engaged in several occupations in order to earn his living. Then again, the per capita income of the Maritimes, being lower than that in other parts of Canada, did not experience the same proportionate fall. Still, the demand for Maritime products, whether of the farm, sea or forest, was affected by the world slump in trade. In the case of Newfoundland, with its highly vulnerable economic position, the effects of the depression were catastrophic. Faced with bankruptcy, the island was forced in 1934 to surrender responsible government and accept direct control by Britain as a condition of financial aid. Ontario and Quebec suffered least. They constituted the industrial heart of the country and produced for a domestic market that was protected by the tariff. This market may have been small, but in it the prices of manufactured goods held firmer than did those of raw materials. Central Canada engaged more in mixed farming than did the west, a circumstance which cushioned the shock of the especially severe fall in the price of wheat. Some sections of the mining industry enjoyed fair prices during the depression. The banks and other financial institutions of Montreal and Toronto and the service industries of the two provinces were able to carry on, although on a greatly reduced scale. Nonetheless, every corporation was badly shaken by the decline in business activity. Such well-known firms as Algoma Steel, Canada Steamship Lines and Abitibi Power and Paper had to be reorganized. The pulp and paper industry was especially hard hit. Thousands of businesses, large and small, went bankrupt.

The west felt most the impact of depression. Markets for British Columbia lumber and fish were drastically cut in the early thirties. The prairies, relying on exports of wheat for a high

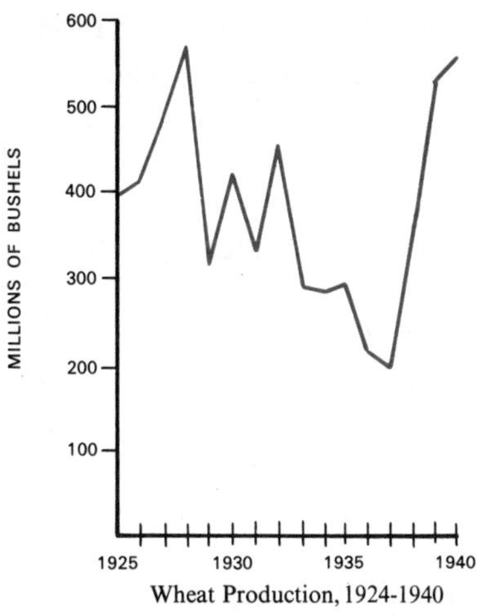

Wheat Production, 1924-1940

proportion of their income, were hit with devastating effect. To add to the general misery, the southern portions of the prairies were visited by an unprecedented drought. For most of the years from 1929 to 1937 a severe dry spell occurred, accompanied by hot winds that stripped the top soil from the land. A Regina journalist described the drought area in 1934:

. . . for a distance of more than fifty miles we passed through a landscape of almost incredible desolation. . . . The land was as lifeless as ashes, and for miles there was scarcely a growing thing to be seen. Where a scanty herbage had struggled up through the dust, flights of grasshoppers had apparently completed the destruction and then, despairing of further sustenance, had flown off to other fields.

The prairie farmer's cash income fell faster and farther than incomes dependent upon salaries and wages. In many cases his earnings were not sufficient to meet depreciation on his buildings and equipment. Thousands of farmers abandoned their farms in despair. During the decade from 1931 to 1941 about 250,000 people moved out of the southern portions of the three prairie provinces. Many went to the cities, others to the United States. Those who remained on the land eked out government relief supplies in a desperate effort to keep body and soul together.

In the cities, manufacturing continued, relying on the demands of the protected domestic market. The prices of goods were maintained, but businessmen could only reduce their overhead by firing workers. Unemployment, in both the primary and secondary industries, grew with each passing year. For the entire decade of the thirties it exceeded 10 percent of the available labour force, and in 1933 it climbed to as high as 22 percent. The younger unemployed relied on government relief, worked on public projects (such as the beginnings of the Trans-Canada Highway), lived in work camps modelled on those in the United States or restlessly "rode the rods" back and forth across Canada, seeking work that did not exist. The despair bred by unemployment gave rise to bitterness and, in some cases, to violence. The unemployed engaged in "sit-down strikes" in the lobbies of post offices, or, as in Regina in 1935, clashed with police in demonstrations that resulted in several fatalities.

As economic stagnation spread, its consequences became more apparent. Railway revenues fell drastically; receipts from taxes declined to such an extent that the provinces had difficulty balancing their budgets; the salaries of civil servants and teachers had to be reduced; incomes from stocks and property fell away; mortgages were foreclosed, and borrowers defaulted on their debts. The depression became an unmitigated calamity for almost every household in Canada.

PRIME MINISTER BENNETT

The depression produced a set of totally new conditions in Canadian politics. Not since the first decades after Confederation had there been such a time of serious economic difficulty, and never had there been a trade slump of such magnitude. It seemed as if the demise of private enterprise was at hand, necessitating strong action by the state. The leaders of the old parties, however, were extremely reluctant to see the state assume more direction in economic affairs at the expense of free enterprise. In addition, the federal structure of Canada was such that the constitutional responsibility for unemployment relief rested with the provinces,

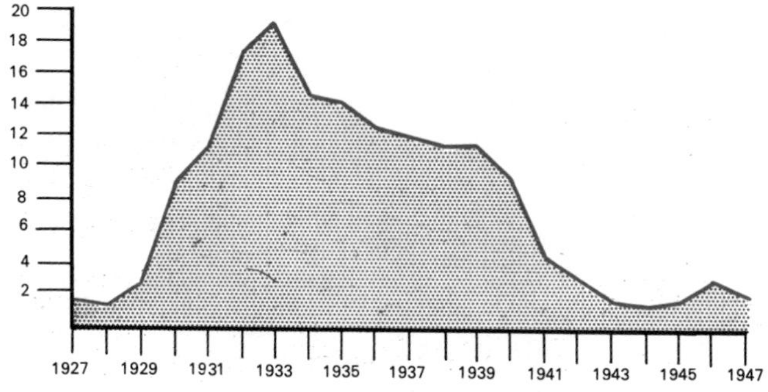

Percentage of Total Labour Force Unemployed, 1927-1947

which, of course, did not have the resources to deal with this particular problem. The catastrophe of the depression was such that some arrangement to cope with the problem had to be worked out.

Prime Minister King minimized the depression and predicted that employment would soon be available. Falling back on a constitutional argument, King stated that it was not the duty of the federal government to extend social assistance to the victims of depression. He reminded the provinces that they bore the constitutional responsibility of providing direct relief and other social assistance. Yet the provinces, because of their declining revenues, found it utterly impossible to carry out a relief program of the nature and size required. When Mackenzie King eventually did take limited steps to help by authorizing relief grants to several of the western provinces, it was pointed out that Ontario, with a Conservative administration, was not being favoured in the same way. Mr. King thereupon made the rejoinder:

> With respect to giving monies out of the Federal Treasury to any Tory government in this country for these alleged unemployment purposes . . . I would not give them a five-cent piece.

The "five-cent piece" speech, besides outraging Canadians by its cynicism, revealed that the Liberal government had no positive policies with which to meet the depression.

The political possibilities of King's slip were immediately seized upon by the new leader of the Conservative party, Richard Bedford Bennett. Elected in 1927 to succeed Arthur Meighen as head of the party, "R.B." was a vigorous personality. Bennett, a New Brunswicker, had gone west as a young lawyer, settling in the expanding town of Calgary. Here he had made a fortune via land speculation and the practice of corporation law. In 1911 Bennett entered parliament, but remained a comparatively obscure member during World War I.

Physically large, with a strong voice, Bennett seemed to radiate power and success. He laid down his views to the House of Commons and to his Conservative colleagues with the force of a schoolmaster lecturing his pupils. In reality Bennett possessed little understanding of the ways of politics. Intensely vain, he believed that any course of action he favoured was automatically beyond criticism. He never felt the need to practise the art of compromise. He was indifferent to the views and advice of other men, the members of his own party included.

In the election campaign of 1930 Bennett attacked the King government claiming that it was old and tired and had no will to meet the depression. In characteristic fashion he declaimed such slogans as "Canada first and then the Empire" and declared his intention of building up Canadian industry behind tariff walls in order to help Canada "blast her way into the markets of the world." The Canadian people, confused and shocked by economic calamity, responded to this positive appeal. Bennett won 137 seats for the Conservatives, and the Liberals were reduced to 88. Farmers' groups and independents accounted for another 20 seats. With the majority behind him, Bennett now undertook to lead Canada out of the depression.

Bennett called a special session of parliament in 1930 to enact a new tariff policy. His program, based on a hallowed Conservative principle, was to raise the Canadian tariff substantially with a view to cutting down imports. By this means he would maintain production and employment in those parts of the economy sheltered by the tariff. This course of action, by helping to restore confidence in the soundness of the economy, would promote recovery. The fact that it would not assist the exporting areas of

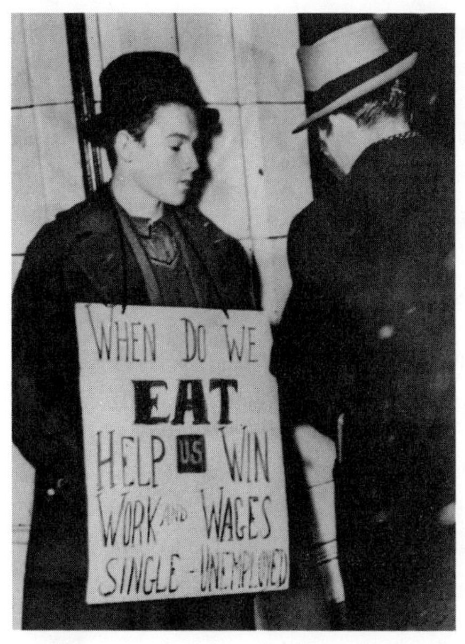

A young man, left unemployed by the depression, begs on a downtown Toronto corner. Even for those lucky enough to have a job, conditions were frequently close to unbearable. The 1934 royal commission investigating price spreads gave some examples: "One man of ten years' experience worked 70 hours per week in a Montreal contract shop, to earn $7 at 10 cents per hour. . . . Hours of employment are often oppressively long. Thirteen hours a day, 60 hours a week, are not uncommon in rush periods."

Canada would be remedied by federal grants and relief payments. Thus, in effect, the favoured areas of the country would support the less-favoured. A high tariff on imports, Bennett argued, would also induce other nations to consider lowering their duties on Canadian exports. He informed the Commons that this would aid the revival of world trade.

Bennett's version of economic nationalism suited the mood of Canada. The recent Hawley-Smoot Tariff in the United States had increased duties on Canadian wheat and livestock to a record level of 48 percent, and Bennett ordered retaliation. It has been estimated that the level of the Canadian tariff was pushed up an average of 10 percent. Almost every branch of secondary manufacturing in Canada secured additional protection from Bennett's tariff policy, and imports came to consist mainly of those items that could not be produced in Canada. (However, Bennett's economics also resulted in an increase in American ownership of the Canadian economy. American companies simply built branch plants in Canada to avoid the Canadian duties on manufactured imports.) Canada's trade deficit with her best customer, the United States, was much reduced. Tariff protection, nonetheless, failed to promote exports and indeed worked great hardship in those areas of Canada which produced for the export trade. Canadian exporters, their costs increased by the tariff, felt more severely than before the downswing of depression. Bennett had indeed protected the domestic market, but this market was not large enough to absorb the production of all sections of the country.

Coming as he did from a Loyalist province and a Loyalist family, Bennett was very conscious of the traditions of a unified British Empire. As a young man he had been inspired by Joseph Chamberlain's vision of a preferential tariff for the Empire and he was in close touch with another Canadian, Lord Beaverbrook, whose English newspapers were editorializing to the same end. In 1932, under the stress of the depression, an Imperial Economic Conference was called in Ottawa to consider the matter of expanding trade within the Commonwealth. Bennett presided at the Conference, happy to be able to forward the traditional Conservative tariff aims of protection and imperial preference. Unfortunately, the conference, attended by all the self-governing dominions, exhibited more discord than unity. Although Bennett preached the virtues of co-operative effort, he was unwilling to forego the protection he had given to Canadian manufacturers. He urged that existing rates of duty be retained and that the conference work upwards from there, increasing tariff levels on imports into the Commonwealth from abroad. The United Kingdom put forward the reverse proposition, in particular asking that British manufactures be admitted into Canada at lower rates.

After weeks of discussion the conference only narrowly avoided failure. In the end a series of separate trade treaties was negotiated between the nine countries attending. Canada received increased preferences in the British market for her foodstuffs, lumber and non-ferrous metals. In return, Britain obtained some concessions for her manufactures, although she had to accept the main elements of Bennett's protective tariff. Bennett had driven a hard bargain at the Ottawa conference, turning the entire meeting into a victory for economic nationalism. During the next ten years Great Britain's and the Commonwealth's

In 1935 British Columbia relief camp strikers arrived 2,000 strong in Regina on the first leg of their trip to Ottawa, where they hoped to force the federal government to provide work. Their journey actually ended in Regina in a bloody riot quelled by police forces.

share of Canada's export trade increased, reversing a trend of the 1920's. Still, the items covered by the Ottawa agreements comprised only a small part of Canada's exports and imports; and the huge markets of the United States and Europe remained closed to Canada, partly because of their high tariffs, but also because of the increased Canadian tariff.

Bennett did not neglect the problem of the social consequences of depression. In an emergency session of parliament in 1932 he had announced a $20 million public works program, followed later by large federal relief grants to the provinces. Special subsidies were awarded to the prairies, where the need for assistance was most pressing. Expenditures on relief increased almost tenfold in the five years of the Bennett regime, highlighting the vital fact that the dominion government alone had the financial resources to meet the gigantic problem of unemployment assistance.

Two other achievements of the Bennett regime—the Bank of

Canada and the Canadian Broadcasting Corporation—have become established features of Canadian life. The Bank of Canada, created in 1934, was the first central bank in Canada's history. It was charged with the task of managing the country's monetary system. The depression had revealed that there were serious shortcomings in the operation of this system, since the government could do little to regulate the flow of credit in the economy. The Bank of Canada was to be a publicly owned "banker's bank," holding part of the gold reserves of the chartered banks and possessing a monopoly on the issue of bank notes. It was to manage Canada's public debt, to advise the government on fiscal matters and to control the external value of the Canadian dollar. Bennett also turned his attention to radio broadcasting, which had been declared to be a federal responsibility by the Judicial Committee of the Privy Council.* The Canadian Radio Broadcasting Commission was set up in 1932 as a publicly owned radio network, broadcasting in English and in French. By 1936 the Commission possessed only three stations. That year, however, it was reorganized as the Canadian Broadcasting Corporation, given larger finances and a more effective board of management. Soon it was operating two national radio networks.

Other matters as well gained government attention. A parliamentary inquiry into the organization of the retail trade, carried out in 1934-35, disclosed that many large Canadian business concerns were making fantastic profits by underpaying the producer, overcharging the consumer and forcing the small businessman to the wall. The Royal Commission on Price Spreads revealed the great difference that existed between the cost of consumer goods and their retail price. It also made it clear that although large profits were being made in certain industries and retail operations, very low wages were being paid for long hours of work. In certain Quebec textile mills, for instance, it was discovered that a weekly wage of three dollars

*The first public broadcasting stations in Canada were established in 1922 and, in the following year, the Canadian National Railways set up the first government-controlled broadcasting department. A young Tyrone Guthrie, later to be the first director of the Shakespearean Festival at Stratford, worked for the C.N.R. Radio Department in 1929, producing a series of Canadian historical dramas.

was being paid for a seventy-two-hour week. Bennett was alarmed by these disclosures, the more so since the depression showed no signs of abating and a general election was in the offing. If his government was going to survive, he would have to offer the voters positive policies to combat the revelations of the Commission.

In a series of six radio addresses early in 1935, the Prime Minister suddenly announced a sweeping program of social security and labour legislation. These measures, patterned after Roosevelt's "New Deal," were designed to correct some of the findings of the price spreads investigation. Bennett accompanied them with an analysis of the capitalist system so critical that it shocked a number of Conservative supporters. (Bennett even went so far as to identify the crash of 1929 as the crash of the capitalist system.) Many Canadians were stunned by Bennett's strictures, coming as they did from a tycoon who had accumulated millions under the free enterprise system and one who had previously strongly defended that system. Parliament subsequently endorsed the Bennett program. A wages and hours act improving labour conditions and eliminating child labour was quickly passed, together with a comprehensive scheme of unemployment insurance. The dominion government undertook to control prices and marketing conditions.

The Bennett "New Deal" was only one issue in the general election of October, 1935. Much of the attention of the electorate focused on the person of the Prime Minister: his arrogant manner and his eleventh-hour conversion to the principle of state intervention. Many voters could not believe that Bennett was sincere in his election-year advocacy of social reform, and the Liberals skilfully exploited this disbelief. They pictured their leader as sane and sensible and electioneered with the slogan, "It's King or Chaos!" Eight provincial premiers, distrusting Bennett, announced their support of the Liberals.

The Conservatives went down to defeat. The party standing in parliament shrank to 39 seats. The Liberals elected 171 members, and the rest of the new House was filled with the representatives of the new protest parties—Social Credit and the Co-operative Commonwealth Federation (C.C.F.)—which had emerged since

1930. Indeed, the support these parties obtained was the most remarkable fact about the 1935 election. The Liberals won about the same percentage of the popular vote that they had in 1930, so that the new parties were the main beneficiaries of the Conservative decline. This indicated an ominous trend away from the old parties.

PROTEST MOVEMENTS IN THE 1930's

The protest parties which made their first appearance in the federal parliament in 1935 showed the mood of Canadians as the depression wore on, a mood best summed up in the word "frustration." The momentum of nation-building had faltered. Economic advance, which had accomplished such an improvement in the material position of many Canadians during the previous decade, had come to a halt. The federal government seemed unable to provide leadership. In addition, its chances of coping with the depression were greatly reduced by the rigid division of legislative powers under the BNA Act, which assigned many economic and social functions to the provinces. In view of the difficulties that limited federal action, it is hardly surprising that new movements appeared in various regions of Canada. The appearance of sectionalism has, indeed, been a characteristic of every economic slump in Canadian history. In the 1930's it was accompanied by an emphasis on a local leader, who promised strong action to cure the ills of the economic system as they applied to his area of the country.

The face of Quebec had been changing during the 1920's as industrialization and urbanization gained headway. In the northern part of the province large mining, hydro-electric and pulp and paper developments drew many habitants away from the farms. By 1921, when for the first time the urban population of the province exceeded the rural, the old picture of an unchanging, agricultural Quebec was fast becoming an illusion. While industrialism brought many *Quebecois* into association with their English-speaking countrymen, it also gave rise to a heightened nationalism. Leadership in Quebec's industrial and financial circles was seen to be in the hands of an English-speaking minority. This condition, partly the result of a lack of technical qualification among French Canadians, was inevitably judged as evidence of discrimination. In addition, French Canadians were disturbed that the possession of their natural resources was passing into the alien hands of English Canadian, American and British interests.

These grievances helped to bring into existence a new party, the *Union Nationale*, dedicated to the preservation of the "rights of Quebec." The new party was authoritarian and advocated a program of nationalization of some industries, combined with sweeping social reform to deal with provincial problems. It was led by a clever, tough-minded lawyer, Maurice Duplessis, and was largely recruited from provincial Conservatives, a spent force in Quebec politics after World War I. The times were propitious for a new party; the corrupt Liberal administration of Alexandre Taschereau was breaking up after long years in office.

Duplessis won a sweeping victory in 1936, gaining 76 of the legislature's 90 seats. This was the beginning of Duplessis' personal dominance of Quebec, a dominance that was to last (with the exception of a period during World War II) until his death twenty-five years later. Once in power, Duplessis soon came to terms with business interests in the province and secured their co-operation. Little was heard of social reform and even less of the program of nationalization. (Several commentators have claimed that Duplessis deliberately helped keep the wages of workers low in order to attract further capital into Quebec.) The new administration developed a close alliance with the Roman Catholic Church and appointed itself the guardian of Quebec's cultural values. It provided much assistance in rural Quebec but brought labour unions under close state control and suppressed all radical opinion.

Quebec, although it supported the *Union Nationale* provincially did not abandon the Liberal party federally. The *Union Nationale*, publicly at least, eschewed taking part in federal politics, and the party never became a force beyond the province. However, Duplessis, wanting to shift Quebec attention away from the unsatisfactory state of provincial affairs, could usually

On the first anniversary of Duplessis' election to office, La Province *of Montreal took a cynical view of the regime's promised programme of social reform. The Premier, casting dirt on the coffin, intones, "Requiescat in pace!"*

be found resisting what he termed the "centralization" of federal policies and insisting on the separateness of Quebec, both legally and culturally. He rejected all national plans that were based on a uniform treatment of the provinces, from the post-1945 tax rental agreements to the project of a Trans-Canada Highway and federal aid to universities.

Ontario also witnessed a demonstration of faith in "provincial rights" during the 1930's, although it was less overt than that in Quebec. In this province economic discontent was skilfully mobilized by the "onion farmer from Elgin County," the boisterous, wise-cracking Mitchell Hepburn. Promising social justice for the small man, Hepburn reorganized the provincial Liberal party, which had stagnated for twenty-nine years in the wilderness of opposition, and led it to victory in 1934.

Hepburn elicited support from farm groups and from the mass of taxpayers who demanded a reduction in provincial expenditures during the depression. In spite of his promises to the Ontario electorate, Hepburn did very little to implement his original plans of reform. Indeed, he showed considerably more enthusiasm for the principle of government regulation of labour union activities. Hepburn's most violent efforts in this field were reserved for such American-led labour unions as the C.I.O., which was endeavouring to organize the province's automobile workers. A strike at the General Motors plant at Oshawa in 1937 occasioned the dispatch of police and the Premier's personal intervention in an effort to destroy the power of the union.

The Hepburn administration, although of the same political complexion as the federal government after 1935, was essentially a sectional movement. Hepburn's personal enmity towards Mackenzie King coloured his approach towards federal policies and made him unable to take a larger view of the economic problems of Canada. He resigned the premiership in 1942, shortly before the Ontario Liberals were swept from office by a rejuvenated Conservative party.

A much more radical protest movement arose in Alberta, a province which considered itself "crucified" by Bennett's tariff policies. As an area that produced primary products for world markets, Alberta was particularly hard hit by the fall in raw material prices. In addition, the people of the province were heavily indebted to banks and financial houses (mostly located in eastern Canada) which had provided development capital. As was the case with the Populists in the United States in an earlier depression, many western farmers felt that economic improvement could only come through the introduction of "cheaper money," that is, easier credit. Alberta offered, in fact, a wonderful opportunity to a politician who would do something for its impoverished farmers.

Such a movement was organized by William ("Bible Bill") Aberhart, a Calgary school principal who was also a popular radio evangelist. In 1932, he chanced upon a book on Social Credit. This is a theory, originated by a Scots engineer, Major Douglas, which states that the basic weakness of capitalism is the divergence between the limited purchasing power of the community and its unlimited ability to produce goods. If purchasing power is increased to the point where it absorbs output, then a satisfactory economic equilibrium will be reached. Douglas proposed to increase individual purchasing power by having governments issue every citizen a "social dividend," or cash payment, which Aberhart stated should be of the order of $25 a month.

During the bitter days of the mid-thirties, Aberhart preached Social Credit the length and breadth of Alberta with all the zeal of the true convert. To farmers who had seen their wheat fields wither and their cattle die of thirst and who were faced with crushing debt payments and no income, there was an irresistible appeal in Aberhart's promise of earthly salvation through Social Credit. "We are going to see that the people of Alberta are properly cared for," Aberhart prophesied, ". . . that they are going to be furnished with the necessities of life. . . ." He fused religion with his political program: "The Spirit of Christ has gripped me. I am only seeking to clothe, feed and shelter starving people." His followers endorsed this message enthusiastically and gave him their absolute trust. "I don't claim to understand the fine points in the system," an old lady is said to have remarked, "but if Mr. Aberhart says it is so, then I am sure everything will be all right."

Aberhart's electioneering was phenomenally successful. Election day in August, 1935, saw the Social Credit movement sweep Alberta, winning 56 out of the 63 seats in the legislature. In the federal election a few weeks later, 17 Social Credit candidates were returned to Ottawa.

Once in power Aberhart found how difficult it was to pursue radical economic theories. Having attacked the chartered banks as the strongholds of "hard money," he now proceeded to pass legislation taxing the operations of their branches in Alberta. But the regulation of banking and currency is a federal responsibility, and in 1937 Ottawa disallowed the Alberta statutes. Other efforts

This was cartoonist Arch Dale's view of Aberhart's "funny money" scheme.

by Aberhart to lighten the debt burden of the people by liquidating interest payments on mortgages and loans were also unsuccessful, since interest is also a subject under federal jurisdiction. An attempt to prevent appeals to the courts regarding the validity of provincial statutes met the same fate. The federal government, in vetoing this measure, described it as taking away the rights "of any citizen of Canada to appeal to the Courts of the land against the exercise of arbitrary power."

The Social Credit challenge to the national financial system failed. In his attempt to implement Social Credit, Aberhart pushed the principle of provincial rights to extreme lengths. He was rebuffed and thereafter settled down to head a government with a conventional legislative program. However, Social Credit had dramatically revealed the financial weakness of the western provinces and had demonstrated the need for a full-scale investigation of federal-provincial relations.

Another party that sought to counter the causes of depression, the Co-operative Commonwealth Federation, was born in the west in the terrible times of the thirties. The party owed its existence to several groups of people. One was a small band of Progressive M.P.'s who had survived the official disappearance of their party. Others were various socialist groups, mostly urban organizations modelled on those of the British Labour party. A third element was a number of university teachers from Toronto and Montreal. The most important element, however, was the various farmers' organizations, who focused much of their resentment on the protective tariff, freight rates and interest charges on mortgages and loans. These, they claimed, were the work of eastern banking and business interests that dominated Ottawa. In 1932 representatives of farm and reform organizations, together with a few trade union spokesmen, met in Calgary to establish a socialist party. The result was the Co-operative Commonwealth Federation. The words of the title possess individual significance. "Co-operative" recalled the farmers' belief in joint action; "Commonwealth" indicated the party's hope for a new social order, in which wealth would be shared more equally; "Federation" showed that the organization was a loose coalition of various economic and social groups.

At a C.C.F. convention in Regina in 1933, delegates approved a party platform. The "Regina Manifesto" called for "a planned socialized economic order" and envisaged nationalization of banks and financial institutions, insurance companies, transportation and electric power. It also demanded greater government support of agriculture, effective conservation of natural resources, official encouragement of co-operatives, government recognition of the principle of collective bargaining, and a large program of social welfare legislation. To meet the existing economic emergency, the Manifesto commended the immediate adoption of vigorous public works measures of social importance. Slum clearance and rural electrification were singled out as activities that would be of permanent benefit to Canadians. Although the C.C.F. program called for the creation of a

The first CCF caucus: left to right, Tommy Douglas, Grant MacNeil, Arthur Heaps, J. S. Woodsworth, M. J. Coldwell, Grace MacInnis and Angus MacInnis. Coldwell succeeded Woodsworth as party leader. Douglas became premier of Saskatchewan (the first socialist to head a government in North America) and later the first leader of the NDP, a party that grew out of the CCF. Mrs. MacInnis, Woodsworth's daughter, was active in both the CCF and NDP. This historic photograph was taken by Karsh.

"National Planning Commission" to supervise Canada's economic growth, the movement was firmly based on democratic principles. Like British socialism, it believed in the parliamentary system, in socialism by evolution rather than revolution. Its chief task, it claimed, would be to create a government that would be truly representative of every Canadian. In this sense it differed from the other protest movements of the 1930's, which were basically, if not entirely, interested in promoting the claims of a particular region.

The guiding spirit behind the C.C.F. was the remarkable James Shaver Woodsworth. An upright figure with a trim beard and an ascetic's face, Woodsworth was a Christian idealist and a passionate reformer. As a Methodist minister in a poor district in north Winnipeg he began to question the basis of the economic and social order of his day and to ponder the human cost of industrialization in turn-of-the-century Canada. During World War I, Woodsworth was dismissed from his post as head of a welfare agency because he urged that wealth as well as manpower should be conscripted. It was at this time that he resigned from the Methodist Church, partly because he could not accept the Church's endorsement of war and partly because he believed that the many middle-class church members were indifferent to the critical economic and social needs of their fellow Canadians.

In Winnipeg, during the general strike of 1919, Woodsworth was arrested for publishing seditious statements (one of which was a quotation from the Book of Isaiah). The charges were later dropped, and Woodsworth was elected from Winnipeg Centre in 1921 as a labour candidate, representing this constituency in the House of Commons until his death in 1942. His lifelong ambition was to bring the farmers and the urban workers together into a mighty reform movement of "Canadian Socialism." The C.C.F. movement was his great attempt to "replace the present capitalist system with its inherent injustice and inhumanity by a social order from which the domination and exploitation of one class by another will be eliminated . . . and in which genuine democratic self-government, based upon economic equality, will be possible."

The C.C.F. made slow headway in its early years. It was unable to gain the official support of organized labour. It was accused of being a communist organization, and its leaders were branded as dangerous radicals. Mackenzie King, quietly appropriating some C.C.F. policies (for instance, old-age pensions), seemed to give Canadians the moderate pace of reform they desired. The new party won modest support in Ontario, but little in Quebec or the Maritime provinces. In the west it figured more prominently. Provincial elections in British Columbia in 1933 returned seven C.C.F. members, and others were elected in Saskatchewan the next year. The party began to attract more attention in the latter stages of World War II, when trade unions were stronger and social reform figured prominently. In 1943 the party captured thirty-four seats in the Ontario legislature and a year later came to power in Saskatchewan.

THE ROWELL-SIROIS COMMISSION

By the mid-1930's, the depression had clearly revealed Canada's difficulty in taking action to meet pressing economic problems. In part, this difficulty stemmed from the fact that in the Canadian federation ten governments, not one, shared responsibility for economic matters. But it also arose from the peculiar interpretation placed on the BNA Act by the highest court in the British Commonwealth, the Judicial Committee of the Privy Council. As the final court of appeal for all Canadian civil cases, the Judicial Committee was in a position to utter the last word on the meaning of the Canadian constitution. In the 1880's the Judicial Committee had begun a trend of interpretation that ran counter to the intentions of the Fathers of Confederation. Provincial sovereignty was established as co-ordinate with that of the federal government and emphasis was laid on Section 92 of the BNA Act, listing provincial subjects, rather than on Section 91, in which the federal government's powers were laid down. By the outset of the depression the Judicial Committee had enlarged the scope of authority of the provinces at the expense of Ottawa. Most economic subjects were considered to touch upon the "property or civil rights" clause or the reference to "matters of a merely local or private nature," both found in Section 92. They were therefore assigned to the jurisdiction of the provinces. Although Ottawa possessed the right to regulate trade and commerce, this power was given a limited interpretation. The federal government's sweeping authority to "make laws for the peace, order and good government" of Canada was held to apply to economic questions only when such an emergency as war arose. That a world depression might also constitute a critical emergency and might require concerted action, led by the federal government, was not recognized by the learned judges of the Privy Council. The Privy Council's judgments on the "New Deal" legislation of R. B. Bennett clearly revealed the trend of its thinking on Canada's constitution. In 1937 five of the Bennett measures were referred by Mackenzie King to the court, which found them to be beyond the powers of the federal parliament.

Co-operation between federal and provincial governments to combat the depression was difficult to attain, irrespective of the Judicial Committee's rulings. The provinces were suspicious of entrusting Ottawa with authority that might never be recovered. Centralization in economic and social affairs could well deal a death blow to provincial autonomy. In addition, some provincial administrations, such as Aberhart's in Alberta and Hepburn's in Ontario, were openly hostile towards Ottawa. As a result agreement on questions of common interest was bound to be difficult, if not impossible.

In 1937 Mackenzie King tried a new approach. Recognizing that the division of financial powers lay at the heart of the problem, he appointed a royal commission to investigate "the economic and financial basis of Confederation" and to make recommendations designed to alter dominion-provincial relations to meet existing conditions. A commission was appointed under Newton W. Rowell, Chief Justice of Ontario, and later under Joseph Sirois, a Quebec lawyer. Aided by a staff of experts, the commission travelled across Canada, hearing views and studying evidence. Its report, issued in three volumes with eighteen books of supporting data, was published in 1940.

The Rowell-Sirois Report is one of the most important documents in British North American history. Its diagnosis of conditions in Canada at the end of the 1930's can be ranked in significance and perception with the survey made by Lord Durham and his staff a century before. Four major recommendations, designed to correct inequalities among the provinces, were made. The first was that the federal government assume the debts of the provinces. In return, the provinces would be asked to surrender three fields of taxation—personal income, corporation income and succession duties. Thus, a uniform system of taxation, valuable in promoting economic development, could be implemented across Canada. In the third place, the commissioners suggested that the statutory subsidies to the provinces (which bore no relation to existing fiscal needs) be abolished and be replaced by "adjustment grants," calculated to give each province the revenue needed to maintain a suitable standard in social services and administration. Finally, the commissioners recommended that the federal government become completely responsible for unemployment relief.

The recommendations, which aimed at a reconstruction of federal and provincial finances in Canada, were too wide-ranging to be adopted at the time. Mackenzie King called a conference in January, 1941, to consider them, but no agreement could be reached. Three provinces—British Columbia, Alberta and Ontario—refused to consider the proposals. King did not press the Report's recommendations further. Canada was at war and it was obviously no time for a controversial reorganization of the division of federal and provincial powers.

However, the Report was not without effect. The recommendation that Ottawa set up a national system of unemployment insurance had already been implemented through an amendment in 1940 to the British North America Act. The wartime tax rental agreements (see p. 452) introduced the principle that the federal government would dominate the major fields of taxation. More important, the Report had expressed a point of view that came to be accepted by Canadians—that the federal government has a right and a responsibility to intervene to assure the economic and social welfare of the people. The notion of the state acting positively for the common welfare was greatly forwarded by the experience of dealing with the depression in Canada (as in the United States). The heavy responsibilities of the central government in World War II were to make this idea even more acceptable to Canadians.

* * *

Beset as Canada was by crippling economic difficulties in the 1930's, even more dangerous events were taking place on the international scene. Far across the Pacific an aggressive militarist state, Japan, had begun her conquest of Asia. On the continent of Europe, Benito Mussolini and Adolf Hitler created totalitarian states and set out to terrorize their weaker neighbours. For Canada, the shock of the great depression was about to merge into the even more harrowing experience of World War II.

CHAPTER 17

A NATION IN ARMS

Twenty years after the Peace Conference of 1919, the world was again at war. Canada, which had long sought to avoid foreign involvement, now found herself committed to a conflict in which the very existence of the North Atlantic community and the democratic ideals it professed were at stake. Her decision to participate in the war was inevitable, given her historic association with Britain and her own belief in a separate national destiny. Domestically, the war strengthened Canada through industrial expansion and also provided conditions under which the federal government successfully reasserted its leadership. At the same time, the war was a severe test of national unity since it raised once more the nightmare of compulsory military service.

With victory won, Canadians turned to the problem of maintaining peace. In this regard, the special international position of Canada, tied both to the Old World and the New, was made apparent. Canada participated, quietly but effectively, in the creation of the United Nations Organization, recognizing that in it lay the best hopes for world peace and security.

THE APPROACH OF WAR

Canada's foreign policy between the wars was almost, but not quite, isolationist in nature. There were many reasons for this circumstance. The geographical location of Canada in North

America rendered her comparatively safe from attack. Geography was complemented by the protection implicitly afforded by the Royal Navy and the Monroe Doctrine. The ever-present example of the United States, which was decidedly isolationist in outlook between the wars, also conditioned Canada's outlook. Inevitably, the appalling economic difficulties of the 1930's directed the gaze of Canadians inwards to the great challenge of developing a viable national economy. In addition, Canada's reliance on world trade predisposed her to follow a cautious foreign policy, a policy that would not disturb vital commercial links with other countries.

Mackenzie King, Prime Minister and Secretary of State for External Affairs for most of the years between the wars (the two offices were not separated until 1946), was the chief architect of Canada's foreign policy. First and foremost among his principles was the belief that no step should be taken that would disturb Canadian unity. In actual practice this meant accepting as few foreign commitments as possible. In relations with other countries King also showed that he was guided by certain general considerations. As a North American, he knew that it was politic to strive for close and friendly associations with the United States. Towards Britain King behaved somewhat ambiguously. Britain's good will was very important since she had always provided the best guarantee of Canadian security. Yet King was on guard lest he be drawn into supporting British imperial commitments that might be incompatible with Canada's best interests. The important rule to King was to ensure, as far as he possibly could, that Britain and the United States pursued policies that were in harmony, and therefore of benefit to Canada.

Canada's relations with the United States were of great importance to her in the inter-war period. It was for this reason that in 1927 King had established in Washington Canada's first foreign mission. Canada's relations with her great neighbour took on a new cordiality after Franklin D. Roosevelt became President.

As Governor of New York State, Roosevelt had become familiar with a number of Canadian-American problems, in particular, the desirability of developing the power and naviga-

Prime Minister King and President Franklin D. Roosevelt symbolically join hands at the opening of the Thousand Islands International Bridge across the St. Lawrence in 1938. Possessing all the personal magnetism and charm so conspicuously lacking in King, Roosevelt was a remarkably popular figure in Canada.

tion potential of the St. Lawrence River. Roosevelt's hopes for the St. Lawrence project were frustrated, but he was successful in his advocacy of closer trade ties with Canada. The Reciprocal Trade Agreements Act of 1934 gave the President considerable discretion to reduce the tariff by negotiating commercial agreements with foreign countries. Concurrently, King was interested in tackling Canada's economic difficulties through an enlargement of her export trade. The result was a trade treaty at the end of 1935 that lowered the American tariff on about seven hundred items that made up two-thirds of Canada's exports to the United States. In return, Canada granted "most-favoured-nation" treatment to the republic. Thus, both countries began to retreat from the extreme protectionism they had adopted at the outset of the Great Depression. Three years later the King government secured additional concessions in the American market, winning lower rates on items that composed about 80 percent of Canada's exports to the United States. The commercial agreements of 1935 and 1938 laid the basis for a pattern of trade that has remained fixed to this day. They also foreshadowed the intimate military and economic co-operation between the United States and Canada that was to develop during World War II.

In 1919 Canada was a charter member of the League of Nations. (See page 377.) Her role in the League over the next few years, however, suggested that she valued her membership more for its indication of her new status in the world than for any contribution she might make to the goals of the League. Although Prime Minister King strongly favoured the League's efforts to mediate international disputes and its crusade for disarmament, he was much less enthusiastic concerning the League's duty (under Article X of the Covenant) to organize force to discipline countries that would not live peacefully with their neighbours. From the earliest sessions at Geneva he took the view that since Canada was not likely to receive any benefits under the collective security scheme she should not be required to underwrite it in a military sense. "We live in a fire-proof house, far from inflammable materials," stated the Canadian delegate to the League in 1924. Indeed, King's efforts at this time were devoted to amending Article X to render it less binding. A Canadian-supported resolution to this effect was defeated in 1923, but it did strongly influence the thinking of many League members on Article X.

Canada's attempt to weaken Article X is a good illustration of her withdrawal into the North American setting. Her negative policy at Geneva stemmed partly from the conviction that the United States' abstention from the League reduced Canada's obligations to serve it. The policy also expressed King's awareness of the suspicion many French Canadians had of the League and its objectives. Essentially, however, King's reluctance to support measures of international control resulted from his unwillingness to see Canada undertake any overseas commitments. Having just succeeded in removing his country from a system of centralized foreign policy within the British Empire, King was determined to avoid being drawn into another arrangement that might limit Canada's prized autonomy. King's viewpoint is understandable, but it was hardly helpful to the concept of a new world order based on mutual obligation and assistance.

The Italian invasion of Ethiopia in 1935 showed the world only too clearly the aggressive nature of fascism. Yet even this demonstration failed to shake King's attitude towards collective security. He was prepared, in company with other democratic states, to join in imposing economic sanctions on Italy in an effort to halt her aggression, but he would have nothing to do with military sanctions. When the Canadian delegate to the League suggested that the embargo be extended to include oil, the one import without which Italy could not continue her Ethiopian campaign, he was publicly repudiated by King.

As Europe moved closer to the brink of war, King remained diplomatically aloof. He refused to express an opinion on Hitler's re-occupation of the Rhineland, the industrial heart of the Kaiser's Germany. The next year, 1937, King cut off a flow of materials and volunteers to the Nationalist side in the Spanish Civil War. He thus supported the futile policy of attempting to isolate the Civil War from the rest of the world. However, at this time, the King government would not agree to prohibit the export of metals and scrap iron to Japan, which had been attacking China since 1932. King claimed that it would be ineffective for a single country to impose sanctions on a wrongdoer. In one sense this was true, but once again an opportunity to make a practical gesture of moral disapproval was lost. During the Munich crisis of 1938 King's attitude was again cautious and noncommittal. He did not consult with the British government and publicly greeted with relief Neville Chamberlain's settlement at Czechoslovakia's expense. From this point on, King continued to maintain "no foreign policy except correct neutrality," and was a passive spectator to the march of events that led to 3 September, 1939.

THE FIGHTING FRONTS

When Canada entered World War II on 10 September, 1939, she was a country virtually unprepared for war. Her permanent fighting forces totalled somewhat less than 10,000 men, while her entire defence budget amounted to only a few million dollars. In

1939 British and Canadian military opinion decided that Canada's participation in the conflict would take the form of economic aid and such specialized military assistance as the provision of convoy escorts and the training of air crews. The Canadian war effort was planned along these lines during the early months of the war. The British Commonwealth Air Training Plan was initiated, and over the next few years Canada trained tens of thousands of pilots, navigators, wireless operators and air gunners at sixty-four flying schools across the dominion. The Royal Canadian Air Force, a mere 4,500 regulars and reserves in 1939, was strengthened, and many squadrons were sent to Britain in the course of five years of war to join in the air struggle against Nazi Germany. The Royal Canadian Navy, the smallest of the services (about 1,000 officers and men), was given the task of assisting in the protection of the North Atlantic convoys. By the end of the war a Canadian Navy of almost 1,000 vessels was responsible for escorting 80 percent of the convoys leaving the New World for Europe.

Yet military forces could not be minimized, and English-speaking Canada was soon clamouring for the despatch of an expeditionary force to Britain. In December, 1939, the vanguard of what was to become the First Canadian Army was transported to England. General A. G. L. McNaughton, the Canadian commander, insisted that his men be kept together as the nucleus of a Canadian force, rather than distributed among the various Allied forces in the different theatres of war. McNaughton likened his troops to "a dagger pointed at the heart of Berlin" and envisaged them as a striking force that would lead the assault on Hitler's *Festung Europa.* (On the eve of the invasion of Europe in 1944, the Canadian Army overseas numbered 250,000 men, of whom 75,000 were at that time fighting in Italy.)

Canadians formed the largest contingent in the first raid on *Festung Europa*, the ill-fated landing in 1942 at Dieppe, on the French Channel coast. Making up the striking force were 5,000 Canadians, together with 1,000 British troops and a small number of American observers. The Dieppe raid, long planned and rehearsed, was designed to throw light on the problems of a full-scale invasion of the continent. Unfortunately, the left wing of the raiding force was delayed in transit and had to land in broad daylight and in full view of the enemy. Landing craft were forced to disgorge Canadian infantry and tanks in several feet of water at the edge of the beach, in the face of a murderous fire from the German coastal batteries. Mine fields at the water's edge claimed many lives. After ten hours of carnage in and around Dieppe, the force was withdrawn, having suffered 3,300 casualties. Although the Canadians suffered terrible losses, their tragic experience at Dieppe was of some value in assisting Allied planners prepare for the later assaults on North Africa (1943) and Europe.

Canadian forces in Britain were well aware that their great test would come with the invasion of Europe. This process began with the invasion of Sicily. The date, 10 July, 1943, marked, in the

On August 19, 1942, 5,000 Canadians and 1,000 British "commando" troops made a powerful raid on the Channel coast of Nazi occupied France in the area of the small resort town of Dieppe. The purpose of the raid was to test the German defences and to provide practical experience that could be used in planning a full-scale invasion of Europe. Dieppe proved to be a costly lesson. The attack was met with fierce resistance and of the 5,000 Canadians who set out only 2,211 returned.

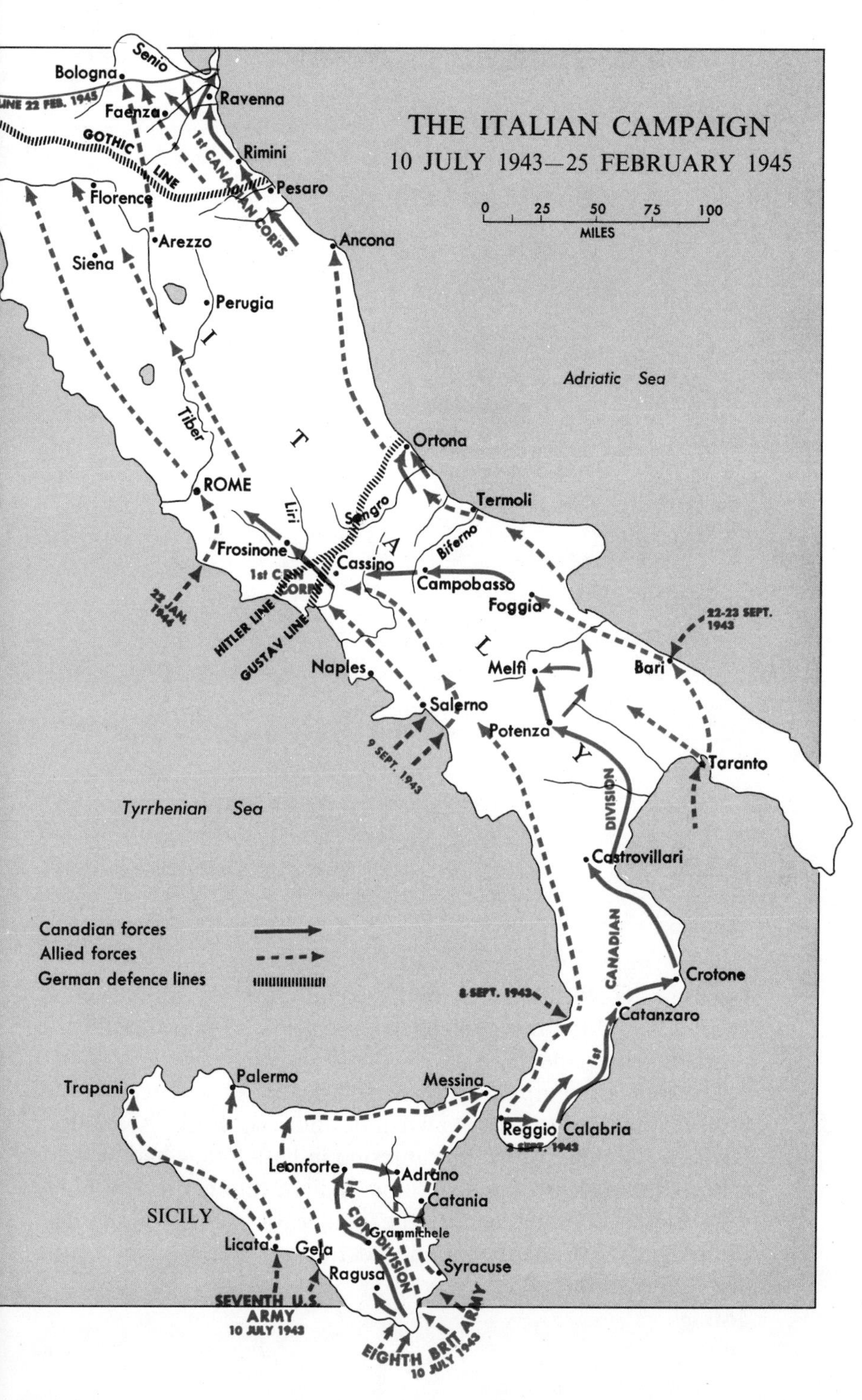
THE ITALIAN CAMPAIGN
10 JULY 1943—25 FEBRUARY 1945
0
25
50
75
100
MILES
Senio
Bologna
LINE 22 FEB. 1945
Ravenna
Faenza
GOTHIC
LINE
1st CANADIAN CORPS
Rimini
Pesaro
Florence
Arezzo
Ancona
Siena
Perugia
I
T
A
L
Y
Tiber
Adriatic Sea
Ortona
ROME
Termoli
Liri
Sangro
Biferno
Frosinone
Cassino
1st CDN CORPS
Campobasso
Foggia
22 JAN. 1944
HITLER LINE
GUSTAV LINE
22-23 SEPT. 1943
Naples
Melfi
Bari
Salerno
Potenza
9 SEPT. 1943
Taranto
Tyrrhenian Sea
DIVISION
Castrovillari
Canadian forces
Allied forces
German defence lines
CANADIAN
Crotone
8 SEPT. 1943
Catanzaro
1st
Trapani
Palermo
Messina
Reggio Calabria
3 SEPT. 1943
Leonforte
Adrano
Catania
1st CDN DIVISION
SICILY
Grammichele
Licata
Gela
Syracuse
Ragusa
SEVENTH U.S. ARMY
10 JULY 1943
EIGHTH BRIT ARMY
10 JULY 1943

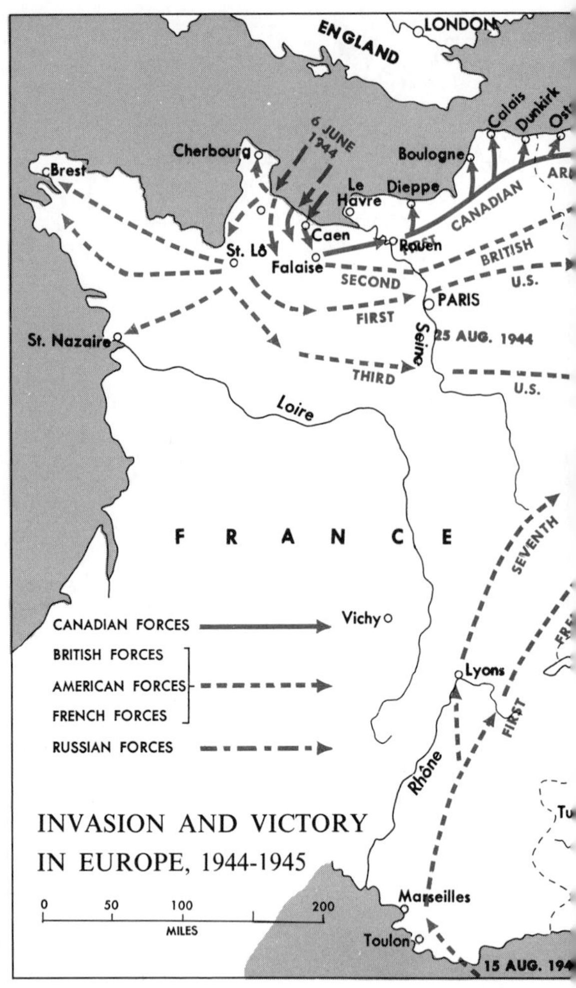

INVASION AND VICTORY IN EUROPE, 1944-1945

words of the official history of the Canadian Army in the Second World War, "the divide between the years of waiting and the years of achievement."

The Sicilian campaign was an invaluable experience for the First Canadian Infantry Division and the Fifth Armoured Division. Highly trained but untested in battle, they had to fight in the choking dust of a scorching Sicilian summer over a hilly, rock-strewn countryside. In the course of a thirty-eight day campaign, the Canadians endured heat stroke, dysentery and

malaria. Yet they marched up to forty miles a day, and outfought some of the toughest troops in the German *Wehrmacht*.

The fall of Mussolini's government in July did not remove Italy from the war, and the Allies were faced with the task of invading the mainland. At this point, General McNaughton resigned as commander-in-chief of Canadian forces overseas, believing that all Canadian forces should be kept together for the invasion of Northwest Europe and not diverted piecemeal into a long Italian campaign. The cabinet in Ottawa, however, decided to continue the arrangement by which certain Canadian units formed part of the British forces in Sicily. On 3 September, 1943, the Canadian spearhead of General Montgomery's Eighth Army landed unopposed on the southernmost tip of Italy. The fighting that followed was one of the severest campaigns of the entire war. The long Italian peninsula, with its rugged mountain chains, narrow, winding roads and numerous, turbulent rivers, afforded excellent terrain for the German defence, and the Allied advance was often painfully slow. During the twenty-month campaign for Sicily and Italy, 91,000 Canadians were engaged at one time or another.

For all its difficulties, the Italian campaign was of lesser importance than the invasion of Europe, which began on 6 June, 1944, with the assault on the Normandy beaches. The Normandy landings made full use of the lessons of Dieppe. A large naval force hovered offshore to provide a heavy bombardment. British, Canadian and American bombers dropped thousands of tons of bombs to "soften up" German coastal defences. The Allies employed landing craft, equipped with artillery that opened fire while the craft were still approaching the shore. There were tanks that "swam" and "flail" tanks to beat a path through minefields. The invasion force, which included 14,000 Canadians, struck Normandy on a fifty-mile front, and everywhere the beaches were won.

While American troops swept out of Normandy to liberate Paris and swing towards the German frontier, and the British headed for Brussels and Antwerp, the First Canadian Army advanced upon the Channel ports and the rocket bomb sites in the Calais area. In its advance it had the satisfaction of capturing Dieppe and avenging the 1942 disaster. In the autumn of 1944 the Canadians were given the exceedingly difficult and bloody task of clearing the Germans from the islands around the mouth of the Scheldt River so that the Allies could use the captured port of Antwerp. In early March, 1945, Canadian infantry began to fight their way over the Rhine into the northwest corner of Germany. Other Canadian forces cleared the Germans out of the northern and western parts of Holland. By 7 May, 1945, the battle for Germany was over. Three hundred and thirty-three

A Sherman tank of the Lord Strathcona Horse loaded with children in the Dutch village of Harderwijk, April 19, 1945. A Canadian officer describing a similar scene wrote: "The scene in a liberated town is quite extraordinary. The place of course is festooned with flags.... The young people wave and shout; the children yell and wave flags; ... the old people stand by the roadside and look happy; and the army rolls through. . . ."

days had elapsed since the landings in Normandy, and during that period the Canadian forces in Europe had suffered over 11,000 fatalities.

THE BATTLE OF PRODUCTION

Canada's participation in World War II was greater than that of the 1914-18 conflict, both in terms of the number of men (and women) enlisted in the fighting forces and in terms of the country's economy. During World War II well over 1,000,000 Canadians served in the armed forces, a figure amounting to almost 10 percent of the 1939 population of Canada. In World War I 630,000 Canadians had served in the forces, a figure that represented 8 percent of the 1914 population. World War II transformed beyond recognition the old Canadian economy based on the export of wheat. In its wake the war left a higher degree of secondary manufacturing and a greater degree of trade with the United States. The period 1939-45, in fact, laid the foundations of today's economy.

In 1939 Canada was still recovering from the disastrous effects of the depression. Ten percent of the labour force was still unemployed. In addition, there were many men who had drifted out of the cities and back to the farms; but they could only be considered as under-employed. The war halted this trend and soon reversed it; throughout the war the number of farm workers dropped steadily. Despite this decline the output of Canadian agriculture rose 30 percent between 1939 and 1945, thanks to greatly improved farming methods and a wider use of mechanical equipment. With Britain desperately short of food, Canada was encouraged to produce a wider range of agricultural products. Thus the prairies became a region of mixed farming, turning to the production of beef, pork, dairy products, flax and oil seeds as well as wheat. This development, which was paralleled by similar diversification in other parts of the country, brought renewed health to Canadian agriculture. Canadian forests yielded timber and pulp and paper that were valuable to the prosecution of the war. Mining made a strong contribution, with Canadian nickel, copper, lead and zinc supplying most Allied requirements. The recently opened uranium mine on Great Bear Lake was taken over by the government, its production going to the Manhattan Project, the Allied program of atomic research.

These wartime developments, important as they were, were

overshadowed by the expansion of Canada's manufacturing capacity. Here, the astounding advance was not in primary manufacturing (smelting and refining, pulp and paper, chemicals) but in secondary manufacturing (the automobile industry, iron and steel production, the electrical industry, textiles, instruments). A rise in secondary manufacturing was practically inevitable. With foreign supplies cut off and restricted, even from the United States, Canada was forced to begin making many items she had formerly purchased abroad. For the first time electronic equipment was manufactured in Canada, as were synthetic rubber, roller bearings, diesel engines and high-octane gasoline. Government and business assisted by pouring larger sums than ever before into research and development. Many of the new industries survived the war and became permanent features of the Canadian economy.

Only about one-third of the country's vast war production was actually used by her own fighting men; the rest went to her Allies, especially Britain. At first Britain was able to pay for the supplies she obtained from Canada, but when her capital resources were exhausted she was forced to borrow. The federal government made large interest-free loans to the United Kingdom and in 1942 provided a non-repayable credit of $1 billion for British purchases in Canada. Others countries also received aid in the form of war supplies. (During World War II the United States was not the only "arsenal of democracy.")

The close trading relations that had been built up between the United States and Canada during the depression were confirmed during the war. As imports from Britain had to be reduced in the early war years, Canada was forced to buy more goods and material (particularly coal, steel and oil) in the United States. As there was little export income, these purchases quickly created a substantial trade deficit and necessitated stringent Canadian exchange regulations. In April, 1941, Prime Minister King journeyed to President Roosevelt's estate on the Hudson River and there concluded the Hyde Park Agreement. Under this arrangement, Canada and the United States sought to complement their war production, each purchasing certain requirements from the other. Thus, Canada bought such items as machine tools and aircraft engines from her neighbour while the United States placed large orders with the sizeable small arms and ammunition industry in Canada. It was also arranged that Canada could charge those supplies she imported to fill British war orders against British lend-lease accounts. (Lend-lease was an imaginative program of American support for Britain devised by Roosevelt. It permitted the transfer of supplies of all kinds to any country whose security was judged vital to the United States, without specific requirements as to repayment.) The Agreement was most valuable in conserving Canada's stock of United States' currency, as well as in encouraging economic co-operation between the two countries. Coupled with heavy American capital investment in Canada during the war, the Hyde Park Agreement further emphasized the trading intimacy between the two countries and spelled out a definite pattern for the future.

Ottawa's direction of the war effort was powerfully exerted through the mechanism of taxation. Heavy tax rates were levied on corporations and individuals in order to meet the tremendous costs of war. In 1942 the federal government reached an agreement with the provinces that permitted effective mobilization of the country's money resources. The provinces surrendered their right to levy personal and corporation income taxes in return for compensation from Ottawa. The 1942 tax-rental agreement was to run for five years; it became the first of a series of such arrangements between Ottawa and the provinces. These tax-rental agreements, by making the federal government the dominant financial partner in the federation, went a long way towards re-establishing federal leadership in Canadian affairs. (This arrangement had been one of the unwritten objectives of the Rowell-Sirois Report and it was to form the basis of post-war federal social and economic planning.)

WAR AND NATIONAL UNITY

Britain went to war on 3 September, 1939, but the Canadian parliament did not meet to consider the question of Canada's participation until 7 September. This was in accord with Prime

Minister King's frequently stated declaration that parliament would decide "the momentous question of peace and war." When parliament met, the government proposed measures for the defence of Canada and announced its desire to join Britain in the conflict. A three-day debate followed, marked by an appeal from some French-Canadian members for neutrality, and an equally-fervent plea by King's Quebec lieutenant, Ernest Lapointe, for his province to take an active part in the war. The three-day session witnessed the political death of J. S. Woodsworth of the C.C.F. Woodsworth made a moving, almost apologetic, speech in which he once again declared his pacifism; two days later his party officially chose to support participation in the war (although only to the extent of economic aid to Britain) under a new leader, M. J. Coldwell. In the end, the government's policy was endorsed by parliament without the necessity of a vote, and King George VI, as King of Canada, was advised to declare war on Germany. On 10 September, 1939, Canada went to war by virtue of her own authority.

The apparent unity of parliament is somewhat misleading, for many French Canadians had accepted the decision to participate most reluctantly. They (and other Canadians) did not feel that Canada's security was menaced by the Third Reich. On the other hand, there were quite a number of English Canadians who were pessimistic about King's capacity to provide leadership in wartime. They believed him to be too cautious, too often influenced by the wish to placate Quebec. They advocated unstinted support of Britain and demanded the formation of a coalition government. The issue that came to symbolize these two attitudes was conscription for overseas service. A generation before, in World War I, compulsory military service had arrayed Quebec in defiant hostility against the rest of Canada. The wound caused by racial controversy had hardly healed when World War II broke out. Was the wound to be reopened, perhaps with fatal results for Canada?

To Mackenzie King this possibility represented the greatest challenge of his career. All his public life he had stressed the necessity for national unity. Now he committed his party to the task of preserving national unity through the disruptive condi-

Two famous French-Canadian nationalists, the indomitable and controversial "Le Chef," *Maurice Duplessis (right), and the equally controversial mayor of Montreal, Camillien Houde. In his day Duplessis was branded "lawless," a "fascist" and a "dictator," but by many he was hailed as the "saviour of Quebec." Houde, at one time leader of the Quebec Conservative party, was mayor of Montreal from 1928 to 1954 except for brief intervals. Between 1940 and 1944 he was interned for open defiance of the 1940 National Registration Act.*

tions of war. At the outbreak of hostilities Mackenzie King announced a pledge by his cabinet to French Canada:

> The present government believes that conscription of men for overseas service will not be a necessary or an effective step. Let me say that so long as this Government may be in power, no such measure will be enacted.

King never admitted any regret in making this pledge, but his words were to haunt him through the political battles of the war years.

King had not long to wait for opposition. It emerged in Quebec, where Maurice Duplessis, whose party success had been built on provincial rights, suddenly announced an election in October, 1939. Duplessis, seeking to strike a colossal blow at the forces of federalism and to strengthen further his position as the spokesman of his race, accused King of planning to use the war to weaken the autonomy of Quebec and the liberties of French

Canadians. He warned the people of his province that the election would be a struggle for autonomy against the apostle of "participation, assimilation and centralization." It was clear that should Duplessis continue in power his administration would seriously hamper the national war effort. Ernest Lapointe and three other federal ministers from Quebec immediately declared that if Duplessis were successful at the polls they would resign from the cabinet, leaving Quebec with no one to present its views in Ottawa. The implication of Lapointe's threat was plain: in the cabinet he could guarantee the cabinet's promise of no conscription; outside it he could not. Lapointe's gamble was successful. Quebec rejected Duplessis, replacing him with a Liberal government. Quebec was willing to protect what there was of national unity by refusing Duplessis' total isolation and accepting Lapointe's limited isolation. For the next five years the Quebec Liberals remained in office and co-operated with Ottawa in furthering the national war effort.

Opposition to King also came from Ontario, where he was accused of timidity. His principal critic was Mitchell Hepburn, who had maintained a bitter personal feud with King for years. Early in 1940 Hepburn proposed a motion condemning the federal government's futile war effort. George Drew, leader of the provincial Conservatives, seconded the motion. In addition, the Conservative opposition in Ottawa repeatedly called for the formation of a national government to mobilize the country's war effort.

King met all his critics (and caught them unawares) by calling a general election for March, 1940. Requesting an unequivocal mandate, he said:

> This war demands Canada's utmost effort. Such an effort can be made only by a government which draws its strength from every section of the country. . . .

The country agreed and gave him a tremendous vote of confidence. The Liberals increased their standing to 178 seats, the largest parliamentary majority since Confederation. King had won the first victory for wartime unity.

The conscription issue, however, was destined to bedevil Canadian politics. In 1940 the government established a military "call-up" for home defence under which men were inducted into the army for training and service within Canada. Two years later, Mackenzie King sensed that Ontario was beginning to seethe with the same pro-conscription sentiment that had destroyed the Liberals in 1917. In April, 1942, King decided to ask the nation in a plebiscite if it was in favour of releasing his government from its repeated pledges that it would not introduce conscription for overseas service. King was cautiously seeking to placate and reassure all of English Canada. He was also intent on silencing the Conservative opposition in parliament, led by R. J. Manion, who were noisily clamouring for conscription. The response was overwhelmingly favourable to King's request—except in Quebec, where barely one-third of the voters approved. French Canada remained uneasy, even after King's immediate (but ambiguous) dictum, "Not necessarily conscription but conscription if necessary."

The manpower problem became critical in 1944 after the invasion of Normandy. The landings in Normandy, the subsequent Canadian advance along the Channel coast and into Holland, and the seemingly endless Italian campaign caused heavy casualties. Colonel J. L. Ralston, the Minister of National Defence, toured the fronts in Italy and northwest Europe in late 1944. He became convinced that the system of voluntary recruiting could not supply the necessary infantry replacements. Ralston was emphatic that the required men (some 15,000 infantry) could only be obtained by sending the home defence draftees overseas. In other words, the remedy was conscription for overseas service. Fearful of what this would do in Quebec, King talked with his cabinet and senior army officers for days, arguing against conscription and desperately seeking some other solution. (King had no intention of sending a single infantryman overseas.) Casting around for a political solution to the crisis, King discreetly discovered that General McNaughton, who had resigned prior to the invasion of Italy, was a declared foe of conscription and confident of finding the necessary reinforcements. King dismissed Ralston on 1 November and informed a

An advertisement placed by an all-party committee in the Toronto Globe and Mail, *April 24, 1942. In English-speaking Canada all the major parties urged their supporters to vote in favour of releasing the government from its pledges on conscription.*

stunned cabinet that General McNaughton was the new Minister of National Defence and that he would produce infantry reinforcements without recourse to conscription.

However, the crisis had not passed. It soon proved impossible to secure enough overseas volunteers from home defence forces. McNaughton made the unflattering discovery that his name and prestige would not produce the required volunteers from among the 70,000 "zombies," as the home service troops were cruelly nicknamed. By late November, 1944, the position of the government was serious, as it still sought in vain to solve the manpower crisis through voluntary enlistment.

King's government was saved by one major factor—the decision of Louis St. Laurent to accept a limited degree of conscription. St. Laurent was an able Quebec corporation lawyer brought into the cabinet by King in 1941 to replace the dead Lapointe as the chief minister from Quebec. His reluctant acquiescence allowed King to come before parliament with an order-in-council sending 16,000 draftees to Europe immediately. St. Laurent could not overcome the opposition of the Quebec members but he could—and did—soften it enough to head off a major Quebec anti-conscription motion of no confidence during the two-week debate on the order-in-council. The main motion authorizing the despatch of 16,000 draftees was finally passed, 143 to 70. Mackenzie King had won another victory for unity. His methods in handling the whole matter of conscription, especially in the 1944 crisis, may well be open to criticism, but they did succeed in maintaining an undivided Canada. French Canadians were decidedly unhappy with conscription, but they accepted the bitter pill with what grace they could muster, for they knew that it had not been forced upon them by a majority bent on asserting its will.

WARTIME DIPLOMACY

Canada's objective during the war was simply to help win the war; thus she was prepared to co-operate to the best of her ability in Anglo-American affairs. Yet at the same time she was insistent that her identity be respected and her contributions recognized. During World War I she had often been preoccupied with asserting national status; in World War II she felt obliged on occasion to oppose all tendencies to take her existence for granted. This problem was most apparent in her relations with Great Britain, where past associations worked to blur Canada's recently achieved sovereignty.

Canada quickly rallied to Britain's side in the struggle against the dictators. For a year, from the fall of France in June, 1940, to the invasion of Russia in June, 1941, Canada was Britain's most important ally. But she was sometimes made aware that Britain was capable of ignoring her efforts in the common cause. King was exasperated, for example, when in a 1944 address Churchill spoke of the war being brought to a close by the sacrifice of Britons and Americans. The Canadian leader burst out:

> This is not all mere chance or oversight, as the matter has been repeatedly brought to his attention. . . . It is the John Bull and his Island attitude of self-sufficiency and unconscious superiority. . . .

Mackenzie King responded vigorously to this British attitude, the "taking for granted style" as he termed it. He recalled Canada's contribution to the war effort before the United States entered the conflict. He coupled a recital of Canada's military and economic achievements with an emphasis on Canadian nationality and separateness. Thus, he was instinctively cool to any suggestion of a central council to direct the affairs of the Commonwealth during the conflict. King was suspicious of the Commonwealth prime ministers' meeting convened in London in 1944 to make military and political decisions, and he attended it very reluctantly. He stated his belief that the various prime ministers would be better employed in leading their countries at home and stressed that he was not in a position to commit the Canadian cabinet.

There was one important attempt during the war to revive the idea of a unified Empire speaking with one voice in foreign affairs. The attempt was made by Lord Halifax, the British Ambassador to the United States, in a 1944 speech to the Toronto Board of Trade. Halifax urged imperial solidarity because he felt the post-war world would be dominated by three titans, Soviet Russia, the United States and China. United, "the British Commonwealth and Empire" might be "the fourth power in that group upon which, under Providence, the peace of the world will henceforth depend." This was essentially the same proposition that Laurier, Borden and King had had to ponder time and again. Canadians, however, were not interested in helping to build a titan. Mackenzie King used the occasion to deliver an effective speech to the Canadian Commons in which he stressed the advantages of informal co-operation among Commonwealth members rather than the creation of any centralized machinery. He also felt that the same principle of voluntary action should be applied in all international relations to prevent the emergence of "power politics by a few great nations leading inevitably to war." Even the new Conservative leader, John Bracken, condemned what he called "the balance of power doctrine."

Relations with the United States also grew more frank as the war progressed. They centred around a major military question – the defence of North America – as well as innumerable problems stemming from wartime co-operation. Matters of defence had come to the fore as the United States was slowly drawn into the war. Her arms shipments to Britain, her transfer of destroyers to the United Kingdom in return for bases in the New World, her common front with the Latin-American countries against the Axis – all these steps made it certain that she would eventually join with Canada in the defence of North America. In August, 1940, Prime Minister King and President Roosevelt met at the border city of Ogdensburg, New York. From their meeting emerged the Permanent Joint Board on Defence, an advisory body to co-ordinate plans for the defence of the northern half of the Western Hemisphere. A number of projects were put into operation. Some of these were directed towards holding strategic areas on the fringe of the continent (e.g. Newfoundland and Labrador), while others established air supply routes to Britain through the Arctic areas of Canada. The entry of Japan into the war led to such projects as the Alaska Highway to link Alaska more closely with Canada's western provinces and the United States. Air bases and weather stations were constructed on both sides of the Rockies to provide staging routes from the United

States to Alaska and the Aleutian Islands. The American activity in continental defence raised many Canadian fears of the loss of national identity, but at the time American efforts had to be accepted as military necessities.

Canada's preoccupation with the pressing demands of war left her little time to consider the problems of peace. Some of these matters had been touched upon at the first Quebec conference in August, 1943, when Churchill, Roosevelt, King and their staffs met in the historic Citadel. Canada was not invited to the preliminary discussions on a world peace organization at Dumbarton Oaks, Washington, D.C., in 1944. However, Canada was asked, along with forty-nine other Allied nations, to attend the San Francisco conference in the late spring of 1945. At this founding conference of the United Nations Organization the

On the terrace at the Citadel during the Quebec Conference of 1943, seated left to right: Prime Minister King, President Roosevelt and Prime Minister Winston Churchill. Like Roosevelt, Churchill enjoyed great respect and affection in Canada. His speeches were received in English Canada with great interest and enthusiasm.

concept of a world assembly received the full endorsement of the Canadian delegation. Prime Minister King, although he accepted the fact that the great powers were intent on dominating the United Nations, nevertheless made a plea for the middle powers. He argued that they should not be excluded from important decisions affecting world peace:

Experience has shown that the contribution of smaller powers is not a negligible one, either to the preserving of the peace or to its restoration....

Although this appeal resulted in some slight changes being made in the composition of the Security Council, it cannot be said that Canada played a leading role in shaping the United Nations. She had to be content to observe, trusting that her intimate relationships with Britain and the United States would allow her some influence in the post-war world.

* * *

Almost before the ink was dry on the charter of the United Nations, the world scene was transformed by the explosion of atomic bombs over Japan. The most destructive weapon in history had now been introduced into international politics. Was there a role for Canada in the age of nuclear power? Canada had supplied uranium for the manufacture of the atomic bomb; could she now offer advice and leadership in the much more difficult problem of maintaining peace in the atomic age?

READINGS

From Prosperity to Depression

The twenty-year interval between the two world wars constituted a dramatic period, first of economic expansion, then of setback and discontent, for Canadian society. The booming prosperity of the 1920's was suddenly shattered by the impact of world depression, cruelly intensified in western Canada by a succession of natural disasters. The evidence that a breakdown in the economic system created serious social evils was made brutally plain to Canadians in all parts of the country. From the disorganization of the "hungry 'thirties" arose anger, frustration and demands for a new social and economic order.

The bitter memories of these years were permanently etched into the Canadian experience, to influence the attitudes of people and governments from those days to these.

The economic growth and confidence of the late 1920's came to an end, symbolically, with the collapse of prices on the New York Stock Exchange on Tuesday, October 29, 1929. During the weeks and months that followed, a creeping paralysis spread over the trade and industry of the Western world. The Canadian parliament concluded its 1929 session in mid-June and did not assemble again until 20 February, 1930. The Speech from the Throne, written by the Liberal government of Mackenzie King, made no mention of the crippling blow which had fallen on the financial markets of North America, but dwelt on the recent phase of prosperity in 1929. The Governor General told the members:

It affords me much pleasure . . . to be able to congratulate you upon the continued prosperity of this country. The year 1929 was the most productive year in the history of Canada. In industries, other than agriculture, employment reached the highest point on record; new construction was the largest known. Mining production was of unequalled value. Manufacturing production surpassed all previous records. There was vast increase in the development of hydro-electric power. The products of our fields and our herds reached higher standards of excellence and quality than at any previous time. The Dominion is already recovering from the seasonal slackness evident at the end of the year, and it is not to be forgotten that the bulk of the 1929 wheat crop still remains in Canadian hands for final disposition. . . .

House of Commons Debates, 20 February, 1930, p. 2.

The Leader of the Opposition, R. B. Bennett, sarcastically commented on the unreal quality of the Speech from the Throne.

I venture to say that in the many years which have elapsed since Confederation it will be . . . difficult to find a speech from the throne so vague, so filled with generalities, and so lacking in the promise of useful legislation. It might indeed be said that instead of being a prospectus, as all speeches from the throne are supposed to be . . ., it was a record of the past, a record of the days that are no more. . . .

. . . I will ask any hon. member of this house if he has been as prosperous in the past year as he was in the preceding years of his life. Is his condition as good? That is the question. Now, let us look at the tests imposed.

One of the tests imposed by the administration in former days was railway earnings. It was proclaimed . . . that the earnings of the railways were a test of the great prosperity of the people. What about 1929? What about January, 1930? How do they compare with previous years? . . .

Then take the next test which they used to impose, the stock market prices. Who has not heard the Prime Minister tell about the high prices of stocks as compared with what they were in previous years? What does he say about them now? . . .

Then you turn to the third test that has been imposed, the cost of living. . . . I find that the cost of living was 160 as compared with 100 in prewar times and it has alternated between 156 and 160 during all the years since the government came into power. . . .

There is one further test to be applied, the test of employment. . . . since the beginning of the year I have traversed Canada from Victoria to the far east and in every city of the Dominion, east and west, there is abnormal unemployment, so that men who are accustomed to give, as I have been, to assist those who are unable to earn sufficient to keep body and soul together, have never before seen such distress as I have seen in all the communities I have visited. . . .

House of Commons Debates, 20 February, 1930, pp. 16-18.

The Depression soon made itself evident in grim reality over much of Canada. The west suffered most for here economic collapse was accompanied by natural disaster. A zone stretching across the southern part of the prairie provinces, the so-called "Palliser's triangle", experienced abnormally low rainfall over much of the thirties. In addition to drought the area was visited by other calamities—hail, wind erosion, grasshopper plagues, rust and plant diseases. The worst years, 1933 and 1936, saw the desolation of vast acreages which had formerly grown abundant wheat crops. Anne Marriott's poem, *The Wind Our Enemy*, describes the coming of the drought.

The wheat in spring was like a giant's bolt of silk
Unrolled over the earth.
When the wind sprang
It rippled as if a great broad snake
Moved under the green sheet
Seeking its outward way to light.
In autumn it was an ocean of flecked gold
Sweet as a biscuit, breaking in crisp waves
That never shattered, never blurred in foam.
That was the last good year. . . .

They said, "Sure, it'll rain next year!"
When that was dry, "Well, next year anyway."
Then, "Next—"
But still the metal hardness of the sky
Softened only in mockery.
When lightning slashed and twanged
And thunder made the hot head surge with pain
Never a drop fell;
Always hard yellow sun conquered the storm.
So the soon sickly-familiar saying grew,
(Watching the futile clouds sneak down the north)
"Jest empties goin' back!"
(Cold laughter bending parched lips in a smile
Bleak eyes denied.)

Anne Marriott, *The Wind Our Enemy* (Toronto: Ryerson, 1939), pp. 2/3.

The dust storms, resulting from a combination of low rainfall, light soils and strong winds, were the most devastating feature of the drought. In the long term these storms were caused by the removal of the grass cover of the southern plains when the area was planted in wheat. Thus the farmers of the 1930's suffered grievously from the over-optimistic settlement of large parts of the prairies in the Laurier years. J. K. Sutherland, a farmer near Hanna, Alberta, has left this vivid account of the dreaded "black blizzard."

The morning is usually fine and clear, with maybe just a gentle breeze blowing. We farmers are all out in the fields ploughing, seeding, summer fallowing—doing any one of a score of jobs and duties that fall to the farmer's lot ere the soil will produce. The breeze comes on just a little stronger, and a few small particles of soil start to drift gently along the top of the cultivated land. These tiny soil particles soon loosen up other little particles. Very soon, with the increasing wind, the whole surface of the field is gently sifting along, always moving, always gathering fresh momentum by rapidly increasing volume. There is nothing spectacular yet. But wait—away off to the northwest a heavy black cloud is forming between sky and earth. Black, yes, black as night. It sweeps towards us rapidly at forty, fifty, sixty miles an hour. We turn, each individual one of us, looking for the nearest shelter. Teams are unhooked as quickly as possible, and if no stable room is near turned with their heads away from the storm. Those of us with tractors either make for shelter or stay with the machines as long as possible.... The air gets colder. The huge black wall is now only a mile away. A minute, and with a blast like the roar of a thousand lions it is upon us. We are alone in a sightless mass of hurtling soil, stinging sand and thumping clods. We lose all sense of direction. Unless one happens to be within hand's reach of a fence progress in any calculated direction is almost impossible. We can only stand buffeted by the blows of a thousand hammers, or drift helpless, choking, blinded. This is the black blizzard.

For hours the tortured soil is torn and ravished until the storm ceases. Then we look out on the fields which we have tilled. They are as smooth as if polished by a giant plane. Here and there a few wheat plants, stricken, stand on roots still remaining in the hard subsoil. With to-morrow's sun they will probably fade and die. Millions in rich top soil is gone forever. That is the black blizzard, the most appalling thing in nature.

Jean Burnet, *Next-Year Country, A Study of Rural Social Organization in Alberta* (Toronto: University of Toronto Press. 1951), pp. 6/7.

The prairie farmer, reeling under natural disasters, was dealt another blow by the falling price of wheat on the world market. A price of 38 cents a bushel (the Winnipeg price of No. 1 Northern in 1932) meant 20½ cents for the farmer at an elevator in Alberta. But there were other costs that the farmer had to bear. James Gray gives some examples.

It is true that this was the historic low, that the average price obtained by the farmers for their 1932 crop was higher. Yet over a wide area of Alberta the actual cash income of the farmers amounted to only a few pennies a bushel for their crop. Joe Nolte of the Stettler area hauled fifty-four bushels into the elevator that winter and got a cash grain-ticket of $2.95 for the load. He took the ticket to the editor of the Stettler *Independent* to record the event for posterity, for, as he pointed out, after deducting threshing expenses he had a net cash return of one cent per bushel. His story was topped by another farmer who harvested thirty-three bushels to the acre and took it to market when the price of No. 1 Northern was twenty-eight and half cents at the elevator. That autumn had been cold and wet and much of the grain was tough and smutty. This caused the second farmer's wheat to be discounted eighteen cents a bushel. Threshing and twine cost seven cents; hauling, three cents a bushel. Thus a bumper crop returned its grower one-half cent per bushel.

James H. Gray, *The Winter Years, The Depression on the Prairies* (Toronto: Macmillan, 1966), pp. 199/200.

By 1933 the human costs of economic depression were becoming only too apparent. One of the most glaring was the army of unemployed transients, moving back and forth across Canada looking for work. They came from prairie farms, from factories in Ontario, from fishing villages in Cape Breton. Most of the time, one observer has reported, "they weren't really going anywhere."

The Bennett government set up a number of relief camps in an effort to provide work for single men. In four years of operation the camps accommodated over 115,000 men. Their purpose was admirable but there was considerable criticism of the way in which they were administered.

The fatal error of the government was in placing the camps under the Department of National Defence and making the *King's Rules and Orders*—K.R. & O.—the procedural Bible. This step guaranteed that whatever grievance did develop in the camps would be bottled up until it reached explosive proportions. No organization of any kind was permitted in any camp, and no petition could be circulated, and no committee could be formed to complain about anything. . . . Anyone who tried to organize a protest in a camp faced expulsion and in some camps that meant being expelled in midwinter at the camp gates a hundred miles from the nearest habitation. Perhaps few of the men in the camps would have joined a Relief Camp Workers' Union if it could have been organized. But the fact that no organization was permitted became a rankling grievance,

Equally to blame for morale trouble in camps was the pay of twenty cents per day. There was something about that twenty cents per day that came to symbolize everything that was wrong with the lives of everybody on relief. It affronted human dignity as little else could have done. It was just the right size to be insulting.

Underlying these main defects of the camp system was a host of picayune grievances. In addition to the twenty cents per day, the men also got a tobacco allowance—based on 1.45 cents per day for each day in camp. Thus before a new-comer was able to get a ten-cent package of tobacco, he had to get seven days of camp life behind him. Because the camps were established as a temporary measure to meet a condition that was expected to pass away next year, many were devoid of recreational facilities. There was no place for a hockey rink or baseball diamond and no equipment for either game. In many remote camps, outside communication ceased when a rickety radio went dead.

James Gray, *The Winter Years, The Depression on the Prairies* (Toronto: Macmillan, 1966), pp. 147/48.

While the plight of the farmer and primary producer was serious enough, conditions of employment for the industrial worker were also desperate in most cities of central Canada. Their economic rewards were documented in the Report of the Royal Commission on Price Spreads, set up by the Bennett government to investigate the large differential between the price that producers received for commodities and the price paid by consumers. In the sober words of the Report:

Wage rates and earnings [in the needle trades] are often exceedingly low. Quebec country home-workers probably cannot average 50 cents per day. Male piece-workers in one large Montreal factory averaged 16 cents per hour, less than the minimum of 18 cents for inexperienced females. One man of ten years' experience worked 70 hours per week in a Montreal contract shop, to earn $7 at 10 cents per hour. One man of four years' experience earned $3 per week, or 5.5 cents per hour in a Quebec country factory. In one Montreal factory, all workers, men and women together, averaged 25 cents per hour. In 1932, out of 115 men in two thoroughly good Toronto union shops, 57 earned for the year less than $800; 88, less than $1,000; only 27 over $1,000; and only 2 over $1,600.

It is bad enough to pay such wages as these. It is adding insult to injury to hand them to the workers, as is often done, in pay envelopes which, thoughtfully provided by banks, bear such encouraging advice as:

Think of tomorrow
Divide your pay in two,
Take what you need to live,
Put the balance in safety.

If the clothing worker takes advantage of this helpful suggestion and 'divides his pay in two' his 'thoughts of tomorrow' would hardly be such as to recommend him to the consideration of a bank director....

In the two Toronto department stores, as was perhaps natural under prevailing conditions, the wages of the female employees in April, 1934, tended to group around the legal minimum of $12.50 per week. In Eaton's 54 percent, and in Simpson's 53 percent of the female store employees received over $10 but less than $13 per week. At that time more than 50 percent of the male store employees in both firms received more than $19 per week.

In the Montreal stores, wage rates were considerably below those in Toronto, with the following percentages of female employees receiving less than $13 per week.

Dupuis Frères	91
Eaton's	69
Simpson's	60
Ogilvy's	56
Morgan's (less than $50 per mo.)	73

Report of the Royal Commission on Price Spreads (Ottawa: King's Printer, 1937), pp. 110, 119.

The Royal Commission recommended increased government regulation of wages, hours of labour and employment practices. It prepared the ground for later legislation of the war and post-war years which gave Canada many of the characteristics of a welfare state.

Economic catastrophe inevitably aroused criticism, protest and visions of a new society. When the traditional parties failed to provide the leadership which the victims of depression demanded, new movements arose to express the discontent. The most exciting was Social Credit in Alberta, created and led by the fiery William Aberhart. Aberhart combined a shrewd grasp of mass psychology with a simplistic interpretation of the workings of the capitalist system. J. A. Irving gives this description of one of Aberhart's most celebrated speeches, delivered six weeks before his victorious election in August, 1935.

With tears in his eyes, he described the pitiable conditions into which the depression had plunged hundreds of thousands of people in Alberta. He promised that a Social Credit government could end all this by giving every adult in the province a monthly dividend of $25. "You remain in the depression," he declared, "because of a shortage of purchasing power, imposed by the banking system. Social Credit offers you the remedy. If you have not suffered enough, it is your God-given right to suffer more. But if you wish to elect your own representatives to implement the remedy, this is your only way out." In closing, Aberhart graphically described the struggle of a deep-sea diver with a devilfish, and compared this struggle to Alberta's terrific struggle with the money octopus. "We still have one hand free," he roared, "with which to strike—to mark our ballot on election day. Let us strike then with all our might at this hideous monster that is sucking the very life blood from our people!"

J. A. Irving, *The Social Credit Movement in Alberta* (Toronto: University of Toronto Press, 1959), p. 291.

The testimony of people who supported Social Credit shows that Aberhart's identification of eastern financial interests as the cause of the economic difficulties of the west made a potent appeal to the suffering. A salesman in an Alberta department store later recalled his reaction.

I lost my job after two years of depression. Listening to Aberhart explain the depression on the radio convinced me that the Eastern financial interests had put on the depression. I've been robbed myself by capitalistic interests very badly. We people in the West were pretty well disgusted with the Eastern financial interests. We felt the East had been milking us long enough. They had kept manufacturing down East. I joined the Social Credit movement as a protest against the rule of the big money interests. . . .

J. A. Irving, *The Social Credit Movement in Alberta* (Toronto: University of Toronto Press, 1959), p. 246.

Another follower describes the emotional effect of Aberhart's victory.

Mr. Aberhart won my complete loyalty because of his sympathy with the poor and unemployed. I've seen him cry. I've seen tears rolling down his cheeks when he was describing the suffering caused among the poor by the depression—through no fault of their own, as he made clear to us. . . . He had a voice that made the pilot lights on your radio jump. You simply had to believe him. Sometimes when I heard him, I used to say to my wife: "This man seems to be in direct contact with the Supreme Being."

J. A. Irving, *The Social Credit Movement in Alberta* (Toronto: University of Toronto Press, 1959), p. 265.

A more penetrating analysis of the economic system was provided by a new socialist party, the Co-operative Commonwealth Federation. The Regina Manifesto, issued at the party's second conference in 1933, was a sweeping indictment of capitalism and a blue print for future economic planning and reconstruction. While some of the points of the Manifesto have still to be realized, others have since passed into legislation and become part of Canada's economic structure.

We aim to replace the present capitalist system, with its inherent injustice and inhumanity, by a social order from which the domination and exploitation of one class by another will be eliminated, in which economic planning will supersede unregulated private enterprise and competition, and in which genuine democratic self-government, based upon economic equality will be possible. The present order is marked by glaring inequalities of wealth and opportunity, by chaotic waste and instability; and in an age of plenty it condemns the great mass of the people to poverty and insecurity. Power has become more and more concentrated into the hands of a small irresponsible minority of financiers and industrialists and to their predatory interests the majority are habitually sacrificed.... We believe that these evils can be removed only in a planned and socialized economy in which our natural resources and the principal means of production and distribution are owned, controlled and operated by the people....

...Control of finance is the first step in the control of the whole economy. The chartered banks must be socialized and removed from the control of private profit-seeking interests; and the national banking system thus established must have at its head a Central Bank to control the flow of credit and the general price level, and to regulate foreign exchange operations....

...Transportation, communications and electric power must come first in a list of industries to be socialized. Others, such as mining, pulp and paper and the distribution of milk, bread, coal and gasoline, in which exploitation, waste, or financial malpractices are particularly prominent must next be brought under social ownership and operation....

With the advance of medical science the maintenance of a healthy population has become a function for which every civilized community should undertake responsibility. Health services should be made at least as freely available as are educational services today. But under a system which is still mainly one of private enterprise the costs of proper medical care, such as the wealthier members of society can easily afford, are at present prohibitive for great masses of the people....

The Regina Manifesto, 1933, in J. M. Bliss (ed.), *Canadian History in Documents, 1763-1966* (Toronto: Ryerson, 1966), pp. 290-294 *passim.*

While the effects of the depression of the 1930's were not really overcome until World War II brought economic recovery to Canada, the prairies were restored to productivity through the skilful application of techniques of soil conservation. The Prairie Farm Rehabilitation Administration (1935) was a remarkably successful venture of the Bennett government to combat erosion and drought in the west lands. James Gray recounts the methods that were employed to change the face of the "dust bowl."

Task forces were sent out from the Lethbridge and Swift Current Experimental Farms in 1936 to direct emergency cultivation to halt the blowing soil. Networks of deeply ridged fields were put together, and when the hollows between the ridges filled up, the fields were gone over again and again. Where weeds had taken over and helped to break the power of the wind, crested wheat grass was seeded into the Russian thistle and stinkweed. It was done with more hope than confidence; but it worked out, for the showers did germinate the seed and in the end the soil blowing was stopped, and for good. New techniques developed at Swift Current made it possible to grow wheat without soil erosion, and new grass mixtures doubled and quadrupled the cattle-carrying capacity of the ranges. The problem of how to turn the Palliser Triangle into a productive cattle-raising and wheat-growing empire has been solved.

Almost three million acres of land in western Saskatchewan and Alberta were taken out of cultivation and restored to grass, then fenced and cross-fenced and converted into community pastures for the farmers in the area. In the course of time, rivers were dammed, huge new irrigation schemes were developed, and the whole face of the West was changed for the better. The land that blew in the Dirty Thirties will never blow again as long as it remains in grass, or is cultivated by wind-proofing methods. . . .

James Gray, *The Winter Years, The Depression on the Prairies* (Toronto: Macmillan, 1966), pp. 213/14.

BIBLIOGRAPHY

*INDICATES VOLUMES AVAILABLE IN PAPERBACK.

Allen, Ralph. *Ordeal by Fire: Canada, 1910-1945* Doubleday Canada Ltd., 1961—a popular, dramatic history of Canada during these years.

Britnell, G. E. *The Wheat Economy*. University of Toronto Press, 1939—a vivid account of the shattered economy of the prairies in the 1930's.

Burnet, Jean. *Next-Year Country*. University of Toronto Press, 1951—a sociological study of Alberta farmers in the depression years.

Canada in World Affairs. Oxford University Press—a series of volumes sponsored by the Canadian Institute of International Affairs (C.I.I.A.) providing a record of Canada's external relations since the late 1930's; covers political, diplomatic, economic and military factors.

I Soward, F. H., *et al. The Pre-War Years*. (1941).

II Dawson, R. M. *Two Years of War, 1939-1941*. (1943).

III Lingard, C. C., and Trotter, R. G. *September, 1941—May, 1944*. (1950).

IV Soward, F. H. *From Normandy to Paris, 1944-1946*. (1950).

Carr, E. H. *International Relations between the Wars*. Macmillan, 1947—the approach of World War II.

Cook, Ramsay. *The Politics of John W. Dafoe and the Free Press*. University of Toronto Press, 1963—the best discussion of the views of the great Winnipeg editor.

Dawson, R. M. *The Conscription Crisis of 1944*. University of Toronto Press, 1961—a short but informative account.

———. *Constitutional Issues in Canada, 1900-1931*. Oxford University Press, 1933—provides material on the 1926 constitutional crisis.

———. *The Development of Dominion Status, 1900-1963*. Oxford University Press, 1937—treats the development of Canadian autonomy in the transition period from Empire to Commonwealth.

———. *The Government of Canada*. University of Toronto Press, 1956—a standard work on the subject.

———. *William Lyon Mackenzie King, A Political Biography*, Vol. I, *1874-1923*. University of Toronto Press, 1958—the first volume of the official biography ending with King's assumption of the prime minister's office.

Drury, E. C. *Farmer Premier, Memoirs of the Honourable E. C. Drury*. McClelland and Stewart, 1966—the story of Drury as leader of the United Farmers of Ontario, and Premier, 1919-23.

*Eayrs, James. *In Defence of Canada*. University of Toronto Press—a fascinating account of defence and Canada's external relations in the years between the wars.

I *From the Great War to the Great Depression*. (1964).

II *Appeasement and Rearmament*. (1965).

Ferns, H. S., and Ostry, B. *The Age of Mackenzie King; The Rise of the Leader*. Heinemann, 1955—a critical account of King's progress to the leadership of the Liberal party by 1919.

*Forsey, E. A. *The Royal Power of Dissolution of Parliament in the British Commonwealth*. Oxford University Press, 1943—another account of the constitutional crisis of 1926, supporting Meighen's stand.

*Glazebrook, G. P. de T. *A History of Canadian External Relations*. 2 vols. Carleton Library (McClelland and Stewart), 1966—the standard history of the subject, providing a full account until 1939, with a bibliographical essay on the later years.

Graham, Roger. *Arthur Meighen*. Clarke, Irwin—an authoritative biography of Meighen.

I *The Door of Opportunity*. (1960).

II *And Fortune Fled*. (1963).

III *No Surrender*. (1965).

*Granatstein, J. L. *Conscription in the Second World War, 1939-1945: A Study in Political Management.* ("The Frontenac Library," No. 1.) Ryerson, 1968—a brief study using representative source material.

Gray, James H. *The Winter Years: The Depression on the Prairies.* Macmillan, 1966—a sensitive record of the depression from the point of view of one who suffered.

Hutchison, Bruce. *The Incredible Canadian.* Longmans, Green, 1952—a colourful sketch of Mackenzie King's life.

Irving, J. A. *The Social Credit Movement in Alberta.* University of Toronto Press, 1959—a good picture of Aberhart and the origins of the movement.

*Laporte, Pierre. *The True Face of Duplessis.* Harvest House, 1960—a portrait of the despotic Premier by a one-time journalist and Quebec Liberal politician.

Lipset, S. M. *Agrarian Socialism.* University of California Press, 1950—the early record of the C.C.F. government in Saskatchewan.

Mallory, J. R. *Social Credit and the Federal Power in Canada.* University of Toronto Press, 1954—the conflict between Alberta and the federal government over Social Credit legislation.

Massey, Vincent. *What's Past is Prologue.* Macmillan, 1963—the memoirs of Massey; good on his experiences as Canada's representative in Washington and London.

Masters, D. C. *The Winnipeg General Strike.* University of Toronto Press, 1950—the only work on the 1919 disturbances in Winnipeg.

McGregor, F. A. *The Fall and Rise of Mackenzie King, 1911-1919.* Macmillan, 1962—covers King's controversial career during World War I.

McHenry, D. E. *The Third Force in Canada.* University of California Press, 1950—a description of the C.C.F. from its founding to 1948.

McKenty, Neil. *Mitch Hepburn.* McClelland and Stewart, 1967—the only biography of Ontario's colourful Premier of the 1930's.

*McNaught, Kenneth. *A Prophet in Politics.* University of Toronto Press, 1959—the life of J. S. Woodsworth, founder of the C.C.F.

*Morton, W. L. *The Progressive Party in Canada.* University of Toronto Press, 1950—the best study of the third party of the 1920's.

Munro, Ross. *Gauntlet to Overlord.* Macmillan, 1945—a war correspondent's account of the Canadian forces in Europe in World War II.

Neatby, H. B. *William Lyon Mackenzie King, The Lonely Heights,* Vol. II, *1924-1932.* University of Toronto Press, 1963—the exciting second volume of King's official biography.

Official History of the Canadian Army in the Second World War. Queen's Printer.

- I Stacey, C. P. *Six Years of War: The Army in Canada, Britain and the Pacific.* (1955).
- II Nicholson, G. W. L. *The Canadians in Italy, 1943-1945.* (1956).
- III Stacey, C. P. *The Victory Campaign: The Operations in North-West Europe, 1944-1945.* (1960).

Pickersgill, J. W. *The Mackenzie King Record,* Vol. I, *1939-1944.* University of Toronto Press, 1960—much the most interesting source on Canadian politics and diplomacy during World War II; based on King's personal diary.

———, and Forster, D. F. *The Mackenzie King Record,* Vol. II, *1944-1945.* University of Toronto Press, 1968—continues the King diary, focusing in this volume on the conscription crisis of World War II.

Power, C. G. (Norman Ward, ed.). *A Party Politician: The Memoirs of Chubby Power*. Macmillan, 1966—throws an interesting light on federal and Quebec politics since 1908.
*Quinn, H. F. *The Union Nationale: A Study in Quebec Nationalism*. University of Toronto Press, 1963—an analysis of Duplessis' party.
The R.C.A.F. Overseas: The First Four Years. Oxford University Press, 1944, and *The R.C.A.F. Overseas: The Fifth Year*. Oxford University Press, 1945—Canada's part in the air war, 1939-1945.
Report of the Royal Commission on Dominion-Provincial Relations, Vol. I. King's Printer, 1940. (An abridged version, *The Rowell-Sirois Report, Book I*, is published in the Carleton Library [McClelland and Stewart], 1963.)—an excellent economic history of Canada since 1867, especially good on the prosperous 1920's and the impact of the depression.
Schull, Joseph. *The Far Distant Ships*. Queen's Printer, 1950—a vivid description of Canada's naval operations in World War II.
Soward, F. H. *Twenty-Five Troubled Years*. Oxford University Press, 1943—a brief account of international tensions in the period between the two world wars.
Stacey, C. P. *The Canadian Army, 1939-1945, An Official Historical Summary*. King's Printer, 1948—a useful account in brief compass.
Swettenham, J. A. *McNaughton:* Vol. I, *1887-1939;* Vol. 2, *1940-1966*. Ryerson, 1968/69—the authorized biography of the great Canadian soldier-scientist.
Watkins, Ernest. *R. B. Bennett: A Biography*. Secker and Warburg, 1963—a rather sketchy life of Bennett.
*Young, Walter D. *A Season of Discontent: The Rise of Third Parties in the Canadian West*. ("The Frontenac Library," No. 2.) Ryerson, 1969—a brief study, using representative source materials, of the origins and fortunes of Progressivism, the C.C.F.-N.D.P., and Social Credit.

5

THE CHALLENGE OF NATIONHOOD IN A CHANGING WORLD

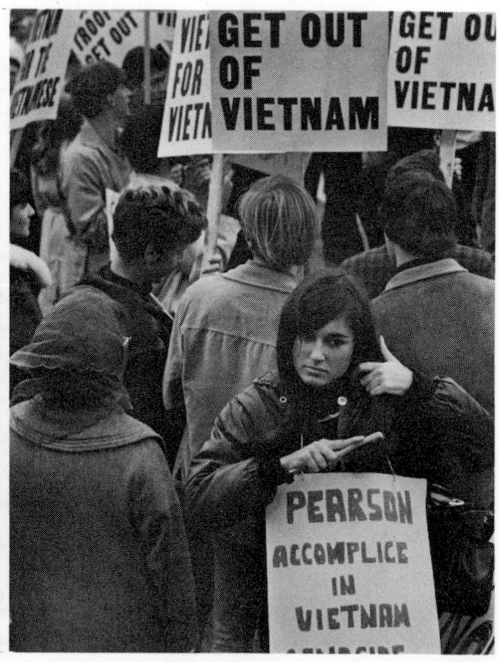

CHAPTER 18

POSTWAR CANADA

The dominant characteristic of Canadian life in the postwar period has been growth: growth in population, growth in industrial production, growth in personal income, and growth in transportation services. During this headlong and exciting growth, the face of Canada has been changed almost beyond recognition in the intangible aspects of its national life. Since World War II, Canada has also changed remarkably. Its educational system serves more people and offers better instruction, and the writers, artists and actors of Canada are more numerous and more confident than ever before. Canadian cities are more exciting places in which to live than they were twenty years ago. In summary, Canadians today live a fuller and richer life as a result of the changes of the last two decades.

Yet the basic problems of Canadian existence remain. Is it possible for a separate Canadian economy to survive beside the most powerful economic system in the world? Can Canada continue to trade all over the world? Can a strong central government function in Canada, given the enormous size of the country, the loyalties of the different regions, the division between the two founding peoples? Can Canada's political system, with all its complexities and frustrations, create an acceptable concept of Canadian nationhood? Canada's unprecedented physical growth in the years since 1945 has not solved these crucial questions.

POPULATION AND SOCIAL CHANGE

Basic to any understanding of Canada in the twenty years after World War II is the country's impressive population growth. For every three Canadians in 1945, there were over five in 1966. In September, 1966, Canada's population passed the 20,000,000 mark. Most of this surging growth came from natural increase. The depression of the thirties and the war had held back marriages and the "catching up" process began after 1945. The "baby boom" continued through the decade of the fifties, producing a population increase of nearly 15 percent in the five years from 1951 to 1956. This rate of increase had been exceeded only once before in Canada's history, in the decade before 1911, when the prairies were being settled. Undoubtedly the good economic conditions of the 1950's supported a growth in the population, but the expansion also derived from a trend towards earlier marriages and an increase in the average size of families. In 1957 the Canadian birth rate stood at 28 per thousand, one of the highest in the world.

After the peak year of 1957, the birth rate in Canada began to decline. It kept on falling until in 1966 it stood at the lowest level in twenty-five years. Partly this decline reflected the low level of births during the depression and the war, but it was also caused by changes in Canadian society. Young people were staying at school longer; more women were working; young married couples were buying automobiles or houses before starting families; rising living standards were cutting down the size of families. It appeared that Canada was once more falling in step with the trend towards smaller families that had occurred all through the Western world since the time of the Industrial Revolution.

Although the growth in Canada's population had slowed down by 1966 (the increase in the first half of the 1960's was only 9 percent), another large population wave was coming over the horizon. It would be composed of the children who were born during the period of the heavy birth rate prior to 1957. Although it was likely that fertility rates would not be as high in the future as they had been in the 1950's, the sheer number of these potential

Several aspects of Canada's postwar development are illustrated above. At the top (left) immigrants are shown on board ship. On the right, a Toronto apartment project towers above a relic of a previous era. On the bottom, the tendrils of two super highways twist their way through suburban Toronto.

parents indicated a very substantial number of Canadian babies over the next ten to fifteen years. The addition of these children to the population promised many changes in Canadian life. A larger population would strengthen the economy in innumerable ways, not least through the growth of the home market. Pressure on educational facilities would continue and the demand for new houses, apartments designed for families, and recreational services would make for further alterations in the face of Canadian cities. It was predicted that by the end of the century Canada might well have 40 million people.

Immigration played a significant role in the expansion of Canada's population after the war. Starting slowly after 1945 with war brides and displaced persons, the flow built up during the decade of the 1950's. In 1957 the movement reached greater dimensions (282,164 persons) than in any year since 1913. During this period immigration accounted for one-quarter of the entire

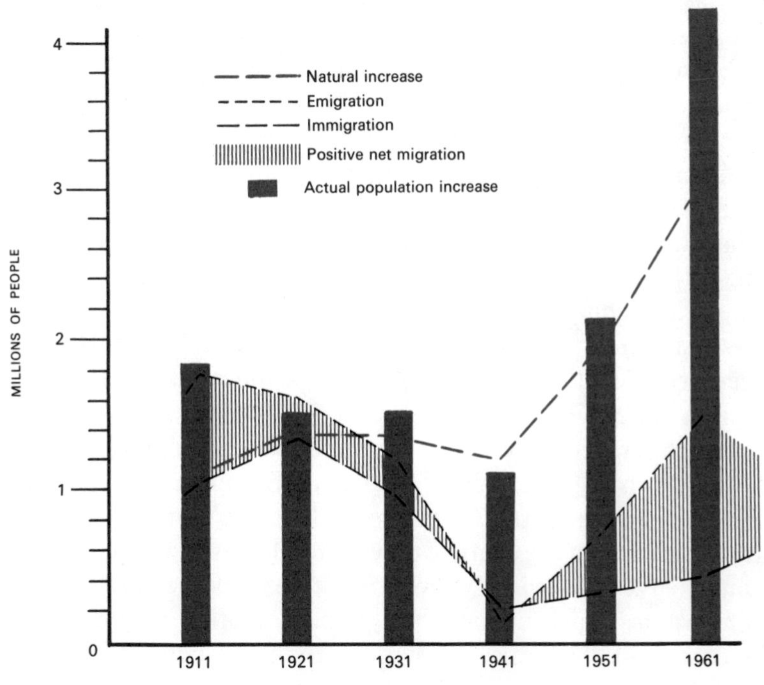

Demographic Trends, 1911-1961

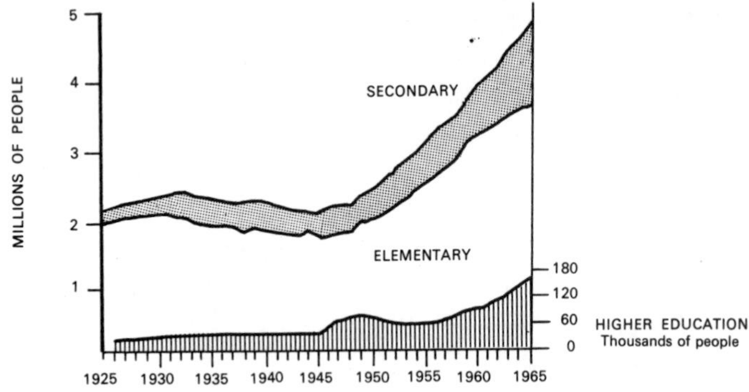

Full-Time Enrolment in Provincial Schools and Colleges, 1925-1965

Canadian population growth. After 1957 the flow of new arrivals slackened, so that by the early sixties immigration was responsible for only one-tenth of the country's growth. Then in the mid-sixties it began to pick up again. The improvement was helped by the federal government's new regulations which removed many existing geographic and ethnic barriers to admittance. After several generations of restricted immigration, Canadà appeared to be returning to a more liberal policy, one that recognized the country's need for trained people and the world's concern for racial equality and human betterment.

In the two decades after the end of World War II, over two and a half million people came to Canada as immigrants. Possibly one-fifth of these went on to other countries but the majority stayed, enriching Canada with their skills, their enterprise and the distinctive flavour of their national cultures. The British Isles provided the largest single group, followed by Italy, the United States, Germany, Greece and Portugal.

One difference between the immigrants of Laurier's time and those who came after World War II is that the latter settled in urban centres in central Canada or in British Columbia, whereas at the opening of the century they had settled in many provinces. Ontario received slightly over 50 percent of the mid-century immigrants, Quebec about 25 percent, British Columbia 10 percent, and the prairie provinces about 12 percent. The remainder, a mere 3 percent, entered the Atlantic provinces. In addition, the typical immigrant of the early 1900's had been a farmer or a labourer; the immigrant of the 1950's was usually a skilled worker or a professional person.

The hundred years since Confederation witnessed remarkable changes in the dispersal of Canada's population. Some regions lost population, others gained. The cities, especially the larger ones, gained most of all.

The growth of more and larger cities was another feature of Canada's expansion in the postwar era. People moved from rural areas into the cities, not simply because industrialization seemed to offer better economic opportunities, but also because technological changes reduced the number of workers needed to work farms or cut trees in the bush. The rural segment of Canada's population fell from 38 percent in 1951 to 26 percent in 1966.

People moved as well from smaller towns and cities to the more dynamic metropolitan centres. The ten largest Canadian cities grew at a rate twice as fast as that of the remainder of the country. By the mid-sixties Montreal was still the largest urban centre, although Toronto, the second largest city, was growing faster. Vancouver remained secure in the third position but Winnipeg was closely challenged by Ottawa for fourth place. Canadians, like so many other people in the Western world, were becoming a nation of city dwellers. Life in the city offered many amenities not present in rural communities but it also necessitated physical and social planning on a scale that Canada had never experienced before.

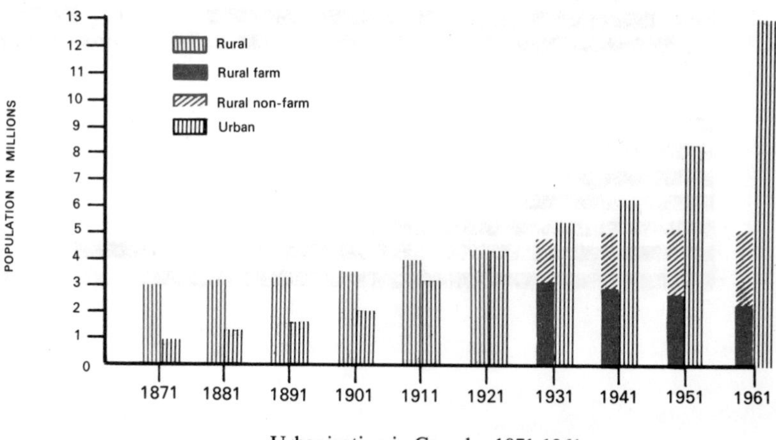

Urbanization in Canada, 1871-1961

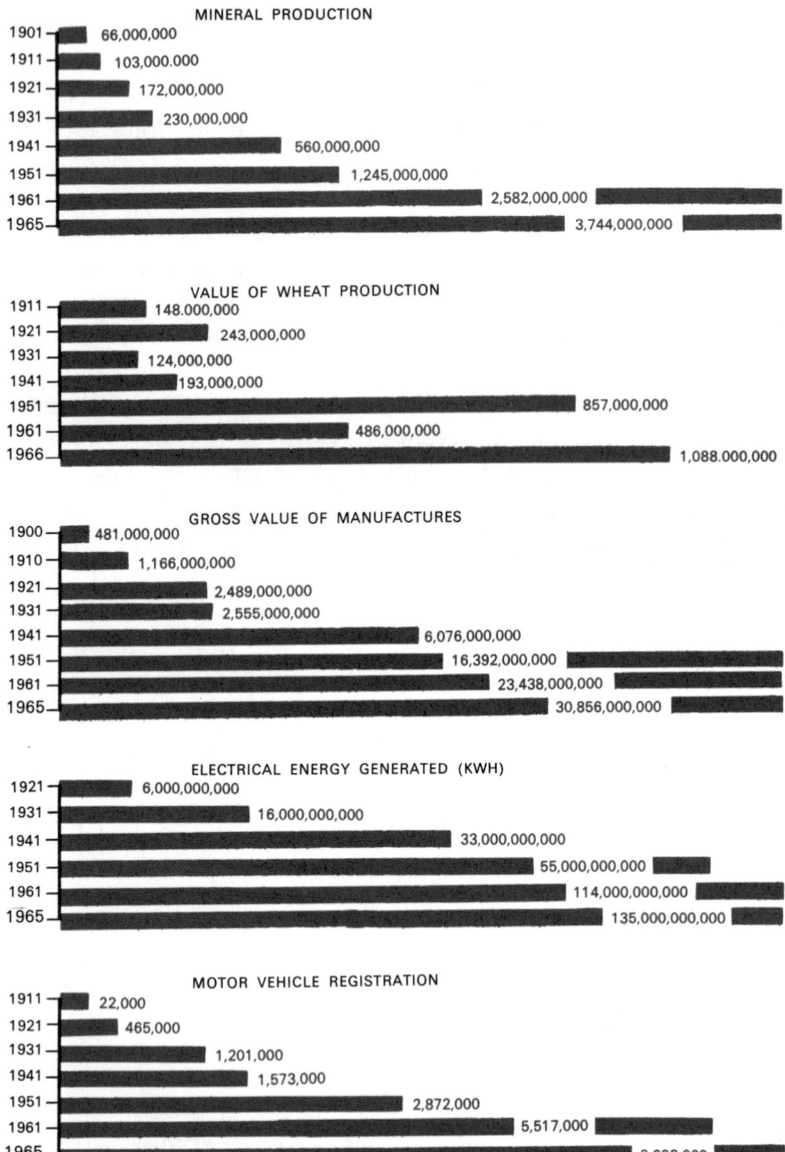

Canada's Economic Growth

THE EXPANSION OF THE ECONOMY

The dynamic growth of Canada's economy between 1945 and 1966 gave Canadians the second highest standard of living in the world. These years also represented the greatest period of economic growth in the history of Canada. Production records were established in every area of economic activity, while the development of new resources proceeded on a scale that would have been undreamed of a generation before. It is no exaggeration to state that Canada, in its material aspects, changed more in these two decades than in all the previous periods of its history.

Although Canadians born after 1945 took prosperity for granted, political leaders and businessmen did not have this view at the end of the war. Memories of the Great Depression were still very real and most people considered that a capitalist system of private property and free enterprise could not proceed without ups and downs in the business cycle. The war had brought prosperity, but could good times continue when wartime demands dried up?

The Canadian government made a bold statement of its hopes for postwar economic expansion in a White Paper issued late in 1945:

> The ultimate aim of all reconstruction policies is the extension of opportunity, welfare and security among the Canadian people. . . . [the] adoption of a high and stable level of employment and income, and thereby higher standards of living, [is] a major aim of Government policy.

The Canadian economy moved easily from war to peace through the infusion of civilian demands that had been held in check during the conflict. The Korean War, which broke out in 1950, revived military demands and set off a worldwide wave of raw material purchases. The United States, in particular, suddenly realized its lack of long-term supplies in basic industrial materials and began to stockpile these commodities. Canadian exports to the United States dramatically increased, while American capital flowed into Canada to develop large resource

projects. There were two short recessions in the Canadian economy during the fifties and the early sixties, but in general the level of economic activity in Canada moved steeply upward. After 1961 the economy "took off" and Canada experienced a period of economic expansion and prosperity.

The gross national product (the value of all the goods and services produced in Canada) was calculated at $5.6 billion on the eve of World War II. The war lifted this figure to $11.8 billion; by 1967 it had climbed to over $60 billion. Some of this increase undoubtedly resulted from the decreasing value of the dollar as a result of inflated prices. However, the dimensions of the expansion of the economy are unmistakable when it is observed that the real output of the country, as expressed in terms of each person employed, rose by almost 50 percent in the period. This represented an annual increase in the gross national product of about 4 percent.

The average weekly industrial wage of Canadians in 1965 was about ninety-three dollars, compared with thirty-two dollars twenty years before. Canadian affluence was vividly demonstrated by automobile sales. While the population of Canada did not quite double between 1946 and 1966, the number of motor vehicles sold in 1966 was more than nine times the figure twenty years before.

Unemployment, which was expected to be a serious problem after the war, virtually disappeared from many regions of Canada. The unemployment rate by the mid-sixties stood at less than 5 percent of the labour force. More and more the unemployed were persons who, because of their location, their lack of opportunity, training or ability were unemployable. In a free economy *total* employment is impossible, but Canada by the mid-sixties had achieved what economists call *full* employment.

Prosperity was attributable, as it had been during every pre-

◀ *Four aspects of contemporary Canada. At the top (right to left) are oil drilling operations in the Rainbow-Zama area of Alberta, the Place Ville Marie in Montreal, and salmon fishing on the coast of British Columbia. The lower photograph is of a potash processing plant at Esterhazy, Saskatchewan, a new industry that has helped to boost that province's economy.*

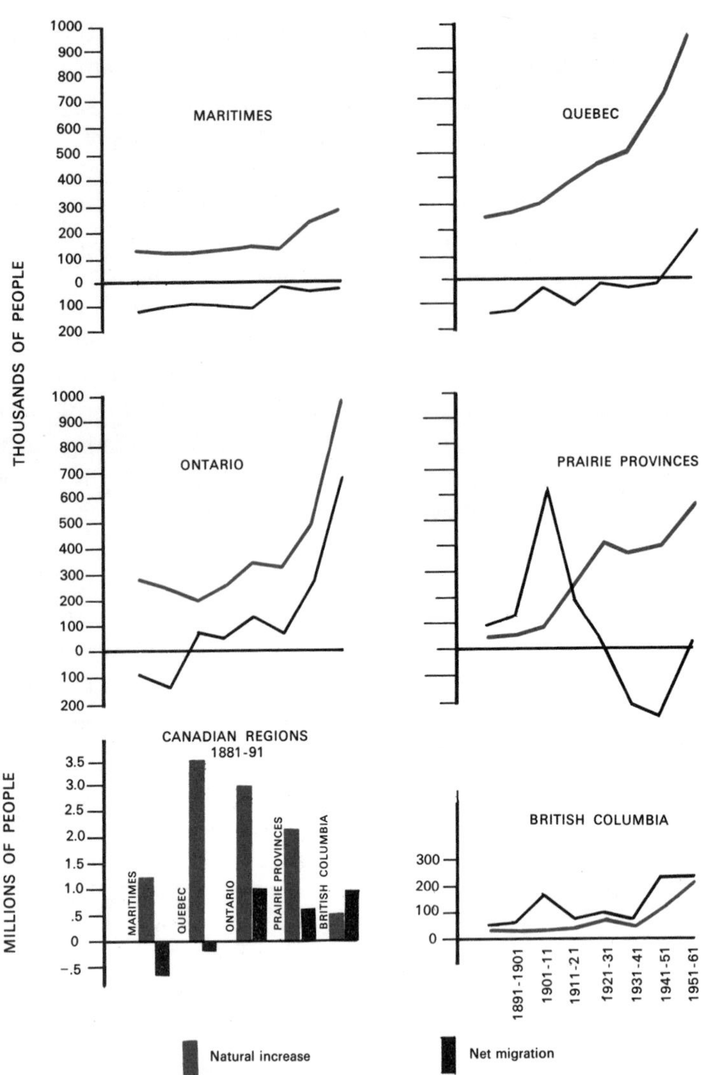

Net Migration and Natural Increase by Provinces and Regions, 1881-1961

vious boom, to the exploitation of natural resources to meet world demands. The interesting feature of the postwar economic expansion, however, lay in the fact that new resources were taking the place of the old. Wheat, which had long been Canada's leading export, now stood third in the trading list, and other farm products were even farther down the list. Newsprint and lumber bulked larger than ever before in Canada's trade, and they were joined by resources that were virtually untapped before the war—oil, iron ore, natural gas, uranium and chemical products. The development of these resources brought a diversification to the Canadian economy and increased the populated area of the country. Although the nation's population remained concentrated in a narrow belt along the American border, there was penetration of the Canadian North by men and machines. New towns sprang up in the wake of this advance. The Ungava peninsula, virtually uninhabited since the days of the fur trade, became the centre of vast iron-mining operations; new mining towns sprang up in northern Ontario and along the route of the Hudson Bay Railway; a great aluminum smelter was built at Kitimat far up the British Columbia coast; construction began on a railway to Great Slave Lake in the Northwest Territories. Oil and gas pipelines paralleled the railway systems in linking the country together; new airfields were built, and many refineries and processing plants established.

The new resources needed to be sold abroad in order to promote Canadian prosperity. Roughly one-fifth of what Canada produced went into foreign trade, so that one dollar in every five in the income of Canadians was derived from this source. (The corresponding figure in the United States was one dollar in every twenty-five). During and after the war Canada stood next in rank behind the United States and Great Britain among the trading nations of the world. Although her comparative position slipped a little after 1954, Canada, nevertheless, exported commodities in 1966 worth over $10 billion, representing a per capita income from exports of $500. She exported a greater proportion of partly-processed goods (pulp and paper, chemicals, iron ore) than she had before the war, a factor which led to a strengthening and diversification of Canadian industry. Between 1946 and 1966, agricultural products declined in importance in Canada's external trade, leading to problems of surpluses in some years. But this trend was checked by extraordinarily large wheat and flour sales to such Communist-bloc countries as China and

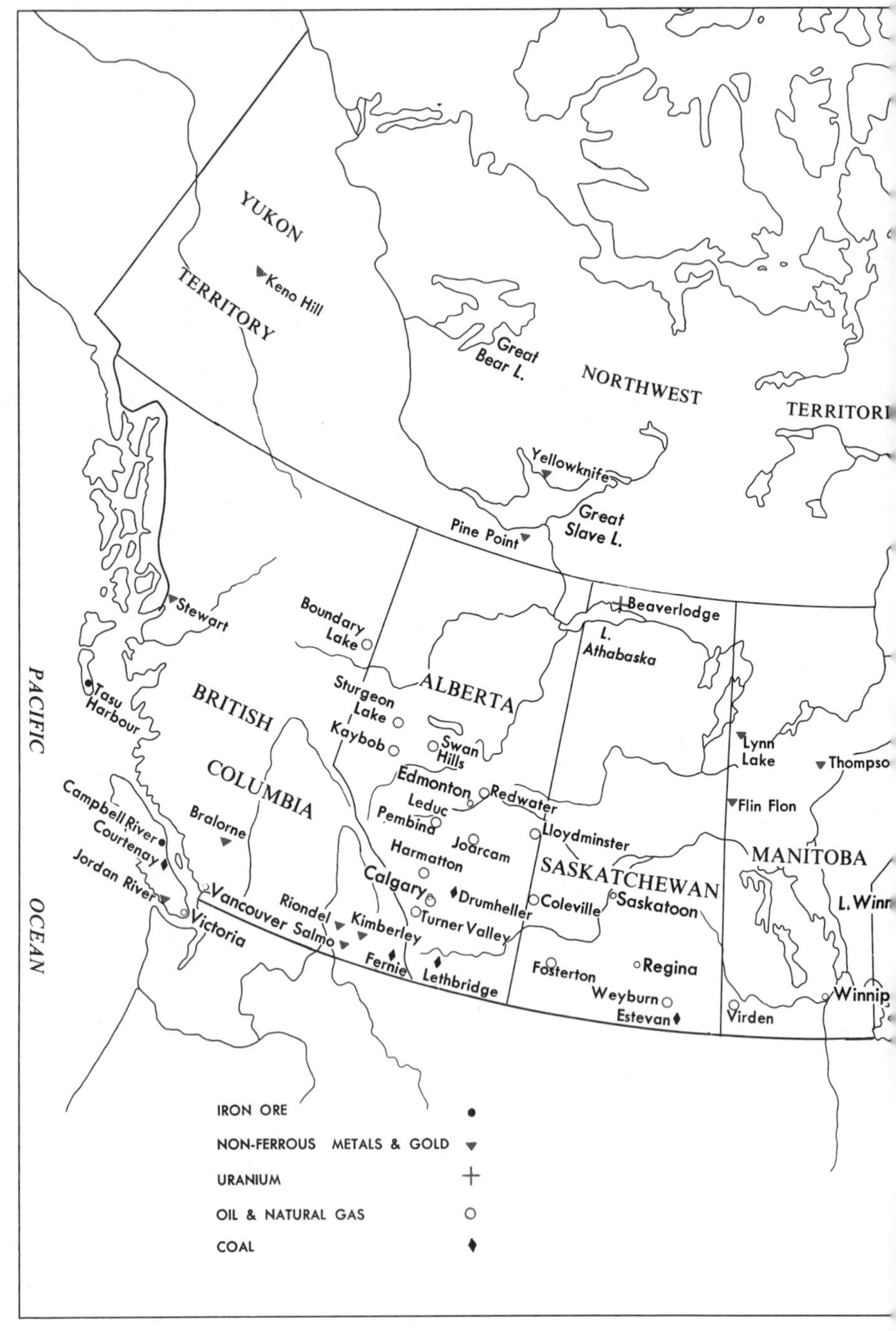
YUKON
TERRITORY
Keno Hill
Great
Bear L.
NORTHWEST
TERRITORI
Yellowknife
Great
Slave L.
Pine Point
Beaverlodge
L.
Athabaska
Stewart
Boundary
Lake
PACIFIC
OCEAN
Tasu
Harbour
BRITISH
COLUMBIA
ALBERTA
Sturgeon
Lake
Kaybob
Swan
Hills
Lynn
Lake
Thompso
Edmonton
Redwater
Leduc
Pembina
Flin Flon
Campbell River
Courtenay
Jordan River
Bralorne
Joarcam
Lloydminster
Harmatton
MANITOBA
SASKATCHEWAN
Calgary
Drumheller
Coleville
Saskatoon
L. Winn
Vancouver
Victoria
Riondel
Salmo
Kimberley
Turner Valley
Fernie
Lethbridge
Fosterton
Regina
Weyburn
Estevan
Virden
Winnip
IRON ORE
NON-FERROUS METALS & GOLD
URANIUM
OIL & NATURAL GAS
COAL

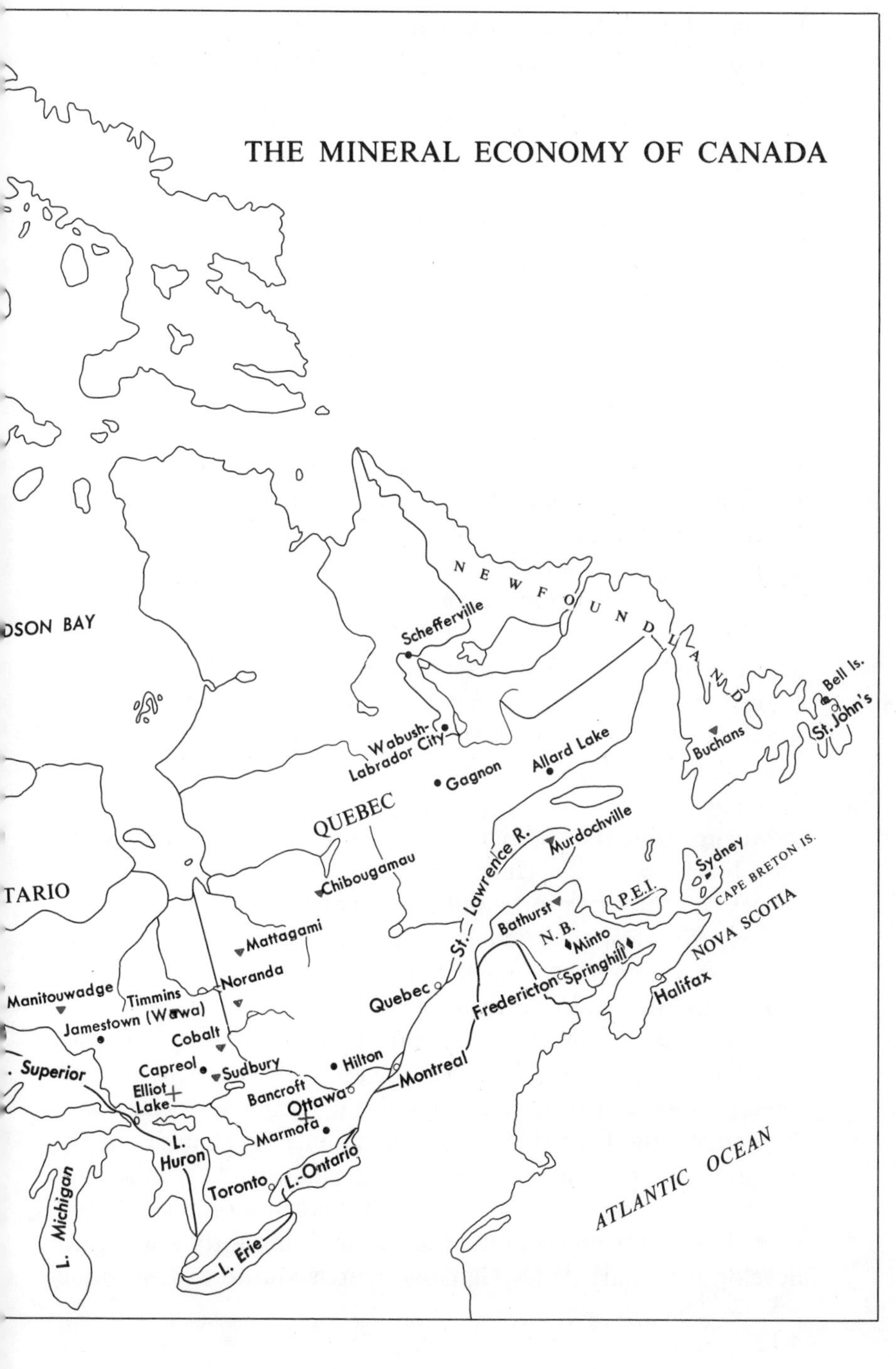
THE MINERAL ECONOMY OF CANADA
DSON BAY
TARIO
QUEBEC
NEWFOUNDLAND
Schefferville
Wabush-Labrador City
Gagnon
Allard Lake
Buchans
Bell Is.
St. John's
Chibougamau
Murdochville
St. Lawrence R.
Sydney
CAPE BRETON IS.
P.E.I.
NOVA SCOTIA
Bathurst
N. B.
Minto
Springhill
Halifax
Fredericton
Mattagami
Noranda
Manitouwadge
Timmins
Jamestown (Wawa)
Cobalt
Quebec
Hilton
Montreal
Capreol
Sudbury
Superior
Elliot Lake
Bancroft
Ottawa
Marmora
L. Huron
Toronto
L. Ontario
L. Michigan
L. Erie
ATLANTIC OCEAN

Russia. These sales, while not halting the relative decline of agriculture, showed dramatically that a buoyant foreign trade could stimulate the entire economy.

The great bulk of Canada's external trade has always been with her partners of the North Atlantic community—Britain and the United States. Before 1939 Canada's imports came mostly from the United States and her exports went mainly to Britain and other parts of the world. The war, by fostering economic co-operation between the United States and Canada and by interfering with North Atlantic trade, built up very close trading relationships between the two North American countries. After 1945 Britain's import restrictions and shortage of American currency prolonged the trend. The phenomenal expansion of the United States economy in the postwar years made that country the fastest-growing market in the world. Canada, situated close by and possessing the resources the United States wanted, was in the strongest possible position to exploit this market. The trade alignment between the two countries was strengthened by the flow of American capital to Canada for the purpose of developing specific Canadian industries, by the "borrowing" of technical "know-how," patents and industrial processes, by the similar tastes of American and Canadian consumers, and by stronger links between the business communities on both sides of the border.

Most of Canada's foreign trade is now conducted across the long border with the United States—between 50 percent and 60 per cent of all exports and about two-thirds of all imports. These proportions are much larger than they were before the war. Canada and the United States are each other's best customers and the trade between them is greater than between any other two countries in the world. This trade is enormously beneficial to each country. Canada sells to a market near at hand and at attractive prices, the materials and goods she is best able to produce; the United States is assured of a dependable supply of the commodities she needs for her vast industrial organization. Yet there are dangers in too great a dependence on one market. Canadian government and business are constantly seeking to develop new markets for Canadian goods and to expand trade

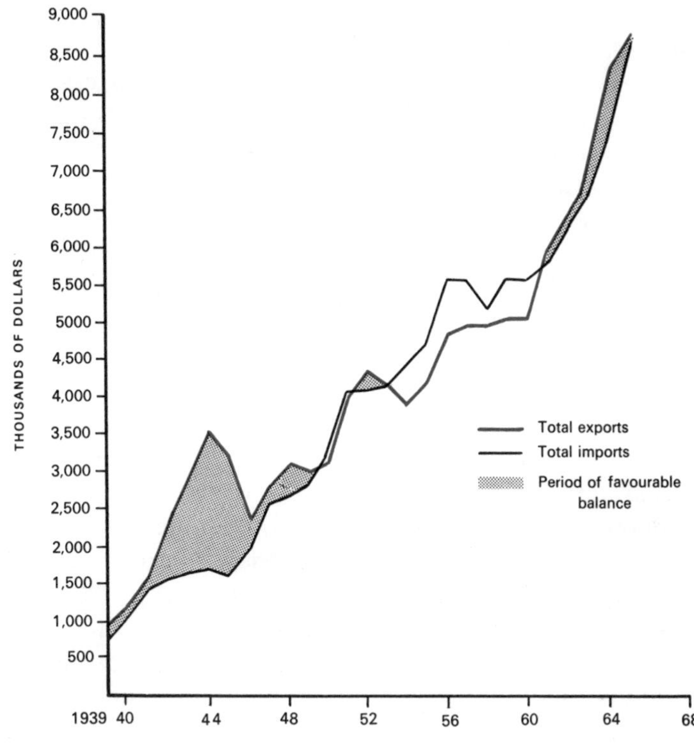

The Balance of Trade,1939-1964

beyond the North American area. For these reasons Canada has always been a supporter of efforts to remove restrictions in international trade. She was a founding member of the General Agreement on Tariffs and Trade (G.A.T.T.), set up by the United Nations in 1947, and during the mid-sixties she took an active part in the "Kennedy Round" of comprehensive negotiations designed to liberalize trade in the North Atlantic area.

Although Canada has enjoyed a surplus on her commodity trade since the 1950's, the total of all her commercial transactions abroad shows a deficit. This is because she has incurred so much indebtedness to foreign countries, especially the United States. She must, for example, pay interest and dividends to non-resident investors. Canadian subsidiaries of American, or other foreign companies, must pay their head offices for various services. Canadians travelling abroad must acquire foreign currency. This indebtedness is partly offset by the large amounts of capital that flow into Canada from abroad. The dimensions of this flow worry many Canadians but foreign capital has unquestionably been the essential stimulant for much of Canada's postwar economic growth.

The close connection between Canadian and American economic life is well illustrated in the trade union movement. This began under the auspices of the American Federation of Labor (A.F.L.), which chartered a number of locals in Canada in the late years of the nineteenth century. With the growth of industry in Canada at the time of World War I, membership in the organized labour movement expanded considerably. Canadian unions were mainly grouped under the Trades and Labour Congress of Canada (T.L.C.), a loose federation of craft unions whose position approximated to that of the A.F.L. The T.L.C. was established in 1886, five years after the A.F.L. Most of the unions in the T.L.C. were linked with their opposite numbers across the border. Yet even this link failed to introduce much of the militant atmosphere of American unionism in the 1930's upon the Canadian scene. Again, the great controversy which rocked American labour over the merits of industrial or craft unions made little impression upon Canada.

The Congress of Industrial Organizations (C.I.O.) established branches in Canada and set up the Canadian Congress of Labour in 1940. After World War II developments in Canadian labour followed those in the United States. The merger between the A.F.L. and the C.I.O. was duplicated in Canada when the Canadian Labour Congress (C.L.C.) was set up in April, 1956. Many types of unions—craft and industrial, national and international—were included within this body. In 1965 the C.L.C. could speak for about 1.2 million members, or 75 percent of all Canadian unionists.

International unions claim about 70 percent of all Canadian union members, but this figure has dropped significantly since 1911, when it was about 90 percent. However, the popular impression that the Canadian labour movement is "colonial," in that it is directed by union leaders in the United States, is not borne out by the facts. The C.L.C. is autonomous and has only a nominal relationship with the A.F.L.-C.I.O. The C.L.C. is not influenced by the latter's views on legislative or political questions. For instance, the C.L.C. has endorsed the New Democratic Party (N.D.P.) as its political arm, a participation in politics which the American organization has never pursued for very long. Canadian unions on many occasions have refused to follow the advice of American labour leaders, who are often too much occupied at home to give much attention to Canada. Very few of the dues paid by Canadian unionists ever leave Canada, and a C.L.C. official has estimated that far larger sums come into Canada from American unions to aid striking Canadian workers.

By the 1960's the Canadian labour movement, like the American, was concerned about the threat of automation. They were, therefore, given much attention to improving the skills of their members and creating new employment opportunities. The unions were also worried about their relative decline in relation to the growth of the labour force. In 1965, for instance, only 30 percent of all non-agricultural workers in Canada belonged to unions. It was apparent that there were hundreds of thousands of office workers, clerks and civil servants who had not been

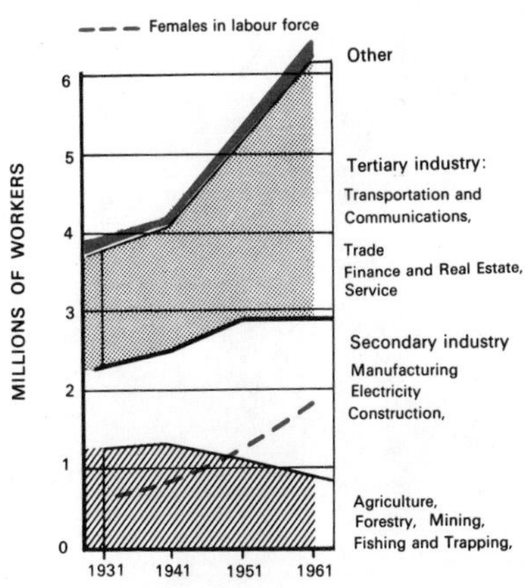

The Labour Force, 1931-1961

drawn into the union movement. On both sides of the border the unions began to try to recruit these people in an effort to strengthen their place in the economic system.

The project that symbolizes Canada's rapid economic advance since World War II, her growing industrialization and the interdependence of the North American economy, is the St. Lawrence Seaway.

In the 1930's President Franklin D. Roosevelt had favoured the construction of extra canals to make the St. Lawrence route navigable to ocean vessels. A treaty with Canada in 1941 authorizing the commencement of the seaway was blocked in Congress, but in the years after 1945 the plan assumed a heightened importance. A shortage of electric power in Ontario and New York drew attention to the desirability of harnessing the potential of the International Rapids of the St. Lawrence, so close to major industrial sites on both sides of the border. The iron ore deposits of the Ungava peninsula required a deep waterway for transport to the steel mills of the lower Great Lakes region. A seaway running almost 2,500 miles into the interior of the continent and navigable by ocean shipping was seen as providing additional routes for American and Canadian trade in time of war. All the evidence seemed to point to the advisability of beginning construction on a joint power and transportation scheme.

While the United States still hesitated, Canada established the St. Lawrence Seaway Authority in 1951 to construct a channel of twenty-seven-foot draught from Montreal to the lower lakes, thus eliminating the old St. Lawrence fourteen-foot canals. Congress hastened to join in the development of hydro-electric power facilities on the St. Lawrence and then, at the last moment, decided to participate in the entire project. The Wiley-Dondero

◀ *Some aspects of Canadian industry are illustrated on the facing page. Top left, lumbering operations in northern Ontario (compare with p. 263); top right, a paper-making machine; left centre, Thompson, a planned community in northern Manitoba that was first settled in October, 1957, to sustain mining operations of the International Nickel Company; lower left, meat-packing plants in Winnipeg, Manitoba; lower right, loading grain on a lake ship at the Lakehead.*

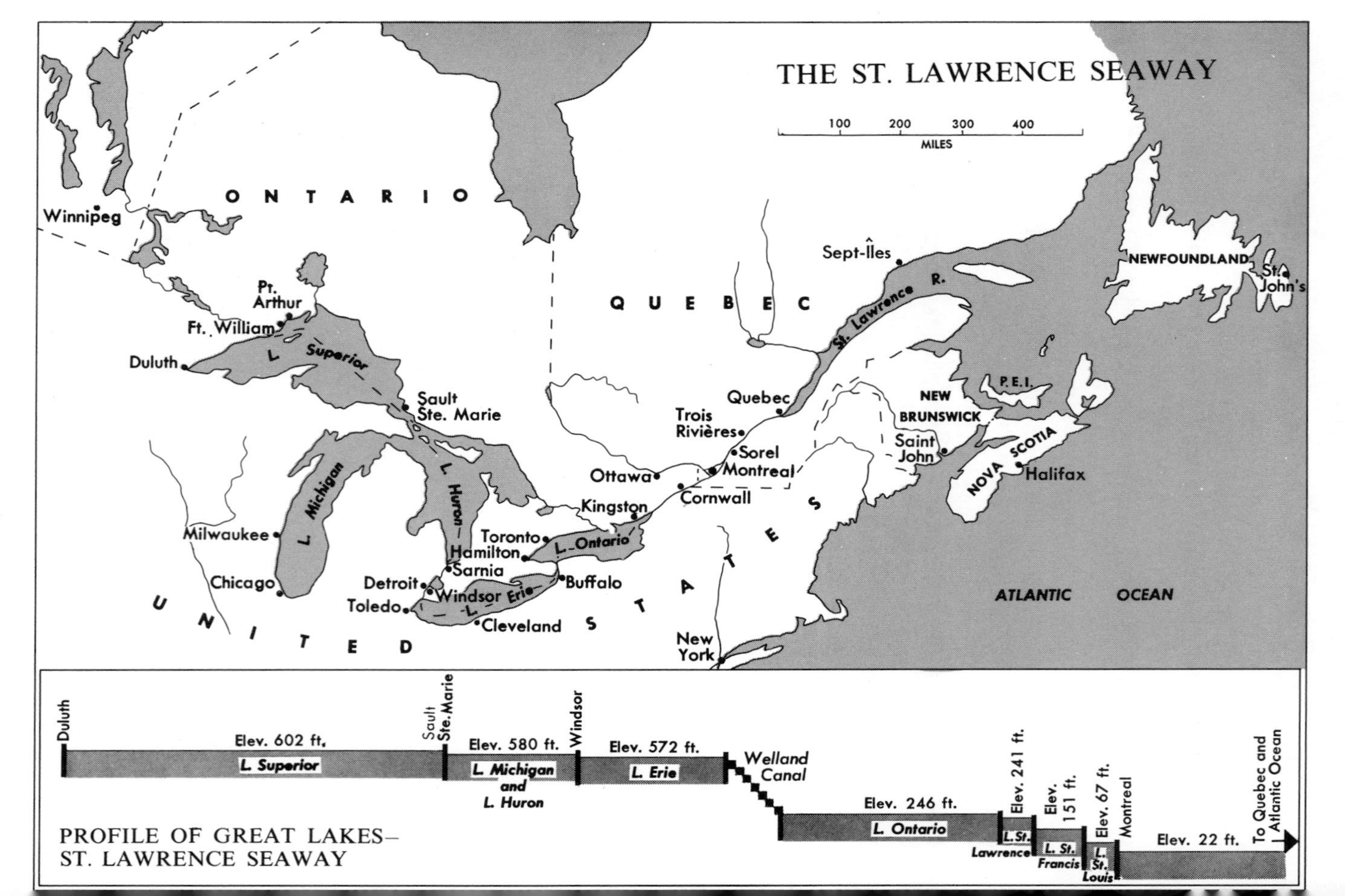
THE ST. LAWRENCE SEAWAY
100
200
300
400
MILES
ONTARIO
QUEBEC
UNITED STATES
Winnipeg
Pt. Arthur
Ft. William
Duluth
L. Superior
Sault Ste. Marie
L. Michigan
L. Huron
Milwaukee
Chicago
Detroit
Windsor
Toledo
L. Erie
Cleveland
Sarnia
Hamilton
Toronto
L. Ontario
Buffalo
Kingston
Ottawa
Cornwall
Montreal
Sorel
Trois Rivières
Quebec
St. Lawrence R.
Sept-Îles
New York
NEW BRUNSWICK
Saint John
P.E.I.
NOVA SCOTIA
Halifax
NEWFOUNDLAND
St. John's
ATLANTIC OCEAN
PROFILE OF GREAT LAKES—ST. LAWRENCE SEAWAY
Duluth
Elev. 602 ft.
L. Superior
Sault Ste. Marie
Elev. 580 ft.
L. Michigan and L. Huron
Windsor
Elev. 572 ft.
L. Erie
Welland Canal
Elev. 246 ft.
L. Ontario
Elev. 241 ft.
L. St. Lawrence
Elev. 151 ft.
L. St. Francis
Elev. 67 ft.
L. St. Louis
Montreal
Elev. 22 ft.
To Quebec and Atlantic Ocean

Act, passed by Congress in 1953, authorized United States' co-operation, provided the canal by-passing the International Rapids section was constructed on the American side of the river. Somewhat reluctantly, Canada accepted this last-minute participation but specified that she must have freedom in the future to construct parallel canals on the Canadian shore if the traffic warranted. An agreement embodying these terms was signed in 1954 and work began, Canada undertaking the larger share of the construction.

The Seaway was formally opened in 1959, and in its first year of operation handled over 30,000,000 tons of cargo, a gain of almost 10,000,000 tons over the last year of the old canals. Seven years later the Seaway was handling 49,000,000 tons of iron ore, grain, coal, scrap iron, steel and oil. It was expected that by 1980 the Seaway would be providing transportation for 75,000,000 tons of cargo moving between the United States and Canada and out to the nations of the world. The Seaway, and the ships which use it, are the practical manifestations of the strong commercial ties that bind the Canadian and United States' economies together.

THE POLITICS OF POSTWAR CANADA

Mackenzie King, whose whole energies had been devoted to leading Canada through the stresses and strains of World War II, fought his last election campaign in 1945. His government was given a comfortable majority, but King was ageing and did not feel able to cope with the complex questions arising from Canada's transition from war to peace. He had already chosen his successor, Louis St. Laurent. St. Laurent was a capable colleague who had done much to promote French-Canadian confidence in the King government. He was appointed Secretary of State for External Affairs in 1946, and he was elected Liberal leader in the summer of 1948. A few months later he succeeded King as prime minister.

Mackenzie King was not spared many years of retirement. He had intended to spend his leisure in writing his memoirs, but at

Mackenzie King at the National Liberal Convention, Ottawa, August 7, 1948, the last such convention he attended. King was a complex, some might say pathetic, personality. The victim of a mother-complex and the adherent of a private, mystical cult through which he attempted to communicate with the dead, he was plagued by loneliness and insecurity. Few Canadians knew anything about the private life of the man with whom they entrusted the leadership of government for over two decades; most were surprised and puzzled when some of the details became known after his death.

the time of his death he was still arranging the vast collection of papers he had accumulated. He died on 22 July, 1950, at his summer home in the Gatineau Hills near Ottawa. King's death marked the passing of an era, for he had dominated Canadian political life since the early twenties. His first achievement had been to rehabilitate the Liberal party after the disruptive strife of 1917 between English and French Canada and to make it again a national party. This he had done through times of social unrest, through years of international turmoil and through the demanding years of World War II. It was not in King's nature to be a bold or inspiring leader. Yet he possessed an approach that was far more appropriate for his country than decisive leadership: a profound. instinctive understanding of the wishes of a multi-racial Canada. He knew how far he could move in one direction to please one group without offending others. He knew the anxieties of the Canadian people in a world menaced by depression and war, and he understood their often inarticulate faith in an independent identity. He relied on their willingness to accept compromise as a way of life. If politics is the art of the possible, then Mackenzie King was a master politician.

If King resembled Macdonald in many of his characteristics, St. Laurent was more akin to Cartier. He possessed the confidence of French Canada to a unique degree, and he understood the national problems of Canada. His bilingualism, combined with a warm Gallic charm, brought him a popular following. St. Laurent was well regarded by members of all parties, although towards the end of his career many Canadians suspected that he was too much influenced by some members of his cabinet, C. D. Howe in particular. St. Laurent often gave the impression of being the amateur in politics, the successful lawyer who had wandered late in life into a new sphere of activity.

An event that had been anticipated ever since Confederation occurred soon after St. Laurent's succession to office—Newfoundland was admitted as the tenth province of Canada.

First claimed for England in 1583, Newfoundland attracted over the centuries a number of inhabitants engaged in the fisheries. The development of mining and newsprint industries in the twentieth century broadened Newfoundland's economy and provided a slightly improved living for its people. The world depression of the 1930's destroyed the basis of this economy, and Newfoundland had to surrender self-government in 1934 and accept British administration and assistance, a humiliating

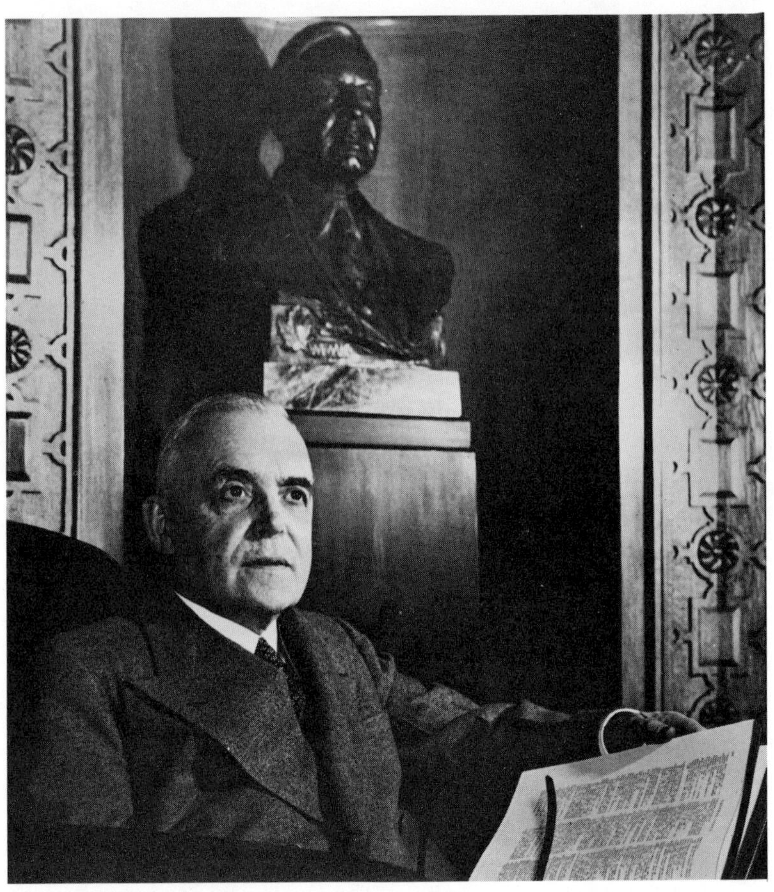

Louis St. Laurent, Mackenzie King's successor as Prime Minister, attracted wide personal popularity among Canadians. For his gracious and friendly manner, he was often affectionately referred to as "Uncle Louis."

step for a community that had gained responsible government in 1855 and dominion status just after World War I.

World War II, with its demands for pulp, paper, minerals and fish, made life much easier in Newfoundland. It also emphasized the strategic importance of the island, lying as it does alongside North Atlantic shipping lanes. At the end of the war, Newfoundland was faced with a difficult decision: should she continue under commission government, should she become once more a separate self-governing member of the Commonwealth; or should she apply for admission to Canada? A national convention was held to debate the issue. A former organizer of a fisherman's union, later a radio personality, Joseph R. Smallwood emerged in the convention as the leading advocate of union with Canada. The convention failed to recommend this course, but Britain decided that the issue should be carried to the people in a referendum. "Joey" Smallwood, confident of his power to persuade the electorate, applauded this decision. The referendum on Newfoundland's future was held in June, 1948. Again, federation with Canada emerged as the electors' second choice. However, since responsible government did not gain a clear majority, a second vote was held in July. This time, 52 percent of the electorate voted to join Canada.

The majority for Confederation was narrow, but both Great Britain and Canada felt it was definite enough. Negotiations for union took place in Ottawa in the autumn of 1948, and the arrangement was effected on 31 March, 1949. The next day Joseph R. Smallwood was appointed premier. By the terms of union Newfoundland received the same financial subsidies as the older Canadian provinces, as well as additional assistance because of her unstable economy and low standard of public services. The federal government took over the island's public debt and the operation of the Newfoundland Railway. Newfoundlanders had to accept the higher Canadian tariff, but their government was provided with special transitional grants while it adjusted to provincial status.

The Liberals, who played such a prominent role in defining Canada's sovereignty between the wars, continued the process after 1945. Several important constitutional steps were taken. (Two changes were made at this time in the terminology of the Commonwealth. The adjective "British" was informally dropped, together with the use of the word "Dominion"*, which had long been objectionable to French Canadians, since to them it connoted subordination.) In 1947 new Letters Patent were issued

*Strictly speaking, the phrase "Dominion of Canada" has never been Canada's formal name, the British North America Act simply stating in its preamble that "there shall be one Dominion, to be known as Canada."

for the governor general of Canada, giving him authority to exercise all the prerogative powers of the Sovereign in respect of Canada. This meant that the highest acts of state (for example, the ratification of treaties) could be authorized by the governor general without the formal approval of the monarch. A long-standing judicial limitation on Canada's constitutional position was removed in 1949 when it was decided to abolish appeals to the Judicial Committee of the Privy Council in London. This step had been projected as far back as 1875 but had proved impossible to accomplish because of legal obstacles and the unwillingness of certain provinces to surrender their right of appeal to this court. In the immediate post-war period, the continuance of appeals to the Privy Council came to be regarded as "a badge of colonialism." With the abolition of the appeal in 1949, the nine justices of the Supreme Court of Canada became the ultimate interpreters of the Canadian constitution.

There was one last matter to be settled before Canada's constitutional autonomy would be complete—amendments to the BNA Act, which, as a British statute, could only be changed by the Westminster parliament. There was no question of Britain's refusing to acquiesce in a transfer of such power to Canada, but rather an inability existed on Canada's part to determine how amendments should be made. A satisfactory amending procedure would have to safeguard provincial and minority rights, and at the same time give the Canadian constitution enough flexibility to meet changing economic and social conditions. A first step in meeting the problem was taken in 1949 when the Canadian parliament obtained the power to amend the BNA Act in purely federal matters. But a procedure for amending the constitution in other fields, some of which are shared by the federal government and the provinces, was impossible to obtain. Some provinces, notably in the prairies and in the Maritimes, did not want to see many sections of the constitution placed in a category where they could only be changed with the unanimous approval of all the provinces and the federal government. This, they felt, would enclose the constitution in a strait-jacket and prevent the federal government from exercising leadership, especially in economic affairs. Other provinces were suspicious of federal action in some of the shared fields and wished to retain provincial control over amendments in these areas. Quebec's desire for a "special status" also created difficulties, as did her claim to speak for persons of the French language living outside Quebec. There were many conferences on the subject following 1949 but no consensus emerged. Instead, it appeared that day-to-day administrative and legislative decisions made by all the governments would determine the shape of the federal system in Canada. Only as a new pattern emerged would it then be possible to devise an amending procedure that reflected the realities of the situation.

St. Laurent led his party to victory in the elections of 1949 and 1953. By the time the election of 1957 approached, the length of their hold on office (since 1935) had become a source of weakness to the Liberals. Ministers who had been in power so long appeared to display arrogance in the Commons. Twelve years after World War II, the government seemed to retain more than a trace of the peremptory manner that had been acquired when it possessed the extraordinary powers necessary during a war. This manner was highlighted in the acrimonious "pipeline debate" of 1956. The St. Laurent government had authorized the construction of a natural gas pipeline from Alberta to eastern Canada, part of it to be built at government expense. American financial interests in the pipeline company aroused misgivings among the opposition parties. The government took the view that its plan was the only feasible way to construct an expensive transcontinental pipeline. Consequently, it refused to meet any opposition suggestions regarding the bill. When the opposition persisted in its criticisms, the government abruptly employed closure, (a procedural device to end debate in parliament) and the bill became law. This method of forcing the bill's passage, however, severely damaged the reputation of the St. Laurent ministry.

The Conservatives vigorously exploited the government's failing popularity. After a succession of ineffectual leaders, a Saskatchewan lawyer, John G. Diefenbaker, was elected to head the party in 1956. Known for his concern for civil rights, Diefenbaker attacked the Liberal ministry time and again in parlia-

These photographs of John Diefenbaker were taken in the course of a brief visit he made with some newsmen to his original family homestead in Saskatchewan. Diefenbaker was intensely proud of his German origin and conscious that he represented that large group of Canadians who were of neither British nor French origin. He was also proud of his family's days as homesteaders in Saskatchewan. Both these factors contributed greatly to his political views.

ment. Above all, Diefenbaker reiterated that the Liberals had been too long in power and had lost touch with the people. The Conservatives toppled the Liberal government in the general election of June, 1957, 112 Conservative candidates being elected to 105 Liberals. John Diefenbaker, who had sat in parliament since 1940, became prime minister.

St. Laurent retired as Liberal leader, and the party chose as his successor Lester B. Pearson, who was nationally known for his work in external affairs. To Pearson fell the task of guiding a shattered Liberal party in the new election that Diefenbaker called for March, 1958. Confident of mounting popularity,

Diefenbaker promised measures that would secure greater Canadian control of the country's natural resources and lessen Canada's economic dependence upon the United States. This program, delivered with a fervent emotionalism, touched the deepest springs of the Canadian consciousness—the will for a separate identity in North America. The result of the 1958 election was a landslide for the Conservatives. The party carried every province except Newfoundland, and won 208 seats, for the largest majority won by any party since Confederation. The Liberals elected only 49 members, the C.C.F., 8. As a federal party Social Credit was completely eliminated. For the first time since the days of Macdonald, the Conservatives dominated Quebec, winning 50 of its 75 seats.

Over the next four years the Diefenbaker government carried out an extensive legislative program. Much of the Conservative legislation was directed to the prime task of maintaining Canada's growth. The need for greater co-operation between management and labour was recognized in the establishment of a National Productivity Council. The effects of a changing economy in reducing employment opportunities for semi-skilled and unskilled workers brought large federal grants to assist technical and vocational training throughout Canada. A great irrigation and power project on the South Saskatchewan River was begun. In the field of radio and television the government set up a new regulatory body, the Board of Broadcast Governors, to supervise the activities of private stations and of the Canadian Broadcasting Corporation. Indians were given voting rights equal to those of other Canadians. Perhaps the accomplishment in which the new Prime Minister took most pride, however, was the Canadian Bill of Rights, enacted by parliament in 1960. Such a measure, to protect freedom of religion, speech and association, had long been urged by Diefenbaker while he was a private member. Unfortunately, the Bill of Rights is not "entrenched" in the constitution; that is, it is only an act of the federal parliament and can, therefore, be changed or repealed in the same manner as any other act of parliament.

The Diefenbaker government suffered a serious check in the election of 1962, a check that had not been unexpected, for there were signs that the Prime Minister's personal popularity, upon which so much of the party's success since 1957 had been based, was steadily waning. In addition, an economic recession, which began about the time the Conservatives first came to power, inevitably reflected against the government.

There were other, less predictable factors that influenced the outcome of the 1962 election. One was the unsettled state of Quebec politics. Maurice Duplessis, after eighteen years of almost dictatorial rule in Quebec, died in September, 1959. His death released a torrent of new forces and ideas in *la belle province.* There were demands for greater French-Canadian control of Quebec's resources, for more industry and more investment. There was devastating criticism of an educational system that paid little attention to scientific studies and business training. The church's traditional role in education was seriously questioned.

Above all, there was the insistent claim that the "French fact" had to be recognized throughout the whole of Canada and not just in Quebec. A French-speaking Canadian, it was argued, should be able to feel at home in every part of his country. He should be able to carry on dealings with the government or the courts in his own language and his children should be able to receive an education in their mother tongue. There were even those in Quebec who wanted the association with the rest of Canada discontinued, since, they claimed, it had only led to the dominance of the English-speaking minority in the province. Moreover, they feared for the long-term survival of French-Canadian culture and felt it could only be maintained by an independent Quebec.

In the first election after Duplessis' death, in 1960, the reactionary *Union Nationale* party was toppled from power, and a Liberal administration under Jean Lesage was installed. His government provided leadership for the forces of change and in 1962 was given a triumphant vote of confidence when it promised to make Quebecois, "*maitres chez nous.*" In the 1962 federal election the "renaissance of Quebec" resulted in 35 Liberals being elected from the province, as compared with only 14 Conservatives.

The emergence of a Social Credit group from Quebec (known popularly as the *Créditistes* to distinguish them from the western members of the party) was another new force in the 1962 federal election. Under the flamboyant leadership of Réal Caouette, the *Créditistes* captured 30 seats, mostly in the poorer farming and mining areas of eastern and northern Quebec.

In 1962 the Conservatives also felt the force of a new party, the successor to the C.C.F. For years there had been a feeling in socialist circles that it was time to construct a new party, more broadly based than the C.C.F. and with a wider appeal. A new party would also avoid the stigma of defeat that seemed to cling to the C.C.F. This feeling led to a 1961 Ottawa convention at which the C.C.F. and the Canadian Labour Congress decided to launch a new party. The proposal generated tremendous excitement among delegates, especially when Premier T. C. Douglas of Saskatchewan agreed to resign office to accept the leadership of the new party. "Tommy" Douglas, a forceful, witty platform orator, possessed the considerable reputation of having led the first socialist government in North America for the first seventeen years of its existence. After some discussion, the successor to the C.C.F. called itself the "New Democratic Party," hoping with this name to win the support of the same elements that backed the Democratic Party in the United States. The N.D.P. won 19 seats in the 1962 election (compared with the 8 won by the C.C.F. in 1958). Its voting strength was drawn mainly from industrial and mining constituencies in Ontario and British Columbia.

The Liberal opposition also made heavy inroads upon the government's parliamentary majority. Indeed, the Liberals more than doubled their standing in the Commons, winning 99 seats. Conservative strength was cut to 116 seats in a House of 265, and John Diefenbaker found himself "in office but not in power." Bolstered by Social Credit votes in the Commons and faced by a divided opposition, the Diefenbaker government survived several votes of confidence, yet it appeared curiously unwilling to deal with the pressing issues of the early 1960's—defence, economic growth and foreign affairs.

It was nuclear weapons that proved to be the nemesis of the

Conservative administration. In 1957, shortly after it had come to power, the Diefenbaker cabinet had come to an agreement with the United States to establish bases for fifty-six Bomarc missiles in Canada. These missiles required nuclear warheads to be effective, but the decision to install them was delayed. One group in the cabinet feared that the acquisition of nuclear weapons would hurt Canada's efforts to promote disarmament and to secure a ban on nuclear tests. The Prime Minister, beset by pro-nuclear and anti-nuclear factions in his cabinet, could not reach a decision. Late in 1962 the United States government lost patience and sharply criticized Canada for not having lived up to its obligations in the joint air defence of North America. This brought the crisis into the open and touched off a revolt within the cabinet. The Minister of National Defence, Douglas Harkness, resigned over the government's failure to arm the Bomarcs; a group of ministers attempted to unseat John Diefenbaker and, when the move failed, some left the cabinet themselves. The Prime Minister appealed to the Conservative caucus for support and won endorsement, but he could not count on the support of parliament. In February, 1963, the Diefenbaker government was defeated in the Commons and forced to call an election. In April it was defeated at the polls.

The Liberals won 129 seats in the ensuing election, securing broad support from the major urban centres across the country. Ninety-five Conservatives were elected, mostly from the prairies and the rural parts of western Ontario. The *Créditistes* did well in Quebec and the N.D.P. managed to hold their own. Diefenbaker left office and Lester Pearson, at the head of a minority government, became the fourteenth prime minister of Canada on 22 April.

Pearson selected a cabinet that included a strong group of former professors and civil servants, and immediately embarked on an ambitious legislative program. A principal aim of the new government was to conciliate French Canadians, and to remove the factors that had led them to feel they constituted a minority permanently opposed to the rest of the country. A royal commission was appointed to examine the way in which the principles of bilingualism and biculturalism operated in Canada. At the same time, the government proposed a new flag for Canada, a distinctive maple leaf design. It was hoped that this flag would win the allegiance of all Canadians. French Canadians favoured the new flag but many people of British origin were unhappy over the abandonment of the Red Ensign. The flag issue created a long debate which the government terminated by using the notorious closure procedure. Along with the new flag, the Union Jack was recognized as the symbol of Canada's membership in the Commonwealth. The maple leaf flag was flown for the first time on Parliament Hill in February, 1965, and it soon won acceptance across Canada as an honoured national symbol.

The Pearson government pushed forward reforms in many fields. The Canada Pension Plan, in conjunction with the Quebec Pension Plan, established a national contributory old age pension scheme. A comprehensive medical insurance plan was also set up. A war on persistent poverty was declared, and the government established the Company of Young Canadians to work with such groups as Indians, slum dwellers and the rural poor. Volunteers sent out by the Company attempted to assist these people to help themselves and to gain self-respect. These measures owed much to the reforming philosophy of the late President John F. Kennedy in the United States. Changes were also made in federal-provincial financial agreements to give the provinces a greater share of tax revenues in order to support their expanding responsibilities. Another measure of long-term significance was a new redistribution act, designed to create constituencies of a more uniform size (about 70,000 people). The new ridings, established by impartial commissions free from political influence, corrected the wide divergence that had previously existed among federal constituencies. The effect of the new act was to give a greater proportion of seats to urban areas. In the field of defence, nuclear warheads were installed on the Canadian missiles on the last day of 1963. The government also moved to integrate the command structure of the three branches of the Canadian armed forces. This step was followed by the unification of the forces, a development the government

Following the Liberal defeat of 1957, Lester B. Pearson succeeded Louis St. Laurent as party leader. Faced with the task of rebuilding a shattered party, he surrounded himself with a remarkably talented group of men, many of whom had hitherto been senior civil servants and prominent businessmen. However, he was never able to attract unqualified support among the voters, even though he was admired for his personal integrity.

claimed would improve Canada's peace-keeping capacity and create a more effective fighting organization.

In a effort to secure a clear majority in parliament, the Pearson administration went to the country on 8 November, 1965. In the election the Liberals added only four seats to the 127 they had had at dissolution, the Conservatives picked up five to hold 97 places, and the N.D.P. also made gains to stand at 21. The Social Credit party and the *Créditistes* lost ground. Significantly, the election revealed that Liberal strength lay in central Canada, while the Conservatives found their strongest base in the prairie provinces.

Though still unable to command an absolute majority of seats in the House of Commons (at least 133 seats), the Pearson government gained in confidence as Canada celebrated her

Centennial Year. The overwhelming success of Expo '67 at Montreal, the genuine enthusiasm and enjoyment shown by all Canadians in the Centennial celebrations, and the Prime Minister's personal success in playing the role of an informal and affable host to the many official Centennial visitors from abroad, helped generate the government's new attitude and a generally improved image across the country.

At the same time, the Conservative Opposition was persistently weakened by an internal controversy over the leadership of John Diefenbaker. "The Chief" fought tenaciously to retain his office, but in September, 1967, a leadership convention was held and Robert Stanfield, Premier of Nova Scotia, was elected the new national leader of the Conservative party. Thus Centennial Year brought renewed vitality to both of Canada's major parties.

In January of 1968 Prime Minister Pearson announced his intention to resign and requested his party to call a leadership convention to choose his successor. The convention held during April chose Pierre Elliott Trudeau as leader of the Liberal party. Several days later Pearson officially resigned and the Governor General called on Trudeau to become Canada's fifteenth Prime Minister.

On 25 June a general election was held, resulting in the Liberals winning a majority of forty-five seats over all the other parties in the Commons, the first time that this situation had occurred in a decade. The Liberals won 155 seats to the Conservatives' 72. The result was largely due to the tremendous popular impact made across Canada by the new Liberal leader. Not yet fifty when he became prime minister, Trudeau was an articulate, former law professor from Montreal, with a particular appeal to young people and the urban middle class. He had been an outspoken critic of Duplessis, urging educational and electoral reforms for Quebec, and had taken a prominent stand against both separatism and a "special status" for Quebec. There was a widespread belief that his assumption of the prime minister's office would bring a fresh "swinging" spirit into Canadian politics. The test lay ahead, however, when, in the cruel glare of public life, his achievements were to be measured

In 1967/68 both major federal parties elected new leaders. The Conservatives chose the capable but rather austere Premier of Nova Scotia, Robert Stanfield (left). The new Liberal leader was Pierre Elliott Trudeau, a wealthy bachelor and former university professor from Montreal.

against the expectations that his magnetic personality had aroused.

* * *

Canada's new strength as an advanced industrial country of 20,000,000 people was accompanied by a new role in international affairs. The Second World War swept Canada out of the quiet waters of North American isolation and placed her in the full current of world politics. The postwar years saw Canada emerge as one of the leaders of the "middle powers," vitally concerned with defining a function that would not simply be that of a follower of the great powers. The efforts Canada made in this direction after 1945 constituted some of the most exciting features of her postwar history. They revealed a sense of maturity and purpose among the Canadian people never exhibited before in facing events beyond the borders of the country.

CHAPTER 19

CANADA AND THE WORLD

The storm of World War II and the harsh reality of the postwar ideological struggle between East and West shattered all the old illusions of Canadian foreign policy. Her North American position no longer offered shelter to Canada and the "fireproof house" of the inter-war years had disappeared with the coming of long-range aircraft and intercontinental missiles. The recognition of these facts made Canadians realize that they could not remain aloof from international affairs.

An indication of the new circumstances in world politics came shortly after the end of the war. On the night of 5 September, 1945, a Russian cipher clerk, Igor Gouzenko, quietly slipped out of the Soviet embassy in Ottawa and went to the R.C.M.P., carrying with him information of a Soviet spy ring in Canada. Investigation revealed that a Soviet military attaché in Ottawa was collecting confidential information from a group of Canadians, including scientists, a member of parliament, an army officer and civil servants. Eventually, eighteen persons were brought to trial, of whom eight were convicted of espionage.

The Gouzenko affair shocked Canadians, not only because it revealed that fellow countrymen had betrayed military and state secrets, but because it demonstrated in dramatic fashion that the Soviet Union, a wartime ally, was already waging a cold war. In a curious way the Gouzenko case brought home to Canadians what was to be the most striking feature of the world after 1945—the new interdependence of nations. The Soviet agents in Canada were part of a spy network that extended to other countries. Information obtained in Canada might not only impair Canada's ability to defend herself, but might also damage the security of the United States or Great Britain. Espionage was merely one example of the many links that bound countries together in common circumstances in the postwar world.

CANADA AND THE UNITED NATIONS

After 1945 Canada threw herself into international affairs in a way she had never done before. Her main purpose was to gain security for herself and for other nations through collective action. The League of Nations had attempted to accomplish this objective but it had collapsed because of the failure of the peace-loving countries to give it their support. Canada herself bore a share of responsibility for the inability of the League to rally its members to stop aggression. The Second World War, on the other hand, demonstrated that collective action could produce results. The coalition of countries that had won the war turned itself into the United Nations, dedicated to the proposition that international peace could only come through the establishment of a collective security system. Canada joined the United Nations in 1945, not because of the status that membership afforded, but because she believed in the aims of the organization and was prepared to support them. "The Canadian people," said St. Laurent, "wish Canada to be a part of the international organization and to do whatever may be required in order to be a full partner in it." As a "middle power" (a country of moderate size, strength and influence) Canada felt that she might best serve in those areas—technical, economic and social—in which she possessed knowledge or experience. When Canada was elected to the U.N. Security Council in 1947, she recognized that she was taking on responsibility for situations occurring far from her shores. Yet these situations might prove vital to Canada, for, in the age of nuclear weapons, they inevitably affected the security and welfare of all countries. Local conflicts could easily explode into general wars, and economic instability all too often threatened peace.

The men who typified Canada's new attitudes in foreign policy were Louis St. Laurent, who presided over the Department of External Affairs when it was first separated from the office of the Prime Minister in 1946, and his successor, Lester B. Pearson, a career diplomat who rose to become Under-Secretary and later Secretary of State for External Affairs. Both men were moved by liberal, internationalist feelings restrained by a shrewd consciousness of what was practicable. Under St. Laurent and Pearson Canada took useful initiatives in diplomacy that gave substance to the role of a middle power.

The concept of collective security depended upon the willingness of the nations involved to use force to punish an offender. Canada, as a member of the United Nations, accepted this course of action in 1950, when the communist government of North Korea launched an invasion of Western-oriented South Korea. The United Nations General Assembly branded the move an act of aggression, and the Security Council called upon United Nations members to aid South Korea. Canada responded without hesitation. She sent an infantry brigade and artillery units (about 22,000 men) to Korea, along with destroyers and fighter and transport aircraft. From late in 1950 until the armistice in 1953, and for almost two years during the uneasy truce that followed the armistice, Canadian forces remained in Korea, taking part in some of the heaviest fighting of a gruelling war. Canada's participation in this first test of collective security in the postwar world revealed dramatically the revolution that had occurred in her foreign policy. It also showed the seriousness with which the country regarded its responsibilities under the United Nations Charter.

The United Nations, in spite of its weaknesses, was Canada's chief hope for securing international stability. On many occasions in the postwar years Canada's position as a middle power allowed her to carry out activities that would have been impossible for a great power or beyond the capacity of a small power. This was particularly true of situations in which feelings of anti-colonialism were present. Canada was not an imperial power;

she was, in fact, a country that had peacefully thrown off imperial control and then remained on friendly terms with the mother country. Thus her participation in international affairs was acceptable both to young nations struggling for freedom and to the colonial powers of western Europe. During the postwar period Canada served on a number of international commissions attempting to solve troublesome disputes. Her soldiers, airmen, communications personnel, observers and diplomats were sent to such scattered points of tension as Kashmir (1949 to present); Palestine and later Israel (1954 to present); Southeast Asia [Vietnam, Laos and Cambodia] (1954 to present); Lebanon (1958/59); the Congo (1960-1964); West New Guinea (1962/63); the Yemen (1963/64); Cyprus (1964 to present); and the India and Pakistan clash over the Rann of Kutch (1965/66). Few of the disputes in these areas were permanently settled, but the presence of outside observers undoubtedly helped on occasion to reduce open hostilities and thus to gain time for efforts directed towards a lasting solution.

"Peace keeping," as this function became known, reached a critical point in 1956, at the time of the Suez crisis. The brief war between Israel and Egypt, which led to an Anglo-French invasion of Egypt, was a severe test for international diplomacy. World opinion was shaken by the resort to arms of two respected powers. For Canada the episode was especially painful: it disclosed a serious divergence of opinion between the United States and Britain. It also gravely disturbed the Commonwealth, whose Asian and African members condemned outright the British intervention. In a rare gesture, Canada abstained from voting on the United States' motion condemning the Franco-British action in Egypt. Lester Pearson, however, presented the General Assembly with a proposal for a "United Nations Emergency Force" (U.N.E.F.). This force was to attempt to bring about a ceasefire in Egypt, and then to remain in the Middle East to patrol the troubled borders between Israel and the Arab States. The General Assembly ratified the plan, and Great Britain and France accepted it as a way of retreating from a situation that had become intolerable. A 6,000-man multinational force was called into being, financed by contributions from United Nations members. A Canadian, Major-General E. L. M. Burns, was appointed first commander of the force. U.N.E.F. remained in existence in the disputed Sinai peninsula, safeguarding a precarious peace in the Middle East until 1967, when it was obliged to withdraw at the insistence of Egypt.

Too many expectations should not be raised by the modest success of peace keeping. Indeed, the limitations of peace keeping were dramatically revealed by the experience of the U.N.E.F. The United Nations force had carried out its work since 1956 on the Egyptian side of the frontier only, as Israel had refused to give consent for the force to patrol on the Israeli side. Furthermore, Egypt took the view that the continued presence of the force on her territory was dependent upon her approval. When Egypt demanded the withdrawal of U.N.E.F. in May, 1967, the UN authorities felt they had no alternative but to comply. The force withdrew and within a month the six-day war broke out between Israel and her Arab neighbours.

It is clear, then, that peace keeping cannot by itself "settle" *international disputes*. At best it can bring some stability to a trouble zone and provide the breathing spell that *may* allow both diplomacy and the healing effects of time to bring about a permanent settlement. The effectiveness of peace keeping is also limited because it cannot be applied to a dispute in which either the United States or the Soviet Union is involved or has strong feelings. It is also costly, requiring the maintenance of expensive military formations for long periods. Indeed, it has imposed a severe financial strain upon the United Nations, since several important member countries have been unwilling to bear their share of the costs. Finally, it has been impossible so far to persuade the major powers that the United Nations should be given a permanent peace keeping force that could be sent immediately to any trouble spot.

THE NECESSITY OF SELF-DEFENCE

In spite of a deep preference for a peaceful world order, based on habits of reason and compromise, Canadians recognized that force was still very much a factor in international affairs. Thus

Canada maintained a much larger defence establishment after World War II than ever before in her peacetime history. After the Korean War the size of the Canadian armed forces remained at about 115,000 men, organized in the three conventional divisions of navy, army and air force. The cost of this establishment steadily climbed as weapons became more complicated and expensive. By the mid-sixties national defence was costing Canada over $1.5 billions a year or 20 percent of the national budget.

The Liberal government after 1963 determined to obtain more value from this expenditure as well as to improve the efficiency of Canada's fighting forces. The first step in the program was to integrate the headquarters of the three services under a single chief of defence staff. Stage two involved the consolidation of eleven commands across the country into six. These were organized on the basis of function: for example, mobile, maritime, air defence, air transport. The final step was to create a single defence force for Canada. Through unification, the size of the armed forces was to be reduced, providing a financial saving that would permit the purchase of better weapons and equipment. In achieving the unification of her armed forces Canada led the way among the countries of the Western alliance.

Canada's principal defence arrangements during the period were associated with two regional groupings—NATO and NORAD. The establishment of NATO owed much to the initiative of Louis St. Laurent, who, while leading the Canadian delegation at the United Nations, became increasingly frustrated by Soviet Russia's obstructionism. Because of the Soviet use of the veto, St. Laurent protested, the Security Council had become "frozen in futility and divided by dissension." The extension of Russian control over much of eastern and central Europe immediately after the war, and the threat of further aggression, led St. Laurent and others to propose an alliance in which like-minded nations would band together for mutual protection. The resulting North Atlantic Treaty was signed at Washington in April, 1949, and was unanimously approved by the Canadian parliament. The members of NATO promised to defend each other in the event of attack, to cooperate and consult on defence

Following World War II significant development took place in the Canadian aircraft industry, particular emphasis being placed on military requirements. Possibly the most advanced work of this kind took place at the Avro Aircraft company near Toronto, which produced the Arrow, a supersonic, all-weather interceptor. In February, 1959, less than a year after the Arrow's first flight, the government cancelled the project, stating that it was too costly for the value. The most unfortunate effect of the cancellation was the dispersal of the extraordinary team of research and engineering personnel who had participated in the project. Several of these men eventually held key positions in the United States space programme.

policy and to assist each other in building up defence forces. The North American members, Canada and the United States, established defence forces in Europe. NATO emphasized that North America had a vital interest in the security of western Europe. The alliance, while it gave Canada explicit peacetime military commitments abroad for the first time in history, also reinforced traditional ties with her two mother countries, Britain and France.

From the first, Canada provided a NATO infantry brigade group (about 6,300 men) in Germany, as well as eight to twelve squadrons of jet aircraft stationed at NATO bases in France (until 1967) and Germany. In addition, a substantial part of Canada's naval force was assigned to NATO command.

For almost twenty years NATO helped to keep the peace in

western Europe. But in the late sixties there were many signs that the organization needed a new set of goals. The nuclear stalemate between the Soviet Union and the West had reduced the possibility of a third world war. An increasing number of contacts were developing across the "iron curtain," indicating a new era of greater cooperation and less hostility between Eastern and Western Europe. The United States' refusal to share control of atomic weapons had angered some of the NATO allies, especially France, who decided in 1966 to reduce her participation in the organization. At the same time the Communist countries of the Warsaw Pact (the "iron curtain" counterpart and response to NATO) also appeared to be following more independent policies.

In spite of these developments Canada continued to view NATO as a pillar of her defensive strength. She sought to re-define her military role within NATO, bearing in mind that it was becoming more and more unlikely that massive nuclear attack (using weapons four times as powerful as the bombs dropped in 1945 on Japan) would ever take place in Europe. It was precisely because the alliance of fifteen states had done its work so well in the past that its continued existence was now questioned. But the Canadian government felt that conditions were not yet stable enough to permit NATO to be dissolved. It was also unprepared to lose influence with the great powers by withdrawing from full participation in NATO. Thus the policy for Canada was plain: continue to support NATO and endeavour to make it as responsive as possible to changes in the military balance of power. There was another objective, as well. From the time of NATO's founding, Canadian leaders had advocated the strengthening of the non-military links between the members. Little had been accomplished in this direction, but Canada remained hopeful that economic and other benefits could be derived from the alliance if the members were to take advantage of NATO's potential.

The close military collaboration that Canada and the United States had worked out between 1940 and 1945 continued after the war. The Cold War and the threat from the U.S.S.R. made the defence of Canada more vital than ever to American security.

The partnership in arms that President Roosevelt and Prime Minister King inaugurated at Ogdensburg in 1940 was continued after 1945 under a reconstituted Permanent Joint Board on Defence. A continental defence system was brought into being. Combined military exercises were one feature of this defence collaboration; another was a network of weather stations and radar defence lines in the Canadian north. Further collaboration was achieved in 1958, when Canada and the United States created NORAD, a North American air defence system headed by an American air force general, with a senior Canadian officer as deputy. Canada's contribution to NORAD consisted of several squadrons of interceptor aircraft, 29 radar sites and two squadrons of Bomarc anti-aircraft missiles at North Bay, Ontario, and La Macaza, Quebec.

Defence policy was frequently a controversial issue among Canadians. It was obvious that in any war between the United States and Soviet Russia, Canada would lie in the direct path of attack. Thus, some Canadians felt that the defence of their country was impossible, and they became apathetic about it. Others felt that since the United States was the main object of Soviet hostility, it was unjust that Canada should be subjected to danger. They became irrationally and often violently anti-American, and opposed Canada's participation in continental defence arrangements. Canadian military men were less convinced than their American counterparts that Russia would ever launch an attack on North America. Similarly, the Canadian government did not see the Cold War in the same black and white terms as did many Americans. It was alert to the possibilities of accommodation and interested in pursuing measures that might strengthen the basis of co-existence. Canadians were often critical of American foreign policy, especially its attitudes toward Asian problems and movements of change in Latin America. There was also the nagging worry that the United States was not prepared to consult Canada in the big decisions of continental defence. The NORAD agreement specified that the fullest joint consultation should take place, but several episodes, most notably the Cuban missile crisis in October, 1962, demonstrated that the United States would act unilaterally in North

American defence when she felt her vital interests were threatened. This American attitude, understandable and inevitable as it may have been, did not make for easy Canadian-American co-operation in defence.

PEOPLE AND POVERTY

Probably a basic cause of unrest in modern times has been the inexorable pressure of a rising population upon the world's food supplies. Although it took many centuries for the earth's population to reach one billion, it took only one more century (1830-1930) for the figure to double and only thirty years again to add another billion people. It is now estimated that in a further forty years the present three billion population will double once more. While modern science, by eliminating disease and prolonging life, has created the phenomenal "population explosion," it also offers the only potential means of providing an expanding world population with the necessities of life in the modern age—food, industrial products, transportation and trade. Through sound economic progress, combined with family planning, conditions may be created that will stabilize population growth in the long run. These are the bare outlines of a problem that is almost too vast for human comprehension.

Overpopulation is much more than a social problem. It has important political and international consequences. As Lester Pearson once remarked:

> Rich nations are not necessarily more peace-loving than poorer nations. But poverty and distress . . . make the risks of war greater.

Poverty restricts literacy and retards the development of an educational system that can provide the leaders for a new country. Poverty can make a nation susceptible to the appeal of extremists and dictators; at the same time, poverty works against the establishment of stability and political freedom.

Poverty is the symbol of the widening gap between standards of living in the underdeveloped, traditional societies of the southern hemisphere and the rich, industrial nations of the north. Eighty percent of mankind has a per capita income of less than $500 a year; in Canada in 1964 the average income was $1825. The existence of this disparity in wealth makes it difficult for the West to establish friendly relations with the majority of the world's population in Asia and Africa. Everywhere the rich countries of the West are regarded with envy or suspicion, even when they are carrying out humanitarian activities in the poorer countries. A "revolution of rising expectations" has swept over the world since the end of World War II. Unfulfilled hopes among the developing nations of Asia, Africa and South America inevitably reflect upon the image of the West in these lands. The ominous element in the situation lies in the fact that the line between rich and poor is also, generally, the line between white and coloured. Thus the poverty of Asia and Africa aggravates the serious racial tensions of the modern world.

Faced with the tragic gap between the world's rich and its poor, the Western nations have recognized their inescapable responsibility to provide aid to underdeveloped countries. The attack on poverty has been launched with several weapons: economic aid, loans, technical assistance, refugee programs and educational services. The United Nations, together with the World Bank and the International Development Association, has channelled a great deal of capital into these activities. The Commonwealth has created its own program, the Colombo Plan, established in Ceylon in 1950 at the first Commonwealth conference ever to be held in Asia. Canada took a leading part in this scheme, making contributions during the first ten years of over $280 millions in cash, as well as gifts of wheat and flour.

Although Canada's program of external aid grew substantially in the sixties, the requests for assistance increased even more rapidly. By the mid-sixties the country was spending about $300 millions a year on foreign aid. This figure represented about $15 per Canadian, not an impressive contribution from the country with the second highest standard of living in the world. One percent of a country's gross national product is considered a desirable degree of foreign aid. Canada spent about one-half of one percent. Although this was a better rate of contribution than in

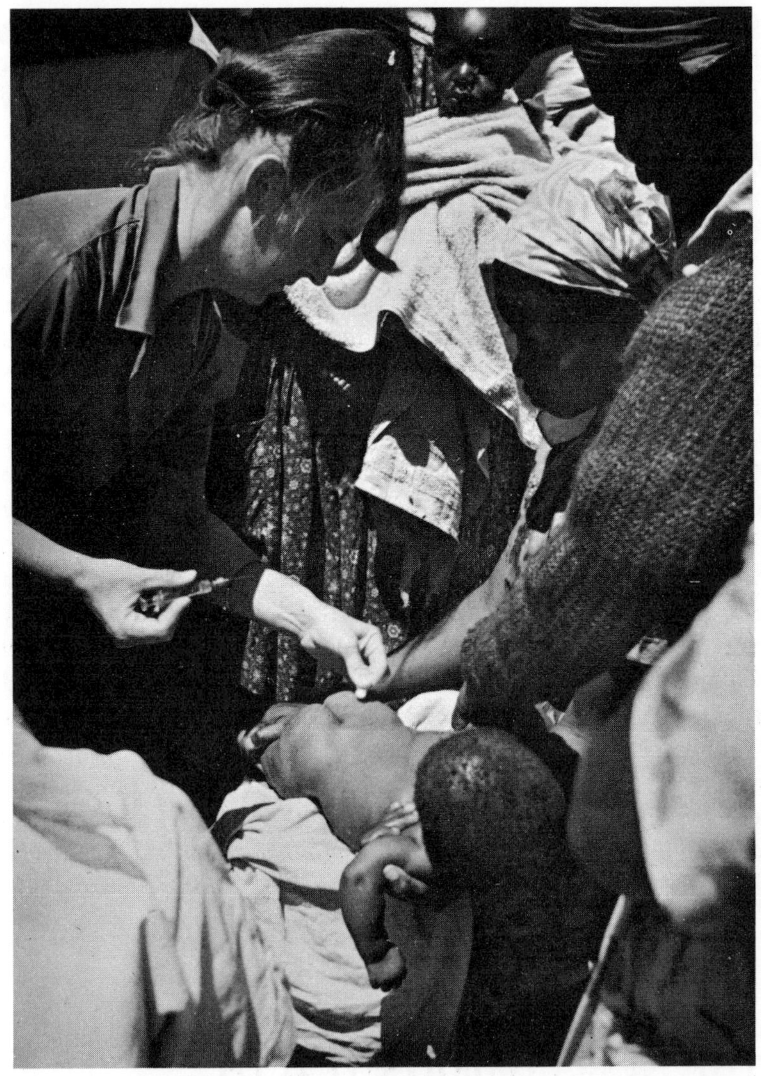

A tense moment. Jeanne d'Arc Grégroire worked as a nurse in Kenya under the auspices of C.U.S.O.

the past, it still did not represent the limit of Canada's capacity to provide help abroad.

Canada's assistance to underdeveloped states was co-ordinated by the External Aid Office in Ottawa, and took many forms. Some of it was for prestige projects, such as the Warsak hydro-electric power dam in the Khyber Pass in Pakistan, or for railways or cement plants. Much of it was for purposes of "self-help"—farm machinery, fertilizers, irrigation projects, pesticides, aircraft for crop spraying—gifts designed to increase agricultural output. Some of it was in wheat and flour for countries such as India, Indonesia, Ghana and South Vietnam.

Under the auspices of the federal government and private organizations such as Canadian University Service Overseas (C.U.S.O.), Canada supplied teachers, physicians, nurses, agricultural specialists, technicians and many other skilled persons to the underdeveloped countries. In 1965, for instance, there were approximately 1,700 Canadians serving abroad in programs. Canada also provided education and training to students from over one hundred foreign countries. In the mid-sixties there were 10,700 of these students studying in Canada, but less than half of them possessed scholarships or other assistance. There was a need for substantially increased aid in this form, especially for graduate and professional study, as a practical gesture of Canada's concern for less wealthy countries. The web of personal relationships thus created would enlarge the horizons of countless Canadians and win the goodwill of Africans and Asians who might later occupy positions of influence in their own countries. On an overcrowded planet in which the fate of all men is increasingly bound together, these intangible benefits of external aid offered hope for the future.

CANADA AND THE NEW COMMONWEALTH

The friendship of the nations composing the Commonwealth was memorably demonstrated in the ordeal of the Second World War. After the fall of France and before the Russian and American entries into the war, the Commonwealth stood virtually alone against Nazi Germany. But the experience of the common struggle did not persuade the members of the Commonwealth to turn their loose, informal organization into one stronger and more centralized. Mackenzie King led the majority of Commonwealth leaders in asserting the advantages of autonomy over the merits of a single voice in world affairs.

After 1945 the Commonwealth underwent dramatic changes. Great Britain, shorn of much of her strength and prestige by the war, suffered a loss of influence. By custom, she remained the senior member and still acted as host for Commonwealth conferences, but she no longer exercised leadership in the organization in the way she had between the wars. Even more striking was the entrance of Asian and African members into the Commonwealth, transforming it from a white man's "club" into a predominantly non-white institution. This process began in 1947, when India and Pakistan gained independence. India's wish to continue in the Commonwealth, as a republic, created an awkward constitutional problem. Mackenzie King, although ill in London during the 1949 meeting of prime ministers that considered this question, devised an arrangement that permitted India's continued membership. Henceforth, the British monarch was to be considered head of the Commonwealth, although not necessarily the head of state of all the member countries. After 1949 the Commonwealth expanded steadily as successive territories of the British Empire emerged from colonial status to independence. By 1966 the Commonwealth had become a multiracial association of twenty-three sovereign and independent states, having a total population of 750 million. Twenty years before, the Commonwealth had been an organization of six "white" countries; now there were nine nations from Africa, five from Asia and three from the West Indies. There were still six members of predominantly European population, for although Eire and South Africa had left, Cyprus and Malta had joined. However, Europeans accounted for only one out of every nine people in the Commonwealth.

Canada placed great store in the benefits of membership in the Commonwealth. She saw it as one of the few successful voluntary international organizations in the world's history. She also regarded it as a useful bridge between Europeans and non-Europeans, whites and non-whites, developed and underdeveloped countries. The Commonwealth represented a cross-section of the world's peoples, its leaders prepared to sit down together to discuss a variety of mutual problems. Knowing from domestic experience about the tensions that can develop between racial groups, Canada realized the imperative need to maintain an organization representing a cross-section of the world's peoples. The Commonwealth offered a means to harmonize conflicting attitudes, first through discussion, then through advice and service. Thus Canada worked very hard to preserve the unity of the Commonwealth, at such times as the Suez crisis and the Rhodesian independence crisis, when it seemed in danger of collapsing. Canada was also interested in using the Commonwealth as an instrument for encouraging economic progress among the poorer members and as a means of providing technical assistance. The Colombo Plan of 1950 was an early (and successful) initiative in these fields.

Canada played a major role in the momentous Commonwealth conference of March, 1961, at which South Africa applied to continue as a member of the Commonwealth after becoming a republic. Although unhappy with South Africa's *apartheid* (meaning roughly, "apart-hood") policy, which maintained racial segregation and white supremacy, the Canadian government, had previously adhered to the principle that the internal affairs of Commonwealth members should not be criticized by other members. On this occasion, however, Prime Minister Diefenbaker told the conference that South Africa's racial policy was not compatible with the Commonwealth ideal of respect and cooperation among the races on a basis of equality. Since her membership was open to review, there was no choice but to reject the application or face the destruction of the Commonwealth. Mr. Diefenbaker's position was a logical sequel, and a sound one, as well, to his lifelong fight for civil rights in Canada, for it recognized that the African and Asian members would be unwilling to remain partners in an organization that included one nation openly practising racial discrimination. South Africa, recognizing that a fundamental conflict existed, decided to withdraw her application for continied membership. By standing with the majority of Commonwealth members in favour of racial equality, Canada had helped to assure the continued existence of the association she valued so highly.

Another development within the Commonwealth held promise of great usefulness in the future. This was the establishment of a permanent Commonwealth secretariat, endorsed at the 1964 conference in London. There had been earlier proposals for centralized administrative machinery that would have allowed the Commonwealth to speak with one voice in world affairs. The last such suggestion had been made by Australia in 1944. At that time Canada, fearing a loss of her autonomy, had opposed the idea and it was never carried further.

In 1964 Canada supported a plan put forward by some African members to create a secretariat in London. Canada now felt confident of her ability to assert her own interests in international affairs. The newer members had never felt the worries of the "old" white Dominions, and instead emphasized the usefulness of undertaking certain tasks in common and with expert assistance. The new secretariat was intended to improve the flow of information among Commonwealth members, to co-ordinate activities in the educational, health and technical fields, and to arrange agendas for Commonwealth conferences. A Canadian, Arnold Smith, was chosen to be the first Secretary-General of the Commonwealth. This was a tribute to the quality of the Canadian diplomatic service as well as to Canada's reputation among both new and old members of the Commonwealth.

* * *

The postwar era was a momentous one for Canada in the field of external affairs. For the first time she gave positive support to the concept of international collective security, both by military action and by helping to keep the peace in troubled areas of the globe. For the first time in her history she voluntarily entered into commitments to help defend her friends in Europe and America. She showed a growing awareness of the needs of other less fortunate societies. She concerned herself with the deepest aspirations of the vast majority of the world's people, struggling to assert the essential dignity of man. In these ways Canada began to develop a distinctive role in international affairs.

At the same time Canada attempted to deal with pressing domestic problems. The maintenance of national unity, a perennial problem, became increasingly difficult and raised significant questions. For example, to what extent could and should bilingualism be achieved? What was the best way in which to preserve French-Canadian culture without destroying the country? Another perennial problem was how to maintain and strengthen both Canadian culture and her economic independence in the face of great pressures issuing from the United States. Indeed, was it reasonable to believe that Canada could remain a fully autonomous and distinctive society in North America? Perhaps, even more to the point, was there anything significantly distinctive about Canada – was there a Canadian identity? These questions, complex and deeply rooted in the country's past, confronted Canadians as they approached the second century of their Confederation.

CHAPTER 20

CANADA'S SECOND CENTURY: PROBLEMS AND PROSPECTS

Canada's second century opened in an atmosphere laden with questions. Is Canada a land of two nations, one with its capital in Quebec and the other with its capital in Ottawa? Is it possible for English and French-speaking Canadians to live together in a single state? Can the federal structure in Canada accommodate the demands of the provinces for greater financial resources and the need for a central government strong enough to carry out nation-wide policies in many fields? Has Canada moved from being a colony in the British Empire to being a satellite in the American "empire"? Will Canada's ever-closer economic ties with the United States finally lead to political union? Are Canadians becoming "mock Americans"? What chance is there, in the face of the overwhelming pressures of the American mass media, for a distinctive Canadian culture to emerge? Do Canadians today possess the same courage and imagination as their fore-fathers showed in the making of Confederation? It is vital that these questions be discussed, not because they can be satisfactorily answered in a single generation but because only through study can answers come at all.

THE "QUIET REVOLUTION" IN QUEBEC

The most arresting feature of the domestic scene in postwar Canada was the emergence of Quebec as a dynamic force in Canadian life. For generations Quebec had been a sleeping giant, the majority of her people living in unchanging rural communities in which life was centred on the Church. Education was based on the classical subjects of the past. The society of Quebec was hierarchical and largely closed to influences from outside. During the years of Quebec's isolation, the rest of Canada had moved on to embrace city living, industrialization and the acquisitive values of twentieth-century Western civilization. The gap between the two parts of Canada widened with every passing year. Then in September, 1959, Premier Maurice Duplessis, whose conservative outlook and almost dictatorial regime had dominated the life of Quebec for close to a quarter of a century, suddenly died. His death seemed to release the key log from a jam. A torrent of new ideas and energies burst forth, questioning old institutions and practices and proposing new ones. This was the "quiet revolution."

The "quiet revolution" had two dominating objectives: one was concerned with the future of Quebec itself, the other with the future of French-speaking persons throughout Canada. Its leaders stressed the need to modernize the institutions of Quebec, to close the gap that existed in personal incomes, in education, in welfare services, between Quebec and the wealthier provinces of English Canada. French Canadians, they declared, had to be more than a docile labour force for the English Canadians who managed Quebec's economy. The ferment of the "quiet revolution" was harnessed by the Liberal party under Jean Lesage, a former federal cabinet minister, to sweep the *Union Nationale* government out of office in 1960. Lesage immediately set to work to purge Quebec of the corruption and patronage that had grown up during the Duplessis years. Into the provincial civil service, he brought young men – intellectuals, social reformers, administrators – to define and implement the goals of the "quiet revolution."

The spirit of reform touched every phase of Quebec life.

Economic planning was begun in an effort to develop the full potential of each region in the province; the immense hydro-electric power facilities (previously owned privately) were brought under provincial government ownership and increased in capacity; plans were launched for an integrated steel industry, and automobile plants; highways were improved and extended. At the same time the Roman Catholic Church was forced to acknowledge the supremacy of the state in education. In particular, the system of classical colleges (private, state-subsidized institutions that provided a continuous program of studies from the secondary level to undergraduate level, concentrating on the traditional humanities in preparation for specialized study at the university level) was challenged as being outmoded. Critics claimed that its curriculum was too narrow and too rigidly bound by tradition, making the colleges unsuited to the needs of the time. New educational programs emphasizing scientific knowledge and business training were begun. In the space of a few years Quebec was provided with an extensive new educational structure. Social welfare was brought under closer control of the state, displacing the Church and private institutions.

Although Lesage won re-election in 1962, there were signs that he had pushed the pace of reform too quickly. He had also failed to convince his people that the gigantic transformation of Quebec justified heavy additional taxation. In June, 1966, Lesage was narrowly defeated by a rejuvenated *Union Nationale* party under Daniel Johnson. As the administration at Quebec City changed, it was clear that there would be only a slowing down and not a halt in the current of reform that had been released in the old province.

The second objective of the "quiet revolution" – to win fuller recognition for the "French fact" in Canada – could not be realized as easily as social and economic reform in Quebec. It depended on the attitudes of other Canadians, many of whom had little acquaintance with French-speaking persons and felt little sympathy towards them. French Canadians felt a strong desire to be accepted as full partners in Canadian life, and not to be considered as just another ethnic minority whose views should be consulted only occasionally. They insisted that the French

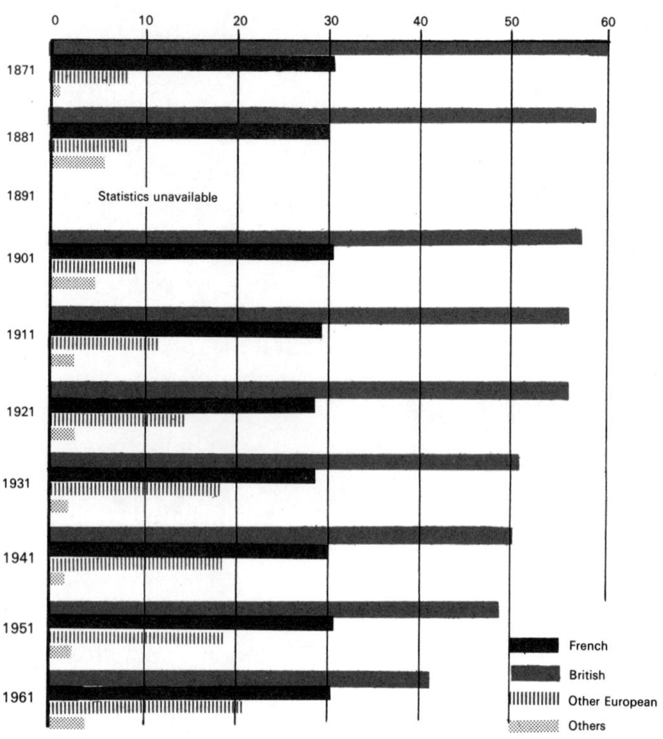

Population by Ethnic Origin, 1871-1961

Canadians should occupy a place of equality because they were one of the "two founding peoples." They felt that Ottawa, the seat of the federal government, should be a city in which French-speaking Canadians could feel at home. For many French Canadians, it often seemed to be like the capital of a foreign country. They wanted greater participation in the federal bureaucracy and greater recognition of bilingualism in education and administration throughout Canada. French Canadians, in short, demanded something better than the status of "second class citizens" in a Canada dominated by English-speaking persons. Their philosophy was the old nationalism of French Canada, given new urgency by the rapidly changing conditions of the mid-twentieth century.

French-Canadian nationalism, in the vigorous way in which it was presented in the 1960's, was bound to create strains in Quebec's relations with the federal government and with the rest of Canada. The governmental responsibilities of the province and its ability to finance them were points at issue. During the Second World War the federal government had introduced new programs, such as family allowances and unemployment insurance, that touched on provincial authority as specified by the BNA Act. Similarly, Ottawa had taken over a number of areas of direct taxation through rental arrangements with the provinces. In the 1960's Quebec, joined by other provinces such as Ontario and British Columbia, began to dispute these arrangements. Quebec felt that it was vital for the maintenance of her identity that she administer social welfare programs, as she had a constitutional right to do. But this field was a costly one, and to support her measures she needed much larger sources of revenue. Thus, she asked for the federal government's withdrawal from a number of fields of taxation in which it had previously been active.

Under the Pearson government, a complex series of administrative and financial arrangements between Ottawa and the provinces were hammered out. These arrangements were described loosely as "co-operative federalism." Under this scheme provinces could participate with the federal government in certain programs or they could "opt out," receiving a fiscal equivalent if they did so. They would then be free to establish their own programs in the area. Quebec took this course in setting up her own pension plan as the counterpart of the Canada Pension Plan in 1966.

"Co-operative federalism" aroused some misgivings, since it appeared to weaken the authority of the federal government. Fears were expressed, for instance, that if the federal government turned over to the provinces too much of its taxation revenues it would lose the power to control the economic health of the country. This was foreseen as a disastrous weakness at times of inflation or depression. Other observers felt that since Quebec was being granted arrangements not desired by other provinces, she would eventually obtain a "special status" in the federation. If the most extreme demands of the Johnson government were conceded (full provincial control over personal income tax, for instance) Quebec would have virtually the powers of an "associate state" in relation to the federal government. Co-equal authority between Quebec and Ottawa would seriously weaken the Canadian federal union and make the central government's leadership in broad national policies unrealizable. To forestall these dangers, Ottawa announced in 1966 that it planned to withdraw from certain shared programs touching on provincial jurisdiction. On the other hand, it would insist on keeping a predominant place in the income tax field, which it regarded as a major instrument of national economic policy. The challenge to the provinces was plain: if they wished to spend money, they must raise it themselves. The 1966 position of the Pearson government showed that the federal system in Canada had become much more decentalized than the authors of the Rowell-Sirois report of 1940 had recommended. There were those who said that this condition made Canada a "truer" federation.

Behind the discussion over Quebec's place in the federation lay a larger question: the ultimate destiny of the approximately 30 percent of Canadians who were French-speaking. The subject came to the fore in 1967, the year of Canada's Centennial, when the President of France, General Charles de Gaulle, on a state visit to Canada, dramatically concluded a Montreal speech with the words, "*Vive le Québec libre.*" Although the General's meaning was ambiguous, he must have known that his words were identical to a popular slogan used by those advocating an independent Quebec.

There were many answers to the question of the future of French-speaking Canadians. Some felt that it was futile to expect a minority group to maintain its language and culture in the overwhelmingly English-language climate of North America. Canada, they said, should adopt the American policy of assimilating minorities in a common society, a "melting pot." Others felt that practical steps had to be taken to recognize the existence of (to use Premier Daniel Johnson's words) "a nation of French speech, whose home is in Quebec." But what did "nation" mean? Did it mean a group of people who shared a common tradition and were united by certain cultural bonds? Or did it mean a

French President Charles de Gaulle (left) with Quebec Premier Daniel Johnson during de Gaulle's dramatic visit to Quebec in 1967. The French President's visit remained controversial long after he had left. Had he been led by some provincial officials into misjudging Quebec's true feelings? Had he intended to encourage outright separatism? To what extent had his reception on the ceremonial drive between Quebec City and Montreal been contrived? Several leading Quebecois, while dissociating themselves from de Gaulle's own policy intentions, spoke of the profound impact his call for a "free Quebec" had had upon them. De Gaulle's subsequent policy of open and frequently provocative encouragement for Quebec nationalism was received in the province with a mixture of pleasure and apprehension.

community entitled to exercise authority over its members – a political state, in fact?

The last notion was very attractive to a small but influential group of intellectuals and professional people in Quebec. The separatists, as they were called, demanded immediate independence, claiming that Quebec's association with the rest of Canada

In the fall of 1967 efforts were made to begin a review of the Canadian constitution. The Premier of Ontario, John Robarts, sponsored the "Confederation of Tomorrow Conference" in Toronto, attended by representatives of the provinces. The main sessions of the conference received extensive, national television coverage for the first time in the history of premiers' meetings. Two premiers who made particularly strong impressions on the Canadian public were J. R. Smallwood of Newfoundland and Daniel Johnson of Quebec, shown in a brief sequence above. Smallwood was an advocate of a strong central government, while Johnson defended Quebec's demands for greater decentralization.

only meant continued subordination. They made light of the arguments that Quebec's secession from Canada would hurt her economically by cutting off foreign investment and forcing large national corporations to leave the province. Essentially their appeal was to the pride and the nationalism of French Canadians. Only in independence, they said, could the full development of the French Canadian community be realized.

The problem of Quebec in the latter part of the twentieth century is the problem of Canada on a smaller scale; how to preserve an identity in a North America that is dominated by the United States giant. There are those who say that the two problems are really one; that Quebec's identity can best be preserved within the Canadian Confederation and that French-speaking Canadians have a special contribution to make to the survival of a united Canada. This was the view of Prime Minister Pearson and his Liberal government after 1963. The concept of partnership received exciting expression in Centennial year with the resounding success of Expo '67 in Montreal. This was an ambitious, co-operative project that combined the artistic flair of French Canada with the practical approach of English-speaking Canadians. As the most popular international exposition in history it gave Canada a new stature all over the world, not the least in the United States.

Those who believed in a united Canada drew assurance from the achievements of the Centennial year. They celebrated the diversity of the country, recognizing in this condition the root strength of Canada. Prime Minister Pearson described his hopes this way in late 1967:

> The future of Canada, indeed its very survival, depends on our success in building a society where diverse races and languages, diverse talents and capacities, diverse energies and interests are not only permitted, but are encouraged to grow and develop side by side.

THE DILEMMA OF CANADIAN CULTURE

After World War I Canada remained culturally a generation behind her southern neighbour. Nevertheless, there was one significant development in the inter-war period. World War I had shown that Marconi's wireless was not a toy but a potent means of mass communication that could be used to link the remotest part of a broad land. The experiment of the Canadian Broadcasting Corporation (established in 1936), in which the federal government took the lead in providing radio communication for the nation, set a pattern for the strengthening of culture in Canada. This primary reliance on government action did not, of course, exclude the operation of private enterprise in broadcasting. By the time World War II began, radio was reaching 90 percent of the Canadian population, carrying programs which educated one region in the problems and ideas of another. Radio provided opportunities for writers, actors and musicians, and gave Canada its first true taste of mass culture. In at least one area, radio drama, the C.B.C. became recognized as a world leader.

In the field of literature the commanding name in the years following World War I was that of E. J. Pratt, a Newfoundlander.

Pratt's first success, a long narrative poem, *The Titanic* (1926), showed that a major poet had appeared. In later poems Pratt retold some epic Canadian stories: the construction of the C.P.R., and the Jesuit martyrdoms. More recently there has been a flowering of Canadian poetry, bringing to prominence such people as A. M. Klein, Irving Layton, Raymond Souster, Saint-Denys Garneau and Leonard Cohen. In the earlier period there was no Canadian novelist equal in stature to the poet Pratt, but the next generation saw at least three Canadian novelists gain international attention—Morley Callaghan, Hugh MacLennan and Gabrielle Roy.

The Group of Seven (the original seven of the name being Lawren Harris, Arthur Lismer, J. E. H. MacDonald, A. Y. Jackson, F. H. Varley, Frank Carmichael and Frank H. Johnston), with their bold representations of Canada's different regions, made a sensational appearance in Canadian art in the early 1920's. Their influence dominated Canadian painting for at least a generation. J. E. H. MacDonald's canvas, *The Solemn Land,* is still, to many people, a symbol of Canada. After 1945 the influx of large numbers of Europeans made itself felt in Canadian arts—painting in particular—and there was an increasing awareness of modern trends. The result was an appreciation of the works of such Canadian painters as Paul-Emile Borduas, Jean Paul Riopelle and Harold Town.

Canadian development in music, as in the other arts, has perhaps been slow, but it has been marked by a number of outstanding figures. Of the older generation, Healey Willan, an Englishman who came to Toronto as a young man, achieved international recognition as a musician, teacher and prolific composer, especially of Church music. After World War II the number of serious composers increased; John Weinzweig, Harry Somers and Pierre Mercure were among the most prominent of this generation. Canada also began to produce some truly outstanding performers at this time. Among any group of international artists the names of Jon Vickers, Maureen Forrester, Glenn Gould, Leopold Simoneau and Teresa Stratas would rank high.

The modern, mass culture phase of Canada's development

The Mall, Simon Fraser University, British Columbia (above), is an example of the striking architecture of the 1960's. Below is J. E. H. MacDonald's painting, "The Solemn Land," typical of the work of the Group of Seven.

dates only from 1945. If achievement since has been stupendous, the problems raised have been equally momentous. More Canadian artists have been able to make a living from their talents, yet the culture that they have been promoting may, in fact, not be Canadian at all. Paradoxically, just as the country was discovering its own cultural roots, it faced (as it still faces) the threat of cultural domination by the United States. Canadian ballet and opera companies, symphony orchestras, poets, novelists, dramatists and directors began to find a market at home for their work, but at every turn they had to resist the powerful temptation of wider recognition and higher income in the United States or in Britain. Perhaps the real change from the inter-war period was to be found in the awareness of this competition, for during the twenties and thirties Canadians read American magazines, listened to American radio programs and devoured the latest American novels without serious consideration of the impact of an American culture upon Canada.

Following World War II, Canadian magazines, in particular, found it increasingly difficult to meet American competition. Various periodicals died, others amalgamated. In the newspaper world the same phenomenon occurred. Canada's cities were served in the sixties by fewer papers than a generation before, and although circulation increased, much of what Canadians read came to the newspapers through American news sources or in the form of syndicated columns. The introduction of television in 1952 opened up new fields for Canadian performers and writers, but again, so strong were American influences that the federal government, via the Board of Broadcast Governors, found it necessary to limit the amount of American material carried by Canadian networks.

World War II accelerated three major social trends, each of which strengthened Canada's cultural life. First, industrialization promoted urbanization, so that the greater part of Canada's population worked and lived in cities where increased cultural and recreational facilities were provided. Second, more children began attending schools for longer periods than ever before. Third, the Royal Commission on National Development in the Arts, Letters and Sciences, popularly known as the Massey

In the field of the performing arts two of the most outstanding companies are the National Ballet of Canada and the Canadian Opera Company. Above is a scene from the National Ballet's production of Les Sylphide. Below, Salome (in the opera of the same name by Richard Strauss) embraces the severed head of John the Baptist. Both these companies present performances in major Canadian cities and tour to smaller centres, often to quite remote areas.

Commission (after its distinguished chairman, Vincent Massey), commented in its report of 1951 on the "prevailing hunger existing throughout the country for a fuller measure of what the writer, the artist and the musician could give." As a result of the Commission's recommendations, various levels of government undertook to expand cultural facilities. In Ottawa, new quarters were provided for the National Gallery of Canada, a new national centre for the performing arts was built and the National Library was formally installed in a handsome, modern building. All over the country this pattern was repeated. For example, Charlottetown built the Fathers of Confederation Memorial Centre; Fredericton established the Beaverbrook Art Gallery; Montreal, the *Place des Arts*; Toronto, the O'Keefe Centre; Winnipeg, a concert hall and arts centre; Vancouver, the Queen Elizabeth Theatre. Professional opera, drama and ballet companies were founded in such cities as Halifax, Montreal, Toronto, Winnipeg and Vancouver, and sent on tour, bringing an unaccustomed richness into the lives of countless Canadians. Perhaps the most significant cultural institution established during these years was the Stratford Shakespearean Festival, which set high standards for all Canadians to meet and quickly achieved international renown. Of great importance was the creation in 1957 of the Canada Council. With a capital endowment, the interest from which was to be dispersed among universities, writers, scholars and artists, the Canada Council did an immeasurable amount to encourage cultural vitality throughout the country. Here again, in typically Canadian fashion, state aid was used to promote the national good.

Yet, the paradox remained that, at the very moment when Canada seemed on the threshold of extending her own culture, she was faced with the threat of domination by the mass culture of the United States. Nor was this the only problem, for French-Canadian culture faced the threat of English-language cultural domination at a time when Quebec's own culture was showing new life and excitement. To survive, both Canadian groups would have to struggle to express themselves, and in that struggle seek to avoid the narrow, parochial nationalism that could so easily blight the flowering of Canada's cultural identity.

LIVING BESIDE AN ECONOMIC GIANT

The Canadian economy has always been highly vulnerable to forces outside its control. From the days of the fur trade, when Canadian beaver were caught to satisfy the demands of European fashion, to the opening of the prairies, when Canadian wheat was planted to meet the urgent requirements of the industrialized nations of western Europe, economic activity in Canada has been shaped by external demand. Canada's increasing economic integration with the United States since 1945 has meant that external demands have come more and more from that country. The American interest north of the 49th parallel has been to develop those sectors of the Canadian economy that will best serve the United States' need for industrial raw materials. Canada has been expected to produce unmanufactured or semi-manufactured goods that will complement, and not compete with, the products of the United States' economy. There has grown up a relationship between the structure of the Canadian and American economies that cannot be changed overnight nor transformed by a regulation issued at Ottawa. These basic truths should be kept in mind as the subject of Canadian-American economic relations is examined.

This subject has represented a worrisome problem to Canadians, especially the aspect concerned with the movement of United States capital into Canada. The economic growth of Canada has always required more capital than can be provided by Canadians. The boom periods in Canadian history have invariably been associated with large inflows of foreign capital. This capital has been used to lay railways, construct factories, develop mines and build hydro-electric power plants. During the nineteenth century most of Canada's capital needs were supplied by Britain, whose industrial wealth made her a lender to the world. During World War I Britain was obliged to sell many of her overseas investments to finance her war effort. The United States, whose investments in Canada had previously been about one-third the size of Britain's, now began to provide much of Canada's capital needs. The oil discoveries made in Alberta after World War II touched off an immense flow of American funds to Canada. By 1965 the United States owned about 73 percent of all non-resident investment in Canada. Much of this sum represented a direct investment in Canadian subsidiaries of companies controlled from the United States, while the rest was composed of purchases of Canadian securities. Britain's investment in Canada in 1965 amounted to 15 percent of the total, Western European countries and Japan providing most of the balance. Total foreign investment in Canada by 1965 came to $34 billions, an amount which had more than doubled in ten years. Canada, in fact, had become one of the world's greatest importers of that scarce commodity—private capital.

American investment was concentrated in what are called the "prime movers" of Canadian growth—the oil and gas industries, minerals, pulp and paper. In the field of petroleum and natural gas, for instance, American ownership accounted for about 70 percent of the industry. In mining and smelting American ownership was over 50 percent; in manufacturing about 40 percent. The Canadian automobile industry was 95 percent American-owned.

The massive flow of American capital to Canada has aroused much concern among Canadians. Is Canada wise in selling the ownership of so much of its natural resources? Do United States subsidiaries in Canada act in conformity with the national interest of Canada? Do they, for instance, try for export markets if this will bring them into competition with their American parents? Are they prevented from trading with countries that may be unfriendly with the United States although not with Canada? Do they allow Canadians to enter their top management positions? Is there a danger that the United States will become dominant in the Canadian economy, and through economic control exert political influence? The fears are interrelated. In essence they touch on the deepest concern in Canadian history—the preservation of Canada's identity and independence.

The "problem" of American investment must, however, be seen in perspective. There is little evidence to show that, over the long run, American subsidiaries in Canada are likely to act any differently than do Canadian companies. Private corporations are moved primarily by the profit motive, whether they are owned

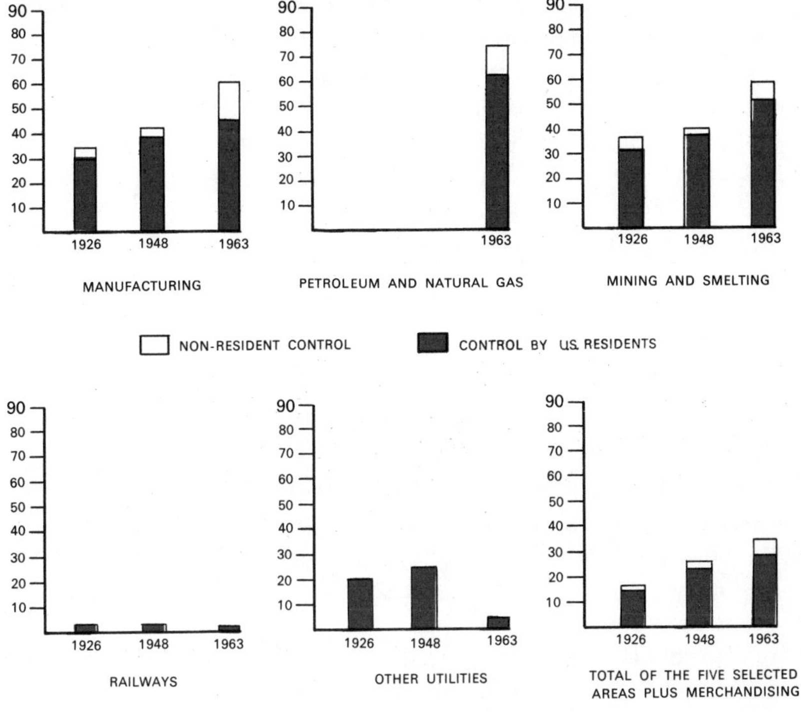

Foreign control is expressed here in terms of a percentage of the equity and debt capital invested by residents as well as non-residents in those companies whose voting stock is controlled by non-residents.

Foreign Control in Selected Areas of Canadian Industry

on Wall Street in New York or Bay Street in Toronto. They are not instruments of a government but free agents, carrying on their activities within the general limits set by the laws of the country in which they are incorporated. In Canada, the federal parliament and the legislatures of the provinces make the laws regulating business activity. These laws are formulated with the object of defining and protecting the welfare of the Canadian people.

The plain fact is that Canada has benefited enormously, all through her history, from the influx of foreign capital. With the capital have also come skills, technological know-how and access to foreign markets that could not otherwise have been obtained. Without the large capital inflow from abroad Canada's industrial expansion and living standards would not approach their present levels. To attempt to discriminate against United States investment in Canada, as Walter Gordon, the Liberal party Finance Minister, did in his first budget in 1963, is a dangerous maneuver that can lead to unfortunate consequences. Such a policy is discriminatory because it singles out one country for attention; it is economically unsound because it disturbs a natural movement of economic forces; it is risky because it invites retaliation. Persisted in, discrimination could discourage American investor interest in Canada, reduce the flow of American capital, and slow down the rate of Canadian economic growth. Such a policy could also poison Canadian-American relations for many years. Few Canadians would be prepared to face all these possible consequences.

The solution to the problem would seem to lie not through discriminatory regulations applied to foreign investment, but through encouraging Canadians to invest more of their own funds in the growing sectors of their economy. Life insurance companies, with tremendous assets at their disposal, clearly should place more than the 5 percent they now do in the common stock of Canadian companies. Over the years the volume of savings by Canadians has steadily increased, both in relation to the national output of Canada and in relationship to total investment. Canadian investment in the United States is valued at over $8 billions, a larger investment on a per capita basis than that of America in Canada. The comparative scale of the two economies inevitably determines that the impact of the one on the other is bound to be spectacular. Yet the Canadian economy is growing stronger and achieving a better balance every year. In the long run these trends may help to reduce Canada's economic dependence on the United States.

The prospects for creating a more secure base for the Canadian economy are bright. The expansion of Canada's internal market, which is bound to come from population growth, the strengthening of Canada's manufacturing to serve this market, the diversification of Canada's resource industries through the discovery of new uses for raw materials and new techniques for exploiting them – these are favourable factors in the future economic growth of Canada.

A ROLE FOR CANADA IN WORLD AFFAIRS

In the years after the Second World War, Canada became more and more a North American nation. Her attitudes and values were conditioned by the restless democracy, the open society, the material abundance that were characteristic of life in North America. Her outlook on the world was profoundly affected by this transformation. As her ties with Britain became weaker, her relations with the United States grew steadily stronger and more compelling. In part, this resulted from the inexorable pull of economic forces, but it also came from the United States' post-1945 position as the leading nation of the Western world. In the great struggle against international communism, the United States was the champion of the West. Her armed forces provided stability and security for all the nations in the Western alliance against their most formidable adversary, the Soviet Union. Canada's role in world affairs was strikingly influenced by her proximity to the United States and by the realization that she shared a common attitude with the Americans on world problems. Thus she developed a special relationship with her great neighbour to the south. Following the Ogdensburg agreement of 1940, Canada had been a formal ally of the United States; after the war Canadian-American links were strengthened further by the establishment of an intricate system of co-operative air and sea defence. This alliance, and all that it signified, became the inescapable reality in Canadian external policy during the decades after the war.

There were some Canadians who questioned the alliance or drew sombre conclusions from it. Neutralism for Canada had supporters, some of whom suggested that Canada should accept no responsibility for the use of nuclear weapons. This position was a denial of Canada's historical experience, which had been determined by the country's continuous involvement in European and North American affairs. Neutralism carried serious threats to the well-being of Canada, for the adoption of this policy would almost certainly have called forth a violent anti-Canadian reaction in the United States. This might well have shown itself in measures limiting Canadian-American trade or in political pressures.

Other Canadians claimed that the preponderance of American power relegated Canada to the role of a satellite. Canada's defence was so vital to the United States, they said, that the latter country would not tolerate any expressions of an independent attitude from Canada. But that situation had never occurred in the past and was unlikely to appear in the future. Over the years Canadians had never shown a disposition to withhold their views when they were not popular in the United States, nor to refrain from acting if they felt their national interests were affected. A "satellite Canada" was not the type of country in which the majority of Canadians wished to live.

The sound structure of a Canadian-American partnership was the only feasible orientation for Canada. Yet such a partnership was clearly an unequal one, encompassing units which had a tenfold disparity in power and influence. This disparity made it difficult to define a role for Canada in the harsh world of international politics.

Canada's role involved frank speaking with the United States when the occasion called for it. As Prime Minister Pearson said:

> No doubt we shall continue to judge each other more critically than we judge anyone else, because we expect more of each other. We know that our friendship is strong enough to stand the test of frankness. . . .

Canadian frankness could be expressed behind the scenes through regular diplomatic channels ("quiet diplomacy") or it could be stated openly as it was in 1965 when Lester Pearson suggested a pause in the United States' bombing attacks on North Vietnam. Through candid speaking Canada could often interject into the complicated process of decision-making in the United States a viewpoint that might have been previously ignored because it came from an unregarded minority group in the United States. Sometimes Canada, through its Commonwealth associations, could express the viewpoints of Asian and African countries directly to Washington. In this capacity Canada acted as an "interpreter," not in the traditional sense between Britain and the United States, but as a bridge between the underdeveloped, unaligned nations and the America of

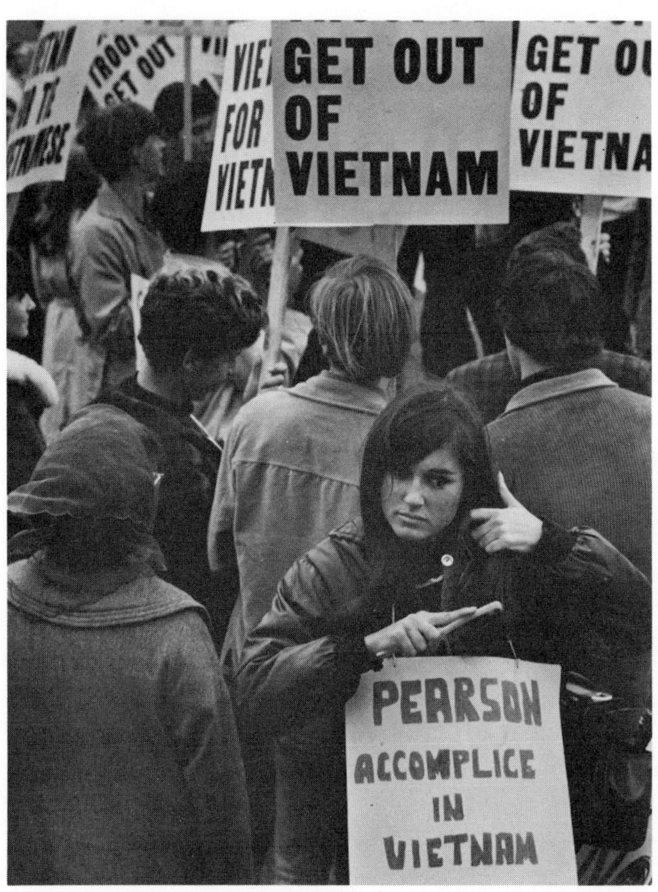

A characteristic of Canadian society, no less than that of other western countries in the late sixties, was the current of protest, particularly among the youth. The war in Vietnam and the government's attitude toward it were among the most popular targets.

wealth and commitment. This was the part Canada played so brilliantly in the Suez crisis, when Canadian initiatives won the support of India and Pakistan, and Great Britain and the United States. Occasionally Canada could put forward a new idea in the constant dialogue with the United States as, for instance, it did in 1948 when it broached the concept of NATO.

Canada's historical experience and social and cultural conditions provide her with distinctive attitudes on world affairs. Conscious of her own limitations and sometimes unsure of her ideological goals, Canada has never cherished dreams of making the world over in her own image. Canadians have, therefore, tended to see issues in shades of grey, not as contrasts in black and white. Canada has never been inspired by "missionary diplomacy," as has the United States during parts of the twentieth century. The Canadian experience in cultural dualism has provided an exercise in "peaceful coexistence" that inevitably carries over into Canadian attitudes towards international relations. The art of compromise, the method of mediation, the capacity for patience – these qualities, evident in domestic affairs, have also been well illustrated in the record of Canadian diplomacy since 1945. Canada, as a smaller power, has tended to look with a certain scepticism on any country or any policy that claims ultimate wisdom. Canada has also been suspicious of actions which suggest that power is being used as an end in itself. These attitudes represent the luxuries of a small country that does not possess the primary responsibility for maintaining world order but is, nevertheless, prepared to make its own contribution to this goal.

There are occasions that lend themselves to the expression of a legitimate Canadian point of view. Yet Canadians in all walks of life should recognize that Canada's right to criticize and to offer advice is not unlimited. The United States, not Canada, has the ultimate responsibility for the defence of the West and this responsibility requires a degree of caution and deliberation that is bound to affect American decisions in foreign policy. The magnitude of the American contribution to defence is also so great that it gives the United States the right to take the dominant share in decisions. American defence expenditures are thirty-six times greater than Canada's, even though the United States' population is only ten times as large. In an ultimate test of strength, such as that which occurred over Cuba in 1962, it will be the decision of the United States that must prevail. On occasions such as these, the basic self-interest of Canada lies in supporting the United States, which has faced the challenge and bears the responsibility of meeting it. Sir Robert Borden put the issue clearly at the Washington Conference in 1921. He said of Americans: "They may not be angels, but they are at least our friends." Momentary irritation at American actions should never be allowed to push this truth out of the minds of Canadians.

CANADIAN NATIONALISM: CLOSED OR OPEN?

Nationalism has itself contributed to Canada's standing in the modern world. Canada has shown how a dependent colony can gain independent status peacefully and gradually. Her example has been followed by colonies of white settlement in the British Empire and later by Asian and African members of the Commonwealth. Canada's nationalism from the first has been based upon the acceptance of cultural diversity within a single political entity. It has been a moderate expression of a movement that in other lands has sometimes assumed violent aspects. Canadian experience has served, and may serve again, as a model of liberal nationalism.

As Canada moved into her second century, however, there were signs that the traditional view of Canadian nationalism was under attack. Some Canadians felt that Canada should assert herself more forcefully, particularly in her dealings with her great neighbour. It was also felt the Canadian economy should be made more self-sufficient by a strengthening of its industrial sector and by encouraging the Canadian people to purchase Canadian products. It was said that high tariffs should be imposed to assist Canadian manufacturing and that the inflow of foreign (particularly American) capital should be cut down. Foreign cultural influences through periodicals, broadcasting and films should be reduced as far as possible. Canadian art should be judged by standards related to the Canadian scene. Through these arrangements, it was argued, Canada would gain the prospect of modest but steady economic growth and a secure opportunity to control her own destiny.

Other Canadians have characterized this vision of Canada as "ultra-nationalist, inward-looking, reactionary, overly sensitive to criticisms of its friends and preoccupying itself with giving visibility to its independence in ways which are artificial and trivial." They have claimed that Canada has the opportunity to move towards a more exciting but dangerous destiny. Foreign competition should not be feared but welcomed because of the spur it can give to one's own efforts. The economy should be expanded by attracting capital and immigrants and techniques from abroad. The major emphasis should be placed on increasing foreign trade and stimulating other countries to do the same. Canadians should be prepared to expose themselves to the best in foreign culture and to measure their achievements by the highest international standards. The goal for Canadian education and cultural life should simply be excellence.

Nationalism of the second type has been described as an "open" nationalism. It is moderate in tone and offers the prospect of growth in response to new conditions. It respects the diversity of peoples within and without the nation. It attempts to reconcile conflicting points of view and to seek solutions by consent rather than by pressure. It emphasizes reason and understanding as the only sound bases of international relations. It is based on the conviction that co-operation between countries in political and economic affairs is not only politically but morally desirable. It is a type of nationalism that offers nations the chance of stability and economic progress.

Whichever form or variation of nationalism Canada chooses to adopt, the decision rests with her people. For over three

The photographs opposite can be said to symbolize two of the major problems that face Canadians. At the top is a view of the federal-provincial constitutional conference that met in Ottawa, February, 1968. At the centre of the horseshoe is Prime Minister Pearson flanked by Pierre Trudeau and Mitchell Sharp. How, in an age when relationships between governments, groups and individuals are becoming increasingly complex, is the Canadian political structure to be developed so that needs of the people are met without stifling the legitimate asperations of different cultural and regional groups? At the bottom is a view of Grise Fiord on Ellesmere Island, Canada's most northern settlement. How can Canada best develop her vast natural resources, especially under the rigorous climatic and geographic conditions that exist in large areas of the country? ▶

hundred and fifty years their ancestors have laboured in the immense northern reaches of North America to create new societies. "To have done great things together in the past, to wish to do more of them, these are the essential conditions for being a people." This is the challenge to Canadians in the second century of their existence as a nation. The experience of the past provides a partial answer, but the last word can only come from Canadians, young and old, English and French-speaking, Easterners and Westerners. They, and they alone, possess the opportunity and the means to realize the potential greatness of their homeland.

READINGS

Canada's Second Century: Questions and the Way Ahead

Composed of people of two major languages and cultures and living all her life in the shadow of great powers, Canada has found it difficult to understand herself and her role in the world. Yet in the years since World War II she has begun, sometimes soberly, sometimes emotionally, to examine her society and institutions and to see how well they fit the rapidly changing conditions of our time. In the process of self-examination Canadians have not only learned a great deal about themselves, but they have begun to discuss their place in the world and to consider the kind of country in which they would like to live. Some of their thoughts are set forth in the selections that follow. These views can be regarded as contributions to the continuing debate on Canada—its nature and destiny.

The Canadian dilemma is first of all a cultural one, arising from the co-existence of two founding races within one state. This condition has, of course, existed for over two centuries and has produced its own history of tensions and conflict. Confederation established workable arrangements to reconcile these differences. Now, one hundred years later, the condition of affairs embodied in the British North America Act is being challenged and even rejected by one of the founding races.

The political rights of French-Canadians (which were usually interpreted as the rights of the province of Quebec) were reiterated over and over again by the long-time premier of Quebec, "*le chef*", Maurice Duplessis. In 1955, at a federal-provincial conference, Duplessis described the powers his province claimed under the constitution and demanded the necessary revenues to carry them out.

> The federative system which necessitates, fundamentally, an attribution of public tasks, must also provide a correlative division of revenue sources. Of what benefit to the provinces would be the most extensive legislative and administrative powers if, on the other hand, they were prevented from collecting the revenues that the exercise of these powers demands? . . .
>
> The Canadian constitution consecrates the exclusive right of the provinces to legislate respecting matters of very great importance, notably in regards to education, hospitals, asylums, institutions and charitable homes, public works within the province, administration of justice and all which touches property and civil rights. A progressive legislation in these domains necessarily entails considerable expense and clearly requires that the provinces have the right to raise the necessary moneys. Fiscal independence is all the more indispensable in the case of a province, such as the Province of Quebec, which is developing itself with giant strides; development which greatly enriches Canada but which exacts, on the part of the province, numerous and additional outlays in particular for new schools, new hospitals, for social legislation and for other provincial purposes.

Proceedings of the Federal Provincial Conference 1955: Ottawa, October 3, 1955 (Ottawa, 1955), pp. 37-8.

Duplessis' Liberal successor, the reforming Jean Lesage, put forward a more general argument for the survival of French-Canadian culture in the speech to the provincial premiers at Charlottetown early in 1963.

> It has always been agreed that two cultures existed in Canada: the French-Canadian culture and the English-Canadian culture. But merely to agree is not enough; this sociological background must be turned into a fact, a living reality. French-Canadian culture must have the means to assert itself and to develop, because as a result of the circumstances and of the neglect of the deeper meaning of Confederation, this culture finds itself at a disadvantage. Now, French-Canadian culture is not just the spoken language, it is also the over-all mentality and the behaviour of a whole group. In order for this culture to be able to develop, in order for it to be able to take root in fertile ground, the presence of those who possess it must be accepted and wanted. Their eventual contribution to the Canadian scene must be

appreciated, and certain prejudices based on phenomena seen from a distance and outside their context must be done away with. The French Canadians must be understood as they are now, and not as too many people used to think they were.

Frank Scott and Michael Oliver (eds.), *Quebec States Her Case* (Toronto: Macmillan, 1964), pp. 16/7.

Provincial autonomy and cultural awareness found a point of union in the separatist movement in Quebec in the early 1960's. Dr. Marcel Chaput, in a book that startled English Canada, *Why I Am a Separatist,* cried out against the "psychological climate," the "brainwashing," which he said French Canadians experienced every day of their lives.

- His country is the whole of Canada, but he is accepted only in Quebec.
- He is told that he belongs to the great French civilization, but simultaneously he hears someone speak of "those damned Frenchmen."
- He is forced to be bilingual; the others are unilingual.
- He hears nothing but praise at school and elsewhere for the beauty of the French language; he is obliged to learn English.
- He is told that Canada is a country which united two cultures; he has difficulty getting service in west Montreal if he uses French. . . .
- He enters the French university only to study from American text-books.
- He is told all about national unity, but he is ordered: "Stay in your province."
- He hears people insist that Canada is an independent country; every day he sees another country's queen on his coinage and on his stamps. . . .

Marcel Chaput, *Why I am a Separatist* (Toronto: Ryerson Press, 1962), p. 28.

The demand for separation was voiced in more strident terms when the Front de Libération Québécois (FLQ) appeared on the scene in 1963. The party presented a highly-coloured interpretation of French-Canada's history to prove that Quebec was a colony enslaved by "Anglo-Saxon imperialists," represented chiefly by the federal government in Ottawa. From its reading of Canadian history the FLQ concluded that the only solution for French Canada lay in violence and terrorism.

Here is the historical background of the problem: On 8 September 1760 Monsieur de Vaudreuil, Governor of New France, signed Montreal's capitulation, thereby sealing its fate. Shortly thereafter England was to take official possession of the French colony and of the 60,000 French Canadians living in it. This was the beginning of a long story of Anglo-Saxon domination over Quebec. Ours was a rich country, and London's capitalists were already counting future gains. In order to establish undisputed Anglo-Saxon supremacy over Quebec, the 60,000 French settlers had at all costs to be anglicized, by one means or another. It seemed easy enough at the time, for what did this handful of men represent bèside the crushing power that was then England? But, suddenly, the American Revolution broke out. For a time it became important to go easy on the French Canadians. Yet the efforts at anglicization were not thereby set aside. One day, the English Canadians went too far; and the 1837 rebellion flared up. It was drowned in blood. Then came the Durham report. Since it was proving impossible, said Lord Durham, to absorb the French Canadians by force, let us go about it in other ways: slow assimilation takes longer, but is just as effective. Union having proved a failure, Confederation was devised—assimilation's perfect tool—its very name embodying a falsehood. Since then, all of Quebec's efforts to get recognition for its people's basic rights have been thwarted by colonialism.

What if today, in 1963, there are over five million of us? Assimilation continues to make its insidious inroads. While in 1940 our numerical strength came close to 40 per cent of the Canadian population, today we only represent 28 per cent of the total. This, we are told, is the only thing that counts. Time plays into their hands, and well do they know it.

Frank Scott and Michael Oliver (eds.), *Quebec States Her Case* (Toronto: Macmillan, 1964), pp. 84/5.

English Canadians were generally taken by surprise at the separatist movement and their attitudes towards the aspirations of Quebec at this time tended to vary widely. Probably one of the most widespread was the feeling that English was the dominant language in Canada and that Quebec was struggling against the currents of the age in seeking to establish its cultural identity around the French language. The Toronto *Globe and Mail* did not see the need for an enquiry into bilingualism when such a study was proposed late in 1962.

If we were now to start probing at the causes of our differences, we could well lose this valuable ground we have already gained. Prejudiced people on both sides of the fence would merely look through the massed evidence to select those portions that substantiated their prejudices, and they would find them. We could end up angry and injured, and farther apart than ever.

A wiser course, in our view, would be to let Quebec complete the task it has set itself. The Province is now in good hands, and the necessary basic reforms have been initiated. If we have patience, the discovery, already made by its leaders, that English is the language of commerce and is as essential to Quebec as to the rest of us, will spread through the populace. We will find wide areas of agreement. French-speaking Canadians will retain their culture, as the Welsh and the Scots have done. We will be able in time to find the unity we seek.

Globe and Mail, Toronto, 20 December, 1962.

The Liberal party under L. B. Pearson recognized the challenge facing Canada in the bilingual crisis. On coming to power in 1963 it set up a royal commission headed by two prominent Canadians, André Laurendeau and A. D. Dunton, to report upon "the existing state of bilingualism and biculturalism" in Canada and to recommend steps to strengthen the concept of an equal partnership between the two founding races. The Commission's first recommendations were for the establishment of bilingual districts in various parts of Canada to ensure French and English language rights in government, the courts and education.

In the course of its analysis of Canadian attitudes towards the bicultural problem the Commission gave this interpretation of the situation in the mid-sixties.

The chief protagonists, whether they are entirely conscious of it or not, are French-speaking Quebec and English-speaking Canada. And it seems to us to be no longer the traditional conflict between a majority and a minority. It is rather a conflict between two majorities: that which is a majority in all Canada, and that which is a majority in the entity of Quebec.

That is to say, French-speaking Quebec acted for a long time as though at least it had accepted the idea of being merely a privileged "ethnic minority". Today, the kind of opinion we met so often in the province regards Quebec practically as an autonomous society, and expects her to be recognized as such.

This attitude goes back to a fundamental expectation for French Canada, that is, to be an equal partner with English-speaking Canada. If this idea is found to be impossible, because such equality is not believed in or is not acceptable, we believe the sense of deception will bring decisive consequences. An important element in French-speaking Quebec is already tempted to go it alone.

Preliminary Report of the Royal Commission on Bilingualism and Biculturalism (Ottawa: Queen's Printer, 1965), p. 135.

The Commission felt that a change of attitude was required on both sides if Canadian unity was to be preserved.

From evidence so far accumulated, it appears to us that English-speaking Canadians as a whole must come to recognize the existence of a vigorous French-speaking society within Canada, and to find out more about the aspirations, frustrations and achievements of French-speaking Canadians, in Quebec and outside it. They must come to understand what it means to be a member of a minority, or of a smaller partner people, and to be ready to give that minority assurances which are unnecessary for a majority. More than a century ago, Sir John A. Macdonald wrote to an English-speaking friend: "Treat them as a nation and they will act as a free people generally do—generously. Call them a faction and they become factious." They have to face the fact that, if Canada is to continue to exist, there must be a true partnership, and that the partnership must be worked out as between equals. They must be prepared to discuss in a forthright, open-minded way the practical implications of such a partnership. . . .

On the same evidence, it seems to us that French-speaking Canadians for their part must be ready to respond positively if there are to be truly significant developments toward a better partnership. It would be necessary for French-speaking Quebecers to restrain their present tendency to concentrate so intensely on their own affairs, and to look so largely inward. Problems affecting all Canada are their problems too. They would need to beware of the kind of thinking that puts "la nation" above all other considerations and values. They too, like the English-speaking, should forget the conquest and any psychological effects they think it left. They would have to avoid blaming English-speaking Canadians for shortcomings which are their own; and at times, to remember that English-speaking Canadians have their feelings too. They, as well as the English-speaking, must remember that, if a partnership works, each party must give as well as get.

Preliminary Report of the Royal Commission on Bilingualism and Biculturalism (Ottawa: Queen's Printer, 1965), pp. 138/39.

One of the younger intellectual leaders of French Canada, Pierre Elliott Trudeau, shared many of the sentiments expressed by the Laurendeau-Dunton commission. As a teacher at the

University of Montreal he courageously and vigorously attacked French-Canadian nationalism and its extremist offspring, separatism.

We have expended a great deal of time and energy proclaiming the rights due our nationality, invoking our divine mission, trumpeting our virtues, bewailing our misfortunes, denouncing our enemies, and avowing our independence; and for all that not one of our workmen is the more skilled, nor a civil servant the more efficient, a financier the richer, a doctor the more advanced, a bishop the more learned, not a single solitary politician the less ignorant. Now, except for a few stubborn eccentrics, there is probably not one French-Canadian intellectual who has not spent at least four hours a week over the last year discussing separatism. That makes how many thousand times two hundred hours spent just flapping our arms? And can any one of them honestly say he has heard a single argument not already expounded *ad nauseam* twenty, forty, and even sixty years ago? I am not even sure we have exorcized any of our original bogey men in sixty years. The Separatists of 1962 that I have met really are, in general, genuinely earnest and nice people; but the few times I have had the opportunity of talking with them at any length, I have almost always been astounded by the totalitarian outlook of some, the anti-Semitism of others, and the complete ignorance of basic economics of all of them. . . .

Several years ago I tried to show that the devotees of the nationalist school of thought among French Canadians, despite their good intentions and courage, were for all practical purposes trying to swim upstream against the course of progress. Over more than half a century "they have laid down a pattern of social thinking impossible to realize and which, from all practical points of view, has left the people without any effective intellectual direction."

Pierre Elliott Trudeau, *Federalism and the French Canadians* (Toronto: Macmillan, 1968), pp. 167/68.

Later as Minister of Justice (a few months before he became Pearson's successor as prime minister), Trudeau emphasized the need to make French Canadians feel at home in every part of Canada. In a speech to the Canadian Bar Association in 1967 he outlined his plan for achieving this goal.

We all agree on the familiar basic rights—freedom of belief and expression, freedom of association, the right to a fair trial and to fair legal procedures generally. We would also expect a guarantee against discrimination on the basis of race, religion, sex, ethnic or national origin. These are the rights commonly protected by bills of rights. They are basic for any society of free men.

But there are rights of special importance to Canada arising, as I have said, from the fact that this country is founded on two distinct linguistic groups. While language is the basic instrument for preserving and developing the cultural integrity of a people, the language provisions of the British North America Act are very limited. I believe that we require a broader definition and more extensive guarantees in the matter of recognition of the two official languages. The right to learn and to use either of the two official languages should be recognized. Without this, we cannot assure every Canadian of an equal opportunity to participate in the political, cultural, economic, and social life of this country. I venture to say that, if we are able to reach agreement on this vital aspect of the over-all problem, we will have found a solution to a basic issue facing Canada today. A constitutional change recognizing broader rights with respect to the two official languages would add a new dimension to Confederation.

Pierre Elliott Trudeau, *Federalism and the French Canadians* (Toronto: Macmillan, 1968), pp. 55/6.

Early in his career Trudeau, in collaboration with Gérard Pelletier (later a minister in the Trudeau government), had founded and directed the small magazine *Cité Libre*. For more than a decade it was an influential forum for the expression of liberal, humanitarian opinion in Quebec. Early in the sixties, however, other voices began to appeal more urgently to some university students and young people in Quebec. One of these was André Major, who while still in his early twenties wrote in another journal, *Liberté*, and subsequently helped to publish a third review, *Parti Pris*. His writings show the strong influence of Marxism-Leninism on some sections of the Quebec nationalist movement and reveal a deep contempt for the approach of moderate French-Canadian thinkers such as Trudeau. The challenge which Major's views present to those of Trudeau is profound. It is a confrontation that continually agitates the minds of the younger generation in Quebec. In 1963 Major wrote in *Liberté* with a burning passion of his determination to create a new society in Quebec.

There are but two human species which have only hate in common: the one which crushes, and the one which refuses to be crushed.

PAUL NIZAN

We are often blamed for speaking or acting with passion. This criticism flatters us, for our passion is one we see as healthy and essential, that of men's liberation. We reject a faltering vision of the world, which thinly disguises complicity with the oppressors. . . .

The hatred we now turn against those who oppress our people was initially turned in on ourselves. We hated in ourselves our sense of estrangement, we hated all that resulted from our collective alienation. Subsequently we understood that inner contradictions are but the reflection of social inconsistencies. Having understood that the root of our disaffection lay outside us, we turned against those who hold the real power in our society. This, then, is what led us to Marxism. Marxism gave us a method of understanding human reality, and a more precise and accurate insight into the world. As a philosophy of overcoming inconsistencies (*dépassement réel des aliénations*) it draws man into daily and practical action. It is the only form of humanism we can possibly accept. In this attitude lies the crucial difference which sets us apart from earlier generations. No longer will we go along with concessions to Capital, with expedient alliances that put us on the side of the oppressors, with mere exchanges of views, or with any form of conciliation. We have made our choice of sides. . . .

The young are beginning to talk, to organize themselves, to set up a framework for action. The old watchdogs are getting restless: why, the children seem not to have taken their lessons to heart! Wise heads come together: surely the ailment is a passing one; all that is needed is to bring the children back to the ways of reason—to the reasons of silence. So, surveys are made, interviews recorded: what do you think of this, or that? But unfortunately, the children have their own very headstrong and very dangerous ideas and attitudes. Messrs. Pelletier and Trudeau become alarmed, they try to convert this straying youth, these wanderers off the path of righteousness. They say to the young revolutionaries 'Careful, now, you're turning rightist, you're wrecking our work'. But the young don't listen, totally absorbed as they are in preparing a future which won't turn to mockery in their hands. Just last summer these hoary gentlemen were heralding the death of separatism. What a laugh ! They still think words can kill. . . .

The old Left just failed to see what Guy Pouliot expressed at the RIN convention, that there was *'an indissoluble connection between unemployment, Anglo-American capitalism, and the* [*English-*] *Canadian Constitution'. From a Marxist point of view it is pointless to think of the liberation of the Quebec proletariat without seeing the need for national liberation, since this proletariat belongs to a dominated language group, to a dominated nation.*

Its liberation will take place at two levels at the same time: the freeing of a proletariat exploited by capitalists, and the freeing of the proletariat that forms part of a nation dominated by another nation, by a foreign capitalism.

Our struggle, doubly inspired, thus aims at a *double* liberation. We shall fight against the Canadian colonialist ranks which immobilize our nation, just as we shall combat the capitalism inherent in those ranks and any Quebec capitalism that may develop along the lines of foreign capitalism.

What I have just set forth is based on principles stated by Lenin in his 'Critical Notes on the Nationalist Question'. . . .

. . . The battle is on, and it may be taken as a fact that a good many of us will fight, arms in hand.

Frank Scott and Michael Oliver (eds.), *Quebec States Her Case* (Toronto: Macmillan, 1964), pp. 74-82 *passim.*

The search for a Canadian identity has been made more difficult over the years by Canada's dependence on two great metropolitan powers, first Great Britain and now the United States. Canadian aspirations, in fact, have often been defined in reaction against influences and pressures coming from abroad. L. B. Pearson, retired from political life and speaking freely as a university professor, put the matter this way in 1968:

In earlier years, it was Downing Street that was our obsession, basically for the same reason—domination of Canada by, and dependance of Canada upon, another government. And we don't like the feeling that we may have merely gone from the colonial frying pan to the continental fire.

Indeed, worrying about the Americans, their friendly pressures, is probably the strongest Canadian unifying force at a time when we are in some doubt about the reality of the separate Canadian identity.

It must mean less if there is to be international co-operation and peace. Independence is relative and limited, even for the most powerful. For us, it can only mean the right to take decisions in our own country through our own institutions.

L. B. Pearson, 37th Conference of the Canadian Institute on Public Affairs, reported in the *Globe and Mail*, Toronto, 29 July, 1968.

What are called "American" influences are often influences arising from modern forms of technology, mass communication or industrial organization. Since she possesses the most powerful economic system in the world, the United States generates many of these currents but their impact is not confined to Canada. They are world-wide in their scope. Canada, because of her economic integration with the United States, is peculiarly sensitive to them. In 1951 a Royal Commission on National Development in the Arts, Letters and Sciences, of which Vincent Massey was chairman, spoke of the problems created by Canada's cultural dependence on the United States.

On this continent, as we have observed, our population stretches in a narrow and not even continuous ribbon along our frontier—fourteen millions along a five thousand mile front. In meeting influences from across the border as pervasive as they are friendly, we have not even the advantages of what soldiers call defence in depth.

From these influences, pervasive and friendly as they are, much that is valuable has come to us . . . gifts of money spent in Canada, grants offered to Canadians for study abroad, the free enjoyment of all the facilities of many institutions which we cannot afford, and the importation of many valuable things which we could not easily produce for ourselves. We have gained much. In this preliminary stocktaking of Canadian cultural life it may be fair to inquire whether we have gained a little too much. . . .

Although during the last generation our periodicals have maintained and greatly strengthened their position, the competition they face has been overwhelming. Canadian magazines with much difficulty have achieved a circulation of nearly forty-two millions a year as against an American circulation in Canada of over eighty-six millions. 'Canada . . . is the only country of any size in the world,' [someone] has observed, 'whose people read more foreign periodicals than they do periodicals published in their own land, local newspapers excluded.'

The American invasion by film, radio and periodical is formidable. Much of what comes to us is good. . . . It has, however, been represented to us that many of the radio programmes have in fact no particular application to Canada or to Canadian conditions and that some of them, including certain children's programmes of the 'crime' and 'horror' type, are positively harmful. News commentaries, too, and even live broadcasts from American sources, are designed for American ears and are almost certain to have an American slant and emphasis by reason of what they include or omit, as well as because of the opinions expressed. . . .

American influences on Canadian life to say the least are impressive. There should be no thought of interfering with the liberty of all Canadians to enjoy them. Cultural exchanges are excellent in themselves. They widen the choice of the consumer and provide stimulating competition for the producer. It cannot be denied, however, that a vast and disproportionate amount of material coming from a single alien source may stifle rather than stimulate our own creative effort; and, passively accepted without any standard of comparison, this may weaken critical faculties. We are now spending millions to maintain a national independence which would be nothing but an empty shell without a vigorous and distinctive cultural life.

Report of the Royal Commission on National Development in the Arts, Letters and Sciences (Ottawa: King's Printer, 1951), 17/18.

The Canadian economy is also subject to powerful pressures from across the border. The United States is Canada's best customer; it supplies most of our capital requirements; it provides management skills, advertising techniques and technological leadership. All these examples of interaction work to Canada's economic advantage and the material well-being of her citizens. Yet there are also disadvantages, as a 1957 report on the state of the Canadian economy pointed out.

The benefits of foreign investment that we have mentioned are very real and tangible. It is more difficult to state in similarly precise terms what the dangers are in the present situation and what conflicts might occur between the interests of Canadians and the interests of the foreign owners of wholly-owned subsidiaries of foreign companies operating in Canada. In the course of the Commission's hearings, concern was expressed over the extent to which our productive resources are controlled by non-residents, mostly Americans. Many Canadians are worried about such a large degree of economic decision-making being in the hands of non-residents or in the hands of Canadian companies controlled by non-residents. This concern has arisen because of the concentration of foreign ownership in certain industries, because of the fact that most of it is centred in one country, the United States, and because most of it is in the form of equities which, in the ordinary course of events, are never likely to be repatriated. . . .

At the root of Canadian concern about foreign investment is undoubtedly a basic, traditional sense of insecurity *vis-a-vis* our friendly, albeit our much larger and more powerful neighbour, the United States. There is concern that as the position of American capital in the dynamic resource and manufacturing sectors becomes ever more dominant, our economy will inevitably become more and more integrated with that of the United States. Behind this is the fear that continuing integration might lead to economic domination by the United States and eventually to the loss of our political independence. This fear of domination by the United States affects to some extent the political climate of life in Canada today.

Report of the Royal Commission on Canada's Economic Prospects (Ottawa: Queen's Printer, 1957), pp. 389/90.

A more recent study for the federal government on foreign ownership in Canadian industry proposed means by which the activities of companies owned outside Canada could be linked more closely with the development of a distinctive Canadian economy.

Canadians want national independence and economic growth. They want to increase the benefits from foreign ownership and reduce the costs. They want a *national* economy that functions efficiently within the world economy. Canadian history bears witness to those aspirations.

It is a function of government to translate those aspirations into objectives for national policy. On the basis of the discussion in the Report to this point, those objectives can be stated as:

- to require foreign-owned subsidiaries in Canada to behave as "good corporate citizens" of Canada, and to perform in ways that are fully consistent with Canada's economic and political interests.
- to improve the overall efficiency of the Canadian economy, and the performance of Canadian corporations, Canadian-owned as well as foreign-owned, in ways which will facilitate the capacity to generate self-sustained economic growth.
- to take positive steps to encourage increased Canadian ownership and control of economic activity, in ways that will facilitate the achievement of greater national independence and continuing economic growth.

Report of the Task Force on the Structure of Canadian Industry (Ottawa: Queen's Printer, 1968). pp. 393/94.

In diplomacy as well Canada has had difficulty in establishing a role for herself which would be independent of the United States. The best way to achieve this, many observers believe, is to act in a disinterested and constructive manner, expounding policies that are in tune with the realities of a particular situation. This has been the secret of Canada's success in international affairs since World War II, states a former member of the Department of External Affairs.

Canada did not acquire influence because of her power; rather she achieved influence—and respect—very largely because we acted as if we were indifferent to prestige and power. In time, the policy-makers in other countries came to recognize the disinterested services of the Canadians and charged us with an increasing number of delicate assignments, such as the reappraisal of the NATO alliance, and membership on most of the United Nations peace-supervisory teams.

Without calling in question our basic commitment to the western alliance, our spokesmen in the United Nations earned for Canada the reputation of being a reasonable nation interested in the extension of areas of agreement and the lowering of international tension. We generally abstained from the exchange of insults that has characterized the Cold War and, by the quiet, persuasive pitch of our pronouncements, invited the representatives of all other powers to approach us in the expectation of a rational, constructive discussion of even the most inflammatory issues. Many nations wished to consult with us about proposed initiatives, and our support was prized. The Canadians acquired a reputation for having helpful ideas; this was probably owing less to the originality of our representatives than to their close contacts with a considerable variety of other delegations; it was also helped by the fact that we were sometimes asked, because of our good reputation, to take the lead in presenting joint resolutions. . . . Through their acceptability, tact, skill, and knowledge the Canadians came to perform a role in the United Nations similar to that of floor leader in the American Congress; the ill-coordinated nature of the representation in the General Assembly made this function particularly useful.

P. V. Lyon, *The Policy Question: A Critical Appraisal of Canada's Role in World Affairs* (Toronto: McClelland and Stewart, 1963), p. 89.

The advantages of "quiet diplomacy", especially in Canada's relations with the United States, were set out by A. D. P. Heeney, former Canadian Ambassador in Washington, and Livingston T. Merchant, former United States Ambassador in Ottawa, who prepared a report on the subject for their governments in 1965. From their experience they concluded:

The need is clear for our two governments to confirm the practice of intimate, timely and continuing consultation on all matters of common concern, at the appropriate level, employing such machinery and procedures as are most effective for this purpose.

As partners in NATO, and sharing responsibility for the air defence of this continent, Canada and the United States have similar policies and share important common obligations. In the conduct and development of their unique bilateral relationship, however, the two countries must have regard for the wider responsibilities and interests of each in the world and their obligations under various treaties and other arrangements to which each is party.

This principle has a particular bearing upon our affairs in relation to the heavy responsibilities borne by the United States, generally as the leader of the free world and specifically under its network of mutual defence treaties around the globe. It is important and reasonable that Canadian authorities should have careful regard for the United States Government's position in this world context and, in the absence of special Canadian interests or obligations, avoid so far as possible, public disagreement especially upon critical issues. This is not to say that the Canadian Government should automatically and uniformly concur in foreign policy decisions taken by the United States Government. Different estimates of efficacy and appropriateness or degree of risk generate honest differences of opinion among the closest allies. The Canadian Government cannot renounce its right to independent judgment and decision in the "vast external realm". On its part, Canada has special relations and obligations, some of which the United States does not share but of which it should take account, in particular with Great Britain and the other states of the Commonwealth, with France, and with certain other nations.

It is in the abiding interest of both countries that, wherever possible, divergent views between the two governments should be expressed and if possible resolved in private, through diplomatic channels. Only a firm mutual resolve and the necessary practical arrangements to keep the totality of the relationship in good and friendly working order can enable our countries to avoid needless frictions and minimize the consequences of disagreement.

A. D. P. Heeney and Livingston T. Merchant, *Canada and the United States, Principles for Partnership* (Ottawa, 1965), pp. 48-50.

Other Canadians have felt that Canada was too closely tied to the United States through defence pacts such as NORAD and NATO which have had the effect of reducing her powers of independent action in non-military fields. This opinion holds that Canada should adopt a neutral policy. Such a policy, it is said, would not result in a loss of influence but would allow the country to use her capabilities more creatively in international affairs. This was the view in 1960 of James M. Minifie, a veteran Washington correspondent for the CBC.

The vivid and memorable act which would set the stage for restoration of Canadian independence would be a Declaration of Neutrality.

It would involve dissolving the smothering alliance of NORAD (the North American Air Defence command), withdrawing from a NATO already wrecked by President de Gaulle, and annulling the Permanent Joint Board on Defence, Canada-United States. It would not involve withdrawing from the Commonwealth; on the contrary it would strengthen the Commonwealth bond by severing the military fetter with a non-Commonwealth nation. Still less would it involve leaving the United Nations. Here again, it would enable fuller participation in the United Nations, bolder initiatives without the "arm-twisting" which currently goes on whenever Canada shows signs of departing from the American line.

It would not be an isolating neutralism. Quite the opposite. It would involve closer identification with internationalism than is possible under the restrictions of NORAD and NATO. Canada could play a particularly important role in this hemisphere, once it had clearly established its freedom from American military control.

J. M. Minifie, *Peacemaker or Powder-Monkey* (Toronto: McClelland and Stewart, 1960), p. 5.

The project which symbolized both the hopes of Canada's second century and the potential results of genuine co-operation between English and French-speaking Canadians, was EXPO 67. Among the innumerable commentaries on EXPO's meaning in Canadian history one only can be cited. Harry J. Boyle, an experienced newspaperman, wrote at the end of Centennial year:

Expo and the centennial year blasted away most of the remaining defeatist elements of colonial thinking. In the loftiest of inspiring ways, as novelist Hugh MacLennan said in an eloquent TV tribute, "Expo washed our senses."

But this all is a prelude. It is the inspiration and the example. We have discovered and reasserted the importance of man the individual. Have we learned enough to insist on making his environment worthy? There's little doubt of the effect on the younger people. They will not in the years ahead accept compromise, that the "cultural hemorrhage" of creative and scientific people to the United States is inevitable and can't be stemmed. They will also challenge theories about economics which insist on placing the stress on unbreakable rules rather than practice, because they have seen where the need of war produces unlimited resources. They feel that money should be expended in the cause of people rather than buildings, war or prestige.

They will not forget, above all, that Expo happened! They know it was a product of inspired imagination but was brought to fruition by artists and scientists, builders and dreamers and by a team of people caught in a common inspiration where it really didn't matter what language you used to express the idea . . . since the ideas and the dedication were more important than anything else.

When that flame was doused at Expo it wasn't really extinguished, because the incandescence of its symbolism has somehow taken the edge off the dark loneliness of our vast space and made it closer and warmer and even a place where Canadians will have less reticence in speaking and working together.

The year 1967 was a dream resolved. The year 1968 is the real challenge.

Harry J. Boyle, in *Weekend Magazine*, no. 52, 1967, p. 5.

BIBLIOGRAPHY

*INDICATES VOLUMES AVAILABLE IN PAPERBACK.

Aitken, Hugh G. J., *et al. The American Economic Impact on Canada.* Duke University Press, 1959—essays on trends in Canada's economic history since 1945.

Barber, Joseph. *Good Fences Make Good Neighbours: Why the United States Provokes Canadians.* McClelland and Stewart, 1958—an analysis of Canadian-American relations since World War II.

Brecher, I., and Reisman, S. S. *Canada-United States Economic Relations.* Queen's Printer, 1957—one of the most valuable studies undertaken for the Gordon Commission on Canada's economic prospects (1957).

Brewin, Andrew. *Stand on Guard: The Search for a Canadian Defence Policy.* McClelland and Stewart, 1965—a critical appraisal of Canada's defence policy from a leading N.D.P. member of parliament.

Canada in World Affairs. Oxford University Press—further volumes in the C.I.I.A. series mentioned in the Bibliography for Part IV; the coverage of topics is broad and the exposition is balanced.

* V Spencer, R. A. *From U.N. to N.A.T.O., 1946-1949.* (1959).
* VI Harrison, W. E. C. *1949-1950.* (1957).
* VII Keirstead, B. S. *September, 1951 to October, 1953.* (1956).
*VIII Masters, D. C. *1953-1955.* (1959).
* IX Eayrs, James. *October, 1955 to June, 1957.* (1959).
X Lloyd, Trevor. *1957-1959.* (1968).
XI Preston, R. A. *1959-1961.* (1965).
XII Lyon, P. V. *1961-1963.* (1968).

**Canada Year Book.* Queen's Printer, annually—the best, single statistical reference for all aspects of Canada's growth in the contemporary world.

**Canada, The Official Handbook of Present Conditions and Recent Progress.* Queen's Printer, annually—a shorter version of the *Canada Year Book.*

Clark, Gerald. *Canada: The Uneasy Neighbour.* D. McKay, 1965—a veteran newspaperman looks at Canadian-American relations.

*Clarkson, Stephen (ed.). *An Independent Foreign Policy for Canada?* McClelland and Stewart, 1968—a collection of short papers discussing the choices open for the development of Canadian foreign policy.

*Cook, Ramsay. *Canada and the French-Canadian Question.* Macmillan, 1966—nine essays on the interpretation of Canadian history and politics, bringing out the role of French Canada.

*Desbarats, Peter. *The State of Quebec: A Journalist's View of the Quiet Revolution.* McClelland and Stewart, 1965—the work of a well-informed observer of the Quebec scene.

*Eayrs, James. *The Art of the Possible: Government and Foreign Policy in Canada.* University of Toronto Press, 1961—an analysis of the way external policy is made in Canada.

————. *Northern Approaches: Canada and the Search for Peace.* Macmillan, 1961—a stimulating group of essays discussing contemporary issues in Canada's external relations.

Fraser, Blair. *The Search for Identity: Canada, 1945-1967.* Doubleday, 1967—an interpretive history of Canada since 1945; the last work of a great journalist.

*Grant, George P. *Lament for a Nation: The Defeat of Canadian Nationalism.* McClelland and Stewart, 1965—the author feels that the Canadian identity can never be maintained against the forces of continentalism in North America.

Hutchison, Bruce. *The Incredible Canadian.* Longmans, Green, 1952—a biography of Mackenzie King.

*Knowles, S. H. *The New Party.* McClelland and Stewart, 1961—the history and viewpoint of the C.C.F.-N.D.P. party.

*Lyon, Peyton V. *The Policy Question: A Critical Appraisal of Canada's Role in World Affairs.* McClelland and Stewart, 1963—the case for Canada's continued involvement in N.A.T.O. and military presence in Europe.

*Macquarrie, Heath. *The Conservative Party.* McClelland and Stewart, 1965—a short history of the Canadian Conservative party.

Massey, Vincent. *On Being Canadian.* Dent, 1948—a great Canadian speaks of Canada's cultural needs just after World War II.

McInnis, Edgar. *The Atlantic Triangle and the Cold War.* University of Toronto Press, 1959—Canada's role in world affairs since World War II.

————, (with F. H. Soward). *Canada and the United Nations.* Manhattan Publishing Company, 1957—an account of Canada in the international organization.

Merchant, Livingston T. (ed.). *Neighbours Taken for Granted: Canada and the United States.* Praeger, 1966—eight hard-hitting essays written by American and Canadian commentators.

Minifee, James M. *Peacemaker or Powder-Monkey: Canada's Role in a Revolutionary World.* McClelland and Stewart, 1960—a provocative presentation of the case for Canadian neutralism in international affairs.

Monthly Review of the Bank of Nova Scotia—a quick way to keep abreast of Canadian economic developments; obtainable without charge at any branch of the Bank.

*Newman, Peter C. *Renegade in Power: The Diefenbaker Years.* McClelland and Stewart, 1963—a best-selling, exciting, but cruel account of John Diefenbaker as prime minister.

————. *The Distemper of Our Times.* McClelland and Stewart, 1968—a sequel to the previous book, concentrating on the Pearson years in the author's now familiar, hard-hitting style.

Park, Julian (ed.). *The Culture of Contemporary Canada.* Ryerson, 1957—a collection of essays on aspects of Canada's cultural life.

*Peacock, Donald. *Journey to Power.* Ryerson, 1968—a popular account of the leadership changes in the two major parties by one who, as a member of the Pearson and Trudeau staffs, was a close observer of the events described.

Pearson, L. B. *Diplomacy in the Nuclear Age.* Saunders, 1959; and *The Four Faces of Peace and the International Outlook.* McClelland and Stewart, 1964—two volumes of Lester Pearson's speeches on world affairs; the first contains his notable address upon receiving the Nobel Peace Prize in 1957.

*Pickersgill, J. W. *The Liberal Party.* McClelland and Stewart, 1962—a short but lively history of the Liberal party.

Roberts, Leslie. *C. D., The Life and Times of Clarence Decatur Howe.* Clarke, Irwin, 1957—the life of the great Canadian businessman and Liberal cabinet member.

Ross, Malcolm (ed.). *The Arts in Canada: A Stock-taking at Mid-century.* Macmillan, 1959—another collection of essays on cultural activities in Canada.

Royal Commission on Canada's Economic Prospects. Queen's Printer: preliminary (short) report, 1956; final report, 1957—the "Gordon Commission" report, a thorough stock-taking of Canada's economic progress since World War II. A useful digest is contained in *Shea, A. A. *Canada, 1980*. McClelland and Stewart, 1960.

Royal Commission on National Development in the Arts, Letters and Sciences. King's Printer, 1951—the "Massey Commission" report, an invaluable assessment of the problems and prospects of Canadian cultural development after World War II.

Russell, Peter (ed.). *Nationalism in Canada*. McGraw-Hill, 1966—a collection of stimulating essays on various aspects of the subject: the land, the people, the federal system, policy and culture.

*Scott, Frank, and Oliver, Michael (eds.). *Quebec States Her Case*. Macmillan, 1964—illustrates French-Canadian opinion during the "quiet revolution."

Sevigny, Pierre. *This Game of Politics*. McClelland and Stewart, 1965—a fascinating account of Conservative politics and Quebec after 1956, written by a member of the Diefenbaker government.

*Sloan, T. S. *Quebec: The Not-So-Quiet Revolution*. Ryerson, 1965—another journalist's impressions of the changes in Quebec in the 1960's.

Smith, J. M. *Canada's Economic Growth and Development from 1939 to 1955*. Queen's Printer, 1957—a short but useful historical account written for the "Gordon Commission".

Swettenham, J. A. *McNaughton*, Vol. 2, *1940-1966*. Ryerson, 1969—the concluding half of the authorized biography.

*Tackaberry, R. B. *Keeping the Peace: A Canadian Military Viewpoint on Peace-Keeping Operations*. Canadian Institute of International Affairs, 1966—a pamphlet describing the record of Canadian peace-keeping and outlining the difficulties in this activity.

Thomson, Dale C. *Louis St. Laurent: Canadian*. Macmillan, 1967—the only biography of St. Laurent.

*Trudeau, Pierre Elliott. *Federalism and the French Canadians*. Macmillan, 1968—nine essays, written over the period 1954-67, providing the most convenient statement of the constitutional views of Canada's fifteenth Prime Minister.

Wood, H. F. *Strange Battle-Ground: The Operations in Korea*. Queen's Printer, 1966—the official history of the Canadian Army in the Korean War.

Young, J. H. *Canadian Commercial Policy*. Queen's Printer, 1957—largely an economic analysis but with some historical material; prepared for the "Gordon Commission."

Young, Walter D. *Democracy and Discontent: Progressivism, Socialism and Social Credit in the Canadian West*. ("The Frontenac Library," No. 2.). Ryerson, 1969—a brief study, using representative source material, of the origins and fortunes of the C.C.F.-N.D.P. and Social Credit.

INDEX

C

D

E

F

M

N

O

P

Q

R

The Publisher wishes to acknowledge with gratitude those who have given permission to use the photographs in this book:

Abitibi Paper Company Ltd., 496; Art Gallery of Ontario, 543; Avro Aircraft, 522; Ken Bell Photography Ltd., 545; British Museum, 17, 22; Fred Bruemmer, 4, 557; Canadian Government Travel Bureau, 9; Canadian Pacific Railway, 288, 291, 292, 334; Canadian Opera Company, Toronto, 545; Canadian Press Picture Service, 540, 557; Capital News Service, Ottawa, 506; Chateau de Ramezy, 170; Cliché des Musées Nationaux, Chateau de Versailles, Paris, 48; Colonial Williamsburg, 27; Department of Highways, Ontario, 480; Glenbow Foundation, Calgary, 296, 320, 322, 333; *Globe and Mail*, Toronto, 401; Imperial Oil Ltd., 486; International Nickel Company of Canada, 496; Karsh, Ottawa, 433; Hans Keusen, 3; *La Presse*, Montreal, 405; *La Province*, Montreal, 428; L'Inventaire des Oeuvres d'Art, Province de Québec, 43, 54; McCord Museum, McGill University, 81, 192, 205, 208, 216, 241, 252, 260, 263, 264, 268, 281, 290, 313, 315, 316, 322, 327, 346; National Film Board, 8, 486, 496; National Gallery of Canada, 101, 112, 188; Provincial Archives, British Columbia, 257; Provincial Archives, Manitoba, 248, 284, 327; Provincial Archives, Nova Scotia, 173, 176; Public Archives of Canada, 39, 64, 76, 77, 80, 96, 103, 110, 127, 130, 134, 135, 137, 141, 143, 145, 147, 150, 155, 159, 161, 166, 183, 194, 208, 211, 215, 216, 245, 249, 256, 272, 276, 279, 302, 303, 304, 306, 308, 333, 340, 344, 349, 357, 363, 367, 369, 373, 376, 395, 399, 444, 449, 461, 500, 502; Public Information Branch, Manitoba, 496; Royal Ontario Museum, 19, 32, 34, 36, 94, 121, 123, 131; Saskatchewan Government Photo, 486; Simon Fraser University, 543; Toronto Public Libraries, 14, 15, 63, 181, 224, 457; *Toronto Star Syndicate*, 421, 423, 454, 480, 512, 514, 539, 553; Travelpic Publications, Niagara Falls, Ont., 51, 57, 67, 74, 139, 221; Turofsky, Toronto, 440; *Winnipeg Free Press*, 431

Every effort has been made to credit picture sources correctly. The Publisher would be grateful for information that would correct any errors or omissions.

2 3 4 5 75 74 73 72